THE BREACH

INSIDE THE IMPEACHMENT AND TRIAL
OF WILLIAM JEFFERSON CLINTON

Peter Baker

A LISA DREW BOOK

SCRIBNER
New York London Toronto Sydney Singapore

SCRIBNER
1230 Avenue of the Americas
New York, NY 10020

DESIGNED BY ERICH HOBBING

Set in Adobe Garamond

Manufactured in the United States of America

1   3   5   7   9   10   8   6   4   2

Library of Congress Cataloging-in-Publication Data

Baker, Peter.
The Breach: inside the impeachment and trial of William Jefferson Clinton/Peter Baker.
p. cm.
"A Lisa Drew book."
Includes bibliographical references and index.
1. Clinton, Bill, 1946—Impeachment.
2. Trials (Impeachment)—United States.
3. Impeachments—United States. I. Title.
KF5076.C57 B35 2000
342.73'062—dc21
00-041963

ISBN 0-684-86813-X

For Susan

And they that shall be of thee shall build the old waste places: thou shalt raise up the foundations of many generations; and thou shalt be called, The repairer of the breach, The restorer of paths to dwell in.

Isaiah 58:12

The American people returned to office a president of one party and a Congress of another. Surely they did not do this to advance the politics of petty bickering and extreme partisanship they plainly deplore. No, they call all us instead to be repairers of the breach and to move on with America's mission. America demands and deserves big things from us, and nothing big ever came from being small.

President Clinton,
second inaugural address,
January 20, 1997

CONTENTS

Cast of Characters   11

Prologue: *"We have to impeach the bastard"*   15

1. *"I don't know how we can get through this"*   23

2. *"You're a damn, damn, damn fool"*   43

3. *". . . go to the White House and tell him he has to resign"*   67

4. *"I don't want them to win"*   93

5. *"How can you be so goddamn stupid?"*   111

6. *"We need to purge the poisons from the system"*   140

7. *"The crazy right has them by the throat"*   160

8. *"Somebody in this room rat-fucked the president last night"*   188

9. *"The pressure got to me"*   217

10. *"There are people in my party who just hate you"*   238

11. *"We are fighting for the presidency of the United States"*   259

12. *"Heavenly Father, we are in trouble"*   279

13. *"There may actually be a case here"*   300

14. *"The horse is stinking up the room"*   327

15. *"This is going to be ninety white men leering at her"*   339

16. *"She's the best witness I ever saw"*   367

17. *"Good God Almighty, take the vote!"*   380

18. *"The most difficult, wrenching, and soul-searching vote"*   395

Epilogue: *"The country didn't want an impeachment"*   413

Acknowledgments   421

Notes   423

Chronology   427

Appendices   433

Index   447

CAST OF CHARACTERS

Bob Barr	House manager, Republican from Georgia
Robert F. Bauer	Counsel to House Minority Leader Richard A. Gephardt and Senate Minority Leader Thomas A. Daschle
Paul Begala	Presidential counselor
Howard L. Berman	House Judiciary Committee member, Democrat from California
Sidney Blumenthal	Special assistant to the president
Mary Bono	House Judiciary Committee member, Republican from California
Rick Boucher	House Judiciary Committee member, Democrat from Virginia
Erskine B. Bowles	White House chief of staff
Lanny A. Breuer	White House special counsel
Juanita Broaddrick	Arkansas nursing home operator who claimed Bill Clinton sexually assaulted her in 1978
Dolly Kyle Browning	Childhood friend of the president who claimed they had a long-standing affair
Edward G. Bryant	House manager, Republican from Tennessee
Dale Bumpers	Former senator, Democrat from Arkansas
Steve Buyer	House manager, Republican from Indiana
Robert C. Byrd	Senator, Democrat from West Virginia
Plato Cacheris	Counsel to Monica S. Lewinsky
Charles T. Canady	House manager, Republican from Florida
Chris Cannon	House manager, Republican from Utah
James Carville	Former consultant to the president
Bill Clinton	President of the United States
Hillary Rodham Clinton	First lady of the United States
Susan M. Collins	Senator, Republican from Maine
John Conyers Jr.	Ranking Democrat, House Judiciary Committee, from Michigan

11

Gregory B. Craig	White House special counsel
Betty Currie	Personal secretary to the president
Lloyd N. Cutler	Former White House counsel
Thomas A. Daschle	Senate minority leader, Democrat from South Dakota
Tom DeLay	House majority whip, Republican from Texas
Pete V. Domenici	Senator, Republican from New Mexico
Rahm Emanuel	Senior adviser to the president
Julian Epstein	Chief counsel and staff director, House Judiciary Committee Democrats
Russell Feingold	Senator, Democrat from Wisconsin
Dianne Feinstein	Senator, Democrat from California
Barney Frank	House Judiciary Committee member, Democrat from Massachusetts
Richard A. Gephardt	House minority leader, Democrat from Missouri
Newt Gingrich	Speaker of the House, Republican from Georgia
Al Gore	Vice president of the United States
Slade Gorton	Senator, Republican from Washington State
Lindsey O. Graham	House manager, Republican from South Carolina
Phil Gramm	Senator, Republican from Texas
Thomas B. Griffith	Senate legal counsel
Tom Harkin	Senator, Democrat from Iowa
Orrin G. Hatch	Senator, Republican from Utah
Asa Hutchinson	House manager, Republican from Arkansas
Henry J. Hyde	Chairman, House Judiciary Committee, lead House manager, Republican from Illinois
Harold M. Ickes	Former White House deputy chief of staff
Norma Holloway Johnson	Federal district judge who oversaw the Starr grand jury
Paula Jones	Former Arkansas clerk who sued President Clinton for sexual harassment
Vernon E. Jordan Jr.	Washington attorney, friend of the president
Mickey Kantor	Former commerce secretary and adviser to the president
David E. Kendall	Personal counsel to the president
Peter T. King	Congressman, Republican from New York
Monica S. Lewinsky	Former White House intern

Joseph I. Lieberman	Senator, Democrat from Connecticut
Bruce R. Lindsey	White House deputy counsel and longtime friend of the president
Bob Livingston	Speaker-designate of the House, Republican from Louisiana
Joe Lockhart	White House press secretary
Trent Lott	Senate majority leader, Republican from Mississippi
Abbe D. Lowell	Chief Democratic investigator, House Judiciary Committee
Terence R. McAuliffe	Fund-raiser and friend of the president
Bill McCollum	House manager, Republican from Florida
Michael McCurry	White House press secretary
Cheryl D. Mills	White House deputy counsel
Thomas E. Mooney Sr.	Chief of staff and general counsel, House Judiciary Committee Republicans
Bill Paxon	Congressman, Republican from New York
John D. Podesta	White House chief of staff
Jack Quinn	Congressman, Republican from New York
William H. Rehnquist	Chief justice of the Supreme Court
James E. Rogan	House manager, Republican from California
Charles F. C. Ruff	White House counsel
Rick Santorum	Senator, Republican from Pennsylvania
David P. Schippers	Chief Republican investigator, House Judiciary Committee
Nicole K. Seligman	Personal counsel to the president
Donna E. Shalala	Secretary of Health and Human Services
Christopher Shays	Congressman, Republican from Connecticut
Douglas B. Sosnik	Senior adviser to the president
Arlen Specter	Senator, Republican from Pennsylvania
Kenneth W. Starr	Independent counsel
Ted Stevens	Senator, Republican from Alaska
Linda R. Tripp	Pentagon colleague and friend who tape-recorded Monica S. Lewinsky
Maxine Waters	House Judiciary Committee member, Democrat from California
Kathleen E. Willey	Former White House aide who claimed an unwelcome advance by the president

"We have to impeach the bastard"

B ob Livingston was looking for a place to escape. He moved wordlessly through the chamber of the House of Representatives, where his fellow congressmen were arguing about whether the president of the United States should be removed from office for the first time in American history for high crimes and misdemeanors. Republicans were crying about the rule of law, Democrats about partisan witch-hunts. Livingston tuned out the raging speeches and brushed past the milling congressmen. Finally he made his way to the door leading to the Republican cloakroom and ducked inside. Here he hoped to find a few moments of peace.

With a row of phone booths, a few worn leather couches, a coffeepot, and a droning television, the L-shaped cloakroom on most days was a useful, if inelegant, hideaway from the monotony of legislative business. At this moment, it was also an effective refuge from the political storm that had swirled around Livingston in the last few days. It was Friday, December 18, 1998, and Livingston stood on the precipice of power, slated to become the next Speaker of the House. And yet he had the look of a haunted man, hiding from the swarm of television cameras staking out his office elsewhere in the Capitol. His tall, lanky form slumped into a chair in the cloakroom. His face was drawn, his eyes looked empty. Just two nights before he had been forced by a pornographer to publicly confess to marital infidelities, and now he presided over impeachment proceedings that had their origins in President Bill Clinton's own sexual indiscretions. As if the situation were not surreal enough, suddenly the country was at war half a world away as Clinton ordered American warships and planes to bombard Saddam Hussein's Iraq.

Pen in hand, Livingston had been scribbling on some paper, trying to work on his speech for the impeachment debate, but he felt it was missing something important. He got up and squeezed himself into one of the cloakroom's phone booths and made a few calls. Finally, the weight of it all just hit him. The world had gone mad, it seemed to Livingston. How could all of this be happening at once? Across the room he spotted an aide walking into the cloakroom and gestured for him to come over.

"We've got to stop this," Livingston said. "This is crazy. We're about to impeach the president of the United States."

Livingston had lost his nerve. He could not go through with it. He instructed his aide to summon the other members of the House Republican leadership for an emergency meeting in an hour. "We're going to have a censure vote."

The import of those words was instantly clear. It meant no impeachment. It meant surrender. At the behest of his party's conservatives, Livingston had been blocking attempts by Clinton's Democratic allies to offer a nonbinding resolution on the floor that would reprimand the president rather than impeach him. If the House were allowed to vote on such a censure measure, moderate Republicans would have a vehicle to express their disapproval of Clinton's behavior without feeling compelled to go along with those seeking to make him the first president impeached in 130 years. Censure would pass and impeachment would fail—at least that was the conventional wisdom. Five days earlier, prodded by House Majority Whip Tom DeLay, the power-broker from Texas who had helped him secure the Speakership in the first place, Livingston had announced he would not permit such a vote. Now, almost literally at the last minute, he was changing his mind.

Livingston's aide, Mark Corallo, was alarmed. A feisty former military man, Corallo was convinced that Clinton was guilty of perjury and obstruction of justice for trying to cover up his affair with onetime White House intern Monica S. Lewinsky. What's more, just that morning Corallo had been told by a friend about an even more explosive allegation contained in the locked vault at the Gerald R. Ford House Office Building where the secret evidence sent by Independent Counsel Kenneth W. Starr was stored, a sensational if uncorroborated charge that Clinton had sexually assaulted a woman more than twenty years earlier when he was the attorney general of Arkansas. Corallo had rushed over to the cloakroom to tell Livingston, when he found the new Speaker dispirited and ready to give up.

"Wait a minute," Corallo told Livingston. "You need to go to the Ford Building and see the evidence."

"No, I've heard about some of it," Livingston replied. "People have told me."

"No. You need to go look. Boss, we have a *rapist* in the White House."

The nation was not yet familiar with the name of Juanita Broaddrick and her harrowing tale of a motel room encounter that had left her with a swollen lip and a terrible secret that two decades later would be splashed out in the nation's newspapers and television sets despite the president's denial. At that point, Broaddrick had refused to speak about it publicly, and her case had only been hinted at cryptically in the newspapers. Livingston had heard the story, at least wisps of it, in the hallways of the Capitol, but he stood quietly and listened as his aide poured forth indignation.

"If you allow a censure vote, he gets away with it," Corallo argued. "He has flouted the law. He has attacked you and everything we stand for. We may take a short-term hit in the polls, but in the long run, we'll be remembered as the guys who stood up for the rule of law."

Livingston thought about it. A tough-minded, fifty-five-year-old former criminal prosecutor, he believed in the rule of law as strongly as anyone. Certainly he had no great affection for Clinton. But this was *the president.* Livingston was, at heart, an institutionalist who had been raised to respect the office. His family tree extended to the beginnings of American democracy, including a forefather who had administered the presidential oath of office to George Washington. Livingston knew impeachment was not something to be undertaken lightly. And after a quarter century of political ladder-climbing, after swallowing his own sense of loyalty to push his friend Newt Gingrich out of the Speaker's chair in a postelection coup, this was hardly what Livingston wanted to do in his first act as the leader of the House. He had dreamed of using his newfound position to trim back government and cut taxes. Those were the driving passions that had fired his two decades in Washington, not partisan thirst for revenge against the likes of Bill Clinton.

Yet Livingston knew that it was too late to turn back. If he could not convince his own aide to halt the barreling locomotive of impeachment, how could he bring along a conservative Republican conference anxious to throw Clinton out of office? Maybe in the days or weeks before, another outcome had still been possible, but no longer. The debate had started; the vote was scheduled for the next day. Besides, Livingston concluded, Corallo was right. However unpleasant it was to deal with, in Livingston's mind the president had committed serious crimes that the House had to confront directly. To let Clinton off, Livingston decided, would set a dangerous precedent that future presidents could do as they pleased with no accountability.

"So what you're saying," Livingston finally said to his anxious aide, "is we have to impeach the bastard."

"Yes, I'm saying we have to impeach the bastard."

"Okay," Livingston sighed. "We won't have a meeting."

Livingston did not tell his congressional colleagues about his eleventh-hour moment of doubt and quickly put it out of his own mind as well. Little did anyone realize that barely twenty-four hours before Clinton would be

impeached, the one man who could have stopped it very nearly did. Small
wonder that he hesitated. The months of scandal and turmoil had taken their
toll in Washington. Lives had been wrecked, careers ruined. The nation's politics had been warped into something almost unrecognizable. All the rules had
been rewritten. A president could be caught enjoying sexual favors in the Oval
Office suite from an intern barely older than his daughter, then lie about it on
national television, cover up his misconduct, and yet soar to record heights in
political popularity polls. A special prosecutor could force a young woman to
divulge her most intimate secrets, haul her mother into a grand jury, and even
compel the Secret Service agents who guard the president to break their
code of silence, all without anyone able to tell him to stop. A Speaker of the
House could seek to use the president's wrongdoing to his advantage in an
election, only to endure a devastating defeat and find himself forced from
power just days later, all the while conducting his own secret, five-year extramarital affair. And now his successor faced his own moment of truth.

For all of the titillation about thongs and cigars, the story of the impeachment and trial of William Jefferson Clinton was not so much about sex as it
was about power. It may have started with an unseemly rendezvous near the
Oval Office, but it mushroomed into the Washington battle of a generation,
ultimately dragging in all three branches of government. It tested the boundaries of America's constitutional framework and challenged the precepts of
nearly every major institution of public life. And the consequences went far
beyond whether Clinton would stay in office or not—for good or ill, the decisions made by the House and Senate would redefine the limits of presidential
and congressional power for decades to come. Just as lawyers and lawmakers
cracked open history books to study the precedents set by Andrew Johnson
and Richard M. Nixon, another set of national leaders in the future will search
for lessons from the six-month showdown between the Democratic president
and the Republican Congress—from August 1998 when Clinton's fate was
thrown into the congressional arena by his admission that he had misled the
nation, through his impeachment by the House in December, and finally to
his eventual acquittal by the Senate in February 1999.

The impeachment and trial had their origins not merely in the lust of
a chief executive or the animosity he generated in his foes, but in a fast-
changing, scandal-soaked Washington culture that had grown coarse and
corrosive over the years. With the advent of the independent-counsel law following Watergate and the political wars that helped destroy the reputations
of Supreme Court nominees Robert H. Bork and Clarence Thomas, House
Speaker Jim Wright, and would-be defense secretary John Tower, attack politics had become more the norm than the aberration, a trend exacerbated by
the development of multiple twenty-four-hour cable news channels hungry

for conflict to fill dead airtime. At the Clinton White House, life under the microscope of a half-dozen special prosecutors had so jaded the president's advisers that when counselor Paul Begala joined the White House staff in 1997, he put an attorney on retainer even before his first day on the job. Was that the fault of Clinton or Starr? The Republicans or the media? There were plenty of directions in which to point fingers.

Clinton opened his second term vowing to bring the parties together, to become the "repairer of the breach." But the last half of his presidency demonstrated that the breach was wider than anyone had ever anticipated. The impeachment and trial represented the triumph of partisanship on both sides of the aisle. Led by the White House, the Democrats made a calculated decision to promote partisanship and then use it as a shield for the president—demonizing his critics, resisting every GOP move, and even manufacturing disagreements where none existed, all to prove the political perfidy of the other side. Despite the private doubts of their own leaders, the Democrats resolved not to seriously consider removing a president who remained at lofty heights in the opinion polls. For their part, Republicans allowed revulsion at Clinton to consume them so much that they turned away from opportunities to work together with the opposition toward a bipartisan conclusion. The clearest lesson from Watergate was that impeachment had to be bipartisan to work, and yet the GOP majority pushed forward with little serious effort to win over Democrats, unwilling to consider any solution short of the ultimate goal. For both sides, impeachment, in the end, turned out to be another campaign to be won. Compromise was for the faint of heart.

In another era, Washington might have found a consensus resolution without the political equivalent of nuclear escalation. There was a time when the powerbrokers in the nation's capital could have settled on a proper course of action and then made it happen behind closed doors—whether the right answer was impeachment, resignation, censure, or some other outcome. In 1974, Barry Goldwater, Hugh Scott, and John J. Rhodes went to the White House to convince Nixon to resign rather than face certain impeachment by the House. In 1987, Democratic leaders agreed to forgo impeachment proceedings against Ronald Reagan for the Iran-contra affair once former senator Howard H. Baker Jr. took over as White House chief of staff, pledging to put things back on track. But by the Clinton era, Washington had become such a polarized place that when the city's "wise men"—former senators, onetime White House officials, and even ex-presidents—tried to intervene to bring the two sides of the Clinton clash together, they were ignored. In the current generation, outsiders such as Bill Clinton and revolutionaries such as Tom DeLay cared little what the party elders inside the Beltway thought.

The Clinton impeachment saga was also the story of real people making it up as they went along, uncertain about what was the right answer. For every James Carville, the consultant who would defend his president to the last by tearing down his attackers, there was an Erskine B. Bowles, the White House chief of staff who wrestled with his own sense of betrayal and despair. For every Tom DeLay, who never wavered from his relentless campaign to drive Clinton from office, there was a Bob Livingston, who struggled with genuine doubts and conflicting imperatives until the bitter end. In hindsight, it would often seem that everything was inevitable—that the House was always bound to impeach and the Senate was always fated to acquit. But that was not the way it felt to those waging the battle at the time. At any number of points, events might easily have turned out differently—including the moment when Livingston entertained second thoughts as the House opened its historic debate.

Robert L. Livingston Jr. grew up in modest circumstances and a broken home in New Orleans, raised by a mother alone from an early age after his father abandoned the family. After dropping out of Tulane University, he signed up with the navy for a four-year hitch, which included a tour aboard ship in the Caribbean during the Cuban missile crisis, before returning to school. Making tuition money as a welder's assistant at the local shipyards, Livingston earned undergraduate and law degrees at Tulane and met a bright young man studying for a doctorate named Newt Gingrich. Livingston went to work for a succession of local, state, and federal prosecutors over the next half-dozen years, cementing his affinity for institutions and order. But the young lawyer did have a wild side. He liked to gamble at an illegal casino and carouse deep into the evening at the dives in the French Quarter. Once when he returned home late, he found his dinner left for him outside the front door by his unamused wife, Bonnie.

By 1976, the political bug had bitten, and with the encouragement of his boss, the Democratic state attorney general, Livingston decided to run for Congress—but as a Republican. He and Bonnie spent their entire life savings of $5,000 in a futile bid in a historically Democratic district, but when the man who had beaten him, Congressman Richard Tonry, resigned a year later amid a vote-fraud scandal, Livingston won the 1977 special election for the seat. In Washington, he quickly earned a reputation as a serious, fiscally conservative, pro-defense legislator who worked hard to steer federal money to the shipyards where he had once labored. After Republicans took over in 1994, Gingrich, his old acquaintance from Tulane, reached past other, more senior members to give Livingston the gavel of the most powerful panel in the House, the Appropriations Committee, which divvies up hundreds of billions of taxpayer dollars each year. Eager to make a point, Livingston showed up at his first meeting as chairman hefting a machete in one hand and an alligator knife in the other—all to show what he planned to do to the bloated federal budget.

But in a town of one-dimensional politicians, Livingston proved to be more complicated. True to its long tradition, the Appropriations Committee under Livingston remained an island of bipartisanship even amid the fervor of Gingrich's revolution. The institutionalist in Livingston cherished relationships across the aisle; sometimes he would break out harmonicas with his friend, Democratic congressman David R. Obey, in the middle of a committee meeting. Yet the rebel in Livingston would lead the charge during the budget battle that shut down the federal government in 1995. "We will never, never give in!" he thundered on the House floor. "We will stay here until doomsday!" The videotape of his defiant outburst was played over and over on television until he became a symbol of Republican intransigence. His own mother later told him never to do that again because he looked like a raving lunatic.

Despite the tension of that showdown, little personal animosity had developed between Clinton and Livingston, as it had with Gingrich and other Republican leaders. When Livingston toppled Gingrich as leader of House Republicans after their disastrous midterm election in November 1998, the new Speaker-designate kept an open mind on impeachment. After his ascension, the first time he met with the top House Democrat, Minority Leader Richard A. Gephardt, Livingston said he was receptive to the idea of censure as an alternative to be offered on the floor. By his second meeting with Gephardt, Livingston was more wary. DeLay had applied considerable pressure, and the new Speaker hedged his bets. At their final meeting in the days before the debate was to begin, Livingston told Gephardt that censure was off the table. By that point, Livingston's own skeletons were about to burst out of their closet—and the embattled Speaker-to-be was telling friends that he had secretly been threatened with exposure by a lobbyist ally of the White House if he blocked censure.

Livingston had thought he had made up his mind a week before the debate began on the floor, when he convened a meeting of the Republican leadership and a few ad hoc advisers. It was the Thursday before what he would later come to call his "week from hell," and he went around the room at the Library of Congress soliciting opinions. "Look, we're down to the wire here and we've got to go forward," he had said. "I want an idea of where you all stand."

For the next hour, they went through the pros and cons of censure, talking about the consequences of impeaching Clinton or failing to. In the end, the decision was clear—they would go forward with impeachment. There was only one dissenter, Anne Northup of Kentucky, who had barely won reelection a month earlier and worried about the political ramifications of taking on a popular president.

Only in the days after that meeting did Livingston learn that his own past adultery would definitely come to light. Only after that was the country suddenly thrust into war. The turmoil made Livingston rethink his decision. Barely an hour before his brief turnaround in the cloakroom on the day the impeachment debate opened, Livingston had met with a Republican congressman from Iowa who urged him to step down as Speaker for the good of the party. The congressman was not there on behalf of a group, but Livingston knew he reflected the sentiments of others in the GOP conference. All of this was swirling through his mind.

After Corallo stiffened his resolve again in the cloakroom, Livingston turned his attention back to his speech. He crossed out lines and scribbled in new ones. He crunched up one draft and threw it in the wastebasket. The next draft was better, coming closer to saying what he wanted to say about the president's behavior and the stakes for the system. Bob Livingston was nothing if not a creature of the system. After a long day of drafting, he met in his office privately with Tom DeLay, who told him to stand strong, that they would get through it together.

Finally, Livingston emerged from his inner office, draft speech in hand, and put on his coat.

"I need a punch line," he told his aides as he walked out the door. "It really needs a punch line."

That night, around two in the morning, Livingston bolted up in bed. He knew what his punch line would be.

CHAPTER ONE

"I don't know how
we can get through this"

Hillary Rodham Clinton looked miserable. Her hair was pulled back, her face clear of any makeup, her eyes ringed red and puffy in that way that suggested she had been crying. She stared vacantly across the room. The people who had surrounded her and her husband for the past seven years had never seen her like this. Even in private, she was always perfectly poised, immaculately coiffed, impeccably dressed, and inalterably in control. Now, however, she appeared to have been to hell and back. To see her like this, thought some of the longtime Clinton loyalists who had rushed back to the White House to help in weathering the worst crisis of her husband's presidency, it seemed as if someone had died.

When one of her husband's original political advisers, James Carville, arrived in the Solarium on the third floor of the White House, summoned back overnight from Brazil at her request, Hillary rushed over to him, clutched his hand, and sat him down next to her.

"You just have to help us get through this," she said. "I don't know how we can get through this."

Neither did anyone else. At that moment, on the afternoon of Monday, August 17, 1998, President Clinton was three floors below them, facing off against Independent Counsel Kenneth Starr in the Map Room of the White House and testifying via closed-circuit television to a federal grand jury about his relationship with a young former intern named Monica Samille Lewinsky and his efforts to cover it up during the sexual-harassment lawsuit filed against him by former Arkansas state clerk Paula Jones. Forced by incontrovertible DNA evidence, Clinton was admitting after seven months of adamant denials that he had fooled around with a woman less than half his age in a private hallway and cubbyhole just off the Oval Office, and he would have to tell the nation later that night. It was not an easy confession to make. Indeed, Clinton had not been able to bring himself to break the news to his own wife. Four nights before, he had sent his lawyer to pave the way for him.

It had to have been the longest walk of David E. Kendall's life, the journey that night, Thursday, August 13, to the residential part of the executive mansion where he had met with the first lady. Kendall, a fastidious yet tough-as-nails attorney from the blue-chip Washington law firm of Williams & Connolly, had represented both Clintons for five years now through every manner of alleged scandal, from Whitewater to Travelgate to Filegate, becoming one of their most trusted confidants. And so it fell to him at that critical moment to play emissary from husband to wife, to disclose the most awful secret of any marriage.

Something had obviously gone on between the president and Lewinsky, Kendall had told the first lady in his soft, understated way. The president was going to have to tell the grand jury about it. Only after Kendall laid the foundation did Clinton speak directly with his wife.

Over the weekend it became clear to others in the White House that the president was about to change his story, and reports citing unnamed sources began appearing in the press, first in the *New York Times* and later the *Washington Post*. Clinton's political advisers began preparing for the inevitable national television address he would have to give to explain himself. Mickey Kantor, a longtime friend who had served as his commerce secretary and now as occasional damage-control adviser, was pushing to have Clinton preempt Starr by addressing the nation on Sunday evening, the night before his grand jury appearance. The lawyers were horrified. A witness never spoke publicly before undergoing an interrogation under oath, they argued; that would only give the prosecution ammunition and possibly aggravate the grand jurors.

No, it had to be Monday night after the session, or perhaps the next morning, depending on how Clinton felt afterward. With the timing settled, the real question then came down to what should be said and how. Everyone agreed that Paul Begala, Carville's spirited and tart-tongued former partner who had come on board at the White House as a free-floating political adviser, would be in charge of putting together a speech for the president, even though no one had told him officially what Clinton would tell the grand jury. The consensus was that Begala would have the best feel for the delicate job. Begala solicited a draft from Robert Shrum, the longtime Kennedy family adviser and wordsmith, who faxed it over to the White House. In this version, Clinton would say, "I have fallen short of what you should expect from a president. I have failed my own religious faith and values. I have let too many people down. I take full responsibility for my actions—for hurting my wife and daughter, for hurting Monica Lewinsky and her family, for hurting friends and staff, and for hurting the country I love." While he would maintain that he "did nothing to obstruct this investigation," he would not mince words in saying he was sorry. "Finally, I also want to apologize to all of you, my fellow citizens," he would say. "I hope you can find it in your heart to accept that apology." That would be it. No rationalization. No nimble word games. And no mention of Starr.

As they studied the Shrum text, Begala and the other Clinton aides concluded that it would be too groveling. After all, Clinton was still the president and needed to avoid appearing weak to the nation's enemies. Neither Begala nor most of the other White House advisers working on the draft realized just how timely that concern was, not having been told about secret plans to launch air strikes within days against terrorists blamed for recent bombings of U.S. embassies in Africa.

Begala spent the weekend coming up with his own passages and phrases intended to have Clinton express his contrition without sacrificing his dignity or antagonizing Starr. In Begala's draft, the president would frankly acknowledge that he had misled the country, would take responsibility for his actions, and would pledge to spend the rest of his administration working on the issues the public cared about to regain the nation's trust. On Saturday night, Begala called up a fellow White House political adviser, Rahm Emanuel, at home and read him the latest draft. Emanuel agreed it was the way to go.

Others sent drafts too. Mark Mellman, a Democratic pollster who worked for many Democratic congressmen, was asked to sketch out some thoughts. Sidney Blumenthal, a fiercely partisan defender of the Clintons first as a journalist for *The New Yorker* and then as a member of their staff, faxed in versions from vacation in Europe that would have the president firmly denounce Starr's politically motivated witch-hunt. But the only draft that counted was the one the president scratched out in his own left-handed scrawl on a yellow legal pad over the weekend. On Monday morning, as Clinton was going through his final preparation session with his lawyers, Kantor arrived at a strategy meeting in the office of White House counsel Charles F. C. Ruff, clutching three pages of now-typed remarks, with more notes from Clinton in the margins.

"I've got what he wants to say," Kantor announced.

There was groaning around the room, where most of the president's political team had gathered, including Begala, Emanuel, Deputy Chief of Staff John D. Podesta, counselor Douglas B. Sosnik, and press secretary Michael D. McCurry. They were flabbergasted. Begala had his latest draft in his coat pocket. When had Clinton had time to write his own speech? Between the long hours of preparations with his lawyers, dealing with his own tortured family situation, and secretly overseeing plans for retaliation against terrorist Osama bin Laden, the president hardly had a lot of free moments. The group decided to have Begala go over the new draft, but it became clear immediately that it was too strident.

Across the building, Clinton was huddling in the Solarium with Kendall and his partner, Nicole K. Seligman, to go over one last time what he would tell the grand jury. Neither Chuck Ruff nor any of the other White House lawyers was allowed to attend because Starr had already shown that they did not have complete attorney-client privilege as lawyers for the government, so it was left entirely to the president's privately paid legal team. Knowing that Starr had a sample of his blood to compare with a semen stain on a navy blue Gap dress Lewinsky had saved, Clinton recognized he had no choice but to admit the obvious, but he refused to use the actual words. Starr's office had insisted on videotaping the session, ostensibly in case one of the grand jurors was absent, and Clinton had no doubt that the tape would ultimately find its way into public view. Any clip of him saying anything explicit, such as "She performed oral sex on me," would be played on television again and again, until it became so instilled in the minds of viewers that it would not only humiliate Clinton but become the single moment defining him in the history books.

The solution he and his lawyers came up with was a prepared statement with carefully chosen words that would make the confession as dignified as possible. Oral sex would be described simply as "inappropriate intimate contact." Phone sex would be called "inappropriate sexual banter." Everyone would know what he was saying.

Clinton and the lawyers also went over fourteen set pieces they had drafted—prepared mini-speeches ranging from four lines to four pages that he could deliver at opportune moments during the session. They knew, for example, that the prosecutors would surely ask the president if it was right or wrong to mislead the Jones lawyers during his civil deposition, and they had rehearsed an answer for him, saying that it was acceptable as long as he was trying to be "literally truthful." Normally, lawyers instruct clients to give short answers under oath, but in this case, Kendall and Seligman knew Clinton would never be able to tell his story for the camera unless he talked right over his inquisitors. Besides, having negotiated a strict four-hour limit to the questioning, the president's team figured he could filibuster long enough to eat up the clock.

The prep session with the lawyers was interrupted when the president's national security team arrived to brief him on another matter. The attorneys picked up their papers and left the room, unaware of what was so important. Once they were gone, National Security Adviser Samuel R. Berger gave Clinton the latest report on plans to bomb a suspected terrorist camp in Afghanistan and a suspected chemical-weapons facility in Sudan.

*   *   *

Around 12:30 P.M., Starr arrived at the White House, where he was met by Kendall, who pulled him aside for a private "walk in the woods." Kendall mentioned a weekend newspaper report suggesting that despite their long adversarial relationship, the president's lawyer actually had great respect for the special prosecutor.

"You know all those nice things I was quoted saying about you?" Kendall asked.

"Yes."

"I didn't say them."

"I didn't think so."

Kendall went on to tell Starr that the president would make a difficult admission to the grand jury that he did in fact have a relationship with Lewinsky but would not get into the specifics. Kendall warned the prosecutor not to push the matter with intrusive questions. "If you get into detail, I will fight you to the knife, both here and publicly," he vowed.

At 12:59 P.M., the president entered the ground-floor Map Room, where Franklin Delano Roosevelt had charted the progress of Allied forces during World War II and where the last map of troop locations that he saw in 1945 before his fateful trip to Warm Springs, Georgia, still hung on the wall more than a half century later. Waiting were Starr and six of his lawyers, a pair of technicians, a court reporter, and a Secret Service agent. Accompanying Clinton were Kendall, Seligman, and Ruff. At 1:03, the cameras were turned on and the oath administered.

From the start, Starr's deputies set a confrontational tone by stressing the importance of the oath and asking Clinton if he comprehended it—in effect challenging the president's basic capacity for honesty before his first answer.

"Do you understand that because you have sworn to tell the truth, the whole truth, and nothing but the truth, that if you were to lie or intentionally mislead the grand jury, you could be prosecuted for perjury and/or obstruction of justice?" asked deputy independent counsel Solomon L. Wisenberg.

"I believe that's correct," Clinton replied evenly.

Wisenberg pressed the point. "Could you please tell the grand jury what that oath means to you for today's testimony?"

"I have sworn an oath to tell the grand jury the truth and that's what I intend to do."

"You understand that it requires you to give the whole truth—that is, a complete answer to each question, sir?"

Clinton tried to remain calm. "I will answer each question as accurately and fully as I can."

The questioning was turned over to another deputy, Robert J. Bittman, who began by asking Clinton if he was ever physically intimate with Lewinsky. The president said he would read a statement, pulled out some paper from his pocket, and put on his reading glasses. The effect of the glasses, combined with the hair that had grayed considerably in office, made Clinton look like an aging man instead of the vital, vigorous leader who had first emerged on the national stage seven years earlier.

"When I was alone with Ms. Lewinsky on certain occasions in early 1996 and once in early 1997, I engaged in conduct that was wrong," he began, reading slowly and deliberately. "These encounters did not consist of sexual intercourse. They did not constitute sexual relations as I understood that term to be defined at my January 17, 1998, deposition. But they did involve inappropriate intimate contact. These inappropriate encounters ended, at my insistence, in early 1997. I also had occasional telephone conversations with Ms. Lewinsky that included inappropriate sexual banter. I regret that what began as a friendship came to include this conduct and I take full responsibility for my actions."

For Ruff, who as the chief lawyer for Clinton in his capacity as president had helped direct his defense for seven months, this was the first time he learned directly that his client had lied to all of them. Ruff had come to the White House the year before to cap a sterling legal career, having served as the final Watergate special prosecutor, U.S. attorney in Washington, chief lawyer for the city government, and defense counsel for such embattled Democrats as Senators John H. Glenn and Charles S. Robb. At fifty-eight, he had spent much of his adult life in a wheelchair after contracting a poliolike disease while teaching law in Africa. Yet never in his career had he been as hampered in representing a client; as a government lawyer without full attorney-client privilege, Ruff had been shut out of the recent grand jury preparations and therefore had never heard the truth from the president's mouth until just then. By this point, that was hardly a shock, but it meant that from now on, Ruff would always have to wonder if he was being lied to.

Undeterred by Kendall's warning, Starr and his prosecutors spent much of the afternoon deconstructing Clinton's opening statement and trying to pin down the president on exactly what he meant and how he could justify his testimony. During the Jones deposition, Clinton had testified he did not recall being alone with Lewinsky except for a few occasions when she brought him papers and the like. Now his first words were "when I was alone with Ms. Lewinsky." In the Jones deposition, he said he had no specific recollection of giving her gifts. Now he was well aware of all sorts of gifts and named them in great detail. In the Jones deposition, he had said he did not have "sexual relations" or a "sexual affair" with Lewinsky. Now he was admitting that they engaged in some sort of sex play without stating exactly what it was, in effect insisting that he did not actually have sexual relations with Lewinsky because he was merely a passive recipient of oral sex and never fondled her as she testified he did.

Clinton jousted with the Starr lawyers every step of the way, insisting that there was no legal inconsistency between his past statements and his new admission, that he had been technically accurate before and did not commit perjury. Wisenberg noted that Clinton allowed his attorney during the Jones deposition to assert that there "is absolutely no sex of any kind in any manner, shape, or form" between Clinton and Lewinsky.

That "was an utterly false statement. Is that correct?" Wisenberg asked.

"It depends on what the meaning of the word *is* is," Clinton responded. "If the—if he—if *is* means is and never has been, that is not—that is one thing. If it means there is none, that was a completely true statement." The president's lawyers winced. They believed he was being somewhat lighthearted about it, but recognized immediately that by quibbling over the tense of the verb, it would reinforce the public criticism of Clinton's slippery style with words.

Convinced the videotape would eventually be made public, Clinton resisted strenuous attempts by Starr's prosecutors to get him to elaborate on his admission, declining to describe his sexual activities with Lewinsky. But with his finger wagging and his eyes narrowed in anger, Clinton lashed out against both the Jones lawyers for their "bogus lawsuit" and the Starr team for trying to "criminalize my private life."

When they asked about his January 17 testimony in the Jones case, Clinton fell back on one of his fourteen prepared set pieces. "My goal in this deposition was to be truthful, but not particularly helpful," he said. "I did not wish to do the work of the Jones lawyers. I deplored what they were doing. I deplored the innocent people they were tormenting and traumatizing. I deplored their illegal leaking. I deplored the fact that they knew, once they knew our evidence, that this was a bogus lawsuit, and that because of the funding they had from my political enemies, they were putting ahead. I deplored it. But I was determined to walk through the minefield of this deposition without violating the law, and I believe I did." As for Starr, Clinton said resentfully, "We have seen this four-year, forty-million-dollar investigation come down to parsing the definition of sex." Never mind that it was Clinton doing the parsing.

While the president was in with Starr and his deputies, the rest of the White House was in a strange state of suspended animation. The waiting was killing everyone; little real work was getting done at the most senior levels. Soon after the grand jury session began, the electronic surveillance equipment that monitored the president's precise location at all times while in the White House showed that he had moved from the Map Room to the medical center. Some of his aides momentarily panicked. Was he all right? Doug Sosnik, the president's counselor and constant companion for most of the past two years, raced from the West Wing over to the residence to find out, only to discover that they had just taken a break and retreated to the medical unit because it was next to the Map Room and had a refrigerator filled with Diet Coke. All over the White House, televisions were tuned to CNN, where a surreal "game clock" in the corner of the screen showed the time elapsed during the grand jury session as if it were a football game. Joe Lockhart, the deputy press secretary, grew so angry that he started throwing things at the television and finally called up CNN correspondent John King to tell him the clock was inaccurate anyway because they had no idea how much time had been spent in breaks. Soon afterward, the clock disappeared from the screen. One small victory, at least.

The political team reconvened in Ruff's office, including Podesta, McCurry, Lockhart, Emanuel, and Begala. Mickey Kantor sauntered in and began delivering a pep talk. The president appreciated everything everyone had done, he announced. Nobody should worry that the president had committed perjury, he added before leaving again.

The other aides were stunned at the presumption. Lockhart was particularly furious. They had spent every waking moment fighting for this president, absorbing his private tirades and being lied to by both the boss and his lawyers. And now this guy from the outside professed to convey the president's feelings toward them? In their minds, Kantor was an enabler who encouraged Clinton's worst instincts and caused more damage than he contained. They had blamed him for spreading stories early in the scandal suggesting the president suffered from sexual addiction, and just in recent days they were certain despite his denials that he had been the one who had leaked news of Clinton's impending confession to the *New York Times*. "Fuck you," someone exclaimed as soon as the door closed behind Kantor. "Who the hell are you?" others piped in.

A more serious fight, though, was beginning to rage over the president's draft. The speech was supposed to be a straightforward admission and apology, but Clinton had written tough attacks on Starr into the text. That would undermine the message of contrition and merely set up a new confrontation. Throughout the rest of the afternoon, the president's advisers maneuvered over the language of the speech, with the political staff united against Kantor, who wandered in and out and professed to represent what Clinton really wanted.

After getting nowhere, Begala, Emanuel, and the others decided to go over Kantor's head. They rushed down the narrow staircase to the first floor of the West Wing and burst into the office of White House Chief of Staff Erskine Bowles, who had tried for seven months to keep out of the scandal-defense business. They were about to screw this up, the other aides told Bowles. He had to come upstairs and help. For once, Bowles agreed to get involved and immediately raced up to Ruff's office to find Kantor.

"How dare you?" Bowles demanded. "We're not going to use this crap!" Bowles was as fired up as few had ever seen the mild-mannered investment banker from North Carolina. But he made no more headway than anyone else had.

When the grand jury session finally ended at 6:25 P.M., Clinton gathered with his lawyers and a few other advisers in the medical unit. Carville was among those waiting for him, positioned there in an effort to have a friendly face greet him upon his emergence from the legal lion's den. The president seemed all right, tired but composed. Given all he had gone through, he did not appear especially worked up. If anything, the adrenaline was still pumping and he seemed relieved. The lawyers reviewed his testimony and tried to figure out if there was anything to clean up. Kendall was particularly aggravated that the Starr team had tried to extend the four-hour time limit while on camera, essentially playing to the grand jury. The president was frustrated that he had not been able to see the grand jurors because of the one-way closed-circuit hookup. He had wanted to take the measure of his audience for perhaps the most important performance of his life and yet could not.

At the moment, though, there was no time for postgame analysis. "Sorry to interrupt you guys," Doug Sosnik interjected, "but we need to make a decision about whether you should go on."

With only five minutes until the evening news began, they had to determine whether Clinton should address the nation that night. If he was going to, Mike McCurry wanted to alert the networks in time to get the announcement on their broadcasts. The expectations for a speech had grown all day in the media, and the White House aides felt they had little choice. Waiting until the next day, they feared, would be seen as a sign that the grand jury testimony went badly. Besides, Clinton was anxious to get on with his vacation to Martha's Vineyard and escape from Washington as soon as possible.

"Well, I feel fine," he said. "What do you guys think?"

"If you feel okay, then we'd probably prefer you go on," said Sosnik.

It was a go. But first, the lawyers said they wanted a chance to debrief their client in private and ushered him off to the Solarium, while Begala, Sosnik, and the other political aides returned to the West Wing to prepare. About a half hour later, Begala headed up to the Solarium to see where things stood.

Eventually 7:30 P.M. rolled around and the rest of the political aides still had not been called to come join the president and his legal team. For seven months, the lawyers had shut out the political advisers from the defense efforts, and now it looked as if it was happening again. They must be working on the speech by themselves, the political aides concluded.

"They fucked us," Sosnik exclaimed.

Podesta, Sosnik, Emanuel, and Carville rushed upstairs to the Solarium to discover the president and the first lady surrounded by his lawyers, prepared to go on national television with both barrels blasting at Starr. It was exactly what they were afraid of when Kantor had first told them there was another draft. Any attack on Starr would detract from the central message they thought the president should deliver—that he had misled the country, that he was wrong to do it, and that he was sorry.

"I was wrong. I have to apologize to the American people," the president agreed. "But this is outrageous what Starr has done. If I don't say that, no one else will. I can't just let this go."

"People aren't going to hang with you because you're opposed to Starr," Emanuel told the president. "They're going to hang with you because of what you're doing for them."

Reaching back to the first crucible many of those in the room had gone through together, Emanuel reminded Clinton of his famous speech the night of the New Hampshire primary in 1992 when he came back to place a strong second despite the Gennifer Flowers and Vietnam draft scandals. Clinton had told his audience that night, "The hits that I took in this election are nothing compared to the hits that the people of this state and this country are taking every day of their lives under this administration." That was the emphasis Clinton should remember now, Emanuel said—the people wanted to know their issues were more important to him than his own.

Everyone in the room felt the same way about Starr, Emanuel added. The speech was not wrong, but it was the wrong time and the wrong messenger. "You shouldn't do it. We'll do it."

Sosnik made the same point. "That's why God invented James Carville," he said, as Carville himself, the president's favorite attack dog, looked on.

But Clinton would not be moved. He raged that Starr and his henchmen were unfair to him, and he felt strongly that if it was left unsaid it would legitimize their actions. The front end of the speech, where he would express his regret, would give him room at the back end to lay out his grievances.

"I did wrong and so did he," Clinton huffed. "Damn it, somebody has to say these things. I don't care if I'm impeached, it's the right thing to do."

The debate raged on for some time. Kendall, still steaming from the way Starr had handled the grand jury session, justified an attack on the independent counsel's conduct because Clinton had to offer some reason why he did not tell the truth to the public for seven months. Harry Thomason, the president's Hollywood producer friend who had urged Clinton back in January to give a fateful finger-wagging denial ("I did not have sexual relations with that woman, Miss Lewinsky"), agreed that the president had every right to declare a zone of privacy in his speech. Kantor felt the president should be allowed to say what he truly felt and tried to fend off those who believed otherwise.

And then there was the first lady, who had by now covered up her hurt again to take on the role of field marshal for the defense. Hillary Clinton despised the prosecutor for once forcing her to testify before the Whitewater grand jury herself—in person at the courthouse, where it would be more publicly humiliating. At some point, the discussion boiled down to a one-on-one match between the first lady and Erskine Bowles. Never before could anyone remember Clinton ignoring Bowles's advice on a significant matter, but on this one the chief of staff was not getting through.

"This is crazy," Bowles said. "This is stupid and wrong." In his experience, Bowles said, he had found that the best thing to do after screwing up was just admit it and say you're sorry. Don't blame it on anybody else.

The room was crowded with so many would-be speechwriters that Kantor finally erupted in exasperation, "This is getting out of control!" he cried, pushing himself back from the table. "We'll never get this done!"

Podesta, Sosnik, and Emanuel decided to leave, hoping if they removed themselves, so would the lawyers. But the lawyers stayed and Begala was left on his own to keep fighting without help. By that time, the die was probably cast. Hillary Clinton had weighed in.

"Well, it's your speech," she told her husband sharply. "You should say what you want to say." Then she turned on her heel and walked out.

The debate was over. Clinton went upstairs to shower and change into a fresh dark suit with a sharp blue tie that he had worn at his first inauguration in 1993. He returned to the Map Room and sat down soberly, placing his palms on his knees, steeling himself. A technician complained the microphone needed to be higher on his lapel, so Begala walked over to move it. Harry Thomason and his wife, Linda Bloodworth-Thomason, positioned themselves in the room outside of camera range so they could cheer Clinton on during the broadcast. In a few moments, the cameras were turned on and the president addressed the nation:

"As you know, in a deposition in January, I was asked questions about my relationship with Monica Lewinsky. While my answers were legally accurate, I did not volunteer information. Indeed, I did have a relationship with Miss Lewinsky that was not appropriate. In fact, it was wrong. It constituted a critical lapse in judgment and a personal failure on my part for which I am solely and completely responsible. But I told the grand jury today and I say to you now that at no time did I ask anyone to lie, to hide or destroy evidence, or to take any other unlawful action.

"I know that my public comments and my silence about this matter gave a false impression. I misled people, including even my wife. I deeply regret that."

At this point, Clinton's tone shifted and his eyes narrowed again in that unmistakable sign of barely contained rage easily recognized by his aides. Any sense of remorse was gone. Now there was only deep-seated resentment. The questions about Lewinsky "were being asked in a politically inspired lawsuit, which has since been dismissed," he said. The independent counsel's investigation began with private business dealings and then "moved on to my staff and friends, then into my private life.

"This has gone on too long, cost too much, and hurt too many innocent people. Now, this matter is between me, the two people I love most—my wife and our daughter—and our God. I must put it right, and I am prepared to do whatever it takes to do so. Nothing is more important to me personally. But it is private, and I intend to reclaim my family life for my family. It's nobody's business but ours. Even presidents have private lives. It is time to stop the pursuit of personal destruction and the prying into private lives and get on with our national life."

In just four minutes, it was over. The rest of Clinton's staff watched from the Solarium, where chicken enchiladas were served. They looked around at each other with knowing expressions. The verdict was clear. It was a disaster.

"What do they expect me to do?" Clinton fumed when told about the negative television analysis. "Roll over and let Starr do this and just take it?"

An unfaithful president was hardly a new story. Grover Cleveland had faced charges of fathering an illegitimate child. Warren G. Harding engaged in regular sexual romps with Nan Britton in the same space just off the Oval Office that Bill Clinton would later find so convenient. Franklin D. Roosevelt had Lucy Mercer. Dwight D. Eisenhower was linked to Kay Summersby. John F. Kennedy fooled around with Marilyn Monroe, Judith Campbell Exner, and a host of others. Lyndon B. Johnson, ever insecure about the Kennedys, even boasted that he was far more of a philanderer than his predecessor, telling associates, "Why, I had more women by accident than he ever had by design."

None, however, had his private indiscretions so thoroughly and publicly excavated as Clinton had. A product of an era when the news media no longer covered up politicians' peccadilloes, Clinton had strayed so often and so flagrantly from his marriage vows while building his political career in Arkansas that he was talked out of his first run for the presidency in 1988 by aide Betsey Wright, who compiled a list of women and suggested he would suffer the same fate as Gary Hart had just months earlier. Four years later, Clinton launched his campaign for the 1992 presidential nomination by confessing to a roomful of reporters in Washington that he had caused problems in his marriage, only to discover that the tactic would not inoculate him once Gennifer Flowers had sold her story of a twelve-year affair to a tabloid. The next six years would produce a regular smorgasbord of tales from Clinton's past, each seemingly more sensational than the last, from the Arkansas state troopers who said they procured women for him to Paula Jones, who claimed he exposed himself to her and requested that she "kiss it." If rumors were to be believed, he had slept with movie stars, a Miss America, the wife of one of his ambassadors, the daughter of a former vice president, a woman on his White House staff, a judge he had appointed to the bench, the stewardesses from his campaign plane, and even prostitutes. It became almost impossible to separate the credible from the ridiculous, although the evidence suggested there was a mix of both.

All of which most of the American public had absorbed largely with indifference until January 21, 1998, when Monica Lewinsky became a household name and the political implosion predicted a decade earlier by Betsey Wright finally came to pass. Starr's investigators, having reached a dry well in searching for provable financial wrongdoing by the first couple, had now turned their attention to Clinton's attempts to cover up his extracurricular love life during legal proceedings spawned by Jones's sexual harassment lawsuit. For days following disclosure of Starr's investigation, even Clinton privately wondered whether his presidency was over. His indignant denials, false though they were, bought him the time he needed for the shock of a president fooling around with an intern to wear off, so that when he finally came around to admitting his deceit, the public had already processed the situation and come to terms with it.

But within the White House, a pallor had set in for seven months and virtually never lifted. The energy of the place was sapped, and top aides squirmed when forced to answer questions about their boss's sexual adventures. It was always clear in the West Wing who had an upcoming date with Starr's grand jury—they would disappear for long stretches to consult with lawyers, and if that were not enough of a clue, their faces always gave it away. Many senior White House officials harbored doubts, but let themselves be convinced that perhaps the president was really telling the truth, that he had "retired" from womanizing, as he once put it.

Beyond the staff, the president himself was never the same after the Lewinsky story broke. He and his aides went to great lengths to tout his ability to "compartmentalize"—to focus on his duties while putting concerns over scandal in "a box" to the side. And Clinton often demonstrated a remarkable ability to ignore his own political peril and concentrate on whatever policy issue might be presented to him. But much of that was for show as well, a poll-tested and focus-group-tested strategy to portray the president as engaged in his job and above the sleaze that obsessed others. In private, Clinton was consumed with the Starr investigation and its collateral damage, sometimes so preoccupied that he appeared lost during meetings. In the months leading up to his August grand jury testimony, aides would occasionally find him in the Oval Office absently moving things around on his desk or playing with the old campaign buttons he kept in the hallway leading to his private dining room. At one meeting with members of the Congressional Black Caucus, the president simply could not answer their questions—it fell to an aide to conduct the meeting while Clinton sat there apparently distracted by his woes. On another occasion, the head of the World Bank left a meeting with the president and later called a senior White House official to say, "It's like he isn't there."

Whatever esprit de corps had once existed in the White House likewise degenerated into political cannibalism, as political advisers intent on saving Clinton's administration were shut out—and sometimes even lied to—by the president's own lawyers, who insisted that secrecy was the best course for their client. "I'm going to kill Chuck," John Podesta used to grumble at moments of frustration with Ruff, the White House counsel. Joe Lockhart would storm out of strategy sessions, warning the lawyers, "If you guys aren't going to shoot straight, I'm going to stop coming to these meetings." Mike McCurry actually did stop coming; anytime he showed up, his colleagues knew it was so that he could yell at the attorneys for hiding critical information from him. On several occasions, McCurry threatened to quit if they kept deceiving him—once, early in the year when they misled him about whether they were using private investigators to research Clinton enemies and, more recently, when Ruff refused to tell him whether Starr had issued a subpoena for the president's testimony. McCurry's protests, though, made no difference. Even after the existence of the subpoena was finally confirmed, David Kendall misled him about whether the president's testimony would be transmitted live to the grand jury at the courthouse or merely videotaped.

Even within the legal team, there were subtle divisions, an "insane asylum of alliances," as one of the lawyers put it. Kendall and Seligman had been the never-say-die soldiers for the Clintons for years, while Ruff was an outsider more concerned about the impact on the White House for presidents to come. Where Ruff's relationship with the president and the first lady was strictly professional, two other lawyers ostensibly under his command, Bruce R. Lindsey and Cheryl D. Mills, had personal connections to the first couple that gave them authority beyond their rank as deputy counsels. Lindsey had been Clinton's friend and consigliere since their Arkansas days, while Mills had earned their loyalty through six years of fiercely defending their interests. Then there were the other outside lawyers widely disliked by the core legal team—Robert S. Bennett, the blustery lead counsel on the Jones case, who scorned Kendall (and vice versa), and Kantor, a longtime Clinton friend whose status as a lawyer on the case appeared designed mainly to cloak him with the protection of attorney-client privilege so the president could have someone to speak with in confidence.

The revelation that the president really had lied—and had sent aides out to repeat his lies on television and to the grand jury—further embittered a demoralized staff. While more jaded advisers such as Podesta and Rahm Emanuel took it in stride, others were deeply hurt. Paul Begala, who had moved from Texas to Washington to help put together a promising second term, was devastated to learn that Clinton had deceived him and let him publicly lie on the president's behalf. Begala took his politics personally and sank into a deep depression, to the point where he vowed never to appear on television again defending the president—and began thinking about whether he should resign altogether. McCurry had never considered himself close to the first family the way Begala did, but he had come into his job as the public face of the Clinton White House with a long career of credibility in Washington and was determined not to sacrifice all that by becoming the Ron Ziegler of his era. McCurry suspected from the beginning that Clinton was not telling the truth, and the press secretary went out of his way to parse his briefings with reporters to leave himself an escape hatch later should his suspicions be borne out—as they ultimately were.

Outside of the Clinton family, though, perhaps no one was more upset than Erskine Bowles. A millionaire investment banker from Charlotte, North Carolina, Bowles was the straight man in the Clinton White House, an upright, no-nonsense administrator who helped banish the political chaos that had dominated the first-term administration. Tall and lanky with a lean, bespectacled, almost owlish face and a lilting Carolinian accent, the fifty-three-year-old Bowles had become the president's alter ego in his second term, mending his bruised relations with the Republican Congress and keeping him company on the golf course. Clinton had leaned heavily on him to take the job in the first place and then to stay when he was itching to leave.

Clinton and Bowles had never met before the 1992 presidential campaign, but they forged a quick and deep bond. Both sons of the New South around the same age, they shared a passion for golf and for bringing the Democratic Party back to the political center. For Bowles, the clincher came in a car ride after a fund-raiser when then-candidate Clinton noticed that something seemed to be wrong. Bowles told him his son, Sam, had had a diabetic seizure that morning, and Bowles was angry at President George Bush for vetoing legislation allowing fetal-tissue research that some believed might find a cure. After becoming president, Clinton repealed the research ban in one of his first acts and gave Bowles the pen used to sign the executive order.

While his own father had once run unsuccessfully for governor of North Carolina, Bowles had never served in government, and yet he abandoned the private sector to come to Washington to work for his new friend, first as head of the Small Business Administration and later as deputy White House chief of staff. He returned home in December 1995, but kept helping out where he could, finding a place in Wyoming for the Clintons to vacation and even handling the delicate assignment of nudging Dick Morris out of the 1996 reelection campaign when reports surfaced about the political consultant's illicit relationship with a $200-an-hour prostitute. After the 1996 election, Clinton prevailed on a reluctant Bowles to come back to the White House, but only with the understanding that it would be a short-term venture. Bowles the businessman found the brittle, scandal-obsessed Washington distasteful and sometimes disorienting, his antipathy showcased in a *New Yorker* cartoon he posted on the wall of his West Wing office. In it, a man roasting in the fires of hell commented, "On the other hand, it's great to be out of Washington."

Yet as the months went by in 1997, the White House enjoyed more policy successes—and Bowles enjoyed the job more. A fiscal conservative who unlike his White House colleagues got along well with House Speaker Newt Gingrich and Senate Majority Leader Trent Lott, Bowles had made balancing the budget his central political passion and within a few months of his return to Washington had worked out a deal with congressional Republicans to erase the federal government's red ink for the first time since man first walked on the moon some three decades earlier. The president wanted Bowles to stay, and in December 1997, returning on *Air Force One* from an uplifting thirty-six-hour Christmas-season visit to Bosnia, Clinton and the first lady pressed their case. Whitewater and other scandals seemed to have receded. Now it was time for a fresh beginning, to turn the second term into a season of real progress.

Bowles returned to Washington from Sarajevo invigorated and dove into the policymaking process that led up to each year's State of the Union address. He was confident he could persuade Congress to pass free-trade legislation known as fast-track, and the administration's domestic and economic gurus had dreamed up a series of exciting ventures, including expanding Medicare for early retirees and providing child care assistance for hard-pressed young parents. With the budget balanced, Bowles became increasingly determined to use the rare moment of opportunity to fix the long-term generational problems of Social Security and Medicare. And with Congress out of town on recess, the White House seized the agenda by rolling out these proposals one at a time in a carefully orchestrated campaign of announcements and media leaks in advance of the formal unveiling in the State of the Union speech.

In a fit of optimism, Bowles told Clinton in mid-January that he would stay on as chief of staff.

Less than a week later, the Monica Lewinsky story broke.

Bowles had known the Paula Jones case still lurked out there. Indeed, he had been the first top aide to see the president when he returned to the White House from the deposition on January 17, 1998. Clinton walked straight from his limousine into the Oval Office to confer with Bowles about an Asian economic crisis. The president seemed fine. But the first warning sign came a few hours later when Clinton called Bowles and abruptly canceled plans for the two to go out for the evening with their wives. That night, Clinton, worried about the extensive questioning about Lewinsky during the deposition, called his secretary, Betty Currie, at home and asked her to come to the office the next day so that they could compare their stories. When the Lewinsky story showed up in the *Washington Post* four days later, Clinton was quick to reassure Bowles with a lie. "Erskine," he told his chief of staff, "I want you to know that this story is not true."

Bowles had to believe him. It was inconceivable that Clinton had really done this. If Bowles did not accept Clinton's word, there was no way he could still work for him. And yet colleagues could see that Bowles was unnerved. Usually an unflappable manager, Bowles liked to tell people that he always tried to stay even-tempered—at, say, 55 on an imaginary scale of 100. But he had allowed himself to go up to 75 in the exciting policy-driven days of early January and quickly plummeted to 35 or lower in the aftermath of the allegations about Lewinsky. On the day the story broke, Bill Richardson, then the ambassador to the United Nations, called Bowles because he had offered Lewinsky a job the previous fall at the indirect behest of the president. Richardson planned to disclose publicly what had happened, he said, and started to explain to Bowles. "I don't want to know a fucking thing about it!" Bowles interrupted. "Don't tell me about it!" Three days later, during a meeting with other top aides in his office on Saturday, January 24, to plot damage control, Bowles grew sickened at the discussion of the situation. "I think I'm going to throw up," he said, and abruptly bolted out of the room, never to return to the meeting. Three days after that, he accompanied the president to Capitol Hill for the State of the Union address, the moment Bowles had once anticipated so eagerly. "When I walk down that aisle, I'm going to be smiling," he told his wife beforehand. "But I'm going to be dying inside. Dying."

For the next seven months, Bowles refused to get involved in the political effort to save the president, almost as if he would not let himself even acknowledge the allegations—or the possibility that they could be true. Other officials would find Bowles waiting with the secretaries outside the Oval Office while Clinton consulted inside with his political team about the investigation. Bowles would not even go in the room. If he got drawn into it, he explained to those who asked him to step in, then how could the White House get anything else done?

By late summer, there was no choice. Bowles had been on vacation in Scotland during the crazed days leading up to the president's grand jury session and returned to Washington only the night before, Sunday, August 16, making a late appearance at the office to get up to speed. There really was a dress, he was told. Apparently, Clinton's DNA was on it. The president was changing his story.

Bowles was distraught. Clinton had lied to him, lied to his face. He had sent him to the grand jury with that lie. Bowles had sometimes been described in the media as the president's best friend—not just his best friend in the White House, but best friend, period—and yet clearly he did not even really know the man. The man he thought he knew—the voracious reader who devoured information before making a considered decision, the caring leader who saw hard-luck stories in the papers and asked aides to help out people in distress without disclosing his role, the politician with the vision to imagine things his staff could not—was not in fact the whole picture. Everyone who knew Bowles saw that he was taking the betrayal hard.

At the White House the morning of the grand jury appearance, though, Bowles did his best to hide it. As he opened the day's 7:30 A.M. staff meeting, he told the president's senior advisers to stay focused on their work and ignore the obvious distractions swirling around them this day. Repeating an aphorism imparted to him during childhood by his father, Bowles reminded the gathering, "It's easy to be there for someone when they're up, but it's the good ones who are there when you're down."

Thomas A. Daschle was driving along a wide-open highway in the middle of nowhere in South Dakota later the same day when the car phone rang. It was Bowles, calling from Washington.

Can you get to a hard line? Bowles asked.

Daschle told him he was still quite some distance from the nearest small town with a pay phone. He would have to try calling back later, around 4 P.M.

Daschle knew without asking what the call was about. As the Senate minority leader, Daschle was the president's chief liaison to the Democrats there, and he had followed the developments in the Lewinsky investigation carefully. Daschle knew that Clinton was testifying before Starr's grand jury. If it played out to its seemingly extreme conclusion, Daschle realized he could be faced with the prospect of a Senate trial on whether Clinton should be removed from office. At four o'clock, he dialed the White House and was put through to Bowles, who asked where he was. Daschle told him and mentioned that he had stopped for an ice cream malt.

"Right now," Bowles sighed, "I'd give you a million dollars to be there drinking that malt."

The chief of staff filled in Daschle on what the president was telling the grand jury and the plans for a late-evening speech to the nation. Daschle thanked Bowles for the heads up and moved on to a hotel, where a few hours later he found himself in front of the television watching as the president admitted he had "misled people, including even my wife," and went on to decry investigators for "prying into personal lives." Daschle called his own wife to gauge her impression and to share his—intense disappointment, both with the substance of the president's message and the manner of its delivery.

Like Daschle, nearly every member of Congress was out of town for the summer recess, watching television and digesting the stunning developments in isolation from each other. Yet even without the Capitol Hill echo chamber, the reaction among many of them was strikingly similar. Senator Orrin G. Hatch, a Utah Republican who had been publicly promising the president that the nation would forgive him if only he confessed all, sat in a television studio watching on a monitor. By the time it was over, he was boiling. "What a jerk!" Hatch exclaimed in frustration. House Minority Leader Dick Gephardt was in Paris, although his staff was refusing to tell clamoring TV bookers where in Europe he was, lest they track him down. When he heard the news the next morning, the Missouri Democrat with the Boy Scout sensibilities could barely contain his disgust and grimly realized that it would soon fall to him to decide whether to try to rescue the president or pressure him to leave for the good of the party and the nation. Senator Joseph I. Lieberman was at a country club in Westchester County near New York City, attending a wedding. Ducking out to search for a television, he found an accommodating waiter who led him outside into the wet darkness and across the street to his own basement apartment so the Connecticut Democrat could watch with his wife. Lieberman immediately thought Clinton's tone was wrong and unconvincing; the more he thought about it as the night wore on, the angrier he grew.

Lawmakers who had been prepared to give Clinton the benefit of the doubt such as Hatch, Gephardt, and Lieberman found themselves bitterly discouraged at his response. In the Capitol office of House Majority Whip Tom DeLay, however, there was never any question of forgiveness. He did not believe for a second that Clinton was genuinely repenting; the president was only confessing because he had been caught. The DNA had forced his hand. For months, DeLay had been denouncing Clinton as a "sexual predator" and accusing him of providing only "the spin, the whole spin, and nothing but the spin." This then, finally, was the moment DeLay had waited for, the moment when Clinton would stand revealed as the liar he always was. He had lied about Gennifer Flowers, about the draft, about smoking marijuana. He had lied to DeLay and other Republicans during the budget battle that led to the shutdown of the federal government in 1995. And now at last was DeLay's chance to make him pay.

It was the waiting that was killing them now. At 5:44 P.M. that Monday, DeLay's policy director, Tony C. Rudy, out in California for the congressional recess, sent an E-mail to press secretary Michael P. Scanlon back in Washington to find out what was happening with Clinton at the grand jury.

"still no word?" he wrote in that casual internal E-mail style in which capitalization, precise spelling, and proper grammar were optional.

"Hes going to admit it," Scanlon wrote back. "the big q is on what level— I still say we need to attack!"

Rudy agreed. "we need to force dems to distance themselves from theliar," he replied. "He looked into americas eyes and lied."

"God bless you Tony Rudy—Are we the only ones with political instincts—This whole thing about not kicking someone when they are down is BS—Not only do you kick him—you kick him until he passes out—then beat him over the head with a baseball bat—then roll him up in an old rug— and throw him off a cliff into the pound surf below!!!!!"

CHAPTER TWO

"You're a damn,
damn, damn fool"

Tom DeLay set about finding a baseball bat and an old rug the next day. After watching the president's speech at his home in northern Virginia outside Washington, DeLay stopped by the Capitol briefly on the morning of Tuesday, August 18, before flying to California for a campaign swing. He had made no public comment the night before on the advice of his press secretary, Mike Scanlon, who had predicted that Clinton the masterful public performer would never hurt himself with a nationally televised speech and so it could be risky to go after him on the same evening. DeLay wasted little time reminding his young aide of that advice.

"He'll never screw up, right, Scanlon?" DeLay said mockingly.

DeLay's reaction to the speech was visceral. As he saw it, attacking Ken Starr was a disgusting move. The tone, the manner, the sense of arrogance, all suggested a man trying to get away with something. DeLay told aides that when he had served in the Texas legislature, if someone lied, he would be ostracized by his own party; in Washington, it seemed, you could lie with impunity and get away with it. DeLay resolved not to let Clinton get away with it. For months, he had held himself back, taking occasional potshots but thinking someone else would emerge to take the lead. By now, though, it seemed clear no one else would. Senate Majority Leader Trent Lott was too restrained, House Majority Leader Dick Armey too weak within his own caucus, House Judiciary Committee chairman Henry J. Hyde too judicious. Even the outspoken Newt Gingrich, who had risen to political stardom by attacking the ethics of then-Speaker Jim Wright, appeared to waffle on how aggressively to press the case against Clinton, lurching back and forth without warning.

By the time his plane landed that afternoon, DeLay had figured out what he wanted to do. He called back to Washington and set up a conference call with his top aides. His staff, like most others, was scattered around the country, many on vacation, but DeLay ordered them to get back to Washington right away. From this day forward, he said, they were going to make it their mission to drive Clinton from office. Not just to impeach him, but to force him to resign. That had to be the goal, because DeLay knew that removal by Congress was improbable at best so long as Democrats controlled more than the thirty-four votes necessary to block the two-thirds majority required for conviction in the Senate.

"This is going to be the most important thing I do in my political career, and I want all of you to dedicate yourselves to it or leave," he told his staff. "As of today, I want a war room. I want a communications strategy. I want a political strategy. I want you to work day and night."

DeLay's pronouncement was greeted with some trepidation within his inner circle. Some DeLay advisers, including Congressman Bill Paxon, a boyish New York Republican and onetime rising star, had been warning him to keep a low profile, lest he find himself the latest critic destroyed by Clinton. But others, including Scanlon and Tony Rudy, encouraged DeLay. If they were going to wage war, they wanted to do it with no holding back. By the end of the day, DeLay had thrown down the gauntlet in public, issuing a statement calling on Clinton to step down.

"For the good of the country, and to put this scandal behind us, the president should resign," DeLay said. "It is bad enough that our president is guilty of having an extramarital sexual relationship with one of his young interns. But it is much more damaging that this president looked the American people in the eye and knowingly lied to us."

DeLay convened a conference call of the House Republican leadership to inform them of his decision to go after Clinton. At the beginning of the call, Gingrich opposed the idea, but by the end, he had flipped and agreed it was the right thing to do, effectively giving DeLay the green light. The decision put the pugnacious fifty-one-year-old congressman from Sugar Land, Texas, on a collision course with the world's most powerful man and guaranteed that the issue would not be brushed aside or finessed with a deal, at least not if he could help it. Born in Laredo, Texas, the son of an oil-drilling contractor who was none too gentle with him, DeLay grew accustomed to rough environments early in life. He became a pest exterminator in Houston, a career choice that became something of a caricature in his later political life—so much so that he chose not to list it on his official biography posted on his Web site, instead simply referring to himself as the onetime owner of "a small business." After a stint in the Texas legislature, DeLay first won his seat in Congress in 1984 and quickly built a reputation for a fiercely conservative, bulldog style that earned him the nickname The Hammer. In 1994 he ran for majority whip, the number-three position in the House, in charge of lining up votes for the Speaker, beating out Gingrich's candidate for the job.

Three years later, DeLay met with conservatives plotting to overthrow Gingrich, but when the coup failed, he acknowledged his role and apologized, saving his job.

DeLay and his staff enjoyed promoting stories about his toughness, a little myth-building that helped increase his influence (he kept a bullwhip prominently on display in his office, near his copy of the Ten Commandments). But The Hammer had secured his place in the House Republican leadership by assiduously catering to all of its members, including moderates and liberals. He turned his office into a full-service constituent center for congressmen, from making sure they got pork-barrel projects to laying out barbecue chicken for them during late-evening sessions. DeLay understood better than most how to play the inside game.

While DeLay hit the television circuit to attack Clinton, his staff returned to Washington to set up the nucleus of an organization designed to oust the president. In a conference room in the Capitol, they created a series of teams, one devoted to communications, another to research, and a third to member services. As they brainstormed, they decided to become the clearinghouse of impeachment for the party, flooding House Republicans with information and providing a central booking agency for members who shared DeLay's conviction and were willing to go public with calls for Clinton to resign. They would put together a list of E-mail addresses and phone numbers to blast-fax statements, while sending two hundred talk-radio shows names of members advocating resignation. A "message of the day" would be sent to every Republican member's office to keep up the pressure. Sample press releases would be written for other congressmen to release in their own names. Their research staff would comb through archives on the Nixon impeachment to figure out how it worked—including everything they could find about young Hillary Rodham's role as a junior lawyer on the staff of the House Judiciary Committee during Watergate, right down to the address of her apartment and details such as her Illinois driver's license and Arkansas bar membership. With Democrats already complaining about the possible cost of an impeachment inquiry, DeLay's aides decided to search for any travel vouchers or other receipts showing expenses by the future first lady during Watergate, although they would quickly find those still under seal.

For all this effort, they would come up with a name. They would call it The Campaign.

"We've got that walk to the helicopter," Doug Sosnik noted. "How are we going to handle it?"

It was the Day After, Tuesday, August 18, and the Clinton White House was suffering a political hangover of the worst kind. Clinton's demoralized political advisers gathered in the morning to plot the images of the day—a strangely comforting ritual. The main event was the first family's departure for Martha's Vineyard, a moment that would be thoroughly scrutinized for any hints about the condition of their marriage. To get to the resort island, the president and first lady would have to travel together by air force jet. To get to Andrews Air Force Base, they would have to travel together by marine helicopter. To get to the helicopter, they would have to stroll across the South Lawn.

Scores of cameras would be waiting for that walk. Usually, the president's aides choreographed every detail of such an event—make sure to put your arm around her, wave to the crowd, play with the dog, whatever. Nothing was left to chance. But on this day none of the aides could bring himself to formulate a proposal, let alone bring it to the president or the first lady. It would be inhuman.

When the family emerged from the Diplomatic Entrance and headed for *Marine One,* the first lady glared straight ahead, her face worn and wounded, refusing to acknowledge her husband's presence and not even bothering with her customary public pretense of nonchalance. The president, holding the blue leash for Buddy, his chocolate Labrador retriever, in his right hand, managed a wan smile for the crowd. It fell to their eighteen-year-old daughter, Chelsea, to provide the image of the day. Positioning herself between her parents, she reached out to grab her father's left hand and her mother's right hand. There was the best picture the White House aides could have wanted but did not for once try to stage—Chelsea as the human bridge, holding her parents together at perhaps the most cataclysmic moment of their twenty-three-year marriage.

When they reached the helicopter, the president reached out to hold the first lady's right elbow as she climbed the stairs, only to have her brush past him unassisted. The president boarded behind her and they buckled in for the short flight to Andrews. No first family can vacation entirely alone, but the entourage of senior officials had been kept to a bare minimum—Doug Sosnik, Mike McCurry, and Capricia Marshall, the White House social secretary and close confidant of both Hillary and Chelsea. As the chopper blades beat the air and the green-and-white aircraft launched itself into the sky, the cabin was dominated by an awkward silence. McCurry tried a little light banter about Martha's Vineyard to ease the tension, and Sosnik joined in the strained chitchat, talking about the sights and activities on the island.

Once they arrived at Andrews, the group boarded a twin-engine DC-9, a backup version of *Air Force One* used whenever the president flew someplace with a short runway that could not accommodate the regular fully loaded Boeing 747. The president settled in at a small table with Sosnik and

McCurry, while Hillary and Chelsea sat behind them, talking quietly between themselves. As the plane soared northeast, the first lady drifted off to sleep while the president read *The General,* a military thriller by Patrick A. Davis, and worked on the *New York Times* crossword. Suddenly Clinton was laughing and showed McCurry the clue for 46 down: four letters meaning "meal for the humble."

The answer: "crow."

"Here's one that's appropriate for today," Clinton joked.

The painful silence between the president and first lady convinced McCurry that they had yet to deal with the obvious threat to their marriage. While others, including even Sosnik, were still unaware of the impending military strikes on Afghanistan and Sudan, Hillary Clinton knew what was coming, and that had been one more thing inhibiting an extended, intimate discussion. Their relationship would have to wait until the immediate crisis passed. But for all her anger, Hillary did call her press secretary, Marsha Berry, before leaving the White House to authorize a statement intended to quiet a little of the clamor: "Clearly, this is not the best day in Mrs. Clinton's life. This is a time that she relies on her strong religious faith. She's committed to her marriage and loves her husband and daughter very much and believes in the president, and her love for him is compassionate and steadfast. She clearly is uncomfortable with her personal life being made so public but is looking forward to going on vacation with her family and having some family time together." Nowhere did the first lady mention the seething rage she felt at her husband's betrayal or her own public humiliation.

When the plane touched down on the island around 5:15 P.M., a throng of several hundred friends and supporters waited to cheer them up, including Vernon E. Jordan Jr., the Washington power lawyer who had gotten ensnared in the scandal by helping Lewinsky find a New York job and a lawyer to draft her false affidavit denying a sexual relationship with the president. Jordan gave each member of the first family a tight bear hug as soon as they reached the tarmac. Chelsea was delighted to find some of her college friends from Stanford University on the runway, realizing it meant she would not have to spend the entire vacation with her mother and father, and she jumped out in front of her parents to work the receiving line like an old pro.

The chill Clinton would feel over the next few days came not just from his wife but from much of the Democratic establishment. While polls showed the public approved of his speech, it had clearly bombed inside the Beltway, even with his own party. Some of the most senior and respected Democrats in Washington were privately livid. While the president was winging his way to Martha's Vineyard, one Democratic congressman, Paul McHale, a former marine who had served in the Persian Gulf War and proudly displayed a military saber on his wall, termed Clinton's affair "morally repugnant" and called on him to resign. No one at the White House was worried about a backbencher like McHale, but they were instantly petrified about what reaction he might set off. Doug Sosnik had told Clinton as far back as February that his fate was in the hands of congressional Democrats. Drawing on the lessons of Watergate, Sosnik stressed that Richard Nixon was forced out of office not by Democrats but by fellow Republicans when they concluded he was guilty and could not survive. Similarly, Sosnik told Clinton, "Republicans are never going to be able to remove you, but Democrats can."

While the House would be the first stop for any impeachment drive, the White House team was more worried about the Senate, where the members were more independent-minded and more readily able to build momentum for resignation. Sosnik, John Podesta, and the others on Clinton's political team had worked for the Senate Democrats, and they divided up the list to call each of the forty-five members to identify who would fight for the president, who was soft, and who could bolt. Their canvass showed that the president was in far more trouble than even the media suspected. At least a dozen Democratic senators appeared on the verge of abandoning the president, including Robert C. Byrd, Joe Lieberman, Bob Graham, Bob Kerrey, Daniel Patrick Moynihan, Richard Bryan, Dianne Feinstein, Ernest F. "Fritz" Hollings, and Russell D. Feingold. Feinstein had stood in the Roosevelt Room on that day in January when Clinton had denied having sex with "that woman," and she felt personally betrayed. "My trust in his credibility has been badly shattered," Feinstein said publicly the day Clinton left on vacation. Privately, she refused to take his phone calls. Even Tom Daschle, the even-tempered leader of the Senate Democrats, was deeply angry. When White House aides called his office to suggest that Clinton talk with Daschle, they were told that the minority leader was not in a frame of mind to take his call. It would be days before Daschle would finally agree to speak with him.

Clinton's problems on Capitol Hill were exacerbated by his long history of rocky relations with congressional Democrats. Perhaps if they had been closer to him, they might have been more willing to rally to his defense. But Democrats in Congress did not trust their president much more than the Republicans did. From the start, they had learned the hard way to watch what Clinton did, not what he said. In the early days of his presidency, he had convinced House Democrats to take the political risk of voting for a highly controversial energy tax as part of his budget plan, then, when the issue moved over to the Senate, he reversed himself and abandoned the so-called BTU tax—and his House allies. As they saw it, he cost them their majority, as Republicans, led by Newt Gingrich, roared into the 1994 midterm elections, captured the Senate, and ended forty years of Democratic control of the

House. They watched with exasperation as Clinton cut deals with Republicans over welfare reform, trade agreements, and the budget, often leaving Hill Democrats out of the picture. And then in the ultimate insult, Clinton on the advice of consultant Dick Morris cemented his reelection in 1996 through a "triangulation" strategy designed to set him apart from both Republicans and congressional Democrats.

Now Clinton could no longer afford to keep his distance from his party. He needed them to come to his rescue. But they were wondering whether *they* should keep their distance from *him.*

It was a question Mike McCurry had never thought he would have to ask the president's personal physician, but there he was on the phone with Dr. E. Connie Mariano: Is the president taking any drugs to suppress his sexual appetite?

The answer came back no. McCurry realized how intrusive this sounded, but the press was asking and he had to be informed before answering. Over the years, the White House had found itself disclosing even the most minor of ailments or treatments because the president's health was a matter of public policy; there could be no legitimate privacy argument anymore. How about any other medications? McCurry asked Mariano. Was anyone treating Clinton for stress or providing marriage therapy?

"We have not and I don't believe any is indicated," Mariano answered. The doctor explained that she treated her patient, not the man she read about in the newspaper. While the White House kept psychiatrists on its list of on-call medical professionals, Mariano said she felt Clinton had plenty of people to vent to and that loving relatives, supportive pastors, and friends were the best type of treatment.

Bill and Hillary Clinton, though, were essentially not talking in the Oyster Pond compound they had borrowed from a Boston developer. The president was left to take long walks on the beach alone with Buddy to contemplate his predicament. On Wednesday, August 19, their second day of "vacation," he celebrated his fifty-second birthday with a small dinner of barbecued chicken and island corn at the Chilmark farm where Vernon Jordan was staying, but then after returning to the compound around 11:30 P.M., he picked up the secure phone installed especially for his use and stayed up until 3 A.M. consulting with aides and military advisers about the upcoming strike against two sites linked to Saudi terrorist Osama bin Laden. By the time Clinton hung up, the missiles were scheduled to slam into their targets in just twelve hours.

The next day, Thursday, August 20, McCurry was in the middle of another briefing where reporters were quizzing him about the state of the presidential marriage when he was handed a note saying Clinton was on his way over to the Martha's Vineyard school that had been converted into a press center. Abruptly interrupting an answer about Lewinsky, who was reappearing at the grand jury that day to contradict Clinton's testimony, McCurry disclosed that the president would arrive any moment to make an announcement about national security and would then return immediately to Washington—setting the room abuzz with speculation about the surprise Clinton had in store. Resignation? Divorce? McCurry had said "national security," but few paid attention.

A few minutes later, at 1:55 P.M., Clinton whisked into the school gymnasium wearing a suit and a solemn expression. "Good afternoon. Today I ordered our armed forces to strike at terrorist-related facilities in Afghanistan and Sudan because of the threat they present to our national security." Three minutes later, he marched back out to head for his plane and Washington, where he could oversee the operation. Clinton had no genuine national-security reason to leave the island, as the White House had set up all the communications equipment he would need to monitor activities and talk with foreign leaders. But Clinton decided it would look more presidential to be in the Oval Office at such a moment—and if it provided a brief escape from his domestic turmoil, so be it.

Just like that, Clinton had changed the subject. He was the commander in chief again, leading the nation against embassy-bombing Middle Eastern terrorists, not the weak-willed husband who was putting the country through a national soap opera because of his personal failings. Administration officials argued they had no choice about when to act because the leaders of bin Laden's organization were gathering that day at the camp in Afghanistan hit by missiles, a rare opportunity to strike at the core of a major terrorist organization. Newt Gingrich, Dick Armey, and Trent Lott rallied behind the president and praised his decision as justified. Yet the timing was so convenient that it drew immediate comparisons to *Wag the Dog,* a Robert De Niro–Dustin Hoffman movie about a president who waged a fake war to distract attention from a sex scandal. "There's an obvious issue that will be raised internationally as to whether there is any diversionary motivation," opined Senator Arlen Specter, a Republican from Pennsylvania. If there was any diversionary motivation, though, it did not work. The president returned to Martha's Vineyard the next day to face the rest of his two-week sentence in purgatory with his wronged wife.

Dick Gephardt had mostly kept quiet in public about the president's admission for more than a week, but now he had no choice. Having returned from Europe, he was scheduled to embark on a three-day campaign swing for fellow Democrats running for the House, and a handful of national political reporters had already been invited to join him long before Clinton's grand jury appearance. Gephardt could not cancel and could not avoid being asked about the hottest political issue in the country.

Gephardt had never been close to Clinton. The son of a milk-truck driver, the fifty-seven-year-old congressman had grown up on the south side of St. Louis and started his political career as a new-breed leader who had broken with old Democratic orthodoxies. After a stint as a city alderman, he won election to Congress in 1976 as an ardent opponent of abortion and a skeptic about the value of new government programs. In 1981, he voted for Ronald Reagan's tax cuts. As he prepared to mount his own bid for president in 1988 in a field that included then-senator Al Gore, though, Gephardt's political center shifted to the left, and he embraced abortion rights and waged a populist crusade on foreign trade. After winning the Iowa caucuses, Gephardt stumbled in New Hampshire and collapsed on Super Tuesday, but when he returned to the Capitol, impressed colleagues rewarded him with the job of House majority leader.

When Clinton arrived in Washington four years later, the new president from Arkansas never bothered to woo the second-highest-ranking Democrat in the House. Gephardt refused to support Clinton's drive to pass the North American Free Trade Agreement (NAFTA) early in his presidency, setting the course for a relationship that would remain distant at best. With Gephardt now thinking of running for president in 2000 against Clinton's loyal lieutenant Vice President Gore, tensions with the White House had only increased. Indeed, the month before the Lewinsky story broke, Gephardt had tested out a campaign speech that implicitly criticized the small-bore politics of the Clinton-Gore team by calling for a party "where principles trump tactics" and that created "a movement for change and not a money machine." Infuriated White House aides retaliated by boycotting a meeting with Gephardt and openly attacking him in the press for "his flip-flops on multiple issues."

So by the time Lewinsky arrived on the scene, there was no reservoir of good will between the two men. Although now a leader of liberals, Gephardt was still something of a conservative "with a small *c*," as one ally put it, when it came to personal behavior and was genuinely offended by Clinton's conduct. Added to that, Gephardt had been working tirelessly to close the gap with the Republicans in the midterm 1998 elections, now just ten weeks away, only to find his labors undermined by a president who could not keep his pants on.

The day before embarking on the campaign swing, Gephardt spent hours on telephone conference calls, listening to other Democratic congressmen vent their frustration at the president and urging them not to react too precipitously. His members were unsatisfied by the president's public apologies and were petrified about what next sensational disclosure might be around the corner once Starr delivered a report to Congress. "Members should feel free to disavow the president and his actions," Gephardt told some of the nervous Democratic congressmen. Huddling with his strategists, Gephardt then tried to figure out what to say when he was asked about Clinton's conduct. In the end, they decided, Gephardt's top priority had to be keeping his own people together, particularly moderates and conservatives within the caucus. That meant he had to maintain a strategic distance from the White House to keep his credibility.

Still, the next day he went a little further than even his own advisers thought he should. During a stop in Scranton, Pennsylvania, on Tuesday, August 25, Gephardt used the "I-word," seemingly opening the door to the possibility of impeachment. "If Congress decides to go forward with an impeachment process, we will be involved in perhaps the most important task the Congress will ever have. We have to, under the Constitution, carefully examine the facts and then make a judgment on whether or not he should be expelled from office." On one level, that was simply common sense; but the signal Gephardt unintentionally sent was that he thought impeachment might be warranted. While it should not be done lightly, he said, "that doesn't mean it can't be done or shouldn't be done; you just better be sure you do it the right way."

Clinton erupted in anger that night when he read in an early version of a story in the *Washington Post* about what Gephardt had said. The headline went further than Gephardt's actual words and fueled the fire: "Gephardt Says Clinton Could Be Impeached." Clinton picked up the phone and tracked down his friend and chief fund-raiser, Terence R. McAuliffe, who was also close to Gephardt.

"You see what your friend Gephardt did?" Clinton yelled into the phone.

McAuliffe did not know the details but tried to calm Clinton down. "Mr. President, it's not true. I haven't talked to him for a couple days, but I guarantee it. There's no way he said that."

McAuliffe called Gephardt the next day and communicated the president's unhappiness. Gephardt, who had been in McAuliffe's wedding, said there had been a misunderstanding but warned that he could not be seen as the president's defender. "Look, we have a role that we have to play here. We don't know what the facts are. We can't be anything but objective."

McAuliffe called Clinton back and relayed the message. But the president had been fuming for hours and had also registered complaints about Gephardt with Jesse Jackson; John Sweeney, the president of the AFL-CIO; and Gerald McEntee, head of the American Federation of State County and Municipal Employees. All three tracked down Gephardt's chief of staff, Steve

Elmendorf, at a labor conference in Hawaii to pass along the president's gripes. Like his boss, Elmendorf conceded that perhaps the comments were not as artful as they could have been, but stressed "we have to hold the moderates." Sweeney and McEntee also called House Minority Whip David E. Bonior of Michigan, who shared their concern. Bonior, who had often clashed with Clinton, nonetheless had made the cold calculation that dumping him would be worse for Democrats than keeping him around. But he was having trouble impressing that on the more wary Gephardt.

The White House did not have a full appreciation for the level of antipathy on the Hill. Earlier that summer, Gephardt had met with small groups of fifteen or twenty members of his caucus to talk over the president's predicament, always taking care to pick a cross-section for each session so that the conservatives known as Blue Dogs could hear how the more liberal members felt and vice versa. The anger that poured out at these meetings was palpable. Gephardt was struck by how negative many of the members were toward the president, and he found it particularly ironic that the harshest were the New Democrats, with whom Clinton had so consciously allied himself, sometimes at the expense of Gephardt and other party leaders. Even before the president's August 17 admission, some of the party's senior congressmen, including Martin Frost of Texas and David Obey of Wisconsin, had told Gephardt or his staff that the minority leader should consider going to Clinton to demand his resignation.

With an impeachment referral from Starr now all but certain, Gephardt had his staff work up lists of members they should worry about, and the results that came back were overwhelming. After poring through whip books, Elmendorf and Gephardt's floor director, George Kundanis, identified 100 of the 206 Democrats as possible votes for impeachment. The staff came up with a second watch list of eighteen House Democrats who deeply disliked Clinton—from liberals such as Neil Abercrombie of Hawaii and George Miller and Fortney H. "Pete" Stark of California, to conservatives such as Ralph M. Hall of Texas, Gene Taylor of Mississippi, and Pat Danner of Missouri. Others they put on that second list were Scotty Baesler of Kentucky, Peter DeFazio of Oregon, Diana DeGette of Colorado, Bob Etheridge of North Carolina, Bob Filner of California, Marcy Kaptur of Ohio, Matthew G. Martinez of California, Carolyn McCarthy of New York, Lynn Rivers of Michigan, David E. Skaggs of Colorado, Louise M. Slaughter of New York, and James A. Traficant Jr. of Ohio. These Democrats were not necessarily proimpeachment votes, but given their personal distaste for Clinton, it was critical to monitor them.

What these meetings and lists demonstrated was that as he faced the most perilous threat of his political career, Clinton had no safety net beneath him.

*   *   *

"Bill, you're a fool! You're a damn, damn, damn fool!"

Clinton was being taken to task by a senator fed up with his sense of victimization. It was a breach of protocol even for a senior member of Congress to call the president by his first name, let alone to curse him, but the Democrats on Capitol Hill were beyond aggravation. And not just those Democrats who did not get along with him—in this case, Senator Patrick J. Leahy was on the phone, a liberal Vermont Democrat and Clinton supporter who shared his outrage at Starr's conduct. Even Leahy's wife could not believe how blunt he was being. "That's the president!" she whispered in horror.

At the urging of his staff, from Martha's Vineyard Clinton had begun making phone calls to key congressional Democrats. The idea had been for him to do in private what they complained he had not done in public—apologize for his actions. But after telling them he was sorry for putting them in such a bad situation, Clinton would invariably launch into a tirade about how unfairly he had been treated. As they hung up the phone, several of the lawmakers were more convinced than ever that Clinton was not truly sorry. He was still too busy nursing his resentment. After listening to one such presidential rant, Senator Joe Lieberman took out a laptop computer at his summer beach house and began tapping out his feelings of disappointment, emotions that were only exacerbated when his ten-year-old daughter told him she was worried she would be laughed at when she returned to school because she had insisted to her classmates the president had told the truth.

Leahy took out his frustration directly on the president. The longtime senator had been watching a movie after dinner while celebrating his wedding anniversary at the family farm in Vermont when Clinton called on Tuesday, August 25. Clinton was defensive and went on at some length about Starr's vendetta.

"Look," Leahy interrupted. "I really don't need to be told that. I'm a former prosecutor myself. I know this is excess. No elected prosecutor, Democrat or Republican, would ever do this." Leahy continued: "But don't even look for sympathy on this. You're going to have to be damn sure your testimony has been honest before the grand jury. People will be very critical of Starr, but they aren't going to excuse your conduct one iota just because of Starr's misuse of the office."

Clinton's tone changed somewhat, and he admitted he had done wrong.

Leahy asked if he had spoken with many other senators.

Not many, not yet, the president responded. He was not really anxious to talk with them at that point.

"Well, you should," Leahy said, and then softened himself. "You realize that even people like myself who are very, very angry at what you did are still your friends."

Friends, though, were in short supply for the president, angry or not—particularly in Martha's Vineyard. By the middle of his second week of "vacation," Clinton was growing stir-crazy and decided to get out for a while. His staff looked around for a short day trip he could make and settled on Worcester, Massachusetts, a short hop away, where he could announce a scholarship program for would-be police officers and a new teacher's guide for detecting troubled youth. No mention would be made of Lewinsky, no new apologies issued. This would be the first test of Clinton in a crowd following his admission, albeit a hand-selected crowd in a friendly region of the country.

"This should be interesting," Clinton said nervously as his small military plane landed at the Massachusetts airfield on Thursday, August 27. He had no idea how it would go or how he would be received. For a politician with a consistently keen instinct for his audience, this was flying blind.

Along the way, Clinton saw signs in crowds lining the motorcade route, including one that said, "Thanks, Mr. President. Thanks to you I've got a job." That provided a momentary uplift, but his face still betrayed the weight of his ordeal. During a series of scripted events, he talked about school violence, international terrorism, and Hurricane Bonnie—anything but the one subject that was at the top of everyone's mind. His speech was uninspired and a little distracted. But flanked loyally all day by Senator Edward M. Kennedy, Clinton found the crowds warm as they gave him standing ovations, and he did his best not to focus on the smaller groups of protesters hoisting signs like "Liar," "Resign," and "Impeach." As he got back on the plane at the end of the day, Clinton was relieved, confessing to aides that he had not known what to expect.

The president, though, had ignored the relentless chant from his staff to address the Lewinsky subject again and offer the more fulsome apology that so many politicians and media pundits back in Washington were demanding. His aides were virtually united in their desire to see him speak out in more remorseful tones—mostly out of conviction that he had no choice, but perhaps a little from their personal need to see more genuine contrition. Clinton had spoken with a few of them individually to apologize for lying to them, including Bowles, Podesta, Emanuel, and Paul Begala, but they had not found his words truly satisfying. Now they were pushing him to take another stab at it with the nation watching, particularly before he left the country in a few days for a state visit to Russia.

Feeling more confident after Worcester, Clinton decided to give it a try the next day, Friday, August 28, during a church service intended to commemorate the thirty-fifth anniversary of Martin Luther King Jr.'s famed "I Have a Dream" speech. Taking the three-page remarks about King prepared by his staff, the president turned over the sheets of paper and began scribbling new lines that would allude, however elliptically, to his own crisis. A few hours later, he got up at Union Chapel in Oak Bluffs, a small, predominantly black town on Martha's Vineyard, to address an audience of four hundred people packed into a sweltering building, including Anita F. Hill, the law professor who had accused Clarence Thomas of sexual harassment, and John Lewis, the civil rights legend who now served as the only black member of the Democratic congressional leadership. After some reminiscences about King's speech and a segue into the economic turmoil in Russia, Clinton pivoted to the topic of forgiveness and ruminated on Nelson Mandela's ability to forgive the white jailers who had stolen away so much of his life.

"All of you know, I'm having to become quite an expert in this business of asking for forgiveness," he said with a smile, triggering a round of applause. "It gets a little easier the more you do it. And if you have a family, an administration, a Congress, and a whole country to ask, you're going to get a lot of practice." At this, the crowd laughed. "But I have to tell you that in these last days, it has come home to me, again, something I first learned as president, but it wasn't burned in my bones, and that is that in order to get it, you have to be willing to give it." More applause. "And all of us—the anger, the resentment, the bitterness, the desire for recrimination against people you believe have wronged you, they harden the heart and deaden the spirit and lead to self-inflicted wounds. And so it is important that we are able to forgive those we believe have wronged us, even as we ask for forgiveness from people we have wronged."

Hillary Clinton did not show up at the Oak Bluffs church that day and showed no sign of forgiveness throughout their island stay. Unable to play golf or work the party circuit for fear of angering her and appearing to the public to be taking his penance too casually, the president puttered around the estate and the small cottage, down from the main house, that had been set up as an office. Desperate for company, he summoned aides a couple of times after midnight to come over and play his favorite card game, hearts. He commiserated with a few friends by phone. "I fucked it up," he told his fundraiser and golfing buddy Terry McAuliffe. "I was mad. You won't believe the questions they asked me. . . . A fucking witch-hunt." People did not understand how this had hurt him, Clinton added. "I've been living with a thousand cuts a day." With his consultant and confidant James Carville, the president confessed his worry about his marriage. "She is not going to forgive me," he moaned.

His assessment seemed on the mark on Sunday, August 30, when the first couple left Martha's Vineyard. At the airport, Hillary Clinton rushed to the plane, leaving the president behind as he bade farewell to onlookers. They only had a single night back in Washington before packing up for another out-of-town trip, this one an overseas mission to Russia, Ireland, and Northern Ireland. The weeklong excursion came at a crucial moment for their hosts—Moscow was in economic and political upheaval following the devaluation of the ruble and President Boris Yeltsin's dismissal of his prime minister, while the peace accord Clinton had helped negotiate in Northern Ireland was foundering after a terrorist attack. Adding to Clinton's headaches as he departed Washington on Monday, August 31, the sky-high U.S. stock market took a serious tumble, with the Dow Jones Industrial Average plummeting 512 points, its second-worst point drop in history. Prosperity had been a major factor in keeping his poll numbers elevated through months of scandal, and if public support started to dip, the politicians in his own party would follow for sure. Perhaps worse, as *Air Force One* crossed the Atlantic, rumors were rampant back in Washington that Bob Woodward or some other investigative reporter was on the verge of breaking a story disclosing that Clinton had had a sexual relationship with a second intern. Even with no tangible evidence to back it up, the scare reinforced the deep anxiety among Democratic lawmakers. No one knew what might be in the next day's newspaper. The president seemed just one sensational allegation away from self-destruction.

Hillary Clinton accompanied the president on the trip to Russia as she normally did on foreign journeys, but for the most part kept a separate schedule. When she did appear with him in public, she remained aloof. At Moscow's Elementary School No. 19, on Tuesday, September 1, she introduced him simply as "Bill Clinton, President of the United States." When he approached the lectern, he touched her shoulder as she passed by him on the way back to her seat, but she simply kept walking, looking down without any gesture in return. "I've been getting along fine," she curtly told reporters.

No one in Clinton's traveling party was looking forward to the joint news conference with Yeltsin the next day. Although there were more than enough important questions about Russia and its financial and political future, White House aides knew the reporters would ask about Monica Lewinsky—after all, it would be their first shot at the president since his August 17 admission. Aides had discussed canceling the news conference, but that was problematic with a foreign host. Besides, they hoped it could rebound to Clinton's benefit because reporters might appear unpatriotic for bringing up a scandal while a president was on foreign soil.

As he entered the ornate St. Catherine's Hall in the Kremlin to a spasm of camera-shutter clicking shortly after 1 P.M. on Wednesday, September 2,

Clinton looked so glum he seemed to be barely breathing. There was none of the usual glimmer in his eyes as they swept the room, taking its measure. There were no smiles of recognition at the aides or reporters he saw, just a deep frown that the camera-conscious politician almost never displayed in public. The only one in the room who looked worse was the ailing Yeltsin, who appeared to border on the comatose. During the preliminaries, Clinton's attention seemed to wander. He sat slumped in his chair, his fingers folded in front of his face, occasionally wiping the exhaustion from his eyes.

The first question from an American reporter made no mention of Lewinsky and asked only about Russia and the stock market tumble back in the United States. The second U.S. reporter turned the subject to Lewinsky, asking whether the reaction to his admission had "given you any cause for concern that you may not be as effective as you should be in leading the country."

Clinton paused as if to collect his thoughts before answering. "I have acknowledged that I made a mistake, said that I regretted it, asked to be forgiven, spent a lot of very valuable time with my family in the last couple of weeks, and said I was going back to work," he said, speaking softly and staring down rather than looking at the audience. "I believe that's what the American people want me to do."

The next U.S. reporter, Laurence McQuillan of Reuters, followed up by asking Yeltsin what he would do if Russian legislators refused to confirm his candidate for prime minister. Thinking that was the full question, Clinton looked over to McCurry and then Secretary of State Madeleine K. Albright in apparent relief. But then McQuillan turned to Clinton: "Mr. President, another Lewinsky question." Clinton's face reddened. Gently and deferentially, McQuillan asked if the president felt the need to offer an apology and whether he worried "that perhaps the tone of your speech was something that didn't quite convey the feelings that you have, particularly your comments in regards to Mr. Starr."

Yeltsin answered his part of the two-pronged question with a single, incoherent sentence: "Well, I must say, we will witness quite a few events for us to be able to achieve all those results." He then stopped as if he had blanked out. No one had a clue what he meant and assumed it was the lead-in to a convoluted answer. But Yeltsin remained silent. "That's all," he finally said.

Clinton recovered a little of his sense of humor. "That's my answer too!" he said, cracking a smile. "That was pretty good."

But Clinton could hardly duck the question, though he offered no explanation for the reaction to his speech. "I read it the other day again, and I thought it was clear that I was expressing my profound regret to all who were hurt and to all who were involved, and my desire not to see any more people hurt by this process and caught up in it. And I was commenting that it seemed to be something that most reasonable people would think had consumed a disproportionate amount of America's time, money, and resources, and attention, and now continued to involve more and more people. And that's what I tried to say."

Despite his quiet demeanor during the news conference, Clinton was enraged as he left the room. "This is chickenshit! This is all the press cares about!" he screamed to his aides when he arrived back in their holding room. Two of the three questions from the American media had been about Lewinsky, even as the Russian economy was collapsing. "There's real things going on in the world, and look at this press corps. It's embarrassing. All they care about is this. They're obsessed with this. This is not where the American public is."

Clinton was not the only one angry. Steny H. Hoyer, a Democratic congressman from Maryland who had accompanied the president to Moscow, found McQuillan later in a hallway and accosted the reporter. "Speaking as an American, I'm outraged!" Hoyer shouted. The media should "drop its obsession" with Lewinsky because the public simply did not care, Hoyer lectured.

Hoyer might not have cared, but some fellow Democrats back home certainly did. Several Democratic senators, including Bob Graham, Russ Feingold, and even Robert G. Torricelli, a staunch Clinton defender from New Jersey, watched Clinton's answers at the televised news conference and grew more aggravated. In fact, Clinton had not moved much at all in his latest formulation. The media and politicians had become fixated on his failure to use words like *sorry* or *apology*, and yet he still stubbornly refused to do so. Instead, he merely recast the meaning of his previous statement to suggest it went beyond what it actually said. The president asserted that he had already "expressed my profound regret to all who were hurt and to all who were involved," when actually on August 17 he had not explicitly apologized to anyone who was hurt. He had acknowledged a couple of weeks earlier that innocent people had been hurt, but attributed that to Starr and his intrusive investigation.

Joe Lieberman, the Democratic senator from Connecticut, was also disheartened. Over the last few days, he had been working to polish thoughts he had written on his laptop on vacation into a fuller speech to deliver on the Senate floor. Lieberman, a fellow New Democrat who had worked with Clinton to push the party to the political center, planned to condemn the president's actions as reprehensible and to call on Congress to censure him. But word quickly got around about his intentions, only in the rumor mills it had been inflated into a call for resignation, and the White House and fellow Democrats began pressing Lieberman to delay and tone it down.

On Monday, August 31, Erskine Bowles had called from the White

House. "I understand you're thinking about giving a speech," he said. "It's up to you to decide that. I hope it won't be that damaging." But Bowles appealed to Lieberman not to give it while Clinton was overseas, particularly while he was in Russia, where the president's news conference with Yeltsin would be dominated by this question if a senator from his own party denounced him beforehand. Lieberman did not want to wait a week until Clinton returned to Washington, but agreed to hold off until he left Moscow for Northern Ireland. Tom Daschle called the same day. "We've got to work on this together," he implored Lieberman. "If one person speaks out, then everyone will be under pressure to speak out. Whatever we do, we should do together." The next day, Daschle delivered the same message at a lunch meeting of the Senate Democrats, their first since Clinton's admission. They had to hang together, he urged. If anybody did feel compelled to speak out, he added, at least they should not call for specific actions, such as resignation, impeachment, or censure.

Lieberman took that last message to heart and rewrote his speech. He intended to give it Friday, but then heard that the Senate might not be in session that day and moved it up to Thursday, September 3, the day after the president's Moscow news conference. When Lieberman took the floor, the chamber was as usual mostly empty. But as he spoke and word spread, one by one senators began trickling in to listen. Lieberman denounced Clinton's actions as "disgraceful" and "immoral," adding that his own outrage had not subsided since the August 17 national address but had evolved into "a larger, graver sense of loss for our country" and its moral foundations. He took direct issue with Clinton and his assertion that even presidents have private lives. "Whether he or we think it fair or not, the reality is in 1998 that a president's private life is public," Lieberman said, particularly a president who "was given fair notice" during his initial presidential campaign.

Lieberman's biggest concern, however, was the message Clinton had sent. "Such behavior is not just inappropriate. It is immoral. And it is harmful, for it sends a message of what is acceptable behavior to the larger American family, particularly to our children, which is as influential as the negative messages communicated by the entertainment culture." Beyond that, the president's lies to the nation and under oath were not understandable moments of panic in an embarrassing situation but an "intentional and premeditated decision" to deceive. Lieberman was walking on the edge of calling for punishment, but quickly retreated. Censure would be "premature" until the Starr report was delivered, he said, while "talk of impeachment and resignation at this time is unjust and unwise." There was the consolation for the White House; he did not lay out a course of action for the president. The dam did not break.

But it was leaking. Senator Bob Kerrey, the Nebraska Democrat who had lost the presidential nomination to Clinton in 1992 and had famously described him as "an unusually good liar," saw Lieberman speaking on the television in his office and rushed to the floor to back him up. "I wish to join him and say that the president has got to go far further than he did in his speech to the nation," Kerrey told his colleagues. "This is not just inappropriate behavior. This is not a private matter. This is far more important for our country and threatens far more than his presidency unless we deal with it in a more honest and, as the senator from Connecticut has said, noncondemning fashion." Senator Daniel Patrick Moynihan, a New York Democrat who had had a long, awkward relationship with Clinton, stood and endorsed Lieberman's comments as well, adding an ominous warning. "In time, not distant time, a point of decision will come to the Congress, a decision will come to the Congress, and it will be for us to discharge our sworn duty," he said, an implicit reference to impeachment. "We take an oath to . . . uphold and defend the Constitution of the United States against all enemies, foreign and domestic—foreign *and* domestic, sir, which acknowledges that we can be our own worst enemies if we do not hew to our best standards."

Word of Lieberman's speech reached the traveling White House party in Ireland, where Clinton was visiting to celebrate the Good Friday peace accord he had helped broker and to keep it from falling apart in the wake of a terrorist bombing that had killed twenty-eight people in the small dairy town of Omagh. Flying in from Moscow, the president had spent the day in Northern Ireland, meeting with both sides and comforting victims of the bombing, including a fourteen-year-old girl who had lost her sight. In a boost to his spirits, Clinton was greeted everywhere he went by large and enthusiastic crowds who saw him as a savior. Because of the time difference, Lieberman did not take the Senate floor until Clinton arrived at Phoenix Park, the U.S. ambassador's residence in Dublin, where he was to stay the night. Exhausted, the president went to sleep fifteen minutes later and was not told about the senator's broadside until the next morning, Friday, September 4.

Deflated once again, Clinton was upset that his old friend would speak out while he was overseas. White House aides groused that Lieberman had rushed to the floor out of fear that another Democratic senator would beat him to the punch and steal the glory. But the president agreed that he could not show pique in public, especially not at another Democrat. This was a moment of maximum danger. Alienating Lieberman any further would give cover to all the other Democrats in the Senate who were itching to take a shot at Clinton. So when a reporter asked him about the speech at a joint appearance with the Irish prime minister, Clinton responded calmly.

"Basically, I agree with what he said," the president said, although he never actually watched the full speech. "I've already said that I made a big mistake, it was indefensible, and I'm sorry about it. So I have nothing else to say except that I can't disagree with anyone else who wants to be critical of what I have already acknowledged was indefensible."

Asked if it was helpful for Lieberman to speak out, Clinton did not take the bait. "But there's nothing that he or anyone else could say in a personally critical way that—I don't imagine—that I would disagree with, since I have already said it myself, to myself. And I'm very sorry about it."

Finally, after nearly three weeks, he had said the words he had refused to say all along: *I'm sorry.* It was the most direct apology yet. And yet it was still not good enough for some. Back home, Senator Feingold endorsed Lieberman's speech and said Clinton still needed to explain himself. Maryland governor Parris N. Glendening, a fellow Democrat, canceled a fund-raiser with the president because he did not want to be seen with him just before an election.

By now, there was no doubt that Starr was planning to send an impeachment referral to the House. Under the law that created the independent counsel, Starr was obliged to provide the House with "any substantial and credible information" that "may constitute grounds for impeachment." As Clinton was jetting back from Ireland on Sunday, September 6, Starr's prosecutors were conducting the last of a series of interviews with Monica Lewinsky as part of an effort to document every sexual encounter she had had with the president—all to show that he had lied under oath when he maintained he never touched her erotically. While his client was away, David Kendall was preparing one last gambit to forestall an impeachment report.

In the true don't-give-an-inch tradition of his law firm, Kendall had prepared a lawsuit that would ask a federal judge to block Starr from transmitting any report to Congress that contained analysis of the evidence, premising the request on the theory that the law only empowered an independent counsel to provide "information." Any interpretation or recommendations were beyond Starr's authority and would usurp the House's "sole Power of Impeachment," Kendall wrote in the brief. During Watergate, before the advent of the independent counsel law, special prosecutor Leon Jaworski had shown his report to the House to U.S. district judge John J. Sirica first to make sure it was simply a straightforward recitation of facts and evidence, not conclusionary in any way. Yet while Kendall's suit was signed and ready to go, he realized he had only a slim hope of succeeding, and Chuck Ruff and Dick Gephardt both advised against it. Such a move would only look like more fancy White House lawyering.

So instead Kendall drafted a letter to Starr and sent it on Labor Day, Monday, September 7, making the same points and asking for a week to review any report before it was submitted to the House. When he saw the letter, Starr interpreted it as a sign of impending litigation on the topic, and so he did two things: he drafted his own response to be sent to Kendall the next day, rejecting the request for an advance peek, and he made sure his staff was ready to move immediately when the House returned to town on Wednesday, September 9.

Hours after Kendall sent his letter to Starr, the president's advisers gathered for a three-hour evening strategy session at the White House to review where they stood. In a rare move, the president walked up the stairs in the West Wing to join the meeting in Ruff's office. The situation had clearly taken a turn for the worse from the day a few months earlier when John Podesta had been so confident that he told congressional Democratic leadership aides not to worry because the public did not care about Clinton's womanizing. "The guy can fuck Miss America and nobody gives a damn," Podesta had told his fellow Democrats. Now people gave a damn, at least on Capitol Hill. Gephardt's August 25 comments had rattled the White House aides. The enthusiastic reaction to Lieberman's speech within the party was disturbing. Each day, another Democrat inched closer to following Paul McHale down the road toward urging resignation. Congresswoman Marcy Kaptur, an Ohio Democrat who had fought Clinton on trade issues in the past, had said that "if he resigned tomorrow, it wouldn't be enough in my judgment." During the White House meeting that night, another House Democrat, James P. Moran Jr. of Virginia, was on CNN telling Larry King that Clinton had lied in court and that impeachment proceedings were "undoubtedly" necessary. Senator Harry Reid, the mild-mannered, bespectacled Democratic whip, was practically in a panic over how the president's problems were dragging him down in an already tough reelection contest in Nevada. Senator Fritz Hollings was telling people around him that Clinton should get out now, and fellow Democrats such as Dianne Feinstein, Russ Feingold, and even the more liberal Patty Murray of Washington State were all entertaining similar thoughts. Lawrence Stein, the chief White House lobbyist on Capitol Hill, had been told that Senator Robert Byrd had already drafted a speech demanding Clinton's resignation.

Bill Richardson, the former U.N. ambassador who had just been installed as secretary of energy and had once served in the House as chief deputy whip, had been calling around to his friends in the Democratic caucus and summarizing the results in memos sent to Podesta. Anxiety seemed to be the order of the day. House Minority Whip David Bonior reported to Richardson that he had to talk several Democratic congressmen out of giving speeches calling on Clinton to resign. Several members reported that Congressman Tim Roemer of Indiana, who was influential among his fellow New Democrats, was off the reservation. Congresswoman Anna G. Eshoo of California complained to Richardson that the president had dragged everyone out on a limb with him and needed to own up to his problems.

Within the White House, Podesta feared that someone on the president's staff would quit in an opportunistic "protest" and bask in the admiration of the news media. "We need to make sure somebody doesn't want to be the hero running into enemy arms," he had warned Doug Sosnik and Rahm Emanuel in a private meeting. The group worried about Mike McCurry, the media-friendly spokesman who was already scheduled to leave his post in early October. Sosnik, whose office was located next to the press secretary's, was assigned the "McCurry Watch" to look for signs of disaffection. To keep the rest of their troops in line, White House officials accustomed to spinning anything even drafted talking points for how they should respond when asked about being betrayed by the boss.

Question: "Do you forgive him for misleading you and the country?"

Answer: "It's been said that 'he who cannot forgive others breaks the bridge over which he must pass himself.' Of course I do."

Clinton, back in Washington really for the first time since his grand jury appearance and nationally televised speech three weeks earlier, soaked in all the ominous reports that Monday night in Ruff's office and recognized that something had to be done. He agreed to summon the House and Senate Democratic leaders to separate meetings in the White House residence to apologize in person; he would do the same with his cabinet. He would also try to recruit someone to lead his defense effort against any impeachment drive, an *überlawyer* as some began to call it. David Kendall and Chuck Ruff were not the political bulldogs he would need now that the matter was heading into the congressional arena. Erskine Bowles had been a steady right hand for budget negotiations but clearly did not possess the political temperament for this sort of mission. The ideal candidate would be a distinguished political figure like former Senate majority leader George J. Mitchell, who could take over as White House chief of staff just as Howard Baker did when Ronald Reagan's presidency was threatened by Iran-contra. But Mitchell had been resisting all entreaties.

The White House team was not sure it could rely on the Democratic congressional leadership either, so Podesta had quietly begun taking steps in case the president was deserted by his own party. Given the strained relationship with Gephardt—not to mention his recent comments on impeachment—Podesta was trying to build his own independent whip operation loyal to Clinton that could rally members without help from the party hierarchy. Through intermediaries, Podesta had reached out to a variety of House Democrats he thought might agree to participate in such a rump group—

particularly influential Old Bulls—and had received commitments from some key members, including Congressman Vic Fazio of California, chairman of the party caucus, who offered to lead the group. But others were more reluctant. Congressman Howard L. Berman, perhaps the most respected Democrat on the House Judiciary Committee, where any impeachment inquiry would start, had declined to participate, saying he could only advise them as long as his role was low-key. Podesta had asked former White House lobbyist Howard Paster to approach Congressman John D. Dingell of Michigan, the dean of the House and its longest-serving member, to see if he would head up the rump Clinton whip group, but Dingell refused. Steve Elmendorf, Gephardt's chief of staff, found out about the behind-the-scenes maneuvering from Paster and complained to Podesta that he should at least keep them informed about such efforts.

As the White House team batted around ideas on this evening, though, the president was still not fully aware of just how politically isolated he was. Unbeknownst to him, one of his own top advisers was quietly sounding out Democrats about approaching the president to resign. Harold M. Ickes, the profane, brass-knuckled New Yorker who had served as Clinton's deputy chief of staff in his first term and masterminded his reelection in 1996 only to be passed over for chief of staff in the second term, was telling senior Democratic officials and allies around town that they needed to consider whether it was time to cut the party's losses and push the president out of office.

Ickes, the namesake son of Franklin D. Roosevelt's famously hard-nosed interior secretary, had remained loyal to the president in the twenty months since his unhappy departure from the White House and had grown even closer to Hillary Clinton. But Ickes considered the current scandal a dire threat to the Democratic hold on the presidency. Impeachment by the House and even conviction by the Senate appeared to be real possibilities, particularly given the mood among Senate Democrats. So Ickes began sounding out key players within the party about resignation. This might be an honorable way out, he told them. If Clinton really was in danger of being removed by Congress, Ickes said, this would avoid a divisive ending and put Gore into the Oval Office early enough to let him repair the damage to the party and give him a fighting chance in 2000. Ickes believed that the party had to have a serious discussion about the option. The party was more important than its leader.

To that end, Ickes talked with leaders of the interest groups that dominate internal Democratic politics, particularly labor unions, people such as John Sweeney of the AFL-CIO, Gerald McEntee of AFSCME, and Sandy Feldman of the American Federation of Teachers. Clinton would probably never agree to step down voluntarily no matter how slim his chances were, but

Ickes told people that the only possible way to convince his ex-boss to give up power would be to put together a coalition of interest groups and key senior members from Congress to go to him as a delegation and tell him there was no way to hold the White House in 2000 unless he resigned. Gore himself might have to be enlisted.

One of the power players Ickes met with was Sweeney, president of the AFL-CIO, still perhaps the single most dominant force within the Democratic Party even after decades of decline. Ickes and Sweeney got together over breakfast at the Washington Hilton Hotel, and the former White House aide presented his case. Sweeney listened, but was not yet ready to abandon Clinton.

"Let's wait and see, Harold," he said. "Let's see how this unfolds."

CHAPTER THREE

"... go to the White House and tell him he has to resign"

The menacing jaws of a *Tyrannosaurus rex* greeted all visitors to Newt Gingrich's private sanctuary, and few guests did not take away at least some sense of irony. In the conference room in the House Speaker's second-floor office suite in the Capitol, Gingrich, a lifelong paleontology buff, kept a glass-encased three-foot skull from the king of dinosaurs, a loan from the Smithsonian Institution. As Gingrich, House Majority Leader Dick Armey, his Democratic counterpart, Dick Gephardt, and other senior lawmakers and aides gathered in what had become known as the Dinosaur Room on the morning of Wednesday, September 9, they faced a menace of a different sort.

With recess over, the House was just now returning to Washington for the first time since President Clinton's admission, and lawmakers were on edge about what it would mean for them with an election just fifty-five days away. While everyone assumed that Ken Starr planned to send the House a report outlining allegations of impeachable offenses by the president, House leaders had done precious little to prepare for its arrival at their doorstep. Gingrich, nervous about the strongly ideological tilt of members on both sides of the House Judiciary Committee, had months ago floated the idea of taking the issue away from the panel and handing it over to a special task force he could more easily control, only to be faced down by Judiciary chairman Henry Hyde, who insisted his committee should not be circumvented.

This meeting, long delayed, could no longer be put off and was itself something of an accommodation. Gingrich and Gephardt did not like each other and only rarely tolerated each other's company. In the nearly four years Gingrich had been Speaker, he and Gephardt had only met privately perhaps three or four times. Joining them this morning were Hyde and the ranking Democrat on the Judiciary Committee, John Conyers Jr. of Michigan, as well as the chief investigators each side had hired in recent months, David P. Schippers by the Republicans and Abbe D. Lowell by the Democrats. Unaccustomed to congressional protocol, Lowell blithely took a seat at the conference table along with the lawmakers, only to realize belatedly that staff members were expected to sit in chairs behind the principals. Trying to cover his faux pas, Lowell grabbed Schippers and pulled him up to the table too.

"This is as serious a thing as we'll ever do," Gingrich said as he opened the meeting.

Gephardt concurred and began by reaching out to Gingrich: "Let it be a way for Congress to look good. I'll go halfway and even more to reach a sensible goal. I don't have any partisan goals or objectives here."

But having pledged his good faith, Gephardt quickly called attention to what he saw as the first sign that Republicans were not prepared to work with Democrats in a bipartisan manner—rumors that Rules Committee chairman Gerald B. H. Solomon of New York was ready with a GOP plan for how to proceed. "We've already heard that Solomon has a draft of procedures and rules and we haven't received it. That's not right," Gephardt said. Watergate should be the model for cooperation between both sides, he added.

Gingrich and Hyde assured him that they wanted to work across party lines. "This will ultimately fail if the Democrats don't get on board," said Hyde. "It is a recipe for failure if it is partisan. While we are the majority party, we retain respect for the minority." This was the most serious undertaking since World War II, he added, and he wanted to work so closely with Conyers that the two Judiciary leaders would "come out looking like statesmen, not political ward-heelers."

The first test of that would come over the question of what to do with whatever material Starr sent. No one in the room had much clue what it might include, and because of the heightened political sensitivities surrounding the case, congressional leaders and aides had avoided even contacting prosecutors to ask. For weeks, House Republican leaders had suggested on television and in the newspapers that they wanted Starr to send some sort of executive summary wrapping up the case, with the idea that it could be released to the public while the rest of the evidence could remain sealed, and they hoped the independent counsel would get the message. But the decision on what to release and when was trickier than that. After a $40 million investigation, many lawmakers believed the public had a right to see whatever Starr sent, particularly given that it dealt with the conduct of the nation's highest elected official. Yet it could be inflammatory and unfair to put it out without some prior review, not only for the president but also for all the other people caught up in the case, including Monica Lewinsky.

On a political level, Gingrich clearly believed that disclosure of the damning details of Clinton's infidelities and deceptions less than two months before an election could only help Republicans at the polls. Gephardt feared that as well, but he worried that keeping it from the public would only result in the most sensational elements of the report seeping out in the newspapers bit by bit over the next eight weeks. Better to get it all out at once and give Democrats a chance to recover, he calculated, rather than have his members subjected to "death by a thousand leaks." What's more, some senior Democrats, including Congressman John Dingell, last of the Old Bulls in his party, were pressing for immediate release lest they be accused of covering up for the president. "My personal view is to get it all out," Gephardt told Gingrich and the rest of the group.

Hyde wanted a more restrained approach. He had instructed his staff of lawyers over the summer to draft proposed rules that would allow him to maintain tight control over any evidence submitted by Starr or developed by the committee's own investigators. In a series of draft resolutions prepared as early as June 9, only the committee would be allowed access to Starr's report and accompanying material until a majority of the panel voted to release it. Moreover, Hyde as chairman and Conyers as ranking Democrat could have the first look at the evidence, and Hyde would have the power to place under seal anything he deemed especially sensitive, keeping it secret even from the rest of the committee.

Just as Gingrich and Hyde split on this question, so too did Gephardt and Conyers. A staunch defender of the president and relentless critic of Starr, Conyers was far more skeptical of any release and wanted prior review of everything before making it public. His view was closer to Hyde's than his own leader's. Where Conyers and Gephardt agreed, though, was in pushing for a twenty-four-hour advance look by Clinton's legal team, embracing the argument advanced by David Kendall in his Labor Day letter to Starr. It was good strategy—either the president's lawyers would be better equipped to defend him or the Democrats could use a refusal to show how unfairly GOP leaders were treating Clinton. That point united Gingrich and Hyde on the other side as well. They were certain that if the White House had prior review, it would use the extra time to inoculate Clinton by leaking the most damaging facts in the most favorable light before the public had a chance to evaluate Starr's report.

Gingrich rebuffed Gephardt's request. Kendall would have the right to publicly refute the charges once they were public, Gingrich said. Besides, the Speaker added, they could trust Hyde. "Henry is conservative about these things and doesn't want this to be Jerry Springer."

Lowell, the Democratic investigator just hired by Gephardt, interjected that all the talk was somewhat premature anyway, since they had no idea in what form Starr would send any material. There might be a summary and there might not. It could just be boxes of grand jury transcripts. Gingrich agreed and said they should authorize the staff to contact Starr and find out what they could about what was coming their way.

Then Gingrich bitterly recalled the ethics investigation into his handling of a college course he had taught. Clearly, he was still bruised from the experience, which nearly cost him his Speakership the year before. "I turned over a million pages in my ethics investigation and I had to pay a three-hundred-thousand-dollar fine," he fumed. "I'm willing to give you more than the Democrats gave me in my investigation. This will be an issue of congressional legacy."

"This will validate the Founders' belief that democracy can work," Hyde added. "If this fails, we will all pay a big price."

Gephardt replied with equally high-minded words, promising to act in good faith. This should not be a political process but a legal one, he said. If the president enjoyed a 90 percent approval rating but had committed impeachable offenses, he should be impeached despite his popularity, Gephardt said. At the same time, if Clinton were at 10 percent yet had not committed high crimes and misdemeanors, then he should not be. This was not about polls, Gephardt said. "If we give in to that, we're doomed."

Around 3:45 P.M., the phone rang in Hyde's committee offices and his top aide, Thomas E. Mooney Sr., took the call. It was Jackie M. Bennett Jr., Starr's deputy independent counsel. Bennett had been noncommittal when Mooney and the other House aides had called him following the meeting in the Dinosaur Room, but now just a few hours later he was more specific about when the report might be on the way. The answer: now.

"I got two vans rolling," the Starr deputy reported.

"Oh?" Mooney asked. "What's in the vans?"

"I got eighteen boxes in each van."

They went back and forth for a moment over whether it was eighteen boxes or thirty-six total. Bennett said it was two identical sets of evidence, one for the Republicans and one for the Democrats, eighteen boxes each, for a combined total of thirty-six. Finally, Mooney asked, "Where are they rolling to?"

"They're rolling to the Capitol."

Jesus Christ! Just like that? The report was on its way? Mooney could not believe it. What kind of warning was this? They had just been on the phone and given no clue. Mooney asked Bennett if Gingrich's office had been contacted. No, came the answer. How about the sergeant at arms? No again. What entrance were the vans coming to? They had not thought about that.

"How far away are you?"

"About ten minutes."

Phones started jangling all around the Capitol as Mooney and the other staff members scrambled to get ready to receive the evidence. It was not as if they could just cart it up to any old office. These were perhaps the most sensitive and important documents to arrive at the Capitol in years, and they had to be kept under the tightest security. The sergeant at arms, Wilson Livingood, had set aside a locked room in the Ford House Office Building to hold the evidence complete with file cabinets and plans for round-the-clock security; he had had the locks changed just the night before. After talking with Mooney, Bennett called Livingood to notify him and Capitol Police officers were immediately dispatched to the Capitol steps. It did not take long for everyone else to find out what was happening. Shocked congressmen in every corner of the Capitol, senior officials at the White House, and everyday citizens across the nation were suddenly watching it live on television as cameras trailed the bizarre caravan of two vans, one blue, the other white, down Pennsylvania Avenue until they arrived at 4 P.M., a surreal show that presidential aides angrily assumed was political theater staged by Starr. By the time Bennett got off the line with Mooney and Livingood to call Abbe Lowell, it was too late.

"Thanks a lot," Lowell replied sarcastically, his television tuned to MSNBC. "I've already gotten that information from Lisa Myers."

In delivering the report and accompanying evidence to the steps of the Capitol, Starr had dropped at the House door the biggest issue it had faced in nearly a quarter century—and he had caught its leaders flat-footed. The House was so unprepared that it had not passed the rules required to deal with the receipt of the report. The Dinosaur Room meeting from earlier in the day resumed an hour after the unexpected delivery as Gingrich, Gephardt, Hyde, and Conyers continued thrashing about for a course of action. Confused by the turn of events, they authorized their aides to contact Starr's people once more to get a briefing about what was in the boxes, all of which would remain sealed and uninspected until the House voted on a set of procedures. In a twenty-minute call, Starr's deputies gave the aides a bare-bones description of what was sent but offered no advice about what to release or guidance about how graphic or sensitive the materials might be.

"I have very nervous members," Gingrich reported to the other House leaders. No one had a clue what was in the report and what they were about to turn loose on the nation.

"We need to do some kind of look-see," Conyers said. "We don't know what we have."

Gingrich did not want to do that. If they reviewed the report before releasing it, he felt, they would take political ownership of its content. "We're damned if we do and damned if we don't," he said aloud. Why not release the report immediately and hold on to the rest of the material in the boxes for review, Gingrich suggested.

Gephardt was unsure. The details that support the president could actually be in those boxes, he noted. That should be released at some point too.

Finally, they seemed to reach a deal—they would release the main report by the end of the week, but Hyde and Conyers would look through the remaining evidence and determine what should be held back before releasing it.

Across the Capitol, Tom DeLay felt bushwhacked. He had not even been invited to the meeting in the Dinosaur Room. Intent on revving up The Campaign now that the Starr report had arrived, DeLay was convinced that Gephardt and the Democrats were only feigning bipartisanship and had no intention of working with Gingrich and Armey on a legitimate impeachment inquiry.

"They're going to fuck us. It's a setup," he told his staff. "They're going to screw us. They're going to leave us and they're going to screw Newt and Dick in the back."

Clinton was a mere spectator in all this. After apologizing to House Democratic leaders in a private meeting at the White House earlier in the day, he flew to Florida for fund-raisers and another stop on the contrition tour—each time growing more expansive and expressive. "I've done my best to be your friend, but I also let you down and I let my family down and I let this country down," he told a group of donors in Orlando. "But I'm trying to make it right. And I'm determined never to let anything like that happen again." Improbably he added, "I hope this will be a time of reconciliation and healing, and I hope that millions of families all over America are in a way growing stronger because of this."

When the cabinet arrived at the White House the next day, Thursday, September 10, no one knew what to expect. Cabinet meetings were rare enough in the Clinton era. Unlike his predecessors, he had never found much utility in them. Indeed, the cabinet had not met in nearly eight months, not since that day in January in the early throes of the Lewinsky scandal when Secretary of State Madeleine Albright and three other secretaries were dispatched to the White House driveway to vouch for the beleaguered president. "I believe that the allegations are completely untrue," Albright had said then. "I'll second that, definitely," Commerce Secretary William Daley had agreed, followed by Health and Human Services Secretary Donna E. Shalala and Education Secretary Richard W. Riley. Now they were being summoned back to hear from their leader why their faith had been misplaced.

One by one, the government department chiefs made their way into the Yellow Oval Room in the private, second-floor residential section of the White House. It was a sizable group, about two dozen, since Clinton had given cabinet rank to a wide range of officials, including his domestic policy adviser, the national drug czar, and the head of the Small Business Administration. But there were few staff members, giving it a more intimate feel than a typical back-to-business meeting. Many of the cabinet officers found themselves strangely nervous. Some stared at their shoes, avoiding eye contact not only with the president but with each other as well. Others wondered whether their colleagues would stand by him. Would Albright resign? Would Shalala? Why wasn't Daley there?

As everyone settled in, Clinton sat in front of the fireplace, while the cabinet members seated themselves in a series of chairs and couches arranged to face him in roughly three rings, almost amphitheater-style. Albright, befitting her rank as secretary of state, sat in the front. Vice President Gore arrived late, after everyone else had sat down, and took a chair to Clinton's right.

The president brought no notes and did not look at his top advisers as he started talking in a quiet, pained voice. Tired from his late-night return from Florida, he began by quoting the Bible, thanking everyone in the room for their support and acknowledging that he had put them in a difficult situation. He thought of the cabinet as something like a family, he said, and so he owed them an apology for what he had put them through. This had not been easy on him either, he assured them, nor for his wife and daughter. He was not proud of what he had done and was paying a price for his mistake. As tears filled his eyes and his senior advisers sat rapt and breathless, Clinton recalled that when he was the governor of Arkansas, he was often described as a "good guy but ineffective." Now he heard himself depicted as the reverse. "It's more important to be a good person than a good president," he said, "and I'm going to spend the rest of my life trying to atone for this."

Opening up in a way none of them had ever seen before, Clinton told his cabinet secretaries that he had grown to feel like a person who was not himself since taking office. He had woken up profoundly angry every day for the last four and a half years, he said, the same time frame that he had been under investigation by Starr and his predecessor. And that, he suggested, had created a behavior pattern that was not justified but could be explained because he was not at peace with himself. His face tightened and he started to sound more agitated as he invoked his critics. Whatever he had done did not merit what they were doing. These people, he said fiercely, really wanted to destroy him.

After about twenty minutes, he stopped, and an awkward silence filled the room. Finally, the secretary of state rose to her feet. For Albright, who was older than Clinton, the whole subject was extremely distasteful; her own marriage had broken up after a husband's infidelity. But she mentioned none of that, instead focusing on her role as ambassador to the world. She had been all around the globe in recent months, Albright told Clinton, and he should know the world's leaders were behind him. And so was she.

That set the tone. One after another, cabinet secretaries got up and said they too were sticking with him. They praised Clinton for the good he had done in office. He would get through this, they said, and so would they. The discussion leaned heavily on religious themes of sin and redemption, atonement and forgiveness. Labor Secretary Alexis M. Herman and Transportation Secretary Rodney Slater both cited Bible passages and told Clinton he was a good president who should not give up. "In due season we shall reap if we do not lose heart," Slater said, borrowing from the book of Galatians. Agriculture Secretary Dan Glickman quoted Proverbs 23:7, "For as he thinketh in his heart, so is he," adding that perhaps out of this Clinton could better understand himself and better lead the country. Interior Secretary Bruce Babbitt talked of going to confession and how a sinner had to believe what he did was not right in order to cleanse his soul. "If you ask God for forgiveness and your family for forgiveness, then as Christians, Lea Ellen and I can forgive you," added James Lee Witt, the director of the Federal Emergency Management Agency and, with his wife, a longtime Clinton associate dating back to Arkansas.

Finally, Shalala could not take it anymore. For her, there was far too much ass-kissing. As a cabinet veteran since the inception of the Clinton administration, she had accepted a lot she had not liked over the last six years, including the retreat on universal health care and the president's signature on a Republican-authored welfare-reform law that she considered repugnant, all in the name of his political survival. But now she was furious. Everyone had worked so hard to get him reelected, yet that coveted second term had been imperiled because Clinton could not control his libido. And nobody in this room was telling him that what he did was simply wrong. Not the lying, the sex. Like everyone else, Shalala had known before she took the job that Clinton had had problems staying faithful to his wife, but this looked to her as if the White House was being infected with the loose morals of the campaign trail. This was not even an affair with a woman his age, which Shalala might have been able to understand. This was abusing his office for his personal gratification with a former intern barely older than his daughter. At fifty-seven, Shalala had spent a lifetime setting standards for young people. As the chancellor of the University of Wisconsin, she had once forced out a tenured professor for hitting on undergraduates. In the world she lived in, people in power were not supposed to take advantage of someone over whom they were in charge.

Others knew of her strong feelings and were even counting on her to share them with the president. Before the meeting, Erskine Bowles, the White House chief of staff, had called to tell her not to hold back. The president still did not get it, Bowles said. Clinton thought it was all just a right-wing conspiracy to get him. "You've got to tell him the truth," Bowles told her. "You've got to be honest."

And so she was. To her, she said, it sounded as if Clinton really believed that only his performance as president should matter, not how he conducted his private life. She asked him to reassure her that he believed character was as important as the policies he enacted, that how a leader behaved was as vital to the job of president as programs and laws.

"I can't believe that is what you're telling us, that is what you believe, that you don't have an obligation to provide moral leadership," Shalala told the president. "I don't care about the lying, but I'm appalled at the behavior."

Clinton seemed taken aback. "By your standard, Richard Nixon would've beaten John Kennedy," he replied sharply.

"You've got to be kidding," she retorted.

Others in the room were stunned by the exchange. It was a strikingly candid back-and-forth between a president and a cabinet secretary in front of so many people. No one else had the temerity to confront Clinton quite like that. And more than a few of Shalala's peers were distinctly uncomfortable that she had done so and privately disapproved.

But others shared similarly wounded sentiments with the president, though delivered with less edge. Maria Echaveste, the deputy chief of staff, and Aida Alvarez, head of the Small Business Administration, expressed their disillusionment as women.

"How could you not see how important you were to us?" Alvarez asked. Women felt a special bond with him because of his policies, she said, but were also quite moved by the pain he had inflicted on his wife and daughter. "We want you to know that we hurt because we're disappointed."

Carol M. Browner, the head of the Environmental Protection Agency, brought up her ten-year-old son. She did not think it was her place to judge the president, she told him, but because of this scandal she had been forced to have excruciatingly difficult conversations with her son about issues she had not expected to discuss with him until he was much older. Her son, who had met the president, had asked extremely graphic questions. As she spoke, Clinton put his hand up to his face, appearing ashamed or perhaps trying to hold back tears.

But then Browner quickly shifted tone and said this episode had given her an opportunity to teach lessons about forgiveness and to explain why she did what she did for a living. She supported what the president had been doing for the country and she wanted to keep doing it. "I wouldn't be here if it weren't for you," she concluded.

By the time it came around to Bob Rubin, there had been plenty of pained and poignant talk. The treasury secretary, the subject of persistent rumors that he might quit, cut through it with a more characteristically blunt assessment.

"You screwed up, you screwed up big time," he told the president. "But, we all screw up sometimes."

Finally, the vice president spoke. He had remained completely loyal in his public pronouncements, never betraying a hint of disapproval of the president to the outside world. But now in this private moment, he sternly told Clinton that he had let everyone down. Gore too quoted the Bible and concluded that now it was time to move on: "Mr. President, I think most of America has forgiven you, but you've got to get your act together."

As the meeting broke up, Clinton and several members of the cabinet lingered to talk less formally for another twenty minutes. Among them was Shalala, who took the approach of the affectionate, if disappointed, older sister whose remonstrations were intended for his own good. If Clinton was angry with her at this point, it did not show. He wrapped his arms around her in a hug.

"You're always tough on me," he said.

"Only when you deserve it," she responded.

On Capitol Hill, restless House Democrats were meeting in full conference for the first time since Starr's report arrived the day before. Dick Gephardt explained the plan to release the report, possibly on the Internet, but also talked about how they were trying to push for a review period for the president first. Several of the African-American Democrats were outraged, including Maxine Waters of California, Sheila Jackson Lee of Texas, and Mel Watt of North Carolina, all members of the Judiciary Committee. This was a railroad, they complained. Waters declared hotly that she intended for the Congressional Black Caucus to serve as "the fairness cops" in this process, defending the president's rights.

The black members were quickly emerging as a powerful force in Clinton's corner. Where other Democrats worried that their wayward president was dragging them down and were all too willing to cut him loose if need be, the African-American representatives expressed no such equivocation. Even though Clinton had often split from the generally more liberal members of the black caucus on important issues such as welfare reform, his popularity within the broader African-American community was strong and enduring. In part, that owed to a sense that, whatever their policy differences, Clinton understood and cared more about the black community than any previous president. It was not lost on them that one of his best friends was Vernon Jordan, a black man now sharing the legal hot seat alongside him. Moreover, many black congressmen and -women saw a parallel in Starr's relentless pursuit of the president and the prosecutorial excesses their constituents suffered every day. Clinton's persecution complex resonated with them.

To white House Democrats, the message was telling as well: No matter how alienated they might feel from Clinton, they had to remember that an important part of their political base back home viewed the case differently. Depending on the demographics of their districts, abandoning Clinton could place them in as much risk as standing by him.

Henry Hyde held out a box of his favorite Monte Cristo cigars to his guests and then fired one up himself. Only David Kendall joined him in puffing on the stogies, much to the unspoken annoyance of almost everyone else in the room. Kendall and Chuck Ruff were in Hyde's office in the Rayburn House Office Building to review their situation and see how much cooperation they could secure. Hyde was nothing if not gracious to his visitors.

The cigar was one of the few small pleasures left in Hyde's life. At seventy-four, he was heading into the twilight of a long and distinguished political career when suddenly he was confronted with a task he clearly did not savor. Growing up a poor Irish Catholic in Wheaton, Illinois, Hyde earned a basketball scholarship to the same school Bill Clinton would later attend, Georgetown University, where Hyde met his future wife, Jeanne Simpson. After serving in the navy during World War II, Hyde practiced law in Chicago, got himself elected to the state legislature, and eventually won his seat in Congress in 1974, representing an affluent district that included Hillary Rodham's suburban hometown of Park Ridge. In the House, Hyde became one of the most revered Republican members, loved for his quick wit and sense of decorum. He also developed into one of the nation's foremost antiabortion champions, sponsoring a law named for him restricting Medicaid funding for the procedure.

Over the last decade, though, Hyde had suffered through prostate surgery and the death of his wife after a forty-five-year marriage, fully recovering from neither. As he lumbered through the Capitol day after day, his gait slowed and his expression worn, Hyde seemed to be evolving more into an elder statesman for the party than the crusader of his youth. When the Lewinsky story first broke, he seemed to go out of his way to discount the possibility of impeachment, noting publicly that no president could be removed from office without a bipartisan consensus. But when Gingrich floated the possibility of taking the matter away from his Judiciary Committee and appointing a special task force, the old Hyde defied the Speaker and forced him to back down. Hyde held no great respect for Clinton and yet seemed to struggle with how to reconcile his personal distaste for sex scandal and his instincts for fairness. "I hate that son of a bitch," he told a fellow Republican member of the Judiciary Committee shortly after the Lewinsky scandal began. "I want to get him. But I want to get him in the right way."

Whether Hyde liked it or not, the issue was now squarely before him. The question was what was "the right way." He resolved to treat the White House as reasonably as possible but did not want to roll over either.

"We're prisoners of the House and the Rules Committee," Hyde explained to Ruff as the lawyers sought insight into how the Starr report would be handled. Indicating Conyers, Hyde said, "We're going to work like Siamese twins if we can." He added, "I'm going to judge these things the way I'd like to be judged."

Ruff asked for time to read the documents before they were made public so they could properly respond. Kendall pointed out that the president was being put in an extremely difficult position.

But Hyde made clear they would get no advance look: "Only by burglary will you get the report sooner than it's going to be released."

"Just give us an hour," Ruff pleaded.

Hyde softened. "We'll see if we can do that."

Around ten o'clock that night, some thirty hours after the report's surprise arrival, Gingrich got together for a late dinner with some of his closest advisers at Bullfeathers, a bar and restaurant near the Capitol with indifferent food and blaring televisions where lawmakers congregated after hours. Over hamburgers and beer, Gingrich asked how they thought the Starr report would play.

"Do you have any idea what the country's going to learn tomorrow?" asked Bob Walker, a former Republican congressman from Pennsylvania and probably Gingrich's best friend in Washington.

"I haven't read a word of it," Gingrich replied. "And no one else has either."

Walker was stunned. How could they release this to the world the next morning without reading it first? Someone should have reviewed it. Gingrich disagreed. Not reviewing it would ensure the integrity of the process, he said. That way, members would not be out there commenting on evidence before the public saw it. And besides, Gingrich added, if Starr included something they did not like, they would not be responsible.

"I stayed up all night working on this thing," Clinton said. "It was hard for me, but I got down in words how I feel."

It was the next morning, Friday, September 11, and the president was standing in the Oval Office holding on to a few slips of paper containing his thoughts on his situation. He did not bother to show them to Doug Sosnik, his close aide, but instead tucked them in his pocket to pull out in a few minutes at a prayer breakfast being held in the East Room. Sosnik knew better than to ask. By this point, he and the other political aides had given up on their internal campaign to convince Clinton to apologize again more effusively. This was a problem they could not fix, they had decided; no amount of speechwriting spin would make Clinton seem genuine if he was not. Only he could come around to true remorse.

Clinton headed over to the prayer breakfast, where he greeted many of the 106 religious leaders who had gathered. The Bill Clinton who got up at the lectern in front of the broad yellow curtains came across as a different man from the embattled politician who lashed out on national television three weeks earlier. His tone was subdued, his voice soft and low, his eyes moist and drooping from exhaustion.

"As you might imagine, I have been on quite a journey these last few weeks to get to the end of this, to the rock-bottom truth of where I am and where we all are," he told the dead-silent audience. "I agree with those who have said that in my first statement after I testified I was not contrite enough. I don't think there is a fancy way to say that I have sinned. It is important to me that everybody who has been hurt know that the sorrow I feel is genuine—first and most important, my family. Also my friends, my staff, my cabinet, Monica Lewinsky and her family, and the American people. I have asked all for their forgiveness." For the first time, he was publicly admitting he was wrong in his speech following the grand jury appearance, that what had happened was his own fault. And despite his mischaracterization, for the first time he was publicly offering an apology of sorts to Lewinsky.

Still, he made clear he was not surrendering in the political fight to come: "I will instruct my lawyers to mount a vigorous defense, using all available appropriate arguments. But legal language must not obscure the fact that I have done wrong."

In fact, his lawyers were already hard at work constructing that vigorous defense. Clinton was not the only one who had worked late into the night. Kendall's partner, Nicole Seligman, had still not gone home since showing up at the office the morning before as she labored over a response to the Starr report that they had not yet seen. A "prebuttal," the Clinton team was calling it, and they planned to release it before the Starr report was even available. The lawyers had been leery of responding to allegations they had not yet read, but in the end the one benefit of newspaper disclosures about Starr's investigation was that the Clinton team had a pretty thorough road map of where the prosecutors were going. Paul Begala and deputy White House counsel Cheryl Mills were dispatched from the West Wing to camp out at the Williams & Connolly office to help write and edit the seventy-eight-page document. To keep it from getting bogged down in legalese, Begala and deputy press secretary Joe Lockhart wrote an introduction that summed up the president's defense in more politically palatable language.

At the Capitol, the House convened at 9 A.M. to consider releasing the report and engaged in an often-emotional discourse. The Republicans argued that it was critical to put the report out promptly to give the public its own opportunity to judge, but many of the Democrats passionately begged for the president to have an advance look, and some flatly objected to producing a report that none of them had read. The three hours of debate were nothing more than mutual venting, however. Immediate release was a foregone conclusion—indeed, House staffers had spent the previous twenty-four hours preparing for the logistical challenges of posting it on the Internet and printing thousands of copies. The vote in the end was bipartisan, 363–63, with only the most diehard Clinton Democrats opposing release.

As soon as the gavel rapped the House session to a close just at noon, House Clerk Robin H. Carle formally took possession of the report beneath the Cannon House Office Building across the street from the Capitol and began the process of providing it to members and the public at large. Sergeant at Arms Wilson Livingood cut the plastic tape on two boxes, pulled out a pair of large black binders, then resealed the boxes. Ninety minutes later, Hyde arrived in the hearing room used by the Judiciary Committee and signed for his copy. "This is a very sober moment," he said. "We are at the beginning of a long climb up a steep mountain. Nobody looks forward to it."

Hyde's lofty rhetoric quickly became lost in a flood of seamy sex. All around the Capitol and beyond, lawmakers, aides, reporters, and curious citizens crowded around computer terminals to pull down pages from congressional Web sites, the first major real-time national Internet experience in the new information age. Within a half hour after Hyde had his copy in hand, the television networks were broadcasting the first patchy details, correspondents literally reading aloud as they went, not having taken even a moment to review first before going on the air. On CNN, viewers watched Candy Crowley leaf through the report, picking out phrases that few would ever have imagined hearing about their leader. "According to Ms. Lewinsky," Crowley read at one point, "the president touched her breasts and genitalia."

The 453-page report outlined eleven counts against Clinton—four alleging that he committed perjury in his January 17 deposition in the Paula Jones case, one alleging perjury in his August 17 grand jury appearance, five alleging obstruction of justice, and one asserting abuse of office. According to the report, the president had lied when he said he had no specific recollection of being alone with Lewinsky, he had lied when he said he could not remember any specific gifts he gave her just three weeks after presenting her with a half dozen Christmas presents, and he had lied when he said he did not engage in "sexual relations" as defined by Jones's lawyers. Starr charged that Clinton orchestrated a broad campaign to illegally impede the Jones lawsuit and the subsequent criminal investigation by coaching his secretary, Betty Currie, to lie, by encouraging Lewinsky to lie in an affidavit in the Jones suit and simultaneously arranging a job for her at the Revlon cosmetics company through his friend Vernon Jordan, by helping Lewinsky to hide gifts that had been subpoenaed, and by lying to aides, knowing they would repeat his false statements to the grand jury. And in a final count drawn from Watergate-style language, Starr maintained Clinton abused his power by making frivolous assertions of executive privilege during the independent counsel's investigation, by refusing to appear before the grand jury for six months, and by lying to the American people when he said he had not had sex with "that woman."

"In view of the enormous trust and responsibility attendant to his high office, the President has a manifest duty to ensure that his conduct at all times complies with the law of the land," Starr wrote. "In sum, perjury and acts that obstruct justice by any citizen—whether in a criminal case, a grand jury investigation, a congressional hearing, a civil trial, or civil discovery— are profoundly serious matters. When such acts are committed by the President of the United States, we believe those acts 'may constitute grounds for an impeachment.'"

The facts laid out by Starr were powerfully corroborated through White House telephone records and entry logs, contemporaneous E-mail messages and calendars, the testimony of Secret Service officers and presidential aides, and, of course, the DNA test on the infamous blue Gap dress. Lewinsky proved to have a meticulous memory for dates and events, and to the extent possible, her recollections before the grand jury or with Starr's interviewers almost invariably matched other available evidence. For example, she remembered that the second time she had met Clinton, in late 1995, he took a call from a congressman with a nickname while she performed fellatio; telephone records later showed that the president had spoken that night with Republican congressman H. L. "Sonny" Callahan of Alabama during the same time Lewinsky was recorded as being in the White House. Another time she recalled being admitted to the Oval Office by a tall, slender Hispanic Secret Service agent; records later showed that an agent fitting that description was on duty, and he testified that he once let in Lewinsky to "deliver papers" to the president. Few reading the report were left with much doubt that events had taken place essentially as Lewinsky described them. She could not simply be making all this up.

The factual analysis, however, was quickly lost amid the salacious details. A narrative part of the report describing the evolution of the Clinton-Lewinsky relationship read more like a bad Harlequin romance than a legal document and described in shockingly intimate detail each of their ten sexual encounters in the Oval Office suite, even noting when one or the other achieved orgasm. Starr felt compelled to put in detail to rebut Clinton's claim that their activities were not "sexual relations," a defense that rested in part on the proposition that he had never so much as fondled Lewinsky. But Starr went further still by documenting their various "phone sex" sessions in which they talked dirty, conversations that did not fall under any definition of sexual relations. The prosecutor went on to inform Congress and the country that Clinton and Lewinsky twice "engaged in oral-anal contact" and that on another occasion the president inserted a cigar into her vagina, then put it in his mouth and said, "It tastes good."

The very word *impeachment* evoked dread images from the Watergate days, and it seemed unthinkable to many that for the second time in a generation the nation had to decide whether to evict its leader for high crimes and misdemeanors. The power to impeach a president derived from several clauses scattered in various parts of the Constitution, without a great deal of elaboration. The central element was contained in a single sentence in Article II, which states, "The President, Vice President and all civil Officers of the United States, shall be removed from Office on Impeachment for, and Conviction of, Treason, Bribery, or other high Crimes and Misdemeanors." Article I, section 2, designates the House as having "the sole Power of Impeachment," and section 3 assigns the Senate the responsibility "to try all Impeachments." The same section stipulates that in such a trial senators are to take an oath, the chief justice presides, and conviction requires a two-thirds vote of those present. Punishment "shall not extend further than to removal from Office, and disqualification to hold and enjoy any Office of honor, Trust or Profit under the United States." However, those convicted would still be subject to separate criminal prosecution. That was as much guidance as the framers provided to those who would have to carry out those duties in the centuries to come—no definition of "high crimes and misdemeanors," no rules of evidence or standards of proof, no explicit instructions about the possibility of lesser penalties.

The history of the drafting of those clauses offered some clues, though at times they were subject to radically different interpretations. The framers adopted the concept of impeachment from the British model but shaped it for the American system of democracy, intending it as a tool to protect the nation from a chief executive whose egregious conduct constituted a threat to the republic. At the Constitutional Convention of 1787, the framers rejected a proposal to subject presidents to impeachment for "maladministration," thus distinguishing the concept from a parliamentary system where prime ministers can be voted out whenever they lose the confidence of legislators. Yet the meaning of "high crimes and misdemeanors" was left deliberately vague. In *Federalist* No. 65, one of the seminal writings on impeachment, Alexander Hamilton suggested they were "those offenses which proceed from the misconduct of public men, or, in other words, from the abuse or violation of some public trust." He went on to emphasize that politics was an inherent and indeed even welcome element in the impeachment process. "The prosecution of them, for this reason, will seldom fail to agitate the passions of the whole community, and to divide it into parties more or less friendly or inimical to the accused." As a result, however, he added that "there will always be the greatest danger that the decision will be regulated more by the comparative strength of parties, than by the real demonstration of innocence or guilt."

In the next two centuries, impeachment was used only sparingly, leaving few precedents to guide the players in the Clinton drama. While only Andrew Johnson and Richard Nixon were seriously threatened with removal, the question came up with several other presidents as well. In 1843, John Tyler had an impeachment resolution introduced against him charging, among other things, that he had misused his veto power, but the House voted 127–84 not to authorize a formal inquiry. The House ignored an attempt by one of its members in 1896 to impeach Grover Cleveland in a dispute over the issuance of government bonds. Even after losing reelection in 1932, Herbert Hoover was still confronted in his final months in office with attempts to impeach him for increasing unemployment, negotiating bad treaties, and mistreating World War I veterans, but the House voted twice to table any investigation. Nearly twenty years later, several congressmen tried to impeach Harry S Truman for seizing the steel mills and firing General Douglas MacArthur, only to have the resolutions referred to the Judiciary Committee, which promptly buried them.

Until now, Andrew Johnson was the only president ever impeached by the House and tried in the Senate. A willful, ornery man, Vice President Johnson had assumed the nation's highest office after the assassination of Abraham Lincoln in the waning days of the Civil War, only to battle with Congress over the pace of Reconstruction. Johnson, who drew fire for his go-easy approach to the vanquished Southern states and unwillingness to guarantee new rights for freed slaves, survived one impeachment attempt before finally pushing Radical Republicans over the edge in 1868 by firing their ally, War Secretary Edwin M. Stanton. Congressional critics filed an impeachment resolution in the House the same day, charging that he had violated the Tenure of Office Act, a clearly unconstitutional law previously passed over Johnson's veto that forbade him from removing cabinet officers without Senate consent. The next day, the Committee on Reconstruction, headed by

Congressman Thaddeus Stevens, recommended approval of the resolution, and two days later the House voted 126–47 to impeach Johnson. Only afterward were actual articles of impeachment drafted, adding the charge that Johnson had maligned Congress in a series of political speeches. A seven-week trial in the Senate, however, ended in acquittal by a single vote.

The Nixon case was more familiar to those involved in the Clinton situation; indeed, many of the lawyers and lawmakers had played supporting roles in the earlier drama, including Hillary Clinton. Long a polarizing figure in American politics, Nixon had faced down impeachment threats stemming from his handling of the Vietnam War as far back as 1972, but revelations of his involvement in the cover-up following the Watergate burglary finally pushed the Judiciary Committee to recommend impeachment on a bipartisan vote in 1974. Nixon resigned before the full House took up the matter, becoming the only president ever forced from office.

Aside from Johnson, the House had impeached just fourteen other federal officials in the nation's history—a cabinet secretary, a senator, and twelve judges. The senator was expelled rather than tried, and the other cases resulted in seven convictions and six acquittals or resignations. As Hamilton had predicted, politics infused many of those cases. The first impeachment of a judge came when President Thomas Jefferson decided to get rid of a jurist appointed by his predecessor, John Adams. The Senate voted strictly along party lines in 1804 to remove Judge John Pickering, who had been accused of drunkenness and insanity. Less than an hour after that vote, the House impeached another member of the bench, Supreme Court Justice Samuel Chase, but this time a number of Jefferson's fellow Republicans in the Senate balked and he was acquitted.

None of this history, however, settled the essential question: What is a high crime? Scholars and lawyers agreed that not every crime was impeachable; no one argued that a president should be removed from office for a speeding ticket or some other petty violation. Yet it was clear that high crimes were also not limited exclusively to grave abuse of office; even the most fervent proponents of this interpretation conceded that murder would be impeachable, even if it had no direct bearing on a president's exercise of the power of his office. So where to draw the line? That was for this new generation in Washington to figure out for itself.

While poorly prepared, both sides had been bracing for this moment for months. Way back in the spring, Hyde had met at a Chicago hotel with a casual friend of his, former mob prosecutor David Schippers, and asked him to come to Washington in case the Judiciary Committee needed an impeachment investigator. Like anyone else, Hyde could see that the Lewinsky scandal was heading his way, and he wanted someone outside of the Washington loop reporting to him. With white hair and beard that made him look like Santa Claus with a badge, the sixty-eight-year-old Schippers brought to the table a long résumé of tough cases, including his investigation of Mafia boss Sam Giancana. The father of ten children, he also sported a Democratic pedigree straight from the wards of Chicago and Robert F. Kennedy's Justice Department, a résumé Hyde made much of, even though Schippers's political views resembled those of conservative Republicans on the national level.

Hired in March for $20,000 a month, Schippers brought with him a team of eight experienced investigators and lawyers, including his son Tom, and they set up shop in the warrens of the Ford Building, far from the main traffic of daily congressional life. Ostensibly they were there at first to conduct oversight hearings on the Justice Department, but they really were in place so they could hit the ground running as soon as Starr decided to send a report to Congress.

By the time Schippers was on board, the Democrats were still trying to find their footing. For guidance, Dick Gephardt turned to a longtime adviser, Robert F. Bauer, one of Washington's smartest and best-connected Democratic lawyers. Bauer, an election law specialist, had gotten to know Gephardt while representing his 1988 presidential campaign. Although virtually invisible to the public, Bauer at forty-six now had the ear of the nation's most important congressional Democrats, representing Gephardt and Tom Daschle simultaneously while also holding accounts of both the House and Senate Democratic campaign committees. Schooled in the politics of scandal from his days defending House Majority Whip Tony Coelho, who was forced to resign in 1989 over financial improprieties, Bauer instinctively knew how serious Clinton's problem was for Gephardt and sent him an eight-page memo on March 30 warning against complacency.

The conventional wisdom promoted by the White House that the Lewinsky affair would never proceed to impeachment was deeply flawed, Bauer argued in the memo. A case put forward by Starr could achieve credibility with a mainstream press distrustful of Clinton and then build momentum. Moreover, Bauer pointed out, removing the president might not be the real goal for Republicans pursuing impeachment. "It can be used to bleed the President of credibility, divert our resources as a party, and weaken our ability to prepare for both this Fall's elections and the Presidential in 2000," Bauer wrote. Gephardt was urged to begin looking for a chief counsel for the Judiciary Committee but not to think of the matter in purely legal terms. "To win, we have to be smart about politics—about message and positioning, and the possession of legal ability in the right quarters is helpful but will not in any way be decisive," Bauer wrote. Perhaps more important was to begin formulating a plan for procedures in any impeachment inquiry, "not because we would ever win on such issues, but because the battle over process will have a major impact on the politics and flow of the entire proceeding. . . . Forcing the Republicans to contend with our criteria for a fair process is good politics, and process in any event is centrally important to our ability to affect the course of events in the House."

Gephardt concurred. Process would be their battleground. The search began for a chief investigator who would help wage that battle. Normally, that prerogative would fall to the ranking Democrat on the Judiciary Committee, but in Gephardt's office John Conyers was viewed as a wildly unpredictable old man. They could never leave a matter as important as this in his hands. Moreover, Gephardt's chief of staff, Steve Elmendorf, did not get along with Conyers's top aide, Julian Epstein, a crafty political operative with *GQ* looks who essentially ran the committee with Conyers's proxy and once was dubbed "Machiavelli in Armani." So Gephardt decided early on that he would have to take charge for the Democrats himself, and he began meeting personally with committee members on June 5 to plot strategy over pizza and Diet Coke.

Tension among the Democrats escalated over the next three months. Conyers and Epstein resented Gephardt inserting himself into their business, but the minority leader steamrollered over them. On Gephardt's instructions, Bauer considered several possible chief investigators, including prominent Democratic attorneys Michael Zeldin, Tom Green, and Abbe Lowell. Zeldin was ruled out because he was perceived as Epstein's favorite and besides, had already been on television too much defending the president, which might compromise the independent image Gephardt wanted. Green turned out to be the candidate of the president, who lobbied on his behalf. Clinton told Conyers directly that he wanted Green and sent Gephardt a backdoor message by promoting the attorney with intermediaries who then passed along his preference to the minority leader. That was enough to sink Green. The choice came down to Lowell, a scrappy forty-six-year-old former Justice Department lawyer who enjoyed the spotlight and had represented clients in virtually every major political investigation in Washington over the last decade, including former House Speaker Jim Wright and former Ways and Means Committee chairman Dan Rostenkowski.

Gephardt, though, continued to run into resistance from Conyers's office. Epstein had taken phone calls from associates warning him about Lowell's ego and volatility. "Abbe is all about Abbe," he was told. Epstein worried that Lowell might come along and make life difficult with a bomb-throwing performance; when impeachment was all over, Lowell could go back to his lucrative private practice, but Epstein would still be on the Hill, still having to work with the Republican majority to get anything accomplished. Epstein shared his concerns with Gephardt's office as well as important Democratic members of the committee such as Barney Frank of Massachusetts and Howard Berman of California. Lowell could be a tinderbox, Epstein warned them.

While Gephardt and Elmendorf pushed to get Lowell on board, Epstein stalled, suggesting more vetting before a decision. Finally, in August, five months after Schippers was hired by the Republicans and with time running short before Starr was expected to send a report, Gephardt pushed Conyers into signing off on Lowell, who was given an $18,000-a-month contract. Democrats would spend the fall charging that Newt Gingrich was secretly masterminding the impeachment and pulling the strings at the Judiciary Committee, but in fact, Dick Gephardt quietly asserted control on his side of the aisle.

Once he was finally installed, Lowell went straight to work. As soon as they were allowed into the vault with the secret information on Friday, September 11, Lowell immediately began devouring it as quickly as possible. This was the evidence not included in the now-public Starr report, answering all the questions that had obsessed Washington for months. Did Betty Currie rat out the president? What did the Secret Service agents see and hear? Lowell and his team devised a system for reviewing the material and marking useful sections with colored adhesive paper—yellow for privacy issues that might merit redaction, pink for exculpatory information helpful to the president, and blue for examples of prosecutorial misconduct by Starr's office. No one bothered to come up with a color for evidence implicating Clinton.

True to Epstein's fears, it did not take long for the pugnacious Lowell to get into a scrap with the Republicans. After complaining vigorously about office space, supplies, and staff contracts—Lowell drove to a store on Capitol Hill to buy pens and pads with money out of his own pocket—the Democratic investigator was outraged to discover that the Republicans had imposed a midnight closing time on the vault. With fewer people at his disposal, Lowell wanted to continue reading through the night and protested in vain.

But Gephardt tried to keep Lowell focused on the big picture. As the chief investigator prepared to dive into the evidence, Gephardt summoned him to issue instructions: "We're relying on you to tell us whether the president's committed an impeachable offense," Gephardt told Lowell. "Because if we conclude that he has, it's going to be my job and Tom Daschle's to go to the White House and tell him he has to resign."

Gregory B. Craig was sitting on the porch having dinner with his wife, Derry, and a few friends when the telephone rang. It was Saturday night, September 12, the day after the Starr report hit the Internet. "This is the White House operator," the voice on the phone said. "Please hold for the president."

On the line came that familiar voice. Greg, asked the president, could you come down to see me? Craig, a Yale Law School acquaintance of the Clintons' and now a high-ranking official in the State Department, knew what this was about. John Podesta, the deputy White House chief of staff, had been talking with him for several weeks about coming on board to coordinate the president's defense in the impeachment proceedings that seemed almost certain to be launched on Capitol Hill. Craig had written a freelance memo offering the White House advice after Joe Lieberman's speech on the Senate floor, but he had not immediately jumped at the chance to join the president's defense team. "You'll forgive me if I'm not overly enthusiastic," he told Podesta the first time he called in late August. At the time, Craig was the director of policy and planning at the State Department, an enviable perch once held by George Kennan.

But when the president called, people answered, and so Craig excused himself from his dinner guests, piled into a car, and drove from his home in northwest Washington down to the White House. This was not the first time he had been drawn into a volatile, high-profile case. As a young lawyer in the early 1980s, Craig was part of the legal team that had defended Ronald Reagan's would-be presidential assassin John W. Hinckley Jr. and won a verdict of not guilty by reason of insanity. After serving as a foreign policy adviser to Ted Kennedy, Craig was tapped to represent the senator during the rape trial of his nephew William Kennedy Smith. That experience helped make Craig attractive to the White House now. So did his telegenic good looks, affability, and infectious smile, all of which would help the White House put a friendlier face out to the public. At fifty-three, Craig actually *looked* like a Kennedy.

Bill and Hillary Clinton had first gotten to know Craig at Yale in the early 1970s. Craig took a seminar on corporate responsibility with Bill Clinton, but Craig was closer in school to Hillary Rodham. He had kept a certain personal distance from Bill Clinton after an eye-opening conversation early in the future president's political career. As Craig related it to colleagues at the White House, he had run across a Little Rock aide to the Arkansas governor who warned ominously that while Clinton was talented enough to be president, he had "no core" and his womanizing was "out of control." Ultimately, the aide had believed, Clinton's personal recklessness could destroy him. All these years later, Craig had a new appreciation for the prediction.

On this warm, late-summer evening, Craig approached the White House gate and told the Secret Service officer he had an appointment. Craig was escorted inside the private residence and brought up to the second floor, where he found Clinton alone. The president took him outside on the Truman Balcony overlooking the South Lawn with a stirring view of the Washington Monument. Clinton looked exhausted. He had not gotten much sleep the last two nights. For the next hour and forty-five minutes they talked. The president was philosophical, emotional. He spoke of making mistakes and seeking forgiveness, much the same as he had at the cabinet meeting and prayer breakfast.

"Look, I can't make any decision about this," Craig finally said. He had to go home and talk about it with his wife. With a family of five children, this move could turn their lives upside down. "I'd like to help you. But I've got to tell you, I too am absolutely livid about what you did."

The reason the president needed someone like Greg Craig became painfully apparent the next morning, Sunday, September 13. In the wake of the Starr report, Podesta and other top aides decided to abandon their usual practice of keeping Clinton's attorneys off the talk shows and instead opted to mount a full-scale television defense. Chuck Ruff, David Kendall, Cheryl Mills, and Special Counsel Lanny A. Breuer—all inside players who eschewed the limelight—were booked on the major Sunday network talk shows, along with Podesta himself. The defense they offered might have been effective in a court of law but immediately fell flat in the court of public opinion. Tom Daschle and other senior Democrats around town watched with increasing exasperation as the lawyers did what lawyers do and fell back on legalistic answers. The president did not lie under oath to Jones's attorneys, they said; he simply evaded and gave technically accurate half-answers. He was not trying to tamper with a witness when he fed false stories to Betty Currie because she had not yet been called to testify. He did not commit perjury because he did not consider oral sex to be "sexual relations."

"I think under that definition, which is a very contorted definition, the president's interpretation was good faith and correct, and he testified according to that," Kendall said on ABC's *This Week*. "Perjury prosecutions normally involve acts. They don't involve interpretations of a contorted definition."

Clinton tried to influence one of the other talk shows directly that morning. Worried that pressure would build on him to resign, he tracked down Senator Orrin Hatch just before the Utah Republican went on the air on CBS's *Face the Nation*. Hatch sat in his car outside the television studio for twenty minutes talking with the president on his cellular phone before going inside.

"Well, was my apology Friday enough?" Clinton asked, referring to his musings at the White House prayer breakfast.

"Yes, Mr. President, it was for me," Hatch answered. "But, you know, true repentance is more than just being sorry. There are the four *R*'s." Hatch, a devout Mormon who had put out recordings of himself singing Christian music, proceeded to outline his understanding of true repentance: the first step was to recognize that such conduct was wrong, the second was to feel remorse for it, the third was to refrain from repeating it, and the fourth was to make restitution.

After hanging up and heading inside, Hatch went on the air and repeated his praise for the president's performance on Friday, saying it might have changed everything had Clinton done that back in January when the story had first broke or even as late as August when he had finally admitted having a relationship with Lewinsky. But Hatch firmly warned Clinton against relying on the legalisms and word-parsing that Kendall and others were voicing on other networks.

"He ought to quit splitting legal hairs," Hatch said. "He is being very badly served with this legal hairsplitting. Nobody believes that. Nobody wants to hear that. What they want to hear is the president who is truly contrite. I think he went a long way last Friday towards that. He ought to continue that. He ought to get rid of this legalism stuff. The American people are a lot smarter than these four-hundred-dollar-an-hour lawyers think they are, and I think they ought to get the heck out."

"So?" asked Dick Gephardt. "Is there really the cigar thing?"

Gephardt was not asking out of prurient interest. He was truly appalled. After escaping Washington for his son's wedding in Atlanta, Gephardt returned to the Capitol on that Sunday to hear the verdict of his investigators: Was there a case there or not? It had been clear as early as Friday evening that Starr's main report did not have more than previously advertised, but Abbe Lowell and his staff spent the weekend poring through thousands of pages of testimony that had not yet been released to make sure.

Yes, Lowell said, the cigar thing was in there. And so was plenty of other untoward behavior by the president. But there was no list of other interns, no explosive revelation that they had found ready to blow up in their faces. Despite all the rumors, the Starr report had showcased the worst of it. More important, Lowell said, he could win this case with a jury in a courtroom. In some instances, Starr had stretched the evidence beyond what it really showed. In others, there was at least a reasonable debate about whether the conduct was really serious enough to be impeachable.

Lowell ranked the allegations for Gephardt. The toughest was the perjury in the Paula Jones deposition. "There's no doubt he wasn't telling the truth," Lowell said. It was blatant. But they could make the case that the whole Lewinsky issue was not material to the case and therefore not perjury as defined under federal statute. In the grand jury, it was a closer call whether Clinton had told the truth, Lowell said, but the president's answers were so careful that the only real way to sustain a perjury charge was to prove that he had another interpretation of *sexual relations* rather than the definition he professed to believe. On obstruction, Lowell concluded, the evidence had significant holes. The most serious charges concerned whether Clinton had instructed Lewinsky or Currie to lie. If that held up, Lowell warned, it could be impeachable. But there was some exculpatory material for the president on those counts, namely Lewinsky's own statement that she was never told directly to lie, and Currie's testimony that she did not feel intimidated when Clinton ran through his false version of events with her. The easiest to dismiss were the charges that Clinton had abused the power of his office by lying to his aides and frivolously asserting executive privilege. Those were just preposterous arguments, Lowell said. Whatever the propriety of Clinton's doing those things, they were hardly high crimes.

What Lowell did not mention to Gephardt was that he was convinced the one person who had clearly lied before the grand jury was Vernon Jordan. None of the committee's Democratic lawyers who had reviewed his testimony considered his story plausible. Still, Lowell had concluded that most of Jordan's statements that seemed to be obvious lies were not about central events.

Gephardt thanked Lowell for the report. Taken as whole, it sounded like reasonably good news. There was no smoking gun. Best of all, there were no more smoking interns.

At 4 P.M. that day on the other side of the Capitol, a group of senior Democratic aides gathered in Tom Daschle's office. Attending were Pete Rouse, Daschle's chief of staff; Ranit Schmelzer, his press secretary; Laura Nichols, Gephardt's communications director; and Bob Bauer, the Washington attorney who was counseling Gephardt and also advising Daschle. The consensus among the group formed quickly: the performance by the president's lawyers on the talk shows earlier that day had been abysmal. If that was the defense Clinton planned to raise, then they would all sink with him. Daschle wanted a statement put out distancing himself. "I want to make clear I won't put up with this line of argument," Daschle told them by phone from home. Gephardt, who had decided to stick close to Daschle throughout the crisis, agreed to put out a critical statement as well.

Bauer provided the link. Since he was advising both men, he coordinated the drafting. The next day, Monday, September 14, the statements were released. Daschle, who put his out shortly after appearing with Clinton at a New York fund-raiser, said, "I certainly agree with those who have grown impatient with hairsplitting over legal technicalities. . . . The president and his advisers must accept that continued legal jousting serves no constructive purpose. It simply stands in the way of what we need to do: move forward and let common sense guide us in doing what is best for the country." Gephardt echoed the point: "The considered judgment of the American people is not going to rise or fall on the fine distinctions of a legal argument but on straight talk and the truth."

CHAPTER FOUR

"I don't want them to win"

They sat in the locked, windowless room in the Ford Building and watched the worst day of President Clinton's life captured on the television set in front of them. Virtually no one in the country had yet seen the videotape of the president's encounter with the grand jury, and freshman congressman Asa Hutchinson had joined Henry Hyde to review it on Sunday, September 13, at the same time Abbe Lowell was briefing Dick Gephardt on the secret evidence. David Schippers, the chief Republican investigator, had already pronounced the tape "dynamite." It would blow Clinton out of the water, he predicted. But as Hutchinson sat through the four hours of sometimes monotonous questioning, he was not so sure. A former federal prosecutor, Hutchinson agreed that portions of the tape were indeed damaging to Clinton. "He lied through his teeth," Hutchinson told Hyde. And yet the totality of watching the whole session was not so dramatic. Clinton was nothing if not nimble and came across sympathetically to an audience. Maybe releasing the tape in its entirety was not such a good idea, Hutchinson said.

No one else on the House Judiciary Committee had seen Bill Clinton up close for as long as Asa Hutchinson. A fellow native of Arkansas, Hutchinson had repeatedly crossed paths over the years with the president he was now charged with investigating—first at law school, later in the courtroom, and eventually in the state's political circles. A tall, slender man with an engaging smile and relentlessly polite Southern manners, Hutchinson stood out from many of his committee colleagues for favoring low-key, sober professionalism over high-pitched political hyperbolics. His youthful face was betrayed by graying hair, and yet he still seemed younger than his forty-seven years.

William Asa Hutchinson II was a late arrival for his parents, who gave up a grocery store in Oklahoma to take up farming in the Ozarks of Arkansas. After the unexpected birth of a fifth child, Tim, they decided to have one more close in age for him to play with, or so went the family lore, and a year later Asa arrived. Asa eventually followed Tim to Bob Jones University, an all-white, conservative, Christian college in South Carolina where they lived under a strict religious code of conduct that banned drinking, smoking, playing cards, dancing, kissing, and even holding hands. Dating was permitted only with a chaperon. While Tim went on to become a minister, Asa chose a more secular route, enrolling in the University of Arkansas law school in 1973, the same year Bill Clinton was taking a faculty job there. After his first year, Hutchinson married Susan Burrell and found himself working in the campaign of Republican congressman John Paul Hammerschmidt, who was fending off a challenge from Professor Clinton.

In 1976, Asa ran unsuccessfully for county justice of the peace, beginning what would turn into a frustrating, twenty-year electoral losing streak, but with Hammerschmidt's help he would secure a presidential appointment in 1982 to become the youngest U.S. attorney in America, at age thirty-one. When a heavily armed terrorist organization called the Covenant, Sword and Arm of the Lord provoked a standoff with two hundred law enforcement agents, Hutchinson put on a flak jacket to help negotiate an end to the crisis, then prosecuted members of the group on racketeering charges. Clinton, then governor, called him at home one day during the impasse to confer about the terrorist group. The two ambitious young politicians later met about a marijuana eradication program. Hutchinson left the meeting with the impression that the governor was enthusiastic about the idea but grew aggravated when he did not see the follow-through he expected.

Their most traumatic encounter, though, came in 1984 when it fell to Hutchinson to prosecute the governor's half brother, Roger Clinton, who had been arrested in a drug sting. After the grand jury indictment, Hutchinson called Bill Clinton to give him a heads-up and allow the governor to make the announcement himself. Roger pleaded guilty to distribution of cocaine and conspiracy to distribute cocaine, and his testimony was used in other cases. Bill and Hillary Clinton sat in the front row during the sentencing, but no ill will toward the prosecutor developed. More than a decade later, after Hutchinson finally won his seat in Congress, he found himself on *Air Force One* with Clinton heading down to Arkansas in April 1997 to examine tornado damage. When Hutchinson asked after Roger, the president answered, "I've said it a lot of times and I'll say it again: I think the way you handled that prosecution probably saved his life."

In a strange twist of fate, Clinton's own legal problems ended up providing the break Hutchinson needed to finally win an election. In 1996, Jim Guy Tucker, then governor of Arkansas, was convicted of bank fraud in a case that stemmed from Ken Starr's investigation of Whitewater. Tucker's resignation opened up the state's top job to the Republican lieutenant governor, who then dropped his plans to run for the Senate. Tim Hutchinson, having succeeded Hammerschmidt in the House, jumped into the Senate race instead, clearing the way for Asa to run for his brother's seat against Ann Henry, a friend of the Clintons' who had hosted their wedding reception at her house. Both Hutchinsons won and they rented a house together in Washington. So now here was the first-term congressman, fresh to the nation's capital and its peculiar ways, assigned to judge the conduct of a man he had worked with and against for a quarter century.

After his initial hesitation to join Clinton's defense team, Greg Craig spent the next several days poking around the White House. On Sunday, September 13, the day after his Truman Balcony chat with Clinton, Craig consulted with Chuck Ruff, who was cordial even though the recruitment of Craig in some ways threatened his position within the White House political structure. On Monday and Tuesday, Craig worked things out with John Podesta. What finally tipped the decision for Craig was the allure of playing a part in history. It was a selfish reason, he admitted to himself, but he also truly thought he could help Hillary Clinton. That made it seem more noble.

Before he would agree to come on board, though, Craig wanted to ensure he was given the authority to do the job right. He did not want to be simply another cog in the vaunted White House spin machine; to be effective, he believed he had to be in charge. As he negotiated with Podesta, Craig insisted on having the ability to call or meet with the president one-on-one whenever he needed to—"walk-in" privileges that precious few in the White House were granted since the early chaotic days of the first term. Craig also wanted an office in the West Wing near the Oval Office just as Podesta and Ruff had, not over in the Old Executive Office Building next door, where most of the lawyers and aides worked. In the byzantine world of the White House, access and real estate were the coins of the realm. For a couple of days, Craig sparred with Ruff over who would be in charge; Ruff did not particularly want Craig to report to the president without him. But Podesta, who had no love lost for Ruff and his secretive ways, ultimately gave Craig what he wanted. Hillary Clinton even surrendered part of her office suite on the second floor of the West Wing to provide space for Craig. While he would come aboard with the title of "special counsel," they devised another, less formal term to reflect what he hoped would be his mandate—Craig would be the "quarterback" of the defense team, a description that was later written into the announcement of his appointment. Also joining the team would be two former White House congressional lobbyists recruited to return in this hour of need, Steven Ricchetti and Susan Brophy.

Craig's demands showed that he was smart enough to insist on assurances of authority and naïve enough to believe them when offered. By this point, the White House was a den of backbiting and recriminations. The atmosphere Craig found when he arrived was almost poisonous. The legal team he joined was isolated and defensive, the political team suspicious and sometimes even hostile. Rahm Emanuel, the president's tough-minded, foulmouthed senior adviser, ignored Craig from the start. Paul Begala, the White House counselor who felt so betrayed by Clinton, was virtually absent, nursing his wounds. Erskine Bowles continued to resist entreaties to get involved in the mission to rescue the president. Ruff and David Kendall were professional and polite, but wary of their turf, a little peeved at the implication that Craig was needed to finish the battle they had been waging so tirelessly for so long. Resentment against Craig bloomed quickly, to the point where White House aides referred to him derisively behind his back as "QB," mocking his football-inspired job description.

While Craig tried to get up to speed, the rest of the White House was trying to reassure nervous Democrats. Ricchetti helped set up a daily 11 A.M. conference call of well-connected Democratic lobbyists and political operatives around town, both to gather information and to keep erstwhile allies from bad-mouthing Clinton to the press. Other senior officials traveled up to Capitol Hill to absorb some of the fury aimed at the president. On the same Tuesday, September 15, that Craig officially started at the White House, Podesta, Bowles, and Doug Sosnik appeared at a luncheon meeting of Senate Democrats for the first time since the release of the Starr report. The three aides listened as one senator after another vented.

Senator Joseph R. Biden Jr., the Delaware Democrat who ran for president himself in 1988, only to be forced out in a plagiarism scandal, expressed the sentiments of many in the room when he told the visiting aides that the caucus would be better off if Clinton resigned. If it were up to them on a secret ballot, Biden said, there was no question how it would come out. But, he acknowledged, it was not up to them, and he recognized that Clinton would not resign.

Dispirited themselves, the aides gamely tried to defend their boss. "Look, he didn't tell the truth," Bowles told the senators. "He didn't tell the truth to me. He didn't tell the truth to you. He didn't tell the truth to the American people." But, Bowles added, it had to be put in perspective—while Clinton was clearly wrong, the will of the people should not be overturned through impeachment. Bowles might have been trying to convince himself as much as his audience.

Biden's statement was not the only dire warning sign the White House was receiving from the other end of Pennsylvania Avenue. Installed in his West Wing office, Craig was conducting his own canvass. He talked with Congressman Tim Roemer of Indiana, identified by Bill Richardson's survey as one of the Democrats to worry about most. "You guys are going to have to focus on the facts of this," Roemer admonished. "The facts are serious." Craig also called an old acquaintance from the Ed Muskie presidential campaign in Iowa in 1972, Kent Conrad, now a senator from North Dakota.

"How are we doing up there?" Craig asked.

"You're about three days away from a delegation of senior Democrats coming up there to ask the president to resign," Conrad replied ominously.

Conrad knew of no specific organized effort; what he was conveying was the sour mood of the place, his sense of where things were heading. For all of his public apologies, Clinton had yet to truly demonstrate remorse for what he had put the country through, particularly in private conversations with senators in which he continued to rail against Starr and the unfairness of it all. Conrad offered Craig a proposal: Tell the president to throw himself on the mercy of the voters. He should go on national television, say he had to decide whether to continue in office or leave, and then ask the public to weigh in. He should say, "I can't continue to govern without your consent." That would be a way of reestablishing his support from the public, a measure of affirmation for his leadership—or, possibly, the other way around. Either way, Conrad said, Clinton could not remain without the American people on his side.

When the Republican members of the Judiciary Committee met privately in Room 2138 of the Rayburn Building on Wednesday, September 16, Asa Hutchinson went in ready for battle. After the collateral damage from releasing the Starr report on the Internet sight unseen, he was convinced that it would be an even bigger mistake to put out the videotape of the president's grand jury testimony. Having seen it with Hyde over the weekend, Hutchinson thought parts of Clinton's testimony would be useful in building a case, but concluded that showing it unedited would dull the impact of the moments that were damaging for Clinton. What they should do, Hutchinson told his colleagues, was release the tape only as part of presentations during hearings, where it could be placed in context. It would have much more impact that way. Releasing the tape now, so early, would draw too much attention to it.

"The videotape should be released, but the issue is timing," Hutchinson argued with his fellow Republicans. "A party-line vote is not going to be helpful, and that's what we're gearing up to do."

Hutchinson argued as passionately as he could, but won few converts. When it came time to decide, he got only four votes—Chris Cannon of Utah, George W. Gekas of Pennsylvania, Ed Pease of Indiana, and himself. Yet party discipline was a powerful force, and once the Republican caucus determined its position, the members felt compelled to go along with the collective decision. In the full committee, when it counted, Hutchinson and the others would vote to release the tape, despite their misgivings.

At 1:30 P.M. that day, aides to Hyde returned a call from *Salon,* a liberal Internet magazine that had made its mark with a staunch defense of the president and relentless attacks on his enemies. The magazine's editor, David Talbott, told Hyde's spokesman, Sam Stratman, that they were preparing to go with a story about a five-year extramarital affair the Judiciary chairman had in the 1960s. Stratman and Paul J. McNulty, a committee lawyer who was helping out with media chores, rushed to Hyde's office to break the news to him. *Salon* planned to report that Hyde had an adulterous relationship with a hairdresser named Cherie Snodgrass starting in 1965 when he was forty-one years old and a year away from first winning a seat in the Illinois legislature. Hyde nodded. It was true. Snodgrass's husband had found out that they were fooling around and had confronted Hyde's wife, putting an end to the affair. But Hyde had managed to patch things up with his wife, and they had remained together until she died years later.

Word that his affair would be publicized crushed Hyde. He turned and stared off into the distance for a moment. It was so long ago, a lifetime. Now he would have to call his four grown children and confess to them before they heard the news elsewhere. He would have to tell them that he was not the paragon of virtue he hoped they saw him as. Nothing he had been through in all his years in politics had hurt like this.

First, though, Stratman and McNulty needed to know what to say to *Salon.* Hyde dictated a statement: "The statute of limitations has long since passed on my youthful indiscretions. Suffice it to say Cherie Snodgrass and I were good friends a long, long time ago. After Mr. Snodgrass confronted my wife, the friendship ended and my marriage remained intact. The only purpose for this being dredged up now is an obvious attempt to intimidate me and it won't work. I intend to fulfill my constitutional duty and deal judiciously with the serious felony allegations presented to Congress in the Starr report."

McNulty thought that it would be hard to describe an affair in Hyde's forties as a "youthful indiscretion" and worried that the press or the Democrats would jump all over that, but he saw pain on Hyde's face and decided not to press the point. Hyde had been around long enough that he must know the right thing to say, McNulty told himself—a naïve assumption, as he would later conclude after the late-night talk-show hosts had a field day with the phrase. Fortunately for Hyde, Newt Gingrich was not parsing the statement. Hyde called Gingrich to offer to resign because of the controversy, but the Speaker told him to forget it. Gingrich could hardly afford to let adultery by itself become an offense meriting resignation; at that moment, rumors were running around the Speaker's office suggesting that Gingrich himself was engaging in an illicit affair with a young House clerk. Gingrich's own chief of staff, Arne Christenson, had heard the gossip but could not bring himself to ask the boss.

Hyde was the third prominent House Republican to have his personal failings aired in recent weeks, following disclosures about Helen Chenoweth of Idaho and Dan Burton of Indiana, and the first instinct among Republicans was to point the finger at the White House. This must all be part of a scorched-earth strategy by the president's defenders to take down his adversaries. *Salon* was seen as a house organ for the White House, particularly Sidney Blumenthal, the journalist-turned-aide who helped spread negative information about Clinton enemies.

In this case, though, there was no hard evidence of White House complicity. A friend of Fred Snodgrass, the betrayed husband of Hyde's paramour, had called dozens of reporters pitching the story of the hypocritical Judiciary chairman about to sit in judgment of a president. At the White House, most of Clinton's top aides recognized immediately that a hit piece on Hyde would only backfire, whether they were responsible or not, and so John Podesta immediately called Hyde's office to deny any known involvement in the story and to vow that he would fire anyone discovered to have played a role. Abner J. Mikva, a former White House counsel for Clinton who had served with Hyde in the Illinois congressional delegation, stepped in to reassure his old friend as well. After checking with Erskine Bowles, Mikva called Hyde to reinforce that the White House was not behind the story.

"I'm the only friend the president's got up here," Hyde responded. "He shouldn't be making trouble for me."

Still, while Hyde was convinced that sympathizers of the president wanted to "dirty up" Republicans like him, he accepted that the White House had no involvement. He could see how the story would come out independently, given the bitterness still felt by Snodgrass. But that did not persuade everyone else in the House Republican caucus, and suspicion of the White House only deepened.

The next day, Asa Hutchinson got a call from a CBS News reporter with an ominous warning. "I'm next target," Hutchinson scratched down on a notepad.

While the drama with *Salon* was unfolding, Clinton confronted the press for the first time since the Starr report was released. As had become almost routine during the scandal, he chose to do so while flanked by a prestigious foreign leader, a circumstance his aides knew would tend to make questions about a sex scandal look petty in comparison to issues of geopolitics. In this case, Clinton had the good fortune to be paired with visiting Czech president Vaclav Havel, the legendary playwright who had led his country to freedom from Communist oppression in the "Velvet Revolution" of 1989. Clinton enjoyed the reflected limelight and Havel's bewilderment at Washington's obsession with such trivialities.

"I don't like to speak about things which I don't understand," the Czech president responded when asked about the Lewinsky case. Standing nearby listening intently was Havel's own second wife, a striking blond nearly two decades his junior.

Coached ahead of time by a worried staff, Clinton remained calm and contrite, refusing to let any of the questions bait him into expressing the pique his aides and friends saw regularly. The president had been particularly upset to learn over the weekend that Chelsea had read the Starr report on the Internet, but he kept that to himself in front of the reporters. "The right thing for all people concerned is not to get mired in all the details here but . . . for me to focus on what I did, to acknowledge it, to atone for it, and then to work on my family—where I still have a lot of work to do, difficult work—and to lead this country," he said. Asked if he would resign, he responded with striking passivity, saying merely that voters "want me to go on and do my job and that's what I intend to do." Likewise, he offered no objection to the release of his grand jury videotape, dismissing the question as "not of so much concern to me."

But Clinton's solicitous tone was belied by a partisan audience. The news conference had been staged in the Dean Acheson auditorium at the State Department, and several dozen employees from the building had been allowed to attend, seated behind reporters in the back of the room. Whenever Clinton addressed the allegations, the administration workers applauded—sending exactly the wrong impression. The State workers were making it sound like a pep rally rather than an apology from the president. Mike McCurry, the custodian of Clinton's public image, smoldered with frustration.

Amid all the focus on contrition, one person Clinton still adamantly refused to apologize to was Paula Jones, whose lawsuit had brought on all this trouble in the first place. But now for the first time in their four-year legal struggle, the former state clerk was signaling to the White House that she would be willing to forgo an apology in exchange for money. Although her suit had been thrown out by a federal judge, she had asked an appeals court to reinstate it. With Clinton politically vulnerable, her lawyers chose this moment to propose new settlement negotiations. In a letter to Clinton attorney Bob Bennett, they offered to drop the appeal for $1 million—and no admission or apology. The president agreed to mull it over.

*   *   *

Several hours after Clinton's news conference with Havel, the Democratic lawyers on the House Judiciary Committee found themselves with an unexpected problem. They were meeting with their Republican counterparts one last time that evening to hammer out what should be withheld from the remaining evidence sent by Starr before it would be released. The dilemma: the Republicans were agreeing to everything.

Under the rules set by the House when it voted to put the Starr report on the Internet the week before, the rest of the evidence submitted by the independent counsel in those eighteen cardboard boxes would automatically become available to the public by September 28 except those parts redacted by the committee before then. Republican and Democratic lawyers had labored late into the night to find all the Social Security numbers, telephone numbers, addresses, personnel records, and other identifying information about witnesses buried in the evidence books and to identify sensitive areas of testimony, such as sexual details or personal information about Lewinsky's weight problems. But as the two sides came to agreement on dozens of proposed redactions, Julian Epstein, the Democratic chief counsel, began to worry. They had to have differences. They had to have split votes. The whole premise governing the Democratic strategy was to paint the Republicans as unfair, to make a case that they were being partisan. After the public backlash against the salacious material in the Starr report, Epstein particularly wanted to have some disagreements so that the Democrats could say the Republicans were only interested in putting out smut—never mind that most Democrats voted along with the GOP majority to release the original Starr report, all equally ignorant of what it might contain.

With harmony threatening to break out, Epstein pulled aside the lawyers handling the negotiations for the Democrats. They needed to find more proposed redactions, he told them, items that were guaranteed to goad the Republicans into rejecting them. The Democratic lawyers made another effort and finally came up with some that the other side would surely object to. They would insist on holding back testimony about Clinton stimulating Lewinsky sexually with a cigar and other such material. The Republicans would not agree, because it seemed to go to the question of whether Clinton had lied to the grand jury when he claimed he never touched her in an erotic way. For Epstein, it was perfect. The Republicans would have to vote along party lines to put out more sexual detail.

When the committee gathered for a closed-door executive session the next day, Thursday, September 17, the plan fell neatly into place. Faced with a series of Democratic motions designed to lure them into the trap, the Republican majority behaved exactly as Epstein had anticipated and rejected eleven redactions or proposals to delay the release of the supplementary material or to give the White House an advance look. That gave the Democrats all they needed to parade out to the cameras and complain that they were being railroaded, as liberal congressman Barney Frank of Massachusetts proceeded to do during the first available break.

"There's no bipartisanship," Frank huffed to reporters waiting outside the closed doors. "They're just deciding what they want to do and doing it."

Republicans grew increasingly agitated at the Democratic spinning. Sam Stratman, Hyde's longtime press secretary, found Jim Jordan in the hallways and angrily confronted him. Jordan had been hired by Gephardt to handle media relations for the committee Democrats after working for the Senate's campaign finance investigation in 1997.

"I've heard about you," the six-foot-six Stratman ripped into Jordan, towering over the much shorter man. "If you can't win on the merits, you're here to blow up the process. It's not going to happen."

"Look around you," Jordan replied. "It's already happened."

During their lunch break, a group of Republican committee members wandered over to the Members' Dining Room, including Asa Hutchinson, Lindsey O. Graham of South Carolina, James E. Rogan of California, Steve Buyer of Indiana, and Mary Bono of California. The discussion soon turned to Clinton's sky-high job-approval ratings. Hutchinson asked Bono, the only female Republican on the committee, why the president's support among women was still so strong.

Bono replied with a reference to Lewinsky's testimony about her encounters with Clinton. "The first thing that popped into my mind," said Bono, "is how many women have four orgasms within thirty minutes?"

The fight over redactions spilled over into a second, unscheduled day of closed meetings on Friday, September 18, before the committee finally agreed to release the following Monday more than three thousand pages of documents as well as the videotape of Clinton's grand jury testimony. Republicans were still steaming over how the Democrats had manufactured a partisan battle. In the end, the two sides had agreed on 155 items to be blacked out of the evidence books, but those were submitted to the committee in a single motion for unanimous consent, while the actual disagreements on 24 other items that Epstein and his team had found were subjected to separate roll call votes. Thus, the Democrats were able to say that every roll call vote had fallen along party lines, even though the parties had actually concurred on 87 percent of the redactions. The Republicans grumbled: they had been outspun.

Republicans had one more thing to worry about from the day's events. During the closed-door debate, Graham had made a cryptic reference that worried his colleagues still stung by the *Salon* article on Hyde earlier in the week. "I'm a sinner too and I'll probably be confessing my sins before this is over," Graham said. Hutchinson went up to him afterward to ask him what he was talking about. Simple, said Graham. "I'm single, I'm not gay, and therefore everything I do is a sin."

As successful as they were in provoking confrontations with Republicans, Julian Epstein and Abbe Lowell were proving equally capable of picking fights with each other. Epstein, accustomed to a virtually free hand in running the committee, was not about to cede control to Lowell, who had been forced upon him by Gephardt and knew nothing about Capitol Hill. Lowell believed he should be given authority to run the investigation as he saw fit.

The uneasy relationship flared up over an issue as arcane as access to the secret-evidence vault. Lowell had groused about Republican restrictions, so Epstein went to Tom Mooney, his Republican counterpart with whom he got along well, and negotiated an agreement that would allow material to be brought in or removed from the room if either of the two men approved it. Lowell was incensed that such a deal was brokered without him, convinced that it undermined him. Epstein cared about working with Mooney. Lowell thought Mooney was manipulating Epstein and called in a fit of pique.

"What the fuck are you doing?" Lowell demanded when he reached Epstein. "You mean if I want to take a pencil in there, I'm going to have to get your written permission?"

"What are you worried about, Abbe? I'll just delegate you the authority," Epstein said. "Abbe, I could give a fuck what you bring in and out. Just don't embarrass us."

Among the Democratic congressmen on the verge of deserting Clinton was Jim Moran of Virginia, a former boxer and stockbroker who had been vocally critical of the president since the August 17 grand jury appearance. Moran had supported Paul Tsongas during the 1992 Democratic nomination contest because he had been told about Clinton's profligate philandering by a staff member at the Democratic Governors' Association, who described the then-governor from Arkansas as trolling for young women at conferences. After the election, Moran believed Clinton had put that behind him and, even when the Lewinsky story broke, gave him the benefit of the doubt. By coincidence, Moran had been at the White House just three nights after the Lewinsky story broke, part of a small group invited for dinner and a movie, a preview screening of *The Apostle,* with stars Robert Duvall and Farrah Fawcett among the guests. Everyone was buzzing about the allegations until the president walked in, when a hush fell over the room—all except one woman, who clearly did not realize who had just arrived because she could be overheard saying, "I would. Wouldn't you?"

Moran left that night convinced that Clinton had not had sex with Lewinsky and the congressman said so publicly. That made him all the angrier when Clinton reversed himself seven months later. "The fact is that he lied to the American people as he did in the court. I think that that is a major problem that is going to undoubtedly necessitate impeachment proceedings," Moran said in a television interview on Monday, September 7. By that Friday, he was talking about resignation. "He should certainly consider any option that would put an end to this and enable the Congress and the country to recover from one of the saddest episodes in American history."

Clinton was distressed. "Why's Moran doing this to me?" the president asked his friend Terry McAuliffe. At a party at the home of White House political director Craig Smith, McAuliffe confronted Moran and demanded to know the same thing. "We can't let Republicans take back everything we won," McAuliffe told him. "You can't play into their hands." The conversation grew so angry that other guests backed away.

Hillary Clinton was upset as well. When she ran across a top Moran adviser, Mame Reilly, at an evening awards banquet, the first lady pressed the same question. "Why is Jim doing what he's doing?"

"He feels really bad about the way the president has treated you," Reilly told her.

"Doesn't he know what he's doing is hurting the country? And hurting me?"

"I think you're the only one who could get him to stop," Reilly answered and offered to have Moran call her.

Reilly called Moran that night, and the next morning, Friday, September 18, he called the White House. "Mame tells me you want to talk to me, you're concerned about what I've been saying," Moran told the first lady. "Hillary, I'm going to be frank with you. Your husband has disappointed me. He's a philanderer and he's shown himself to be a liar. As much as I respect his ability and commitment to public service, I'm just terribly disappointed. And I'm offended at what he's done to you, not to mention all the people who supported him. . . . If you were my sister, I think I'd just grab him, pull him behind the house, and break his nose."

Hillary sounded touched. "Oh, Jim, I love you emotional, Irish Catholic–type guys. If I had had a big brother like you, maybe my life would have turned out very different." But he should realize that she was still behind Bill. "I'm the field general of this operation. I believe in my husband. I believe in what he has accomplished and what he'll be able to accomplish once this is all over. He is my best friend. And I still believe in him."

Moran noticed that she did not say she believed the president, but that she believed *in* him. In any case, she went on to frame the debate and point the finger again at Clinton's enemies. "Much of this is coming from right-wing elements that have been opposed to my husband for what he's been trying to do all his life. And I don't want them to win. And you shouldn't want them to win either. And I think it's important for the country that they not win."

After fifteen minutes or so, Moran hung up, impressed by the first lady's poise. He still thought her husband was a lout, but he respected her request to tone it down. From now on, he would stop speaking out so much.

Now that the grand jury videotape was about to be broadcast to the world, the highest-ranking officials at the White House resolved finally to find out what was actually on it. Only three of the president's advisers had been allowed in the room at the time of the testimony in August—David Kendall, Nicole Seligman, and Chuck Ruff—and they had been characteristically closemouthed afterward. In the hours and days following the session, the president's political advisers tried in vain to learn what Clinton had been asked, how he had answered, and whether there were any particularly dramatic moments or big surprises. But the lawyers refused to tell them, trying to set another leak trap for Starr's office—if only the three of them in the room knew for sure what had actually happened, they reasoned, any disclosures in the newspapers would have to have come from the prosecutors, in violation of grand jury secrecy rules.

Now the time had come to force the issue. On Saturday, September 19, just forty-eight hours before the tape would air, Seligman was invited over to the White House to brief political aides such as Mike McCurry, Doug Sosnik, and Joe Lockhart. She brought her notes from the interview—the only record the Clinton team had, since they were not given their own copy of the videotape or transcript—and read through them for the political aides in Ruff's office.

What were the highlights? the aides asked. What were the contentious moments? The gossip mill suggested Clinton had flown into a blind rage.

He was feisty, Seligman said, even angry at times. But it was controlled, directed anger. Contrary to the rumors, he did not get up and storm out. He did not shout or scream or carry on. He did get indignant and quarrel with the prosecutors from time to time, accusing them of asking "trick questions" and colluding through Linda Tripp with the Paula Jones team in their "bogus lawsuit." Overall, he stuck to the script and came across as a human being pained by what he had done and embarrassed to be put into this situation by vengeful prosecutors.

The political aides realized this could work to their benefit and a strategy

quickly fell in place. In the two days they had left, they would play the
expectations game as if they were on the campaign trail. In hotly contested
primary elections, a candidate's strategists often publicly overstate how well
they think their opponent will do, while underestimating their own chances;
that way, when election night returns prove better than forecasted, their candidate appears stronger than assumed and their rival weaker. In this case, Clinton aides reasoned, if viewers were told to expect an out-of-control president
but instead saw what Seligman described, it could rebound against the
Republicans. Doug Sosnik spoke with several reporters around town that
weekend to stoke expectations. "I don't know, I haven't seen it, but they set the
bar, and if he didn't do that, they haven't met the test," Sosnik would tell
them. David Kendall was dispatched that same Saturday to give a preview
briefing to the *New York Times* on condition that he not be identified as the
source. The next day's story reported that on the tape Clinton's "moments of
remorse are mixed with flashes of fury at the prosecutors." The Clinton
team may not have created the initial expectations of presidential outbursts,
but it encouraged them for its own purposes.

In a basement recording studio in the Rayburn Building the next morning, Monday, September 21, a technician for Fox News loaded a videotape
released by the Judiciary Committee into a pool transmission that would
feed more than a half dozen television networks. At 9:25 A.M., the president's
testimony went out unedited for millions of Americans to watch and judge
for themselves, in living rooms, office suites, and even on the massive jumbo-
sized screen in Times Square. What they saw was not the explosive confrontation they had been promised, but instead a sometimes methodical,
sometimes monotonous four-hour-and-twelve-minute question-and-answer
session punctuated by occasional bursts of glaring, finger-wagging pique by
Clinton. Normally, any sign of emotion by a president in public is magnified
in the media hotbox—a glint of irritation at a news conference can be ana-
lyzed for days as a sign of deep-seated anger—and the moments of indignation shown by Clinton during his testimony were strikingly unusual for a
politician who had long since learned to contain his volcanic temper in the
public eye. But the public had been told to expect more. Instead, it saw a
man under fire who mostly remained calm, so that the "flashes of fury" came
across as understandable exasperation.

In New York to deliver a twenty-four-minute speech on terrorism to the
United Nations, Clinton did not watch his own August performance. He sat
in a holding room waiting to be introduced to the General Assembly, with the
television turned off. Sosnik and McCurry had accompanied him, but as
much as they wanted to flip on the TV to see how it was progressing, they
resisted until the president left the room. Sosnik soon called down to the

White House to see how it was being received and was told that people were offended by the release. It seemed to be spinning the president's way.

Clinton was welcomed with several standing ovations by the foreign leaders gathered in the U.N. chamber. Like Vaclav Havel, they did not understand what the fuss was about and wanted to show support for the embattled leader. As he left the building, Clinton got an update from Sosnik on how the grand jury tape was playing.

"Well, I think a lot of people are still waiting for all these outbursts," Sosnik reported with a smile.

Clinton related what an ambassador from a Latin American country had told him in the chamber: "We have coups in our country too, but they're with guns."

"Look, you're either on offense or you're on defense. The press only gets that one side is wrong and the other is right."

Newt Gingrich was lecturing Henry Hyde on how to handle the impeachment situation. Nuance did not sell, Gingrich said. It was Wednesday, September 23, two days after the grand jury tape had been released, and the two Republicans were about to head into another meeting with their Democratic counterparts to discuss what sort of inquiry, if any, the House should begin. Public opinion had hardened in Clinton's favor since the release of the tape, and now, unlike their initial encounter in the Dinosaur Room, Gingrich was ready to play hardball.

As they sat down with the Democrats in Gingrich's office, however, it was clear that Dick Gephardt was playing offense too. The session got off to a testy start as he complained about being shut out on the redactions. Hyde, on defense, shot back that the Democrats had not been excluded. The two sides had disagreed on only about 2 percent of the redactions, he said, exaggerating the point for effect. He also expressed irritation at the press for characterizing him as nothing more than the subcommittee chairman for the Speaker. Gingrich tried to turn the tables and challenged Gephardt to state what he would do. The minority leader, keeping the initiative, came back immediately with a proposal he had prepared with advisers before the meeting. Any inquiry should be modeled on Watergate rules and be limited to thirty days, he said. The ulterior motive was simple: the Democrats could say they wanted to look into the issue but also wanted to close it down quickly, appealing to broader public sentiment.

The plan was a joke and the Democrats knew it, Gingrich said. There were too many things to look into. The president had been protecting his confidant Bruce Lindsey from testifying because he was the key to the case, Gingrich said. They had an obligation to wait to see if the Supreme Court would uphold Clinton's claim of executive privilege to prevent Lindsey from testifying. They might also want to look into Whitewater and the allegations of hush money paid to former associate attorney general Webster Hubbell, the Clinton-Gore campaign's fund-raising excesses from 1996, and even the controversial transfers of sensitive satellite technology to China.

"It could go on eight to nine months if you let it be opened up to anything else," Gephardt protested.

During Watergate, Peter W. Rodino Jr., the Democratic chairman of the Judiciary Committee, had followed leads wherever they went, Gingrich responded. So would they.

Gone were the bipartisan platitudes of the Dinosaur Room meeting two weeks earlier. Unlike that session just prior to the delivery of the Starr report, Gingrich and Gephardt split up after their session for separate meetings with the media. Asked by reporters about the possibility of censure or some other form of "plea bargain" by the president, Gingrich brusquely dismissed the notion, saying it "simply puts the cart before the horse." Gephardt was just as happy to be rebuffed. It would give him more evidence to make the case that the Republicans were being partisan. Every split vote played into a strategy that Democrats had been employing for months, even before Clinton's grand jury session—painting him as the victim, not the villain.

"We're going to win by losing," Gephardt told Abbe Lowell as they left Gingrich's office.

While Gephardt was trying to find a way to make impeachment go away in thirty days, Clinton was swallowing his pride to try to make the underlying case that had spawned it go away just as quickly. Clinton's attorney, Bob Bennett, called up Paula Jones's lawyers on the same Wednesday and offered to pay $500,000 to settle the suit, half of their $1 million demand from earlier in the month. It was an extraordinary move, but Clinton and his advisers calculated that, to clear the decks for any deal with the House, they needed to eliminate the threat of the Jones suit being restored by an appeals court. Prominent congressional Republicans had been demanding that the president admit that he lied under oath before they would consider a deal short of impeachment, but he could hardly concede anything close to that as long as the suit remained active. Bennett believed that the Eighth U.S. Circuit Court of Appeals, which had not looked sympathetically on Clinton's side earlier in the case, might well overrule the lower court and reinstate the lawsuit in light of the subsequent revelations of misconduct by the defendant. It was time to end the suit if they could.

Jones's lawyers welcomed the counteroffer without committing one way or the other. They would take it back to their client for consultations, they said.

In seeking to resolve the case once and for all, the Clinton team also hoped to forestall any new allegations. Chuck Ruff and the others never knew where the next explosive accusation might come from, and the Jones case always seemed to threaten some new disclosure. Buried deep inside the appendices Starr sent the House was the hint of one such time bomb: Jane Doe No. 5. That was the designation used by Jones's lawyers for Juanita Broaddrick, a nursing home operator from tiny Van Buren, Arkansas, who had met Clinton some twenty years earlier when he was the state attorney general attending a conference in Little Rock. She told a few friends at the time that a meeting in her hotel room had turned into a horrifying rape by the future governor. When contacted by the Jones team, Broaddrick denied the story under oath. All of this had been mentioned in court documents filed during the Jones case earlier in the year, although it got little attention in the media because of its lurid and unsubstantiated nature. But a little-noticed aside in the just-released Starr documents revealed that Broaddrick had since recanted her denial in an interview with the Office of the Independent Counsel. After mentioning her sworn statement in the Jones case, the report added parenthetically: "On April 8, 1998, however, Jane Doe No. 5 stated to OIC investigators that this affidavit was false." Beyond that, there was no elaboration.

Ruff was concerned. He had heard murmurings about Jane Doe No. 5 and the cryptic reference. On the same day Gingrich and Gephardt met, Ruff called Abbe Lowell. What was out there? Ruff asked.

Lowell tried to reassure him. The Republicans were not pushing it, he said. Lowell did not think the committee planned to release the Starr investigation interview with Broaddrick. They were probably okay.

Ruff hung up the phone, still worried. They would have to make sure they were fully prepared in any case. The problem with these situations was that while Ruff often found a defense he could raise, he would never get to the bottom of what had really happened between Clinton and these women behind closed doors.

Ruff was not the only one still afraid of the emergence of other women. So were Democrats in Congress. The next day, Thursday, September 24, Tom Daschle invited Lowell to the regular luncheon of Democratic senators to brief them on impeachment. The senators were curious about what the evidence actually showed as opposed to how it was portrayed by Starr. Bob Torricelli and Carl Levin of Michigan were particularly intense about Starr's handling of the matter. Joe Lieberman asked about the precedent of impeachment starting in one Congress and continuing into the next after an election. Dianne Feinstein wanted the inquiry to focus on perjury, calling that the only issue of real significance. Richard J. Durbin of Illinois asked what was the difference between crimes and impeachable offenses.

But the real question on many of their minds came toward the end, when
Ted Kennedy, himself famous for a lifetime of womanizing, complained that
Clinton was still a moving target. Are there any other shoes to drop?
Kennedy asked. What he wanted to know without saying so explicitly was
whether there were other women out there. No one really knew the answer.

The meeting ended on a fractious note. Robert Byrd, the imperious senator from West Virginia, became irritated that they were even discussing the
case. Why were they having these meetings and talking about evidence when
they could become jurors? Byrd demanded. Daschle replied that they were
not prejudging anything, only trying to keep up to speed, given that they
might have little time to evaluate information if charges were sent by the
House. Byrd was not assuaged.

By the time the House Judiciary Committee met in executive session
again at 10:20 A.M. the next day, Friday, September 25, to consider the final
round of documents to release, the Republicans had learned their lesson.
This time, they made sure to offer even the redactions everyone agreed on as
separate motions to get the recorded unanimous votes. One of the items to
be withheld by mutual accord was the FBI interview of Juanita Broaddrick.
With no serious rifts over redactions, the Democrats offered a series of other
motions designed to generate party-line votes, such as proposals to let Clinton's team have an advance look at the documents before they became public. When the eight-hour closed session finally ended, however, thirteen of
the twenty-five roll call votes were unanimous and another virtually so.
Republicans emerged spinning the day as a model of bipartisanship.

CHAPTER FIVE

"How can you be so goddamn stupid?"

Bob Bauer wanted to meet somewhere discreet, somewhere out of the way where no one would know them. Lloyd N. Cutler suggested lunch at the Metropolitan Club. An exclusive 135-year-old establishment whose membership rolls had included at least a half dozen presidents, the Metropolitan Club with its kelly-green card room, private squash court, barbershop, and fifteen-thousand-volume library had long been a refuge for Washington's power elite, "an island of stability and respecter of precedence in the disturbing sea that washes around it," as the legendary presidential adviser Clark Clifford once put it. Located two blocks from the White House, it was not exactly out of the way. As Bauer and his host made their way across the dining room on Wednesday, September 23, Cutler seemed to stop at virtually every other table to shake someone's hand. So much for secret negotiations.

But the real sponsors of this day's lunch had built in an extra layer of protection to guard their identities. They had sent Bauer and Cutler in their stead, proxies to discuss how to resolve the constitutional crisis gripping the capital. Bauer represented Dick Gephardt, who wanted to explore the possibility of securing a deal in which Congress would censure the president for his misconduct and end the impeachment proceedings. Cutler in effect represented President Clinton, who was equally eager for censure as a way out of his dilemma but could not say so publicly for fear that his ready acceptance would kill its chances with congressional conservatives intent on punishing him.

No one wanted his fingerprints on this one. When Gephardt's office called the White House to suggest a meeting, John Podesta had instructed the minority leader to deal with Cutler, an eighty-year-old éminence grise of the Washington establishment with long connections in the upper reaches of both parties. Having served both Jimmy Carter and Clinton as White House counsel, Cutler was now back at his private law firm and could play intermediary in the censure talks with full deniability—if word spilled out, everyone could say Cutler was just a free agent and the White House was not bargaining, when in fact he was not and it was. Similarly, Gephardt did not want it known that he was trying to broker a deal, so he worked through his own private lawyer.

Over lunch, Bauer laid out Gephardt's thoughts for Cutler. What about some sort of financial penalty to accompany censure by Congress? What about Cutler trying to broker a deal with Ken Starr?

Cutler listened politely, but did little to tip his hand. He made clear that he was not there as the president's official attorney, and if he ever did talk with Starr on Clinton's behalf, it would not be in his capacity as a lawyer. That said, the two attorneys discussed what sort of agreement Clinton and Starr could come to. Bauer said he had an associate who had scoured through the law books and found an obscure false-statements infraction that Clinton could theoretically acknowledge without actually pleading guilty to a crime. They discussed whether it would be constitutional for Congress to penalize the president in any way other than impeachment and removal. Finally, Cutler asked Bauer if he would put something in writing for him. Bauer agreed.

The plan Bauer produced on Gephardt's behalf was comprehensive but hardly simple. To satisfy the variety of often conflicting impulses generated by the long-running controversy, Bauer constructed an elaborate mechanism intended not only to sanction Clinton but to clean up the damage he had done to the institution of the presidency. And in keeping with the clandestine nature of the talks, Bauer came up with a little subterfuge of his own to disguise the real sponsor of the plan. When it came time to submit it to the House legal staff to be translated into formal legislative language, Bauer routed the plan through another congressman's office, a willing Vic Fazio of California, so that Gephardt's name would not show up anywhere on the document in case it ever became public.

Under the proposal, lawmakers would condemn Clinton by issuing a finding that "the President engaged in misconduct unbecoming the stature and high responsibility of the office that the President holds." Citing the Starr report, the resolution concluded that Clinton "engaged in an improper relationship with an individual in the employ of the President of the United States," gave her "unusual and inappropriate assistance" in finding a job, and "failed in clear terms to encourage that individual to provide completely truthful and forthcoming testimony about her relationship with the President in a civil action in which the President was also a defendant." Rather than determine whether Clinton committed perjury or obstruction, the Gephardt plan would sidestep the legalities by asserting merely that Clinton "failed to provide completely truthful and forthcoming testimony" in the Paula Jones case, and in his subsequent appearance before the grand jury, "relied instead on evasive and technical formulations in answering certain inquiries of the Independent Counsel."

"Beginning in January 1998 through August 17, 1998," it concluded, "the conduct of the President of the United States in the civil deposition, before the grand jury and in numerous public statements made directly or, by his encouragement, by the President's aides (A) weakened the bond of trust with the American people essential to the discharge of the President's duties; (B) needlessly prolonged public concern over these matters, delaying and undermining the ability of the country to conduct other business; and (C) added substantially to the cost of the investigation of the Independent Counsel."

As penalty for these actions, the proposal would strip Clinton of his government pension for five years after leaving office in January 2001. Under the payment scales then in effect, former presidents received $152,000 a year in pension, meaning Clinton would have to give up more than $750,000 over the five years. Left unaffected by the Gephardt plan would be other postpresidency benefits, including round-the-clock Secret Service protection and allotments for office space, staff, and expenses that ranged from $300,000 to $550,000 a year. Like any other financial sanctions envisioned as part of "censure-plus," as the concept had been termed, Clinton would have to agree to abide by it voluntarily since Congress was prohibited by the Constitution from passing a "bill of attainder" punishing a single individual. But unlike other ideas floated in public, the notion of taking away his pension had the appeal of ensuring that the penalty would come directly from Clinton's own pocket. A simple fine, many feared, could be paid out of the president's legal expense fund—or worse, out of personal savings and investments that had been generated almost entirely by Hillary Clinton, the family's main breadwinner during their years in Arkansas at a time when he made just $35,000 a year as governor. Only in recent days had it occurred to some Democrats that simply fining the president might make his wife pay for his misdeeds.

But Gephardt did not want merely to hold the president responsible. He worried that in the cover-up, Clinton had done grievous damage to the office by misusing White House lawyers to mount a personal defense and by claiming privileges that were later rejected by the courts. If left unaddressed, Gephardt feared, future presidents would pay the price. Thus, his proposal would create a bipartisan Joint Committee for the Study of Presidential Privileges to settle on the proper boundaries of executive privilege and perhaps even formally establish a "protective function privilege," a legal right to confidentiality that the Secret Service had invented in an unsuccessful bid to prevent agents who guarded the president from revealing what they saw or heard while in his presence. The resolution would also order the Office of

Government Ethics to develop new standards for the president's use of the White House Counsel's Office "to assure that Government resources are committed to official purposes only, and not the personal requirements, including personal defense, of the President."

The last part of Gephardt's plan, though, was the most complicated—and the most cumbersome. Clinton worried about making a deal without guaranteeing that Starr would finally go away. In an effort to force Clinton and Starr to reach their own agreement, Gephardt's resolution would urge the two sides to resolve any issues related to the Lewinsky matter by the time the president delivered his next State of the Union address in January. Within thirty days of that deadline, Starr would have to report the status of any negotiations, and if no deal had been struck, Congress would vote on whether it believed the investigation should proceed. If Congress voted no and Starr went forward anyway, lawmakers would then vote on whether to terminate funding for the independent counsel's office. "This is, in other words, a Congressionally mediated plea bargaining arrangement designed to put pressure on Starr, but also to allow for a vote on his investigation," Bauer wrote in a cover letter that accompanied the plan when he faxed the completed version to Gephardt's office on Thursday, October 1.

Gephardt liked the thrust of the plan. At least there was something to work with. A copy was faxed to Cutler for his review.

Even if Gephardt and Clinton could work out a mutually acceptable deal, though, there was still the matter of the Republicans. As part of The Campaign, Tom DeLay had vowed to do everything he could to kill censure and maintained a steady drumbeat of correspondence to GOP congressmen lobbying against it. On Thursday, September 24, the day after Bauer and Cutler met for lunch at the Metropolitan Club, DeLay sent a "Dear Colleague" letter to fellow Republicans citing statements by a pair of law professors criticizing the concept of censure. "Even constitutional scholars agree: censure is not within our powers," DeLay wrote. A week later, on Thursday, October 1, just as Bauer was faxing his completed plan to Gephardt's office, DeLay sent the GOP conference another such missive, this time reproducing an op-ed piece in the *Wall Street Journal* and adding a note: "Any talk of censure or 'censure-plus' should be stopped."

Censure was not the only angle Gephardt was pursuing. Even if he could find a resolution to sell to Republicans, he would first have to deal with the more immediate question of whether the House should open a formal impeachment inquiry. Given Starr's report and the eagerness of many Republicans to go after Clinton, Gephardt had little doubt that an investigation would be opened, so the trick was deciding what the Democrats should do about it and then trying to herd his rambunctious caucus onto the same path.

Gephardt convened a meeting of Judiciary Committee Democrats in his office on Tuesday, September 29, to develop a unified strategy. The dilemma was dicey and the timing treacherous. In Gephardt's mind, the Democrats could not simply oppose the opening of an impeachment inquiry; with just a month before the election, the perception that Democrats were covering up for a president from their own party would become the singular issue in the campaign. But neither could they go along with the Republicans in simply agreeing to launch an inquiry, even if it was justified; not only would that legitimize the investigation, but it would divide the Democratic caucus right down the middle and still leave many of Gephardt's members vulnerable at the polls. Any Democrat who voted against the inquiry would have a harder time explaining why, if his own party leaders supported it, while those who voted for it risked alienating their political base at a moment when they needed that base the most.

The answer, then, was to draft a Democratic version of an inquiry resolution that would give his members political cover—one that would make it look as if the Democrats were taking the matter seriously but would restrict the process in such a way that the Republicans would be sure to reject it. If Gephardt could get a party-line vote out of it, he would make Republican "partisanship" the issue. Win by losing.

First, Gephardt would have to navigate the treacherous currents within his own party. The White House and a sizable share of his troops in the House, particularly the Congressional Black Caucus, wanted no inquiry whatsoever, believing it unwarranted and a surrender to right-wing forces that had been out to get Clinton. Another group within Gephardt's caucus thought the full-blown investigation sought by the Republicans was merited and opposed any limits on it. The politics of the election played a significant role in where members stood. Those with marginal districts, areas with lots of suburbs and moderate Republican voters or conservative Southern communities where Clinton was anathema to begin with, were pushing for an inquiry. Those from urban areas, particularly districts with heavy concentrations of black voters or union members, key elements of the party's core constituency, were more likely to resist. Putting together an alternative that would stitch together those factions would be tricky.

To do so, the Democrats turned to Rick Boucher, a low-key, moderate member of the Judiciary Committee from the "Fighting Ninth" district in far southwest Virginia, where voters were about as conservative as they came while still voting for Democrats. Boucher was a smart, thoughtful, and thoroughly inoffensive eight-term congressman who worked well with others and was the only Southern, white, Protestant male on the Democratic side of the committee. The rest of the panel showcased the diversity of the party—five African-Americans, four Jews, six Northeasterners—and tended to be significantly more liberal. To reach out to the conservative Blue Dogs, Julian Epstein, the committee's chief Democratic counsel, figured they would need an ambassador who spoke their language, and so he approached Boucher early to recruit him for the role. The problem was that several of the other members saw themselves as the future stars in the history books and were pressing to introduce the alternative inquiry resolution themselves. Congresswoman Zoe Lofgren of California and Congressman Bobby Scott of Virginia had already written their own versions. To smooth over the egos, Gephardt had Boucher work with the most vocal hard-liners as part of a "drafting committee" that had been meeting every day by the time they all gathered in their leader's office that Tuesday—Lofgren, Scott, Maxine Waters of California, Jerrold Nadler of New York, William D. Delahunt of Massachusetts, and Sheila Jackson Lee of Texas.

In this group of lawyers who loved to talk, the discussion quickly bogged down in circuitous debates about small points: Should there be "whereas" clauses? Should they set a standard of proof that should be met before proceeding further? Should they even call their proposal an "inquiry"? Should there be deadlines and, if so, when? Scott pushed to create a series of internal deadlines within the inquiry structure so that certain things had to happen by certain dates, rather than merely setting out a single target end date.

In the end, Boucher and Epstein came up with a two-stage inquiry—the committee would first set a standard for what would constitute an impeachable offense before moving on to consider the specific facts in the Clinton investigation. Under any circumstance, the inquiry would conclude by November 25 with a House vote on whether to impeach, throw out the case, or apply some alternative sanction.

Henry Hyde was working on his own blueprint for how to proceed. The simplest and safest course was to do what his predecessor Peter Rodino did in Watergate, and so Hyde crafted an inquiry proposal that was adapted nearly word for word from the one used in 1974 to investigate Richard Nixon. There would be no limits on the subject areas that could be explored or the time that could be expended. Both Hyde and Conyers would have subpoena power, although the full committee could overrule either. Clinton's lawyers would be allowed to attend all hearings, respond to evidence gathered by the panel, cross-examine witnesses, make objections about the relevance of evidence, and submit exculpatory material.

Hyde unveiled his plan the next day, Wednesday, September 30, but if he thought he would satisfy the Democrats by acceding to their repeated demands for "Rodino-style rules," he quickly learned otherwise. The White House and its congressional allies immediately decried the plan as a wide-open fishing expedition. The trick for Democrats at this point was to keep the focus on procedures and make the issue about fairness, as outlined in Bob Bauer's memo to Gephardt some six months earlier. While Hyde put the finishing touches on his plan, Asa Hutchinson ran into Bobby Scott on the House floor. "I hope you don't give us a fair process," he told Hutchinson, "because if you do, I might have to vote to impeach the SOB."

On the same day that Hyde was producing his inquiry plan, Clinton's lawyer in the Paula Jones case, Bob Bennett, visited the White House to persuade the president to ratchet up the settlement proposal. Clinton was not an easy sell; he had been infuriated when he saw Jones's attorneys on the Sunday television talk shows over the weekend asserting that any payment of money would be tantamount to an admission of guilt. But he put aside his pique and signed off on increasing the offer to $700,000—exactly the amount Jones had demanded in her original lawsuit in May 1994.

The next day, the settlement talks took an unexpected detour. A quirky New York real estate magnate named Abe Hirschfeld entered the picture on Thursday, October 1, making an unsolicited offer of $1 million if Jones would settle. Jones was immediately enthralled—with that much money, she could pay off her lawyers and still have plenty left over. And if she could get the $1 million from Hirschfeld as well as the $700,000 from the president, all the better. At the White House, however, Hirschfeld quickly became the skunk in the garden. The tycoon was an eccentric who fancied himself a political heavyweight even though he had lost his bids for public office. Then there was the problem of the 123 counts of state tax evasion filed against him. The president simply could not get involved with someone like that. Clinton was in enough trouble as it was.

The president found himself stymied on another front as well. In recent days, he had become infatuated with a plan intended to undercut any impeachment inquiry before it got started. His allies could collect the signatures of thirty-four Democratic senators on a letter stating that they would vote against conviction based on the evidence presented by Starr, guaranteeing acquittal and making any further proceedings moot. Clinton grew excited about the idea during late-night phone calls with Senators Bob Torricelli and John Breaux of Louisiana. But when the president's aides learned about it, they were aghast, recognizing that it would be seen as political gimmickry and expose Senate Democrats to charges of prejudging the case. Finally, Tom Daschle stepped in and put a halt to the plan, telling Clinton it would be improper and imprudent. Besides, Daschle and his aides were not at all confident they could get thirty-four signatures; making the effort and then failing to collect enough would be a political disaster.

Further complicating the president's problems was the impending departure of some of his key lieutenants. Mike McCurry, his witty and widely respected press secretary, would not be talking Clinton out of any more jams. McCurry had taken advantage of a lull in the Starr investigation during the summer before the grand jury session to announce that he would resign in mid-October when Congress was done; now he moved up his departure date to October 1, the same day Hirschfeld made his offer. The next day, Clinton's senior adviser Rahm Emanuel, who had turned down an attractive job offer back in his hometown of Chicago early in the year rather than leave as the Lewinsky scandal was unfolding, announced that it was now time to go. Two days after that, Erskine Bowles told reporters that he planned to leave as soon as the budget negotiations were wrapped up later in the month.

No one was quitting in protest, at least officially. But in effect, Bowles and McCurry really were. Both had the advantage of credibility when they said they were leaving for other reasons, since everyone knew they had wanted to go months before and had only stayed out of a reluctance to jump ship at a moment of crisis. Yet few other top aides were quite as disenchanted with Clinton. He had squandered everything they had tried to do. Bowles told colleagues that he was convinced Clinton would never have confessed had his DNA not been found on Lewinsky's dress. Both Bowles and McCurry still liked the president on some level, supported his goals, and did not want to kick him when he was down. But the bottom line was they just could not work for him anymore.

Emanuel was a different story. He was mad at the president too, mostly for being stupid, but he did not take the Lewinsky affair as personally. A blow job was just a blow job. It was hardly worth getting worked up about. And unlike Bowles, Emanuel was a street fighter who rarely shied away from a good scrap. "Rahm-bo," as his friends called him, liked to shout at people and mix it up. But Emanuel had been there at the creation, one of the few aides still left from the early days in 1991 when they were trying to elect a little-known governor from Arkansas. After seven years, he was exhausted and ready to make some money for his growing family.

For his part, Paul Begala had decided to stay. During a fishing vacation with his wife in Utah following the president's August 17 admission, the disillusioned counselor had come close to quitting. Clinton had made a fool out of him. Before Begala had gone out to defend the president publicly in the early days of the scandal, he had made sure to check with the lawyers and was assured that Clinton's denial included oral sex. No one made any of the semantical distinctions that Clinton would later raise before the grand jury.

Now knowing the truth, Begala could not stand even to look at the president. "I'm a Catholic," he explained again and again to fellow White House aides. Had it not been for the impending impeachment drive, Begala would have bolted. But as Republicans moved to launch an inquiry, the anguished aide determined he had to stay for one last fight. Impeachment, he thought, was too extreme.

Whatever their motivations, the departures of McCurry, Bowles, and Emanuel stripped the president of some of his strongest assets at a critical juncture. And some of those left behind fumed at them for jumping ship. Doug Sosnik, who would take Emanuel's title as senior adviser and had already become a constant companion to the president, did not blame McCurry because he had announced his plans three months earlier. But Sosnik was furious at Bowles and Emanuel for abandoning them at this danger point. Indeed, Sosnik generally stopped speaking to either one.

As the Judiciary Committee approached its decision on whether to launch a formal impeachment inquiry, members on both sides grew increasingly nervous about their chief investigators. Neither of them had ever done anything like this before; they did not know Capitol Hill. How would they come across?

At a 5 P.M. meeting of the Judiciary Republicans on Thursday, October 1, Hyde asked David Schippers to preview what he planned to tell the full committee the following Monday. Schippers, sitting in a wingback chair in the corner with a script in his lap, went over it in a low-key, matter-of-fact way that left several of the members alarmed. It did not sound clear or organized at all to them. At that point, the members were summoned to the House chamber for a vote and while milling around the floor they compared notes. If Schippers did that on Monday, they agreed, they were dead.

Congressman Bill McCollum, a hard-charging senior member from Florida, called over to the committee offices. He got one of the lawyers, Paul McNulty, on the phone and shared the group's concern. "There's some really worried people here," he said. From the panic in McCollum's voice, McNulty feared they were on the verge of a mutiny. He tracked down Tom Mooney shortly after 7 P.M. and the two of them found Schippers. The Republican members gathered again the next morning, Friday, October 2, before the full committee was to meet. This time Schippers gave a full-dress, forty-five-minute version of his presentation, with flair and passion, calming the nerves of the antsy congressmen.

Like Schippers, Abbe Lowell was finding his ability questioned as the chief investigator for the Democrats. The day after Schippers reassured his members, Lowell came under fire from his own. At a meeting on Saturday,

October 3, some of the Democratic members seemed shocked that Lowell would be handling their side of the presentation. Zoe Lofgren of California suggested that they hire Laurence Tribe, the famed Harvard constitutional law professor, to do it instead. Maxine Waters agreed. "Don't take offense," she told Lowell. "You're smart. But you have to admit you're not very telegenic. You're too pale, too pasty."

By this time, of course, it was far too late to hire someone else, so the members would have to live with Lowell. Instead, they issued a flurry of sometimes-conflicting instructions: Don't draw conclusions. Don't say we need an inquiry. Don't say the facts are unclear. Don't preempt us on constitutional standards. Don't go too long. Don't go too short.

Lowell had had difficult clients before, but never sixteen at once.

Just as one rich eccentric had inserted himself into the fray a few days earlier, another chose this moment to seek attention. Larry Flynt, the gaudy publisher of *Hustler* magazine, paid $85,000 to take out a full-page ad in the *Washington Post* on Sunday, October 4, offering $1 million for "documentary evidence of illicit sexual relations" with a member of Congress or high-ranking government official. While many congressmen laughed it off, others privately reacted with dread.

Shortly before nine o'clock the next morning, Monday, October 5, a standing-room-only crowd filed into Room 2141 in the Rayburn House Office Building, the same chamber where the Judiciary Committee had voted to impeach Richard Nixon in 1974. Hanging on the wall above the dais were two oil portraits—on the left, Peter Rodino, the Democratic chairman from that era, and on the right, Henry Hyde, the Republican chairman now facing his own challenge twenty-four years later. The parallels and ironies were lost on no one as the panel began considering whether to open the first impeachment inquiry since Watergate.

Hyde labored to strike an evenhanded tone as he opened the meeting, insisting the panel's task was simply to follow its duty and examine the evidence. "Let me be clear about this—we are not here today to decide whether or not to impeach Mr. Clinton," he said. "We are not here to pass judgment on anyone. We are here to ask and answer this one simple question: Based upon what we now know, do we have a duty to look further or to look away?"

Conyers, by contrast, came out swinging. The real villain, he insisted, was Starr, not Clinton. "Even worse than an extramarital relationship is the use of federal prosecutors and federal agents to expose an extramarital relationship," Conyers declared. "Yes, there is a threat to society here, but it is from the tactics of a win-at-all-costs prosecutor determined to sink a president of the opposition party." The only remaining member left from the committee that had voted to impeach Nixon, Conyers added that there was no comparison between the two scandals. "This is not Watergate," he said. "It is an extramarital affair."

As the rest of the members made their opening statements, it quickly became evident that most saw things through a purely political lens, with rare exceptions. Congressman Charles E. Schumer, a sharp-tongued New York Democrat who was running for the Senate, was one of the few Democrats to acknowledge that Clinton was guilty of more than adultery, even if Schumer did not think it rose to the level of impeachment. "To me, it's clear that the president lied when he testified before the grand jury—not to cover a crime, but to cover embarrassing personal behavior." On the Republican side, the junior members seemed to struggle. Asa Hutchinson said he agreed that this was no Watergate. "But are not the important questions the same?" he asked. "Is the rule of law less significant today than twenty-five years ago? Is unchecked perjury, if proven, less of a threat to our judicial system today than when Watergate was the example?" Lindsey Graham appeared the most torn. "The truth is, I have no clue what I am going to do yet," he said, offering a folksy homily in what amounted to his public debut. "Now, I can tell you that and look you in the eye and honestly mean it. I don't know if censure is appropriate, we should just drop it, or we should throw him out of office." He offered a pithy summation of the issue: "Is this Watergate or *Peyton Place*? I don't know."

After lunch came time for the opening presentations by the two chief investigators, each fully aware that skeptics on his own side were waiting for him to stumble. Perhaps more than the opening statements by the committee members, the presentations by David Schippers and Abbe Lowell made clear how quickly the issue was becoming polarized along party lines. In 1974, the Democratic chief counsel, John Doar, worked hand in hand with his Republican counterpart, Albert Jenner, dispassionately sifting through evidence for months to figure out where it all led before finally joining together to recommend Nixon's impeachment. That would never happen with Schippers and Lowell, given that each had already drawn hard-and-fast conclusions from the Starr report. They spent their time at the witness table on this afternoon acting as advocates rather than conveyors of facts. Schippers essentially adopted Starr's view of the case, while Lowell generally embraced Clinton's.

Although stemming from sexual misconduct, Schippers told the committee, the case was built on "allegations of an ongoing series of deliberate and direct assaults by Mr. Clinton upon the justice system of the United States." Schippers repackaged Starr's eleven potentially impeachable offenses into fifteen, counting more examples of lies separately while dropping Starr's assertion that the president committed high crimes by invoking executive

privilege improperly and refusing for months to appear before the grand
jury. With his grandfatherly appearance, Schippers made an impressive public introduction. But unfamiliar with the etiquette of Capitol Hill, the mob-
busting Chicago attorney strayed beyond his role as a staff person at the end
by offering his personal thoughts "as a citizen of the United States who happens to be a father and a grandfather:

"To paraphrase Sir Thomas More in Robert Bolt's excellent play *A Man
for All Seasons,* the laws of this country are the great barriers that protect the
citizens from the winds of evil and tyranny. If we permit one of those laws to
fall, who will be able to stand in the winds that follow? Members of the committee, you're not being watched only by the individuals in this room or even
by the immense television audience throughout the world. Fifteen generations of Americans, our fellow Americans, many of whom are reposing in
military cemeteries throughout the world, are looking down on and judging
what you do today."

That set off the Democrats. It was not Schippers's job to lecture the committee. He was staff, hired to carry out their instructions, not to offer personal opinions. Conyers insisted that Schippers's final statement be stricken
from the record. Hyde agreed it crossed the line and ordered it expunged.

Younger and more familiar with Washington ways, if not necessarily Capitol Hill, Lowell made less of an impression on the committee members with
a presentation that had been drafted to suit sixteen would-be authors. But he
laid the groundwork for the central theme of the Democratic argument—that
for all the "renaming or relisting or further subdividing the grounds" by
Republicans, the case came down to lying about sex. Lowell pointedly
attacked Starr's handling of the investigation, saying the committee should
review the independent counsel's reliance on Linda Tripp, his treatment of
Lewinsky, and the torrent of leaks that had appeared in the newspapers.

"This preliminary review indicates that the charges are often overstated;
based on strained definitions of what is an offense under the law; are often not
supported by the actual evidence in the boxes; and are sometimes . . . the
product of zeal to make the case rather than to state the law," Lowell declared.

The committee then moved to the inquiry resolution itself and the
Democratic alternative. Rick Boucher's substitute called for opening the
inquiry on October 12 by developing a standard for impeachment and
deciding by October 23 whether Starr's allegations reached that level even if
they were true. If they did, hearings into the facts of the case would begin
October 26. The committee would have until November 17 to make a recommendation on whether to impeach the president, dismiss the charges, or
impose some other form of sanction, and the full House would have to act by
November 23.

Although they did not say so aloud, the Democratic strategy was the same used in 1974 by the minority Republicans, who also sought time limits and insisted that standards for impeachment be set first, only to be rebuffed by the majority. For weeks, committee Democrats had been demanding that the House follow the Rodino model, but now they were adopting the opposite approach. While Hyde hoped to finish by the end of the year, he was quick to reject the idea of establishing a formal schedule, mindful of warnings from Senator Fred D. Thompson, a Tennessee Republican who believed the White House simply ran out the clock on his campaign finance investigation in 1997 after an end-of-the-year deadline had been set. Furthermore, Hyde knew the committee was unlikely ever to settle on a consensus definition of high crimes and misdemeanors. "It's like pornography," he said. "You know it when you see it, but you have trouble defining it."

The vote on the Boucher proposal fell along strict party lines, 21–16 against. Congressman Howard Berman, the California Democrat who had declined to formally join the White House whip team to preserve his independence, then offered his own compromise version, this one also requiring the committee to decide whether Starr's report met the threshold for a full impeachment inquiry but imposing no time limits. Congressman Barney Frank, the sharp-tongued liberal from Massachusetts, spoke out immediately for the plan—both because he thought it was a smart counterproposal and because he knew if he embraced it from the start, that would keep Republicans from accepting it. It did not matter, however. The Republicans had already resolved not to agree to any limits. The committee rejected Berman's motion and then approved Hyde's plan on the same 21–16 roll call.

Having unified the largely liberal Democrats on the Judiciary Committee, Dick Gephardt and his group now turned to trying to sell their alternative to the broader and ideologically more divergent full caucus. Boucher was the emissary. At 8 A.M. on Tuesday, October 6, the morning after the committee vote, Boucher showed up for doughnuts and coffee at the office of Congressman Gary Condit, a conservative Democrat from California. Laying in wait for him there were about twenty members of the Blue Dogs, and despite their political kinship with Boucher, the reception was hostile. Condit, Pat Danner of Missouri, and Ralph Hall and Charles W. Stenholm of Texas all spoke out forcefully. People in their districts were upset at the president's conduct, they said, and Congress had to investigate thoroughly. They did not want some fig-leaf, half-assed inquiry.

Boucher left the meeting and reported back to Gephardt. Their alternative plan may have worked in committee, but it clearly would not fly on the floor. If they could not do something to swing some votes, they could lose fifty Democrats or more on the final vote, which would imbue the Hyde inquiry with bipartisan legitimacy and put the burden on those Democrats who voted no to explain themselves back home. Gephardt sent Boucher back to the drawing board with instructions: come up with a new plan to sell to their caucus.

That night, Asa Hutchinson went to a party thrown by Fox News at the Capital Grille restaurant on Pennsylvania Avenue, where he ran into an old acquaintance from Arkansas—Dick Morris, who helped mastermind Clinton's political comeback after the 1994 midterm debacle, only to be forced out when he was caught with a prostitute. Morris, as flamboyant with his politics as with his toe-sucking sexual adventures, did not fail to entertain.

Are you still on good terms with the president? Hutchinson asked, mildly curious.

"Well, he fired me, Asa," Morris said bitterly. "He canned me and then he got his people leaking dirt on me, following me around."

In fact, Morris had become so disaffected from the White House that he had been publicly throwing around allegations of a "secret police" and suggesting in one interview that Clinton might have cheated on the first lady because she did not like men. White House aides had been waging a private campaign to discredit Morris with his onetime friend, the president. Clinton confidant Bruce Lindsey had taken to circling Morris's more outrageous statements in the newspapers and leaving them on the president's desk. Clinton would shake his head when he read the clips. "He's lost his mind," Clinton told aides. "He's a lunatic."

His break with the president complete, Morris began offering Hutchinson freelance strategic advice on how Republicans should run the impeachment effort. Forget about simply building a case that Clinton lied, Morris said. The public had already accepted that he did that but did not want to impeach him for it. Americans did not want to have their private lives investigated and to have a scarlet *A* stitched to their coats. The Republicans could win in a courtroom but not in the public arena, and that was where this was being fought. Instead, Morris suggested calling attention to the damage done to the system of law as well as the more sinister elements of the case, the "secret police" employed by the president against women who might make allegations of sexual misconduct.

"You know, I told Clinton he needed to be looking out for this months ago, but he didn't take my advice," Morris went on. "He didn't want to cash in on it. So now I'm selling it to you guys."

That was Morris—still a political mercenary. Never mind that he helped keep Clinton in the White House for a second term; now he was going around offering strategic tips to those trying to remove him from office. "Morris never learned one of the first rules of politics," Hutchinson observed to his aide Chris Battle in the car as they left the party. "If you're going to challenge the king, you had better kill him, you had better take off his head."

It was a lesson, Hutchinson knew, that he should remember himself.

At the White House, Clinton was deeply unhappy with the idea of his own party offering an inquiry proposal, even a truncated one designed for tactical positioning. It was simply outrageous. Democrats, he told aides, should hold the line against any inquiry and take their case to the American public. The polls showed that voters were on his side on this, and he made sure to point that out to nearly every House Democrat he talked with.

At 8 A.M. on Wednesday, October 7, the day before the full House was scheduled to vote, Clinton called Rick Boucher at home for advice on what he ought to tell Democratic members.

"Tell them to vote their conscience," Boucher suggested.

A couple of hours later, Clinton invited reporters into the Oval Office. "I think everybody should cast a vote on principle and conscience," he said. "It's up to others to decide what happens to me, and ultimately it's going to be up to the American people to make a clear statement there." At a separate, closed meeting with twenty-five freshman House Democrats at the White House, the first lady made a similar point, telling the members that the Clintons would support them no matter how they voted. But Hillary Clinton brought more edge to the discussion, attacking the Republican inquiry proposal as a poor copy of the process used during Watergate and advancing the case for the Democratic alternative. She had been making similar points with her husband's lawyers, pushing them to make constitutional standards for impeachment more of an issue.

By the time the House Democratic caucus met, Boucher had redrafted the alternative plan in an effort to woo the Blue Dogs, moving it closer to Howard Berman's model. He had taken out the internal deadlines and stretched the final target date from November to the end of December. The committee would only have to make a preliminary determination that Starr's allegations, if true, would constitute high crimes and misdemeanors before proceeding with a formal inquiry. That was about as much give as Boucher could offer the conservatives in his party, and, in fact, it was so much latitude that a variety of Clinton advisers and congressional Democrats frantically worried that Gephardt and Boucher had gone too far. Surely, they thought, the Republicans would call their bluff and simply accept the plan.

James Carville, the president's most vocal public defender, called Rahm Emanuel at the White House to complain vigorously that they were making a mistake of epic proportions. If the Republicans agreed to the Democratic plan, it would destroy Carville's whole line of attack—and by extension the president's defense. His entire argument was that the impeachment drive was a partisan witch-hunt; a bipartisan agreement would remove all the arrows from his quiver.

"How can you be so goddamn stupid?" Carville asked.

Emanuel reassured him. Don't worry, they won't take it. "Their stupidity will never allow them," he said.

Gephardt and Boucher were applauded by the caucus when they presented the plan. But many of the Blue Dogs and some moderates, while mollified by Boucher's revisions, still wanted more running room to vote as they pleased and felt pressure because Clinton seemed to be making it a test of loyalty. Congressman Jim Moran of Virginia said at the caucus meeting that opposing the Republican inquiry plan would be the death of the Democratic Party in the coming election, just as the Republicans had been demolished by Watergate in 1974. They had to get the president to back off.

Congressman Vic Fazio arrived at the White House several hours later on a mission—to convince the president to drop his opposition to the impeachment inquiry. The chairman of the House Democratic caucus, Fazio had concluded that turning the vote into a showdown would tear the party apart and force scores of vulnerable congressmen into making a hazardous choice just four weeks before an election. The moderates thought the president would listen to Fazio since earlier in the year Clinton had sounded out the California Democrat about becoming his chief of staff and had more recently considered him to lead his impeachment defense. By now, though, Fazio realized it was probably hopeless. He had been trying to get an appointment to see the president since Monday but kept being put off and now was being granted an audience less than twenty-four hours before the floor vote. The White House probably knew why he was coming, and Fazio suspected the two-day delay was no accident.

When Fazio arrived at the Oval Office, Clinton was having lunch. As they began to talk, the president sat in a chair opposite his desk sipping his soup. Fazio told Clinton that he was there to strongly recommend that the president not make this an important vote and instead give House Democrats a pass to support the Hyde inquiry. This was the last vote before the election, Fazio noted. Not only would backing off be helpful to Clinton's allies in the caucus, it would also focus more attention on the vote everyone knew would eventually come—the question of impeachment itself. After the election, Fazio noted, Clinton might have to go to some of these same wavering members and ask them to make a far more courageous vote. Fazio suggested the president say something like, "I know the process is proceeding and I intend to protect my interests and fight against the unfair impeachment. But this is not the vote that matters. I'm going to ask my friends and supporters to support me on the ultimate vote and not impede this procedural step."

Clinton shook his head. He did not want to confuse the issue, and he certainly did not want to give any ground, he said. Polls showing that the public supported him and opposed impeachment should be reason enough for Democrats to stick with him—it was in their own interest to do so. The president was so intense that Fazio found it hard to get a word in. Whenever Clinton dipped his spoon in the soup, the congressman would seize the opportunity to interject. But Clinton would not budge.

Neither would Hyde. Just like the president, the Judiciary chairman came under considerable pressure not to make the inquiry vote a test of partisan loyalties. Several committee Republicans, including Asa Hutchinson, Lindsey Graham, and Charles T. Canady of Florida tried separately to convince Hyde to do what James Carville feared they would—call the Democrats' bluff and accept their inquiry plan. "Henry, can't we limit this?" Canady asked him. "What are we going to lose?"

But Hyde was convinced that Starr still planned to send evidence related to other possibly impeachable offenses. Over the years, the independent counsel had investigated everything from the Whitewater land deal to the improper collection of FBI files at the White House. In his report to the House the month before, Starr had written that he was still looking into whether anyone connected with Clinton had tried to intimidate another woman linked to the president, Kathleen E. Willey, a former White House volunteer who had accused him of kissing and groping her in the Oval Office in 1993. "He's got more, I know he has more," Hyde kept saying.

The chairman was getting heat from the other side too. After announcing that he hoped to complete the inquiry by New Year's, even though he would not commit to such a deadline in writing, Hyde found David Schippers in his office griping that they could never finish by then. They needed at least until the summer of 1999, Schippers said.

"Well, I had to give them some sort of deadline," Hyde explained.

"Well, okay," Schippers replied, "but don't hold us to it."

This was not about polls, Gephardt had declared in the Dinosaur Room a month earlier, but when the moment of decision came, there was the president's former pollster briefing House Democrats the morning of Thursday, October 8, just before they were to head out to the floor to debate the impeachment inquiry. Stan Greenberg, who had worked for Clinton's 1992 campaign, delivered the same message the president had imparted to Vic Fazio, telling the nervous Democrats that they would not pay a political price for opposing the Republican plan, even in rural districts in the South. Four focus groups taken by Greenberg in Cleveland, Ohio, and Towson, Maryland, on September 14, three days after the Starr report was posted on the Internet, revealed a deep skepticism about impeachment in key demographic groups, especially women, who were the core of the party's support. A Democrat who supported a thirty-day inquiry would have an advantage of 18 percentage points over a Republican who voted for an open-ended investigation, Greenberg reported.

As the congressmen filed out and headed over to the floor, they grew energized. If the debate had been civil in the committee three days earlier, by the time it reached the full House it took on an angrier cast. Hyde opened the debate offering reassurances. While he did not want to formalize the restrictions involved in the Democratic alternative plan, he embraced the philosophy behind it. "Believe me, nobody wants to end this any sooner than I do," Hyde told the House. "But the Constitution demands that we take the amount of time necessary to do the right thing in the right way. A rush to judgment doesn't serve anybody's interests, certainly not the public's interests." As for wandering off into every possible area for investigation, he vowed, "I will use all my strength to ensure that this inquiry does not become a fishing expedition."

Reassured by the poll numbers, feisty Democrats were in no mood to accept Hyde's word and began firing up the rhetoric. Congressman Gary L. Ackerman of New York stood to suggest that the House adjourn to the witch-burning town of Salem. Another New Yorker, Jerrold Nadler, called the Republican inquiry a "thinly veiled coup d'état." Congresswoman Nancy Pelosi of California reminded House Republicans that they had elected Gingrich as Speaker even though he admitted making false statements during his ethics investigation. So many Democrats were itching to sound off that Congresswoman Rosa DeLauro of Connecticut privately approached Julian Epstein, the Judiciary Democratic aide who was helping manage the clock, and told him she had forty women who wanted to speak. Epstein came up with an idea: All the women should line up and approach the microphone one by one to ask for permission to submit written comments to the record since they were not given enough time to speak under the Republican floor rules. The image of women shut out of the debate would carry a powerful message to the country about the unfairness of the process while reinforcing that the president still had the support of female lawmakers despite his abhorrent conduct with women. Gephardt loved the plan, and more than a dozen women trooped up to the microphone in a parade of defiance.

"I rise against this pre-Halloween witch-hunt," snarled one, Congresswoman Corrine Brown of Florida.

The polarizing debate did nothing to win over Republicans, but it did bring a number of edgy Democrats back into the fold. The Boucher alternative was voted down on a 236–198 vote that fell largely along party lines, while the Hyde proposal passed 258–176. In all, thirty-one Democrats agreed to go along with Hyde's inquiry—far less than the fifty that some White House and congressional strategists had feared, and less than a third of the one hundred identified by Gephardt back in August as possible votes for impeachment. The House had agreed to open only the third serious impeachment investigation of a president in American history, and yet for the Clinton camp it was something of a victory. They had held their Democratic losses to a minimum and succeeded in setting up the inquiry from the moment it was launched as a partisan exercise by the Republicans.

At the White House, Greg Craig won a $20 pool by guessing there would be only thirty-four defections, the most optimistic estimate among his fatalistic colleagues. The president himself publicly struck a note of serene acceptance. "It is not in my hands, it is in the hands of Congress and the people of this country, ultimately in the hands of God," he told reporters. "Personally, I am fine. I have surrendered this." But out of public view, he had anything but surrendered. In fact, he was fuming about the thirty-one Democrats who abandoned him. An aide gave him a list of the names and he pored over it, offering an instant analysis of the political situation of each of the defectors. This one didn't have to vote against me, he raged; I got 55 percent in his district last time. Same with this one. And that one doesn't have a real opponent in next month's election.

Although the competing inquiry plans were not that different, neither Clinton nor Hyde had given in, despite substantial pressure from his own allies, guaranteeing the partisan vote. As a result, two things were beginning to happen. First, the Republicans had won the larger debate about whether the charges leveled against the president merited an inquiry. The bipartisan consensus now was that it did. All but five members of the House had voted to investigate Clinton; where they had divided was over how to conduct the investigation. Admittedly, some of the more liberal Democrats went along with their party's inquiry plan even though they felt none was justified, but that showed how the political landscape had been shaped to make further investigation the accepted course.

Second, however, the Democrats had won a different victory. They had transformed the issue, at least within their own caucus, from Clinton's behavior to that of the Republicans. The outrage expressed on the floor this day was no longer directed at their own president, as it was when Joe Lieberman had spoken in the Senate a month earlier. Now it was directed at the majority party. It was becoming us versus them, which was exactly what

Democratic leaders knew they needed. Win by losing, Gephardt had said. Nothing unifies like a common enemy. The big question now was which party would pay a price at the ballot box. Would Democrats be punished for seeming to side with a dishonorable president or would they be able to convince voters that Republicans were acting unfairly out of partisan spite?

The Republicans had killed Gephardt's inquiry proposal, but the Democrats killed his censure idea. In the days since he had had Bob Bauer draft a secret plan to reprimand the president and strip him of his pension for five years, Gephardt had privately been trying to sell the concept within his own party without success. Lloyd Cutler never got back to Bauer, and White House aides privately dismissed Gephardt's proposed sanctions as too severe. Worse still, the minority leader found that Democratic congressmen would not buy into the formula—elected officials did not like setting a precedent where their pensions could be taken away for bad conduct. Tom DeLay did not even have to rally his GOP shock troops to bury the plan because Gephardt abandoned it himself once he realized he could not muster his own party behind it. Any possibility of censure, he decided, would have to wait until after the election.

As it was, the White House was plagued by confusion on censure. Cutler was taking direction from Podesta and Ruff, but the president had not made clear exactly what he would be willing to accept. Then there was Hillary Clinton; some aides were told she was adamantly against any censure-plus plan that involved a financial penalty, even though the president at times seemed open to it. Besides, they knew, any censure deal had to be worked out not with Democrats but Republicans, and they were not talking. The situation was exacerbated by the strategic vacuum in the West Wing—Erskine Bowles, Rahm Emanuel, and Mike McCurry were either gone or on their way out, Paul Begala had removed himself from much of the day-to-day skirmishing as he struggled with his Catholic conscience, a burned-out Doug Sosnik had left for a long vacation, and those left behind were exhausted physically, mentally, and emotionally.

Greg Craig, trying to fill the void, spent his days on scouting missions on Capitol Hill, hoping to find a way to beat impeachment before it got out of committee. On Friday, October 9, the day after the House voted to launch an inquiry, Craig went to see Congressman Martin Meehan, one of the more independent-minded Democrats on the Judiciary Committee and a White House ally on campaign finance reform. "Do we have any shot at any Republicans?" Craig asked. "What about Asa Hutchinson? What about Lindsey Graham?"

"You're not going to get Asa Hutchinson in a million years," Meehan answered. Meehan had been turned off during deliberations on campaign finance by Hutchinson's insistence on promoting his own bill rather than working together. On impeachment, Hutchinson only wanted to *look* neutral, Meehan told Craig. The president would not get any committee Republicans, he declared.

Craig did not want to believe it. The White House team was still optimistic about the committee Republicans. All they needed to do was get three to switch and they would bury this thing before it ever got to the floor. Hutchinson and Graham had been meeting regularly with a couple of their Democratic colleagues on the committee, Howard Berman and Bill Delahunt, in what they called "the breakfast club," an effort to find bipartisan accommodation. "We think we can get Lindsey Graham," Craig told Meehan. "We're having a dialogue with Asa Hutchinson."

The president was reaching out too. With everything swirling around him, he sometimes seemed frighteningly lonely and isolated. A couple of days later, on Sunday, October 11, Clinton's agriculture secretary, Dan Glickman, called the White House around 6 P.M. to leave a message with the operator for the president: "Just tell him I'm thinking of him." Clinton called back just three minutes later, anxious to talk. It occurred to Glickman that the president was obviously alone, sitting around the White House without anyone else on a Sunday evening.

"What can we do about this group in the House?" Clinton asked.

Glickman had never been close to Clinton, but clearly the president would now turn wherever he could. Glickman had served eighteen years in the House and had many friends there. He told Clinton he would make some calls and see what he could figure out.

Indeed, the concerted effort to project the image of a president focused entirely on his job was still something of a façade. During the day, Clinton kept up an active schedule. But by night, often sitting by himself in the White House residence, Hillary keeping her distance, he surrendered to his distress, watching hours of television news or talk shows and phoning allies at home to vent and seek solace. In the bedrooms of senior Democrats around town, anytime the telephone rang at 11 P.M., midnight, or even later, they knew who it would be even before picking up the receiver. The president would talk late into the night, alternately bemoaning how this had decimated his family and lashing out at Starr, Republicans, and the conspiracy to entrap him. The next morning, Clinton would often arrive at the Oval Office with some suggested new strategy or piece of political intelligence to pass along to aides, who were then charged with vetting the ideas—and deducing among themselves who had planted the ideas with the president in the dead of night.

*   *   *

The uncertainty and anxiety within the Republican fold was growing. One night in mid-October, Newt Gingrich was back at Bullfeathers, the Capitol Hill bar where he met with advisers the night before the Starr report was released. Across the room he saw two fellow Republicans walk in, Steve Buyer and Mary Bono, both members of the Judiciary Committee. Gingrich wandered over and joined them at their table. He might have expected light companionship from two junior members. What he got was a double serving of anxiety.

"I'm very concerned about this. What are we doing here?" Bono asked the Speaker.

The widow of the late celebrity congressman Sonny Bono, she had just won his seat following his death in a ski accident earlier in the year, and Gingrich had immediately put her on the Judiciary Committee in the apparent hope that she might soften the harder edges of the panel's otherwise all-male Republican contingent. At the moment, though, it was the Speaker's hard-edged approach that she was worried about. She thought there ought to be a meeting among the key Republicans to decide what their strategy would be. She was discouraged by what she had seen from the party leadership and concerned that Gingrich viewed impeachment only as a political tool for the election. The Republicans on the committee had a responsibility to evaluate the case seriously, she told him. She did not feel the leadership understood how hard it was for them.

Buyer was equally candid with Gingrich. A Persian Gulf War veteran finishing his third term in the House, Buyer complained that the leadership had mishandled the impeachment issue from the beginning and was in danger of being burned badly. As Buyer saw it, Gephardt had suckered Gingrich into releasing all the evidence, including the grand jury videotape, without consulting all the Republicans on the committee. As a result, the public had concluded that Republicans were acting vindictively. Buyer told Gingrich that he was deeply disappointed that the Starr report was not sent immediately to the Judiciary Committee.

"This is white-hot," Buyer told the Speaker. Stay out of it and let the committee do its business, Buyer advised. "I'll tell you what's bothered me. This is *evidence*. This is about the president's fitness to serve and should be viewed that way." He was looking at it as a lawyer, Buyer said, but the leadership was looking at it like politicians. "My district is the heartland of America," Buyer added, "and it takes a lot to move these folks. If their emotions are stirred, the lesson is, don't touch it."

Gingrich listened politely, but did not agree. This was good politics, he insisted. They were going to pick up twenty-two seats and strengthen their control of the House, he predicted. That was the most important goal at the moment.

*   *   *

Despite the vote to authorize the impeachment inquiry, Clinton scored several dramatic political victories on the policy front over the next few weeks that would play an important role in determining whether he would survive. After months of haggling over the first surplus budget in three decades, the president engaged in a bit of brinksmanship with Republican congressional leaders, who were so anxious to go home and campaign that they accepted what many in their rank and file viewed as a bad deal. Eight spending bills were rolled into a mammoth, forty-pound, four-thousand-page package that busted spending caps and was forced through on quick floor votes before members could even digest the highlights summary, much less the fine print. Clinton got many of his priorities, including money for the International Monetary Fund and the start of a program to hire one hundred thousand schoolteachers. Aides crowed that the president could still flex his political muscle even at a time of supposed mortal weakness.

What was consciously overlooked in the jubilation at the White House was that the vast bulk of the domestic agenda put together by Erskine Bowles and his team in the heady days of January had long since been tossed overboard, including antitobacco legislation, Medicare coverage for younger retirees, campaign finance reform, child care tax breaks for working parents, a health care patient's bill of rights, and an increase in the minimum wage. Clinton managed to look good in the endgame of the budget talks only because a week before the finale his aides got together, crossed everything off the priority list that was clearly dead, and drew up a list of a dozen programs that already appeared likely to be funded. Once again playing the expectations game, the White House released the truncated list publicly, and when Republicans went along with most, as already seemed likely, it was cast as a tremendous victory.

Still, in the context of the moment, the details hardly mattered. What mattered were the visuals. What mattered were the emotions. For a week, Clinton appeared at repeated campaign-style rallies alongside his party's congressional leaders, Gephardt and Daschle, fighting for some poll-tested policies popular with the voting public. On Thursday, October 15, the day he wrapped up the budget negotiations, the president loped out of the Oval Office for a triumphant victory appearance on the South Lawn and then boarded a helicopter to fly off to the Eastern Shore of Maryland to try to broker a settlement among squabbling leaders in the Middle East. The image could not be more powerful—while the Republicans focused on scandal, the president was sticking to his day job, winning a budget fight and making peace around the world. When he emerged eight days later from the Wye River Conference Center in Maryland with a dramatic deal between Israeli prime minister Benjamin Netanyahu and Palestinian leader Yasser Arafat, it only reinforced the message to the public, and just eleven days before the midterm congressional elections. To make matters worse for the Republicans, radio talk-show hosts like Rush Limbaugh and other conservatives began bashing the congressional leadership every day for what they saw as a capitulation to Clinton on the budget.

While he could broker peace in the Middle East, Clinton could still not find a way to negotiate a truce with Paula Jones. The unwelcome $1-million bounty from Abe Hirschfeld, the New York millionaire, had bollixed up the talks. On Saturday, October 17, Jones lawyer James A. Fisher proposed to Clinton's lawyer, Bob Bennett, that they settle the case for $2 million—half from Hirschfeld and half from the president. Bennett called back the next day to dismiss the suggestion and to threaten to take the president's last $700,000 offer off the table as well. The impasse meant that the two sides would return to court at least one more time. On Tuesday, October 20, both legal teams presented arguments to the Eighth U.S. Circuit Court of Appeals in St. Paul, Minnesota, over whether Jones's lawsuit should be reinstated. Based on their questioning, two of the three judges on the panel seemed to be leaning toward reviving the case. Bennett flew back from St. Paul determined to find a way around the settlement standoff.

Greg Craig and the president's other lawyers were trying to figure out the rules of engagement on the main battlefield. With most members of Congress out of town campaigning for reelection, the attorneys took advantage of the momentary respite to meet with senior Judiciary Committee officials at 2 P.M. on Wednesday, October 21. Tom Mooney, Hyde's chief aide, passed out copies of the resolution and procedures, emphasizing that they had been adopted verbatim from Watergate, when he worked for the minority staff.

Chuck Ruff, of course, was another Watergate veteran, having served as the final special prosecutor on crimes emerging from the scandal, but he saw the precedents differently. One issue he was most concerned about was interviewing witnesses in closed-door depositions. Would the president's counsel be allowed to participate?

"St. Clair made the same request in 1974 and it was denied," Mooney said, referring to Nixon's lawyer, James St. Clair. The president's lawyers would be allowed to question witnesses in public hearings.

That would moot the president's rights if all testimony was taken by deposition rather than in open hearings, Ruff complained.

But witnesses might feel a "chilling effect" if they saw White House lawyers hovering over them at depositions, Mooney countered.

And so it went, each side interpreting Watergate to its own favor, embracing its lessons when they were useful and dismissing them when they were not. Each camp was using the meeting to set up the other for future advantage. Mooney asked Ruff how they could expedite the process, looking for the White House to agree to stipulate to the record, meaning it would not challenge the facts compiled by Starr. If the president refused, the Republicans could blame any delays in completing the inquiry on him.

Ruff tried to deflect the issue. The White House favored both fairness and speed, he said. As defense lawyers, they needed to know two things—the scope of the charges against their client and the standards for what would be considered an impeachable offense. They needed to know exactly what they were going to be fighting about, Ruff said—just Lewinsky or other matters as well? They were already seeing the case shift before their eyes, Ruff complained. Starr had listed eleven charges against them, David Schippers, fifteen. Abbe Lowell, the Democratic investigator, summed up the case in four central allegations.

Which was it to be? Ruff asked. "Everything depends on that."

"Our focus now is on the Starr referral and we are not trolling for additional issues," Mooney said. At the same time, he noted, Starr had said more might be coming, and if additional credible information was sent to the committee, it would have to be looked at.

Ruff pressed. In Watergate, he said, a lot of time was spent gathering information, but they did not change the issues a week at a time. The president's team needed to know today: Was it defending just the Lewinsky allegations or other issues as well?

Mooney again would not commit. "Our focus is on Lewinsky, but I can't tell you that we're limiting the investigation."

The discussion moved on to standards, which Mooney again brushed off. What the Democrats wanted was unprecedented, he said. There had never been a vote on a precise definition of high crimes and misdemeanors. "I don't think we can do this in some kind of advisory opinion," Mooney said.

"We have a real disagreement on this," said Ruff. "This is the heart and soul of the matter."

Greg Craig spoke up, making a formal request for witnesses to testify about standards. "Here is our official letter making the request," he said, handing copies out.

Mooney took the letter but pointed out that Congressman Charles Canady's subcommittee already planned to hold a hearing on standards on November 9. That should deal with the issue adequately. Mooney tried to turn the subject back to more favorable territory: "If we need information from the White House or the president, can we call and get it expedited?"

Yes, Ruff answered, they could just call him.

"Do you have any exculpatory material you want to submit?" Mooney asked. That was another pointed question: If the White House said no, the Republicans would be able to say that the president did not even have any evidence to contest the charges against him.

Craig recognized the trapdoor and tried to sidestep it: "That depends on what the charges are."

The meeting broke up cordially with no real resolution of differences, but plenty of political points made. The president's lawyers had set up the Republicans on the issues of fairness and surprise charges, while the committee staff had set up the defense team on the issues of exculpatory evidence and expediting the inquiry. As they headed out of the room to where the reporters were waiting, the White House lawyers decided Craig would speak for the team. When he got to the microphone, Craig executed the next part of the plan, complaining vigorously that the president was not being treated fairly.

"You cannot investigate conduct without standards," he said. "That's like a game being played with the rules being made by one side as the game goes along. You can't investigate charges without telling who is charged what it is that they're being charged with. It's like attacking a man who is blindfolded and handcuffed. These are not fair procedures."

Back in Hyde's office, his staff had gathered to fill in the chairman on their meeting when Craig's image came on the television screen. They stopped to listen and were stunned that he came out swinging. They had thought the meeting had turned out amicably, that they had forged the beginning of a constructive working relationship, and yet as soon as it was over, here the White House group was back on the attack. As he watched, Hyde's jaw dropped and the cigar fell out of his mouth.

"What's going on here?" he demanded of his staff. "I thought you told me the meeting went well."

Paul McNulty, the committee lawyer who had been tapped to handle public statements during the inquiry, was quickly dispatched to the microphones to rebut Craig. "The standard is high crimes and misdemeanors," he said. "The real question is what are the facts." McNulty reflected the exasperation of the Republicans: "At some point the president's defenders have got to get away from this partisan attack on process."

McNulty had not read Bob Bauer's memo to Dick Gephardt from six months earlier—process was exactly what the president's defenders intended to focus on. For the Republicans, though, the lesson was clear. No matter how friendly White House officials might seem behind closed doors, their public strategy was already set—attack the accusers, demonize the investigators, complain about partisanship while doing everything to foment it. As

Hyde and his aides brooded about the day, they resolved not to let themselves be caught off guard again.

With the inquiry now launched, the first stop for congressional investigators was Starr's electronically locked headquarters six blocks from the White House to see what he had not told them. Quite a lot, as it turned out. Rummaging through Starr's file cabinets, the House lawyers discovered interviews with Monica Lewinsky's hairdressers, childhood friends, and college lovers. There were files from Kathleen Willey's dentist, her mail carrier, the woman who had bought her house, and the funeral home director who had buried her late husband. Starr's investigators had tracked down Vernon Jordan's chauffeur and at least three people who worked at a Parcel Plus store near the Watergate where Lewinsky would go to log on to the Internet. They had scanned Lewinsky's library records at the Pentagon (she had checked out just one book) and seemingly quizzed almost everyone who had ever worked at the Clinton White House, including the painters, the custodians, the men who washed the Oval Office windows, and the doorman who talked about the weather with the president in the elevator every day. A presidential valet told them that Clinton kept a box in his bathroom to deposit clothes he wanted to give away.

None of this Starr had included in the eighteen boxes of evidence he had shipped to Congress that day in September. The congressional investigators were granted access to the secret warrens of Starr's office only after a joint request by Hyde and Conyers. The sheer volume of material collected by the independent counsel was stunning. House investigators counted more than 320 grand jury transcripts or FBI interviews (known by their form numbers as 302's) stored in Starr's office that never made their way to Capitol Hill. There seemed to be virtually no tip, lead, or rumor that had not found its way to the prosecutors, and they had wandered down numerous undisclosed rabbit trails searching for misconduct by Clinton and his allies. The Democratic lawyers finally concluded that Starr must not have sent all this because it would prove to be powerful evidence of how overzealous his pursuit of the president had become. Most of it was extraneous to the case, but the Democrats did find a few nuggets they hoped would be useful. For one thing, some executives at the Revlon cosmetics company had testified that Jordan did not pressure them to hire Lewinsky. For another, there were tape recordings surreptitiously made by literary agent Lucianne Goldberg of her telephone conversations with Linda Tripp, a delicious bit of irony that might also help call more attention to the extensive plotting that had gone into setting up Clinton.

Republicans, however, were most taken by the numerous tentacles of scandal that surrounded the president. Starr's files were a treasure trove for

Clinton foes who had long suspected he was a sleazy, lying skirt-chaser using the powers of his office to cover up his indiscretions. Like many FBI raw files, the Starr archive contained untold wild allegations, sometimes based on nothing more than the hearsay claims of third-party witnesses. Much of the most sensational material came from interviews with the Jones attorneys, including the names of twenty-one different women they suspected had had a sexual relationship with Clinton. Number six on their list, of course, was Lewinsky, and information about a half dozen others had previously come out in court papers filed during the Jones case, including Marilyn Jo Jenkins, an Arkansas utility official; Beth Coulson, a former Clinton-appointed state judge; Shelia Davis Lawrence, widow of one of the president's late ambassadors; and Dolly Kyle Browning, a high school friend of Clinton's. Unlike most of the others, who denied any untoward behavior, Browning claimed she had carried on a three-decade, on-and-off affair with Clinton. But many more cases had never been publicly disclosed. One woman was alleged to have been asked by Clinton to give him oral sex in a car while he was the state attorney general (a claim she denied). A former Arkansas state employee said that during a presentation, then-governor Clinton walked behind her and rubbed his pelvis up against her repeatedly. A woman identified as a third cousin of Clinton's supposedly told her drug counselor during treatment in Arkansas that she was abused by Clinton when she was baby-sitting at the Governor's Mansion in Little Rock. A young woman from Arkansas was even identified as Clinton's "current girlfriend" in Washington.

Starr's agents showed special interest in the state employee because of her involvement in separate court proceedings. After the woman was placed on a witness list in the Jones lawsuit, according to the files reviewed by the congressional investigators, her case was transferred to a federal judge who once was a partner at a law firm closely associated with Clinton. The judge, according to the papers, ruled against the woman, and Starr's office apparently tried to find out whether there was any connection. The independent counsel's files also included a statement by a man who alleged that he knew of another man who, along with Roger Clinton, once threw cocaine intended for Bill Clinton over the fence of the Governor's Mansion.

All of this the congressional investigators from both parties committed to paper, in the form of top secret memos distributed to a few key officials inside the committee. But they were not sure what to make of it. Experienced lawyers and law enforcement agents knew that anyone could make any claim, even the most patently absurd, and it could end up in FBI files. Clearly, Starr's office was a magnet for anyone with a beef against Clinton to phone in some charge or another—allegations that were duly logged no matter how seemingly implausible. And yet much of this uncorroborated evidence fit what David Schippers and his GOP investigators saw as a pattern, and they were more willing to suspend their disbelief. When it came to Clinton, truth had already proven stranger than fiction.

The question became what, if any of this, was relevant and what, if anything, should be done with it. Hyde had made clear he did not want to lead an investigation into Clinton's sex life. But Schippers was intrigued. He saw elements of conspiracy and obstruction in the various stories in the Starr files. Curious things seemed to happen to people who might testify to Clinton's shenanigans. One woman after another subpoenaed in the Jones suit reported that Clinton's lawyers had helped them try to avoid testifying by providing similarly drafted motions to quash the subpoenas. Perhaps, Schippers thought, there was something to this theory that the president engaged in a conspiracy to silence women he had once sought sexually.

CHAPTER SIX

"We need to purge the poisons from the system"

Newt Gingrich woke up on election day confident that by the time his head next hit the pillow, the Republicans would pick up seats, strengthen their hold on the House, and embolden the drive to impeach the president. After two years of marathon campaigning that had taken him to 237 congressional districts in forty-eight states and helped pump some $66 million into party coffers, Gingrich was certain he had done everything he could to set up his side for significant gains. He headed off with his wife, Marianne, on the morning of Tuesday, November 3, to cast their ballots at the Holy Family Catholic Church, where he brushed off a question about whether he would run for president. Within a few hours, he was on the telephone in a conference call with Republican congressmen around the country, boldly predicting a splendid day and a gain of some twenty seats.

Few others on that phone call were quite so optimistic. Even before the polls closed, troubling signs appeared—reports of high turnout in a Kentucky district that could only mean more Democrats were voting than anticipated, trouble in a Mississippi race that had been expected to be a solid win, panicked calls to party headquarters from Indiana and Illinois. As the sun set over the East Coast, ominous returns started spilling into the Speaker's election headquarters in Atlanta. Congressman Jon D. Fox had lost in a suburban Philadelphia district that had swung back and forth between the parties in recent years. So had New Jersey's Michael Pappas, who had once sung the praises of the independent counsel on the House floor with a nursery rhyme that began, "Twinkle, twinkle, Kenneth Starr." In North Carolina, the Republican incumbent senator, Lauch Faircloth, a conservative who had made a reputation as a chief Clinton critic, was sinking fast. Another archenemy of the White House, Senator Al D'Amato, was taking a nosedive in New York, where Hillary Clinton had campaigned extensively in retribution for his Whitewater hearings.

More numbers flowed in. Congresswoman Anne Northup was holding her own in Kentucky; that was reassuring. But the Republican candidate who had been expected to pick up the seat of retiring Indiana Democrat Lee Hamilton was flaming out. Another Republican candidate was losing to Tammy Baldwin, an openly lesbian Democrat in Wisconsin. Once-promising races in Michigan were in the tank. Even centrist Republicans were having trouble holding their own. As the clock ticked on, precincts began reporting in from the mountain and Western states. John Ensign, the rising star Republican congressman from Nevada who was supposed to unseat Democratic senator Harry Reid, found himself falling just short.

Gingrich spent most of the evening huddling with his advisers in a war room in the Atlanta conference center adjoining the hotel where his victory celebration was being held. Around 9:30 P.M., he marched the long halls that led over to the ballroom where his supporters were cheering his own comfortable reelection victory. A sign proclaimed, "It's a Brave Newt World."

Gingrich chose to focus on his own win. "This is the earliest night ever," he exulted. "We've had some very long evenings in here. And it's so much more fun to be able to claim victory this early and have all evening to party."

There was no party and little fun at the National Republican Congressional Committee offices back in Washington, however. Members from around the country were calling in a panic. The committee chairman, John Linder, was in Georgia with Gingrich, and so with no one really in charge, his predecessor, Congressman Bill Paxon, tried to organize a response, handing out assignments and calming people down. But the incongruous image of a boisterous Speaker and his crowd celebrating in Georgia while the party appeared to be crashing elsewhere only exacerbated the anxiety. Few were comforted by Gingrich's upbeat assessment in one television interview after another that the Republicans were doing well because they were about to retain their majority for the third election in a row, the first time they had done so in seven decades. By 10:30 P.M., Republicans seemed to be just breaking even and possibly worse. They could be losing ground—and maybe even the majority. Wasn't this the same Speaker who had so brashly promised a twenty-seat Republican gain just a few hours before?

In Georgia, Gingrich was preparing for a live television interview when his political guru Joe Gaylord kneeled in front of him to give him the latest.

"This is bad," Gaylord said.

"How bad?"

"Well, I don't *think* we're going to lose control."

As the evening wore on, Gingrich, who had started his day so high, began to realize that he would now have to worry about whether he could hang on to his job even if the Republicans did remain in charge. With the opening of the next Congress, the House would vote on its Speaker in what is usually a routine coronation of the candidate selected by the majority party at its own conference. Typically, every member of the majority votes for its candidate once the issue goes to the floor, no matter where he or she stood during internal nomination fights. But if enough Republicans were to defect by voting present or not voting, Gingrich would fall short of a majority and lose. Theoretically, the dissident Republicans could even join forces with Democrats to elect a Speaker more to their liking, presumably a moderate Republican. Or more realistically, just the prospect would force other GOP leaders to revolt before the vote rather than take the chance of such a humiliation. It did not take much to imagine such a scenario—after all, two years earlier, nine Republicans had refused to support Gingrich on the floor, either voting present or casting ballots for another Republican, leaving the Speaker to squeak by with just three votes to spare.

As this new reality sank in for Gingrich, a few West Coast races were being called. Republican Linda Smith lost her challenge to Democratic senator Patty Murray in Washington State, and the seat of retiring California congressman Frank Riggs slipped out of GOP hands. But they picked up Vic Fazio's old seat, and two of their most vulnerable California Republican incumbents, Brian Bilbray and Jim Rogan, managed to pull out tight races. Rogan, closely watched because he sat on the Judiciary Committee, wound up with 50.8 percent of the vote. Gingrich, reassured that the Republicans would at least keep the majority, went to bed at 2 A.M.

At the White House, the plan had been to watch election results in the family theater in the East Wing. But Clinton stopped by his chief of staff's office to check out the early returns. Craig Smith, the White House political director, had fired up a computer and was racing around the Internet in search of vote totals. Clinton, for all of his mastery of the rhetoric of the information age, was a virtual Luddite when it came to computers, but as Craig showed him how to zip through district-by-district results on the Web, Clinton became entranced with the technology. A kid with a new toy, he even gave instant analysis to the aides gathered around, offering assessments on why each candidate won or lost and thoughts on what that might mean for the larger picture.

Eventually, Clinton's fund-raiser and friend Terry McAuliffe called up from the White House theater, where the sausage pizzas, beers, and sodas had been set up for the viewing party.

"We've got everybody here," McAuliffe told Craig Smith.

But the president did not want to leave. "He's on the computer," Smith reported back, "and wants everybody to come up here."

So the entire party moved over to the West Wing, including aides such as

John Podesta, Doug Sosnik, and communications director Ann Lewis, as well as outside allies such as pollster Mark Penn; union leaders John Sweeney and Gerald McEntee; former Texas governor Ann Richards; Hillary Clinton's former chief of staff Margaret A. Williams; former deputy White House chief of staff Harold Ickes; and Ellen Malcolm and Mary Beth Cahill from Emily's List, the Democratic fund-raising organization for women supporting abortion rights. The first lady, who was scheduled to attend the party, opted out, in keeping with her chilly relations with the president since his August admission. Instead, she stayed in the theater with a few friends and watched a new Oprah Winfrey movie, *Beloved.*

But if Hillary had yet to fully forgive him, it seemed to Clinton that the country had. Accurately or not, the election had been cast as a referendum on impeachment, and the numbers flying across the computer screen were a clear repudiation of Gingrich and the House Republican effort to oust the president. Voters saw it the way he did, Clinton believed, as a partisan vendetta.

Around midnight, when it looked as if the Democrats might even take back the House, McAuliffe called his friend Dick Gephardt in St. Louis and handed the phone to Clinton. The pair talked briefly about the prospect of "Speaker Gephardt." Two old rivals, they momentarily forgot their past differences and shared in the joy of the moment. For Gephardt, it was like a dreamworld. Like Gingrich, he had started the morning expecting Republican gains; in fact, his pollster, Mark Mellman, had just that day predicted a net GOP increase of five to ten seats. Win by losing, indeed.

Clinton did not want to go to sleep. He stayed up until past 2 A.M. watching results, until finally McAuliffe and Smith were the last to leave. In the end, Democrats picked up five seats, not enough to win the House, but a smashing upset nonetheless, and one that Clinton hoped could mean only one thing—the end of impeachment.

The president hugged McAuliffe as he walked out. "Terry, I can't thank you enough. We made it through."

For weeks leading up to the election, Clinton and some of the people around him had given counterintuitive advice to Democratic candidates: run on impeachment. For all of the hand-wringing among so many party strategists, the president and his operatives had concluded early on that impeachment would be a boon at the ballot box, not the other way around. Exhausted by the scandal, voters would punish Republicans for launching the inquiry, they argued, not Democrats for defending a morally suspect president.

Stan Greenberg, Clinton's 1992 campaign pollster who had addressed the House Democrats the morning of the impeachment inquiry vote, summed up the strategy aptly in an October 19 preelection memo later sent to candidates entitled "Gaining the Edge." Contrary to their instincts, Greenberg wrote, "Democratic candidates should want their election campaigns to engage the impeachment issue. Do not run from it. The impeachment inquiry is an opportunity." Based on polling conducted October 14 and 15, just a week after the House vote, Greenberg argued that Democrats had positioned themselves skillfully for the fall election. Voters, he found, would flock to Democrats who wanted to end any inquiry by the end of the year or proposed censuring the president rather than impeaching him. To make his point, Greenberg outlined four scenarios where the Democrat could use impeachment on the campaign trail to a Republican's disadvantage. Between them, they showed Democrats winning by 18 to 33 percentage points.

"What these scenarios suggest is that Democrats should want the impeachment issue to feature in this election, whether or not the Republicans want to talk about this issue," Greenberg instructed candidates. "Indeed, their silence ought to be a signal that they understand their disadvantage. Above all, Democratic candidates should welcome a full-blown debate or exchange with their Republican opponent." The Democratic position would appeal not only to party regulars, he added. "Democrats are in a position to energize the base and win over independents at the same time."

Other Democratic consultants were pushing the same message, particularly Clinton's current pollster, Mark Penn. The White House wanted to show that impeachment was a winning issue, and senior Democratic officials were eager for a demonstration project that would test the theory. Jay Inslee, a former congressman who was running against Rick White, a Republican incumbent in Washington State, provided it. Within eight hours of the House vote to open an inquiry, Inslee cut an ad tackling the dicey subject head-on, asserting that Clinton should "be censured, not impeached" and complaining that "Rick White's vote on impeachment will drag us through months and months of more mud and politics. Enough is enough. It's time to get on with the nation's business." Inslee soon jumped out to take the lead, and Clinton tried to persuade other candidates to adopt the same strategy, though most remained reluctant. The president and first lady also quietly worked to energize core Democrats angry at impeachment, taping 250 radio spots and telephone messages aimed at African-American and Latino communities.

Most Republican candidates were trying to run from the issue. Their base was already depressed by the conservative talk-show bashing of the budget deal. Strategists advising Republican candidates urged them to avoid a campaign premised simply on taking advantage of Clinton's weakness. Consultant Ralph Reed, the pragmatic former executive director of the Christian Coalition, warned in a September 23 memo that "if we rely entirely on the scandal, we will come up short on Election Day."

Gingrich had never been entirely certain how to handle the issue. Most of the time he stayed away from it, believing that Clinton would fall of his own weight and fearing that inserting himself into the controversy would only make it easier for the White House to change the subject to him. Gingrich had advised other Republicans to keep quiet about the scandal and let Clinton's fellow Democrats beat him up, as they were wont to do anyway. And yet Gingrich believed Clinton was a liar who ought to be exposed. "For Bill Clinton, the truth is transactional," he had told advisers as far back as the government shutdown in 1995. As the Lewinsky scandal deepened, Gingrich simply could not resist commenting at times. In the spring, he declared that the president had presided over the "most systematic, deliberate obstruction-of-justice cover-up and effort to avoid the truth we have ever seen in American history" and vowed that "I will never again, as long as I am Speaker, make a speech without commenting on this topic." It was an impetuous promise. Within a few weeks, he had dropped the issue from his stump speech.

As the election came down to the wire, Gingrich changed his mind again. His polls showed morality at the top of voters' concerns and indicated that Republicans were viewed as better able to deal with the issue. On his campaign plane jetting across the country, his consultant Joe Gaylord read him the scripts for three thirty-second television advertisements raising the Lewinsky issue. "That's great," Gingrich said, signing off on the strategy. The ads were produced by the National Republican Congressional Committee (NRCC) and tested in focus groups in Charlotte and Cincinnati. One featured the infamous video footage of Clinton's finger-wagging denial that he had had sex with "that woman," while another featured a woman asking rhetorically what viewers had told their children about the whole affair. "In every election, there is a big question to think about," said one of the ads. "This year, the question is: Should we reward . . . Bill Clinton? And should we reward not telling the truth?"

NRCC's "Operation Breakout" tried to fly under the radar screen of the national political press, with ads placed in only selected key races across the country where they might do the most good in turning out base Republican voters. But once reporters found out about them, they became the image of choice on network television, played over and over to the point where most voters across the country had seen them on the news. By virtue of the intense media focus, the anti-Clinton theme supplanted any other campaign messages and became the voice for the entire Republican election effort. And contrary to expectations, the voters energized by the ads were not Republicans but core Democrats outraged at the attack on their president.

Republican candidates around the country began to panic. Many of them called congressional leaders such as Tom DeLay, begging them not to run the ads in their districts. Even DeLay, the leader of the drive to impeach Clinton, thought the project was badly handled. They should have been running on Clinton and his misconduct, DeLay told advisers, but should have been doing so for weeks, not at the last minute in some desperate stab at finding an issue that would sell. Even Gingrich's former adviser Frank Luntz, architect of the Contract with America and the 1994 Republican takeover, argued that impeachment was a losing campaign strategy. "It could have been our night," he wrote in a postelection report circulated to GOP leaders. "We squandered this opportunity in a haze of anti-Clinton, pro-scandal rhetoric that reminded voters of all the things they hated about Washington." Luntz, who had been effectively exiled from Gingrich's inner circle, complained that Republicans came across as "self-righteous" and offered an "anemic" message designed to appeal only to "first wives."

The result was a loss that went far beyond the few seats that actually changed hands. In the end, Democrats picked up five seats, narrowing the margin in the House to 223 to 211, plus an independent who usually sided with the Democrats. That meant the Republican leadership could afford to lose no more than five votes on any given issue, a governing majority so fragile as to seem almost unworkable. The Democratic victory defied historical trends; going all the way back to the early nineteenth century, the president's party had always lost seats in the sixth year of his administration, usually several dozen. The last time a president's party grabbed more seats in such a "six-year itch" election was 1822, when popular James Monroe was in the White House presiding over the Era of Good Feelings.

"This is just horseshit!" Bob Livingston was shouting into the phone. "This is not a good day!"

The morning after the election, Wednesday, November 4, Gingrich had decided to try to quiet discontent within his caucus by convening a series of telephone conference calls. In his first one of the day with fellow House Republican leaders, the Speaker presented a sunny picture of what had happened. They were still in control, he emphasized. Every committee would still be in the hands of Republicans. They had defied history in keeping a GOP majority for the third consecutive election.

But Livingston was not buying the spin. The generally amiable chairman of the Appropriations Committee had a quick temper that was now erupting. He had spent months raising money and campaigning for colleagues, but they had no message; they ran a campaign devoid of any real issues. They should have been talking about all they had accomplished, about their reform of the Internal Revenue Service, their tax-cutting plan, their telecommunications industry overhaul. Instead, all they did was talk about Clinton. Livingston was fed up and so were others.

Fairly or not, Gingrich was being held responsible for the debacle. The blunder with the ads, his election-day boast of a twenty-seat pickup, and his initial we-really-won assertions all infuriated Republican congressmen. It did not help matters when he went on television the morning after the election and blamed the media for focusing too much on impeachment and the scandal—never mind the ads and his own vow the previous April never to make a speech again without mentioning misconduct in the White House. By his second conference call the day after the election, this one with the general membership of the House Republican caucus, Gingrich was bridling at the criticism and trying to shift blame. The real reasons they had suffered losses, he told his colleagues, were racist radio ads aired by Democrats intended to drive up black turnout and the failure of Senate Republicans to pass House-authored tax cuts. He was not the one who had focused so obsessively on Clinton's scandals, Gingrich insisted. He had tried to promote a real message of Republican progress on issues, but it just could not penetrate the wall-to-wall all-Monica-all-the-time fixation of the television networks.

While many Republicans were jumping ship, Gingrich found that day that he could count on support from one GOP leader. "I'm not going to let them run you out of town," DeLay told him privately.

Henry Hyde spent the morning after the election in Chicago, where he had watched morosely as the results came in the night before. He had hoped the public would speak out in outrage at what Clinton had done. The public had spoken out, Hyde realized, but he just did not like what they had to say. By the time he arrived at the Hilton Hotel at O'Hare Airport around 10 A.M. to meet with senior aides and investigators who had flown in from Washington, Hyde was determined to put the election out of his mind. There was no point in recapitulating what had happened. Republicans still had the majority, he told himself, so he tried to proceed as if nothing had changed.

"Okay," he said, lighting up one of his staple cigars as he sat down in the hotel meeting room with aides Tom Mooney, David Schippers, Mitch Glazier, and Sam Stratman. "I promised you we'd go over the requests for admission. Where are they?"

The aides looked around at one another. They had drafted a list of 103 questions to put to Clinton in the form of "requests for admission"—an interrogatory of sorts intended to narrow the issues and pinpoint where the factual disputes were concentrated. Copies had been brought to discuss with Hyde, but his staff hardly figured that would be the first order of business the morning after such a cataclysmic political event. They had been wondering what the election would mean for impeachment. They half expected Hyde to come in and say, "Forget it, it's over."

When no one said anything, Glazier went ahead and handed out copies of the 103 questions. Someone finally raised the issue of the election, however, and Hyde tried to brush it off. "Why should an election make a difference?" Hyde asked. "We have a duty."

For all of his outward unflappability, though, Hyde knew how disastrous the election setback was and recognized that he had to get impeachment off the table one way or the other as quickly as he could. He had already pledged to try to finish by the end of the year, and now he committed to himself to carry through on that no matter what. After all, his mandate would expire with the old Congress at the beginning of January anyway, and the inquiry would have to be reauthorized by the next House, a daunting prospect now with five fewer Republican seats in the new year. The only way to get through this, then, was to conduct an abbreviated inquiry—no long fishing expeditions, no extensive hearings, no endless parades of witnesses. And so he and his advisers decided at the airport hotel that they would call just one major witness: Ken Starr himself.

Hyde started reading through the list of 103 questions prepared by Glazier and the rest of the staff. With his red pen, he started crossing through one after the other. They were all about sex—emphasizing all the wrong things, trying to be inflammatory, rather than seeking information.

"What are all of these questions about sex?" Hyde demanded.

"Mr. Chairman, this is a sexual harassment case," answered Glazier. "If you're talking about perjury and what he lied about, then you really have to ask these exact same questions you would ask him if he were a defendant in a sexual harassment case."

"Look," Hyde replied, "this case is not about sex. It's about obstruction. If we want to get that across, we have to ask the questions we need but we can't emphasize that." Hyde did not want to be known as the sex investigator. "Everyone's going to be talking about how the Judiciary Committee is obsessed with sex."

Glazier had been sensitive to that concern and had tried to get around it by asking questions in a somewhat obtuse way, such as Did you engage in the kind of activity described on page so-and-so, line such-and-such, of the Starr report? He was essentially asking Clinton if he had touched Lewinsky's breasts or genitalia, as she had testified, but without using graphic words. Hyde was not persuaded: "Isn't this just a cheap shot?" The chairman wanted the questions to be staid, to read as if they came from a blue-chip, downtown law firm, not a partisan legislative committee. Hyde came up with an alternative formulation for asking some of the perjury questions without dwelling on the sexual nature of the issues—they would ask Clinton, Did you lie in your deposition when you testified this way or that, and then quote his own words.

By the time Hyde put down his red pen, just eighty-one questions were left, most of them fairly straightforward and sedate. In standard legalese, they asked the president to "admit or deny" a variety of events in the time line put together by Starr, including phone calls to Vernon Jordan, conversations with Betty Currie, and various meetings with Lewinsky. After Hyde scratched out twenty-two of the most salacious questions, the word *sex* or *sexual* appeared just five times and always in quotations attributed to Clinton. Nowhere in the final version of the questions did Hyde directly ask about Clinton's sexual activities with Lewinsky. But it included some zingers, such as the very first question: "Do you admit or deny that you are the chief law enforcement officer of the United States of America?" In case that had not driven home the point hard enough, another question asked, "Do you admit or deny that pursuant to Article II, section 2 of the Constitution you have a duty to 'take care that the laws be faithfully executed'?" (The committee staff actually got it wrong—the "faithfully executed" clause appeared in section 3, not section 2.)

Around 3 P.M., Hyde got his fellow Republican members of the Judiciary Committee on a conference call to inform them of his decisions. They would press forward with the investigation but try to wrap it up in the next eight weeks, he told them. They would call Starr and submit the eighty-one questions to the president. Fresh off the disastrous elections, the other Republicans sounded nervous and uncertain, but no one challenged Hyde. If he still wanted to forge ahead, they would too.

"We've got a duty to do," Hyde told his fellow committee members. "We're all disappointed over the election results. The Constitution requires that we fulfill our obligations. We will fulfill our obligations and let the chips fall where they may."

The next day, Thursday, November 5, Hyde held a news conference in Chicago to announce the plan to call Starr and submit the questions to Clinton. While it looked as if Hyde was scaling back the inquiry, he insisted that had been his intent all along. "We could just look away from this awful mess and let it disappear," he said. "But our duty demands that we look further. It requires that we search out the truth, face it squarely. It insists that we uphold the rule of law." As for witnesses like Lewinsky, he said it was unnecessary to call them. "We have their testimony. We don't need to reinvent the wheel."

Hyde, who had been rebuffing Republicans calling him in Chicago to urge him to run for Speaker, tried to wrap up the news conference without getting into the brewing leadership fight involving Gingrich. But Hyde could not escape the room fast enough. When a reporter asked what message had been delivered by the Tuesday election, Hyde sounded as peeved as some of Gingrich's worst critics.

"You can't win a campaign without issues and without an agenda," Hyde answered. "And I think we did conduct a status-quo, don't-rock-the-boat, stall-ball campaign. And it cost us."

"And who's to blame for that?" a reporter asked. "Is it the Speaker?"

"Well," Hyde answered, "leadership takes credit when things go right. They ought to take the blame when things go wrong."

Hyde started for the door again as reporters shouted after him: Should Gingrich remain as Speaker?

Hyde paused at the doorway, smiled mischievously, and called out, "Good morning!" before ducking out.

Hyde thought he was carefully staying out of the leadership fight, but in fact his flippant final answer spoke volumes. In Washington, it was seen as a repudiation by one of the Old Bulls of the House. In Georgia, Gingrich saw it the same way. Hyde's few words about leadership taking blame struck home. Maybe Hyde was right, the Speaker wondered. Maybe he really should take the blame now that things had gone so horribly wrong.

Not long after Hyde's news conference, the news grew worse for Gingrich. Bob Livingston called that afternoon. "Look, I'm thinking about running," he told the Speaker. "I wasn't thinking about it a week ago or a few days ago, but I'm thinking about it now."

The two talked for a few minutes about Livingston's complaints, but the conversation quickly degenerated into a quarrel about who was responsible for the budget deal that had helped depress conservative turnout in the election. They hung up.

Gingrich kept working the phones from Atlanta, surveying the political landscape one member at a time. That Livingston might run against him was bad enough. That Hyde had seemed to desert him was crushing. But in some ways, perhaps the hardest blow came in a telephone conversation with one of the newest members of the House, Mary Bono. Gingrich had played mentor first to Sonny Bono when he came to Washington and later to his widow when she decided to run for the seat following Sonny's death. The Speaker had helped her raise money, included her in his trips to California, and given her prestigious assignments in the House, including the Judiciary Committee. He was counting on her support.

When he got her on the phone, Gingrich explained to Bono that a coup might be under way and he was looking for help. Bono hesitated. She was feeling vulnerable after weeks in the impeachment bubble. Gingrich did not seem to understand just how brutal it had been for members of the committee.

While she wished she could pledge her unwavering support to the Speaker, her first instinct was to reserve judgment.

"Newt," she said, "I'm going to stand back and see how it plays out. You might be better off to resign."

The suggestion was stunning for Gingrich. Bono did not mean it viciously. She told him she thought it would be better both for him as a friend and for the party. But for Gingrich, it was an unexpected blow.

Bono reminded Gingrich of a conversation they had once had when he had corrected her after she said loyalty should flow both ways; there were times, he had instructed her, when you had to make a tough decision that might not seem loyal.

"Newt, remember what you taught me?" Bono asked.

"Boy," he answered, "you learned your lesson well."

Livingston had been working the phones too, and the message he had received was consistent and strong. A genuine tide was rising against Gingrich, and the only question was whether Livingston would have the temerity to ride it. Within twenty-four hours, Livingston's congressional office had been transformed into a war room. The chairman himself had been on the phone almost constantly since 7 A.M. the morning after the election, and his own brain trust had immediately swung into gear. Congressman Michael P. Forbes of New York, a Livingston protégé, showed up to help man the phones, write letters, craft memos, and anything else that needed doing. Other allies, including Congressmen Ron Packard, Howard P. "Buck" McKeon, and Sonny Callahan, dispatched their own aides to Livingston's office to help. Even a few Republican aides from the Senate side migrated over.

Outside his own circle, members were telling Livingston that they needed someone new, someone who could right their capsizing caucus and lead them into an uncertain future. Longtime Gingrich critics such as Congressmen Matt Salmon of Arizona and Christopher Shays of Connecticut were saying they would not vote for the Speaker. In addition to the encouragement from members, Livingston was also hearing from other important figures in Republican circles, including fund-raisers, lobbyists, and elected officials outside the Beltway. Among them was Texas governor George W. Bush, then contemplating a run for the White House in 2000. Bush told Livingston that he could not formally endorse him, but said if he did run for president, he did not want to lose because of something Gingrich did. The message there was clear enough too.

Livingston was an ironic candidate for rebel leader. A longtime congressman who had worked loyally in the trenches for years, he had been on the verge of retirement just eight months earlier until he was talked out of it. Among those who beseeched him to change his mind was Gingrich. But Livingston had grown increasingly sour on his old friend. During the 1998 election cycle, Livingston had traveled the country for other candidates, given away some $600,000 of his campaign treasury, and raised another $2 million—but not so that Gingrich could obsess about interns in thongs. For months, Livingston had been dismayed at how Gingrich waffled, one day hitting the scandal issue hard, the next vowing to never mention it. By election day, Livingston had concluded that the strategy to go after Clinton was an abomination.

Still in Georgia, Gingrich was unsure where to turn. The situation began to look desperate enough that he even reached out to Bill Paxon, the young New York congressman who had been involved in the abortive coup against him the year before. In the swirl of the week, Paxon's name had surfaced as a possible challenger to Gingrich—even though he had not run for reelection. The authors of this rather fanciful scenario noted that nothing in the Constitution required the Speaker of the House to actually be a member. Around eleven o'clock Thursday night, Paxon picked up the telephone and dialed Gingrich's home north of Atlanta.

He had heard this rumor, Paxon told Gingrich, and was calling just to make clear he had no interest in challenging the Speaker. Paxon had made his decision to give up politics and was sticking with it.

If this provided any relief for the beleaguered Gingrich, it did not show. He sounded worried. He began telling Paxon about some of the conversations he had been having with rank-and-file Republicans, members who seemed tentative toward him, not just the hotheads and malcontents but even younger loyalists such as Bono, Jo Ann Emerson of Missouri, and J. D. Hayworth of Arizona. What had Paxon heard? Gingrich asked.

"Well, I've heard from some members and you've got some problems," Paxon replied.

Paxon was stunned at how Gingrich sounded. This was a lonely man, Paxon thought, so isolated that he was willing to confide even in a known rival. Normally, Paxon would be the last person Gingrich would be opening up to. In all their years in the House together, in all the legislative fights and leadership meetings, Paxon had never heard Gingrich sound uncertain of himself—uncertain of specific issues or which way to go tactically, yes, but never uncertain of himself. As Paxon put down the phone, he looked at his wife, Susan Molinari, a former congresswoman. "If somebody runs," Paxon told her, "he's dead."

Not much later, maybe eleven-thirty or so, the phone at the Paxon house rang. It was Bob Walker, the former congressman and Gingrich's political alter ego. Walker had some advice for Livingston and wanted Paxon to convey it. Now working as a lobbyist in Washington, Walker warned darkly that "downtown could be a cold place for those who run and lose, and it could be warm if he didn't run." Paxon assumed Gingrich had asked his friend to call. And the message was equally clear: Livingston would never be able to work in private-sector Washington if he took a shot at the king and missed.

Livingston did not know about the call when he woke up early on Friday, November 6, but he had had second thoughts overnight anyway. Maybe he would not run. Instead, he would lay down the law with Gingrich. He got hold of his secretary and started dictating terms of surrender—sixteen conditions that Gingrich would have to accept in order to keep Livingston from challenging him. Livingston insisted on more order in the budget process, regular weekly meetings with the Democrats, longer workweeks and fewer vacations. Most important, he demanded complete control over his own committee—no more Gingrich end runs, no more secret deals with the White House without his involvement. If he was to stay as Appropriations chairman and not run for Speaker, Livingston told Gingrich, he would have to be allowed to "run the committee as I see fit and in the best interest of the Republican majority, but without being subject to the dictates of any other Member of Congress."

Livingston had the three-page letter marked "personal and confidential" and faxed to Gingrich in Georgia, then gave him two hours to respond. This was political hardball at its toughest. "Look," he told Gingrich in a telephone call, "I don't want to run against you. But I've got to run my committee." If Gingrich agreed to these sixteen rules, Livingston told him, then fine, he would not run.

Gingrich was momentarily encouraged, thinking Livingston would not take him on. Then he saw the list. "This is ridiculous," Gingrich told an aide. "We're not going to sign this." He began working the phones again, taking the temperature, seeking advice. One of those he called was Congressman J. C. Watts, the charismatic former Oklahoma football star and the only African-American in the House Republican caucus.

"How do you deal with this kind of situation?" Gingrich asked plaintively.

"In football, when your team loses, they bench you, the quarterback," Watts said. "It's painful—I've been there—but that's just the way it is."

Gingrich also heard from Bill Archer, the tough-minded Ways and Means Committee chairman from Texas, who had told him the day before he would stand by him. Having slept on it, Archer said, he had changed his mind: "You might want to give second thought to this."

Livingston's list of demands was supposed to remain private, but within a few hours, he looked up to see his press secretary, Mark Corallo, rush into the office. "He released the fucking letter," Corallo said. Reporters had copies. Livingston and his staff assumed that Gingrich had leaked it since they did not believe their side had put it out.

"Fuck," said Livingston. It had been more than three hours at this point. Livingston's deadline had passed without a response. Maybe this leak *was* the response. Livingston summoned his entire staff into his office and had his district staff in Louisiana patched in by speakerphone.

"All right, everyone," he said. "I want everyone to go around the room and tell me why I should or shouldn't do this."

The district staff enthusiastically urged him to run, but others raised the obvious concerns. No one had ever taken on a sitting Speaker like this before. Gingrich had given him the Appropriations chairmanship in the first place. It would be tough on his family. Finally, Corallo challenged him to figure out whether he had it "in your gut to take on Newt Gingrich, a guy who will go down in history."

Livingston thought he did, but he had one more person he had to consult. He kicked his staff out of his office and picked up the phone again. This time he dialed New Orleans and got former archbishop Philip Hannan on the line. Hannan was a friend who had paid a surprise visit to Livingston the previous February when he was thinking about quitting Congress and had coaxed him into sticking it out for another two years. This time Hannan gave similar advice: go for it.

Livingston called his aides back into his office. "We're doing this. I'm running."

The first thing he had to do was call Gingrich to let him know. It was a moment Livingston dreaded, but it had to be done. The letter with the sixteen demands was off the table, Livingston told Gingrich around 11 A.M. "It's revoked."

Gingrich would not accept that. He was still trying to work something out: "We're getting you an answer."

Too late. "I'm not interested. I'm going."

Bill Paxon arrived at Livingston's door about a half hour later. "Come on in. Sit down," Livingston told the younger man. As Paxon took a seat, Livingston turned to a secretary in the office with him and issued a few final editing instructions as he worked to polish his speech. The secretary left and Livingston shifted his gaze out the window of his office and stared for a few moments before saying anything.

"Hardest decision I ever had to make," he said finally.

Paxon thought he knew but asked anyway. What decision?

"I just told Newt I'm going to run." Livingston looked out the window again, then back at Paxon. "What do you think?"

Paxon remembered the phone call from Bob Walker the night before. "Well, apparently I'm forty-five minutes too late."

Paxon told Livingston why he had come and described the message from the Gingrich camp. He was not there to encourage or discourage, Paxon added. He did not intend to be doing Gingrich's dirty work by passing along threats, but he had committed at least to telling Livingston what people were saying so he could evaluate for himself.

Livingston seemed unbothered. Yes, he said, he had thought a lot about that. He knew the possible ramifications to his postcongressional career if he ran and lost, but he felt confident he would be okay. He had been in Congress a long time and had a lot of friends in this town. In fact, while he did not mention it, he had heard directly from Walker, who had told him that if he lost a challenge to Gingrich, potential clients might be suspicious of Livingston's ability to deal with a Republican leadership he had unsuccessfully challenged.

Okay, Paxon said, but what about the rest? Are you ready for what the Gingrich people could do to you? Paxon paused. "Just so you know, your life will be an open book."

Livingston looked stunned. It appeared that thought had not really occurred to him. He put his head down on his desk for a few moments, lost in some trance Paxon did not understand. Paxon knew nothing about any personal indiscretions in the older man's past, but he became instantly worried as he saw Livingston's reaction. As Livingston lifted his head from the desk, his face looked drained of blood.

Before Paxon could pursue the subject any further, Livingston's wife, Bonnie, walked into the office, followed by his chief of staff, Allen Martin. They were there to plan the big announcement, now scheduled for just two hours away. As Paxon excused himself, he caught Livingston's attention when Bonnie was not looking, pointed to Martin, and silently mouthed the words, "You better talk with him."

Two hours later, Livingston was on the lawn of the Capitol, surrounded by hastily gathered supporters waving hastily printed signs, courtesy of friends at the American Conservative Union who were rallied to provide the political props necessary for the anti-Gingrich revolt. Accompanied by Bonnie and their daughter Susie, Livingston was armed with a speech that until the last minute had a hole in it because his staff could not find a missing list of issues he wanted to mention, such as preserving Social Security, lowering taxes, and strengthening national defense. It was also missing kind words about the man Livingston was seeking to dethrone. His aides had convinced him to take out a section praising Gingrich's strengths, but now before the microphone, he ad-libbed them back in.

As Livingston described him, Gingrich was a "wonderful human being," a "man of Churchillian proportions," and an "intellectual giant with many talents that exceed anything I can aspire to." Hardly the words of a bitter rival. Yet Livingston argued that, just as Britain had turned away from Winston Churchill in peacetime, it was time to move on from the larger-than-life leadership of Gingrich to a more nuts-and-bolts manager committed to "making the trains run on time."

"Revolutionizing takes some talents—many talents," Livingston said. "My friend Newt Gingrich brought those talents to bear and put the Republicans in the majority. Day-to-day governing takes others. I believe I have those talents."

For Gingrich, back at home in Georgia, the announcement by Livingston was a sharp blow. But behind the emotion of the moment, Gingrich knew Livingston was only a symptom of the larger problem. All around him were people looking out for their own interests, readily willing to speak out against him if it suited them. The party was on the verge of chaos. Even if he could beat back Livingston within the Republican conference—and that was an open question given the passions of the moment—Gingrich knew that perhaps a dozen Republicans were already talking about refusing to vote for him as Speaker when it came time for the full House to vote. The idea of going hat in hand to some of the same people who had caused him so much grief over the last two years was just too much to take. Even more unpalatable was having to do it again and again, assuming he remained Speaker and was forced to hold together a fragile GOP majority on every major vote.

Gingrich had one other unspoken pressure. The rumors his staff had heard earlier in the fall were true. For some five years, he had been carrying on an extramarital affair of his own with a young House clerk, Callista Bisek, who worked as a scheduler for the Agriculture Committee. Gingrich's marital life had been turbulent for decades. In 1981, he had divorced his first wife, his former high school geometry teacher, after she discovered she had cancer; he and his second wife, Marianne, had split up and reconciled periodically over the last seventeen years. Aware of his own glass house, Gingrich in his attacks on Clinton through 1998 had tried not to talk about the immorality of the president's infidelity and to focus instead on allegations of illegality, namely perjury and obstruction of justice. Yet he knew if his affair became public, it would invite unavoidable comparisons and accusations of hypocrisy. In the last few weeks, he had seen fellow Republicans Henry Hyde, Dan Burton, and Helen Chenoweth all exposed for past extramarital affairs. Gingrich believed the White House was capable of anything. Yet how much this weighed on him, how much he factored this into the equation, went unstated in his conversations with some of his closest advisers in the days after the election.

Still working the phone in his congressional district office that Friday, Gingrich hung up after another unsupportive conversation with a fellow Republican. "I just don't think I can be this kind of Speaker," he said, discouraged.

"Then don't do it," said his friend and consultant Joe Gaylord. "Give it up."

Gingrich agreed. It was time to quit. When the next Congress took office in January, he would not stand for reelection as Speaker and would resign his seat. Gingrich called Washington and got his chief of staff, Arne Christenson, on the phone. "This isn't going to work," Gingrich said. "I'm just not going to be able to govern this place with the situation the way it is." At that moment, Bob Walker arrived at the Speaker's office at the Capitol ready to plunge into the campaign to get him reelected. Christenson told him what was happening.

I'm here to help you line up votes, Walker told Gingrich on the speakerphone in Christenson's office.

The Speaker laughed. No, he said, I'm going to join you in the private sector. I've decided not to run for Speaker.

"Can't we talk about it?" Walker asked. This was not a decision to make in isolation in Georgia. Come back to Washington and sit down face-to-face. The whip counts look good. Besides, Walker said, you are absolutely essential to the ongoing movement. You're the visionary, the strategist, the only one left on the Hill to push our agenda.

"If it's an agenda that can't survive without the personalities," Gingrich replied, "it's probably something that can't be sustained anyway."

By this point, Vin Weber, another former congressman and close Gingrich friend who was at a conference at George Washington University across town, had been patched into the call, but he sensed that Gingrich's mind was made up and did not try to talk him out of it. After a series of other calls to friends, advisers, aides, and fellow House leaders, Gingrich finally got the entire Republican membership on a conference call to disclose his decision around 7 P.M. "We have to get the bitterness out," he told them. "It is clear that as long as I'm around, that won't happen." Clearly disillusioned by his fate, Gingrich bemoaned the strife that had overtaken his party. "We need to purge the poisons from the system." He left little doubt about his feelings toward the Republicans who had rebelled against him that week. "The ones you see on TV are hateful," he told his once-faithful following. "I am willing to lead, but I won't allow cannibalism."

Gingrich's choice of words carried extra irony that perhaps he did not realize at the moment. In his downfall, he sounded like two of the adversaries he had long targeted. It was Clinton who, while preparing for his second inauguration in January 1997, said that he wanted to use his second term to "help flush the poison from the atmosphere." And it was Jim Wright, the Democratic House Speaker forced to resign by ethics charges brought by Gingrich, who in his own emotional departure speech in 1989 pleaded with colleagues to "bring this period of mindless cannibalism to an end."

Clinton learned the news of Gingrich's abrupt fall from grace while visiting friends and supporters in Arkansas. Just as he arrived at the house where he was attending a reception, aides Bruce Lindsey and Doug Sosnik walked up to his car to let him know about the head-spinning developments. Here the man who had been trying to force him out of office had instead been taken down as a result of the whole Lewinsky scandal.

Yet whatever momentary pleasure Clinton might have felt at the Speaker's demise must have been tempered by the realization that losing Gingrich meant depriving himself of his favorite target. Clinton had succeeded in rehabilitating himself after the disastrous 1994 midterm elections in large part by playing off Gingrich's excesses. Gingrich had made himself into an enormously useful whipping boy for the Democrats, a potent symbol easily understood by a public that barely tuned in to Washington politics anymore. That was why Gingrich's name had been used in so many Democratic ads in races where he was not running. Bringing in another, more reasonable-sounding Republican such as Livingston might actually be the worst thing for Clinton's future.

Clinton authorized a statement to be issued in his name and was careful to be gracious, not gloating. But when his staff tried to coordinate with Dick Gephardt's office, the conversation quickly turned into a shouting match. Unlike Clinton, Gephardt despised the Speaker and saw no reason to mourn his passing. Gephardt's chief of staff, Steve Elmendorf, and communications director, Laura Nichols, had a heated argument with Paul Begala over the phone about the tone of the president's statement. It was outrageous, they said. Gingrich had gone out of his way to screw over Gephardt, and it would be disingenuous to make nice at the end. The disagreement escalated to the point where Gephardt and Clinton finally got on the phone themselves to hash it out. The president agreed to take out a paragraph hailing the balanced-budget agreement he had reached with Gingrich in 1997, but insisted on praising Gingrich's internationalist foreign policy and leaving the overall tone conciliatory.

Gingrich was a "worthy adversary," Clinton said in the version that was eventually released to the media. "Despite our profound differences, I appreciate those times we were able to work together in the national interest, especially Speaker Gingrich's strong support for America's continuing leadership for freedom, peace, and prosperity in the world." There was no mention of the balanced budget. Gephardt kept the edge in his statement. "The American people sent a strong message that the Republican Congress was a failure," he said, adding, "The Speaker's resignation is the reaction to that message."

Down in Georgia, Gingrich had other things to think about. Suddenly, he had a future to plan. Hyde called and sounded distressed. This was all so sudden. At least Gingrich should remain in the House and help them out. "You'll still be able to do a lot and come back," Hyde said.

Gingrich would have none of that. He could not return to the backbench.

Hyde asked why Gingrich would not run again and heard the answer he feared: "What you said on television didn't help."

Hyde felt guilty. He had been disappointed in the Speaker's strategy for the fall campaigns, but had not wanted to push him out. Hyde had tried to stay out of the leadership battle.

Weary, Gingrich headed home, where he was soon joined by nearly a dozen friends and aides for beer and a barbecue dinner. Gingrich was strangely calm about the day's events. Sipping a Foster's lager, he reverted to his history-professor mode, analyzing his place in twentieth-century politics, reflecting on how an army brat had managed to rise to power, reform welfare, and balance the budget. He had always liked to see himself as a latter-day Churchill and knew that for all his victories in World War II, Churchill finished his career being tossed out unceremoniously as well.

CHAPTER SEVEN

*"The crazy right
has them by the throat"*

Distracted, disoriented, and demoralized, the Republican members of the
House Judiciary Committee returned to Washington on Monday,
November 9, to find virtually no leadership left in their party and no energy
left in their grand adventure. The president was the one accused of violating
his oath of office, and yet their own leader was the one taken down on the
battlefield. What did that mean for the rest of them? Should they give up?
Were they courting disaster if they pressed forward? Where was the balance
between duty and self-preservation? And given the impeachment fervor
within their own political base, what course would be safest politically
anyway? In the junior ranks, Lindsey Graham, for one, had always assumed
they would reach a deal and it would be over; now it was dawning on him that
they meant him and his colleagues.

One thing was evident: the leadership, or what was left of it, had no
appetite for pressing ahead. Several of the committee members had heard
from advisers to Newt Gingrich or Bob Livingston that they wanted the
issue off the political table—Gingrich did not want it to be his last act as
Speaker and Livingston did not want it to be his first. Neither one was saying
so publicly, but the signals from their surrogates were clear enough. Congressman Jim Rogan, who barely mustered a majority in his reelection, had
been approached on the House floor by leadership aides. Henry Hyde told
his staff that he had gotten the same message: get rid of it.

The chairman convened a meeting of the Judiciary Republicans in the
Rayburn Building conference room that Monday morning. They would
hold hearings by mid-November, Hyde told the group, and then try to be on
the floor of the House by December 1. No dragging it out. Starr would be
the only real witness, and everything would be wrapped up quickly.

David Schippers, the aggressive chief investigator, could not believe what
he was hearing. They were lying down. Unaccustomed to the culture of the

Capitol, Schippers erupted and did something no regular aide would dare do—he started shouting his frustration at the congressmen.

"Look, you lost some seats in the election," Schippers lectured the politicians. "But I've got people on this. They've taken psychological hits, physical hits. . . . You want me to go back there and tell them we're going to have a half-assed inquiry?"

"No, no, Dave," Hyde said. "Don't misunderstand me. If you've got more—"

"We're getting more!"

Hyde explained that they had to finish quickly. Given the election result, it was clear the next Congress would not reauthorize the inquiry in January, meaning they only had eight weeks left under the best of circumstances. And Hyde hinted that the issue could even be taken away from the committee and given to some other group to decide what to do.

But Schippers succeeded in steeling the nerves of some of the nervous members. They had to stay the course, consequences be damned. Congressman Chris Cannon, a hard-charging panel member from Utah, leaned over to Schippers and whispered, "If you want a son of a bitch, I'll go with you."

Finally, Rogan spoke up. No one had more to worry about politically than he did. A freshman who had won his seat by just a hair two years earlier in a southern California district that included the liberal bastion of Hollywood, Rogan survived a scare in the elections the week before. In his district, impeachment could easily spell the end of his congressional career before it really got started.

"If anybody understands the potential for fallout, it's me," Rogan told his colleagues. "I won 50.8 percent of the vote. If they're going to make an example out of anyone, it's me." Then he tried a joke to lighten the mood. "In '96, we weren't impeaching him. I got 50.1 percent. In 1998, we are impeaching him and I got 50.8 percent. So obviously it's a political winner."

People around the table laughed, and the tension was broken. If Rogan was still willing to press ahead, his colleagues thought, then they should be too.

In fact, with the exception of Rogan and one or two others, the committee was significantly insulated from the political forces that shaped the new conventional wisdom in Washington. The Republicans who served on Judiciary tended to be more conservative than their House GOP colleagues, just as the committee's Democrats tended to be among the most liberal. Judiciary members on both sides of the aisle were from relatively safe districts and did not have to worry about possible threats to their political careers for failing to seek a middle ground. In the campaign that had just passed, not a single committee member was defeated for reelection despite all the controversy surrounding impeachment. Indeed, of the twenty Republican committee members who sought reelection, nine did not even draw a Democratic challenger, and all but three garnered at least 60 percent of the vote (Rogan, Bob Barr of Georgia, and Steve Chabot of Ohio were the exceptions). Similarly, six of the fifteen Democratic members who sought another term faced no Republican opponent, and only one (Mel Watt of North Carolina) fell below 60 percent. If anything, their constituent calls cheered them on in whichever hard-line direction they were already inclined to pursue; compromise might be the only course of action that could prove dangerous, because theoretically it could prompt a primary challenge in two years.

After bucking themselves up at their private caucus, the Republican members emerged from the conference room and headed out to the hearing room to join the Democrats for the panel's first meeting since the election. Charles Canady, chairman of the subcommittee on the Constitution, led a daylong dialogue about the standards for impeachment, featuring a series of nineteen expert witnesses offering their views of the framers' intent and the applicability in the current situation. The arguments were reasonably predictable—the GOP experts insisted that the allegations involving Clinton were "at the core" of what high crimes were thought to be, while the Democratic academics maintained that "the very heavy artillery of impeachment" would be a disproportionate response to the president's misdeeds. With the assistance of White House aide Sidney Blumenthal, the Democrats had tried to stack the deck in the days leading up to the hearing by recruiting more than four hundred historians and more than four hundred law school professors to sign statements opposing impeachment because the charges lodged against Clinton did not add up to high crimes.

The most important indicator from the meeting, however, came not from the witness table but from the dais. Rejuvenated by their private discussion in the conference room, the Republican members came across as determined as ever. Rather than softening their tone and looking for a way out, Canady and his colleagues asserted flatly that perjury and obstruction of justice by a president subverted the integrity of the legal system. "A president who engages in such behavior," Canady declared, "must be called to account for setting a dangerous example of lawlessness and corruption. He must be called to account for subverting the respect for law, which is the foundation of our Constitution."

The Democrats in the room were taken aback. The election, it seemed, had not taught the Republicans anything. It began to sink in that the fight was not really over.

"You're right," Abbe Lowell told Dick Gephardt in his office the next day, Tuesday, November 10. "They want impeachment and no alternative."

"This means back to partisan warfare," said Steve Elmendorf, Gephardt's chief of staff.

Gephardt was grim. The problem, he said, was that no one was left to rein in the hard-liners on the Judiciary Committee. "It is not Livingston's baby," Gephardt told his aides. "Newt's sworn it off. Without him, there's no leader to stop it."

In the days since the election, Gephardt had recommitted himself to the House and figuring a way out of the current predicament. Aside from forcing Gingrich's overthrow, the campaign results had redirected the minority leader's political future as well. Had the Democrats lost ten or more seats, as so many analysts had expected, Gephardt would likely be preparing to run for president in 2000. But because they gained seats and now stood so close to retaking power in the House, he had concluded that he should aim for the Speakership rather than the White House. Two days after the election, he had met with his closest political advisers at Loew's L'Enfant Plaza Hotel, and the unanimous opinion around the table was that he could not leave his members in the lurch now.

After meeting with his aides, Gephardt gathered later in the day with eight Democratic committee members who expressed their alarm at the turn of events at the subcommittee hearing the day before. Gephardt counseled caution. "Let's revert to the fairness strategy," he said, and keep attacking the Republicans for not playing straight. That was the issue that would resonate with the American public, not defending Clinton directly. But they needed to be careful in their approach to Starr when he appeared before the committee as a witness the next week.

"Don't expect a knockout punch," Gephardt warned. "We want a draw, which is victory." As long as Starr did not score a major blow, then the dynamics would remain unchanged and popular opinion would remain with the Democrats. To that end, they needed to begin working toward an alternative solution with censure, Gephardt said, and should not drag out the inquiry or be blamed for delays.

John Conyers and Lowell began reviewing how they would handle assignments for the questioning of Starr. Each member should focus on a specific area of interest, coordinated by the staff for a coherent attack. Lowell would shoulder the major burden of questioning with a half-hour time slot.

Bobby Scott argued that they should be calling their own witnesses. Several other hard-liners in the room agreed. They needed to explore the origins of this conspiracy against the president, subpoena people like Linda Tripp, Lucianne Goldberg, Starr's deputies, and some of those conservative lawyers who helped set up this whole sting. History would not look kindly if they were not thorough, Scott insisted.

"People are going to look back at this and say we made a mistake," Scott said. "They're going to look back at this as the way to conduct impeachments."

"We want them to look back at this as the way *not* to conduct impeachments," shot back Julian Epstein, the chief counsel. The last thing they wanted were television cameras showing the public a deliberate and thoughtful process, he added. Their goal was to make it look more political.

The firebrands on the committee also expressed their discontent with Lowell, Gephardt's handpicked man, and agitated again to replace him with a better-known lawyer or simply to let the White House lawyers cross-examine Starr by themselves. Lowell had been scrapping for weeks with some of the more aggressive Democratic committee members. A fight over his attempts to negotiate deposition rules with the Republicans had led to shouting. An aide to Congresswoman Zoe Lofgren had left a voice-mail message for Lowell threatening to have him fired. Exasperated as the barbs flew his way in Gephardt's office, Lowell finally protested. He had a background as a real trial attorney, he pointed out. He could handle this. "Give me a chance to do my job."

With the election over, Washington powerbroker Lloyd Cutler thought there was now a mandate to end the impeachment drive and resumed his efforts to negotiate a deal. While he had worked with Gephardt's lawyer before the election, Cutler was focusing much of his attention on finding a sympathetic Republican who might influence the congressional leadership, someone like Howard Baker, the former Senate majority leader made famous during Watergate; Kenneth M. Duberstein, the last Reagan White House chief of staff; or Bob Michel, the former House minority leader.

Cutler was not getting very far, though. He and Baker saw each other often, but the former senator made clear he was not interested in helping. In fact, his wife, Nancy Kassebaum Baker, another Republican former senator, thought Clinton should resign, and while Baker did not share that view, he did see plenty of merit for an impeachment investigation. In his mind, Clinton was guilty of criminal offenses—indeed, more patently guilty of technical violations of the law than even Nixon—and by Baker's reading of the Constitution those crimes were impeachable. The Clinton camp tried a more direct approach to Baker through Guy Smith, a White House aide from Tennessee who had home-state connections to the senator. But when Smith called up, Baker said tersely that he had no advice. Baker's friends were appalled at the nakedness of the appeal.

With the other Washington "wise men" not providing much help, Cutler decided to call Hyde directly. Cutler and Hyde had known and liked each other for years. Cutler had once represented the longtime Illinois congressman in filing a friend-of-the-court brief opposing term limits. When Cutler phoned, Hyde knew he was hearing in effect from the White House. That was fine with Hyde. For all of his stout talk with his troops about duty, privately he was prepared to deal. He did not think the House would impeach Clinton. "Charlie, don't worry about it," he told Democratic congressman Charles Schumer in the Members' Dining Room around the same time he was hearing from Cutler. "The committee will report out the articles, but they'll die on the House floor." Given that expectation, if there was an honorable way out, Hyde was ready to take it. On Tuesday, November 10, the day after his postelection pep talk to committee Republicans, Hyde met privately with Cutler in his office to talk about censure. Maintaining his political cover, Cutler noted he was not there as Clinton's official lawyer and then went through the precedents that seemed to allow censure. He wanted to submit a memo on the constitutional issues. Hyde was receptive but noncommittal. It would be up to the leadership to decide whether censure could be introduced on the House floor, he said.

Still basking in the glow of the campaign triumph and Gingrich's self-destruction, Clinton was no longer so sure he even had to accept being reprimanded by Congress and considered censure-plus—the notion of paying some financial penalty on top of whatever resolution lawmakers passed—off the table entirely. The consensus around the White House was that the Republicans would have to find a way to make it all go away, and soon. Impeachment was now their albatross, not his.

Despite the warning signs at the Judiciary subcommittee hearing, Clinton and his staff invited several dozen allies to the White House the day after Cutler met with Hyde, Wednesday, November 11, for a Veterans Day party to thank them for all they had done on his behalf. It was not billed as a victory celebration, but it had that feeling. Among those who showed up for the happy-hour reception were the regulars from the daily 11 A.M. strategy conference calls that the White House had instituted, Democratic lawyers and lobbyists such as Peter J. Kadzik, Lanny J. Davis, Anne Wexler, Richard Ben-Veniste, Jim Hamilton, Mike Berman, and Kiki Moore. Over warm fruit punch and stale pretzels, they mingled in John Podesta's office and on the adjoining patio, relishing stories from election night and confidently predicting the demise of impeachment. The public was sick of the scandal, and the opinion polls had translated to real victories at the ballot box. While the assembled operatives were generally careful enough not to say it too explicitly, the dominant feeling was that they were out of the woods. Halfway through, the president joined them, still dressed in golfing clothes from a holiday outing on the links. He was in good spirits as he worked the crowd.

Things were moving Clinton's way on other fronts as well. Within forty-eight hours of the Veterans Day celebration, he managed to reach a long-elusive deal with Paula Jones. The breakthrough came when Jones's attorneys, themselves fed up with their client's stubborn refusal to make concessions, told her they would quit the case. That persuaded her to drop her flirtation with the mercurial Abe Hirschfeld and his $1 million pixie dust, clearing the way for Clinton's lawyer, Bob Bennett, to resume serious negotiations. On Thursday, November 12, he spoke to the president three times about the status of their talks, interrupting Clinton's consultations with national security advisers about whether to attack Iraq for its intransigence in U.N. arms inspections. Clinton gave the go-ahead to settle for $850,000. The next day, Friday, November 13, Jones's new attorney, William N. McMillan III, the husband of her friend Susan Carpenter-McMillan, signed a four-page agreement authorizing the dismissal of her appeal in return for the money.

Just like that, the case that had turned Clinton's life upside down—not to mention the nation's politics—finally ended. After four and a half years of scorched-earth legal warfare that had led to the examination of every corner of the president's shadow world and, ultimately, to the prospect of impeachment and removal from office, *Jones* v. *Clinton* was over. Clinton had managed to get out of it without admitting or apologizing for anything, but the steep cost of the settlement—$150,000 more than Jones had originally sought in 1994—led many to consider it an implicit confession of guilt. And the real cost of the suit, to Clinton, to the presidency, and to the country, was immeasurable.

On the same day the suit was settled, Clinton agreed to consider ways to make the impeachment threat go away as well. Having gotten nowhere with his censure deal before the election, Gephardt decided to renew his efforts, and this time he dispensed with Lloyd Cutler and the other middlemen. To figure out what the president might be willing to accept in terms of censure, Gephardt requested a private meeting between the two men, a session kept secret by sneaking the minority leader into the White House out of the view of the watchful press corps, distracted by the Jones settlement. One thing made clear by the session was that Clinton was not interested in parting with his pension for five years, as Gephardt had proposed a month earlier. They would have to find some other, more reasonable formula.

For all of the bravado of his fellow Republicans, Asa Hutchinson was not at all sure where things were headed, nor where they *should* go. The evidence against Clinton seemed compelling, but was it enough? Had the president committed such an egregious offense that he deserved to be shown the door? David Schippers's presentation of the facts before the election had been convincing, and Hutchinson thought that if the president's lawyers did not refute them it would be hard not to support articles of impeachment. In effect, the burden of proof had shifted in his mind from the accusers to the defense. But as an experienced lawyer, he was struggling to keep an open mind.

As part of that effort, Hutchinson asked two of the Democratic committee investigators, Kevin Simpson and Steven Reich, for their assessments of the case, and he agreed to go to breakfast with Abbe Lowell. They met at 8 A.M. on Monday, November 16, at La Colline, a haven for lobbyists on the Senate side of Capitol Hill. Lowell thought Hutchinson was persuadable, and that if he came out against impeachment, it would make it easier for other Republicans to follow. As the food arrived, Lowell pressed his point, walking Hutchinson through his analysis of the grand jury testimony and the constitutional theory. It was a lawyer-to-lawyer discussion of the substance that both found bracing.

Lowell argued that the president's deceptions about Lewinsky during the Jones case were immaterial.

"I would think it is material if it forestalls her from finding other evidence," Hutchinson responded.

"But there's no other evidence to find," Lowell parried.

They went back and forth about whether the president endorsed the truthfulness of his Jones deposition during his grand jury testimony. Hutchinson thought he did; Lowell maintained he did not. They debated whether Clinton could have been witness-tampering if Betty Currie insisted that she felt no pressure. Hutchinson thought he could; Lowell argued he could not.

As it always did, the conversation circled back to what to do about all this. Lowell pushed Hutchinson to consider censure. "If you're positive the president has done this terrible stuff, then how is it better for you to have a divided vote in the committee and a divided vote in the House and lose in the Senate than to have three hundred and fifty people come together for a bipartisan censure in the House? If you're trying to send a message, why isn't that the message you're trying to send?"

"Censure may be the way this ends," Hutchinson replied. "But it can't be the way it begins."

The next day, Tuesday, November 17, the Judiciary Committee released the tapes that had started it all, Linda Tripp's surreptitious recordings of her phone conversations with Monica Lewinsky—in all, thirty-seven tapes containing about twenty-two hours of talking. For the first time since the scandal had erupted ten months earlier, the nation finally heard Lewinsky's voice, albeit disembodied, and cable television networks spent much of the day playing the choicest snippets.

While news coverage focused on the gossipy chitchat between the two women—and Tripp's patent manipulation of the younger woman—Gephardt was quietly working on a censure plan. Following his meeting with Clinton, Gephardt recognized that financial sanctions were off the table, so he wanted to start drafting an official resolution of reprimand that would satisfy fellow Democrats and could be presented as an alternative to any articles of impeachment. Congressman Rick Boucher was again tapped to handle this tricky assignment. With his moderate mien and his deep Southern voice, the Virginia Democrat had proven to be an effective public face for the party during the October debate over the inquiry. And once again, the Democrats were badly divided over how to proceed. Some wanted censure only if it truly hurt the president; others were against it on principle or out of loyalty to Clinton. And many Democratic committee members were intent on attaching their names publicly as author of the effort to secure their places in history. Determined to keep the team together, Gephardt invited three other Democratic congressmen to his 5 P.M. meeting with Boucher that Tuesday—Bill Delahunt, who had been working with some Republicans through their "breakfast club"; Sheila Jackson Lee, who was among the fiercest of the president's defenders; and Paul McHale, the first congressional Democrat publicly to call on Clinton to resign.

To unite the caucus behind a single censure motion would require the support of the four divergent members whom Gephardt had gathered in his office. After some initial discussion, Gephardt seemed satisfied that there was a chance of success and asked the four to begin working on language. Boucher and the others retired to the conference room. Boucher had brought with him a draft censure resolution he had cobbled together with Congressman Howard Berman. Delahunt had his own draft. But McHale complained that both were too weak and let Clinton off the hook for his "reprehensible conduct."

In the interests of keeping McHale at the table, Boucher backed off: "Fine, let's start over."

"Why don't I go back to the office and see if I can synthesize these ideas?" suggested Julian Epstein, the Democratic committee chief counsel. Epstein knew that the key to preserving party harmony on this was to remember the lessons from the inquiry debate—keep it short, clear, and simple. Over the next few hours, he crafted a version that met those criteria and brought it back to Boucher. It would conclude that Clinton's affair with Lewinsky was wrong, that he had lied about it, and that he had impeded the discovery of the truth. Boucher liked it. But that would not be the end of the process; a lot of other committee Democrats felt they too should be part of the drafting and complained at being excluded from the meeting in Gephardt's office.

The main drama of the week, and perhaps the entire House inquiry, was to be the appearance of Kenneth Winston Starr before the Judiciary Committee.

This was the moment everyone had been anticipating. When his report had first arrived on Capitol Hill, some committee Democrats had practically salivated at the idea of calling Starr to testify before them, only to change their minds just as quickly when the Republicans called their bluff and made him their only real witness. The Democrats had wanted to put Starr on trial, to call him to task for his excesses and change the subject from Clinton's behavior, but in the interim they began to realize that the independent counsel was better as a mostly silent figure they could paint as a zealot. The real Starr was a skilled appellate attorney, a former solicitor general, and a former appeals court judge. He might not be so easy to rattle, and if he came across as smoothly as others did in such high-profile hearings—Iran-contra's Oliver L. North leapt to mind—then the dynamics of the case could suddenly reverse.

For their part, the Republicans were no more interested in soliciting straight factual information from Starr than the Democrats. Their goal was to rehabilitate him and give him a chance to lay out his case against the president before a national television audience. In case their sympathies were not plain already, committee aides distributed talking points to Republican members for use in defending Starr publicly. A ten-page paper titled "Positive Points About Independent Counsel Ken Starr" began this way: "Judge Starr is one of the country's premier lawyers, and his record is unblemished." An accompanying sixty-four-page tome called "Response to Recent Attacks on Judge Starr's Investigation" concluded in the first paragraph that "none of these attacks has any merit."

From the moment Starr took his seat at the witness table facing the dais in Rayburn's Room 2141 on Thursday, November 19, the hearing quickly degenerated into partisan bickering. No sooner had Hyde explained the rules of the day than Democrats started peppering him with complaints. Bill Delahunt, a former prosecutor, introduced a motion to give the president's lawyer more time to interrogate the independent counsel, but Hyde dismissed it without giving Delahunt a chance to speak. When Hyde relented and gave him the floor, the Massachusetts Democrat refused to yield back to Hyde when he wanted to ask a question. Congressman Mel Watt raised a point of order.

"I don't yield for any points of order," Hyde said dismissively. In the ensuing squabble, Hyde lost his patience. "You are disrupting the continuity of this meeting with these adversarial—"

"We're disrupting a railroad, it seems like, Mr. Chairman!" Watt shot back. "That's what we're disrupting here."

The Democrats, knowing full well they would lose, pressed for a roll call vote on the issue of giving Clinton's lawyers more time. Predictably, the motion failed on a straight party-line 21–16 tally, giving the Democrats what they really wanted—another piece of evidence to argue that they were being steamrollered. Win by losing.

John Conyers did not wait for Starr to utter his first word before attacking him as a "federally paid sex policeman" who had "ignored his ethical obligations" and allowed "rogue attorneys and investigators to trap a young woman in a hotel room." Seated at the witness table alone in a classic Washington gray suit and red tie, Starr faced Conyers impassively, registering no sign of pique. When Conyers finished, Starr was asked to stand and take the oath, but his soft "I do" could barely be heard over the mass clicking noises that came from the battery of media cameras trained on him. Starr then launched into a two-hour-and-fifteen-minute opening statement that walked the committee through his litany of allegations—this time with none of the graphic detail of his written report but a sharper focus on the issue of truth-telling.

"No one is entitled to lie under oath simply because he or she does not like the questions or because he believes the case is frivolous or that it is financially motivated or politically motivated," Starr said, refuting the president's contentions during his grand jury appearance.

But for the first time in public, the independent counsel exonerated Clinton in connection with other matters he had investigated, including the Whitewater financial dealings that had originally prompted the probe four years earlier, as well as the firing of the White House travel office workers in 1993, and the improper collection of FBI files that had become public in 1996. While Starr disclosed that he had drafted an impeachment referral stemming from Whitewater a year ago, he had ultimately rejected it because the evidence was too thin. The revelations came and went with little notice, an ironic anticlimax given the years investigators had spent rooting around those scandals.

For Starr, though, this was a chance to exonerate himself. After being vilified by the White House and its allies for months, after watching his dreams of a seat on the Supreme Court disappear, after seeing himself caricatured as the Inspector Javert of the 1990s, the fifty-two-year-old former judge could finally present his case in person, refuting the idea that he was a "constitutional monster." He was dispassionate to the point of monotony, using words like *thus* and *therefore* and *indeed*.

"We go to court and not on the talk-show circuit," Starr said, trying to sound principled rather than defensive. "And our record shows that there is a bright line between the law and politics, between courts and polls. It leaves the polls to the politicians and the spin doctors. We are officers of the court who live in the world of law. We have presented our cases in court, and with very rare exception, we have won." He added later, "I am not a man of politics, of public relations, or of polls—which I suppose is patently obvious by now."

What was obvious to the Democrats was that Starr was trying to recast himself as a reasoned prosecutor on the trail of an errant president. Their job was not to let him. Abbe Lowell handled the bulk of the attack for the Democratic side in a sharp-edged hour of questioning about Starr's previous contacts with the Jones lawyers, his failure to report possible conflicts to Attorney General Janet Reno when he asked permission to investigate the Lewinsky matter, and his tactics in forcing the young former intern to cooperate. Like most of the Democratic members who would follow him, Lowell barely bothered to ask about the evidence against the president or challenge its veracity, but focused almost exclusively on Starr's conduct.

The independent counsel had gone through videotaped practice sessions for weeks preparing for such a confrontation, and he kept his cool. "I must take gentle issue," Starr said in response to one accusatory question. "I utterly disagree, with all respect, with your premise," he said to another. He filibustered through answers so long that he controlled the rhythm of the back-and-forth. Lowell, who got bogged down early in a series of questions comparing Starr with Watergate special prosecutor Leon Jaworski, tried several times to interrupt, fearing his time would run out.

Unlike Lowell, each committee member was restricted to five minutes to question Starr, with the interrogation flipping back and forth from Republican to Democrat. As a result, the members could barely get a line of inquiry going before being cut off. Before the session, the Democrats had tried to prepare by coming up with a sequence of questions and assigning different topics to different members in hopes of creating a coherent interrogation, but that flopped. The committee's notoriously independent-minded Democrats had no desire to act in concert. Some of the Democrats, including Bobby Scott, Chuck Schumer, and Marty Meehan, effectively just gave five-minute speeches without really asking Starr anything. The Republicans, for their part, lobbed softballs, giving Starr a chance to steady himself between each Democratic volley.

The real marquee matchup did not come until the evening. This was the moment David Kendall had waited for. After four years of dueling with Starr, the former civil rights attorney had a crack at turning the microscope around and examining the prosecutor. There had been some debate at the White House whether this was really a good idea. Perhaps Kendall had too much invested personally, and given his widely panned talk-show appearance after the Starr report had come out, a number of Clinton advisers were convinced he should not be the public face for the president. Kendall had a fingernails-on-chalkboard effect on congressional Republicans, and a fair number of Democrats as well. Greg Craig wanted the job of tackling Starr and quietly lobbied for the assignment, but he was no match for Kendall in the only circle of power in the White House that mattered on this issue—the triumvirate of Bill Clinton, Hillary Clinton, and Bruce Lindsey. To them, Kendall was the ultimate loyalist, a fierce, take-no-prisoners street fighter who would give their enemies the pounding they deserved, "someone I could count on and trust implicitly," as the first lady had put it in a magazine interview a few months earlier. Besides, no one else, least of all Craig, knew the record as intimately as Kendall.

The showdown began in prime time at 8:35 P.M., more than ten hours after Starr had first taken his seat at the witness table. Everyone in the room was exhausted, it seemed, except Kendall, who had been a bundle of nervous energy all day, like a boxer before the big match. "Oh, I'm ready," he kept telling colleagues. "Can't we get more time? I want more time. I need more time."

Kendall was determined to confront Starr from a position of strength. As he sat down at the table to cross-examine the independent counsel, Kendall noticed that the chair seemed too low, so he quickly reached under the table, grabbed his briefcase and sat on top of it to get a better angle on his nemesis. "Let me begin," he said, reading from his prepared text, "with the simple but powerful truth that nothing in this overkill of investigation amounts to a justification for the impeachment of the president of the United States." Then Kendall addressed the witness.

"Mr. Starr, good evening."

"Good evening," Starr replied. "How are you, David?"

"I'm very well, Ken."

Laughter rippled through the hearing room at the pleasantries and psuedo-friendly use of first names by the longtime adversaries.

From the beginning, Kendall elicited an admission that shocked some in the room—not only had Starr not attended any of Lewinsky's grand jury sessions or FBI interviews, he had never so much as met his star witness. Nor, it turned out, had he participated in or watched the questioning of any of the major figures in the case, such as Betty Currie or Vernon Jordan. To drive home another point, Kendall asked Starr to confirm that he had cleared the president in the Whitewater, FBI files, and travel office scandals. But Kendall was not about to make the same mistake other Democrats had made, and he promptly cut off Starr when he began a laborious explanation of why he had not reported those conclusions earlier.

"Mr. Starr," Kendall interrupted, "I have only thirty minutes. If I could, I think you've adequately answered my question." Turning to another point of attack, Kendall then asked Starr if his office had investigated the adoption of a Romanian child by Julie Hiatt Steele, a onetime friend of Kathleen Willey who had disputed her story of a sexual advance by the president.

For the first time all day, Starr took umbrage. "Mr. Kendall," he said sternly, jabbing his finger for emphasis, "my investigators work very hard and diligently to find relevant evidence. I believe that the questions—and I've conducted no specific investigation—and you've just spent a good deal of time establishing that I don't go with my FBI agents on every single interview—"

Kendall tried to interrupt.

"May I finish?" Starr cut back in. "You asked the question." By now, it was no longer "David" and "Ken." The serene smile on Starr's face had vanished, replaced by an unhappy scowl. "There is an enormous amount of misinformation and false information that is being bandied about with respect to that particular witness and the circumstances of questioning."

Kendall and Starr interrupted each other a few more times before the president's lawyer moved to one of his favorite topics, the allegations that prosecutors had violated grand jury secrecy rules by leaking information about the investigation to the media. "Mr. Starr, in fact, there has been no case remotely similar to this in terms of the massive leaking from the prosecutor's office, and I think we know that."

Kendall had gotten under Starr's skin again. "I totally disagree with that. That's an accusation and it's an unfair accusation. I completely reject it."

As the two bickered, the clock expired. Hyde used the opportunity to needle the president's lawyer for ignoring the case against his client. "Mr. Kendall, your time is up. You may want to get into the facts." Hyde offered another fifteen minutes, Kendall asked for sixty, and they compromised on thirty.

Kendall continued grilling Starr on his media relations policy, but the prosecutor tried to turn the accusation back at the White House, implying that the leaks had really come from defense lawyers who had learned about grand jury testimony through cooperation among witnesses' attorneys. Starr noted that the DNA test results from Lewinsky's dress never leaked to the press: "Those were never in the public domain, because you did not have a witness in your joint defense arrangements who you could debrief and tell you."

Kendall returned to Lewinsky and asked about her first confrontation with Starr's agents at the Virginia hotel. "One of the reasons your agents held Ms. Lewinsky—"

"I have to interrupt. That premise is false."

"I was not meaning to be offensive. Let me rephrase it."

"That is false and you know it to be false."

"Well, I'll rephrase the question."

"She was not held."

"Her own psychological state will speak for itself," Kendall said. "As to how she felt, it's in the record in her testimony."

"You said she was held," Starr shot back. "You didn't say how she felt. You said she was held, and I think that's unfair to our investigators."

Finally, Kendall's time ran out. If nothing else, he had succeeded in rattling the unflappable Ken Starr. Whether his relentless questioning on issues other than the case against the president had had much impact was another question. It was clear it had not influenced the committee Republicans. For the next thirty minutes, David Schippers did what he could to help "Judge Starr," as he called him deferentially, leading him through a friendly disquisition intended not to elicit information but to rebut criticism. Schippers noted that the Democrats had excoriated him for not attending witness interviews. "But you did have experienced, highly experienced professional agents and prosecutors present at each and every one of those occasions, did you not?"

"I did."

"And you relied upon the integrity, the honesty, and the decency of those agents and investigators, did you not?"

"I did, and very proudly so."

Schippers left no doubt where he stood. At one point he asked Starr, "You have a completely unblemished career for your entire life as a lawyer and you're looked upon in the profession as a man of honor, integrity, and decency. Is that right?" And Schippers concluded with a testimonial to the prosecutor. "I've been an attorney for almost forty years. I want to say I'm proud to be in the same room with you and your staff."

Starr's aides in the audience rose to their feet and began applauding. And then so did the Republican members of the committee, including Hyde, while the Democrats remained glued to their chairs—a graphic illustration of the partisan divide that had swallowed up the Judiciary Committee. Not only had that month's elections not curbed the GOP appetite for impeachment, what middle ground there might have been had all but disappeared. Congressmen do not ordinarily applaud witnesses, particularly along party lines. But the Republicans were overwhelmed by the moment, impressed by Starr's marathon performance after more than twelve grueling hours in the hot seat, and for the first time since the election disaster felt revitalized about their case. Lindsey Graham, who had not thought much of Starr up to this point, came away with newfound respect for the special prosecutor. But Asa Hutchinson, who remained in his seat during the ovation, silently fretted that this was a bad move for lawmakers charged with taking an impartial look at the evidence. By cheering Starr on, he felt, they were playing into the hands of Democrats who wanted to make out the House Republicans as nothing more than the handmaidens for a reckless prosecutor.

The confrontation over Starr was not the end of this long day, however. At 11:25 P.M., after kicking out the reporters and cameras, the committee convened in executive session to debate whether to approve its first four subpoenas. The Republican investigators wanted to force testimony by Bruce Lindsey, the longtime Clinton friend and aide; Bob Bennett, the president's attorney in the Jones case; Nathan Landow, the Democratic fund-raiser from Maryland; and Daniel Gecker, the Richmond-based attorney for Kathleen Willey. Lindsey, widely thought of as the chief fixer and keeper of secrets in the Clinton White House, had never testified about the Lewinsky matter, thanks to the long fights over executive privilege. Republican investigators wanted to ask Bennett about the origin of Lewinsky's false affidavit, but they also were interested in talking to him, Landow, and Gecker about the Willey case. Starr had just sent the committee more evidence related to Willey's situation, and the panel's GOP investigators hoped to pursue it to construct a broader case against the president than simply his actions regarding Lewinsky. Willey had suggested in court papers that Landow had tried to discourage her from testifying about her encounter with the president, and committee investigators were interested in reports that Bennett had encouraged Gecker to employ a friend of his as counsel for Willey, actions they thought might add up to a pattern of obstruction in the Jones case.

But the committee Democrats were alarmed at the prospect of forcing lawyers to testify and began complaining as soon as the doors were shut. "Without the attorney-client privilege, you really don't have the right to an attorney," Barney Frank said. "An attorney who is not in any way protected from disclosing everything you tell him or her is not much of an attorney. I think it would be a very grave error for the committee to proceed."

The Republicans had history on their side. Congress had traditionally not recognized common-law privileges such as attorney-client confidentiality, but only those privileges contained in the Constitution, such as the Fifth Amendment right to refuse to provide self-incriminating testimony. "I don't think that anybody who has evidence of whether or not the president committed an impeachable offense, whether that be an attorney or anybody else, should be allowed to not give this committee testimony," said Congressman F. James Sensenbrenner Jr. of Wisconsin.

Howard Berman shot back, "Suppose for a second it is the ethics committee and a member of Congress is the target of an ethics committee investigation."

Sensenbrenner was unmoved. There is "a significant legal difference between the two," he insisted.

Still, Hutchinson felt uneasy with what his fellow Republicans were trying to do. The investigators should be allowed to question the witnesses, and if any of them claimed attorney-client privilege, the matter ought to come back to the committee to decide whether to hold him in contempt, he suggested. "If it is a frivolous claim, which there could be frivolous claims of attorney-client privilege, I would not abide by it. But if it was a legitimate claim of a conversation," Hutchinson said, trying to strike a middle ground, "then I would want to say I would not be holding him in contempt for that."

Neither side persuaded the other, however. While the Lindsey deposition was approved by unanimous consent because he worked for the government and did not enjoy the same attorney-client privilege as private lawyers, the committee voted to subpoena Bennett and Gecker on straight party-line 21–16 votes. A couple of Democrats joined the Republicans in voting 23–14 for the Landow subpoena.

Breaking at 12:36 A.M., the worn-down committee members were famished. Steve Buyer, Lindsey Graham, and Mary Bono decided to get a late dinner. When Abbe Lowell walked up, they complimented him on his interrogation of Starr and invited him to join them. The three Republican committee members, the Democratic investigator, and a few aides piled into their cars and headed off into the darkness looking for late-night food, a rarity in the nation's capital. They eventually settled into a booth at Georgetown's Au Pied de Cochon, where they ordered eggs, orange juice, and coffee.

With jackets off and ties loosened, they put aside the tension of the day and talked more like real people, commiserating about how little time they were spending with their families and agreeing how great it was to escape briefly from the pressure cooker on the Hill. Buyer said he felt like he had been on a submarine for six months and had finally hit port. Impressed by Lowell's performance, the Republicans asked him about his background and teased him about how little money he must be making per hour compared with his private practice. Lowell, always anxious to press a point, tried to show the committee members how the evidence did not add up, but it was far too intense for two in the morning.

"Stop being a lawyer," Bono admonished him.

Yet the Republicans around the table did not sound wedded to Starr's case. They talked about censure as a serious option and casually tossed out possible language, although they worried that finding wording acceptable to both sides would be difficult. Lindsey Graham suggested he did not think lying at a civil deposition would be impeachable in the first place.

When Lowell got home around three in the morning, he was excited. Perhaps a line of communication had been opened. Maybe these guys could be reasoned with. Lowell later filled in Dick Gephardt with an optimistic report.

"There are people we can talk to," Lowell said.

Gephardt remained dubious. "They're not in control," he told Lowell. "The power of the crazy right has them by the throat and they're going to direct the way this goes."

*   *   *

Starr's marathon performance before the committee not only bolstered ambivalent Republicans, but also impressed the public. For the first time in his four years in office, Starr had been able to present himself at length to the American people without being filtered through the lens of White House characterizations. He did not come across as the maniacal zealot depicted by James Carville and company for all those years, but rather as a quiet, dignified, and mostly unruffled lawyer. Instant poll numbers showed high approval for Starr among those who tuned in.

Yet that was not enough to make much of a difference in larger public attitudes; while most of those interviewed by pollsters gave Starr high marks, it did not change their overall opposition to impeachment. Worse for Starr, whatever modest public redemption he had achieved was instantly trumped by a defection from within his own ranks. The day after the hearing, on Friday, November 20, Samuel Dash, the legendary Watergate investigator, quit as Starr's ethics adviser and claimed the independent counsel had crossed the line of objectivity by appearing as an advocate before the Judiciary Committee. Starr replied that he had had no choice but to accept the committee's invitation, but the damage was done: all Democrats had to say was that Starr's own ethics adviser had resigned because the special prosecutor had abused his office. That spoke for itself.

The next Monday, November 23, committee investigators took their first and only deposition of the entire impeachment inquiry. For three and a half hours behind closed doors, they questioned Dan Gecker, Kathleen Willey's lawyer, about his contacts with the president's attorneys. Gecker testified that Clinton counsel Bob Bennett had suggested Willey avoid testifying by invoking her Fifth Amendment right against self-incrimination, a suggestion the president's lawyer attributed to a judge overseeing her deposition in the Jones case. Gecker also told committee investigators that Bennett had tried to get Willey to hire his longtime friend, criminal defense attorney Plato Cacheris, promising that money would not be a problem. In exchange, Gecker said, Bennett suggested they could share information in a joint defense agreement. While Republican investigators thought those actions could be seen as obstruction, Gecker did not cast them in a venal light, and the matter was essentially dropped as soon as the deposition was over.

As they studied the figures on the piece of paper, Tom DeLay's top aides looked at each other in shock. The numbers told a remarkable story: the president was just three votes away from being impeached.

Starr's performance had evidently had an energizing effect among House Republicans, an impact DeLay had encouraged by distributing copies of the independent counsel's opening statement to every GOP congressman. Now the sentiment was showing up in an unofficial vote count taken by DeLay's office. Of the 228 Republicans in the House, DeLay's counters came up with only thirty they thought might vote against impeachment, a number that was shaved to just twenty when the issue was narrowed to a single charge of perjury. About five Democrats were thought to be ready to cross party lines to vote for impeachment, and if a couple others on the fence were to come as well, that would mean 215 votes for the anti-Clinton forces, three shy of the 218 needed for a majority. While obstruction of justice appeared out of reach, impeachment on perjury was suddenly a very real possibility. Despite the election, The Campaign was still alive.

To come up with these numbers, DeLay's staff had mounted a rogue operation. Tony Rudy, now DeLay's deputy chief of staff, and a few other aides had taken it upon themselves to conduct an informal survey without anyone's permission, gambling that if there was enough sentiment for impeachment within the conference, it would show the members that this could genuinely happen. For such an unauthorized mission, they could not use the formal machinery of the whip structure—the Republicans had sixty-seven members involved in the normal whipping operation—so instead they called friends around the Hill, aides in key offices, campaign contributors, confidants of swing members, drinking buddies, even fellow players from their fantasy-football league. What they came up with was not as reliable as an official whip survey, but it felt credible to those who kept tabs on the pulse of the conference for a living.

DeLay was not entirely surprised. A week or so earlier, he had conducted a conference call with some forty deputy whips and was happy to discover a strong current against censure and in favor of continuing with impeachment. Here they were, just three weeks after a disastrous election, and yet the House Republicans were ready to go after Clinton anyway. Having done their unauthorized survey, DeLay's aides then violated another internal protocol: they leaked it. There at the top of the front page of the *Washington Post* on Wednesday, November 25, blared the headline "Perjury Charge Faces Close Vote." With any luck, they hoped, the recognition that impeachment was alive would give it new legitimacy and make the survey something of a self-fulfilling prophecy.

Other senior House GOP officials, however, were stunned, not so much by the numbers as by the brazenness of those who had collected them. Scott Palmer, chief of staff to Deputy Whip J. Dennis Hastert of Illinois, erupted in anger at how the organization had been abused. Vote counts were never supposed to be leaked—particularly one that had not been sanctioned in the first place. He had never given permission for such a survey, he steamed. Palmer, a longtime Hill aide who cared deeply about the integrity of the institution, argued during a "come to Jesus" meeting in DeLay's office that they should put a halt to this corruption of the system right away.

"This is the wrong thing to do," Palmer insisted. "You're going to put members in a bad position. We'll be imposing our will on them in a very sensitive situation. The whip organization isn't designed for this kind of situation. Using the whip organization at this point would destroy it."

Rudy and some of his fellow aides fought back, arguing that they were in a battle to the death with Clinton and could not let DeLay lose. They had to use every possible tactic to win. If they were going to go down, at least they should go down swinging.

"We have to figure out what's best for Tom, and what's best for Tom is to win," declared Rudy's ally, press secretary Mike Scanlon.

But DeLay's chief of staff, Susan Hirschmann, agreed with Palmer and persuaded DeLay as well. There would be no formal whipping. This was not a routine bill where they could exert party discipline; for many members, impeachment would be a question of conscience, and they would resent pressure from their leaders. DeLay would have to figure out another way of winning them to his side.

By now, though, he was already working through the subterranean tunnels of politics to build up momentum for impeachment. In addition to constantly distributing anti-Clinton information to House Republicans and keeping up a steady drumbeat of public criticism of the president, DeLay was using a network of conservative talk shows and party fund-raisers to generate pressure within the GOP. He would go on as many as ten radio talk shows a day, and his staff would blast-fax talking points and tip sheets to perhaps two hundred such programs at a time, revving up the conservative audiences that would then turn up the heat on their local congressmen. Similarly, major campaign contributors and local party officials were encouraged to talk with members about impeachment. DeLay was careful enough not to contact his colleagues directly, for fear of giving the White House ammunition to say he was strong-arming members, but he recognized better than most the various pathways of modern American politics that do not emanate from the nation's capital.

DeLay was about to get some unexpected help from an unlikely source— the White House itself. With the Starr hearing behind them, Clinton's lawyers turned their attention to answering the eighty-one questions Hyde had sent the president after the election. Any thought of refusing to respond had by now dissipated, and instead, the White House team was fully engaged in editing a package to best present the president's case. No one in the Clinton camp had any illusions that the questions were anything but a setup; most of the inquiries had been posed during the Starr investigation, and so in their minds the only real purpose for asking them again was to get the president to repeat politically damaging assertions.

David Kendall, Nicole Seligman, and the other lawyers at Williams & Connolly prepared the first draft of the answers in characteristic fashion—defiant in the extreme, full of lawyerly niggling over words and details, almost hostile in tone. Paul Begala and the political advisers were assigned the task of neutralizing the in-your-face language without increasing the president's legal exposure. For days they labored over the drafts, looking for ways to soften answers and humanize the language. Eventually, the legal and political teams gathered in Podesta's office to go over the document before it went out. Begala had succeeded in massaging it so it was less confrontational. He had also written an introduction for Clinton to sign that was intended to minimize the damage from the legal arguments his attorneys were making: "I have asked my attorneys to participate actively, but the fact that there is a legal defense to the various allegations cannot obscure the hard truth, as I have said repeatedly, that my conduct was wrong. It was also wrong to mislead people about what happened and I deeply regret that."

But the Begala scrub, while toning it down significantly, still left a document filled with argumentative and quibbling answers. The tenor was set with the first one.

Question: "Do you admit or deny that you are the chief law enforcement officer of the United States of America?"

Answer: "The President is frequently referred to as the chief law enforcement officer, although nothing in the Constitution specifically designates the president as such. Article II Section 1 of the United States Constitution states that 'the executive power shall be vested in a president of the United States of America,' and the law enforcement function is a component of the executive power."

Others went along the same vein. More than twenty times Clinton said he did not recall or did not know something mentioned in the questions. Asked if he swore an oath to tell the truth, the whole truth, and nothing but the truth during his deposition in the Jones case, Clinton answered, "I do not recall the precise wording of the oath"—a phrase at least one of the political aides tried unsuccessfully to excise from the draft. Clinton went on to say he believed that he had "to answer the questions truthfully." In other words, the president would not acknowledge an obligation to provide "the whole truth" because even his lawyers knew that his testimony in the Jones case was anything but.

Beyond the quarrelsome language, the responses broke no new factual ground as the president stuck by his story, no matter how far-fetched the committee Republicans considered it: he did not lie under oath when he denied having "sexual relations" with Lewinsky because he meant intercourse; he did not ask or encourage anyone else to lie under oath; he did not direct Betty Currie to pick up the gifts from Lewinsky; he led Currie through a series of falsehoods not to coach her possible testimony but merely "to get as much information as quickly as I could."

The White House delivered the answers on a day calculated to minimize attention to them—Friday, November 27, the day after Thanksgiving. As a cigar-chomping Clinton enjoyed a round of golf, the answers were sent over to the Rayburn Building without his signature. Peeved, the committee aides insisted on a signed copy. After all, the response was to be considered sworn testimony under oath. Kendall, decked out in a tuxedo for an evening event, returned to the White House with a notary to get the signature, then met a young committee aide outside the White House gate around 8:30 P.M. to hand it over.

The answers landed like an unguided missile on Capitol Hill. Hyde and the other committee members saw the president's response as flagrant disrespect for them and the House as a whole. The momentum DeLay had begun to detect among Republicans only accelerated. Any inclination to give the president a break, to extend the hand of forgiveness, or even to cut their own losses following the election debacle seemed to die at this point. In its place emerged a determination to find a strong case against Clinton no matter where it came from. Even Lindsey Graham, who had almost seemed to be looking for a way to excuse the president, seethed as he read the answers and asked, "How can we nail this guy?"

After months of nonstop work and crisis at the White House, John Podesta finally got a chance to jog more during the Thanksgiving holiday weekend following delivery of the answers. Running helped clear his head. Things that were hard to see in the frenetic dozen-meetings-a-day pace of the White House suddenly became obvious. And somewhere on the jogging path in Washington's scenic and almost serene Rock Creek Park on this holiday weekend, it finally became plain to Podesta: They were fucked. There was no way to turn this around.

For weeks, the political smoke detectors at the White House had remained silent. Most of the president's aides remained confident, even cocky, following the election and embraced pollster Mark Penn's faith that public opinion alone would weigh down impeachment until the Republicans gave up. There was no need for the White House to do anything; when your enemy was busy self-destructing, stay out of the way.

But Podesta had picked up on some troubling signs. For years the president's chief firefighter through every manner of scandal, Podesta had now been elevated to replace Erskine Bowles as White House chief of staff. Shortly after the election, he went to see Bob Livingston to talk about getting rid of impeachment but found the new Speaker to be discouraging. Just as significantly, Podesta had noticed that the White House had not been able to get liberal, anti-impeachment Republican congressmen such as Jack Quinn and Mike Forbes of New York to be more publicly vocal in trying to kill momentum for the drive to evict the president. Podesta arrived back at the White House on the morning of Monday, November 30, and began sounding the alarms.

"This thing is rigged," he announced grimly at a staff meeting. "We are going to lose."

Most of the dozen aides in the room were flabbergasted. Was he crazy? they asked. Several had been out of town for a few days and wondered what had changed so drastically in their absence. They knew Podesta had his dark side—colleagues joked that he would sometimes be replaced by his evil twin, "Skippy"—and some thought that he was simply in a dour mood.

The other aides began arguing with Podesta. He was being too pessimistic. They had won the election. Surely the Republicans recognized that. Besides, what could they do if he was right? The only option might be to push off the impeachment vote into the next Congress, scheduled to take office in January, when Democrats would have five more seats. They could argue that holding an impeachment vote before the end of December as Hyde was projecting would be illegitimate because it was now a lame-duck House.

The problem was that the White House and the Democrats had forced the end-of-the-year deadline on Hyde in the first place. Joe Lockhart, who had taken over as press secretary after Mike McCurry's departure, noted that for the last five or six weeks all he had been saying was "Let's end it." Now he would have to go out and say, "Let's extend it"? They could not do that. Greg Craig added that if the name of the game was to win, it would be better to get the House vote over quickly; the spectacle of House Republicans jamming through impeachment would guarantee acquittal in the Senate, he said.

The others were still skeptical of Podesta's ominous analysis. Only one other person in the room, communications aide Jonathan Prince, echoed Podesta's assessment. "They're on a glide path toward impeachment," he said.

Despite Hyde's vow not to go trolling for new allegations, he acquiesced as David Schippers and other Republican investigators began looking under all sorts of rocks in the search for impeachable offenses that would not just involve the former intern. On the same Thanksgiving weekend of Podesta's jogging trail epiphany, Schippers drove down to Fredericksburg, Virginia, to meet with Kathleen Willey and her lawyer for about four hours. Willey had already gone on *60 Minutes* to describe how she went to see Clinton in the Oval Office in November 1993 seeking a job, only to find him kissing her and placing her hand on his aroused crotch. What Schippers wanted to know was what had happened afterward. Willey told him about a series of frightening incidents that led her to believe she was in danger. Her tires had been punctured. Her cat turned up missing, and an animal skull later turned up in her yard. One day, a stranger jogging by her house stopped to ask whether she had found the cat or fixed her car, then asked after her children by name. "Don't you get the message?" she said the man had asked.

Schippers was impressed. Willey, he thought, was one of the most believable witnesses he had ever met. Her story was powerful and could fit into a pattern of potential obstruction that they could include in any articles of impeachment.

That same weekend, while back in Arkansas for the Thanksgiving holiday, Asa Hutchinson drove over to the small town of Greenwood to meet with Juanita Broaddrick at her lawyer's office. With her husband and attorney on hand, Hutchinson hardly dwelled on the alleged assault itself and concentrated instead on whether she had ever felt pressured to keep quiet about what Clinton had done to her. As bitter as she was toward him, though, Broaddrick said no one connected with the president had ever tried to ensure her silence. Hutchinson left disturbed by the woman's allegation but he felt that they could not include it in their inquiry if there was no obstruction-of-justice angle.

Undeterred, Schippers pursued other angles as well. He was particularly intrigued by the campaign finance scandals of 1996. He had heard that Justice Department prosecutors had given immunity to Johnny Chung, the Chinese-American businessman who had befriended the Clintons, steered money from Beijing into Democratic coffers, and compared the White House to a subway where "you have to put in coins to open the gates." Schippers wanted to know where things stood with Chung and decided to push Justice to turn over two critical memos written by Louis J. Freeh, the FBI director, and Charles G. LaBella, the head of the Justice campaign finance task force, that made the case for appointment of an independent counsel to investigate the situation.

After some jockeying, the Justice officials reluctantly agreed to help. Because the Freeh and LaBella memos were sealed, they needed permission from the judge overseeing the campaign finance investigation, but on the same Friday after Thanksgiving that the White House delivered its answers to the eighty-one questions, Chief U.S. District Judge Norma Holloway Johnson rejected the Justice request, ruling that the department had failed to demonstrate a compelling need to break the court-ordered seal. The Judiciary Committee investigators were dumbfounded. The committee's lawyers obtained a draft of the brief filed by the Justice attorneys (the final version was under seal) and concluded that it was shoddily drafted. No wonder they had lost. Maybe they were even *trying* to lose. When Justice officials said they would file a motion asking the judge to reconsider, the committee attorneys were convinced that that would get them nowhere. Three of them, Mitch Glazier, William E. Moschella, and Sharee Freeman, stayed up all night drafting their own motion to the judge.

Amid the flurry over campaign finance, the committee conducted a nine-hour hearing into the consequences of perjury—essentially an extended argument by the Republicans that lying under oath, even about sex, was a serious crime that could and did land people in jail. The star witnesses of the hearing on Tuesday, December 1, were two such convicted perjurers. Pam Parsons, a former basketball coach at the University of South Carolina, had pleaded guilty to lying during a libel suit about whether she had ever been at a gay bar. Barbara Battalino, once a doctor for the Veterans Administration, had pleaded guilty after falsely denying under oath that she had had a sexual encounter with a patient.

"Because a president is not a king, he or she must abide by the same laws as the rest of us," Battalino told the committee.

But one Republican witness backfired on the Judiciary majority. Former congressman Charles E. Wiggins, who was Richard Nixon's most able GOP defender on the same committee a quarter-century earlier and now served as a senior federal appeals court judge, testified that while Clinton certainly committed impeachable offenses, the House should not impeach him anyway because the misconduct was "not of the gravity to remove him from office." Instead, he suggested a million-dollar fine and censure.

Undaunted, the committee went ahead and endorsed Schippers's interest in expanding the investigation into campaign finance, voting 20–15 to issue subpoenas for the disputed documents as well as for Starr's files on former Democratic fund-raiser John Huang and to Freeh and LaBella for their testimony. The committee's lawyers then went over to the courthouse to renew their case before Judge Johnson. Furious that once again the Republicans had not bothered to consult them, the committee Democrats authorized Abbe Lowell to file papers arguing against releasing the documents. A brief was drafted that would seek to intervene on behalf of the Democrats, but Tom Mooney, the Republican staff chief, heard about it and got Lowell on the telephone. A staff member could not go to court and work against a decision made by the full committee, even if some of the members did not like it.

"Abbe, I don't want to hear that you stood up in court and opposed this committee's position," Mooney warned.

Lowell backed off. As it was, when the two sides arrived in her courtroom, the judge had already made up her mind and did not bother to solicit any oral arguments; she simply reversed her previous decision and agreed to let the House have limited access to the memos. Each side could send a single staff member to read the memos, but no copies could be made and no notes taken.

Johnson disclosed her decision publicly the next day, Wednesday, December 2, and two committee lawyers went over right away to review the documents. Schippers went for the Republicans, but Lowell could not go himself because he had represented a minor character involved in the investigation. Instead, he sent one of his investigators, Kevin Simpson, who had worked for the Senate Democrats during the campaign finance probe in 1997. Even that decision, though, stirred up more internal animosity among the Democrats. Julian Epstein, the party's committee chief counsel, was angry that Simpson was picked without consulting him.

The memos suggested there was evidence of abuses and that the president and some of his close advisers engaged in a "pattern of conduct worthy of investigation." LaBella offered a stinging critique of the "gamesmanship" and legal "contortions" of Justice Department officials resisting the appointment of a special prosecutor and urged a probe of the "entire landscape" of campaign finance. But the memos did not contain enough to accuse the president of specific criminal violations without more information.

As they left the courthouse, Simpson turned to Schippers. "See anything that jazzes you?"

"Nah," Schippers responded.

In fact, Schippers thought the memos offered tantalizing leads. He reported back to Hyde: interesting stuff, but it would require a lot more time and resources than they had at the moment to see where it would lead.

That was enough for Hyde. In the last couple of days, he had come under withering fire from Democrats for reopening the much investigated campaign finance scandal. And so during a conference call with fellow committee Republicans the next morning, Thursday, December 3, Hyde announced they would not address fund-raising allegations during the inquiry. After just forty-eight hours, the depositions of Freeh and LaBella were canceled and the subpoena to Starr for the Huang documents was withdrawn. Schippers was furious. He could not believe Hyde would just abruptly call it quits like that on such an important area. The chairman did not even bother to tell him first.

Greg Craig continued to search for another way out but was not finding any avenues. At 5 P.M. on Tuesday, December 1, after the Judiciary Committee completed its hearing on perjury, he went over to the Longworth House Office Building and met with Lindsey Graham, the Republican who had struggled most publicly with the issue. Craig had agreed to come talk with Graham in response to a November 21 letter from the congressman to David Kendall seeking a meeting with the president's legal team, but the White House special counsel was a little wary. Craig feared that it was all a setup, that Graham intended to use the meeting to grandstand later to the media, depicting himself as a reasonable Republican who had tried to get the recalcitrant White House to see the error of its ways, only to be rebuffed. Yet Craig decided there was no way to turn down the invitation. Besides, Graham had already indicated that he would likely vote against an article of impeachment generated by the president's testimony in the civil case, and Craig hoped that perhaps Graham could bring along a few more Republicans such as Mary Bono, Ed Pease of Indiana, and Bill Jenkins of Tennessee to defeat at least that one charge.

For all of his trepidation, when Craig sat down on Graham's couch, he was pleasantly surprised at how well they got along. It was not a setup after all. The two men launched into a rather engaging, professional discussion about the evidence, just two litigating lawyers talking about where the strengths and weaknesses of the case were. Graham repeated his doubts about the civil perjury charge, while Craig conceded that the president's coaching of Betty Currie bothered him too. They talked about what it would take to end the crisis. Graham insisted that the president would have to make a full admission in exchange for being censured and not impeached. Craig mentioned that any deal would have to include an end to Starr's probe.

Craig knew how hard it would be to put together such a package and did not hold out any strong hopes. Still, he had to be somewhat encouraged by Graham's assessment of the political prospects for any articles of impeachment once they passed out of the committee. "It looks like you've got the votes to beat this in the House," Graham offered.

Craig heard a different assessment just two days later. At ten-thirty on the morning of Thursday, December 3, he went to see Vin Weber, the former Republican congressman and close adviser to Newt Gingrich. While Gingrich had disappeared from the landscape, he was still technically serving as Speaker until Bob Livingston was formally installed in January and might yet play a role when the time came. Even if he did not, Weber understood the dynamics of the current ruling class in the House better than most.

As they sat in Weber's downtown office, where the ex-politician had carved out a lucrative lobbying trade in the nation's capital representing Microsoft and other corporate powerhouses, Craig asked about the motivations of the Republicans. The process seemed dangerously close to spinning out of control, Craig said. What could they do?

Weber did not like what was going on in the House either; it was not good for the country. But he was at a loss on what to suggest. If Gingrich were still in charge, Weber said, he could offer ways of getting into the Speaker's head. But larger forces were now at work, and Gingrich no longer had control over them. Weber had chewed over the problem with other so-called wise men around town—people such as Lloyd Cutler, Ken Duberstein, and Bob Michel—but nobody could figure out how to get through to the people on Capitol Hill. The advice of the wise men went unheeded.

"I wish I could tell you something," Weber told Craig. "It's not that I don't want to be helpful. But I'm not sure how you could stop this."

CHAPTER EIGHT

"Somebody in this room
rat-fucked the president last night"

The young lawyer sat down at his desk and punched the password into the computer: "RODINO." Admitted into the secure electronic vault of the House Judiciary Committee, he pulled up the file named simply "Articles." Mitch Glazier, a thirty-two-year-old graduate of Vanderbilt Law School who, for the last three years, had been toiling at the committee on the intricacies of intellectual property law, federal rules of civil procedure, and Title 28, now found himself assigned by Henry Hyde to draft the first charges to be lodged against a president since Peter Rodino's three articles of impeachment against Richard Nixon some twenty-four years earlier. As with so much else throughout the fall of 1998, Hyde was trying to pattern his efforts after those of his predecessor during Watergate. With that mandate in mind, Glazier had been locked alone in his basement office in the Rayburn Building until midnight for days on end, surviving on pepperoni pizza while he studied the Rodino articles and tried to shape a new generation of impeachment counts around their model.

Replicating the Watergate articles seemed to be the only real choice. There was little other precedent to follow. When Andrew Johnson was impeached in 1868, the House passed a resolution containing just a single sentence: "Resolved, That Andrew Johnson, President of the United States, be impeached of high crimes and misdemeanors in office." Only after the House voted were more specifics drawn up in the form of eleven articles— nine of them generated by a single action, Johnson's firing of Secretary of War Edwin Stanton, while a tenth accused the president of defaming Congress by making critical speeches, and an eleventh was essentially a potpourri recasting the previous charges. None of that was much help to Glazier. The three articles passed by Rodino's committee were somewhat more detailed, though still hardly as specific as a prosecutor's indictment or the impeachment articles generally filed against federal judges. One article alleged

188

obstruction of justice stemming from the Watergate burglary and listed nine examples. Another accused Nixon of abuse of power for using the FBI, CIA, and IRS to violate the constitutional rights of his enemies. The third charged that he had assumed to himself "the exercise of the sole power of impeachment vested by the Constitution in the House of Representatives" by defying committee subpoenas seeking evidence. Each Rodino article used the same language at the start and the finish, including two final paragraphs:

"In all of this, Richard M. Nixon has acted in a manner contrary to his trust as President and subversive of constitutional government, to the great prejudice of the cause of law and justice and to the manifest injury of the people of the United States.

"Wherefore Richard M. Nixon, by such conduct, warrants impeachment and trial, and removal from office."

Glazier was struck by some of the surface similarities—how Nixon was accused of lying to the public, defying Congress during the impeachment inquiry and so on. As he sat down to put together articles against Clinton, Glazier adopted the Rodino format—the same three-paragraph introduction, the same wording at the start of each article accusing Clinton of violating his oath "to faithfully execute the office of President of the United States," and the same two paragraphs at the end asserting that his misconduct "warrants impeachment and trial, and removal from office." The Democrats could hardly complain if the Republicans lifted the framework they themselves had first constructed, Glazier reasoned. What did not occur to him or Hyde was that by so consciously mimicking the Watergate format, they were implicitly raising the bar for the substance of the charges as well—lying under oath and covering up an affair might pale in comparison to paying hush money and using the CIA to thwart an FBI investigation of political espionage.

With the shell of the articles on his computer screen, Glazier turned to the trickier question of how to fill the blank spaces in the middle—what to actually accuse Clinton of and how to package the charges. Everyone had his or her own idea. Congressman Bob Barr, a Georgia firebrand who campaigned for impeachment even before the Lewinsky scandal, drafted a version piling everything into a single article. Others suggested as many as ten articles, à la Andrew Johnson. Working with Hyde's inspiration, Glazier came up with two articles, one on perjury and the other on obstruction of justice. Like the Nixon articles, Glazier did not use the word *perjury* but instead said that Clinton "purposely made or caused to be made false or misleading statements under oath"—a pivotal distinction. Under federal law, proving perjury is harder than simply showing that a witness or defendant lied under oath; the lie has to be "material," or important, to the case at hand. The Rodino committee had been careful not to say that specific crimes had been committed; it was not the job of the House to fit elements of a criminal statute.

Glazier took his two proposed articles to Hyde for his review, which to the young lawyer felt like presenting a brief to an appellate court judge. Hyde took his red pen and scribbled his thoughts on how the articles should be drafted, but in general liked the direction. Over the next few days he invited other Republican members to his office to read the draft, but in the interests of maintaining secrecy would not let them take copies. As they read it over, several members insisted on taking the allegation that Clinton had inappropriately asserted executive privilege and making it into a separate article alleging abuse of power; that would draw the historical link with Nixon, they thought. So Glazier broke it out and created an Article III focusing on the misuse of the privilege and the misuse of the office of White House counsel in asserting it. In this draft article, Glazier also charged Clinton with "deceiving the American people concerning his improper and reprehensible relationship" with Lewinsky, "interfering with an agency of the United States" (meaning Starr's office), and jeopardizing Jones's ability "to exercise her access to justice."

Hyde gave copies of the draft articles to one committee Republican he wanted to play a central role in the writing, Congressman Charles Canady, a Yale-trained lawyer who had made a specialty out of constitutional issues and led the November subcommittee hearing on standards of impeachment. On Wednesday, December 2, Canady sat down with the latest copy and played editor, marking up the draft to suggest both substantive and stylistic changes. Wherever Lewinsky's name appeared in the articles, he crossed it out and substituted the phrase "a certain subordinate employee" to make it sound more serious and at the same time emphasize her status as an intern. In Article II, where Glazier had included among the examples of wrongdoing Clinton's months-long refusal to appear before a grand jury before finally succumbing, Canady drew seven lines through the text indicating that should be dropped. And at the end of each article, where it said Clinton "warrants impeachment and trial and removal from office," Canady added the phrase "and is thereby disqualified from holding and enjoying any office of honor, trust or profit under the United States pursuant to Article I, Section 3 of the United States Constitution." No one had bothered to try to bar Nixon from running for office again, but Canady figured it was a precaution that ought to be taken against a president who once dubbed himself the Comeback Kid.

Over the next few days, the Republicans were divided over how specific to be in the articles and drafted alternate versions—one with general descriptions of what Clinton had lied about and the other with more details. As of 3 P.M. on Thursday, December 3, the long version listed nine false statements from his Jones deposition and six from his grand jury testimony. By this point, the draft also included a couple of new allegations—in Article I, it brought in Kathleen Willey and accused Clinton of lying about his conduct with her, while in Article III, it charged that the president had "failed to respond truthfully and fully, under oath" to the eighty-one questions submitted by the committee the month before. But the Republicans still could not come to consensus. On Saturday, December 5, they put together another rough draft shrinking the resolution back to two articles, getting rid of the Willey and executive privilege provisions, and including the answers to the eighty-one questions in a catchall perjury article. By 1 P.M. the next day, Sunday, December 6, they were back at three articles again—including a short version and a long version.

With the start of a new and critical week, the issue was coming down to the wire. The White House, after equivocating on whether to call witnesses, had decided to accept Hyde's offer to present a two-day defense to the committee and would start on Tuesday, December 8. Hyde was trying to keep control over the situation. As if the Democrats and the White House were not enough of a handful, he also had a restless bunch of Republican members. And then there was his handpicked chief investigator, increasingly seen by even some of the committee Republicans as a rogue operator undermining the case by chasing unrelated Clinton scandals. David Schippers had been trying to develop more of the myriad allegations that swirled around Clinton, only to be frustrated by the lack of time. With just a few days before the articles were to be considered, Schippers went to Hyde with a plan to introduce new evidence. He would use his final presentation before the committee to call several powerful witnesses who could tell the panel, and the country, just what sort of man Bill Clinton really was—Kathleen Willey, Juanita Broaddrick, and Dolly Kyle Browning. Broaddrick had balked at the notion of going public with her twenty-year-old rape allegation, but Schippers told Hyde that he was sure she would come forward if the chairman asked her to. Her corroborating witnesses were powerful, and even though Broaddrick alleged no obstruction, her account could prove Clinton lied during his Jones deposition when he denied ever harassing any woman, Schippers said. Browning, in particular, was raring to go and had flown to Washington to testify. Schippers believed his investigators had turned up solid proof that Clinton had lied under oath about his conversation with Browning at a high school reunion a few years back.

"Henry, she's here. You don't have to subpoena her," Schippers said. "She's going to blow this son of a bitch sky-high."

Hyde put his foot down. He had given Schippers plenty of rope to conduct the investigation, but now it was over. Schippers's presentation to the committee was supposed to be a final summation, not an examination of witnesses. Hyde said he would never let the Democrats get away with doing this. Besides, he said, calling in Clinton's former paramours would turn the process into a three-ring circus. If they were to call these witnesses now, Hyde told Schippers, the White House would say they were being unfair to the president.

"For Christ's sake!" Schippers exploded. "No matter what you do, they'll say that about you."

Equally hot inside the Rayburn Building was Congressman Bill McCollum, the intense Republican from Florida. After reviewing the draft impeachment articles developed by Mitch Glazier, he noticed one word conspicuously missing: *perjury.* In a meeting of the GOP members in the Rayburn conference room, McCollum demanded to know why they were not calling a spade a spade.

Schippers said he and the staff felt that "false and misleading statements" covered a broader range of presidential wrongdoing and would be the strongest way to bring the case. "False statements," after all, was the way the Nixon articles phrased the crime.

McCollum was not satisfied. They had to use the word *perjury,* he insisted. A false statement could be something not specifically related to a court case, such as lying in a federal job application. *Perjury* meant it was a lie in court, a far more serious issue. That was what this president had done, McCollum went on; he had undermined the judicial system.

Hyde accepted McCollum's idea and told the staff to include it. The lawyers were unhappy with the instruction. By calling it perjury, they were only setting a higher bar for themselves to clear to prove their case. Not every lie under oath was perjury, and now they were opening the door for the White House to defend Clinton on the issue of whether his testimony fit the technical legal requirements of the perjury statute. Using the false-statements standard would keep the focus on the truthfulness of his testimony. But on Hyde's order, the lawyers did not have much choice. Looking for a way to hedge, they made it an adjective rather than a noun—instead of "perjury," Clinton would now be accused of providing "perjurious, false and misleading testimony," in the hope that the narrow distinction would somehow make a difference.

McCollum advocated another revision of the draft articles as well. Several Republicans wanted to separate the president's testimony in the Paula Jones case from his statements before the grand jury, splitting the current Article I in two. Lindsey Graham had already made clear that he did not want to vote to impeach Clinton for lying in the Jones civil deposition when the president had been ambushed with unexpected questions; it seemed less serious than lying to a grand jury after being publicly warned not to. His committee colleagues wanted to divide the issue so that Graham could still vote for grand jury perjury. In fact, though, Graham had signaled that he would vote for a catchall perjury article even if it included the civil deposition. Floor tactics were the real motivation for the change—the committee Republicans wanted to make sure moderate colleagues who were not on the panel did not have an excuse to vote against grand jury perjury when it came to a vote of the full House.

So now the Republicans had four articles. Article I accused Clinton of perjury before the grand jury on August 17, 1998, by lying about "the nature and details of his relationship with a subordinate Government employee," about the truthfulness of his earlier testimony in the Jones deposition, about the untrue statement he had allowed his attorney to make during that deposition, and about "his corrupt efforts" to influence testimony and hide evidence. Article II accused Clinton of perjury in the Jones case, first in his answers to written interrogatories on December 23, 1997, when he denied having sexual relations with any subordinate federal government employee and then again in the January 17, 1998, deposition. Article III accused him of obstruction of justice, citing seven examples, including his encouragement of Lewinsky to file a false affidavit, his efforts to find her a job to keep her quiet about their affair, his coaching of Betty Currie, and his involvement in hiding the gifts. Article IV accused him of abusing the power of his office by lying to the American public, lying to aides and cabinet secretaries who would repeat those false statements publicly, "frivolously and improperly" asserting executive privilege to impede Starr's investigation, and making "perjurious, false and misleading sworn statements" in response to the eighty-one questions posed by the Judiciary Committee.

The Republicans made no real attempt to involve Democrats in the drafting of these articles on the assumption that it was hopeless. But the Democrats were busy with their own editing process. After much agonizing and internal debate over the wording, they were putting the last touches on a censure resolution they hoped would hold their caucus together and still appeal to moderate Republicans when it came time for a floor vote.

The resolution produced by Rick Boucher would conclude that Clinton "made false statements" and "wrongly took steps to delay discovery of the truth" without conceding that those actions amounted to perjury or obstruction of justice. It would note that Clinton remained liable for criminal prosecution and would require him to sign the resolution as an acknowledgment of his misconduct. Noting that the president has a duty to "set an example of high moral standards," the censure would assert that "William Jefferson Clinton has egregiously failed in this obligation, and through his actions has violated the trust of the American people, lessened their esteem for the office of President and dishonored the office which they have entrusted to him."

The House Republicans and Democrats were not the only ones busy at work on documents that would condemn the president. So was his own staff.

With the denouement in the Judiciary Committee approaching and the outcome seemingly certain, the White House team was focusing on what to do on the House floor. The president's advisers clearly knew that many of the moderate Republicans who held the key were not yet satisfied that Clinton had been sufficiently contrite. Over the weekend, before the committee was to open its debate, a group of aides bantered back and forth about various options. Finally they agreed Clinton should make another stab at conceding wrongdoing, but this time focus not so much on his personal behavior as on his deceptive testimony in the Jones case. He could not credibly continue to insist his answers were somehow truthful, if misleading. If they could have him admit that, it might win over those like Lindsey Graham who were looking for a reason to vote no.

The problem was that Clinton would never admit a crime, nor would David Kendall let him. Kendall was the guardian of the president's legal liability beyond the congressional impeachment proceedings and forever resisted any strategies that could endanger his client in a criminal court after his term in office was over. Kendall felt he had made a mistake by letting political considerations force Clinton into agreeing to testify before the grand jury back in August, and he was determined not to let that happen again.

"You guys are not going to be here two years from now when I'm in a trial defending the president," Kendall told political aides repeatedly.

"I don't care," Paul Begala would testily reply, revealing the depth of his disillusionment with the president. "I don't work for Bill Clinton. I work for the people of the United States. I don't care if he goes to prison the day he leaves office. But until then I want him doing his job."

The trick became finding language that would let the president give ground without it crumbling beneath him. Steve Ricchetti, the congressional lobbyist who had since been promoted to deputy chief of staff, and the group of aides decided to try it in the form of a letter to every member of the House and handed the assignment of working up a first draft to Jonathan Prince, the communications aide who had warned that the Republicans were on a "glide path to impeachment."

"Let me begin with this unvarnished fact: my relationship with Ms. Lewinsky and my efforts to hide it were terribly wrong," the first version began. "In the weeks since August 17, it has become more and more clear to me just how much damage my conduct has caused—to the American people, to my staff, to my friends, and above all, to my family." In this draft, Clinton would go on to apologize again, explicitly and unambiguously. "I let a lot of people down. I know it. I am sorry for it. And I understand that I must be held accountable for it." For the first time, the president would directly accept censure as a punishment for his wrongdoing and the possibility of criminal prosecution after his presidency. "I am ready to accept a sanction that is commensurate with the damage I have caused. I deserve it. Let me also be clear that I expect to be treated, and should be treated, no differently than any American citizen if the Independent Counsel chooses to pursue this matter after January 20, 2001."

While defending his grand jury testimony as "accurate and responsive," the staff draft would have Clinton acknowledge for the first time that he was wrong to try to mislead Paula Jones's lawyers, even if his answers were not perjury. "I walked a very fine line, and I understand that some may think I crossed it. I do not believe I did, but that is no excuse. My relationship with Ms. Lewinsky was wrong, and my approach to questions about it in the Jones deposition was wrong as well."

Prince showed the draft to Cheryl Mills, Greg Craig, Chuck Ruff, and John Podesta, and soon the editing began. By 8:30 A.M. on Monday, December 7, Clinton's lawyers had deleted the concession that his "approach to questions" was as wrong as his original dalliance with Lewinsky, fearing that could make him more vulnerable to a perjury charge. By 10 A.M., it had been argued back in. By 11 A.M. the next day, at Kendall's insistence, aides were debating whether to take out the line about Clinton expecting to be treated the same in court after his presidency. By 1:50 P.M. the next day, that was gone. Then the group started having second thoughts about venue—maybe it should not be a letter after all, but rather a speech in the Rose Garden. After all, the real audience was the American people, and what could be more powerful than the master communicator himself? Begala, whose carefully written speech had been cast aside on August 17, was brought in to try his hand once again.

While the White House political staff focused on convincing millions, Ruff was focused on an audience of one: Henry Hyde. For three months now, the president's chief lawyer had failed to make any headway through official channels, so on the eve of the final committee hearings he agreed to try the back door. Lloyd Cutler, once again playing intermediary, set up a secret meeting between the White House counsel and the Judiciary Committee chairman, a summit so confidential that Ruff did not tell even some of his fellow attorneys, and Hyde hid it from top aides Tom Mooney and David Schippers. On Monday, December 7, the day before the president's team was scheduled to open its defense before the committee, Ruff, Hyde, and Cutler got together on neutral territory, the conference room of a Washington hotel where a spread of shrimp and other food was laid out. To avoid impeachment, Ruff offered to have the president accept censure. It could be a bipartisan ending of the kind Ruff knew Hyde instinctively wanted. But Hyde set terms the lawyer knew Clinton would never agree to. Hyde wanted Clinton practically to admit committing a crime. The conversation was cordial, and Ruff came away convinced that Hyde wanted to find a middle ground, but it seemed unobtainable.

Hyde was not ready to give up, though. After returning from the hotel and thinking over the discussion, he called Ruff directly at the White House with an even more startling proposal: if the president would drop his opposition to impeachment by the House, Hyde would negotiate a reasonable censure deal in the Senate with Majority Leader Trent Lott and Judiciary chairman Orrin Hatch. Constitutionally, the Senate was the place to resolve sanctions, Hyde maintained. As part of the arrangement, Hyde threw in a sweetener: he would work out an end to Starr's investigation as well, removing the threat of criminal prosecution after Clinton left office. All the president would have to do would be to let himself be impeached.

Ruff could hardly believe what he was hearing. Accept impeachment? Ruff was stunned at the presumption, and when he told colleagues at an impeachment strategy meeting the next morning, they were too. How preposterous. How out of step with the public. Ruff never bothered to bring it to the president to ask him. He called Hyde back later that day. Thanks but no thanks.

Hyde was frustrated. He was quietly trying to help, but the White House was not meeting him halfway. All they were doing was putting weakly worded censure proposals on the table, language that would never fly with anyone in his caucus. They were not giving him anything to work with. Hyde figured he would have to vote for impeachment himself no matter what. But if Clinton put a serious compromise on the table, a sincere apology with details about his misconduct, Hyde had agreed to work one-on-one with Lindsey Graham, the most undecided committee Republican, as well as a few others to meet their concerns. That would free scores of nervous moderate Republicans from an impeachment vote they did not want to cast on the floor, and Hyde would have been satisfied. If only Clinton would give in a little.

"Listen," the congressman told the president. "I think you're in very serious trouble. You're going to be impeached if the vote is held."

Clinton appeared taken aback. He and the first lady were hosting one of the numerous annual Christmas parties at the White House, this one for all 535 members of Congress, when Tim Roemer appeared in the receiving line with that stark message. It was the evening of Monday, December 7, just a few hours after the secret Ruff-Hyde meeting, and the executive mansion was filled with elaborate decorations and delicacies, a joyful tableau that seemed to clash with the political tension in town this season. Normally guests engaged in light chitchat during the sixty seconds or so they had the president's attention as they went through the assembly line of having their picture taken with the first couple. So when Roemer, a Democratic congressman from Indiana, showed up in line with a dire warning, Clinton immediately took notice.

"I might have two or three ideas," Roemer offered.

The president said he wanted to hear them. Call when you get home tonight, Clinton instructed.

Clinton knew to take what Roemer said seriously. Soundings on Capitol Hill had indicated as far back as August that Roemer was one of those disaffected Democrats close to abandoning him, and Roemer had warned Greg Craig to focus on the facts because they were serious, then joined Republicans in voting to open the impeachment inquiry in October. A leader of the more conservative wing of the party, Roemer was also one of the more thoughtful members of Congress, with better friendships on the other side of the aisle than most Democrats. After he got back to his house in Virginia that night, Roemer dialed the White House and the operator told him the president was expecting the call but would have to try back in a few minutes. At about 11:30 P.M., Clinton did so, and the two talked for the next half hour.

The president did not seem to have a sense of how quickly things were shifting in the House, how the process was evolving from an assessment of facts and guilt to one of politics and pressure on Republicans through their base constituencies. Voters in Republican districts felt adamantly about the issue and were contacting their representatives; that was having a seismic impact on the dynamics of the fight. Roemer made some suggestions about what the president should do, people he should contact, things he might say.

Clinton was defensive, talking about his enemies and their history of vindictiveness against him. It all went back to his first race for president in 1992, when the Republicans had tried to destroy him, he said.

That was the wrong attitude, Roemer felt, and told Clinton so bluntly: "Get over it. You're ten days away from a vote. This is not about you being a victim. You made mistakes—you have to understand that. It's not just a conspiracy out to get you."

Instead of the sometimes astringent David Kendall, the soothing Greg Craig would lead off the president's defense before the Judiciary Committee. By this point, the committee itself was a lost cause for the president, and so the real target over the next two days of hearings would be the moderate Republicans who did not serve on the panel but would control the fate of impeachment once it reached the House floor, the ones hearing from their anti-Clinton constituents back home. Whatever his strengths in court, Kendall would not be the right messenger for that audience. For Craig, it was at last the chance to do what he had wanted when he first came on board in September, to rally to the president's defense at the moment of maximum peril. Yet it was not to be quite the way he had envisioned. Throughout much of the fall, Craig had pushed to call witnesses who could testify about the facts of the case or the origins of the Starr investigation, but got nowhere either within the White House or on Capitol Hill. So when he showed up at the committee hearing room in the Rayburn Building on the morning of Tuesday, December 8, to open the president's defense, he was left with no one to put at the witness table but a panel of prosecutors and legal experts who would try to dissect Starr's case and argue why it did not amount to high crimes and misdemeanors but possessed no firsthand knowledge of the events at issue.

With their eyes on the moderates, Craig and the others decided to soften the edges of their defense, dispense with the attack-the-accuser style, and offer as much conciliation as they could. The theme the White House lawyers came up with for their presentation boiled down to three words: it ain't Watergate. The witnesses Craig brought along included James Hamilton, who had served as a lawyer working on the congressional investigation into Richard Nixon; Richard Ben-Veniste, a former Watergate prosecutor; and three members of the Judiciary Committee who had voted to impeach Nixon in the same room twenty-four years earlier: Elizabeth Holtzman of New York, Robert F. Drinan of Massachusetts, and Wayne Owens of Utah— "three ghosts of impeachment past," as Owens put it. In case that were not enough to make the point, the closer the next day would be Chuck Ruff, the last of the Watergate special prosecutors.

Craig opened by trying to acknowledge Clinton's misdeeds, while placing them in context. "Just as no fancy language can obscure the simple fact that what the president did was morally wrong, no amount of rhetoric can change the legal reality that there are no grounds for impeachment. As surely as we all know that what he did is sinful, we also know it is not impeachable." Just as the speechwriters were trying to get the president to do himself, Craig went on to give some ground on Clinton's behavior under oath. "I am willing to concede that in the Jones deposition, the president's testimony was evasive, incomplete, misleading, even maddening, but it was not perjury."

But Craig's effort to reach out to the committee without incendiary rhetoric was quickly dashed by his own witness panel. Sean Wilentz, a Princeton history professor, jabbed the Republicans for casting such trivial allegations as high crimes and misdemeanors. "If you believe they do rise to that level, you will vote for impeachment and take your risk at going down in history with the zealots and the fanatics," Wilentz told the committee. "If you understand that the charges do not rise to the level of impeachment, or if you are at all unsure, and yet you vote in favor of impeachment anyway for some other reason, history will track you down and condemn you for your cravenness."

Republicans were steaming. This professor from an ivory tower had just called them "zealots" and "fanatics" in their own hearing room. Ruff and Craig winced. Whatever good will Craig might have engendered with his measured introduction was quickly lost. Instead, he found himself being peppered with questions, an eventuality he had not prepared for. Craig had thought the committee members would question his witnesses, not the lawyer who introduced them. But now Craig was on the spot, deflecting barbed GOP inquiries. Several Republicans took note of his concession that the president was evasive and "maddening" and pressed Craig to explain why that was not the same thing as lying under oath.

"Now, Mr. Craig, did he lie to the American people when he said, 'I never had sex with that woman'?" demanded Bob Inglis, a lame-duck conservative Republican from South Carolina who had just lost a bid for the Senate and would leave Congress in the next few weeks. "Did he lie?"

"He certainly misled and deceived—" Craig started to answer.

Inglis cut in. "Well, wait a minute, now. Did he lie?"

"—the American people. He misled them and did not tell the truth at that moment."

Inglis was not satisfied. "Did he lie to the American people when he said, 'I never had sex with that woman'?"

"You know, he doesn't believe he did. And because of the—"

"He doesn't—"

"May I explain, Congressman?"

"He doesn't believe that he lied?"

"No, he does not believe that he lied, because his notion of what sex is, is what the dictionary definition is. It is in fact something you may not agree with, but in his own mind, his definition was not—"

Inglis was virtually apoplectic. "This is an amazing thing, that you now sit before us and you're taking back all of his—all of his apologies. You're taking them all back, aren't you?"

"No, I'm not."

In their seats behind him, Craig's fellow White House lawyers grew increasingly nervous. Craig was not supposed to respond to questions; Ruff would do that at the close of their case the next day. "Tell them Ruff is coming!" the other lawyers whispered at Craig. He tried, but it was not enough to satisfy the committee members.

Still, while Craig was getting battered, the White House team was about to get an important break. Hyde, who cherished his reputation for fairness and hated that it had been ripped apart, decided to let the Democrats offer their censure resolution for a vote in committee. He did not think it had any chance to pass—he had already come down formally against it himself—but it would at least keep the Democrats from bellyaching that they did not get the chance. As the hearing droned on that Tuesday, Hyde's chief aide, Tom Mooney, found Julian Epstein, his Democratic counterpart, and told him the committee would consider and vote on the articles of impeachment Thursday and Friday, staying all night if they had to. If you want censure, Mooney added, then John Conyers would have to send a letter formally requesting it. This was a major breakthrough, Epstein realized. If Hyde allowed a vote on censure in committee, it established a precedent for allowing a vote on the floor.

After the day's hearings ended, Clinton attended a dinner where he was feted with leaders from Northern Ireland as peacemakers for their role in forging the Good Friday accords. Across the ballroom at the Omni Shoreham Hotel, Clinton spotted Congressman Peter T. King, a maverick Republican from New York who had been outspoken in his opposition to impeachment and had been working with White House aides to battle Tom DeLay and The Campaign. Clinton and King had gotten to know each other well during years of work on the Northern Ireland conflict. King had become so identified with the Catholic cause there that Irish nationalist leader Gerry Adams liked to call him "Sinn Fein's congressman in Washington."

Clinton told Susan Brophy, his legislative liaison who was sitting at King's table, to arrange a meeting at 10 P.M. following the dinner. When they met backstage, Clinton and King talked for a few minutes about the Irish peace process and the recent troubles that had emerged in Belfast, then the president turned to impeachment and asked what could be done. The president said he had noticed that Al D'Amato, the New York senator just defeated for reelection, had come out against impeachment and wondered whether King had anything to do with that.

Yes, he had asked Al to make the statement as a personal favor, King replied, and in return promised to pass along this message to the president: "Tell your friend in the White House even though he came into New York four times against me, I'm still doing this for him."

Clinton laughed. "I've always liked Al," he said, overlooking the enmity he had harbored during D'Amato's Senate Whitewater hearings and his jubilation when the senator lost reelection the month before. King suggested Clinton should call D'Amato the next day to thank him. Maybe that would motivate the senator to call his friends in the New York House delegation. Clinton agreed.

Then King laid out his assessment of the situation for the president. The vote was still very much in play, but Clinton had to find a way to reach out to the undecided Republicans. The combination of DeLay pushing for impeachment and the impression that the president was defying Congress with his answers to the eighty-one questions had made the vote closer than it would have otherwise been.

Clinton grew irritated. His answers to the eighty-one questions were honest, he insisted. The president was clearly aggravated that anyone could suggest otherwise. He stated in those answers that his previous sworn testimony had been true and misleading, which was not a crime, he explained. He went on for several minutes in defense of his testimony and response to Congress.

Like Tim Roemer the night before, King finally interrupted. "With all respect, Mr. President, I know you believe this, but most members of Congress think it's bullshit. Whether it's fair or not, the reality is that these undecided Republicans think you are trying to screw the Congress, and you must accept that." Clinton had to figure out what undecided Republicans wanted him to say, because at this point he probably only had one more shot at it, King said.

Clinton grew emotional again. "Don't the people in Congress realize what I have gone through the last three months? Do they think this has been a walk in the park? I'm not just trying to save my ass. . . . Just because I come to work every day and keep my head up doesn't mean this isn't tearing me apart. I have to act that way because I am the president." Clinton, sitting in a chair opposite King, grabbed the congressman's knee several times to emphasize his point.

King said he sympathized. But the president should reach out to some moderate Republicans, such as Congressmen Michael N. Castle of Delaware, who was interested in finding a censure solution, and Jack Quinn of New York, who had always been supportive of Clinton.

The president said he was convinced that if he telephoned members, some Republicans would claim he was trying to pressure them. They would have news conferences and Clinton would be embarrassed.

That shouldn't be the case with Castle, King said, given that he and Clinton knew each other when they were both governors of their small states.

Clinton reminisced for a moment about how in the late 1980s he and Castle had worked across party lines together on education initiatives with Congress and how much he had enjoyed that. During the final markup of legislation in the House, Clinton recalled sitting in to help the drafting.

"I don't even know if that was legal," the president joked.

"Make sure Ken Starr doesn't hear about that or he'll go after you on that also," King said, laughing.

But Clinton looked at him as if he did not hear, so King repeated that Castle would be key because he regularly spoke with nine or ten moderates.

Eventually, the talk turned to the Senate and what a trial there might look like. The president gave a sardonic prediction of a trial supervised by the senator from West Virginia. "Bob Byrd has been waiting for this all his life," Clinton said, strangely amused at the prospect. "He can give long speeches about the Constitution and impeachment. I can just see him walking around the Senate. He'll just love it."

Clinton mentioned that he heard that Larry Flynt, the publisher of *Hustler* magazine who had been advertising a $1 million bounty for evidence of congressional adultery, was going to make sensational disclosures about Republicans, including some on the House Judiciary Committee.

King said he had heard eleven or twelve might be named.

That would be terrible, Clinton replied. He said he did not want anyone else to go through what he had.

I'm afraid that's where it's leading, King replied.

Then, as if not wanting the evening to finish on such a sober topic as impeachment, Clinton abruptly switched the subject to football.

"Isn't Doug Flutie great?" he asked.

On the second day of the White House defense on Wednesday, December 9, the Clinton team had a small surprise in store for the Republicans—one of their own. In recent days, the president's advisers had been hunting around the country for a prominent Republican to join them at the witness table—anyone with an *R* after his name. They considered former senators Warren Rudman and Jack Danforth. Greg Craig called Lowell P. Weicker Jr., a maverick who served on the Watergate investigating committee while in the Senate, but he did not accept the invitation. Finally the White House recruited William F. Weld, a Justice Department official in the Reagan administration who just recently stepped down as the Republican governor of Massachusetts. In keeping with the Watergate theme, Weld had worked on the House staff during the Nixon impeachment alongside Hillary Clinton. Predictably unpredictable, though, Weld had a little surprise for his friends at the White House too. When his turn at the microphone came up, he presented a plan to punish Clinton short of impeachment. In addition to censure, Weld suggested, Congress should force the president to agree to pay a fine of hundreds of thousands of dollars, sign an acknowledgment of wrongdoing, and take his chances with possible prosecution in criminal court. White House aides looked at each other when Weld rolled it out, but they were not unhappy. If he wanted to play broker, that was fine with them.

Besides, by this point, the White House had all but dispensed with the public fiction that it was agnostic on censure. It had become an article of conventional wisdom in Washington that Clinton would eagerly accept it, even if the covert negotiations involving Ruff, Hyde, and Lloyd Cutler remained a closely guarded secret. After Weld and other experts were finished, Ruff took over the presentation to the Judiciary Committee and for the first time in a public forum openly invited censure. In a discussion of the charge of grand jury perjury, Ruff said it boiled down to a he-said, she-said conflict over whether Clinton touched certain parts of Lewinsky's body. "If you believe he acted in this fashion, you ought to censure him in whatever fashion seems most appropriate," Ruff said, "but you cannot overturn the will of the people, even if you find that there is clear and convincing evidence—which I do not think you can—that the president was wrong and Monica Lewinsky was right on that point."

In making his case before the committee, Ruff provided a sharp contrast to the image of an acid-tongued Clinton defender. He was low-key, thoughtful, deferential—the anti-Carville. "I truly do not mean to speak unkindly of the independent counsel," he said at one point. Ruff walked the committee members through the case as he saw it, pointing out the holes he had found while offering concessions much like Craig's "maddening" description of the day before.

Congressman Jim Sensenbrenner, the second-ranking Judiciary Republican, pressed Ruff right from the start to say whether the president had lied under oath—yes or no. Ruff resolutely refused to be drawn in, choosing his own, more deliberate words to characterize the president's statements.

"But did he lie?" Sensenbrenner demanded.

"I have no doubt that he walked up to a line that he thought he understood," answered Ruff, who appeared uncomfortable trying to walk a line of his own. "Reasonable people—and you maybe have reached this conclusion—could determine that he crossed over that line and that what for him was truthful but misleading or nonresponsive and misleading or evasive was, in fact, false. But in his mind—and that's the heart and soul of perjury—he thought and he believed that what he was doing was being evasive but truthful."

By conceding that "reasonable people" could see Clinton's testimony as perjury, Ruff had employed the artful language the speechwriters had been trying to get the president to use. Ruff had presented the strongest case to date for the president and impressed even some of Clinton's critics. "If you guys win, it will be because of this man," Hyde told Julian Epstein during a break.

For a moment, it appeared as if Hyde might be rethinking the matter. If so, it did not last long. Toward the end of the day, even before Ruff was finished testifying, GOP committee aides started handing out copies of their draft articles of impeachment. Congressman Bobby Scott had set the trap earlier in the week by complaining that Democrats needed to see the proposed articles well in advance of voting on them. Having let themselves be goaded into handing out the articles before concluding the White House defense hearing, Republicans were offering the Democrats another powerful argument in the partisan defense—how fair could the majority have been when they passed around the impeachment articles without even hearing all of the testimony? That did not stop the Democrats from producing their own proposal amid the hearings. Rick Boucher's censure resolution was also given out to the members and the media before the meeting was over. Hyde's favorable appraisal of Ruff aside, the actual hearings had done nothing to change anyone's mind in either camp.

When Tom DeLay heard that Hyde had informally agreed to give the Democrats a vote on censure, he went into a rage. How could Hyde have done that? What was he thinking? He had just knocked out the legs from under them. This would give the Democrats an excuse to argue for a floor vote on censure—and a powerful weapon to use to attack the Republican leadership if it refused.

"Are you kidding?" DeLay demanded when his aides told him. "Get your asses down there and find out what's going on."

DeLay aides Tony Rudy and Mike Scanlon rushed over to the Rayburn Building as the hearing was still going on and began corralling Republican committee staff members in a last-ditch effort to get Hyde to change his mind. But it was too late. Within a few minutes, Hyde publicly announced his decision to allow the censure vote.

If DeLay had known what Asa Hutchinson was doing, he would have been even more concerned. On his own, Hutchinson was looking for a possible out. During the hearings, he had run into Howard Berman, the California Democrat who had been part of the "breakfast club" with Hutchinson, and suggested that one alternative might be for the judge in the Paula Jones case, U.S. District Judge Susan Webber Wright, to step in and punish Clinton using civil sanctions such as a large fine.

"Howard, if the judge would hold a hearing on contempt—there has to be accountability—that would be a form of accountability, and then we wouldn't have to have the impeachment," Hutchinson said.

Berman seized on the idea as a reasonable compromise. Clinton would still be taken to task without the disproportionate response of impeachment. "Well, what should we do? Get on the phone with the judge?"

But Hutchinson instantly retreated. He was more thinking aloud than proposing a specific solution. The plan was clearly unworkable; the legislature could hardly intervene with the judiciary to get an executive sanctioned. Besides, Hutchinson realized, it was probably too late.

With all minds on the Judiciary Committee seemingly made up by now, the summations by two opposing investigators on Thursday, December 10, were aimed instead at the general public and the thirty or so swing House Republicans who would decide the issue on the floor.

Abbe Lowell went first. Feeling that too many cooks had spoiled his earlier presentations to the committee, Lowell decided against showing his plans to all sixteen members of the Democratic caucus. Thus liberated, Lowell came up with a sharper, more coherent closing argument that attacked the majority's conclusions in large part by calling the prosecution's own witnesses as his own. For the first time, he questioned Monica Lewinsky's credibility, quoting grand jury testimony from friends and others that showed she had lied to them about some aspects of her relationship, such as a false claim that she had once had lunch with Hillary Clinton. He quoted a decade-old statement by Hyde during the Iran-contra scandal that not all lying was necessarily the same. And he mocked the notion that Clinton was lying when he said he could not recall certain things by showing the committee a wickedly effective, MTV-style video montage of the various times Starr had claimed a poor memory during his own appearance before the panel a month earlier.

Lowell labored to undercut the comparisons to Watergate when, he noted, the charges against Nixon were proved by secret tapes showing he misused the CIA, FBI, and IRS to cover up attempts to sabotage the opposition party. "Here," Lowell said sarcastically, "the charge stands on tapes of Monica Lewinsky and Linda Tripp talking about going shopping."

Lowell's presentation impressed even some Republicans, who thought he did an effective job of poking holes in the case. "I want you to know you unnerved us," Hyde told him during a break. "You gave us a lot to think about."

David Schippers, who was so effective in his initial appearances before the committee, did not go over as well this time. Like Lowell, he made use of a video, showing Clinton weaving and dodging at his Jones deposition. But where Lowell had established an engaging rhythm, Schippers spent much of his time before the committee reviewing phone logs and other small details. Yet rather than let the evidence speak for itself, Schippers could not help throwing in scornful asides aimed at the president. "Life was so much simpler before they found that dress, wasn't it?" he said at one point. At another, Schippers ridiculed how Clinton described his phone sex calls with Lewinsky. "If what happened on those phone calls is 'banter,' then Buckingham Palace is a cabin."

Schippers also outraged Democrats on the panel—and distressed at least a few Republicans—by asserting that he had found other evidence of wrongdoing by the president that he had not pursued, either because of time or concerns by Starr or the Justice Department that it would interfere with ongoing investigations. Denied permission by Hyde to introduce some of this in his presentation, Schippers said only that he had found "very promising leads," including "incidents involving probable direct and deliberate obstruction of justice, witness tampering, perjury, and abuse of power" without describing what he was talking about, prompting complaints of McCarthy-like tactics.

Still, for Republicans on the committee, the accumulation of evidence he did present on the Lewinsky matter and the way he pieced it together helped ratify their conviction that the president was guilty of the charges against him. "If you don't impeach, as a consequence of the conduct that I have just portrayed, then no House of Representatives will ever be able to impeach again. The bar will be so high that only a convicted felon or a traitor will need to be concerned. . . . If this isn't enough, what is? How far can the standard be lowered without completely compromising the credibility of the office for all time?"

That night, while the committee members began reading opening statements on Capitol Hill, Clinton's advisers gathered in the Yellow Oval Room in the second-floor living quarters of the White House for one of his weekly political strategy sessions. These meetings had started during the 1996 reelection campaign, usually on Wednesday evenings, and continued even after the campaign was over to deal with all sorts of political planning. Aside from the political staff at the White House, they included outside advisers such as pollster Mark Penn and sometimes Washington-savvy administration officials such as Energy Secretary Bill Richardson. Through much of the fall, the meetings had an unreal feel to them because the president and his advisers talked about everything related to politics with the exception of the one issue that dominated the nation's political arena—Clinton's own survival.

On this night, however, some of the president's aides felt they had no choice but to force him to confront it directly. They were a day away from a committee vote on the articles of impeachment, a vote they knew they would lose. After that, they were headed to the House floor and time would be short. The final vote would probably take place within a week or so and Clinton was scheduled to be out of the country for four days in the Middle East. All the signs were pointing to a serious erosion of the president's position among House Republican moderates. They had been relying on Congressman Pete King's advice that the moderates would come around, but it did not seem to be happening. The undecided Republicans were looking for something to grab on to, some rationale to vote no, and the White House had to give it to them. To do that, Clinton would have to make another speech, show again that he was genuinely contrite, and offer a concession that they could accept.

Paul Begala had been working on the speech intended to walk this delicate line. In a draft he wrote, Clinton would adopt Ruff's formulation and say, "My conduct was terribly wrong. Not a day goes by that I do not think about my failures of character and spirit. Not a day goes by that I do not feel profoundly sorry for what I did and what I said. And I understand today how reasonable people could read from my testimony in the Jones case and conclude I crossed the line. I tried not to, but that is no excuse." In this rendering, the president would go on to implicitly invite censure as a reasonable punishment. "I expect to be held accountable for my conduct. I am living through the painful private consequences of my actions, but I know there should be public consequences as well. I am ready to accept those consequences."

The aides decided not to bring up the matter at the meeting itself—too large a group—but pulled the president aside afterward to discuss their proposal. Asking Chuck Ruff to join them, John Podesta, Doug Sosnik, Joe Lockhart, and Begala walked over to the president's study with Clinton. They had steeled themselves for emotional resistance from the president.

"Look, there's an incredible feeding frenzy out there," Podesta told the president. "We think you should do this if you feel like you can."

To the aides' amazement, Clinton nodded and agreed, "No, that's fine. I think you're right."

Clinton was so agreeable, the meeting broke up after just a few minutes. The president wanted a night to sleep on it, so his aides did not show him the draft but decided to go over it with him in the morning. Someone joked that it would probably show up in the morning paper. Clinton headed off to help Chelsea with a college assignment on the Jesuits, while the aides headed back over to the West Wing. From their perspective, it was a major advance. Clinton had come to the same conclusion without a wrenching battle. Maybe this could burst the bubble and release the pressure the same way Joe Lieberman's speech ultimately did back in September.

They had little time to revel in their internal victory, however. A short time later, while Lockhart was back in his office talking on the phone with Podesta, his pager went off. It was NBC. "Let me call you right back," Lockhart told Podesta, then added as a joke, "I'll probably tell you they have it."

It was no joke. They did have it. Somehow the network had obtained a draft of Begala's speech and was going to post it on its MSNBC Web site and air it on *Rivera Live,* one of the evening talk shows on its cable channel CNBC.

Lockhart called Podesta back and said, "Somebody fucked us."

Podesta was infuriated. How could this happen? It had to be somebody who disagreed that Clinton should make another speech and was trying to undermine the idea by leaking it. Either way, Podesta was determined to hunt down the violator and hang him by his toenails. Aides who had seen a copy of the draft were called at home or summoned back to the White House—"Come, don't call, to Podesta's office right away," said the message on one aide's pager. One by one that night, Podesta interrogated them about what they had done with their copies of the draft. By the end of the evening, though, the identity of the culprit was not entirely clear. While there was plenty of speculation, the theories boiled down to two—either hard-line Clinton defender Sidney Blumenthal had leaked it deliberately or someone at pollster Mark Penn's office had by accident. Nobody was admitting to it.

Begala felt miserable. "What we've done," he moaned that night, "is fucked ourselves."

As Podesta searched for a leak, Clinton was back at the residence calling Congressman Jack Quinn at home, as Pete King had recommended. If any Republican was to be on Clinton's side, it would be Quinn, a liberal, pro-labor third-termer from Buffalo described by some as the president's best friend in the House GOP. Quinn was a regular in the small stable of Republicans relied on by the White House for critical votes. He had supported the president's crime bill and family leave legislation, helped rescue his Americorps program, and pushed through a minimum-wage hike. As a practical matter, Quinn was playing politics the only way he could in one of the two most Democratic districts in the nation represented by a Republican, a district where Clinton beat Bob Dole by nearly two to one in 1996. Quinn had grown personally close to the president as well; Quinn had once watched a Super Bowl with him and the two had a running joke about the congressman switching parties. After the election, Quinn had signaled that he would back Clinton in the coming impeachment battle, telling a reporter, "If I had to vote today, I would vote no."

So when Clinton found Quinn at home in Buffalo that night around eleven o'clock, the president did not bother to ask for his vote and instead solicited his assessment of where things stood. Had Quinn seen Chuck Ruff at the committee the day before? "We felt it went pretty well," Clinton said. "Did you see it?"

"I saw parts of the hearing," Quinn answered. "Mr. Ruff looked okay. He made some good points." Quinn was noncommittal but gave Clinton no reason to think he was contemplating a defection. After a few minutes, the president got off the phone, apparently thinking Quinn was still with him.

The next morning, Friday, December 11, a grim-faced John Podesta attended the impeachment strategy session at the White House. He did not always come, but he intended to make a point today. The general buzz of conversation came to an abrupt halt when he spoke.

"Somebody in this room rat-fucked the president last night," Podesta said angrily.

The leak of the speech draft had destroyed the whole purpose of the statement. It was all over television, it was in the newspapers. If the president went forward with it as written, it would look manufactured, another production of a slick White House spin machine, sending him out there for a cynical attempt to escape impeachment. Whoever had let this out of the building had no business hurting the president this way, Podesta told the assembled aides. From now on, information was going to be much more restricted. These meetings were going to be smaller. Fewer aides would be allowed to attend.

The larger question was what to do about the speech. Clinton was as furious as Podesta about the leak and uncertain whether he would go ahead with a statement. He promised to let his aides know later in the day.

In the Rayburn Building on Capitol Hill that morning, the Judiciary Committee was finishing up opening statements. An air of disbelief hung over the room. "Wake up, America!" Democratic congressman Robert Wexler of Florida shouted. "They are about to impeach our president!"

The initial statements by all thirty-seven members made clear that the vote was locked in stone—the remaining suspense lay only in the details and the positioning for the later showdown on the floor. "You know this may be as far as we get," Henry Hyde told David Schippers as they walked into the hearing room that morning, "but at least we'll get them out of committee."

At a lunchtime meeting in their conference room, the committee Democrats were still bickering among themselves. The same dissidents who thought their caucus had not pushed hard enough for witnesses during the hearings were now pushing to propose amendments to the articles during the markup. They wanted to strike certain sections or insist on more specifics in the list of charges. Bobby Scott wanted to amend the articles to describe a constitutional standard for impeachment. Mel Watt and Maxine Waters wanted to know why they were not putting up more of a fight. Julian Epstein, the committee counsel, explained that he had had to agree not to have a messy fight over amendments in order to ensure a vote on censure. Watt got in his face. "Next time you make an agreement, let the rest of us know," he snapped.

The senior Democratic committee members endorsed Epstein's no-amendments strategy. They could not improve the articles, so it was best simply to point out their flaws. "Maxine, what do you want to do?" Barney Frank challenged Waters at one point. "Just because something's out there, you don't have to shoot at it. How could we make this better?"

The meeting ended with members grumbling as they headed back out to the dais to do battle. And feisty they were. Hyde had barely opened the debate on Article I, the grand jury perjury count, before Democrats began pelting him with requests that the resolution lay out specifically what Clinton said that was perjurious.

"What are those words?" demanded Congressman Jerrold Nadler of New York. "What words specifically?"

Hyde brushed him off. "I can only refer you to Mr. Schippers's report yesterday discussing this, and I'll try to get a copy of it and reread it to you."

But Nadler would not be dismissed. The Schippers presentation, he complained, contained "many multiple allegations" and did not clarify the matter.

Hyde tried again. "The words were set out in detail in the presentation yesterday—"

"Then you ought to be able to tell me what they are," Nadler shot back.

"Well, I'm looking for a copy. My copy—I didn't commit them to memory. I'm not quite that acute and I'm waiting for somebody—"

Hyde had blown it. The Republican staff had anticipated the Democrats would try this tactic and prepared one paragraph for each member to read outlining the specific false statements they were alleging. Tom Mooney, the staff director, had warned the GOP committee members that the minority would demand specifics because that was exactly what they had done to the Democratic majority when he had worked as a junior aide on the Judiciary Committee during the Watergate hearings twenty-four years earlier. But the members did not bother to study the heavy briefing books they had been given.

With Nadler hammering away and Hyde stumbling, his aides tried to regain control. "Mr. Chairman, he's out of order," Mooney kept whispering to Hyde, urging him to cut off Nadler. Mitch Glazier, the GOP lawyer who had done much of the drafting of the articles, whispered that each of the members would address the issue in a synchronized way.

But Hyde was not listening. "Give me the lies," he kept telling his staff.

Finally, they found one of the briefing papers and shoved it in front of him. It was exactly the wrong one to hand him—it dealt entirely with the discussion about whether oral sex counted as "sexual relations" and whether the president had lied when he testified he did not kiss or touch Lewinsky's breasts or genitalia.

Embarrassed, Hyde stopped reading. "There's so much here that I really don't care to read, but it's available and you—"

A couple of Republican members, Charles Canady and Bob Goodlatte of Virginia, cut in and tried to prod Hyde into reestablishing regular order, but it was too late. The damage had been done. Once again, the Republicans had played right into the Democrats' hands. In fact, the Republicans were correct that the impeachment articles they had drafted against Clinton were no less specific than the ones against Nixon. More important, as a matter of political strategy, the Republicans had deliberately left out graphic details to emphasize the lies, not the sex. Yet when pressed by the Democrats, Hyde found himself reading aloud the very sex-based questions he had hoped to avoid. The Democrats smiled at their successful ambush.

"Where the president touched her, after he acknowledged having sex, whether it started in November or February—those are not issues on which people think you undo two democratic elections and throw an elected official out of office," Barney Frank declared triumphantly.

For the next several hours, the debate played out in the committee room and on television screens across the country. For all of the anger and recriminations that had suffused the process until this point, the discussion proved to be surprisingly civil. At one point, Maxine Waters even praised Hyde, telling him, "I think you're the fairest chairman I've ever met." But the substance of the debate centered almost entirely on whether the articles should be more specific rather than on the merits of the charges or the constitutional questions. In effect, the battle was being fought on Democratic terms.

Congressman Jim Rogan, the California Republican, understood that and expressed his frustration: "Once again, we are treated to the spectacle of a debate solely over procedure and never about disputing the facts of the case."

As the day wore on, the telephone rang back in the Democratic cloakroom to let the president's allies know that he had decided to go ahead and make a short statement from the Rose Garden. Around 3:30 P.M., Congressman Howard Berman, the California Democrat, went to find Lindsey Graham, who had been so vocal in expressing his wish for Clinton to come clean. "I want you to write down what the president has to say to be a fulsome and complete apology," Berman challenged him in a back room.

Graham found a couple sheets of Judiciary Committee stationery and began scribbling with a pencil:

1. Admit giving intentional false testimony under oath at deposition & GJ about relationship with Ms. Lewinsky & its particulars.
2. President wrongfully sought to influence prospective witnesses by suggesting false stories and improperly sought to influence their future participation in pending legal action.

Berman took a look at it but decided not to pass it along to anyone at the White House—Graham was asking the president to confess to a crime and Berman knew that would never happen. Some fellow Republicans were no happier with Graham's eleventh-hour flirtation with the White House. Bob Barr, the fervent Clinton critic from Georgia, flew into a rage when he overheard Graham telling staff director Tom Mooney about the conversation with Berman.

"Jesus Christ, Lindsey, why are you playing into their hands?" he demanded. "You're abandoning ship!"

This was where he had been all along and Barr knew that, Graham snapped back. "You do what you need to do and I'll do what I need to do." Besides, Graham added, "He's not going to do it. He will not meet the conditions of these words."

The two went back and forth for several minutes. Barr was in Graham's face, and for a moment the two appeared on the verge of fisticuffs. Mooney, worried that the confrontation might turn physical, hovered nearby in case he had to break it up.

Barr need not have worried. Clinton was not about to take Graham's advice. A few minutes later, shortly after 4 P.M., he emerged from the Oval Office and walked alone to a lectern with the presidential seal set up in the Rose Garden. In the Judiciary Committee chambers, Hyde was asked to recess the meeting to hear what Clinton had to say, but he declined, reasoning that they should not let the president dictate how they ran their proceeding. Nonetheless, all but seven of the committee members got up from their seats and wandered into the back rooms to watch on television.

Clinton spoke slowly and soberly. "What I want the American people to know, what I want the Congress to know, is that I am profoundly sorry for all I have done wrong in words and deeds. I never should have misled the country, the Congress, my friends, or my family. Quite simply, I gave in to my shame." He paused as he let that sink in. "I have been condemned by my accusers with harsh words. And while it's hard to hear yourself called deceitful and manipulative, I remember Ben Franklin's admonition that our critics are our friends, for they do show us our faults. Mere words cannot fully express the profound remorse I feel for what our country is going through and for what members of both parties in Congress are now forced to deal with. These past months have been a torturous process of coming to terms with what I did. I understand that accountability demands consequences and I'm prepared to accept them. Painful as the condemnation of the Congress would be, it would pale in comparison to the consequences of the pain I have caused my family." Again, he paused for emphasis and stressed each of the next five words. "There is no greater agony."

When he was done four minutes later, Clinton ignored a question shouted from the press corps about whether reasonable people might conclude he committed perjury—Ruff's formulation—and disappeared back into the Oval Office. On Capitol Hill, in the side room where the Democratic committee members watched, his statement was greeted by silence.

There were no cheers, no affirmations of support, not even so much as head nodding. Democratic members such as Howard Berman and Chuck Schumer and staff lawyers such as Abbe Lowell and Julian Epstein knew Clinton had not cleared the bar; if anything, they were convinced, he had only made matters worse. Some of them were mad at him for even trying if it was not going to be a more serious effort.

In the Republican conference room, Lindsey Graham had stood right at the foot of the television, watching and worrying. Every eye in the room seemed to be on him, and he was nervous at the thought that maybe Clinton would actually make a meaningful statement, forcing the Republican congressman to live up to his word and vote against the articles of impeachment. After it was over, Graham felt relieved. Clinton had not made it a difficult choice. Graham could go ahead and vote yes. Several other Republican congressmen in the room teased him.

"You got off the hook," said Lamar Smith of Texas.

"All right," added Bob Inglis of South Carolina. "This one's for you."

"He just can't get there, can he?" Graham murmured a moment later as he emerged from the conference room. "Too bad for the country. Too bad for him."

The members shuffled back to their seats. The speechifying had continued while they were in the back, but for all intents and purposes it was now over. The committee quickly adopted an amendment from Jim Rogan adding the words "one or more of the following" before the general descriptions of what Clinton had lied about, so that members could vote yes as long as they believed that any of the four charges were proven. And then, just like that, at 4:24 P.M., nine minutes after the president finished speaking in the Rose Garden, the committee voted to impeach him for "providing perjurious, false and misleading testimony to the grand jury."

"The clerk will call the roll," Hyde intoned.

"Mr. Sensenbrenner," the clerk called out.

"Aye," Sensenbrenner answered.

"Mr. Sensenbrenner votes aye," the clerk repeated. "Mr. McCollum."

"Aye."

And so on down the row it went until every Republican in the room had voted, except Hyde, who as chairman waited until the end. Then the clerk went down the list of Democrats and came up with the same singsong ritual in reverse.

"Mr. Conyers."

"No."

"Mr. Conyers votes no. Mr. Frank."

"No."

"Mr. Chairman, there are twenty-one ayes and sixteen noes." A straight party-line vote.

"And Article I is agreed to," Hyde announced.

The room was briefly quiet. There was no surprise in the outcome, and yet still a sense of shock, of disbelief, settled in the hearing room. Over the next few hours, the debate would go on, but it had lost its power. The outcome was settled. At 6:30 P.M., the committee voted 20–17 to approve Article II, with the only switch being Graham, who had said all along that he would not impeach the president for his civil testimony. At 9:15 P.M., the panel voted 21–16, again on straight party lines, for Article III, the obstruction count. Then Hyde recessed for the night, leaving the fourth and most problematic article until the next morning. The Republicans expressed no joy or excitement, only grim satisfaction; the Democrats, mostly resignation. The Democrats had done what they could, but the real battle was to be fought elsewhere, on different terrain. They had laid the groundwork. They had made the issue as partisan as they could. And in doing so, they had provided the president with his best shot at victory.

Asa Hutchinson woke up at five o'clock the next morning, Saturday, December 12, still pondering the consequences of what had been done the day before and looking ahead to the final day of deliberations with deep misgivings. The committee had one final count to consider, Article IV, accusing President Clinton of abusing the power of his office by lying to the American people, lying to aides and cabinet secretaries, who then repeated his falsehoods to the public, "frivolously and corruptly" asserting executive privilege to impede Starr's investigation, and lying to Congress in his responses to the eighty-one questions sent to him by Hyde the month before. For Hutchinson, though, it was too much. Most of the lies being cited were not under oath. This was going too far. He resolved to vote no.

As it turned out, he was not the only one. By the time the Republican committee caucus convened in the conference room in the Rayburn Building before the full panel was to meet, several of the members had reservations. George Gekas, a veteran congressman from Pennsylvania, had privately been crusading behind the scenes for weeks to drop the executive privilege count on the grounds that he did not want to weaken the presidency. Even if Clinton was wrong to assert it, every chief executive ought to have the option of asserting a privilege that is his to assert. Gekas had drawn little support at first. When he told Hyde that he planned to try to amend any impeachment articles to drop the executive privilege allegation, the chairman told him, "I won't support it, but you can try." Yet Gekas had slowly picked up allies. Several Republicans had been won over after Chuck Ruff testified earlier in the week that he and the other White House attorneys had recommended that Clinton invoke the privilege. Besides, by rejecting some of the charges against Clinton, the Republicans concluded they would show they were not just tools for Starr or the GOP leadership. When they gathered in the conference room that morning, even Hyde said he would go along with the Gekas proposal.

In addition to deleting the privilege count, the Republicans decided to remove the charges that Clinton had lied to the public and his aides. While everyone was convinced Clinton had done those things, they were persuaded by the argument that those were not actions worthy of impeachment. What politician would want to set the precedent that lying to the public by itself merited dismissal from office? They would have a tough enough time convincing moderates in their own party, let alone Democrats, that the president's other offenses amounted to high crimes. Better to exercise some restraint, they decided, or at least to look as if they were. That left only the president's answers to the eighty-one questions, but there was a strong consensus to leave those in. For one thing, Clinton was explicitly warned when the questionnaire was sent to him that the answers would be under oath and that failing to respond truthfully would be considered perjury. For another, the president's apparent arrogance in answering them dismissively was what had aroused such anger among House Republicans.

When the full committee got started at 9:40 A.M. that Saturday, Gekas explained the reversal. "We ought to give, in my judgment and the judgment of many, the benefit of the doubt in the assertion of executive privilege."

The Democrats were unsure how to respond. They obviously agreed that the items Gekas wanted to strike were not impeachable, but they realized they were still left with an article they did not support, and worse, one that might be more palatable to the swing moderate members on the floor. As Congressman Jerrold Nadler put it, the Gekas amendment was "changing the absolutely indefensible to the still absolutely indefensible, but on fewer grounds." The White House by this point had withdrawn from the committee deliberations altogether and was entirely focused on the upcoming floor fight. In fact, it had initially decided against sending anyone to the Rayburn Building to attend the final hearing this Saturday. When three aides, Adam Goldberg, Don Goldberg, and Jim Kennedy, had decided on their own to go, they were upbraided by deputy counsel Cheryl Mills. "Why are you going up there? We don't want to give this credibility."

But ignoring it would not make it go away. Over the next five hours, there was little debate about the Gekas amendment or even the remaining allegation involving the president's answers to the eighty-one questions. Instead, Republicans labored to explain themselves while Democrats warned darkly about the ramifications of the panel's actions. "We are not being vengeful," insisted Congressman Howard Coble from North Carolina, an older Republican. "There's no lynch-mob mentality over here, and for the benefit of the gentleman who said that last night, I've had knots in my gut all week because of this. I approached this, my friends, with a very heavy heart and I'll have knots in my gut next week when we cast votes. I don't take it lightly. I don't take it gleefully at all. It's a hard chore for all of us, on that side as well as on this side."

Barney Frank seized on that to make a larger point. The Republicans had been stressing that impeachment was simply the equivalent of an indictment, he complained, when in fact it was ultimately about removing the president from office. By downplaying the significance of the action, Frank said, the majority was trying to make it easier for members struggling with the implications of their vote. "Why has he got knots in his stomach?" Frank asked rhetorically. "Just because he's sending this over to the Senate to decide? He has knots in his stomach, as he courageously articulated, because he understands what we are doing. He understands that you are trying to undo the election."

John Conyers put it more starkly: "This does sometimes to some people begin to take on the appearance of a coup. It's frightening, it's staggering. This is not in a developing country. We're talking about a polite, paper-exchanging, voting process in which we rip out the forty-second president of the United States."

The Gekas amendment paring down the article passed easily, 29–5. Every Republican except Chris Cannon of Utah supported it, along with most Democrats. But Waters and fellow Democrats Robert Wexler, Sheila Jackson Lee of Texas, and Thomas Barrett of Wisconsin voted against it on principle, while Frank, Zoe Lofgren, and Marty Meehan voted "present" rather than make a choice. The final vote approving the amended article itself was more predictable—again 21–16, on straight party lines. When the roll was read at 2:45 P.M., Clinton was in international airspace, having left that morning for a four-day trip to the Middle East to seal the progress made in the Wye negotiations in October.

With all four articles now passed, the debate over the Democratic censure resolution seemed hopelessly anticlimactic. But the Democrats wanted to show the nation that they had a more reasonable alternative and hopefully build a wave of public support that would force Bob Livingston and the rest of the GOP leadership to allow censure to be debated on the floor. More than three hours of debate, though, did nothing to change any votes on the committee. At 6:10 P.M., Rick Boucher's resolution was voted down 22–14. Bobby Scott was the lone Democrat joining a unanimous Republican caucus, though for the opposite reason—he believed that censure was not justified. Similarly, Waters voted present. Ten minutes later, the committee recessed. It was done. The matter was now out of its hands.

CHAPTER NINE

"The pressure got to me"

For The Campaign to succeed, Tom DeLay now had to kill censure for good. To kill censure, he had to force Bob Livingston's hand. Even as the Judiciary Committee finished its work on its articles of impeachment, DeLay maneuvered behind the scenes to do just that.

It was Saturday, December 12, the same afternoon the committee was voting on its fourth article and Rick Boucher's censure resolution. DeLay was still steaming at how he had been sandbagged during the committee deliberations when Henry Hyde allowed the Democrats to introduce their motion to reprimand Clinton rather than impeach him. Hyde's decision had handed the Democrats the politically potent argument that since the committee was allowed to vote on censure, so should the full House. Even before the panel had finished debating Boucher's motion, Dick Gephardt had already written a letter urging the Republican leadership "to allow everyone an opportunity to vote their conscience," meaning censure. The last thing DeLay wanted to do was give weak-kneed Republicans an alternative to voting for impeachment or to allow Democrats a political escape route to avoid the consequences of voting against impeachment. The mistake DeLay and his aides had made during the committee deliberations, they decided, was allowing the censure option to remain viable until momentum for it grew. The trick now was to take it off the table right away.

As the incoming Speaker of the House, it would fall to Livingston, not DeLay, to decide whether to allow a censure vote on the floor. But the majority whip had been lobbying quietly for weeks, telling Livingston at private meetings that the vast bulk of the Republican caucus opposed censure and warning that permitting such a resolution to be introduced could even endanger his formal election to the Speakership. Livingston, who shortly after the election had told Gephardt that "all options are on the table," had now come around to DeLay's way of thinking. "I just don't think it's going to be possible," he had told Gephardt just three days before the committee finished its work that Saturday.

But the pressure on Livingston from all sides was building. In recent days, his chief of staff, Allen Martin, had received a telephone call that the two men took as a barely veiled threat. Butler Derrick, a former Democratic congressman from South Carolina who was working with the White House to lobby former House colleagues, had rung up Martin and offered congratulations for Livingston's impending ascension to Speaker. As Livingston later related it to friends, Derrick had told Martin something to the effect of "You are going to consider censure, right?" and then quickly asked, "Bob can stand scrutiny, can't he?" Livingston knew instantly that, in fact, he could not withstand scrutiny. He had cheated on his wife more than once, and if that came out, it could destroy him politically and personally. Derrick would later deny saying that, let alone trying to intimidate the incoming Speaker. But that was the way Livingston took it, and the perceived danger was weighing heavily on him. What if he did oppose censure? Did that mean his past infidelities would be dredged up? Was he the target of a White House attack machine? Would he be publicly humiliated the way Hyde, Dan Burton, and Helen Chenoweth had been?

DeLay knew Livingston felt pressure and wanted to lock in the new Speaker's opposition to a censure vote as soon as possible, lest he cave in to the Democrats the way Hyde had. So as the Judiciary Committee was finishing its work that Saturday, congressional aide Kathryn Lehman, a refugee from Newt Gingrich's departing staff who had just agreed to join DeLay's office, sat hunched over a computer in the committee's back room drafting a series of three letters that would do the job. The first was to be sent to Livingston and Gingrich and signed by Hyde stating his opposition to allowing a censure vote on the floor. "It is my view that a resolution or amendment proposing censure of the President in lieu of impeachment violates the rules of the House, threatens separation of powers, and fails to meet constitutional muster," Lehman wrote in the two-page letter intended for Hyde's signature. The second letter was to be sent to Hyde from Livingston, a much shorter return message essentially endorsing the first letter. "As a constitutional matter, I share your view that censure of the President would violate the careful balance of separation of powers and the scheme laid out by the Framers to address the issue of executive misconduct," said the reply intended for the future Speaker. The third was the coup de grâce, a four-sentence declaration by Gingrich to Hyde that he would summon the full House back to Washington to take up impeachment next Thursday at 10 A.M. and would not allow censure to be considered on the floor. "As I carry out my duties, I plan to follow your advice with respect to this matter," said the letter written in Gingrich's name. Although he had ceded authority to his successor, Gingrich had to sign off on the matter because he was still officially Speaker until Livingston's installation.

As soon as the committee was done for the day, Lehman set about getting the three signatures DeLay needed. Even though he had just allowed a censure vote in his own committee, Hyde signed the letter drafted for him after being assured that it was the decision of the leadership. Lehman rushed over to Livingston's office, where she met a Judiciary aide formally delivering the Hyde letter—only to find the door locked and the new Speaker nowhere to be found. Panicking, Lehman got a Capitol Police officer to let them inside the office, where they waited anxiously until Allen Martin, Livingston's top aide, arrived. Lehman pressed him to sign Livingston's name on the response letter she had drafted. Even though Livingston had agreed over the phone, Martin hesitated.

"What's wrong?" Lehman asked.

"It's such an important thing," Martin said.

"That's why we need you to sign it. You've known Mr. Livingston a long time. Does he change his mind?"

"No, he doesn't."

"Well, it's really important that we get it out now."

Martin took the pen and signed Livingston's name to the letter. Martin asked if he should put his own initials next to Livingston's signature to indicate that he had been the one who really signed it. Lehman said no.

Like Livingston, Gingrich had agreed by phone to the letter written in his name but was not around when it came time to put it out. Lehman signed it herself, tracing his signature from a sample of stationery she had from her tenure in the Speaker's office. The three letters were then released to the news media barely an hour after the Judiciary Committee adjourned at 6:20 P.M. To the public, it looked as if Hyde, Livingston, and Gingrich had consulted and determined the proper course of action. In fact, it was all DeLay. His name appeared on none of the letters, but he had accomplished his immediate goal: he had strangled censure and left no fingerprints.

Still in Israel, where he was dealing with issues of war and peace, Clinton was consumed with what was happening to him back home. He had long since resigned himself to the likelihood that the Judiciary Committee would vote out articles, and so there was little shock about that, more a determination to win the next battle on the House floor. Censure had been the answer, he knew, and with Republicans now vowing to block consideration of it, the only route left was to focus public pressure on congressional leaders.

At a news conference with Israeli prime minister Benjamin Netanyahu in Jerusalem the next day, Sunday, December 13, the emotionally drained and frequently angry Clinton was the picture of calm, answering the questions he knew would come his way with a stoic equilibrium. He tried to shame the

Republican leaders into allowing a censure vote. "You ought to ask them whether they're opposed to it because they think that it might pass, since, apparently, somewhere around three-quarters of the American people think that's the right thing to do."

Asked if he would follow Nixon's example and resign to avoid an impeachment vote by the full House, Clinton did his best to leave no room for doubts about his determination: "I have no intention of resigning. It's never crossed my mind."

Clinton answered the question even before it was put to him by political leaders back home. On the Sunday television talk shows, taped hours later because of the time difference, Clinton was urged to step down by three House leaders, DeLay, Hyde, and Majority Leader Dick Armey. "He could really be heroic if he did that. He would be the savior of his party," Hyde said. "I would just hope that the president would put the American people ahead of his own ambitions and resign," added DeLay. The entreaties came on different shows in response to obvious questions by the hosts and, unlike the censure letters the night before, were not orchestrated in advance by the leaders or their staffs. Indeed, DeLay had been warned not to go on the show by his friend Congressman Bill Paxon, who told him he would risk becoming the public face of impeachment again. But at the White House, it seemed to be clear evidence of a strategy by the Republicans—first to downplay the importance of impeachment by the House, characterizing it as merely an indictment, then after the vote to point to the impeachment as a reason for the president to resign. Clinton's aides resolved to try to defuse any momentum for resignation. That was the larger threat to his survival.

But the president was not yet ready to give up in the House. While the rest of the Middle East slept, Clinton worked the phones. It was still early enough back home to get in a few calls and try to figure out where he was. At 2:25 A.M. Israeli time (7:25 P.M. the night before in Washington), the president rang up Pete King, the New York congressman who had been helping him try to corral other GOP defectors.

"I know you must be going through hell," King told him. "I'm thinking of you."

Clinton thanked him and asked about the undecided Republicans. King told him that Al D'Amato had been speaking with Congressman Sherwood L. Boehlert, another middle-of-the-road New York Republican, who expressed concern that if impeachment was defeated, the president would be getting away with something that other people would be indicted for.

At that, Clinton bristled. "I never committed perjury," he insisted, urging King to tell Boehlert that all the expert witnesses concurred, including former Republican prosecutors.

King agreed to call and then mentioned another moderate New Yorker he had information about. Congressman John M. McHugh was against impeachment if given the option to vote for censure, but without that alternative, he would probably have to vote to impeach, King told the president.

"Well, how many votes do we have?" Clinton asked.

Well, King said, at least six or seven. In addition to himself, there was John Porter, Chris Shays, Mark Souder.

Clinton interrupted. "How about Forbes? Is he with us?"

Mike Forbes very much wanted to vote against impeachment, King replied, but he was under tremendous pressure from his mentor, Bob Livingston.

"How about Jack Quinn?"

King thought Quinn was getting "a bit nervous" but would still stand with Clinton. The president agreed with that assessment, telling King about his phone conversation with Quinn the other night.

As they talked, the president seemed fervent, focused on what was happening, but not allowing himself to admit how serious the predicament had become. They went through some more names—Mike Castle, who was leading the explorations into censure for the House Republican moderates, Bob Ney, Frank Riggs, Anne Northup. Clinton knew exactly how many votes he had gotten in each of their districts and came up with reasons why this one or that one would stick with him, how if he could only explain to them that he had not done what he was accused of, everything would turn out okay. Clinton said he thought he could hold his Democratic losses to three or four and would need fifteen Republicans, though he wanted to get eighteen. Two-thirds of the Democrats who had voted with the Republicans to launch the inquiry back in October were now circulating a letter opposing impeachment, Clinton said. King filled him in on some new poll numbers showing that 58 percent of Americans supported censure. That was wrong, Clinton interjected. The number was 70 percent.

They hung up at 7:46 P.M. Washington time. King was even more worried. Clinton did not seem to understand just how perilous his situation really was.

Up in Buffalo the next morning, Monday, December 14, Jack Quinn, the president's Republican friend, convened a previously scheduled 10 A.M. meeting of his local labor roundtable, a group of union leaders from his district who advised him from time to time. Just the existence of such a council indicated that Quinn was no ordinary Republican. But by now, he knew what he was going to do on the big vote and knew his union supporters would not like it—he had to vote for impeachment. Quinn had gotten little sleep in recent days, and his wife found him pacing in the backyard, wrestling with the decision. He had talked it through ad infinitum with his family. In the end, he concluded he had jumped too fast the month before when he said he would vote against impeachment. He had not really focused on the evidence. Without the option of censure on the table, what other choice did he have to hold the president accountable?

As the thirty or so labor leaders filed into his district office and snacked on doughnuts, Quinn found himself in a box. He had promised White House lobbyist Susan Brophy over the weekend that he would not announce any decision without informing her first, but he had not been able to find Brophy that morning. The union leaders would surely ask, but he could not tell them and he could not cancel the meeting. So after much talk about the minimum wage and the Davis-Bacon Act, a man from the AFL-CIO finally got up and asked the question of the hour: "What are you doing on impeachment?" Quinn danced as nimbly as he could about how hard a decision it was, without giving a definitive answer.

His father was not fooled. "You're voting for impeachment, aren't you?" he asked in the car afterward.

"Yes."

"Anybody in that room knew that."

Across the country, several dozen swing Republicans were grappling with the same decision. Because Congress was still in recess, the 435 members of the House were scattered in districts far and wide, unable to compare notes in the cloakroom or talk things through on the floor. All of them knew it could easily be the most important vote of their political careers—and that those careers could possibly hang in the balance. All of them knew that history would judge them as much as their constituents. The key was a small bloc of thirty-four mostly moderate Republicans who had not committed one way or the other, particularly in the centrist New York delegation. They were approaching their deliberations in different ways. Some secluded themselves in their homes or offices, studying evidence books or searching their souls. Others reveled in the media attention available to any who accepted it—endless rounds on Geraldo, Chris Matthews, CNN, Fox, MSNBC, even the big gorillas in Washington politics, the Sunday network talk shows. They read *The Federalist* papers, they consulted advisers and relatives, they stopped to talk with voters in the street.

They received no shortage of input. The telephones at the Capitol and in their district offices rarely stopped ringing. Voice-mail boxes were filled to capacity and fax machines churned out one missive after another. The congressional E-mail system was so overloaded that the server periodically went on the blink. Congresswoman Constance A. Morella of Maryland, perhaps the most liberal Republican in the House, received twelve thousand E-mail messages over the weekend. Heather Wilson, the newest member of the House thanks to a special election in New Mexico less than six months earlier, was fielding a thousand phone calls a day at her offices. Much of this was orchestrated by the predictable groups, the labor unions and liberal advocacy groups on the left and the conservative Christian organizations on the right. But many of the calls were from genuinely outraged voters—outraged at Clinton for his abuses in office, outraged at Starr for poking around in someone's sex life, outraged at the Republican Congress for wasting its time on something so trivial, or outraged at opposition Democrats who were willing to sell their souls for the president's survival.

One quarter not heard from much was the White House. While Clinton's aides and friendly former congressmen were reaching out to the undecided Republicans, they were not employing the full arsenal at the president's command. Clinton himself was afraid to call Republicans uninvited for fear of looking as if he was improperly applying pressure, and Vice President Gore was largely limiting his calls to Democrats. Some aides had urged senior White House officials to put together an off-the-books private organization to drum up grassroots pressure on Congress, but John Podesta opted to leave that to allies such as the labor unions and the liberal civil rights organization People for the American Way. Cabinet secretaries with long experience on Capitol Hill, including Energy Secretary Bill Richardson and Agriculture Secretary Dan Glickman, were pushing for a more aggressive effort to organize moderate Republicans, but the president resisted because Pete King had advised against such overt lobbying. At one point, Podesta called Richardson to tell him to stop calling House Republicans. "I'm asking you to chill," the chief of staff instructed.

Like Clinton, DeLay recognized that he could not be seen exerting direct pressure. But he was not about to let up when The Campaign was so close to fruition. Besides his public statements advocating impeachment, DeLay had privately been coaching Hyde since the election, advising him on media relations and assisting with logistics. DeLay had sent copies of Starr's November 19 statement before the Judiciary Committee to each member of the Republican conference and was organizing committee members to do what he could not do himself—whip their fellow congressmen as the vote on the floor approached. The committee staff was provided with whip cards and taught how to divide up the caucus to focus on key congressmen who would move whole blocs of members. DeLay's aides were also enlisting prominent Republican fund-raisers and party officials to help persuade those on the fence. They had obtained a list of every campaign treasurer for every Republican congressman in case they needed it, although they were holding off using it since events were moving in DeLay's direction already. Improvisation was the name of the game. When word reached him that lame-duck congressman Jon Fox, who had lost reelection the previous month and was traveling with the president on his Middle East trip, was leaning against impeachment, DeLay knew better than to call himself. Instead, he enlisted Rabbi Daniel Lapin, founder of a conservative organization outside Seattle called Toward Tradition, whose mission was to ally Jewish and Christian Americans in the cultural wars. DeLay asked Lapin to lobby Fox, as well as several other wavering Republicans. Lapin tracked down Fox and told him the country would be better off morally by getting rid of a leader who used the Oval Office for sex while talking on the phone with congressmen about foreign policy.

For some of the undecided House Republicans, even those who had earlier declared themselves against impeachment, the last few weeks had forced them to focus more intently on the evidence as it became increasingly clear they would have to cast a vote. They could no longer simply brush it off on the assumption that the election meant the issue would never reach them. They had to read some of the material. They had to figure out how they would explain a no vote. They watched as colleagues they trusted and respected came to the same conclusion: Clinton was guilty and should go. A certain peer-pressure momentum began to build.

For some, the evidence played little or no apparent role. They would announce their decision to vote to impeach but cite no specifics. Benjamin A. Gilman, the chairman of the House International Relations Committee, decided to vote for two of the four articles but could not explain why those two charges were stronger except to say that he did not "see sufficient evidence" in the others. Even Congressman Tom Campbell of California, a courtly, thoughtful Stanford Law School professor who had bucked Newt Gingrich in the past, could not identify which of the president's statements to the grand jury constituted perjury and instead simply referred reporters to Starr's report. "I couldn't say off the top of my head" whether there were three specific statements that amounted to perjury or not, he said in answer to a question.

As they searched for a decision, the undecideds were well aware of the poll numbers. The public rather firmly did not want Clinton impeached, as much as they did not like or admire him personally anymore. A survey taken for the *Washington Post* and ABC News on Tuesday, December 15, was typical of the findings—60 percent opposed impeachment, compared with 39 percent who favored it. Voters favored censure over impeachment 57 percent to 36 percent. Still, although his job approval ratings continued to defy gravity, the weeks of attention to Clinton's misadventures had taken a toll, driving up his negative personal ratings to the second-highest level ever in this

When President Clinton decided to admit his affair with Monica Lewinsky to the grand jury and a national television audience on August 17, 1998, he let his lawyer be the first to inform Hillary Rodham Clinton. *(CNN)*

As the first family left for Martha's Vineyard the day after Clinton's testimony, the first lady refused to hold the president's hand, prompting daughter Chelsea to play the bridge between her parents. *(Robert A. Reeder,* The Washington Post*)*

Key Democrats were more distraught than they publicly let on. White House Chief of Staff Erskine B. Bowles *(left)*, once a close friend and golfing partner of the president, was devastated to learn that Clinton had lied to him. "I think I'm going to throw up," Bowles said as he bolted from a strategy meeting, never to return. *(Brian K. Diggs, Associated Press)*

As Independent Counsel Kenneth W. Starr's staff delivered his impeachment report to Congress on September 9, 1998 *(Lucian Perkins,* The Washington Post*)*, House Minority Leader Richard A. Gephardt *(right)* feared that he might have to go to the White House to seek Clinton's resignation. *(Susan Biddle,* The Washington Post*)*

House Speaker Newt Gingrich, who was carrying on his own secret extramarital affair, thought Clinton's troubles would be a political boon but was forced out of power after Republicans lost five seats in the election on November 3, 1998. *(John Bazemore, Associated Press)*

House Majority Whip Tom DeLay *(left)* stepped into the leadership vacuum and, behind the scenes, persuaded incoming speaker Bob Livingston *(right)* to block a Democratic censure alternative. *(Karen Cooper, Liaison Agency)*

Ken Starr collected many more sensational allegations about the president
that he did not include in his report or mention during his testimony to the House Judiciary
Committee on November 19, 1998. *(Lucian Perkins,* The Washington Post*)*

Special White House counsel Gregory B.
Craig was initially reluctant
to join the president's defense team.
(Lucian Perkins, The Washington Post*)*

White House counsel Charles F. C. Ruff
conducted secret talks with Henry Hyde to
try to avoid impeachment.
(Lucian Perkins, The Washington Post*)*

Bob Livingston, who felt he had been threatened by a Clinton ally and then disclosed his own past adultery, stunned the nation by resigning just before the president's impeachment on December 19, 1998.
(Associated Press)

Clinton appeared on the South Lawn with fellow Democrats a few hours later to head off new pressure from within his own party for him to step down as well.
(Robert A. Reeder, The Washington Post*)*

Henry Hyde delivered the articles of impeachment to the secretary of the Senate and assembled a thirteen-member team of "managers" to prosecute Clinton in a Senate trial, but privately doubted the wisdom of calling witnesses. *(James A. Parcell, The Washington Post)*

Chief Justice William H. Rehnquist, taking the oath from Senator Strom Thurmond *(above left),* was warned by Senate officials not to play too active a role. *(Senate Television)*

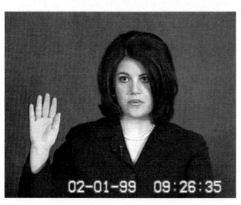

02-01-99   09:26:35

02-02-99   10:19:35

02-03-99   09:45:59

Managers Lindsey Graham, Asa Hutchinson, James E. Rogan, and Edward G. Bryant *(top, left to right)* deposed the only trial witnesses, Monica Lewinsky, Vernon E. Jordan Jr., and Sidney Blumenthal *(above left, above, left)*. Graham and Rogan secretly lobbied Henry Hyde to replace Bryant as Lewinsky's interrogator. *(Karen Cooper, Liaison Agency; Senate Television; Senate Television; Senate Television)*

Senate Majority Leader Trent Lott *(right)* once chased after an angry Senate Minority Leader Thomas A. Daschle *(left)* when Daschle stormed out of Lott's office, but the two worked closely to "copilot" the impeachment trial to a safe landing for the politically skittish Senate. *(Ray Lustig,* The Washington Post*)*

President Clinton emerged from the Oval Office to address the nation after the Senate acquit-- ted him on February 12, 1999, calling for "a time for reconciliation and renewal." Privately, he was vowing revenge on his Republican enemies. And at the same time he was drafting his public statement, Hillary Clinton was meeting with an adviser to plot the beginning of her own political rebirth in the form of a campaign for the Senate. *(Juana Arias,* The Washington Post*)*

poll; 56 percent had an "unfavorable impression of Clinton as a person," just one point below the all-time worst four months earlier, after he testified before the grand jury and admitted that he had misled the nation about his relationship with Lewinsky.

What those overall numbers did not reflect, however, was the arithmetic in individual members' districts. Gerrymandering over the years meant that Republican districts were generally more conservative than the nation as a whole, meaning that, for many, considerably more than 39 percent back home supported impeachment. Moreover, as they calculated the consequences of an impeachment vote, the most serious threat to many moderate Republicans appeared to be not the possibility of losing in a general election, but the prospect of facing a conservative challenger in a party primary. Even if just 39 percent of the voters as a whole supported impeachment, they would almost certainly represent a large majority among Republican primary voters, and angry conservatives would be far more motivated to turn out.

Reassured by pollster Mark Penn, Clinton was trying to play on the broad public support for censure. On that Monday, December 14, while Jack Quinn was making up his mind, both the president and vice president appealed for compromise. "I don't believe it's in the interest of the United States or the American people to go through this impeachment process with a trial in the Senate," Clinton said while visiting Gaza in the Middle East. Gore chimed in back in Washington, "What the leadership of the Congress has done is to prevent any kind of compromise along the lines that the American people want to see. And instead, they threaten to put the country through this long ordeal." But the tide was breaking rapidly against the absent president. The same day, three Republican congressmen on the White House target list disclosed that they would vote to impeach Clinton. When combined with other recent announcements, that meant he had already lost twelve of those key thirty-four members. If the White House lost five Democrats, as officials expected, then it had to pick up sixteen Republicans. At the moment, they were nowhere to be found.

At 7 P.M., Jack Quinn finally got in touch with Susan Brophy, the White House lobbyist, to tell her he planned to vote against the president when the articles of impeachment came to the floor later in the week. He explained that the more he learned about the seriousness of the charges, the more he realized that his conscience told him he had to vote yes.

Stunned, Brophy pleaded with him to change his mind. "Jack, if you go, you're going to take everybody with you."

But Quinn would not be persuaded. Brophy desperately turned to the only option left. "Can't you wait?" she asked. "You can do it and cripple us if you do it" right away. Put off the announcement until Wednesday or Thursday. That might minimize the damage and allow other moderates to come to different decisions in the meantime, she hoped.

Quinn said no, he could not do that. He knew he would take political hits in his liberal-leaning district and figured he had to get the news out as early as he could to give constituents a chance to vent over the next few days. Besides, he knew what would happen if he gave the White House another two or three days—the president would call, the vice president would call, it would be emotionally excruciating. Why make his life any more miserable?

After they got off the phone, Brophy sank into the cushions of a couch in Deputy Chief of Staff Steve Ricchetti's office and cried. Back in Buffalo, Quinn made two more calls—one to Peggy Taylor, the national AFL-CIO lobbyist, to explain his decision to her, and the other to Pete King, his fellow New York Republican congressman. He told King that he had not knuckled under to the party leadership; in fact, he had not even heard from DeLay or Dick Armey. He was not being threatened with a primary opponent back home. But King got the sense that Quinn felt overwhelmed by the fervent opposition to Clinton among his friends and relatives—decent people offended by what the president had done. Quinn had not expected that and had never been exposed to that sort of intensity.

"The pressure got to me," Quinn told King.

At the White House, no one was buying that. It must have been DeLay who had gotten to Quinn—that was the only explanation. The notion that the evidence suddenly changed his mind just did not wash; no new evidence had emerged since Quinn had first said he would vote against impeachment in November. For the president's aides, there was no other possible reason for him to flip-flop but rank politics. And the message was clear to every other Republican who might be thinking of standing with Clinton: don't defy Tom DeLay. They alternated between rage at Quinn and deep depression.

Clinton was still in Israel, but someone had to tell him the bad news. By now, it was the middle of the night in the Middle East, so the task waited until morning. Doug Sosnik got the report by telephone and entered the president's Jerusalem hotel suite before the first event of Tuesday, December 15. Quinn's gone south on us, he told the president. Clinton knew instantly what that meant: It was over. He was going to be impeached. It hit Clinton "like a punch in the stomach," Sosnik later told a colleague.

Clinton had braced himself for this moment. In a way, he had been ready for this outcome longer than any of his aides. He had had a fatalistic feeling about it at times, and so, on some level, this was not exactly a surprise. And yet it was still a powerful realization to be confronted with the inevitability of it, to know that everything he had worked for over a quarter century would come down to this historic judgment, that he would be only the second president ever impeached. Clinton was not given much chance to absorb the development. At that point, National Security Adviser Sandy Berger, press secretary Joe Lockhart, and other aides walked into his suite to brief him about where things stood with the Israeli prime minister and the Palestinian leader. They also needed to talk with him about another national crisis that few outside that room knew was about to erupt—an impending plan to bomb Iraq in retaliation for its intransigence in not cooperating with United Nations weapons inspections. To his aides, Clinton seemed momentarily lost in disbelief, his face registering an expression that appeared to say, "How can all this be happening?"

The scene turned even more surreal on *Air Force One* during the twelve-hour flight home to Washington later in the day. About two hours into the flight, somewhere over Europe, Clinton conducted a decisive meeting of his foreign policy team. Berger and Secretary of State Madeleine Albright were with him on the plane, while Gore, Podesta, and Defense Secretary Bill Cohen were patched through by a secure telephone link. The question was whether to bomb Iraq for violating its agreements on arms inspections. The president had ordered such a strike a month earlier, only to recall the warplanes at the last minute to give diplomacy another chance—an abort decision opposed at the time by both Albright and Cohen. Now the United Nations was reporting that Saddam Hussein had failed to live up to his latest promises. The president went around the group soliciting opinions: they were unanimous in recommending the attack. The November decision to back down meant they had no choice now but to go through with it; otherwise American credibility would be destroyed. And they would have to begin right away before the Muslim holy month of Ramadan, when it might alienate Arab allies to launch a strike. The subject turned to the more delicate issue: How could they explain this to the public? How could they keep this from looking like a *Wag the Dog* scenario intended to divert attention from the president's political problems? After some discussion, Clinton decided in essence that they could not. All they could do was go forward and hope to make their case for why the decision was justified. After the meeting broke up, the president gave Berger the order to set the attack in motion.

As he cruised through international airspace, Clinton's domestic position was crumbling even further. Nine more key, uncommitted House Republicans were stepping up to microphones to announce that they too would vote for impeachment. Aides back at the White House were calling regularly to update the delegation on the jet about the latest defection. Every hour or so, Lockhart stuck his head into the plane's conference room, where the president was sitting. "We just lost Nancy Johnson," he would say, or, "We just lost Mike Forbes." This wore thin rather quickly.

Finally, in a fit of gallows humor, Lockhart returned to the conference room.

"We just lost Gephardt," he said.

No one thought it was funny.

"You've got to be kidding me!"

Bob Livingston, the ramrod-straight former navy sailor, believed in supporting his commander in chief, but he could hardly believe his ears when the secretary of defense, Bill Cohen, a former Republican senator no less, called up to say that the United States might be going to war with Iraq. It seemed unthinkable that the president would order troops into combat the day before the House of Representatives was scheduled to open a floor debate on whether to impeach him. It could not be a coincidence. Clinton had blinked only a month ago, so why was he suddenly all hot to hit Saddam Hussein now? Surely, Clinton would not order a military strike to help fend off the pending impeachment vote, Livingston thought, yet there seemed to be no other logical explanation.

Around 10 A.M. on Tuesday, December 15, Clinton called Livingston himself to talk about the still-secret plans to attack Iraq. After discussing the military and international implications, the conversation came to the obvious domestic considerations. The new Speaker knew that going forward with the impeachment debate on the same day as a military strike—legitimate or otherwise—would be problematic at best, but he did not commit. A few hours later, he called Clinton back. Out of respect for the military and in deference to national security, Livingston said he would postpone the impeachment vote—but not for long.

"Mr. President, I don't think we're going to be able to put this off for more than a day or so. We'll be going forward."

"Yeah, I thought so." Clinton sounded resigned.

Sensing Livingston's unease, the president had Cohen as well as his CIA director, George J. Tenet, and his chairman of the Joint Chiefs of Staff, Hugh Shelton, call up the Speaker-designate to explain the need for the operation. The top officials insisted to Livingston that the strike was justified and not motivated by political concerns.

"This is necessary," Cohen said.

"Look, I've got to be skeptical," Livingston replied.

That night around midnight, Livingston was at home in bed when a telephone call of a wholly different sort roused him. It was his district director back in Louisiana. There was a problem: the media was gathering around a woman the congressman used to know, and rumor had it that she might be ready to sign a contract with *Hustler* publisher Larry Flynt to disclose details about their extramarital affair. Livingston knew that it was all about to come out. But as he pulled the covers back over himself, Livingston could not help but think about the call from Butler Derrick, the former Democratic congressman, and what sure sounded like intimidation. *Bob can stand scrutiny, can't he?* It did not seem like a coincidence to Livingston that he should hear of this new threat to his career and his family from Flynt just twelve hours after telling Clinton that he would push forward with impeachment despite the looming war with Iraq.

Most of Capitol Hill remained unaware of the military machinations that Tuesday, and some Republicans were still futilely focusing their peacemaking efforts on the censure front. Bob Dole, the former senator who had failed to dislodge Clinton in the 1996 election, signed a column in that morning's *New York Times* proposing his rival be reprimanded rather than removed. Congressman Amo Houghton of New York was preparing for a meeting with the president the next day to present his idea for a $500,000 fine in lieu of impeachment. Congressman Mike Castle, a leader of Republican moderates in the House and a friend of Clinton's from the days when both were governors, sent Livingston and Gingrich a letter urging a censure resolution combined with a $2 million fine, half the cost of Starr's investigation into the Lewinsky matter. But it was too late. DeLay had crushed the possibility of a censure vote on the floor. Even Castle believed his cause was hopeless, and rather than try to sell his proposal to fellow moderates after sending the letter, he immediately turned his attention to deciding how he would vote on the articles of impeachment.

With the momentum against Clinton, his few remaining GOP supporters began having second thoughts too. Congressman Chris Shays, a moderate Connecticut Republican who had worked closely with the White House on issues such as campaign finance reform, was publicly rethinking his announced opposition to impeachment. In recent days, he had watched a number of his friends in the caucus, thoughtful Republicans, people he respected, peel off and come out for the articles. While he was under no pressure in Washington, he was feeling quite a bit of political heat back home in his district, where local town Republican committees were fervently urging him to change his mind. Some local GOP activists even threatened him with a primary challenge should he side with Clinton. And Shays was increasingly offended by the arrogance of Clinton's stiff-arm approach to the Judiciary Committee inquiry, particularly his answers to the eighty-one questions.

Seeking reinforcement for his view that the case developed by Starr was not strong enough to throw a president out of office, Shays turned to a onetime mentor, Lowell Weicker, the former Republican senator who later went on to

be elected governor of Connecticut as an independent. Surely Weicker, a liberal rebel not unlike himself, would reassure Shays. But just as Greg Craig had
been rebuffed by Weicker during the committee hearings, so too would
Shays be surprised at the answer he got. "If you're the chief law enforcement
officer and you don't enforce the law, that's it," Weicker told him.

Shays, no stranger to the theatricality of politics, decided to hold a town
hall meeting in the coastal town of Norwalk to let his constituents tell him
directly what they thought. On the night of Tuesday, December 15, more
than two thousand people packed the town hall, and police turned away at
least another five hundred. Actor Paul Newman was among those who got
into the building but still had to watch on television because the auditorium
was filled to capacity. So many cars approached the town hall that Interstate
95 was jammed. For more than four hours, Shays got what he wanted—a
vigorous discourse and the national spotlight. Like a talk-show host, Shays
took comments from hundreds of citizens, alternating between pro and con.
He heard from Republicans and Democrats, ministers and high school students, homemakers and college professors. His adrenaline was racing so
much that he could hardly go to sleep when it finally came to an end after 2
A.M. Instead, he piled his family into his car and drove halfway back to Washington in the dark of night.

"Sweetie," he told his wife in the car, "I have to tell you: I heard good
arguments on both sides. They kind of canceled each other out."

If the meeting did not settle the matter for Shays, it did provide something of a national forum on the issue. With live television coverage, the dialogue proved to be a microcosm of the debate playing out across the country.
More people who turned out for the event opposed impeachment than
favored it—1,100 versus 800, according to the sign-in sheets—but the passion on both sides was overwhelming and the arguments often heartfelt.

Another House Republican struggling at the time was Congressman
Mark Edward Souder from Indiana. While Souder was a committed conservative and self-described "right-wing Christian," he and the moderate Shays
had talked and found they shared similar experiences. Like Shays, Souder
had already said publicly that he was against impeachment and yet now felt
compelled to reevaluate his position. And like Shays, the pressure Souder was
feeling came not from DeLay's office but from back home in his district.
After he made his public comments opposing impeachment, Souder lost
three-quarters of his campaign finance committee. His wife was assailed by a
clerk at the grocery store and she no longer wanted to go out to eat in restau-
rants. His mother and mother-in-law had both gotten grief in public. The
two-term congressman was stunned by the intensity of the emotion out
there, at least among the Republican base.

While Shays met with his constituents in Connecticut, Souder was back in Washington sitting down with two fellow Indiana congressmen who both sat on the Judiciary Committee. As part of the committee whip operation DeLay had helped set up, Steve Buyer and Ed Pease had asked to see Souder and arrived around 10 P.M. to explain why they were voting to impeach and to see whether they could change his mind. Under the rules, committee members were not supposed to discuss the evidence that was not made public with other House members until midnight that evening, but they went ahead and described a frightening array of secret material that remained under lock and key in the Ford Building vault. Among the allegations Souder should know about, they said, was an Arkansas woman called Jane Doe No. 5 who said Clinton had raped her some twenty years earlier. Souder had to go down and look at that material, the two congressmen implored him.

After his visitors left, Souder tried to reach Shays in Connecticut while he was at the town meeting, but could not get through. He found Shays by cellular phone in his car the next morning. "We have to see the redacted material," Souder told him.

Shays and Souder went over to the Ford Building around noon that Wednesday, December 16, and asked to be admitted to the sealed room. They signed their names, were admitted by Capitol Police officers standing guard, and found the Jane Doe No. 5 documents that laid out the Juanita Broaddrick case. If Broaddrick was to be believed, then the president of the United States was not merely an adulterer who exploited a young intern in his employ but a sexual predator who had forced himself violently on an unwilling woman. Both Shays and Souder found Broaddrick's story believable, particularly her explanation that she had not come forward at the time because she was already having an extramarital affair and believed she should never have let Clinton come up to her hotel room in the first place. After reading the documents, the two congressmen sat down with Susan Bogart, one of the committee Republican investigators who had talked with Broaddrick, and asked for her assessment. Bogart described in chilling detail her conversation with Broaddrick.

Shays and Souder then found Hyde and David Schippers talking with a group of other House Republicans who were studying the evidence and joined the conversation. Why was this not part of the public case against the president? they asked. Why was this inquiry so rushed that these and other charges of sexual misconduct were not thoroughly investigated? Schippers reacted testily to the insinuation. After all, he had been the one begging for more time to introduce evidence about Broaddrick and the other Jane Does.

Several other Republican congressmen who were gathered in the room at the time, including Mike Castle, Heather Wilson, and Jay Dickey of

Arkansas, heard their two colleagues cross-examining Hyde about Jane Doe No. 5 and were shocked to learn of the case for the first time. Others who still had not heard about it found out not long afterward during a 5 P.M. closed-door meeting of the entire Republican conference, when a fired-up Steve Buyer stood up to challenge members to go look at the secret evidence. This case, he declared loudly, was not just about what was in the public record but what was in the private record as well. The secret evidence showed a pattern of reprehensible behavior involving women and a practice of obstruction to keep them quiet, Buyer said. In particular, he mentioned Jane Doe No. 5 and her sensational accusation.

"Let me tell you something," Buyer told his colleagues hotly. "We're over here every day, and if you're undecided on the information that's already out there, you have an obligation to yourself and your country to get over there and look at that information."

Over the course of the next seventy-two hours, forty-five House Republicans would do just that, signing into the vault to examine the evidence that was not released publicly. Most of them had already signaled that they were likely to vote for impeachment, so the exact impact of this secret material was hard to gauge. But if nothing else, the outrage over the Jane Doe No. 5 allegations certainly helped reinforce their conclusions and remove any lingering doubts.

Even Chris Shays was momentarily persuaded. "Betsy," he told his wife, "I think I'm going to be voting for impeachment. You won't believe what I just saw."

Exhausted from his trip to the Middle East, Clinton was nonetheless up with the sun on Wednesday, December 16, to prepare for a battle of a far different kind. He had only arrived back at the White House at 11:43 P.M. the night before and had spent nearly two more hours consulting with aides and by phone with Dick Gephardt and Tom Daschle. While he slept, the USS Enterprise and at least eight other navy warships were moving into position to rain down massive destruction on Iraq. Although not scheduled to attend, Clinton decided to drop in at a 7:30 A.M. meeting in the Situation Room, where his senior advisers were going over the plans and timetables. The missiles would begin slamming down into select targets at 5 P.M. Washington time, and the plan called for the president to go on national television shortly afterward to explain the situation.

After reviewing the plans, Clinton wandered over to the 8 A.M. senior staff meeting in John Podesta's office, where most of the aides were unaware of the impending attack and the main topic was the forthcoming impeachment debate. The president rarely attended these meetings, and as he walked in, the assembled staff stood and applauded, ostensibly in recognition of his successful peace mission to the Middle East but perhaps less consciously in support of a leader they knew to be undergoing an extraordinary ordeal. Clinton looked awful. The bags under his eyes were even more pronounced than usual.

Clinton gave a short speech intended to rally his despairing aides and to thank them for their hard work in the difficult days to come. "Don't stop fighting," he said. "The American people are with us. I haven't stopped. Keep up the work."

Most aides thought he was referring to impeachment. But Greg Craig thought something odd was going on. Why was the president at work so early after having returned home so late the night before? When the meeting broke up, he wandered over to Podesta to ask what was going on. Podesta answered with his finger, tracing the arc of a bomb falling from the sky. Craig got it.

Word began to spread around town, and Craig soon called Julian Epstein, the Judiciary Democratic chief counsel, to let him know. Epstein was furious. This was going to blow up their entire strategy on impeachment. "Why the fuck do we learn about this an hour before everyone else learns about this?" he shouted at Craig. "You give me an hour to get ready for this shit?"

Craig said it was a national security matter. The White House staff did not keep him filled in on things like that either.

That was just a tiny taste of the explosion that would follow. Most members of the House were only now returning to town for what they thought would be the opening of the impeachment debate the next day, and the news of what was about to unfold in the Persian Gulf struck with the political force of a Tomahawk cruise missile. DeLay and Livingston were not the only Republicans who immediately concluded that the military operation must be part of a political scheme designed to buy Clinton time to hang on to office. Even Republicans normally inclined to back Clinton's policy with Iraq found themselves suspicious à la *Wag the Dog,* and some decided the suspicion itself demonstrated how the trust between the president and the Congress had been shattered beyond repair.

Democrats were seething too. Livingston told Gephardt at a 1 P.M. meeting that he would delay the vote for a day but would not commit to holding off until hostilities in the Gulf were completely over. The members of Gephardt's caucus were apoplectic that the Republicans would even entertain the notion of going forward while the country was at war. The thought of undercutting the commander in chief at such a critical moment seemed almost treasonous.

At 5 P.M., the Republican caucus gathered in a basement room on Capitol Hill while televisions showed the streaks of tracer lights across a green background over Baghdad. Antiaircraft guns had just begun firing into the sky to defend the besieged capital, and at 5:06 P.M. (1:06 A.M. Iraqi time), the first of two hundred American cruise missiles smashed down on targets around the city. With a stack of pizzas available for hungry Republicans, dozens of congressmen spoke out, angrily insisting that the vote had to go forward or reluctantly urging that they hold off. Among those determined to brook no postponement was DeLay. Livingston did not at first disclose that he had already committed to Clinton and Gephardt to delay the debate by a day and instead let his members vent. After an hour, word came that the president was about to address the nation, and a television was wheeled in so the members could watch. In a telling sign of how wide the partisan breach had opened in Washington, Livingston felt compelled to admonish his Republican colleagues not to boo or hiss at the screen because reporters waiting outside the closed doors might overhear and portray that as a sign of disrespect for the president.

From the Oval Office, a haggard-looking Clinton explained to a national television audience that he had ordered the attack to prevent the spread of chemical, biological, and nuclear weapons. He addressed the question of timing only obliquely near the end of his fifteen-minute speech. "Saddam Hussein and the other enemies of peace may have thought that the serious debate currently before the House of Representatives would distract Americans or weaken our resolve to face him down. But once more, the United States has proven that, although we are never eager to use force, when we must act in America's vital interests, we will do so."

The Republicans in the conference room were unimpressed. They still wanted to go forward as scheduled. Congress continued to meet during the Civil War, some pointed out, and elections were still held during World War II. They suspected Clinton only wanted to delay long enough to push the decision into the next Congress, which would take office in January, when he would have five more Democrats in the House. The subtext of the discussion was that for once they had the momentum and did not want to let up lest they lose it.

Finally, though, Nancy Johnson, a pragmatic congresswoman from Connecticut who only that week had announced she would vote for impeachment, rose to say that a delay would not change her decision or the outcome. "This conference will impeach the president," she declared. That calmed some nerves. Congressman Jim Greenwood of Pennsylvania, another moderate who had been on the fence, suggested that, since this was their new Speaker's first crisis, they owed it to Livingston to defer to his judgment.

After two and a half hours of heated debate, Livingston emerged from the Republican conference to announce what he had already decided a day earlier:

The House would delay its impeachment debate for a day. Pressed by reporters, Livingston would not say what he thought privately, that the whole military operation was a political sham by a president on the brink of impeachment. But other Republicans were not so reticent. "While I have been assured by administration officials that there is no connection with the impeachment process in the House of Representatives, I cannot support this military action in the Persian Gulf at this time," Senate Majority Leader Trent Lott said in a statement to the media. "Both the timing and the policy are subject to question." Dick Armey, the House majority leader, said, "After months of lies, the president has given millions of people around the world reason to doubt that he has sent Americans into battle for the right reasons."

As the defense secretary and the only Republican in the cabinet, Bill Cohen volunteered to refute such insinuations at an extraordinary closed meeting with congressmen on the floor of the House later that evening. Joined by George Tenet of the CIA and Hugh Shelton of the Joint Chiefs of Staff, Cohen spent ninety minutes describing for the members the rationale for the attack and its timing. Cohen, who had risen to national prominence as a member of the House Judiciary Committee some twenty-four years earlier by voting to impeach Nixon, offered his word that the strike was not politically motivated.

From behind a table a few feet away, DeLay stood and demanded, "Is there any reason why we shouldn't go ahead" with the impeachment debate?

Cohen tried to duck, saying it was not for him to dictate how the House conducted its business.

DeLay persisted. Was there "any national security reason the House cannot proceed" while the military was in combat?

"It's been the tradition throughout history that when we have people out there with the risk of dying, it's good to have good bipartisan support," a visibly exasperated Cohen responded, prompting applause around the chamber. "Unity and bipartisan support is important for the morale of the troops."

The House convened at 10 A.M. on Thursday, December 17, emotions roiling on all sides. Democrats were still outraged that the Republicans were even thinking of going ahead with the impeachment debate after just a day's delay, while the Republicans chafed at having their motives questioned once again. On the floor, some GOP members put forth a resolution supporting the troops to make clear that their criticism of the commander in chief should not be misread, a statement approved 417–5. And Newt Gingrich emerged from his self-imposed political hibernation to try to reframe the dialogue away from questioning the attack, in contrast to Lott and Armey. "We have a chance today to say to the world: no matter what our constitutional process, whether it is an election eve or it is the eve of a constitutional vote, no matter what our debates at home, we are, as a nation, prepared to lead the world," he said on the House floor. At the White House, Clinton was vindicated for insisting on praising Gingrich's internationalism in the statement issued after his resignation announcement the month before.

From the lectern in the House chamber, Livingston announced that the impeachment debate would begin the next morning even if the bombing continued. "This is a terribly unpopular measure and no one wants to deal with impeachment, but it is before us and we must deal with it," he told his colleagues, noting that Watergate proceedings went forward during the Vietnam War. "There's no way to know when the troops will have completed their mission." That was the public explanation. Privately, he believed they simply could not wait a week to vote in the midst of Christmas, and he worried there would be no way for them to regroup after the New Year.

The Democrats were in full attack mode and staged a rally off the floor to highlight the impropriety of impeaching a commander in chief while he directed armed conflict with another country.

"That is wrong!" shouted Dick Gephardt. "That is wrong! That is wrong! That is wrong!"

If his colleagues thought the worn look on Livingston's face indicated the stress of the impeachment-and-war debate, they had barely begun to scratch the surface. The public battle Livingston was waging with Gephardt and the president barely compared with the anguish he was going through in private. He was assuming the mantle of leadership at a time when he would be charged with presiding over the impeachment of a president for crimes that had their origin in the same human frailty he possessed. The possibility that he might be exposed had naturally occurred to him when he decided to run for Speaker—a friend even warned him before the election that someone seemed to be nosing around in Louisiana. But in a classic case of self-denial, Livingston assumed that no one would ever actually follow through, and he refused to think about it. Now he had no choice. His past had come back to haunt him—possibly, he thought, at the instigation of the White House or its allies. Livingston decided the only course was to come clean. Amid all the broader debate on war and peace, he found a few moments to fill in DeLay about his dilemma and then marched into a meeting of the House GOP leadership to confess.

"I've been Larry Flynted," he announced.

In a matter-of-fact tone, Livingston explained that he had had some "personal relationships" in the past with women other than his wife and that he was sure one of them was about to go public with her story in *Hustler* maga-

zine. While he did not offer to resign, he hinted that was an option if the situation warranted. Then he went around the room, asking each of the leaders, "What do you think?"

Armey, the burly House majority leader who had been largely invisible
through much of the impeachment saga, spoke up first and said it should not
matter. They should not be deterred from doing their duty. The other leaders
followed suit. Any qualms they had about following an admitted adulterer
into an impeachment debate generated by a president's sexual dalliances
were left unspoken. Livingston had their loyalty, at least for now.

The Speaker-to-be found a somewhat more volatile crowd two hours later
when he met with the full Republican conference. The members thought
they had been called together to plot strategy for the opening debate in the
morning, and for ninety minutes they did just that. Livingston even delivered another lecture about how to behave once they went to the floor: "Look,
this is one of the toughest times this country has faced. We can't let this
country think this is a railroad job. Our decorum matters. Don't let yourself
be goaded into showing disrespect for the president."

Finally, Livingston's press secretary, Mark Corallo, stepped into the room
and approached his boss. "The press has got it," he whispered to Livingston.
"They're beginning to run the story."

Livingston steeled himself and signaled to Congressman J. C. Watts, the
chairman of the conference, who was presiding over the meeting. Watts had
been in the earlier meeting and knew what was coming when he introduced
Livingston. The Speaker-to-be pulled a two-page statement out of his pocket
and began reading: "I have on occasion strayed from my marriage, and doing
so nearly cost me my marriage and my family. I sought marriage and spiritual
counseling and have received forgiveness from my wife and family, for which
I am eternally grateful. This chapter was a small but painful part of the past
in an otherwise wonderful marriage."

The room erupted in disbelief and astonishment. How could this be happening? First war, now this? The Republican members were beside themselves.
One exasperated congressman, Donald Manzullo from Illinois, jumped to his
feet and asked how Livingston could do this to them. Why had he not disclosed this before? Manzullo demanded.

In the next row, Charles Canady, the bookish Floridian on the Judiciary
Committee, leapt up too and got in Manzullo's face, telling him to shut up.
"Take it easy," Canady said. "Things will work out."

DeLay came to Livingston's defense, as did others, all pointing out that
cheating on your wife was different from lying under oath.

"My fate is in your hands," Livingston told the group.

CHAPTER TEN

"There are people in my party who just hate you"

The galleries were strangely empty when members began gathering on the floor of the House of Representatives at 9 A.M. on Friday, December 18, 1998. The drawings of the impeachment of Andrew Johnson always featured galleries jam-packed with spectators, hanging over the railings and hanging on every word, conveying the impression that the nation's future really stood in the balance. But 130 years later, only two of the fourteen sections reserved for the public and dignitaries overlooking the House floor were filled, as people who wanted to watch were kept waiting in a line outside the Capitol. Members milled around on the floor, more edgy than solemn. Without knowing any better, a casual visitor might assume this was the markup for a highway bill in which congressmen had plenty of pork at stake, but not the judgment of history. It would take a while for that to sink in.

Shortly after 9 A.M., Congressman Ray LaHood, an Illinois Republican tapped by Newt Gingrich and Bob Livingston to preside over the debate because neither wanted the dubious distinction for himself, gaveled the chamber to order. The chaplain, the Reverend James David Ford, led the lawmakers in a short prayer: "Where there is hatred, let us sow love; where there is injury, pardon; where there is discord, union; where there is doubt, faith; where there is despair, hope; where there is darkness, light; where there is sadness, joy."

There was, to be sure, plenty of injury, discord, and even hatred this day just one week before Christmas and little prospect for pardon, union, or love. Feelings on both sides of the aisle were raw, and the sense of grievance overwhelming. For the Democrats, it seemed unfathomable that this day had come, that they were there to impeach their president over what amounted to a peccadillo, that the majority was so hell-bent on doing so that it would not even wait until U.S. troops were out of harm's way, that their own party had been rendered so impotent that they were reduced to planning a five-minute walkout to protest. For the Republicans, the shock had not dissipated from the revelation the night before that their own new leader had been unfaithful to his wife, a disclosure that for some fed into the doubts they harbored over what they were about to do and for others hardened their hearts out of the conviction that they had somehow been victimized again by White House dirty tricks. Nearly eleven months after the news of Clinton's affair with Monica Lewinsky had first roiled national politics, despite all the power of the president's office, despite all the efforts of the gray-haired wise men who once ruled Washington and hoped to avert this constitutional confrontation, the moment of decision had arrived. Was Clinton a capable leader who had understandably stumbled and was now being persecuted by his political enemies? Or was he a scoundrel who had so dishonored the presidency that he no longer deserved to hold it?

As the session was getting under way, Tom DeLay summoned nearly twenty members of his staff to his conference room just off the floor. "We all have to understand what we are about to do," he told his aides. "It's not about winning or losing. It's not about politics. This is a very serious moment. We need to pray for strength." Everyone in the room joined hands. His head bowed, DeLay prayed for the country, for the members, and even for the president. Tears streaked down his cheeks. "Please know that we're not happy about doing this," he said. "We see this as our responsibility."

On the floor, a clerk, Paul Hays, read the four articles aloud in their entirety, booming out the stark accusations in his deep baritone. *"Willfully corrupted." "Disrepute on the presidency." "Betrayed his trust as president."* For each article, the clerk concluded, "Wherefore, William Jefferson Clinton, by such conduct, warrants impeachment and trial, and removal from office and disqualification to hold and enjoy any office of honor, trust, or profit under the United States."

Before beginning the two-day debate, LaHood tried to set down some ground rules. "While the impeachment matter is pending on the floor," he announced from the rostrum, "the chair would remind members that although the personal conduct of the president is at issue, the rules prohibit members from engaging in generally personal abusive language toward the president and, also, from engaging in comparisons to personal conduct of sitting members of either House of Congress." In other words, Democrats should not talk about Livingston's affairs or, for that matter, Gingrich's ethics case. Hoots of derision arose from the Democratic side of the chamber as LaHood read his announcement. Livingston sat on the Republican side, his hands folded, his face impassive. Gingrich was nowhere to be seen.

With all this, it was 9:50 A.M. before the articles themselves were addressed, and Henry Hyde tried to defuse the Democratic argument from the start.

"The question before this House is rather simple," he said, standing at a lectern and facing the rostrum. "It is not a question of sex. Sexual misconduct and adultery are private acts and are none of Congress's business. It is not even a question of lying about sex. The matter before the House is a question of lying under oath. This is a public act, not a private act. This is called perjury. The matter before the House is a question of the willful, premeditated, deliberate corruption of the nation's system of justice."

Without dwelling on the details of the allegations, Hyde issued a rhetorical call to arms to defend the "rule of law," invoking the spirit of the Ten Commandments, Mosaic law, Roman law, the Magna Carta, Bunker Hill, Concord and Lexington, Abraham Lincoln, and the soldiers who fought and won World War II. "What we are telling you today are not the ravings of some vindictive political crusade, but a reaffirmation of a set of values that are tarnished and dim these days, but it is given to us to restore them so our Founding Fathers would be proud," he said. Finishing with a flourish, he added, "Listen, it is your country. The president is our flag bearer. He stands out in front of our people and the flag is falling. Catch the falling flag as we keep our appointment with history."

The Republican members jumped to their feet to applaud, while the Democrats sat and stewed. *The Ten Commandments? The falling flag?* It was all too much for many of them. And yet, they worried. Hyde had a mesmerizing effect at times, and if he struck them as a little grandiloquent, he presented the public with a noble face for what they saw as an ignoble cause.

Dick Gephardt took the lectern on the other side of the aisle to open the Democratic side of the argument, but he decided to hold on to what he felt was the moral high ground of the day—the timing of the debate. "Mr. Speaker, this vote today is taking place on the wrong day, and we are doing it in the wrong way." By moving forward, he warned, "we send the wrong message to Saddam Hussein, to the British, to the Chinese, and to the Russians." Having made his point, Gephardt then reached out to the Republicans with an implicit reference to Livingston's crisis and tried to tie it into what the GOP caucus was doing to the president. "The events of the last days sadden me. We are now at the height of a cycle of the politics of negative attacks, character assassination, personal smears of good people, decent people, worthy people. It is no wonder to me and to you that the people of our country today are cynical and indifferent and apathetic about our government and about our country. The politics of smear and slash and burn must end." At this, members on both sides of the aisle stood and applauded, a rare moment of unity on a divisive day. Livingston remained in his seat, motionless.

As he went on, Gephardt never addressed the charges against Clinton, but instead maintained that the punishment did not fit the crime and complained they were not given a chance even to vote on censure. Gephardt was revving up his own troops at this point, stoking their sense of outrage, and they responded. "All we are asking for is that we get to vote our conscience," he said, to which the Democrats gave him a standing ovation. "In your effort to uphold the Constitution, you are trampling the Constitution." The Democrats were wild by now, on their feet and clapping.

The Democratic theme held that the Republicans were acting out of anger, but the anger this day was deep on both sides of the aisle. Over more than twelve hours, 261 members lashed out at Clinton or the Republican leadership. Indeed, some of the harshest rhetoric came from the Democrats. "The majority may well have blood on its hands by starting this proceeding today," asserted Congressman Martin Frost of Texas, the newly installed head of the Democratic caucus, prompting hisses from the GOP side. "Monica Lewinsky is not Watergate! Let he who has no sin in this chamber cast the first vote!" shouted Congressman Robert Menendez of New Jersey, another member of the Democratic leadership team, in an obvious reference to Livingston. What the House was doing was a "constitutional assassination," in the words of Congresswoman Rosa DeLauro of Connecticut, or "a Republican coup d'état," as John Conyers, Maxine Waters, and a half dozen others put it.

The Republicans tried to be more restrained in their rhetoric, focusing largely on the concepts of duty or the weight of the evidence, all the while laboring desperately not to project an image of extremism. "The only way to avoid impeachment is to leave your common sense at the door," said Lindsey Graham. Asa Hutchinson stressed that by covering up his affair with Lewinsky, Clinton had impeded Paula Jones, "a fellow Arkansan," in her lawful right to seek redress in court. "It is not for the president or his lawyers to determine who can or cannot seek justice."

The electricity crackled in the chamber and fairly exploded outside it. During a floor speech, Congressman Bob Barr, the Georgia conservative, quoted John F. Kennedy to say, "Americans are free to disagree with the law but not to disobey it." Democrats fumed at the citation, none more so than the slain president's nephew, Congressman Patrick J. Kennedy of Rhode Island. Flush with rage, Kennedy found Barr a short while afterward in the Speaker's Lobby, an ornate area just off the House floor where members often congregated between votes.

"You quoted my uncle and you went to a White Citizens Council meeting!" Kennedy shouted across the room. "Anybody who has been to a racist group has no right invoking my uncle's memory!" News accounts in recent days had disclosed that Barr spoke about impeachment earlier in the year to a group called the Council of Conservative Citizens, an outgrowth of the old white Citizens Councils that fought integration in the South. In the aftermath of those reports, Barr had maintained that he did not know the organization's history and renounced its racist views.

"You're wrong," Barr told Kennedy. Then, the fifty-year-old Republican chided the thirty-one-year-old. "Young man, you are showing a lack of decorum."

"I'm a duly elected representative of my constituents and I am entitled to say what I want," Kennedy huffed.

"I'm impressed," Barr replied mockingly. "I'm *duly* impressed."

Kennedy stormed off and spent the rest of the day railing about "that racist." Barr later dismissed him as "some punk."

Through all of this, Gingrich remained virtually invisible. At 12:45 P.M., he wandered into the chamber, walked along the back wall for a few moments, and then quickly left again. The lame-duck Speaker wanted no part of this anymore. His would-be successor, Livingston, kept quiet through the day's debate as well, hiding out from the cameras and writing his speech. He had his own crisis to confront. That morning, he had had a visit from a fellow Republican urging him to give up the Speakership in the wake of his admission. "You really ought to consider standing down from the election," Congressman Greg Ganske, a former plastic surgeon from Iowa, told him. Ganske said he had come to his conclusion after sleeping on it overnight and did not represent anyone but himself, yet Livingston knew his sentiments were shared by others. Within a few hours, Livingston was closeted away in the Republican cloakroom, entertaining his brief moment of doubt when he considered allowing the president to be censured after all, only to steel himself to go forward at the urging of the aide who came to tell him about Juanita Broaddrick and the "rapist in the White House."

Down Pennsylvania Avenue, Clinton was going through the motions of a normal day, refusing to dignify the proceedings by appearing even remotely interested in them. It was a show, of course, but he went about it relentlessly. He arrived at the Oval Office for work at 9:30 A.M. and received a briefing from National Security Adviser Sandy Berger about the bombing of Iraq, then consulted by telephone with British prime minister Tony Blair.

At ten-fifteen, though, just twenty-five minutes after the debate had begun on the House floor, impeachment rudely intruded. Waiting to see the president was Chris Shays, the moderate Republican congressman who had held the town meeting in Connecticut earlier in the week. Shays was originally supposed to come down to the White House on Wednesday, but his meeting with the president was postponed in part because of the onset of the war with Iraq. Shays also wanted to put it off until he had made up his mind because he did not want his final decision influenced by Clinton's notable powers of persuasion. In the last forty-eight hours, he had struggled with what he had learned about the Juanita Broaddrick story, but had ultimately put aside his feelings of disgust after concluding that no accusations of perjury or obstruction were involved in her case. Given that, Shays concluded he had no choice but to vote against impeachment.

The news did little to brighten the president's day, however. Clinton received Shays in a library in the White House residence out of deference to the congressman, who did not want to meet in the Oval Office with its trappings of power—and a now famous adjoining corridor that might prove distracting.

"Mr. President," Shays began, "my constituents want you impeached. And, Mr. President, my constituents don't want you impeached." It seemed an apt summary of what he had heard in Norwalk the other night and a fair representation of the larger public mood. For about ten minutes, Shays described his feelings about the case and the sentiments he had heard in that jam-packed town hall. He quoted Franklin D. Roosevelt's aphorism about the White House: "I never forget that I live in a house owned by all the American people and that I have been given their trust."

Clinton responded with a forty-five-minute monologue about how he was not guilty as charged and how his actions had been twisted into a nefarious conspiracy rather than an all-too-human lapse. From time to time, Shays interjected a question. Among them was the allegation foremost on his mind—the Broaddrick episode. Clinton denied her account.

After an hour, the congressman got up to leave. The president returned to his schedule: A meeting with European officials to discuss trade. A briefing by his economic advisers to review the 2000 fiscal year budget. And a session with his advisory council on AIDS.

Having agonized over what to do, having almost given in to the pro-censure sentiment, Livingston returned to his office. He was still struggling with his speech. He had written a draft and then thrown it away. He had given another version to a secretary at seven-thirty to type up, but still felt unsatisfied.

Sometime after 9:30 P.M., Tom DeLay showed up with three aides. DeLay was increasingly concerned about the brewing Republican discontent over Livingston's revelations and had brought his team to plot strategy. Livingston asked DeLay to come into his office alone, leaving the aides outside. Behind closed doors, Livingston talked at some length about his plight, and DeLay offered a brutally honest assessment of his situation: There were a lot of angry members, DeLay told Livingston. They needed to figure out how to ride it out. But Livingston was not sure. With a margin of just six seats, Livingston was coming to the same realization Gingrich had six weeks earlier.

He thought he could still win the Speakership—he might even be able to pick up some Democratic friends, he figured, to offset any Republican defections—but the question was whether he could effectively govern. Whoever would be Speaker would find it incredibly tough even without additional problems; Gingrich had lost his credibility, and now Livingston feared he might have lost his own moral authority.

"Well, maybe I shouldn't even run," Livingston said dejectedly.

"Oh, no, no," DeLay replied. "You can't do that."

It would be tough, but he could win and he could govern. DeLay promised to be there for him. Whatever he needed would be taken care of, the whip said. Livingston thanked him and DeLay got up to leave, hoping he had just averted another disaster. "Everything's going to be fine," DeLay reassured Livingston's aides on the way out. "I know he's shaken, but the members are with him. Yeah, there's a few who are a little disappointed, a little upset. All we have to do is put our arms around them, look them in the eye, and tell them everything will be fine." DeLay, wearing a dark suit and black wool overcoat, folded his arms in front of him to demonstrate what he meant. He then turned on his heel and left, trailed by his retinue of aides. To Livingston's staff, it was a strange scene, one they would later dub their "Godfather moment," with DeLay cast in the role of Don Corleone.

But Livingston was not fine. By now it was around midnight and his aides were trying to buck him up. Everything would work out, they told him. This was a short-lived story. It was Christmas, a time of renewal and hope. Livingston managed a weak smile. He turned his attention back to his speech. "It's a good speech," he told his aides. "But it needs a punch line." He kept muttering that. "It needs a punch line."

At 2 A.M., Livingston woke up from a fitful sleep with a realization. He could not call for impeachment without calling on Clinton to resign, he decided. And Livingston could not suggest the president step down unless he did so too. Somehow, someone in all this needed to set a standard. If Livingston resigned, then he would show Clinton for what he truly was.

"You can't! You can't do it. You're going to kill the party. You're going to kill the majority."

DeLay was in tears when Livingston gave him the news the next morning. DeLay had just finished with the weights and stationary bicycle at the House gym shortly after 8 A.M. on Saturday, December 19, when Livingston tracked him down by phone and told him he needed to see him urgently. Forgoing his shower, DeLay threw on his clothes and rushed out to find the would-be Speaker in his Appropriations Committee office. DeLay pleaded with Livingston to reconsider. Without him, the party would lose control of the House.

"No, it won't." Livingston went on to give the same logic Gingrich had just two months earlier: it was such a narrow majority, it would be an incredibly tough job under any circumstances.

DeLay tried again to talk him out of it, but came around to see his point. "You're right," he said finally. "Well, who do you think can do it?"

Livingston had already given that some thought. "Denny Hastert," he said, naming DeLay's chief deputy whip.

A mild-mannered, bearlike former wrestling coach from Illinois, Hastert was widely liked on both sides of the aisle and might have a chance of pulling together a rambunctious caucus. Within a few minutes, DeLay had found Hastert on the floor and ushered him into a side room with a copying machine adjacent to the Republican cloakroom.

"You've got to run," DeLay said. "Livingston's out."

Hastert was taken off guard and reluctant. "I need to pray about this. I need to talk to my wife about this."

Once again, Tom Daschle was getting in the way of Clinton's plans for how to handle the impeachment crisis. After nixing Clinton's idea to collect the signatures of thirty-four senators opposing impeachment back in the fall, the Senate minority leader now found himself having to quash another ill-considered plan emanating from the White House. This time, he had been asked to come down to the White House for a show of support along with Gephardt after the House impeachment vote. Daschle had no real doubt by this point that he would stand by Clinton in any Senate trial, but the idea of appearing beside him in public at such a delicate moment would destroy the senator's credibility as a future juror. Not only would it look bad to the public, signaling that Senate Democrats were not even willing to listen to the evidence and had already made up their minds, perhaps more importantly it might antagonize Robert Byrd and several of the other senators in the Democratic caucus who might come to the same conclusion. The last thing Daschle wanted was to alienate Byrd and push him into the impeachment camp. If Byrd bolted, so might others. Daschle rejected Clinton's request and refused to come to the White House.

Gephardt was not all that enthusiastic about the idea either. But the internal dynamics of his caucus were quite different. In his case, the loudest voices were pushing for a show of solidarity with the president, no matter how impolitic it might be. While the president's strategists wanted the party leadership to come down to the White House, Charles Rangel, a gravel-voiced congressman from Harlem, was eager to arrange a much bigger rally and kept pushing even when House leaders rebuffed him. Rangel's big chance came that morning when Hillary Clinton came to address the Democratic caucus in the Cannon House Office Building.

The first lady's decision to speak to the caucus, even if behind closed doors, was a late breakthrough for the White House aides who had been desperately praying for her to step in and help rescue her husband. Only she had the moral authority to defend the president and offer him forgiveness, and many of the House Democrats had been waiting to take their cue from her. By the time she arrived at the Cannon Building with John Podesta and Greg Craig around 8:30 A.M.—entering through a back door to avoid being photographed—the members had long since made up their minds about how to vote. But she could energize them about their decision to stick with the president.

"I love and care deeply about my husband," she told the Democrats in their private meeting, from which reporters were barred. That she chose to say those simple words carried great power in that room, even if no one really knew the actual state of their post-Monica marriage. "We have committed our lives to the values of quality of opportunity and a better life for the children of America," the first lady went on. She thanked the House Democrats for standing up for the Constitution and for not being afraid to stick with "the commander in chief, the president, the man I love." The Democrats, who had given her a standing ovation upon her arrival, leapt to their feet again. More than a few choked up.

As the first lady finished, Rangel seized the moment. He had gone to the caucus chairman, Martin Frost, before the meeting to ask for permission to address the group and propose they go down to the White House en masse after the vote, but Frost had refused, reasoning that it was a bad idea for anyone beyond the House leaders to go down. So when Rangel stood up after Hillary Clinton's remarks, Frost refused to recognize him. Rangel marched down to one of the microphones set up in the audience and began speaking anyway, laying out his plan and asking the first lady what she thought of the idea. She liked it, as Rangel knew she would. Come on down, she said.

Tension flooded the House chamber as members from both parties gathered on the floor a few minutes later, just after 9 A.M., for the second and final day of debate. Even the Pledge of Allegiance stirred up emotions in the chamber. "With liberty and justice for all," the recitation ended, whereupon a single voice from the Democratic side of the aisle called out, "All!" Within moments, others took up the chant. "All!" they cried. "All!"

At 9:30 A.M., Livingston crossed the floor and found John Conyers, who controlled the clock for the Democrats. I'm going to speak next, Livingston said, and I might take extra time, but please don't cut me off. "You won't regret it," Livingston said cryptically.

He then approached the lectern on the Republican side of the aisle. He gripped the podium, glanced down at his notes, and looked up again to scan the faces in the audience. The members hushed to hear what the new Speaker had to say, and he began predictably enough, talking about the rule of law and the seriousness of perjury. He said he deeply regretted the hostility that had arisen in the impeachment battle and wished he could have written a different first chapter to "the intended Livingston Speakership." Few in the audience picked up on the adjective. Within a few minutes, he addressed himself directly to the president, confident that Clinton would be watching on television.

"Sir," Livingston said, "you have done great damage to this nation over this past year, and while your defenders are contending that further impeachment proceedings would only protract and exacerbate the damage to this country, I say that you have the power to terminate that damage and heal the wounds that you have created. You, sir, may resign your post."

Cries of anger erupted from the Democratic side of the aisle. "No!" some shouted. "No!" Congresswoman Zoe Lofgren sat at the table near the front of the chamber with her arms crossed and a fierce scowl etched on her face. Congressman Marty Meehan, sitting in the row in front of her, booed and turned to a colleague to say, "Can you believe this guy? *He* should resign." Maxine Waters picked up the thought, and jumped to her feet.

"You resign!" she shouted at Livingston, slamming her open palm down on the table in front of her repeatedly. "You resign! You resign!"

Others picked up the mantra, disrupting the chamber, while Conyers, tipped off that there might be more to this, stood and flapped his arms up and down, signaling his fellow Democrats to be quiet.

"The House will be in order!" called out Ray LaHood, the presiding officer, as he banged his gavel.

Calm restored, Livingston continued. "I can only challenge you in such fashion that I am willing to heed my own words," he said, still addressing the president. Begging forgiveness for his mistakes, he said he had hoped to be a good Speaker. "But I cannot do that job or be the kind of leader that I would like to be under current circumstances. So I must set the example that I hope President Clinton will follow. I will not stand for Speaker of the House on January sixth."

It seemed for a moment as if all the air had been sucked out of the chamber. No one moved at first, no one knew how to respond. "You resign!" the Democrats had shouted moments before, and now Livingston had done just that. Rarely in Washington did a major political earthquake strike without some warning, but this was that unique event that had caught nearly everyone by surprise. Dick Armey and other GOP leaders leapt up and surrounded Livingston as he departed the room, while members on both sides of the aisle rose to their feet and applauded, unsure what else to do. Just a few feet from where Livingston had spoken, Congressman Mark Foley, a Florida Republican, cried openly. The first one to chase after Livingston to his office at the Appropriations Committee was Congressman Jesse Jackson Jr., the son of the civil rights leader, who represented Illinois in the House. Jackson was crying too and wrapped his arms around the tall Republican in a tight bear hug.

"Bob, don't do this," he implored.

In his own office just off the floor, Gephardt had been sitting behind his desk in shirtsleeves, reading aloud the speech he planned to deliver that morning. He had been working on it for some time, even rereading John F. Kennedy's *Profiles in Courage* for its account of a key senator in the Andrew Johnson trial. Gephardt had heard a rumor about Livingston a few minutes before, but had discounted it. Suddenly, Dan Turton, a floor assistant, burst into the office and told everyone to turn up the volume on the bank of four television sets next to the desk. Gephardt turned to his right and watched four images of Livingston declare that he would not take office as Speaker. The minority leader was dumbfounded. Everything was spiraling out of control. Missiles were raining down on Baghdad, the president was about to be impeached, and now the next leader of the House of Representatives was stepping down to atone for adultery. Gephardt immediately thought it was the wrong decision, that Livingston should not do it. It was bad for the nation and bad for the institution. What's more, Gephardt worried that the Democrats had made themselves look terrible, almost as if they had goaded Livingston into doing it.

Congressman Joseph P. Kennedy II of Massachusetts and other Democrats rushed into Gephardt's office, urging him to go out to the floor and speak immediately. "Dick, you've got to get out there," said Kennedy. "They're calling for you. This has to stop." Conyers even announced on the floor that next up to speak would be Gephardt. But the minority leader refused to go. This was a moment of great import and he wanted to make sure he got it right. Gephardt dispatched Turton to inform Conyers that he was not coming out yet and assigned aides Laura Nichols and Erik Smith to throw out his first speech and start drafting an entirely new one. The one line he told them he wanted to keep was his conclusion: "May God have mercy on this Congress, and may Congress have the wisdom and the courage and the goodness to save itself today."

At the White House, the shock at Livingston's announcement was flavored with a gut-churning sense of panic. Aides who turned up the volume on the television in John Podesta's office when they saw Livingston suddenly feared that it could alter the political dynamics and stoke public pressure for

Clinton to resign too. They had braced themselves for the inevitability of impeachment with the comforting knowledge that the president still seemed assured of remaining in office as long as the situation was polarized along party lines. Yet if Livingston stepped down, maybe people would want a clean slate and demand that Clinton go too. It did not seem far-fetched at the time. It seemed like a real moment of danger.

Clinton had been in the residence when it happened and rushed over to the Oval Office to watch in the adjoining dining room with Podesta and Doug Sosnik. None of them could believe that a second House Speaker had fallen as a result of all this. At that moment, press secretary Joe Lockhart rushed in and insisted they had to move immediately to stanch any new resignation drive. "I've got to go out and say something," Lockhart said. "We can't leave this hanging."

The president said the Livingston resignation was bad for the country, and Lockhart asked him to talk out loud about it so he would know what to tell the media. Lockhart scribbled down the president's words on a White House stationery card he had grabbed: "POTUS likes and respect Live enjoyed working as chmn of Appropriations Committee strongly disagree with pol of pers-destruction . . . whether Dems or Republican. Politics of personal destruction has to stop wishes he would reconsider." Lockhart rushed out of the room to deliver a variation on those themes to reporters in the briefing room.

Suddenly the virtues of Charlie Rangel's proposed rally around the president to be held later in the day became far clearer to White House aides. Surrounding Clinton with his fellow Democrats would keep him from looking like a lonely, latter-day Richard Nixon talking to the paintings on the wall. This was a town that could smell weakness. They wanted him to appear vigorous, unbowed and resolute, supported, not abandoned, by his allies. The picture of a president with loyal members of his party would convey an image to the country of business-as-usual politics in which impeachment was simply another partisan fight. And by emphasizing that the House Democrats were unabashedly sticking with Clinton, they hoped to send a signal to Senate Democrats that they should do the same, for as long as they held most of their forty-five members of the upper chamber, there would never be a two-thirds vote for conviction.

Back in the House chamber, prepared speeches now seemed so inadequate to the moment that they were largely tossed aside. If ever members spoke from the heart, this was the time. Even hard-charging Tom DeLay found his eyes again filled with tears as he got up to speak about Livingston.

"There is no greater American in my mind, at least today, than the gentleman from Louisiana because he understood what this debate was all about,"

DeLay told the House, his voice quavering as the low-grade chattering around the chamber came to an abrupt halt. "It was about honor and decency and integrity and the truth, everything that we honor in this country." After four months, The Campaign was on the verge of victory, and yet the collateral damage now included two Speakers from his own party.

For the Democrats, their leader absent, toiling away in a back room in search of the right phrase, it fell to the unlikely Jerrold Nadler, the hefty, bombastic congressman from New York City's Upper West Side, who had hectored Henry Hyde during the committee debate, to give voice to the emotion of the day. "Mr. Speaker, I am even more depressed today than I thought I would be yesterday. I believe the resignation of the gentleman from Louisiana, while offered in good faith, was wrong!" Nadler declared at the top of his lungs. Democrats spontaneously stood and applauded. "It is a surrender, it is a surrender to a developing sexual McCarthyism!"

Hyde lumbered up to the lectern. "My friends, those of us who are sinners must feel especially wretched today, losing Bob Livingston under such sad circumstances," he said, a not-so-veiled reference to his own thirty-year-old infidelity. But Hyde stressed the difference between private and public acts, between what Livingston had admitted doing and what Clinton still would not. "When the chief law enforcement officer trivializes, ignores, shreds, minimizes the sanctity of the oath, then justice is wounded, and you are wounded, and your children are wounded."

In the midst of all this, Livingston reappeared on the floor and quietly found a seat in the third row on the far side of the chamber. Congressman Thomas M. Davis III, a Virginia Republican and new member of the House leadership, came over, shook his hand, and sat next to him. Others came by with a pat on the back or a whispered encouragement.

At 11:30 A.M., nearly two hours after Livingston had dropped his bombshell, Gephardt finally emerged from seclusion and approached the microphone in the well of the chamber. He started by calling Livingston "a worthy and good and honorable man," prompting a standing ovation on both sides of the aisle. Gephardt, the boyish-looking congressman who after twenty-two years was now becoming something of an elder statesman in the House, looked over to Livingston, who nodded slightly in acknowledgment. "I believe his decision to retire is a terrible capitulation to the negative forces that are consuming our political system and our country, and I pray with all my heart that he will reconsider this decision." That triggered another bipartisan ovation. "We need to stop destroying imperfect people at the altar of an unobtainable morality. We need to start living up to the standards which the public in its infinite wisdom understands, that imperfect people must strive towards, but too often fall short. We are now rapidly descending into a politics where life imitates farce, fratricide dominates our public debate and America is held hostage to tactics of smear and fear." Then Gephardt pleaded with great passion for the Republicans to join the Democrats for a bipartisan censure of the president that would begin to heal the wounds. "We are on the brink of the abyss. The only way we stop this insanity is through the force of our own will. The only way we stop this spiral is for all of us to finally say, 'Enough.'"

This time Gephardt brought only his own caucus to their feet, but they remained upright and cheering for many long minutes. They clapped and whooped and hollered as if he had just won an election. To many of them, it was the best speech that the often-overscripted Gephardt had ever given in his career—poignant, powerful, and to the point. In effect, Gephardt had vented for them, and as he moved down the aisle to leave the chamber, he was surrounded by congratulating colleagues.

While heartening the Democrats, though, Gephardt's forceful words did not move any Republican votes. Barely an hour later, the House rejected Gephardt's parliamentary maneuver to force a vote on censure, 230–204. Acting on their prearranged plans, the Democrats then marched out of the chamber as voting began on Article I, gathering on the steps of the Capitol to stage a brief protest rally, then turning around and parading back in before the fifteen-minute voting period expired. As the congressmen inserted their voting cards and pressed the buttons—green for yes, red for no—there were few outward clues to the gravity of the occasion. It was not silent or somber. Indeed, the chamber echoed with the chatter of a hundred casual conversations and some laughter, as members milled around and passed the time between votes as if trudging their way through an appropriations bill. Strangely, it seemed more like a bus terminal than a funeral parlor.

When the vote tally came in at 1:25 P.M., Ray LaHood could barely be heard above the din as he announced the result.

"The article of impeachment is adopted," he declared.

With that, William Jefferson Clinton became only the second president—and the first elected chief executive—ever impeached by the House of Representatives. No matter what happened next, no matter how the Senate received the case, that vote had seared the word *impeached* onto Clinton's legacy. For a man who had plotted his whole life to win the White House and then, once he did, obsessed about his place in history, there could be no greater punishment. In better times, Clinton used to complain to friends that he wished he had been a wartime leader so that he could have had the opportunity to earn admission to the pantheon of America's greatest presidents. Deprived of that, he had hoped to go down in history as another Theodore Roosevelt. Now he might be remembered as another Andrew Johnson.

As everyone had expected, the vote on the charge of grand jury perjury split sharply along party lines—228 for and 206 against. Five members of each party broke ranks, including Pete King, the president's Republican ally, Chris Shays, who had met with Clinton the day before, and Mark Souder, who had joined Shays to study the secret evidence. Voting no with them were fellow Republicans Connie Morella of Maryland and Amo Houghton of New York. The Democratic defectors canceled them out: Paul McHale, the retiring congressman from Pennsylvania who had been the first Democrat to call for Clinton's resignation, plus four Southern conservatives, Charlie Stenholm and Ralph Hall of Texas, Gene Taylor of Mississippi, and Virgil H. Goode Jr. of Virginia.

The House then moved immediately to Article II, which accused Clinton of committing perjury in his deposition in the Paula Jones lawsuit. Even to his own lawyers, the factual evidence that Clinton lied under oath was far stronger in his civil testimony than in the grand jury testimony cited in Article I, and yet a couple dozen Republicans had decided to sacrifice this second article. Lindsey Graham had set the stage for that by voting against it in committee. On the floor over the last three days, many Republicans had approached Graham and other colleagues on the Judiciary Committee and said they wanted to split the difference. Many were already sure they would vote against Article IV, the abuse of power charge, because it seemed so overreaching, but they wanted to vote against two articles to show voters back home that they had given careful consideration to the case and were not knee-jerk partisans. So if they could only have two of the four, the committee members were asked, which two did they want? After consulting with David Schippers, their investigator, Graham, Bill McCollum, Jim Rogan, Steve Buyer, and others spread the word: give us Articles I and III. The third article, alleging obstruction, was the broadest of the group. If they lost the Jones perjury article, Schippers advised the GOP committee members, they could still bootstrap it into the obstruction count during the Senate trial.

So at 1:42 P.M., the House rejected Article II, 229–205, a sacrifice to political strategy. This time, twenty-eight Republicans left the fold. Seventeen minutes later, the House passed Article III, 221–212, giving Schippers the obstruction count he wanted. Mark Souder, still bothered by the Juanita Broaddrick allegations, voted for this article, while eight other Republicans who had supported Article I switched to vote no. At 2:15 P.M., Article IV went down to crashing defeat, 285–148, amid a Republican jailbreak that saw fully a third of the caucus buck the party line.

As the first vote was being taken, Clinton was in the Oval Office conferring with the Reverend Tony Campolo, one of three ministers he had asked to counsel him about his personal failings. Doug Sosnik sent Betty Currie in with a note to let Clinton know the roll call had begun, but by the time the pastoral session was over, the president had missed the vote entirely. To watch the final three votes, Clinton retired along with Sosnik and John Podesta to the adjoining dining room, scene of so many meetings with Monica Lewinsky that would ultimately lead to this day. Clinton remained stoic. As the vote on Article IV arrived, so did Vice President Gore.

"It's not fair, what they've done to you," Gore told him.

Clinton did not think so either. This was not about what *he* had done; this was about what *they* had done. The president defiantly refused to feel shamed by being impeached. He was the victim, not the culprit. And yet, while he was determined not to show it in public, this was as painful a day as he had ever had in his life. His friend and fund-raiser Terry McAuliffe, who had made it his mission to buck up Clinton during moments of despair, called to see how he was doing. The president launched into a fifteen-minute tirade about how people did not understand how this was tearing away at him.

"I have a knot in my gut," he told McAuliffe, about what this had done to his family.

Within an hour, a ragtag caravan of two buses and assorted cars began depositing Charlie Rangel and eighty other House Democrats at the White House to rally around their besieged leader. They gathered first without the media in the East Room, milling around the incongruously festive Christmas decorations. Because the room was decked out for holiday parties, no stage could be set up in the usual spot underneath the gold curtains, and no chairs could be brought in for the audience to sit. Instead, Clinton and the others who would address the group stationed themselves in the southeastern corner of the room and the congressmen simply crowded around them. The mood seemed more like an Irish wake than a Protestant funeral, a strange blend of gallows humor and sympathy for the dead. The lawmakers and White House aides chatted amiably and laughed nervously, not sure how one was supposed to act when one's president had been impeached. When Clinton entered, he accepted condolences and encouragement alike.

"The House people have good instincts on this, and that's how the history books will be written," Julian Epstein, the Judiciary counsel, told the president.

Clinton looked exhausted and emotionally spent, but not outwardly distraught. He gave the impression of someone who had already digested his fate and was turning over in his mind how to go on.

While all eyes were on the president, some of Clinton's aides did a double take when they saw who else had shown up. Hillary Clinton, who had been so effective at firing up the troops that morning, arrived at the East Room to shake hands and stand by her husband's side. Senior White House officials were surprised—she had not been listed for the event and had not given any indication that she planned to attend. None of the president's men would even think of asking her to, even if they believed she would agree. That she had chosen to come on her own, after months of barely speaking to Clinton, was a much welcomed development.

The speeches that followed sounded more like election-eve invigoration than election-night concessions. There was none of the morose meanderings of a Nixon as he flashed his fingers and boarded *Marine One* to depart the White House for good. Gephardt captured the spirit of the crowd with another passionate speech urging defiance.

"You cannot, you must not, you cannot, you must not, you cannot, you must not resign," he implored the president. "We will stay with you and fight with you until this madness is over."

Gore told the assembled Democrats that he and Gephardt had arrived in Congress on the same day twenty-two years earlier, and in all that time he had never heard a finer speech than that delivered on the floor by the minority leader earlier that day. "History will judge you as heroes," Gore assured the congressmen. There was a lot of hugging—Clinton, his eyes watering noticeably, embraced Gephardt, the man who was once ready to toss Clinton overboard if he had to. So did Gore, Gephardt's onetime ostensible rival for the next presidential nomination.

When it came time for Clinton to talk, he was somber but not broken. "I was proud to see you stand up for the Constitution today," he told the congressmen. Reflecting on Livingston's decision, the president said, "It broke my heart," and echoed Gephardt's plea from earlier in the day. "We need to take the hatred out of our public life." And yet he could not conceal his own bitterness. He told a story about the 1994 elections and the difference between Democrats and Republicans—Democrats think government achieves important goals, he said, while Republicans just like the power. "That's what this thing is about. It's about power." He also offered one more apology to the Democrats who had placed their own careers on the line to defend him, however reluctantly. "I would give anything if you had not been in the position you were in today, and if I had not acted in such a way as to put you there."

After the East Room event, Clinton walked across the Colonnade to the Oval Office with Gore, Gephardt, and Podesta to prepare to head out onto the South Lawn and address the nation. Once again, to the surprise of the president's aides, Hillary Clinton followed along. Apparently she intended to stand with him in public as well as in private.

When the scores of rank-and-file House Democrats had taken their place on the South Lawn, Clinton hugged his secretary Betty Currie, wiped his teary eyes, wrapped an arm around his wife, and at 4:15 P.M. marched out of the Oval Office to a spot just a few yards from the patch of grass where an awestruck Boys Nation teenager from Arkansas had shaken hands with John F. Kennedy more than three decades earlier. Shaking hands as he made his way through the crowd, Clinton put aside emotion and forced a smile intended to make him appear almost nonchalant, but his puffy left eye gave him away. His companions tried awkwardly to keep the mood almost casual, as if they were simply going out to address the latest wrinkle in a budget fight. The program reinforced the sense of a campaign-style event—three speakers would go first and then the president, surrounded by a phalanx from his own party to cheer him on. With the television cameras rolling, they would bash the other party and take their case to the public.

Podesta briefly thanked the members for coming, and then Gephardt decried what he called "a partisan vote that was a disgrace to our country and our Constitution." But it was Gore who unknowingly peeled back a bit of the president's protective layer that day, offering unmodulated praise that had Clinton tearing up and biting his lip just a step behind the vice president.

"What happened as a result does a great disservice to a man I believe will be regarded in the history books as one of our greatest presidents," Gore intoned as aides winced at a phrase they instantly knew could come back to haunt the vice president in the 2000 race to succeed Clinton. "There is no doubt in my mind that the verdict of history will undo the unworthy judgment rendered a short while ago in the United States Capitol." To the applause of the gathered Democrats, Gore introduced Clinton as "my friend, America's great president."

Clinton stepped up to the blue-topped lectern with the presidential seal, placed his hands on its sides, and stared forward. Intuitively conscious of the camera and how it caught him, the president mostly kept his chin up and his expression confident and poised, although as soon as he looked down for a second, a crescendo of shutters fired away, capturing a moment that in the morning newspapers would make him look somber and dejected, despite his best efforts. Standing near a magnolia tree planted by Andrew Jackson, the only president ever censured by the Senate, Clinton now pleaded for the same fate.

"I have accepted responsibility for what I did wrong in my personal life," he said as the first lady nodded, "and I have invited members of Congress to work with us to find a reasonable, bipartisan, and proportionate response. That approach was rejected today by Republicans in the House. But I hope it will be embraced in the Senate." In keeping with his stick-to-policy strategy, he quickly rattled off the issues he wanted to work on with the other party, from Social Security and Medicare to education and patients' rights. "We must stop the politics of personal destruction. We must get rid of the poisonous venom of excessive partisanship, obsessive animosity, and uncontrolled anger. That is not what America deserves." He then turned to the most important message of his brief appearance. Asserting that he had spent six years working to bring the parties together, he said, "It's what I intend to do for two more, until the last hour of the last day of my term." He would not resign, he was saying, not under any circumstances.

"I ask the American people to move with me, to go on from here, to rise above the rancor, to overcome the pain and division, to be a repairer of the breach, all of us, to make this country as one America, what it can and must be for our children in the new century about to dawn."

As the Democrats around him applauded, Clinton took Hillary's hand and headed back for the White House. *His* White House. They would not drive him out.

Stunned or not, House Republicans did not mourn for Bob Livingston for long. Even as he was making his unexpected announcement, some members were racing around the floor, trying to encourage Henry Hyde or Dick Armey to run for Speaker. Congressman Bill Paxon, DeLay's adviser, did not wait for the speech to end either before ushering Denny Hastert into the whip's office.

"You either have to run or you have to leave," Paxon told him. Having turned down a draft to run for majority leader after the November election, Hastert could not turn down a top post twice and stay.

Hastert went to a phone booth to call his wife. Paxon did not wait and started spreading the word that Hastert would be the next Speaker. A group of lobbyist-lieutenants quickly assembled in DeLay's office to begin organizing, including several veteran Paxon advisers and Hastert's best friend, lobbyist Dan Mattoon, who left his four children with a neighbor and rushed to the Capitol after watching Livingston's speech on television. Livingston and Gingrich weighed in on Hastert's behalf as well, and any momentary opposition quickly dissipated. But Hastert himself was still reluctant. He came back to DeLay and Paxon and told them that his wife did not want him to run. Paxon raced off to a phone and called the Hastert home himself, only to find that the Illinois congressman's wife was in fact supportive. The real hesitation, it seemed, was in Hastert himself. DeLay and Paxon confronted Hastert with what they had learned and he agreed to give it some more thought. Retreating to a side room off the floor, Hastert prayed alone for about fifteen minutes. Finally, he emerged to tell DeLay and Paxon that he would do it.

While support was solidifying for Hastert, however, the situation was still chaotic enough for imaginations to run wild. After the vote on Article I, Charlie Rangel, the liberal Democrat organizing the White House rally, found Pete King, the maverick Republican who had defied his party on impeachment, and asked to see him off the floor. They walked through the Speaker's Lobby into a hallway, where Rangel laid out an idea: What if King ran for Speaker with the support of the Democrats and a handful of his Republican allies? Given all that had happened, the House could use a coalition leadership, suggested Rangel, who did not mention it but presumably thought that shared power might mean a chairmanship for himself, given his standing as the ranking Democrat on the powerful Ways and Means Committee.

It was clearly a ludicrous notion. Even if such a coup were feasible, it would only work once before the Republicans regrouped and tossed King out at the next opportunity. To King the proposal drove home the insanity of the day, showing just how far things had unraveled. He told Rangel he would think about it, but never brought it up again, fearing that the image of a liberal Democrat offering him the Speakership would only confirm to conservative critics within his own party that he was a traitor siding with the enemy camp.

It was all a moot point by now anyway. The fix was already in for Hastert. Some Republicans had even approached Livingston, asking him to reconsider, and he started to waver, thinking maybe he should not step down after all. DeLay quashed that thought. "It's over," he told Livingston. Indeed, DeLay and Paxon had quickly rounded up enough votes to install Hastert without opposition. At a Republican conference meeting shortly after the last impeachment vote, they had petitions for Hastert already printed and Gingrich lined up to speak on his behalf. As soon as Gingrich was done, operatives positioned at the end of each row handed out the petitions. Hastert walked out with sixty or seventy signatures and, for all intents and purposes, the Speakership. The Campaign won and Hastert installed, DeLay left for the airport and Houston. "This is Denny's hour," he said.

Hastert seemed a little dizzy at the development. After one of the quickest political ascensions in modern times, Hastert was preparing to go home when a pair of Capitol Police officers arrived and informed him they would drive him. Hastert demurred. The officers insisted. "Sir," one said firmly, "we'll be driving you home." Only at that point did it sink in that the former wrestling coach was now the third-ranking official in the United States.

There was unfinished business at the White House too. After returning to the Oval Office, the newly impeached commander in chief met again with his national security team and decided to call a halt to the bombing runs over Iraq. The strike had already been extended one night longer than originally planned because bomb-damage assessments had indicated that initial runs had missed critical targets. With Ramadan arriving, Clinton did not want to risk antagonizing the Arab world by prolonging it. At 6 P.M., he summoned television cameras into the Roosevelt Room for his second nationally televised address of the afternoon to announce the cessation of hostilities. To his enemies, it was one more piece of proof that the raids were simply political—as soon as impeachment was voted, he called them off. To his supporters, it was evidence that the president was able to remain focused on the job at hand and not shirk his duties because of his political problems. Either way, it was a whipsaw ending to a neck-breaking day. "There will never be another day like this," John Podesta told Doug Sosnik as night fell.

At 6:30 P.M., Clinton called Pete King to thank him for all he had done on his behalf. It was a short conversation, maybe ten minutes, but the president sounded composed. History, he said, would show that King did the right thing. Then he asked after King's wife, who was sick with pneumonia. She got on the phone briefly to hear his get-well wishes.

"Mr. President," King said when he got the phone back, "you should realize there are people in my party who just hate you."

CHAPTER ELEVEN

"We are fighting for the presidency of the United States"

The calls were ominous. Unless he left the president alone, Lindsey Graham was warned, he would be "outed" as gay. Some of the threats were telephoned anonymously to his district office in South Carolina. Another came in a conversation with a home state reporter who told him that Larry Flynt planned to claim Graham was secretly homosexual. The forty-three-year-old unmarried congressman had fretted privately with fellow Republicans during the fall that he would "probably be confessing my sins before this is over," but this was going too far. A conservative from a conservative state, Graham knew that even such whispers could hurt him, and he quickly denied being gay. At least some of his critics accepted that, judging by other anonymous messages coming into his office at the same time—these callers threatened to expose various affairs he was supposed to be having with certain women.

With Flynt's $1 million bounty still on the table and Bob Livingston's scalp on his belt, it was clear all the old rules had been discarded. Elected officials could be accused of being gay, they could be accused of being womanizers, and they could even be accused of being both at the same time. The microscope that had uncovered Clinton's sins threatened everyone. Nor did the vote by the House end the anxiety for Graham or most of the other Republicans on the Judiciary Committee. They had another task ahead of them. Under the Constitution, the House was charged with prosecuting the president in a Senate trial, and Henry Hyde had assembled a team of twelve other "managers," as they were to be called, to join him in handling the case. He originally came up with a list of eight, but several committee members lobbied to be included and so he was left with an unwieldy baker's dozen. Hyde flirted with appointing one of the few Democrats who had voted for impeachment on the floor to present a bipartisan team, but Dick Gephardt did not want anyone from his caucus to participate because it would lend legitimacy to the prosecution. For newly appointed managers like Graham, the assignment meant a shot at history—but also the risk of watching their personal lives exposed or false rumors peddled so widely they became accepted as truth.

Asa Hutchinson had been lucky back in September when he was warned he would be the "next target" after Hyde's old infidelity was disclosed; nothing ever came of it. Bob Barr, though, knew Flynt had lawyers scouring through his divorce records for evidence of unfaithfulness. Among the women Graham had been linked to in the gossip trade was Mary Bono, one of the committee Republicans who had not joined the team of managers. Hailing from the celebrity world, Bono faced numerous such rumors. Among others, she had been accused in the *National Enquirer* of having cheated on her late husband. Bono grew so infuriated at the charge that she hired a lawyer and paid him $5,000 to explore a possible lawsuit. She also was said to be dating Congressman Steve Buyer, her fellow committee Republican, who had joined Hyde's team of managers.

In the cloakrooms, no one appeared more nervous to his Republican colleagues than Buyer. A forty-year-old former army lawyer who had served during the Persian Gulf War in 1990 providing legal advice at a prisoner-of-war camp, Buyer had first won his seat in the House two years later in the same election that elevated Clinton to the presidency. Buyer could be alternately charming and prickly but impressed compatriots as a serious legislator with a strong interest in military issues. Deservedly or not, he also had something of a reputation for flirting with attractive female congressional aides. And by befriending the recently widowed Bono, he had raised more than a few eyebrows among fellow Republicans, who figured that, even if nothing was going on, it was reckless to invite speculation. Both Buyer and Bono denied to associates that they were anything more than friends, but Buyer began to worry that Flynt had targeted him.

Fearing the worst, he decided to confess all to his wife, Joni. Buyer made a mental list of all the situations he had been in that could be compromising and disclosed it to her. While he did not tell friends in the House exactly how he had strayed, he left them with the distinct impression that he had good reason to worry. "Look, there were all these accusations out there," Buyer told a fellow committee member. "I was so nervous. I was so uptight. I even talked to my wife." Joni accepted what he told her and told him not to worry, that she had been unfairly impugned when she was younger, Buyer related. Then, with obvious relief, he sighed, "I'm a free man."

Trent Lott and Tom Daschle were determined to avoid the ugliness of the House proceeding. They wanted none of the rank partisanship and personal destruction they had witnessed on the other side of the Capitol. Shortly after the House vote, the two spoke by phone and were relieved to find each other of like minds. The two party leaders had not talked much since the November election, and Daschle was nervous about how aggressive Lott would feel, particularly given his outburst against the military strike on Iraq. Lott had no great love for Clinton—"You can't trust this guy about anything," he told advisers—but the majority leader knew how to count and was convinced the Senate would not convict. Lott had been horrified to hear at a meeting with Senate lawyers on December 7 that a trial could drag on for more than four months. Nothing constructive could be accomplished by that, he concluded, only the same sort of political meltdown that the House had just experienced. Lott resolved to keep that from happening in the Senate. In their conversation, Daschle agreed to help "copilot the plane" to a safe landing.

Lott and Daschle were an unlikely pair of copilots. Although each had spent the last three decades on Capitol Hill and cared deeply about its institutions, they approached their jobs in drastically different fashions. Tall and exuberant with immaculately combed hair that never seemed to move even in a stiff wind, Lott led his caucus much like the former male cheerleader he had been on the sidelines at Ole Miss—constantly smiling, clapping his hands, and egging on colleagues to do what he wanted. Daschle, shorter and bookish-looking in his round-framed glasses, came across as Lott's studious cousin who seemed a little embarrassed by him and yet could not help liking the gregarious older man. Where Lott had a way of trying to dominate a room and relished establishing control of any situation, Daschle used the little end of the gavel when he ran meetings, preferring to sit back and listen until the group had collectively talked its way through a problem. Their paths to this point, though, were remarkably similar. Both had come to the capital from backwater states as young congressional aides, won election to the House, and later moved on to the Senate, where they beat tough competition to lead their respective party caucuses. Despite the partisanship that often flavored debate in the Senate, Lott and Daschle got along far better than either of their staffs wished.

Lott, fifty-seven, the son of a pipe fitter at a shipbuilding plant, earned bachelor's and law degrees from the University of Mississippi and came to Washington in 1968 to work for a conservative Democratic congressman, William M. Colmer, who retired four years later and left his seat to his brash young assistant. In making his initial run in 1972, though, Lott switched parties and ran as a Republican, a rarity in those days in the Old South area around his hometown of Pascagoula. The dicey issue of impeachment confronted him almost right away as a junior member of the House Judiciary Committee, where he voted against throwing Richard Nixon out of office.

During his years in the House, Lott worked closely with other firebrands, including Newt Gingrich, and won election to the Senate in 1988. After the 1994 election, Lott organized a conservative revolt to oust Bob Dole's whip, Alan Simpson, by a single vote. After succeeding Dole as majority leader in 1996, though, Lott demonstrated a pragmatic streak, showing that he knew how to cut deals if he did not have the votes.

Daschle, fifty-one, grew up in small-town South Dakota, earned a degree from the state university, and served for three years as an air force intelligence officer. He too found his way to Washington on the strength of a staff pass, going to work for Senator James Abourezk in 1972. Daschle was elected to the House six years later and to the Senate eight years after that. In 1994, while Lott was toppling Simpson, Daschle achieved an underdog victory of his own, edging past Senator Chris Dodd of Connecticut for the post of minority leader, also by a single vote. His soft-spoken, consensus-driven style proved popular in a caucus that bridled at overbearing leaders, to the point where Dodd would soon say that his colleagues had made the right choice in picking Daschle over him. While Daschle tried to work closely with the White House, he also liked to assert his independence. In his first Sunday television talk-show appearance after winning the leadership job, Daschle made a point of saying, "We want to work with the White House, not for them."

Both Lott and Daschle spent the days after their phone conversation reaching out to their own caucuses. With the Senate out of session and its members scattered around the country, the two leaders could only touch base with their colleagues one at a time in a marathon series of calls. Daschle, who spoke with all forty-four other Democratic senators before Christmas, termed it "a sequential caucus." While both detected considerable desire to dispose of the issue as quickly as possible, Lott also heard an earful from senators who were insisting on nothing short of a full trial with witnesses, while Daschle was picking up enough anger at Clinton from his caucus to be concerned. Daschle's survey suggested that if the vote were held then, there would not be twelve Democratic votes for conviction, the minimum needed assuming the fifty-five Republicans remained unified. But senators were holding back, careful not to commit. Some, including Robert Byrd and Harry Reid of Nevada, the minority whip, were particularly incensed at what was now being called the "pep rally" on the South Lawn of the White House following the impeachment, finding it unseemly. When it came time for an up-or-down vote, Daschle thought he would lose five or six Democrats—including Byrd and possibly Senators Bob Kerrey of Nebraska, Daniel Patrick Moynihan of New York, Russ Feingold of Wisconsin, Bob Graham of Florida, and either of two newcomers from conservative, anti-Clinton states, Evan Bayh of Indiana or John Edwards of North Carolina. In a worst-case scenario, if momentum really turned against the president, Daschle counted up to twenty Democratic votes he thought could go against Clinton. That was unlikely, he believed, but not impossible.

Another bipartisan pair of senators was consulting by phone in the days after the House vote as well. Joe Lieberman, the righteous Democratic senator from Connecticut who had been so offended by Clinton's conduct the previous fall, had grown just as dismayed at the partisanship in the House and now wanted to find a way to bring the controversy to a decorous end. He called his friend Republican senator Slade Gorton from Washington State, another former state attorney general. Lieberman had worked with Gorton in the past and considered him a fellow pragmatist who would set aside ideology in search of a reasonable solution; he also knew that Gorton was close to Lott. As it turned out, Gorton felt the same way about the Lewinsky case and had been planning to call Lieberman. They agreed to work on a plan to short-circuit a trial.

Lieberman and Gorton were not the only ones trying to broker a middle-ground solution. With White House encouragement, two former presidents joined the discussion. After a phone call from Vice President Gore, Jimmy Carter teamed up with his Republican predecessor, Gerald R. Ford, who had spoken with Chuck Ruff. In an opinion piece in the *New York Times* on Monday, December 21, two days after the House vote, they proposed a deal in which the Senate would censure the president and Clinton would acknowledge that he did not tell the truth under oath, with the understanding that an admission could not be used against him in a criminal trial. On the same day, four House Republicans who had voted for impeachment just forty-eight hours earlier embraced essentially the same solution in a letter to Lott. "We are not convinced, and do not want our votes interpreted to mean that we view removal from office as the only reasonable conclusion of this case," Congressmen Sherwood Boehlert, Mike Castle, Ben Gilman, and Jim Greenwood wrote. Their letter did not explain why they had voted against the Democratic move to censure Clinton in the House, lending ammunition to White House aides who suspected they were forced to vote for impeachment against their will.

Byrd weighed in as well. The stern Democratic senator from West Virginia signaled that he was open to "some other solution" than a full trial—just so long as Clinton and his advisers kept out of it. "To a very large degree, we are now navigating in previously uncharted waters, but one thing is clear," Byrd said. "For the good of our nation, there must be no 'deal' involving the White House or any entity beyond the current membership of the U.S. Senate." By "current," he meant that George Mitchell and Bob Dole should keep their noses out of it as well.

*   *   *

How did it feel to be the first impeached president in 130 years?

"Not bad," Clinton answered casually.

In the hours and days after the House vote, Clinton was determined not to show any wounds. Hosting friends at a holiday party at the White House, he made light of his situation, telling jokes and asserting that in ten or twenty years it would become clear he was on the right side of history. Proceeding with parties such as the one in the State Dining Room, all decked out in holiday colors, was Clinton's way of getting through a painful period. If he treated it like business as usual—or, rather, politics as usual—then it lessened the sting. Indeed, the friends and college classmates who surrounded him at these events seemed more distressed than he did. Or at least more than he let on.

Still, signs of the rage that smoldered inside occasionally showed through. Clinton told his friends that he "purged" himself regularly of his anger by turning to a wide array of advisers, including Jim Wright and Nelson Mandela. A Louisiana minister had urged him to remain the "light" in the face of the "dark" forces of the Republican Congress and not to fight them directly because when light mixed with darkness, it only became gray. The lesson Clinton had drawn from such advice was to leave his battle to lawyers and allies. If he engaged himself, Clinton told his guests, he risked losing the support of the American people, who had stuck with him because they believed he remained focused on his job, not survival. But he now recognized the trade-offs involved in that approach. By going forward with his trip to the Middle East instead of staying to lobby swing Republicans, he had made it easier for the House to impeach him. Clinton said his biggest mistake came in the heady days immediately after the November election when he did not lock in the moderate Republicans who wanted to vote against impeachment by pressuring them to commit publicly.

The surrogates the president had relied on were reevaluating their strategy now as well. The largely unspoken secret among his lawyers was that even they believed Clinton had lied under oath in the Paula Jones deposition. As attorneys, they could make the case that his testimony about Monica Lewinsky was not material to the lawsuit and therefore did not constitute perjury as defined by federal statute. But they knew as well as anyone that the president did not tell the truth, the whole truth, and nothing but the truth. Greg Craig, for one, could understand how Clinton might not have understood the definition of *sexual relations* used at the deposition because even the judge appeared confused. However, Craig believed the president's assertion that he had no specific recollection of being alone with Lewinsky was a bald-faced lie. There was no getting around that.

As a result, for all the despair surrounding the impeachment vote in the

House, Craig and the other presidential attorneys were able to find a silver lining—the rejection of Article II, the civil perjury count. The House Republicans did them an enormous favor by knocking out the one charge that was hardest to defend against. The main reason the White House team had not mounted much of a factual defense during the House hearings was that Craig and the others calculated there was no way to defend the president's testimony in the Jones case. The grand jury perjury and the obstruction allegations were different. The disputed testimony before the grand jury was far more ambiguous than in the civil deposition and dealt with narrower questions, such as what month the relationship had actually started and whether the president had actually touched certain parts of Lewinsky's body. Similarly, many of the events labeled as obstruction by the House had alternative explanations that could at least raise reasonable doubt—Betty Currie testified that it was Lewinsky's idea to hide the gifts, not the president's, for example, and no one had testified to an explicit link between the job search and the false affidavit. Unlike in the civil testimony, a basis for a factual defense existed in both remaining articles of impeachment.

Meeting a few days after the impeachment vote, Craig and the other lawyers decided to recalibrate their strategy now that Article II was no longer on the table. If the Senate did hold a trial, they decided, they would put on a real factual defense for the first time. They would not simply argue that Alexander Hamilton and James Madison would never have wanted a president thrown out of office for this type of conduct; they would talk about the evidence and try to make the case that the prosecutors had not established proof that Clinton did what they said he did.

Over the next few days, Craig and the others pored through the evidence books and pulled out material that undercut the House charges against the president. Craig, bearing color-coded documents, then met with a few select reporters from major newspapers to privately spotlight the holes in the case. The White House, he told them, was not afraid of the facts. Not any more, at least. Other White House aides burned when they heard what Craig had done—he had telegraphed their new strategy in the media and made it easier for the opposition. Press secretary Joe Lockhart fumed at the leak, and Doug Sosnik was assigned to take Craig to the woodshed.

Either way, the president's team was still searching for ways to avoid a trial altogether. The most obvious way to head off a trial would be a motion to dismiss the case, which could be filed the day the Senate opened its proceedings and would require only a simple majority. Assuming he could hold the forty-five Democrats, Clinton would have to win over just six Republicans to toss out the charges—a number that did not seem out of reach, considering the number of moderates who had expressed distaste at the prospect of a trial. Even if they could not get an absolute majority, they would presumably garner at least thirty-four votes, demonstrating from the outset that there was no chance for a two-thirds vote for conviction and possibly spurring on the Republican leadership to cut short the trial.

Another tactic under consideration at the White House was a constitutional challenge to the legitimacy of the House vote because it had occurred after the election and before the new Congress was to be sworn in. Bruce Ackerman, a Yale Law School professor, had raised such an attack on a "lame-duck" impeachment when he had appeared before the Judiciary Committee as a Clinton defense witness earlier in the month. Now the president's lawyers, particularly Craig and David Kendall, were intrigued about whether he might be right. If they could get Chief Justice William H. Rehnquist, acting as presiding officer at a Senate trial, to throw out the articles of impeachment based on that argument, it would force the House to take another vote, this time with five more Democrats. That would not make a difference in the grand jury charge, but they might be able to defeat the obstruction of justice article on a second try. Since it only passed 221–212, a swing of five votes would change that to 216–217. Narrowing the case in the Senate to just a single article would make their job that much easier.

White House aides raised other possible motions they could file as well. They suggested a motion barring Asa Hutchinson from serving as a manager because his brother, Senator Tim Hutchinson, was serving as a member of the "jury." It did not take long to rule that idea out, however, after a little research showed that such conflicts of interest were allowed during the Andrew Johnson trial. In 1868, the Senate permitted the participation of one senator who was Johnson's son-in-law and another who was the Senate's president pro tempore and under the line of succession at the time would have taken over as president in the event of a conviction.

Aside from tactics, the president's team was also reevaluating its messengers. While unhappy with Craig's backdoor contacts with reporters, his fellow White House aides decided he should play a more public role, given that he had been the most effective advocate for the president on television. But that was not enough. Craig and most of the others involved in constructing the White House defense had Senate experience and knew they would be better off if they had someone of stature who could relate to the senators as a peer. When Johnson had gone on trial 131 years earlier, his attorney general had resigned and signed up as his chief defense lawyer. The leading candidate for Clinton was George Mitchell, the former Senate majority leader, who had declined to come on board in the fall. Mitchell had an odd history with Clinton. The president had wanted to put him on the Supreme Court a few years back, but the former senator "played Hamlet," in the view of the White

House, and never committed. After Clinton won reelection, however, Mitchell wanted to be secretary of state in the second term, only to lose out to Madeleine Albright. Still, as the president's emissary, Mitchell had played the critical role in forcing peace in Northern Ireland, an achievement Clinton considered among his most important legacies.

When the White House contacted him again about coming to Clinton's rescue in his worst domestic political crisis, Mitchell was still reluctant but agreed to think about it. Steve Ricchetti, the deputy chief of staff, assigned Special Counsel Lanny Breuer to be his liaison and to prepare the briefing books that would get Mitchell ready to join the defense team.

"The chief justice has less of a role than he might imagine." The Senate's chief lawyer tried to be delicate. The Senate's parliamentarian was more blunt about it: William Rehnquist should leave the decisions to the Senate.

While Lott and Daschle were working their caucuses, their aides were busy preparing as well. Senate legal counsel Thomas B. Griffith, parliamentarian Bob Dove, Lott chief of staff David Hoppe, and Daschle aide William V. Corr began a marathon round of meetings with House officials, White House lawyers, and others to figure out what everyone wanted and to make sure they understood who was really in charge—the Senate. The most sensitive meeting was with the chief justice's right-hand aide.

At 9:30 A.M. on Tuesday, December 22, just three days after the House vote, the Senate officials met in the office of the sergeant at arms with Rehnquist chief of staff Jim Duff. Under the Constitution, the chief justice would preside over the trial, but the precise parameters of that role were fuzzy since only one other chief justice had ever served in that capacity. Rehnquist was intimately familiar with that precedent, having written a book about impeachment called *Grand Inquests,* which reconstructed the Andrew Johnson trial. But acting on behalf of Lott and Daschle, Griffith and the others wanted Rehnquist to understand that the senators were not looking for a heavy hand from the rostrum. While a Republican appointee, Griffith was a pragmatic lawyer who shunned ideology in favor of his broader mission of protecting the prerogatives of his institution. Griffith was worried Rehnquist would take it upon himself to rule on a White House motion to dismiss, something he knew the senators would strenuously object to. So Griffith and the others reminded Duff that the Senate could overturn any rulings by Rehnquist on a simple majority vote, and that, in any case, they believed he should rule only on evidentiary and "incidental" questions, neither of which would cover a dismissal motion. Duff was sympathetic without offering commitments. Another tricky issue involved setting the ground rules for the trial. Duff said the chief justice wanted to hold pretrial conferences with both parties, much as any judge in a normal trial might, but Griffith and the others were reluctant to involve him. It was the Senate's show, they said.

All of this amounted to a calculated bluff. Griffith and the others knew the Senate could never overrule Rehnquist because he wore the black robe. If the Republican majority were to reverse a ruling by the chief justice, particularly a known conservative such as Rehnquist, it would be seen as a strictly political move to tamper with the judgments of an independent presiding officer. That was why Griffith and the others wanted to lay down markers at the beginning in the hope that Rehnquist would not force such a confrontation.

In case the message that he would not really be in charge was not clear enough, the chief justice would soon get a pointed reminder. Visiting the Senate chamber to familiarize himself with the layout and the equipment soon after Griffith's meeting with Duff, Rehnquist noticed the microphone while trying out the chair at the top of the rostrum.

"How do I activate the microphone?" Rehnquist asked.

"You don't," answered the sergeant at arms, James W. Ziglar. That too was controlled by Senate officials.

Over the Christmas holiday, Lieberman and Gorton devised a mechanism for wrapping up the case in a hurry. Their plan would allow each side a day to present opening arguments, followed by a day of questioning by senators. Then on the fourth day, the Senate would begin debating in open session whether the charges, if true as presented, rose to the level of high crimes and misdemeanors. With each senator allowed up to ten minutes to speak, the deliberations could stretch into a fifth and sixth day, but at that point, only if two-thirds of the senators agreed—the same margin required for conviction by the Constitution—would the trial move to a second phase that would involve witnesses and more extended debate. Otherwise, the Senate would adjourn the trial and then, after the chief justice had left the presiding chair, move to consider a bipartisan resolution censuring the president.

Lieberman committed the plan to writing in a December 28 memo and sent it to Gorton. "The above procedure completes the trial within a week, and debate and votes on a censure resolution within no more than another week, allowing the nation and the Senate to return to our normal business without having brought the sordid details of this case onto the Senate floor," Lieberman wrote, never imagining that two-thirds of his colleagues might vote to continue to a full-fledged trial. "The above procedure does not, however, excuse the President's misconduct or minimize the damage it has caused to the country and the presidency."

Lieberman and Gorton presented this idea to Lott and seemed to win him over. He liked the brevity. He liked the idea that there would be an early vote.

There was no use in dragging it on for weeks if everyone knew the outcome was fixed. Daschle liked the plan too, as did the White House. But as Lott began circulating it, he quickly ran into a wall of opposition from Henry Hyde and the managers as well as a number of his Senate Republican colleagues—not just conservatives, such as Don Nickles, the majority whip from Oklahoma, and Phil Gramm, the feisty former Democrat from Texas, but key moderates as well. Senator Arlen Specter, an iconoclastic moderate from Pennsylvania who earlier had publicly advocated abandoning impeachment proceedings and simply letting Clinton take his chances in criminal court after leaving office, told Lott on the phone that if the Senate did proceed with a trial, it should do it right, including calling witnesses.

Lott unwittingly provoked more criticism of any potential bipartisan deal within his own ranks by telling the Associated Press the next day that no new testimony needed to be taken to evaluate the case. "Are witnesses required? I don't think so. I think the record is there to be reviewed, read, presented in a form that [House prosecutors] choose." He added, "That would be sufficient."

The fax machine in Greg Craig's office began whirring at 1:49 P.M. that same day, Tuesday, December 29. While Craig and the other White House defense lawyers were thrilled with the Gorton-Lieberman plan, they knew they had to be prepared to fight on other fronts in case it did not work. In recent days, Craig had been conferring about the lame-duck argument with Bruce Ackerman, who had taught him at Yale. That afternoon, the law professor sent down a forty-seven-page paper intended to help the White House make the case that Clinton's impeachment should not force the Senate to conduct a trial. Ackerman's paper maintained that the two articles of impeachment would expire with the end of the 105th Congress on January 3 like any other legislation passed in one house but not the other. Unless the newly elected House reauthorized them, there was no basis for a trial. To back up his thesis, Ackerman relied on the Twentieth Amendment to the Constitution, which was adopted in 1933 to curtail lame-duck legislative activity by moving up the beginning of the next congressional session after each election. "If this lame-duck impeachment is allowed to go forward, a terrible precedent will be created for the future," Ackerman wrote in the paper sent to Craig. "Whenever the opposition party controls the House, a setback at the polls will tempt them to begin a lame-duck impeachment process against their political opponent in the White House."

The problem was that other specialists disputed Ackerman's analysis—including the Congressional Research Service and Charles Tiefer, a former House lawyer who wrote the book on congressional procedures. As recently as a decade earlier, the House had impeached a judge in one session (albeit before the election) and the Senate went forward with a trial in the next session without the impeachment being revoted.

As he read through Ackerman's paper, Craig and his colleagues were still mulling over several other possible tactics as well. In addition to a basic motion to dismiss, they were drafting motions intended to challenge the validity of the articles of impeachment on the grounds that they were improperly vague and bundled multiple allegations into the same charge, even though they were not dramatically different from the articles of impeachment advanced against Nixon in 1974. Theoretically, Craig and other White House lawyers reasoned, Rehnquist could throw out the two articles against Clinton if he found them poorly drafted, and given his jurisprudential background, the chief justice might be more of a stickler for getting the details right.

At the same time, Hyde was meeting with his fellow managers to discuss plans for the trial, and the group came away determined to call witnesses. The chairman was particularly peeved at Lott's public comments about no need for witnesses. While Hyde was not sure they were needed either, he could not believe the Senate majority leader was trying to tell the prosecutors how to put on their case. Hyde dispatched a three-page letter to Lott the next day, Wednesday, December 30, expressing his irritation: "The Senate should hear from live witnesses. Indeed, federal courts have long recognized the importance of live testimony in their rulings and their instructions to juries. I believe that a fair presentation of the evidence and a full defense by the president can be expeditious. We need not sacrifice substance and duty for speed."

Lott first heard about the letter from reporters and found himself as aggravated at the lack of warning as Hyde had been at the majority leader's earlier comment. Lott called Hyde at home to complain about the ambush. "If you have any problems, take them up with me, not in the press," Lott griped.

Hyde agreed. "It's a good idea—if we have problems, we should talk about it before we air it out in public." Perhaps the letter had been too harsh, and it should certainly have been withheld from the press until it was delivered, Hyde felt, but he wanted to make sure to get Lott's attention.

He had it now. For Lott, the managers were already developing into another constituency to juggle on top of the myriad factions within his own Senate caucus. By impeaching Clinton, the managers had become folk heroes among conservative Republican core voters and Lott knew he could not afford to alienate the party's base. At the same time he was looking for a speedy end to the trial, Lott was concluding that he also had to find a way to mollify the managers.

*   *   *

The prospect of a protracted trial was weighing heavily on the White House. Personally, physically, and psychologically, the bone-weary staff could not bear the notion that it might drag on much longer. The longer it lasted, the higher the "opportunity cost" in lost legislation—all the more critical now in trying to rehabilitate the impeached president's legacy before he left office— and the greater the chance that some new disaster could befall the Clinton White House. Another intern could be discovered, more evidence of obstruction might turn up, Juanita Broaddrick could go public with her allegation of rape—anything seemed possible. Given the partisan polarization, the trial seemed unlikely to threaten Clinton's presidency, but the one thing Clinton's legal and political advisers had learned over the last year was to beware when the situation appeared under control because that was usually when the roof would cave in.

Another opportunity cost of a long trial turned out to be George Mitchell. Steve Ricchetti, the deputy chief of staff, and Lanny Breuer, the special counsel, had been wooing him for weeks, and Mitchell sat down with the president's lawyers several times—always at Williams & Connolly, to avoid being spotted by the White House press corps, which hovered around the West Wing. But finally in early January, he told Ricchetti he would not come on board in an official capacity. Mitchell explained that politics had ruined his previous marriage, and now that he had a new wife and a new child, he wanted to devote his time to them. The thought of an ordeal that would consume him for months was unappealing. Besides, Mitchell knew his own negatives as well as anyone and rattled them off for the White House team—he was not well liked among the Republicans, who saw him as excessively partisan. Moreover, he did not want to step on Daschle's toes, one more reason why he preferred meeting in secret at Williams & Connolly. But Mitchell was willing to help and offered sharp analysis of the situation: how Lott had to juggle the fire-breathers within his own caucus, including his whip, Don Nickles, who was to Lott what Lott once was to Bob Dole; how the Gorton-Lieberman plan was likely to play with certain groups of senators; how Pat Moynihan, the Democratic senator from New York, was really trying to help the president even if he looked to be shafting him. One point Mitchell emphasized was that senators in both parties simply did not like Clinton, and the Democrats in particular were irate that they had to clean up his political mess.

The tips from Mitchell helped the White House aides finalize their central strategy for any Senate trial. Whatever they did with motions, factual rebuttals, or witnesses would be governed by one simple imperative—holding together the Democratic caucus. Republicans in this trial would be irrelevant, they knew, because, as Doug Sosnik had warned Clinton almost a year earlier, only Democrats could force him from office. The president would place his fate in Daschle's hands and do whatever the minority leader told him to do. The arguments to be presented on the floor would be calibrated entirely to appeal to Democratic senators. And most of all, the Clinton lawyers would aim their powers of persuasion at a single senator, Robert Byrd. If they could avoid alienating him, they believed, the White House could head off any wholesale defections and guarantee that Clinton would finish his term.

"Why do we need witnesses?"

The question hung in the air in the conference room at the Rayburn Building. It came not from a White House defense attorney or even a skeptical senator but from Henry Hyde. The head of the House prosecution team was meeting with his managers on Monday, January 4, and asking them the same question everyone kept asking him.

Despite his public outburst against Lott, Hyde was deeply skeptical about the desirability of witnesses in a Senate trial. They had thousands of pages of testimony under oath already. The president's attorneys had not really disputed any of it, so why "reinvent the wheel," as Hyde had put it shortly after the November election when he had decided against calling witnesses during House hearings. Bringing witnesses to the well of the Senate, Hyde thought, would be more about show business than the profound constitutional duties they had before them. He was especially leery of Lewinsky appearing on the floor of the Senate. If she pranced out there, it would have sex written all over it and completely undercut everything they were trying to do with the case, he said.

"What are we going to accomplish with these witnesses?" Hyde asked his fellow managers.

The power of the story, several replied. The transcripts had the hard, cold facts, but could not bring the tale of deceit and manipulation to life the way witnesses could. "If a tree falls in the forest, no one hears," said Lindsey Graham. "We want people to hear us."

Hyde remained leery, and he was not the only one. Charles Canady and George Gekas, among others, expressed reservations. "It's bad to put Monica on," Gekas kept saying. "She can't add anything to the record, and she could recant part of her testimony and hurt us."

Hyde relented and put his trust in a quartet of managers he had designated as his evidence team—Asa Hutchinson, Jim Rogan, Bob Barr, and Congressman Edward G. Bryant of Tennessee. If they were so convinced that witnesses were necessary, then Hyde agreed to consider their plan for how they would run the trial. But he took care to emphasize the enormity of the task before them. This could not be a circus. "We are fighting for the presidency of the United States. The stakes could not be higher."

The next day, on Tuesday, January 5, Hutchinson finished a preliminary trial plan along with the rest of the evidence team and sent a copy to Hyde. They envisioned at least sixteen witnesses, who would testify to everything from the facts of the case to the nuances of the relevant sections of law. Under the plan, the managers would open the trial with a presentation about the president's oath of office, his constitutional responsibility to enforce the law, and a history of the Jones lawsuit. Their first witness would be U.S. district judge Susan Webber Wright, who would testify about her orders permitting the Jones lawyers to question Clinton about Lewinsky and about what she saw and heard while personally supervising the president's deposition, now almost a year before. The managers would then call expert witnesses on sexual harassment law and the impact of perjury. Their first choice was Robert Bonner, a former federal prosecutor, judge, and head of Drug Enforcement Administration, but they also listed as possibilities FBI director Louis Freeh and even New York mayor Rudolph Giuliani, a former U.S. attorney. Optional witnesses at this point of their presentation would be the forewoman of the grand jury in the Lewinsky case, a lawyer from Starr's office, and one of the judges who had assigned Starr to investigate the president's actions in the Jones case.

Next on the stand would be Lewinsky herself, plus one or more Secret Service agents, and then Clinton advisers John Podesta, Sidney Blumenthal, and Dick Morris, who would testify about what the president had told them regarding the former White House intern. The court reporter who had videotaped Clinton's deposition in the Jones lawsuit would be called to testify about whether the president appeared to be paying attention when his attorney said there was "no sex of any kind, in any manner, shape, or form" between Clinton and Lewinsky. Moving on to the obstruction allegations, the managers would put on another expert witness about prosecutions of public officials, again listing Giuliani as their preference. Then would come Betty Currie, Vernon Jordan, and Revlon chief Ronald O. Perelman to talk about the gifts, witness coaching, and job search. Finally, even though the articles passed by the House dealt entirely with Lewinsky, the trial plan would conclude by focusing on the president's "pattern and practice of intimidation and use of false affidavits," with Kathleen Willey and her lawyer, Daniel Gecker, as the first two witnesses, to be followed by "other corroborating witnesses yet to be interviewed." David Schippers was not yet ready to surrender other avenues that he was forced to abandon during the House proceedings, and he had an ally in Lindsey Graham, who thought the president's history with women other than Lewinsky proved that he was more sinister than simply a weak-willed husband in a midlife crisis.

*   *   *

The managers were ready with their plan, but the senators were not. While hundreds of members of the new 106th Congress were on airplanes heading back to Washington to be sworn in, Lott and Daschle had yet to figure out what to do once they arrived. The Gorton-Lieberman plan now looked dead, buried by the reluctance of Senate Republicans to give short shrift to the managers and their case against Clinton. Daschle had drafted three possible scenarios, ranging from one that called for just a single day of presentations from each side followed by an immediate vote, to an extended schedule with a month of witnesses and final votes not taken until April 16. At the moment, anything looked possible.

On the day that Congress returned to town, Wednesday, January 6, Lott decided to meet with Hyde to try to figure out what the House team really wanted. Lott asked Senator Mitch McConnell of Kentucky, the incoming chairman of the Rules and Administration Committee, to join him, along with Senate lawyer Tom Griffith and the majority leader's counsel, Mike Wallace, a longtime friend from Mississippi hired to help through the trial. They met at 8:30 A.M. in Lott's hideaway, a summit of sorts between the country's two most important Republicans at the moment—each with conflicting interests and ambitions.

Hyde moved straight into his pitch. He said he understood the Senate would run the show and that the House managers were just guests, but emphasized that they could not simply be dismissed out of hand. "The managers are passionately committed to a fair trial," Hyde said. "They have put their careers on the line for this and they feel betrayed."

If they were not guaranteed a fair trial, Hyde suggested, his team might just "quit and walk out." That was part bluff, part recognition that his managers were already quite hot and it would be a trick to restrain them. Hyde said he needed an "irreducible minimum" of fifteen witnesses, but tried to reassure Lott that the managers did not want to embarrass the Senate. Lewinsky would be called only for the limited purpose of reaffirming her grand jury testimony as it related to perjury—meaning no explicit description of sex play with the president—and for a more extended discussion of the events that had led to the obstruction charge.

"The White House would be crazy to cross-examine her," Hyde said.

But if that calmed Lott, what he heard next could not have. Schippers, who had accompanied Hyde and was still intent on broadening the case beyond Lewinsky, suggested that some of the other witnesses might include Kathleen Willey and Dolly Kyle Browning. Those two could demonstrate other examples of perjury and obstruction, Schippers said. Other witnesses Schippers mentioned were Susan Webber Wright and Dan Gecker. Still, Schippers said the "irreducible minimum" of fifteen witnesses could actually be reduced, perhaps even down to five or six if both sides stipulated to the record as compiled by Starr and the Judiciary Committee.

One other thing the managers wanted—the right for Schippers to address the Senate on the floor. He was their lawyer. Otherwise, the case would be left entirely in the hands of thirteen politicians who had not been in a court-room in many years, if at all, going up against the elite of the Washington bar. In the impeachment trials of some judges, the House had hired lawyers to present the cases to senators, but that had always been in committee, not on the floor. Lott did not think for a second that Robert Byrd would stand for a lawyer addressing them on behalf of the House.

"We can't do that," Lott told Hyde flatly.

But the senators tried to reassure Hyde that the case would not be buried without consideration. One way or the other, McConnell said, there would be an up-or-down vote on the articles themselves. "It honors the Constitu-tion and does credit to the House," he said before the meeting broke up.

That promise reflected advice Lott was secretly receiving from a select group of political consultants and pollsters he had convened to help guide him through the minefield ahead. On the same morning Lott was huddling with Hyde, this rump group began meeting clandestinely to figure out the best way for the majority leader to proceed without fracturing the Republican Party. Even if acquittal was a foregone conclusion, ending the trial without a final up-or-down vote would spark a revolt by conservative voters who despised Clin-ton, these advisers told Lott's staff. Among those joining the strategy sessions with Lott's senior aides were former White House aide Tom Griscom, politi-cal consultants Ed Rogers and Ed Gillespie, and pollster Frank Luntz. They mapped out plans to get together at the Capitol every morning throughout the trial to help shape Lott's message, but even the existence of the meetings would be kept confidential, and the senator himself would never attend, to avoid look-ing as if he was allowing politics to dictate how to handle the case.

As it was, Lott had enough meetings to keep him busy. With senators back in town for the first time since the House vote, the Republican confer-ence convened for a marathon closed-door session that started in the morn-ing in the Mike Mansfield Room of the Capitol and then after lunch moved to the Lyndon B. Johnson Room. Their first opportunity to talk directly with one another led to a sort of political group-therapy session where many of the senators poured out anxieties about their predicament. Lott, still singed by the internal uprising against the Gorton-Lieberman plan, tried to calm the crowd.

"We've got to be fair," he told his fellow senators. "We've got to be consis-tent with what the House needs and we've got to be acceptable to Demo-crats." He emphasized that he would not let the Senate head down the same

path as the House. "We're not going to slide into a circus. We don't need witnesses. We should have the evidence and the votes."

The political consequences of a protracted trial were never far from the
surface. Several senators discussed the need to look out for freshmen senators
up for reelection in 2000. But one of those vulnerable incumbents objected
in a passionate speech that emboldened the nervous conference. "I'm more
interested in how the history books judge me than the election," declared
Senator Rick Santorum, a young and devoted conservative from Pennsylvania. "If you're trying to help me, don't help me."

With time running out, Lott left the meeting and spoke with Daschle.
The trial was slated to open the next day, and no one had a clue what to do.
The two leaders decided to appoint a small committee to wade through the
morass. Eschewing the conservatives most eager to convict the president,
Lott picked three independent-minded senators for his side—two Old Bulls,
Appropriations Committee chairman Ted Stevens of Alaska and Budget
Committee chairman Pete V. Domenici of New Mexico, plus Watergate veteran Fred Thompson of Tennessee. For the Democrats, Daschle likewise
steered away from Clinton defenders in tapping two of the senators most
critical of the president, Joe Lieberman and Joe Biden of Delaware. For the
last slot, he recruited Carl Levin of Michigan, who was more traditionally
partisan but also one of the Senate's smartest lawyers. The selection of the
group seemed designed to guarantee that each party would be tough on its
own side in the interest of finding a middle-ground solution.

The Gang of Six, as they quickly became dubbed, gathered for the first
time that afternoon at five o'clock in Lott's hideaway office to consult with
Senate lawyers about procedures. They decided to meet with both sides that
night and summoned the House managers over for a 6:15 P.M. meeting.
Hyde brought his evidence team—Asa Hutchinson, Jim Rogan, and Ed
Bryant—but got an immediate cold shoulder. From the start, the senators
made clear that the House team had no chance of winning. They would
never get the two-thirds vote they needed for conviction, and so, a lengthy
trial was just a "self-indulgent process," as Biden put it.

The assessment was bipartisan. Stevens, a crusty, seventy-five-year-old
former World War II pilot known for perhaps the most volatile temper in the
Senate, delivered it the most bluntly. "The president isn't going to be
removed," Stevens said firmly. "I can produce thirty-four affidavits of senators tomorrow that would show that they won't vote for conviction."

Hyde was upset. "Well, if that's the situation, there's no point in our being
here." Hyde began shifting in his chair as if he were about to leave.

"Now, Henry!" Stevens shouted, slapping his open palm down on the
table. "Let's talk this through!"

Hyde settled back in the chair, but he and the others were stunned by the harsh reception from their own Republican colleagues. Hutchinson could not imagine that the senators were already passing judgment on the outcome of the case without hearing a word of evidence. During his days as a prosecutor, he knew when he picked a jury that a number of members had likely already made up their minds, but at least during the voir dire they observed the etiquette of *pretending* to be neutral.

Hyde tried to dispel the impression that he and his team were merely reckless partisans out for political blood and figured the best way to do that was to let his young lieutenants speak for themselves. "We're not in this for the politics," Hyde insisted to the senators. Pointing to Rogan, he said, "He carried his district by less than a percent. Some of these members are doing this at great political cost. But I want you to hear from these, my colleagues."

Hyde then introduced the other managers, giving biographical information about each. He described both Bryant and Hutchinson as former U.S. attorneys, at which point Stevens interrupted, "I'm one too."

"I'm a former defendant," Hyde added lightly, a reference to a savings and loan lawsuit he was once involved in. The assembled lawmakers smiled and the mood eased slightly.

One by one, Rogan, Bryant, and Hutchinson discussed their involvement in the case. They said it was distasteful and they were not happy about having to be there, but they genuinely believed weighty allegations were at stake. They highlighted the evidence that troubled them most. When they started the House process, the managers said, no one thought it would even get out of committee, yet as the facts came spilling out, that changed. When they left the committee for the floor, no one thought the full House would pass the articles, yet that too changed. They should be given the same chance to present their case to the Senate.

The senators were still skeptical. What else did the House team need besides transcripts?

There was no comparison between transcripts and real witnesses, Hutchinson replied. The human reaction of the grand jurors to Lewinsky showed that; some jurors reached out to her in an almost motherly way, he recalled.

Well, the senators asked, what did the managers *really* need?

Hutchinson looked over at Hyde and asked if he should go through his trial plan. Hyde nodded. So Hutchinson walked through his order of proof, witness by witness, to show the senators how the managers planned to put the case together. The senators on both sides of the aisle were impressed. Until then, it was easy to look on the managers as crusaders caught up in a political jihad, but that was not the way they came across that night. They were articulate, prepared, earnest. The senators and their aides got the impression for the first time that maybe this was for real. The managers made a good accounting of themselves, if not necessarily of their case, Thompson thought. Lieberman felt the managers had made him think about the case in a different way. This was not just political, he concluded; they really believed that this president should not continue in office.

From there, the senators and their staffs retired to Stevens's office in the Appropriations Committee suite. The White House lawyers were up next, but they could not make it to Capitol Hill until 9 P.M., so the Senate delegation took off their suit coats, loosened their ties, broke open some red wine, and ordered Domino's pizza, including a special kosher pie for Lieberman. By the time Chuck Ruff, Greg Craig, and David Kendall showed up, the pizza was gone, so the group gathered in the committee conference room and got down to business. Unlike the meeting with the managers, where the Republican senators took the lead, Carl Levin essentially ran this session with his fellow Democrats. Joe Biden, who had left after the managers' meeting for a television interview, returned in the middle.

The senators were hoping the White House would simply agree to stipulate to the record and not call any witnesses, but Ruff was not about to make any commitments when he did not even know what the rules would be. Asked how many witnesses he would need, Ruff took a tough approach, saying there was no way to say at this point because it depended entirely on what the managers would do. They had never had any chance to gather evidence either during the Starr investigation or the House proceedings, Ruff pointed out. They would need a period of discovery, and only then could they decide how many witnesses they might require. It was an eminently reasonable position legally, but not politically.

Stevens blew up. "Bullshit!" he shouted, again banging his hand down as he had done with Hyde a couple hours earlier. "You know as well as I do that you're not going to call a single witness. You don't need to. You've got the votes!"

CHAPTER TWELVE

"Heavenly Father, we are in trouble"

The sergeant at arms moved to the center aisle of the Senate chamber and called out like some medieval town crier in a twentieth-century business suit. "Hear, ye! Hear, ye! Hear, ye!" declared Jim Ziglar. "All persons are commanded to keep silent, on pain of imprisonment, while the House of Representatives is exhibiting to the Senate of the United States articles of impeachment against William Jefferson Clinton, president of the United States."

All one hundred members of the United States Senate sat in their seats, tense and rigid, unusually attentive to every little detail, consumed by the gravity of the task awaiting them on this day, Thursday, January 7, 1999. The chamber that usually bustled with the motion of horse-trading legislators and aides and clerks was unnaturally still. The galleries were filled with tourists, officials, relatives, reporters, and even historians coincidentally in town for a conference. This was a room absorbed with history. All of the senators knew the legacy of the desk where he or she sat—Robert C. Smith of New Hampshire sat at the desk used by the great orator Daniel Webster and later by the abolitionist Charles Sumner, who was caned after an antislavery speech. Thad Cochran of Mississippi sat at Jefferson Davis's desk, still showing the scars from when Union soldiers took bayonets to it. Ted Kennedy sat at the desk once used by his slain brother, John F. Kennedy. Now the descendants of those great senators knew their legacy would be to sit in judgment of a president for the first time since Andrew Johnson was put on trial in the same chamber. Suddenly, it all seemed so real. Most senators had figured the House would never impeach Clinton. Even once it did, many of the senators assumed some deal would be cut in the dead of winter to forestall an actual trial. But they were wrong, and now they had no choice but to confront the issue.

With no precedent other than the Johnson trial, everyone was following the only script available to them, down to the letter. Just as Charles Sumner and Benjamin F. Wade and Edward G. Ross did in 1868, the senators remained mute at their desks. And just like Thaddeus Stevens before them, Henry Hyde and his fellow managers marched across the marbled floors of the Capitol and into the Senate chamber to lodge their charges. Other than the clicking of cameras, they heard no sounds as they moved through the stately building.

"Mr. President," the silver-haired Hyde said from the well of the Senate, "the managers on the part of the House of Representatives are here present and ready to present the articles of impeachment, which have been preferred by the House of Representatives against William Jefferson Clinton, president of the United States."

His voice deliberately emotionless and his eyes fixed on the papers before him, Hyde recited the two articles passed by the House. Each ended the same way. "In doing this," Hyde intoned, "William Jefferson Clinton has undermined the integrity of his office, has brought disrepute on the presidency, has betrayed his trust as president, and has acted in a manner subversive of the rule of law and justice, to the manifest injury of the people of the United States. Wherefore, William Jefferson Clinton, by such conduct, warrants impeachment and trial, and removal from office and disqualification to hold and enjoy any office of honor, trust, or profit under the United States."

Impeachment. Trial. The words hung in the air in case anyone had not quite come to grips with what was about to transpire. His part of the ritual opening complete, Hyde asked for "leave to withdraw," and the line of thirteen men from the House marched back up the center aisle and out of the chamber. "That's probably the most respect we'll be shown by the Senate in this entire process," Hyde remarked to his fellow managers.

That was the end of the formalities for the moment, and the senators got up from their desks to mill around the chamber. Lott and Daschle crossed the aisle and began talking again about how to proceed. A few other senators joined in, and then a few more, until the conversation mushroomed into a veritable mob of legislators, dozens of Republicans and Democrats bunched together in the well throwing out ideas and trying to hear one another. Finally, Senator Don Nickles, the Republican whip, suggested that rather than gather separately, the two party caucuses should meet together in the Old Senate Chamber, all one hundred senators in the same room at the same time, alone, without reporters or cameras, so that they could work something out rather than keep talking past each other. While the full Senate did not normally meet behind closed doors except on rare occasions involving national security, the notion of a joint caucus immediately intrigued many of the senators standing around the chamber, who saw it as a way of averting the bloody partisan confrontation that had consumed the House.

Lott particularly liked the idea. Daschle was open to it, but wanted time to consult his colleagues and said something he hoped would be noncommittal. Republicans took it as assent and thought they had an agreement. Not for long, though. It soon became clear that Daschle was not ready for such a joint meeting. Even as the huddle on the floor was breaking up, so too was the Gang of Six, who had been tapped to work with the House managers and the White House lawyers. They had planned to meet again at 11 A.M. but got the word first that they had been disbanded. Blame was quickly spread. Some thought Lott had pulled the plug because he was receiving grief from other senators irked that he had turned over responsibility to just three of them; others pointed at Daschle on the assumption that he did not genuinely want to work with the Republicans if that would mean a full trial.

The mistrust was evident at a private meeting of the Republican conference after the huddle on the floor. Lott described the meetings held over the last twenty-four hours by the Gang of Six and then announced that Daschle no longer wanted that group to do any more. The managers wanted fifteen to eighteen witnesses, Lott told his colleagues, while the White House wanted a month's delay for discovery. Ted Stevens warned about what that would mean. "Any discovery will trigger Pandora's box," he said, opening them up to all sorts of delays and tangents. His compatriots from the Gang of Six, Fred Thompson and Pete Domenici, both told the conference they were impressed by the managers but that they had urged them to winnow their witness list.

"Why do we need witnesses?" Lott asked. The question unnerved some of the conservatives in the caucus, who could see that their leader cared less about having a thorough airing of the case than he did about getting through it as quickly as possible. But Lott still had not been completely persuaded that the managers should have witnesses. If there were fifty-one votes for it, he would be there, but he knew how fragile his majority was. At the moment, he was sure he did not have fifty-one votes. "We've got to stay together or we'll get creamed," he told his colleagues. "If not, they'll pass the motion to dismiss."

There was more back-and-forth about witnesses and how to keep the House in line. Some of the hard-liners grew agitated at all the defensiveness.

"We're not on trial here," insisted one.

"Yes, we are," Lott shot back.

The senators filed back into the chamber shortly before 1 P.M. for the actual ceremonial opening of the trial. With the charges now officially presented by the House, the chief justice had been summoned to the Capitol and was prepared to take over as the presiding officer. At 1:19 P.M., a welcoming committee composed of six senators formally escorted William Rehnquist into the chamber, and he ascended the stairs to the top of the dais. Rehnquist was dressed in his customary judicial black robe, adorned with four gold braids on each sleeve, a touch he had adopted a few years earlier from the costume worn by the Lord Chancellor in a production he had seen of Gilbert and Sullivan's *Iolanthe*. That the chief justice was dressed in comic-opera regalia at the impeachment trial of the president drew plenty of amused snickers among the senators and their aides.

At the top of the rostrum, Rehnquist met Strom Thurmond, who at ninety-six was the oldest senator in American history and the Senate president pro tempore charged with swearing in the chief justice. In his role as president of the Senate, Vice President Gore could have performed the duty, but decided against it for obvious reasons, leaving the task to Thurmond. At six foot two, Rehnquist towered over Thurmond, who was hunched and leaning on the desk.

"Senators, I attend the Senate in conformity with your notice, for the purpose of joining with you for the trial of the president of the United States, and I am now ready to take the oath," Rehnquist announced, raising his right hand in the air and putting his left on a Bible.

"Do you solemnly swear that in all things appertaining to the trial of the impeachment of William Jefferson Clinton, president of the United States, now pending, you will do impartial justice according to the Constitution and laws, so help you God?" Thurmond asked in a halting voice.

"I do."

Thurmond shuffled off the rostrum and Rehnquist took his place. The chief justice asked the senators to raise their hands and repeated the same oath swearing to "do impartial justice."

"I do," came the reply from one hundred voices.

The senators then filed down the aisle, one by one, in alphabetical order, to sign a book affirming their pledge with a black-ink Parker Vector pen inscribed for the occasion. The pen, however, had a rather unfortunate typographical error: "*Untied* States Senate," it said. Untied, indeed. They had no idea what to do next. Having formally opened an impeachment trial, the Senate was supposed to then issue a summons to the president notifying him of the charges and setting out the terms of his response. But as yet, the senators had come up with no plan for how to move forward, and so no summons was issued. Instead, after the oath was administered, the Senate simply recessed to return to the various huddles around the Capitol.

Among those in the chamber who felt the weight of history as they raised their right hands was Senator Susan M. Collins, a first-term Republican from Maine who was already desperately searching for an exit strategy. Collins, one of only nine women in the Senate, had established the same reputation for independent thinking as her mentor and predecessor, Bill Cohen, and ranked by far as one of the most liberal members in the current

GOP lineup. She supported abortion rights, opposed the death penalty, and once spoke out for a gay rights law in her home state. In the Senate, she had taken on the powerful tobacco industry and often tried to reach across the aisle to work with Democrats, much like Cohen, who now served as Clinton's defense secretary.

Collins, forty-six, had grown up in the tiny Maine town of Caribou, the daughter of a lumber dealer and a religious educator who had schooled her early on about politics. Both mother and father had served as mayor of her hometown. After working for Cohen in Washington for twelve years, she had returned to Maine and eventually launched her own political career, winning Cohen's seat as her first elected position when he retired from the Senate in 1996. Unlike some of her Republican colleagues who had long ago made up their minds on Bill Clinton, Collins felt torn as the trial loomed. She could not get over Clinton's recklessness—it was as if he could not stop doing wrong, could not tell the truth, almost like a sociopath who wanted to be caught. She initially thought he would resign and that it would never come to the Senate, but eventually concluded that Clinton had no shame.

As the trial began, Collins resolved to put aside her anger to take a fresh look at the evidence. "I look at the faces of my colleagues, wondering could we indeed do 'impartial justice'?" she wrote in her diary that night. "Could we cast aside partisan labels and hear the evidence, not as Republicans and Democrats, but as American jurors? Could we meet the challenge before us? The oath is intended to be transformational. It transforms the Senate from a body of partisan politicians into an impartial jury sworn to seek the truth."

Yet she was already wondering what would happen if she came to the conclusion that the evidence was not enough. A former aide sent her an article over Christmas by Joseph Isenbergh, a University of Chicago professor who offered the novel idea that the Senate could vote first on conviction and then separately on removal—in essence, allowing senators to make the judgment that Clinton did the things he was accused of doing while concluding that it was not enough to merit eviction from office. The article noted that the Senate had taken such a two-stage vote on an impeachment as early as 1804, at a time when the constitutional framers' thoughts on such issues were far more current than now. Collins was intrigued and filed the article away for future reference.

At the moment, though, the issue at hand was how to start the trial, not end it. Around the Capitol, small groups of senators convened to advance one idea or another. As the day wore on, Republicans became frustrated that the bipartisan caucus suggested on the floor by Don Nickles had not come together because Daschle had not signed off on it, so Lott decided to go forward with the GOP-drafted procedural plan and simply force it through on the strength of his majority. He scheduled a vote for 5 P.M. and went to the Republican cloakroom to tell his senators, but the noise made it hard to hear and people were confused about what they would be voting for. Connie Mack, the Florida Republican who chaired the party's conference, grabbed Lott by the arm and told him he should call a formal meeting of all the GOP senators.

At 2:30 P.M., the Republicans gathered to hear Lott describe their strategy. Daschle was balking at the joint caucus and pushing the Gorton-Lieberman plan again, the majority leader explained, so they would go to the floor and put the two competing plans to a test, which the GOP would presumably win. Lott explained their version of the procedures—the House managers would get five days to present their case, the senators would get two days to pose questions, motions to dismiss the case and to subpoena witnesses would be allowed, and the trial would end by February 5.

Some of the moderates began grumbling. Forcing a partisan vote would be a disaster, they said. It would start off the trial in the same way the House impeachment inquiry was started, coloring it permanently with the hue of partisan politics. At the back of the room, Senator Olympia Snowe stood up. Snowe shared the same moderate-to-liberal instincts of Susan Collins, her junior colleague from Maine, but carried more authority because of her longer tenure. "I'm not voting with you," she declared. "I won't do it. This is a mistake. We should not give up this easily. We should have a bipartisan meeting in the morning." She had talked with several Democrats, she said, and they were receptive to the idea.

Lott's majority was beginning to dissolve. Ted Stevens, the crusty Appropriations chairman who had tried to broker a deal with the managers, concurred with Snowe. He was a juror, he said, and so was everyone else in the room. Their role as jurors was not to play legislator as if this were a spending bill. They ought to keep the idea of the bipartisan caucus alive because Lott could not afford to rely entirely on his majority. "I'm not going to vote with you at some point," Stevens warned.

Collins, Arlen Specter, and John Chafee of Rhode Island were also pushing Lott to give the joint caucus another chance. The arithmetic was not hard; with that many Republicans balking, that meant that Lott did not even have fifty-one votes to force through his procedural plan on the floor. The room was tense. Lott's leadership was on the line. After the budget deal he had brokered with Clinton the previous fall, after his flirtation with the Gorton-Lieberman truncated-trial plan, after his unilateral negotiations with the Democrats, many of the Republican senators did not trust their leader. In turn, Lott was growing aggravated with his splintered caucus. Each of them had his or her own idea about the way things should run and had no appreciation for what he had been trying to do.

"Look, I've stuck my neck out for bipartisanshit," he blurted out in frustration. "Ship!" he quickly corrected. He meant to say bipartisan*ship*. The room laughed at the Freudian slip. Maybe he had gotten it right the first time? Lott continued undaunted, "I stuck my neck out and some of you chopped it off."

The mood remained prickly. Pat Roberts from Kansas got up to make the point that the public did not care what they were doing. Voters were not paying attention. He had asked his staff to record what was happening across the television spectrum at 1:30 P.M., and the senator then gave a rib-tickling rendition of what the country was actually watching—Luke loves Laura, a storm front moving in on North Carolina, that sort of thing. "I'm sorry," he said, "but we've got to quit peeing down each other's legs."

Daschle was sitting in the outer lobby of Lott's office, waiting to talk things over with the majority leader and unaware of the grief his counterpart was taking in the Republican meeting. A television set was carrying live the latest in the endless stream of press availabilities by senators at the media stakeout in the corridor. On the screen at the moment was Republican Jon Kyl of Arizona, who as it turned out was excoriating Daschle for rejecting the proposed bipartisan caucus. Daschle watched in astonishment. That wasn't at all what had happened. What kind of good faith was this? He was being blamed for the breakdown in negotiations after all he had done to find a bipartisan accommodation? Frustration boiled up inside and Daschle stormed out of the office.

"Tell Senator Lott we've gone to the floor," he snapped to one of the Republican aides as he left.

As soon as he returned and heard what had happened, Lott rushed out of his office to find Daschle to try to smooth things over. He found him on the floor and the two sat down together to talk. Contrary to what Kyl had said, Daschle told Lott that he was willing to hold the joint caucus meeting. Daschle wanted a deal as much as the other side did. Lott was happy to hear it. Given Olympia Snowe's over-my-dead-body speech, he knew he had to find a way of getting out of the scheduled vote.

One more thing, Daschle said. "All these misunderstandings are impeding our ability to do this. The only way we're going to resolve this is if you and I go to the gallery together." By that, Daschle meant the press gallery so that they could announce the joint caucus together.

At 5:30 P.M., the two appeared side by side in front of the television cameras and expressed a little of the difficulty they were facing. "Senator Daschle and I are not dictators," Lott told the reporters. "We are leaders that are getting some latitude by our conferences and our caucuses, but we have to bring along ninety-eight other senators. We are struggling very hard to do that."

Still, Lott was flush with the momentary victory. He had headed off a potentially calamitous confrontation with the Democrats, not to mention a possible insurrection within his own ranks, while paving the way for a possible bipartisan consensus on how to proceed with the trial. On day one, at least, the situation had not blown up. As they prepared to leave the press gallery, a broadly grinning Lott grabbed Daschle's hand and thrust it in the air triumphantly, almost as if they were political ticket-mates who had just won an election.

Downstairs in the Republican cloakroom, about a dozen senators were watching the performance on television. Rick Santorum, the Pennsylvania conservative who had moved over from the House in the 1994 election and remained close to the revolutionaries there, exploded in anger and complained loudly about what he had just seen. Lott was caving in to the Democrats! Again! Santorum threw his hands in the air, then threw his whole body around in aggravation and finally stalked out of the room.

So it was that Lott had quelled a storm on one side only to ignite another one on the opposite flank. At 5:45 P.M., he convened the Republican conference again to try to explain what he had done and heard more grousing from his troops. Several of them got up to say that the House team did not want the twenty-four hours of opening arguments Lott was planning to offer them; they wanted witnesses like a real trial. The Senate Republicans were undermining their own compatriots from the House, several complained. But others thought the managers were asking for trouble. They did not understand the dynamics in the Senate. Someone had better go over there and straighten them out.

Lott agreed and decided to talk to the managers himself, on their turf. And he had another idea—Santorum should go with him. Santorum, for all his pique at the way things were unfolding, understood the realities of the situation, and would serve as an emissary the managers could trust. If Santorum told them that there was no assurance of witnesses, they would have to listen.

Across Capitol Hill at the Rayburn Building, the managers were already meeting in the Judiciary Committee conference room and venting their disgust at what was happening.

"I'm not going to be part of a show trial," growled Chris Cannon, manager from Utah. Cannon reported that he had spoken earlier that day with both of his state's Republican senators, Orrin Hatch and Robert F. Bennett. Despite their supportive comments before the television cameras, both told him on the phone to give up the idea of a full trial with witnesses. Cannon was riled up. How could they say one thing in public and then stick the dagger into the managers' backs in private? He thought of Hatch like a brother, and now to have him effectively telling Cannon to roll over?

As the managers were sharing their gripes, Lott and Santorum arrived uninvited and unannounced. The majority leader of the Senate seldom deigned to come over to House turf to meet with anyone less than the Speaker himself. The two senators sat down at the conference table, flanking Hyde, Lott on the left and Santorum on the right. They were there to explain where things stood, they said. Lott laid out his proposal for the managers: Each side would get twenty-four hours over five days to present its case without witnesses. The senators would have two days for a question-and-answer session, and then motions to call witnesses or dismiss the case would be considered. If witnesses were rejected, final votes would take place by February 5. If they were called, the votes would happen by February 12.

To the managers, it was clear what twenty-four hours meant. It meant the Senate would give them a fig-leaf trial designed mostly to cover the senators' own posteriors. After twenty-four hours of arguments from each side, the senators could declare that the case was adequately presented and that witnesses were unnecessary.

"Some of us have a problem with what's going on," Hyde told Lott, and then turned to Cannon. "Chris?"

Cannon lived up to his name. "This deal is designed to screw us!" he exploded. They were cutting the managers off at the knees. This was a whitewash. Cannon was steaming mad and held nothing back out of deference to the most powerful senator. Where Lott tried to be gracious, Cannon was pugnacious. "We're a coequal house here! The worst thing that could happen here is you could give us rules that we will not follow!"

Hyde let the confrontation play out. To some in the room, he seemed testy, almost fatalistic, like an actor who had already read to the end of the script to see that the final scene did not go well for him. But several others joined in Cannon's assault on Lott, including Bob Barr and Jim Rogan.

"I have a problem calling this a trial," Barr said.

"That's just semantical," Lott retorted.

More than semantical, one of the managers shot back. This was not a trial.

Lott tried to empathize with the managers. "I was in the House. I was where you guys are. I sat on the Judiciary Committee during Watergate. I'm not against you guys." He enlisted Santorum to reinforce the point. "Look, I brought Rick along because I thought you'd really respect Rick's judgment."

Santorum backed up Lott. "Trent's one of us. He's not here to try to cut anybody off. But he's got to run the Senate. He's not the Speaker. He's the majority leader, he has to lead." Santorum tried to reason with the managers. He still spent a lot of time with his former colleagues in the House, still came over to use the House gym three times a week. "I want you to have witnesses. I want this to work. But I think this is the best we can do." He tried a baseball analogy. "We don't know how we're going to get to home plate. This is a way of getting to second base."

The senators were getting nowhere. Finally, the managers asked Lott and Santorum to leave the room so they could speak candidly among themselves. Unaccustomed to being kicked out of meetings, Lott nonetheless politely stepped out. While he cooled his heels for the next fifteen minutes, the managers thrashed about for what to do. Some argued they should just walk out. They should not dignify a sham. Hyde, though, had no interest in such a protest. They had a job to do, no matter how unpleasant the Senate was making it. For now, at least, they decided to hold out for witnesses and take eight hours for opening arguments—no more.

"Eight hours?" Lott asked incredulously when he was readmitted to the conference room. "You need fifty hours!"

"You're putting us in a box," Santorum said.

You're putting *us* in a box, one of the managers replied.

At this point, Hyde the conciliator tried one last time to find a middle ground. "Well, we can go twelve hours." But as he looked around the table, he was met with disapproving glares from his fellow managers and quickly reversed himself. "Well, no, we'll go eight hours."

Lott surrendered for the moment. "All right," he sighed. "I'll go back and see if I can sell this to Daschle. We just want to look after you." But Lott warned the managers that however many hours they got for opening arguments, "Don't use all your time arguing for witnesses. I'd make your case."

"Heavenly Father," began Senator Daniel K. Akaka, delivering the opening prayer, "we are in trouble and we need your help. We've come to a point where we don't know what to do."

Amid much tension and uncertainty, the senators had gathered at nine-thirty the next morning, Friday, January 8, under the half-dome ceiling of the Old Senate Chamber, located down the hall from their modern home and now used mainly as a museum stop for tourists. Smaller and more intimate than the current chamber, the room, with its massive chandelier, gilt eagle and shield, spittoons, and feathered quills, harkened back to its antebellum heyday, when it hosted the Senate from 1810 to 1859 and witnessed such larger-than-life figures as Daniel Webster, Henry Clay, and John C. Calhoun debate the future of the young nation. In this room, the Missouri Compromise was brokered, abolitionist Senator Charles Sumner was beaten by a cane-wielding Southern congressman, and President Andrew Jackson was censured for refusing to turn over a document related to the Bank of the United States.

Within three years of Jackson's reprimand in 1834, his fellow Democrats had recaptured control of the Senate and expunged the censure.

That history was not lost on senators as they found seats in the room now, instinctively arranging themselves along party lines as they did in the regular chamber, Republicans on the right and Democrats on the left, even though seats were not assigned. Folding chairs were brought in to accommodate the growth of the Senate in the last 140 years, but there were no television cameras, no microphones, no sound systems. In fact, some of the senators in the back had a hard time hearing the soft-spoken Akaka as the Hawaii Democrat led them in a brief prayer at Lott's request.

Fearing that their most partisan members could make a difficult situation even worse, Lott and Daschle had privately collaborated to stack the deck. The night before, they had agreed to steer the meeting into a more productive direction by opening it with statements by three members from each caucus who would command the respect of their peers and were serious about finding accommodation. By agreement of both sides, Robert Byrd was tapped to go first to set the historical and constitutional stage for his younger brethren. At eighty-one, Byrd occupied a unique perch in the firmament of the U.S. Senate. Byrd had served in Congress for forty-six years—forty of them in the Senate—and was one of only three Americans elected to seven consecutive terms in the upper body. Silver-haired, punctilious, and proud, Byrd looked the part of the old-school senator and played it too, seeing himself as the guardian of the body's prerogatives and principles. He had literally written the history of the Senate in a four-volume set. Byrd had been appalled by everything that had happened regarding Monica Lewinsky, from the original affair to the president's dissembling to the proceedings in the House. He told colleagues he had watched literally every minute of the House hearings, and did nothing to hide his disgust.

"The White House has sullied itself," he told his fellow senators. "The House has fallen into the black pit of partisan self-indulgence. The Senate is teetering on the brink of that same black pit."

As Byrd stood in the front of the chamber, his hands shook with age, the pages of his speech flapping in a way that distracted from the gravity of his words. Books that he had brought up front and stacked behind him to make points about impeachment kept falling over.

"We look very bad," Byrd went on. "We appear to be dithering and posturing and slowly disintegrating into the political quicksand." To avoid the fate of others tarnished by the scandal, he added, "We can start by disdaining any more of the salacious muck which has already soiled the gowns of too many. If we can come together in a dignified way to orderly and expeditiously dispose of this matter, then perhaps we can yet salvage a bit of respect and trust from the American people for all of us, for the Senate, and for their institutions of government."

After about twenty minutes, Byrd finally finished and sat down. Few liked following Byrd, but Connie Mack went ahead, since he had a story that involved his colleague from West Virginia. As a young Republican House member, Mack had been a conservative scrapper, and after being elected to the Senate, he needed time to realize that it was a different place, one less partisan and more collegial. Once, he recalled, Byrd had chided him for some perceived transgression on the floor, and Mack had flared with anger. Yet in the time it took him to travel from his office to the floor to issue a scathing rebuttal, he realized he ought not be defensive. The lesson, he said, reading from notes, was that the senators ought to open up to one another and express their true fears about what lay ahead.

Joe Lieberman went next, recounting a fable to make his point: A scorpion asked a frog for a ride across the water. The frog asked how he could be sure he would not be stung. Trust me, the scorpion said. The frog did and gave the ride. The scorpion stung him anyway. "Why?" asked the wounded frog. "I couldn't help it," the scorpion replied. "It's in my nature."

The senators, Lieberman went on, needed to overcome their own partisan natures. They all shared similar goals—they wanted to fulfill their constitutional responsibility, they wanted to make sure it was a fair trial, and they wanted to make sure it would not damage the Senate or the country. "There will not be sixty-seven votes on this set of facts," he said. "We must do what is necessary to achieve this result, then move on." Lieberman's stark assessment was an important signal to the other senators. If there were any hope of reaching a two-thirds vote, it would depend on Democrats such as Lieberman, and if he had already concluded that the president would be acquitted, that could become a self-fulfilling prophecy.

His original proposal with Slade Gorton now dead, Lieberman told the Senate that he was no longer pushing for a test vote. The key issue, he said, was whether witnesses would be called. They should not if they were not necessary because they would prolong the trial and bring the Senate into the sordid sexual details they so fervently wanted to avoid. "This is a political trial and we are politicians," Lieberman said. They had to convince the managers that they would be treated fairly. "This is a sad chapter begun by the president's abysmal conduct. The president's conduct has left wounds in the country. Partisanship in the House has deepened these wounds."

Gorton rose and echoed Lieberman's points about the larger goals, but now he split with his friend on the issue of witnesses. He too had thought the existing record was adequate, he said, but had changed his mind. "We need to give the prosecutors some rein," Gorton said. He then set forth the

Republican plan that would set aside time for motions, presentations, lists of witnesses, and proffers from the two sides about their need for discovery, leaving until later the question of whether testimony would be taken.

Chris Dodd stood next, recalling the caning of Charles Sumner and how it had poisoned the atmosphere in the Senate, inhibiting it from dealing with the national crisis brewing at the time and leading to the Civil War—and then noted that the attack had been generated in part out of an allegation of an affair. Lieberman had spoken for the Senate last September when he castigated Clinton from the floor, Dodd said, and now the Senate should again follow his lead.

More down-to-earth was Mitch McConnell, who headed the National Republican Senatorial Committee and squarely put the politics of impeachment on the table. "The Senate has a tendency to think about the next election," he said. "The impeachment trial will have no effect on the 2000 election. Put that away. . . . Byrd is right. The Senate is on trial because we're sure of the outcome."

By this point, senators had stopped coming to the front of the room and were simply standing at their nineteenth-century polished-wood desks to speak. The prepared remarks had long since been discarded, and they were talking with each other as colleagues and friends thrown into a desperate situation and searching together for a way out. Without the amplification of a sound system, without the omnipresent television cameras, without reporters scribbling down every word, the senators for once saw themselves as statesmen seeking the common good rather than as strategists obsessed with the gamesmanship of the moment.

Phil Gramm seemed an unlikely candidate for statesman. A Democrat turned Republican, Gramm had carved out a reputation as a Texas brawler, happily bashing liberals and pushing his own party's leadership to stand up for conservative values. Joe Biden once apologized for calling him "barbed-wire Gramm" on the floor, only to have Gramm tell him, "No, no. Keep doing it. They like it back home." So as he stood at his desk in the Old Senate Chamber, Gramm surprised many in the chamber by quoting in his inimitable Texas twang none other than Daniel Webster, noting that the senator from New England gave his famed "Union First" speech 150 years ago in this same chamber, speaking "not as a Massachusetts man, nor as a Northern man, but as an American." Gramm talked about the oath they had taken to do impartial justice and what that would mean for a trial. To do impartial justice, he believed strongly that the House managers deserved a chance to present their case, including witnesses. If the president asked for witnesses, was there anyone who would not allow him to call them? Gramm asked. Neither should they handcuff the House.

But in fact, Gramm went on, as the senators haggled over how to proceed, they were not so far apart. Under the existing rules that governed impeachment trials in the Senate, any party could make a motion seeking witnesses, which would then be decided by a majority of senators. The only way to stop the managers from making such a motion would be to change those rules, Gramm said, and everyone knew that would not happen because it would require a two-thirds vote, or sixty-seven senators, which neither side at that point could muster. So at the moment the question of witnesses was, he said, moot. Why not throw out both the Republican and Democratic resolutions and write one together?

Sitting on the other side of the chamber, Ted Kennedy was struck by Gramm's point—and more than a little bit taken with his invocation of Webster. The aging liberal lion, who had fought plenty of partisan battles of his own during three decades in the Senate yet also knew how to work across the aisle when it suited his purposes, stood and seconded Gramm. They did essentially agree on how to move forward, at least for now, he said. The witness question did not have to be settled at this moment. They could go ahead with opening arguments from both sides and then decide how to proceed from there.

"We can get to second base together," Kennedy said, echoing the metaphor Rick Santorum had used with the managers the night before. "Let's worry about how to get from second base to home plate later."

Senators murmured to each other. Gramm and Kennedy were on the same page. If two of the most partisan, ideologically opposite senators could see their way to a middle ground, then they should lock it in. As other senators stood to offer their thoughts, Lott interjected and closed off discussion. "If we've got an agreement between Gramm and Kennedy, we ought to be able to wrap this up," he said quickly. "Let's not talk ourselves out of something."

Around the chamber, senators thumped their desks in approval. "Hear, hear!" some called out. "Seal the deal!"

Lott pronounced the two-hour meeting over, grabbed Daschle by the arm, and started to walk off. For the second time in two days, Lott had seized the moment to preserve bipartisanship and force the one hundred independent-minded senators to keep paddling in the same direction. He had kept the situation from falling apart for another few hours. But as senators got up and left the chamber in an excited buzz, the few aides in the room shot looks of panic at each other. Tom Griffith, the chief Senate lawyer, turned to his deputy and asked, "What agreement?"

The much hailed pact in the Old Senate Chamber was in fact something of a chimera. The two sides had said some words that sounded alike, but there was no agreement as such. A resolution still had to be written translating the bipartisan bonhomie into real nuts-and-bolts rules for how the trial would work, and that would prove to be anything but a pro forma exercise. Then the senators would have to actually read the measure and vote on it. Some Republicans were quietly aggravated at how quickly Lott had declared the fight over; Democrats such as Senator Tom Harkin of Iowa were upset with Kennedy for effectively giving in. There was still plenty of room for disaster.

Lott's chief of staff, Dave Hoppe, gathered Griffith and the other lawyers, Mike Wallace for Lott and Bob Bauer for Daschle, in his office along with other aides and the four senators tapped by the majority leader to haggle over the details—Lieberman, Gorton, Kennedy, and Gramm. The next few hours were pure chaos, as the negotiations took on a life of their own. Bauer, the Democratic lawyer, seemed to be doing much of the battling with Gorton and Gramm. At one point, sympathetic to concerns expressed by Chuck Ruff at the White House, Bauer made a proposal that locked in the president's right to additional discovery. The Republicans were happy enough with that proposal because it actually moved beyond Kennedy's "second base" and in their eyes strengthened the case for witnesses. But when Marty Paone, a Daschle aide, walked in, he became alarmed and quickly pulled the other Democrats out of the room.

"What are you doing?" he asked. "We just had a meeting where they decided to punt on that."

With Hoppe's permission, the group then moved up to Lott's private office to consult. Daschle joined them. "We'll deal with the issue of subpoenas later," he agreed. He instructed his negotiators to go back downstairs and tell the Republicans that was as far as they would go.

Gramm and Kennedy, the new political odd couple of the Senate, likewise scrapped over the issue of allowing in new evidence. The Texan insisted the House managers had to have the right at some point to try to introduce more material. "You can't muzzle the House," he said.

Kennedy shot back that what they had talked about in the Old Senate Chamber did not envision opening up the trial to new allegations. "That's not the way we're going to deal with it," Kennedy said before walking out of the meeting.

When he returned with a new draft of his own, Gramm was equally dissatisfied: "This doesn't look right."

Others got involved. More meetings were held. Senators Fred Thompson, Mike DeWine, Jon Kyl, and Ted Stevens moved in and out. Lott and Daschle were brought in. With the afternoon dwindling away and anxiety rising, negotiators finally came up with the breakthrough just minutes before the Senate was scheduled to reconvene on the floor at 4 P.M. to vote. The compromise: House managers would be allowed to make their presentation about the need for witnesses before the Senate voted on any motion to dismiss. That was enough to satisfy some of the hard-liners looking out for the managers' interest. The deal was finally done.

On the floor back in their regular chamber, the senators barely had time to read the freshly printed resolution as Lott presented it. Under the plan, the managers and the White House would file various briefs over the next few days, and then beginning next Thursday, January 14, each side would have up to twenty-four hours spread over three days to present opening arguments. The Senate would then conduct a two-day question-and-answer period in which members could make inquiries only in writing through the chief justice. At that point, motions to dismiss the case or, alternatively, to call witnesses would be in order. That would be the moment when the senators would be forced to revisit the same roadblock they had decided to drive around this morning. But the details were lost on many senators. What mattered was that, for the moment at least, they were in agreement. One by one, the clerk called their names and one by one they rose at their desks and called out, "Aye." The plan passed 100–0, in stark contrast to the largely party-line vote that had launched impeachment proceedings in the House just three months earlier. As he made his way off the floor, Lott smiled in satisfaction—and relief. He had survived another day.

"You're giving them a shot to argue black babies on the floor of the Senate!"

At the White House, John Podesta was furious. Bipartisanship was all well and good for the Senate, but for his boss it was a disaster in the making. And in case the president's allies among the Senate Democrats failed to understand that, Podesta was on the telephone delivering testy, profanity-laden tirades to make the point crystal clear. The unanimous procedural agreement, in his view, gave carte blanche to the House managers to dredge up any scurrilous innuendo against the president, from the numerous Jane Does identified during the Paula Jones case right down to the recurrent but unproven rumors that in Arkansas he had fathered children by black prostitutes—a rumor resuscitated in recent days by a tabloid newspaper and Internet gossip Matt Drudge, only to be eviscerated when a DNA test showed that a young boy was not Clinton's son.

While publicly White House officials had bemoaned the partisanship in the House, it had actually served their strategy quite nicely. The last thing they wanted was for the Senate to treat this matter seriously and give it credence by working together. The 100–0 vote to start the trial meant legitimacy. It meant that the White House could not complain that the proceeding was rigged against the president because, in fact, every Democrat had gone along with the resolution. Clinton instinctively felt he was being screwed. He got on the telephone with several Democratic senators and railed about what a mistake it was for them to go along with the Republicans. How could they do that to him?

For those the president did not get in touch with, Podesta played enforcer. When he reached Bob Bauer, Daschle's lawyer, Podesta angrily mocked the backslapping self-congratulations of senators appearing on television, "preening their little unity dance," as he put it. "I hope they feel good about it," he said sarcastically. Fuming, Podesta also rang up Joel P. Johnson, another Daschle adviser, to vent: "We don't know what kind of crap they've collected from his enemies, and you're going to let it all flop out there on the floor."

Both Daschle advisers urged Podesta to calm down and assured him things would work out fine. They believed that Republican senators would never allow the managers to do that because they were petrified of appearing to be on a partisan witch-hunt.

"Trust us," Johnson told Podesta.

The trial was now on and the show about to start. Briefs were being written and filed, presentations drafted, assignments made, and strategies developed. One thing both sides needed to do was familiarize themselves with the battlefield. Neither the White House lawyers nor the House members had spent any time on the Senate floor and had no idea how a trial would work logistically. So on Monday, January 11, each side was brought to the chamber for a tour. The managers arrived at 11 A.M. and were shown where they would speak and where they would sit. Alarm bells went off immediately. Their table, according to the sergeant at arms, Jim Ziglar, would be to Rehnquist's right—just in front of the Democratic senators. And who would be in the front row next to their table? None other than Chuck Schumer, the New Yorker who had fought them in the House Judiciary Committee before taking his seat in the Senate.

Hyde and the others were not at all pleased about this and asked Ziglar if they could switch sides. They would feel more comfortable on the Republican side of the chamber.

Sorry, Ziglar replied, but that was the way it had worked during the Andrew Johnson trial and tradition was being stuck to assiduously.

Chuck Ruff and the White House team arrived at 3 P.M. for their own tour and were equally chagrined to discover that they would be stationed right in front of the Republicans, with Strom Thurmond staring over their shoulders. The president's lawyers asked Ziglar the same question: Could they switch sides?

Sorry, Ziglar repeated.

Other managers had more serious concerns on their minds as they checked out the "courtroom." Bob Barr had nudged Hyde into putting him on the evidence team, the group of managers who would do the heavy lifting in presenting the case and arguing the facts. But the other members, Asa Hutchinson, Jim Rogan, and Ed Bryant, were worried that would backfire. Barr was such a lightning rod that he generated antipathy among Democrats and some moderate Republicans. Hutchinson and Rogan had both received friendly warnings from senators who said, "If Barr's one of the main presenters, you might as well just turn off the lights in the Senate," as one told Rogan. Hutchinson and Rogan had already brought their concerns to Hyde, grabbing him outside the rest room after a managers' meeting. A few days went by without any result, though, and so now, touring the Senate floor, Bryant decided to take a stab at it. He grabbed Bill McCollum and brought him over to Hyde. McCollum should be on the evidence team rather than Barr, Bryant told Hyde.

After touring the floor, the managers met back in their House office building. Hyde swallowed his discomfort and decided he had to do something about Barr. The young guys were right. Barr would hurt their cause, and they had to focus on that. Still, Hyde tried to soften the blow. Turning to Barr, he said, "I've got something special for you to do." Bill McCollum would serve on the evidence team, while Barr would respond to any trial motions filed by the White House.

Hyde had given no advance notice of his move, and everyone else around the table suddenly held his breath, unsure what the next moment would bring. After all these months together, it may have been the tensest point they had encountered internally.

But the combustible Barr did not explode. He did not even complain. "Henry," he said graciously, "I'll do whatever you want me to do."

Relief swept through the room. It was not, however, to be the end of Barr's bad day. That night, *Hustler's* Larry Flynt announced on Geraldo Rivera's CNBC television show that he had turned up evidence of hypocrisy by Barr—during a divorce proceeding, the Georgia congressman had refused to answer questions about whether he had cheated with a woman who later became his third wife. Flynt had a news conference in Los Angeles later that night and also provided an affidavit from Barr's ex-wife alleging that the vocally antiabortion Republican had paid her to have an abortion in 1983 after they already had two children, even driving her to the clinic himself. Flynt had paid the ex-wife for the allegations and Barr denied ever encouraging anyone to have an abortion.

While Hyde was giving Barr the task of responding to any White House motions, the president's team was deciding not to file any. Although the lawyers had drafted a motion to dismiss the case, Daschle and other Senate Democrats warned the White House not to submit it. Having bought into a process on a 100–0 vote, the Democratic senators felt some obligation to hear the case, at least the opening arguments, before voting to get rid of it. All of the other motions considered by the White House team—the lame-duck argument, the bundling argument, the vagueness argument—likewise appeared more costly than beneficial. They would lose those and only give the Republicans ammunition to claim that the president was still trying to weasel his way out through fancy lawyering. Better at this stage, they decided, to let the process play itself out. Besides, the lame-duck argument might have been mooted because the newly elected House had ratified the appointment of the managers.

Asa Hutchinson spent the day shuttling from one meeting to another. In the morning, he and a couple other managers met with Republican senators Arlen Specter, Jon Kyl, and Jeff Sessions to talk about witnesses. Specter had been talking with Lott on the subject and volunteered to play intermediary with the House team, but could not get any Democrats to join him. He asked Joe Lieberman, who begged off, saying Daschle would not let him participate, and he asked Chuck Ruff, who said if the Senate Democrats were not involved, then he would not come either. Specter advised the managers to discard any expert witnesses and focus on the conflicts in the facts that needed to be resolved. "The tenor and the tone—that's what's important," he told Hutchinson and the others.

The managers, however, were still focused on witnesses who would expand their case, not pare it back. Along with Lindsey Graham, Hutchinson also met that day with Kathleen Willey in Jim Rogan's office to gauge whether she might be called to testify. Willey seemed like a strong witness to Hutchinson, believable in her account of her meeting with the president. But the further her tale went, the more disjointed and conspiratorial it became, Hutchinson thought. Moreover, the original case against Clinton regarding Lewinsky relied so heavily in the beginning on Linda Tripp, yet Tripp's testimony contradicted Willey's about whether the encounter with the president was welcome or not. So Tripp was attacking Willey's veracity; Willey was attacking Tripp's. It was all too circuitous. After a bit, Hutchinson excused himself and left the room.

Lott met with a dozen other Republican senators in his hideaway the next morning, Tuesday, January 12, to prepare for the beginning of opening arguments. They talked about how the camera in the chamber would work, whether to open final deliberations, and what to do about all the senators who seemed to have prejudged the case. They were also worried about the annual State of the Union speech. Clinton was scheduled to address a joint session of Congress a week from then, and it seemed unthinkable to have a president go through with such a ritual at the same time he was on trial for high crimes and misdemeanors. But it was not clear what to do about it—if they disinvited him, Clinton would just make that an issue against them and simply give his speech from the Oval Office.

Arlen Specter said they should go ahead with business as usual and do what they would normally do. Jeff Sessions argued that they should not let Clinton address them in person but make him submit it in writing, as presidents did before Woodrow Wilson first journeyed down Pennsylvania Avenue to deliver his report orally. Don Nickles said they should let Clinton do whatever he wanted, but the senator added that did not mean he would have to show up to listen.

Specter, meantime, wanted Clinton to come up to Capitol Hill in a different context—as a witness in the trial. "We should call the president," he said. "We have the power to do that."

That was actually a matter of some debate. Constitutional scholars remained divided over whether the Congress had the authority to summon the president to testify before it; some felt it would violate the separation-of-powers doctrine. Andrew Johnson was not compelled to appear in person at his impeachment trial. Gerald Ford while president testified before a congressional committee examining his decision to pardon Nixon, but he appeared voluntarily. The only thing that could force Clinton to come would be the pressure of public opinion, and there was no sign of that.

Indeed, in case the Republican senators needed a reminder of where the public stood on their current endeavor, they got a sharp wake-up call during their conference meeting on this Tuesday. Linda DiVall, a longtime Republican pollster, delivered a presentation of her findings and analysis from the 1998 midterm elections, and the trends were not promising. Republicans had lost the moderate vote decisively, and those voters who focused on issues such as education, health care, the economy, and Social Security broke for the Democrats, DiVall told the senators. The Republicans, it was clear, needed an agenda and this trial was not it.

"Make no mistake," DiVall said. "Impeachment politics are driving down the perceptions of the party."

The same day, a financial officer at a Washington law firm cut a check for $850,000, slipped it into an overnight envelope, and officially put an end to *Jones* v. *Clinton*. Most painful to the president was that he was actually forced to use personal money for some of the payment. His fund-raiser, Terry McAuliffe, and other advisers had told him he would not have to pay a dime of the settlement, only to discover that they could not tap into his legal defense fund because its bylaws permitted payments only for attorney fees and legal expenses. Bob Bennett, Clinton's lawyer in the Jones case, succeeded in convincing one of the president's insurers, Chubb Group Insurance, to fork over $475,000 but failed to persuade the other one, State Farm, to contribute. As a result, the final $375,000 was withdrawn from a blind trust that contained the first family's assets—money that had been made by the first lady when she was a lawyer in Arkansas. The irony was lost on no one. Hillary Clinton had to pay for Bill Clinton's problems with women financially as well as emotionally.

CHAPTER THIRTEEN

"There may actually be a case here"

"Be easy on us," Asa Hutchinson requested. "We're a little rusty."
"Don't worry," William Rehnquist replied. "I haven't practiced law in thirty years, so we'll all be a little rusty."

On the dreary and drizzly winter day that the trial was to begin in earnest, Thursday, January 14, the House managers and the White House lawyers were summoned to meet with the chief justice. Neither side realized the other would be there. They gathered around 12:45 P.M. in the President's Room just behind the Senate chamber, where the chief justice and his clerks had set up shop for the duration of the trial. A stiff-backed chair had been brought in for the chief justice, and his clerks carted over piles of papers from the court to work on during breaks. With colorful floor tile, gilded mirrors, and fresco paintings by Italian artist Constantino Brumidi, the room was officially set aside for the president to use, and from 1861 to 1933 chief executives often came to sign legislation here at the end of congressional sessions. While here in March 1865, Abraham Lincoln learned that Confederate general Robert E. Lee had asked to meet with Union general Ulysses S. Grant, a prelude to the surrender of the South. A century later, Lyndon B. Johnson signed the Voting Rights Act of 1965 here, a rare moment in modern times when the room was put to its original use. Bill Clinton had stopped by after his inauguration in 1993 and used it as a holding room prior to State of the Union addresses, but otherwise had little interest in forays to congressional territory, a diffidence that had now come back to haunt him.

Greg Craig had been excited at the news that Rehnquist wanted to see the White House lawyers. Any attorney would relish the opportunity to confer with the nation's top jurist. Who knew what morsel of wisdom he might offer at the outset of this most extraordinary trial? However, when Craig arrived in a procession led by Chuck Ruff in his wheelchair, defense lawyers found themselves at the end of a long line of House managers already waiting to be admitted. One by one, the prosecutors and defenders were brought before the chief justice, whose black robe with the gold braids was slightly askew. Rehnquist made eye contact with each one and greeted them ever so properly. "Yes, how do you do, Mr. Manager Hyde?" "Yes, how do you do, Mr. Manager Hutchinson?" The same took place with the president's team. "Yes, how do you do, White House Counsel Ruff?" "Yes, how do you do, Counsel Craig?"

After the introductions, the advocates waited uncomfortably, the thirteen House managers lined up on one side of the room and the White House lawyers on the other. Craig figured Rehnquist was searching for just the right thing to say, given the gravity of their undertaking and his appreciation for history. Finally the chief justice looked up.

"Well, let's begin," Rehnquist said. Then, as if he were a referee at a boxing match, he added, "Fight fair."

To those in the room, of course, it had been anything but a fair fight to this point. Craig and the rest of the White House team believed they had been bulldozed in the House by a vindictive Republican majority out of pure hatred for President Clinton. With Tom DeLay leading the charge, the Republicans had disregarded history and precedent, dispensed with due process, and strong-armed reluctant moderates into a purely partisan impeachment. The Republicans were just as convinced that the White House had not fought fair. Rather than defend Clinton, the president's partisans had pilloried anyone who dared criticize him, from Starr to Hyde to DeLay. Theirs was a fire-bombing strategy that observed no limits imposed by decency or decorum. So when they entered the Senate chamber shortly before 1 P.M. that afternoon, neither side was sure how things would work in this second phase. As David Kendall had told associates, it was as if all of them were in parachutes plunging through the night sky into the murky darkness below. The senators felt the same way. "My heart is pounding not because of nervousness but rather because of the enormity of the task before me," Susan Collins wrote in her diary. "Everyone seems to feel the same way. Tension and expectation fill the air."

Having failed to convince the Senate sergeant at arms to let them switch places, the House managers took their seats around the black-topped table to Rehnquist's right, just in front of the Democratic senators, and the White House lawyers sat at the table to the chief justice's left, in front of the Republican senators. Craig, Kendall, and Ruff were joined at the defense table by Nicole Seligman, Cheryl Mills, Lanny Breuer, and, in a surprise, Bruce Lindsey. Although officially one of the president's lawyers, Lindsey had remained largely invisible during the impeachment process and could theoretically be called as a witness during the Senate trial. The White House team had no intention of putting Lindsey at the lectern to address the Senate. He was there to help with strategy—and to be the president's eyes and ears.

This first day was to be devoted to the prosecution. Hyde, who had originally agreed to let his number two on the committee, Jim Sensenbrenner, open their presentation, thought better of the idea and decided to speak first himself. He would not talk long, just eight or nine minutes, but it was important to frame the case properly from the start, and Sensenbrenner, a plodding, nasal-toned Midwesterner, was not the man to do that. Indeed, Sensenbrenner recognized he was no trial lawyer. "Did I ever tell you about the time I handled an uncontested divorce case and lost?" he asked fellow managers.

Hyde lifted himself to his feet and shuffled the short distance from the prosecution table to the lectern. Approaching the well, he bowed his head slightly at Rehnquist: "Mr. Chief Justice." Then Hyde turned to face the Senate and set his papers down. "Members of the Senate, what you do over the next few weeks will forever affect the meaning of those two words 'I do.' You are now stewards of the oath. Its significance in public service and our cherished system of justice will never be the same after this. Depending on what you decide, it will either be strengthened in its power to achieve justice or it will go the way of so much of our moral infrastructure and become a mere convention, full of sound and fury, signifying nothing."

From the altitude of Hyde's short opening, the Senate quickly became bogged down in Sensenbrenner's monotonous hourlong summary of the case, which he had written a few days earlier while watching football on television. Although Sensenbrenner tried to dismiss the notion that theirs was a case about private wrongdoing rather than public misconduct, it quickly became clear that he had not captured the imagination of the Senate. On his notepad a few feet away, Asa Hutchinson scrawled, "Good but 15 min into—he's lost the Senate audience." Another fifteen minutes later, Hutchinson jotted down another note: "Sen Stevens is asleep."

Staying awake would become a premium for the senators, particularly the older ones. They had to sit at their desks and listen, for hours on end, without saying a word themselves. Under the rules, they had essentially no speaking role on the floor. Even during the question-and-answer period that would come later in the trial, they were required to submit inquiries in writing to the chief justice, who would read them aloud. On this day, as the arguments opened, all one hundred senators were on hand from start to finish, a far cry from their ordinary experience. Senators rarely spend much time on the floor unless they have a bill of their own to steer to passage. And they rarely leave the talking to anyone else.

As the managers began laying out their case, Senators Bob Kerrey, Joe Biden, and Arlen Specter took laborious notes. Rick Santorum chewed gum. Senator Paul D. Wellstone of Minnesota got up several times to stretch an aching back. Tom Harkin, who had dismissed the case as a "pile of dung" on a weekend talk show, shook his head in disagreement at various points in the argument. But otherwise it was a solemn, serious group that seemed, for once, to be paying attention to what was unfolding in front of them.

Another break from tradition was the presence of four large, flat-screen, high-definition television screens, two on each side of Rehnquist (plus a small one installed underneath his desk out of view of the senators). Never before had televisions appeared on the floor of the Senate, and Robert Byrd, the self-appointed guardian of custom in the chamber, had erupted in righteous indignation when he learned that the lawyers wanted to use them for their presentations. Told that the televisions were necessary to show the videotaped clips of the president's testimony, Byrd eventually relented, but insisted on having them covered when they were not in use so as not to offend convention more than necessary.

The problem with that solution became clear just after Sensenbrenner sat down and turned over the lectern to Ed Bryant, the manager from Tennessee, who started his presentation by showing Clinton taking the oath of office as president from Rehnquist. Or rather by *trying* to show Clinton taking the oath. While the image appeared on television sets across the country, no visual actually showed up on the screens inside the Senate chamber because the four machines had overheated while under Byrd's coverings.

The rest of the managers' presentation went smoother. Bryant, Hutchinson, and Jim Rogan spent the afternoon introducing the senators to the details of the case with a series of charts and handouts. Hutchinson captivated the senators by spinning out the tale of obstruction day by day, and sometimes minute by minute, methodically recounting each meeting, each phone call, each court action, and how they all seemed to fit together into a pattern of illegal behavior. Hutchinson related how Clinton did little to help Monica Lewinsky find the job she so desperately wanted until after her name showed up on a witness list in the Paula Jones case on December 5, 1997. Just six days later, on December 11, the judge in the case agreed that the president could be questioned about his relationships with women who worked for the government. That same day, December 11, Hutchinson pointed out, Clinton talked with Vernon Jordan about finding a job for Lewinsky in New York and suddenly the task became a high priority for the president's friend.

"Let's look at the chain of events," Hutchinson told the senators. "The witness list came in. The judge's order came in. That triggered the president to action. And the president triggered Vernon Jordan into action. That chain reaction here is what moved the job search along."

Only after getting Jordan on the case did the president feel comfortable enough to tell Lewinsky that she might be called as a witness to answer questions about their relationship, Hutchinson went on. And when Clinton did call her at two in the morning on December 17, he suggested she could avoid testifying if she swore out an affidavit. She could always say she was delivering papers to him or visiting Betty Currie, Clinton told her that night, recalling the cover stories they had used to try to avoid detection in the past. Hutchinson noted how Jordan had simultaneously found Lewinsky a lawyer to help her execute such an affidavit and then trolled New York corporate boardrooms until he found her a job at Revlon by intervening directly with the head of its holding company, Ron Perelman. "Mission accomplished," Jordan reported back to Clinton after the Revlon job offer came through, a line Hutchinson had blown up into large letters at the top of each of his blue-and-yellow charts.

Hutchinson likewise wove in the other episodes that led to the obstruction charge, how Clinton coached Currie as the Lewinsky story was first breaking, how presidential gifts that had been subpoenaed by the Jones lawyers came to be hidden under Currie's bed at home, how Clinton lied to aides he knew were going to be summoned to testify before the grand jury to pass along his falsehoods. "The seven pillars of this obstruction case were personally constructed by the president of the United States," Hutchinson concluded. "It was done with the intent that the truth and evidence would be suppressed in a civil rights case pending against him. The goal was to win, and he was not going to let the judicial system stand in his way."

Rogan wrapped up the day with a review of the perjury count against the president, using the now working televisions to show the senators a blizzard of video clips of Clinton's statements under oath and to the public, including his finger-wagging "I did not have sexual relations with that woman" declaration on national television. Perhaps most powerful was the juxtaposition of key moments in the president's Jones lawsuit deposition and his later attempts before the grand jury to explain that earlier testimony. Rogan showed Clinton seemingly watching intently during the Jones session as his attorney declared "there is absolutely no sex of any kind, in any manner, shape, or form" between the president and Lewinsky. Then Rogan played Clinton's explanation before the grand jury seven months later that he was not really paying attention when his attorney said that, and besides, "It depends on what the meaning of the word *is* is." In case the senators did not fully appreciate it, Rogan played the two clips again. Either Clinton was not paying attention when the attorney said it, or he was paying such close attention that he picked out the use of the present tense and relied on the literal meaning of the word *is* to justify the veracity of the statement.

"Now, I am a former prosecutor," Rogan added, "and that is like the murderer who says, 'I have an ironclad alibi. I wasn't at the crime scene; I was home with my mother eating apple pie. But if I was there, it is a clear case of self-defense.'"

By the time the managers wrapped up at 7 P.M. that day, the mood at the trial had dramatically changed. For all of the saturation coverage of the Lewinsky scandal over the previous twelve months, most of the senators had never focused on the details and were only now hearing for the first time how all the evidence added up. For many of them, it was a shock, especially for Democrats, who in their own minds had instinctively dismissed the case as weak. Listening to Hutchinson outline the sequence of events, building his case for obstruction brick by brick, the senators were struck by the power of the evidence. Senators milling around the Democratic cloakroom afterward were morose and grim-faced. Senator Russ Feingold, the Wisconsin Democrat, walked out of the chamber thinking, There may actually be a case here. Fellow Democratic senator Dick Durbin of Illinois thought to himself that he might actually have to vote for conviction.

Daschle was worried. If momentum built, he could have trouble holding his caucus together. Daschle had prepared for this moment by recruiting a crew of Democratic lawyers to help puncture holes in the prosecution case, and now they swung into action, poring through the day's presentations to find weaknesses to identify in a memo to be distributed the next morning to every Democratic senator. The team was led by Bob Bauer, Daschle's longtime lawyer, who had advised Dick Gephardt through the House proceedings, and included two of Abbe Lowell's investigators from the House Judiciary Committee, Kevin Simpson and Steven Reich. Lowell himself would have been too controversial to enlist, Daschle's advisers decided, because he had made himself into such a high-profile advocate by the end of the committee hearings. As it was, bringing Simpson and Reich over had prompted retaliation by the Judiciary Republicans. Annoyed that the two Democratic lawyers were still being paid from House funds while working on the Senate side, Jon Dudas, the deputy committee counsel, kicked Simpson and Reich out of their offices, changed the locks, and threatened to file an ethics complaint.

Sensitive to the dispute and leery of having it appear that the Democratic leadership was pressuring senators, Bauer and his team decided they would list no authorship on the memos they would begin producing daily to rebut the House managers. The first of these "blind memos," as they were called, was titled "Factual Inaccuracies in House Managers' Presentation (Day One)," and its five pages took issue with various assertions made by Sensenbrenner and Hutchinson on the floor that Thursday.

But a piece of paper could not alter the impressions held by many senators. In the Republican cloakroom, the conservatives were heartened and some of the early skeptics were reevaluating their initial assessments. Senator Ted Stevens, the cranky Old Bull who had told the managers just a week earlier they had no chance, gushed to reporters that Hutchinson had done a "tremendous job of connecting the dots." Susan Collins used almost identical language in her diary that night: "The star of the day . . . is Asa Hutchinson. . . . His tour-de-force makes a powerful case for the obstruction of justice charge. . . . I learn much that is new as Asa connected the dots on the road map."

At the White House, where aides were practically cheering after listening to Sensenbrenner's droning presentation—"Is that the best they could do?" they crowed to one another—the mood had turned somber by the time Hutchinson was through. As the president's advisers assessed it, Hutchinson came across as reasonable and thorough. Their whole strategy was premised on the notion that the managers would overplay their hand and the White House would be able to use it against them. But Hutchinson had demolished that in a single smooth afternoon performance.

To the lawyers for the president, Hutchinson's performance was too smooth. From where they were sitting on the floor, they kept hearing him make what they thought were factual slipups. And one in particular stood out: Hutchinson suggested that Vernon Jordan stepped up his job search for Lewinsky on December 11, 1997, after the judge in the Jones case issued her order allowing Clinton's relationships with other women to be explored. What Chuck Ruff, Greg Craig, and the other White House lawyers knew was that Jordan had already left the country by the time the judge's order was handed down that day. He was somewhere over the Atlantic on his way to Amsterdam, so her order could not have had the influence that Hutchinson suggested. As the Clinton lawyers discussed that flub, they decided to keep it to themselves for now. It would be far more powerful to wait and use Hutchinson's mistake against him when it came time for them to present their defense next week.

Still, Hutchinson was the man of the hour. While conviction remained unlikely, strategists on both sides now felt that if anyone had a chance of altering the odds, it would be the personable prosecutor from Clinton's own home state. That evening, as the senators digested what they had heard, Hutchinson headed over to nearby Union Station for dinner with Peter Jennings. How much life had changed for this low-profile politician who had lost his first four races for public office before finally winning an election and now, barely two years into Congress, was supping with the anchor of *ABC World News Tonight*—at the broadcaster's request, no less. Jennings was already at B. Smith's restaurant when Hutchinson arrived for their 8:30 P.M. appointment. Linda Douglass, the ABC reporter who covered Congress, was a little late, and as she arrived, she saw none other than Betty Currie walking in. Douglas invited her over to the table to meet Jennings and Hutchinson.

Introduced to Hutchinson, Currie said lightly, "I see my name came up a lot."

The other big sensation of the day was Jim Rogan, the forty-one-year-old manager from southern California who, despite his bare majority in the election the previous fall, had developed into one of the president's fiercest critics. In his debut on the Senate floor that afternoon, Rogan had impressed many of the senators as he passionately denounced Clinton's conduct. Rogan was a political scrapper, perhaps the unlikeliest of prosecutors. A former Democrat who had emerged from the same sort of hardscrabble childhood as the president, Rogan credited Clinton with inspiring him to go to law school two decades earlier. They would recognize each other's story line—both were born to broken homes and suffered from alcoholic stepfathers, all the while quietly dreaming of growing up to become president of the United States. On the night Clinton was elected in 1992, a friend turned to Rogan and said, "That guy's story is your story." And yet perhaps it was the similarity of their backgrounds that led Rogan to take an unforgiving attitude toward Clinton's misconduct. Tough times, he believed, were no justification for shameful behavior.

Rogan was born to an unmarried cocktail waitress and raised by his chain-smoking longshoreman grandfather until he died, then by his grandmother until she died, and finally by a great-aunt until she died. Reunited with his welfare-dependent mother at age twelve, Rogan had led a Jekyll-and-Hyde adolescence—one minute a troublemaker who smoked pot, skipped class, and got thrown out of school, and the next an underage political junkie who idolized Democrats and grew obsessed with collecting campaign buttons and photos. Without ever finishing high school, he enrolled in a community college and managed to earn his way into the University of California at Berkeley and UCLA School of Law, financing his education by working the bar at a club so tough he packed a handgun while serving drinks. His decision to study law was reinforced after attending a midterm Democratic convention in Memphis in December 1978, when Rogan met a young politician who caught his fancy. With dark, shaggy hair that covered his ears, Bill Clinton did not look all that much older than Rogan, but he was now governor-elect of Arkansas. Rogan introduced himself to the rising Democratic star, who asked if he was interested in politics. Rogan said yes, he might want to run someday. Well, Clinton told him, law school was a good background for politics—and a good fallback if politics did not work out.

Rogan would not see Clinton in person again until inauguration day, 1997, when the Californian was entering Congress. In the interim, he had converted to a conservative Republican after serving as a deputy district attorney in Los Angeles putting away gang murderers, rapists, child molesters, and drug dealers. He had developed a flair for theater in the courtroom, often to powerful effect. During closing arguments in the trial of a drunken driver, Rogan had never said a word but instead lined up ten glasses on the rail of the jury box and poured ten cans of beer into them until he had demonstrated just how much the defendant had consumed. Then he held up four fingers to represent the four victims and snapped his fingers to symbolize their lives being snuffed out. The jury convicted within forty-five minutes. Rogan's crime-fighting exploits were noticed. In 1990, the governor of California appointed him a local judge, the youngest in the state at the time, and after a few years he got himself elected to the State Assembly. In 1996, he won a seat in Congress, prevailing in a district where Hollywood influence might normally ensure a more liberal representative. When he arrived in Washington, he wrote a note of praise to Clinton for giving defeated challenger Bob Dole a Presidential Medal of Freedom following the election and told the president he had never forgotten meeting him at the 1978 convention. A week or so later, a White House courier arrived at Rogan's office with a handwritten response from Clinton reminiscing about that day.

But as a politician, Rogan had by then developed a deep distrust of Clinton—he had become convinced the president would not keep his word, would tell people one thing and do another, would claim credit for actions that were not really his. During the 1996 election, he grew to see Clinton as a demagogue for accusing Republicans of wanting to destroy Social Security and Medicare, a charge his own Democratic opponent in California parroted. And now embroiled in the impeachment trial, Rogan marveled at Clinton's ability to say something blatantly untrue and yet appear so sincere. As a prosecutor, he had seen this trait in some defendants so convinced of their own lies that they could pass polygraph tests. As a child of a broken home, he had seen it in a close relative who would look him straight in the eye and lie without blinking.

For all of his courtroom experience, the impeachment trial was like none that Rogan or anyone else had ever prosecuted. Special rules were needed. At Lott's request, Susan Collins issued a nine-point tip sheet on decorum during the proceedings—always stand when Rehnquist enters the room, address him as "Mr. Chief Justice," and never walk between him and the lawyers. Yet while dignity reigned on the floor, the corridors in the Capitol quickly took on an almost carnival-like atmosphere. Whenever the trial recessed for a break, House managers, senators, and to a lesser extent, White House lawyers rushed to the media stakeout to face the battery of television cameras and microphones. One after the other, members of the jury offered running commentary on what they were hearing inside, while prosecutors tried to amplify their case and defense lawyers labored to rebut it. The proceeding had become such an international spectacle that Capitol Police instituted unusual security precautions in case of a terrorist attack. Perhaps most disconcerting to the few lawmakers who noticed them were the black duffel bags surreptitiously deposited at strategic points near the Senate chamber. Inside were dozens of gas masks. Just in case.

It was something of a madhouse behind the chamber as well. The House team had established a headquarters in the Marble Room, where senators normally relax, read, or even sleep during the tedium of floor sessions. Everything in the room except for the furniture and the blue carpet was made out of marble. It quickly took on the frenetic hustle-bustle of a hospital emergency room, with lawyers and lawmakers coming and going, televisions blaring from the side, computers and tables set everywhere, and reams of documents scattered throughout. Lindsey Graham could often be found pacing up and down the room, mumbling to himself as he tried out lines for his presentation. Every so often he would grab a staff member. "Let me try this out on you," he would say, then offer some pithy zinger. "You like that? You like that?"

By the second day of their opening arguments, however, it became clear that in the chaos of their headquarters, the thirteen managers were not consulting fully with each other about their presentations. On Friday, January 15, five managers offered four hours of arguments that began to sound numbingly familiar. Bill McCollum started out by summing up the evidence, followed by George Gekas, Steve Chabot, Chris Cannon, and Bob Barr discussing the legal issues of the case in what became a law school seminar on perjury and obstruction of justice. It got to the point where they were even using the same lines. Around the chamber, senators strained to remain engaged. Daschle stared off in the distance. Lott leafed idly through the books of evidence. Bob Torricelli and Chuck Schumer sat slumped in their chairs, their hands on their faces. Even most of the managers were not in the chamber as the arguments droned on. At the defense table, the lawyers exchanged furtive smiles and notes on yellow Post-it pads.

Everyone woke up late in the afternoon, though, when they saw someone leap to his feet at the back of the chamber. "Mr. Chief Justice, I object," called out Tom Harkin, the Iowa Democrat and staunch Clinton supporter. Bob Barr had been close to finishing the day's final presentation when he addressed the senators as "you, the distinguished jurors in this case." That term, *jurors,* had gotten under Harkin's skin all week. They were not just ordinary jurors confined to ruling on guilt or innocence, he felt; they were senators empowered to take into account other factors such as the good of the nation. The last thing Daschle wanted was for Democrats to be lodging objections. Far better, he thought, to play it safe and avoid stirring the waters. At Daschle's request, Harkin had agreed not to do anything on the floor without checking with him first, but then as Barr was going on, the senator's pique got the better of him. In his seat a few rows away, Daschle moaned softly to himself.

Harkin began reading a lengthy justification for his position, citing the Constitution, the Senate rules, and *The Federalist* papers. The Republicans were momentarily panicked. Sitting on the backbench, Eric Ueland, an aide to Senator Don Nickles, cried out to the GOP senators in a loud whisper, "Regular order! Regular order!" Another aide rushed up to chief legal counsel Tom Griffith and exclaimed, "Harkin's speaking! Stop him!" Finally, Senator Judd Gregg, a New Hampshire Republican, rose to his feet to object to the length of the objection, putting an end to Harkin's monologue.

But Rehnquist sided with the Democrat on the crux of his complaint. "The Senate is not simply a jury; it is a court in this case," the chief justice proclaimed. "Therefore, counsel should refrain from referring to the senators as *jurors.*"

While Harkin and other Democrats gloated, Lott was exasperated. How could this have happened? They had lost the first ruling in the case. A few minutes later, when the session ended for the day, Lott summoned Griffith over to the well of the Senate and asked how Rehnquist's ruling could be overruled. A transcript was shortly produced, and Griffith studied it along with Parliamentarian Bob Dove, Lott's lawyer Mike Wallace, and Rehnquist aide Jim Duff, among others, but they concluded that the chief justice had it right. Griffith took the determination to Lott's chief aide, Dave Hoppe, who agreed to drop the issue. But Lott and other Republicans continued to smolder.

Harkin was the hero of the moment to the Democrats, but he was not done. During a break that same afternoon, he retreated to his hideaway office in the Capitol along with fellow liberal senator Paul Wellstone and fretted about the strength of the managers' case. "As I was looking down at the floor," Harkin told Wellstone, "all the guys sitting on the House side, these are guys we know. I've served with Hyde. I've served with Sensenbrenner. We see them across the table when we deal in conference. I look at the White House side and we don't know any of these guys. We don't know Ruff, we don't know Craig, we don't know Kendall. . . . We need somebody who can really connect with senators." Like a former senator.

Harkin picked up the telephone and called over to the White House. The only senior official he could find was Paul Begala, the presidential counselor. "Sounds great," Begala said. "Why don't you bounce it off Daschle?"

After the floor session ended, Harkin headed over to Daschle's office, where Democratic senators were gathering each day after the trial to hash out what to do next. As the meeting was breaking up, Harkin huddled with Daschle and Harry Reid, the Democratic whip. They had been thinking the same thing—Daschle had been wondering whether his predecessor, George Mitchell, would do it, while Reid had in mind the astronaut-turned-senator John H. Glenn of Ohio, who had recently retired. Harkin suggested Dale Bumpers, another just-retired Democratic senator and a powerful orator from Clinton's home state of Arkansas. Daschle assigned Harkin to call all three to see if any would do it.

If the first two days of the prosecution case were spent scouring through the weeds of evidence, the final day on Saturday, January 16, brought the Senate back to more elevated terrain, with talk of honor, principle, and patriotism. Steve Buyer, Charles Canady, and George Gekas made the constitutional arguments that Clinton's misdeeds qualified as high crimes worthy of removal, but it was the odd couple of Lindsey Graham and Henry Hyde who caught the attention of the "triers of fact and law," as the senators were now being called.

Graham was the Matlock of the House team, spinning folksy homilies in his South Carolina drawl. Unlike the methodical Asa Hutchinson or the roaring Jim Rogan, Graham relied not on a prepared script but scrawled notes and his own stream-of-consciousness improvisation. His was a talk, a conversation even, not a speech. Occasionally, he wandered away from the lectern, Oprah-like, a microphone clipped to his lapel. He empathized with senators sitting through what he agreed might seem like "a snoozer." In his sometimes rambling yet captivating way, Graham tried to undercut two of the strongest arguments from the other side—that the president's misdeeds had no broader consequences that required a constitutional solution and that the country could not stand the upheaval that would result from replacing its president. "To set aside an election is a very scary thought in a democracy," Graham acknowledged, but he stressed that the nation had calmly absorbed what was happening. "If you convict him, it will be traumatic, and if you remove him, it will be traumatic, but we will survive." Graham then tried to place the Paula Jones lawsuit and sexual harassment laws in the context of civil rights, something the president had defended passionately for his whole career. "When those rights had to be applied to him, he failed miserably," Graham said. The Supreme Court had ruled unanimously that he had to answer to Jones, but "when he chose to lie, when he chose to manipulate the evidence to witnesses against him and get his friends to go lie for him, he, in fact, I think, vetoed that decision."

Graham compared Clinton's case with that of federal judges impeached and convicted for perjury and similar charges. "The question becomes, if a federal judge could be thrown out of office for lying and trying to fix a friend's son's case, can the president of the United States be removed from office for trying to fix his case? You could not live with yourself, knowing that you were going to leave a perjurer as a judge on the bench. Ladies and gentlemen, as hard as it may be, for the same reasons, cleanse this office."

Hyde provided the lofty counterpoint to the down-home Graham. Silver-haired and well-practiced at the art of soaring political oratory, Hyde liked to summon the ghosts of Anglo-American icons and invoke concepts like "sacred honor" and "bedrock principle." As he had done on the floor of the House a month earlier, he cited the Ten Commandments, Roman law, and the Magna Carta and framed the choice before the Senate as a question of patriotism. "We must never tolerate one law for the ruler and another for the ruled," Hyde intoned. "If we do, we break faith with our ancestors from Bunker Hill, Lexington, Concord, to Flanders Fields, Normandy, Hiroshima, Panmunjom, Saigon, and Desert Storm."

Hyde even resorted to the time-honored tool of the politicians mastered by Ronald Reagan—the letter from a constituent. In this case, Hyde read a note sent by a third-grader from Chicago, who wrote that Clinton should be forced to write a hundred-word essay by hand because "I do not believe the president tells the truth anymore right now." The boy's father added a postscript disclosing that he had forced his son to write the letter as punishment after he had lied and defended himself by saying that the president had lied too. "Some of us have been called Clinton haters," Hyde said. "I must tell you distinguished senators that this impeachment trial is not, for those of us from the House, a question of hating anyone. This is not a question of who we hate, it's a question of what we love. And among the things we love are the rule of law, equal justice before the law, and honor in our public life. All of us are trying as hard as we can to do our duty as we see it—no more and no less."

The problem for the managers was that they did not always see eye to eye on what that duty should be. After leaving the floor that evening, they gathered to discuss strategy, including whether to call Clinton as a witness. The constitutionality of issuing a subpoena to a president to testify in a congressional proceeding was dubious at best, so most of the discussion centered on whether they should ask the Senate to invite Clinton to come voluntarily.

Rogan and Bill McCollum argued strongly for calling the president. He was the one person who knew the most about all of the events in dispute. He owed it to the Senate to appear and answer for his actions. Even if they could not subpoena him, ratcheting up the pressure might compel him to come to avoid appearing afraid. Rogan had already been tapped by Hyde to prepare for questioning the president, and he was anxious for the opportunity.

Asa Hutchinson dissented. Under the separation-of-powers doctrine, he said, it would be inappropriate to do anything to pressure a president to appear before Congress. Besides, he added, it would look too political and simply backlash in favor of the Democrats.

At that moment, the Democrats would have welcomed anything that would work to their benefit. As they left the floor, the Democratic senators looked like war-weary soldiers who had been strafed by the enemy. Gathering in Daschle's conference room after the floor session, a number of rattled senators worried that the managers were scoring points, particularly after Graham's presentation that afternoon. "This guy's killing us," complained Bob Bauer, Daschle's lawyer. Graham had successfully minimized the significance of removing the president; he had made the unthinkable thinkable. The Democrats had also cringed when Graham described Clinton as a champion of civil rights who had failed when it came to his own case. "Oh, fuck, that was powerful," Kevin Simpson, the Democratic investigator, told colleagues. And the comparison with the judges who had been removed for perjury had unnerved several of the Democratic senators—that was an argument that really cut.

Bauer opened the meeting by proposing two ways that they should hit back at Hyde for his Flanders Fields analogies on the grounds that he went way too far in suggesting the Senate had to convict Clinton to honor its war dead. "This can't be compared to the sacrifice of troops at Normandy," Bauer told the group.

But it quickly became apparent that the senators had no fight in them. "I'm not comfortable with this," said Dick Durbin. "Why don't we just say, 'You can't judge the score by halftime'?" suggested Chuck Schumer.

The others around the table nodded their agreement. That was the way to go—cut their losses and hope the White House could mount an effective comeback next week.

Despite the success of the joint caucus in the Old Senate Chamber that had produced the trial rules a week earlier, both Democrats and Republicans had decided to keep meeting separately for the remainder of the trial, once again reinforcing the party-line nature of the proceeding. Daschle, who in normal times convened his caucus once a week, was now holding meetings every morning at ten o'clock in an effort to keep his troops on board. The closed-door sessions over the last week, though, had revealed the depth of the party's frustration with Clinton. Resentment flavored the discussion as senators chewed through the case in detail for the first time. A lot of what the Republicans had been saying about Clinton resonated with the Democrats—they did not like him much either, let alone trust him. By several counts, seven or eight of the forty-five Democratic senators got up at these caucus meetings and suggested they would have been better off had the president stepped down.

"Clinton should have resigned," Senator Fritz Hollings told the caucus one day. "If he had an ounce of honor, he would have done it a long time ago. But he didn't, so we're stuck with him." Wearing sunglasses because of recent eye surgery, the seventy-seven-year-old conservative from South Carolina did not bother to hide his disdain for Clinton. "Let's get this thing over with," he said, and then paused. "Where's Dianne?" he asked, looking around the room for Dianne Feinstein from California. Spotting her, Hollings continued his tirade against Clinton. "And then after this is all over with, I think what he ought to do is go back to San Francisco where they don't recognize *funny* people like him."

The other senators laughed, including Feinstein. "I can't believe, Fritz, you're doing this to me after I backed you in the last election!" she shot back.

At the White House, a sense of foreboding hung over the strategy sessions that weekend as the president's advisers tried to figure out how to present his defense in a way that would appeal to senatorial skeptics. Despite what the pundits were saying, the White House was not at all sure it could count on acquittal. While their heads told them there were not twelve Democrats who would defect, their hearts were seized with fear born of the recognition that nothing had gone according to plan so far in this crisis. Who knew what might happen now? The managers were clearly on a roll, and the Clinton team had to find a way to put a stop to it. As the lawyers reminded the president's political aides, the prosecution in any trial appears strong after it has presented its own case. But the aides realized that Tom Harkin was right and they needed another way to communicate with the senators, particularly the Democrats. They had to rally the Democrats.

Harkin had heard back from John Glenn's office that he was out of the country and would not be available. George Mitchell once again turned down the job in a telephone call on Sunday, January 17. About an hour later, Dale Bumpers called Harkin back. "Oh, God, I can't do that," he said once Harkin explained what he wanted.

"I'm just telling you, we need you," Harkin implored. "The country needs you. The president needs you."

Bumpers told him he would think about it and hung up. Bumpers, seventy-three, who had served as governor of Arkansas before Clinton did, had just stepped down from the Senate after twenty-four years of service. Known as a staunch liberal who crusaded against profligate military spending, he was generally popular on both sides of the aisle, although some Republicans considered him a demagogue. But Bumpers was not really close to Clinton. In fact, for years the two were wary rivals for the mantle of top dog in a small state. While he was governor, Clinton even suspected Bumpers of spreading stories in Arkansas about his womanizing. To overcome Bumpers's resistance, Harkin decided more pressure was needed and tracked down Terry McAuliffe, the president's friend, at the steam room of a gym the next day, Monday, January 18, to arrange for Clinton to call Bumpers personally. The president did, but Bumpers was still reluctant.

"I'm not the right man for the job," Bumpers told Clinton. They were from the same state, he pointed out. It would not have any credibility.

Clinton persisted. Think about it, will you? A few hours later, Clinton called again to see if he would agree.

Bumpers put him off again. "Let me meditate tonight and see what I could put together."

After hanging up, Bumpers deposited himself in a recliner in his suburban Maryland home and spent the next three or four hours scribbling on a notepad. The next morning, he called Bruce Lindsey and accepted the assignment.

In the meantime, Greg Craig was pursuing another idea. Since some of the Democratic senators had been appalled during caucus meetings when they were told about the unfair impeachment process in the House, he figured the White House should recruit some of the Democrats from the House Judiciary Committee to join the defense team to tell the whole Senate how the president had been railroaded. Craig and the others at the White House came up with three House Democrats to add to the team—John Conyers, Rick Boucher, and Tom Barrett from Wisconsin. The Clinton aides had been impressed with Boucher and Barrett and felt they had to have Conyers as the senior Democrat on the committee.

Yet the idea collapsed before it could be developed. Word of the plan leaked out even before the White House had bothered to ask the House members whether they would be willing. Conyers and Barrett agreed to join the team anyway, but when John Podesta reached Boucher at 8 A.M. on Tuesday, January 19, the Virginia congressman said no. After all the time he had spent on this painful issue in the House, Boucher had felt an enormous sense of relief to be freed of the responsibility. Besides, he reasoned, how could he adequately prepare with just a few days' notice? Podesta thanked him politely, but when word got around the White House, other aides fumed and vowed to take revenge.

It made no difference. While White House aides thought Daschle had cleared the idea of recruiting House members with Robert Byrd, in fact the powerful senator objected vehemently to the plan once he learned about it during the Democrats' closed-door caucus meeting later that Tuesday morning, just hours before the defense team was to take the floor and open its case. It was wholly inappropriate for members of the House to play a role on the defense team of the chief executive, Byrd declared. Other senators tried to reason with him. Clinton had a right to choose whomever he wanted. "This is his defense," some argued.

"You don't understand how strongly I feel about this," Byrd roared back. "It hits me *right here,*" he said, fiercely chopping his hand at his own chest. "Right here!"

Even though Byrd was outnumbered, Daschle quickly realized it was better to pull the plug and told the White House to drop the House Democrats. In keeping with their don't-irritate-Byrd strategy, the president's advisers promptly did just that. But it was one more blowup they did not need.

More internal tension would be generated when the presidential lawyers sat down to go over their assignments for the coming week's arguments. Chuck Ruff told the group that he would open their presentation but keep it relatively brief so as to avoid upstaging the president's State of the Union address scheduled for later the same evening. White House aides had given some thought to giving up their time on the first day of defense arguments and leaving the message entirely to Clinton and his annual policy address, but decided on this middle-ground course instead. On the second day, Ruff told the group, Craig would present the defense against the perjury count, and Cheryl Mills would handle half of the obstruction charges, leaving the rest of that count to David Kendall on the third day. Dale Bumpers would close. Left out were Nicole Seligman and Lanny Breuer, who were told they might get to handle motions and witnesses later in the trial. Seligman reacted calmly to the decision, but Breuer was distraught at what he saw as a betrayal by Ruff, his former law partner at Covington & Burling.

At thirty-three, Mills had been a tough behind-the-scenes operator in the Clinton White House since its inception, earning the unwavering trust of the first family with her give-no-ground approach. But she had spent only two years at a law firm before joining the Clinton camp and had none of the extensive courtroom experience of Breuer, a forty-year-old former New York prosecutor, or Seligman, who at forty-two had helped defend Oliver North during Iran-contra and had handled other high-profile Washington cases. Aside from her smarts and her tight relationship with the Clintons, though, Mills brought something to the lectern none of the other lawyers did—she was African-American, which would stand in silent contrast to the thirteen white men prosecuting the president and allow her to counter the damaging points made by Lindsey Graham about Clinton's failure to live up to civil rights laws.

Just before 1 P.M. on that Tuesday, Ruff wheeled himself onto the floor of the Senate and, after the opening prayer, rolled over to the well to begin the president's defense. The lectern had been removed to accommodate his wheelchair and a small table set up to his left on which to put his papers and a glass of water. He also put down a copy of *The Federalist* papers. Ruff attached a microphone to his lapel, but it would fall off repeatedly until he gave up and held it in his hand. For all of his years of experience at the intersection of law and politics in Washington, Ruff seemed atypically nervous at first, his left hand shaking as he talked. He had worked late into the night at home writing his presentation by himself without consulting the other lawyers and had kept his drafts so secret that even the client had no idea what Ruff would say this day. The night before, Clinton had called Mills to ask what Ruff planned to tell the Senate, she told a colleague; Mills had to confess she did not know either.

Ruff knew he had to undercut the managers' credibility and spent much of the next few hours methodically pulling at the loose threads of their case in hopes of unraveling the entire quilt. While the managers had impressed their audience with measured professionalism, it fell to Ruff to recast them as overzealous advocates willing to shade the truth and draw unsubstantiated conclusions from flimsy evidence. "What you have before you," Ruff told the senators, "is the product of nothing more than a rush to judgment." The managers had concocted a "witches' brew of charges" and constructed their case "out of sealing wax and string and spiders' webs" on top of "shifting sand castles of speculation."

Ruff gave several examples of what he called "prosecutorial fudging." The knockout blow: Vernon Jordan could not have been motivated to intensify his job search for Lewinsky on December 11, 1997, by a court order allowing women such as her to be questioned in the Jones lawsuit because the judge made her ruling during a conference call that began at 6:33 P.M., nearly forty minutes after Jordan had gotten on a plane for Amsterdam. "Beware of the prosecutor who feels it necessary to deceive the court," Ruff warned solemnly, with Asa Hutchinson's own chart mounted on the easel to his side.

If this had been a regular courtroom, the jury might have gasped at the revelation. In this case, it cemented Ruff's standing with the Senate. Relentlessly sober, the president's trial lawyer offered a striking contrast to the orations of the politician-managers. Theater was not his style. He had brought the copy of *The Federalist* papers with him to hold up as a prop, but decided when he came to that section of his presentation simply to read the desired citations from his notes instead. While rarely scintillating, he projected a sense of gravitas that played well in the chamber. After all the shouting of the last twelve months, here was a grown-up, reminding the country of what was really at stake.

"We are not here to defend William Clinton the man," he said. "He, like all of us, will find his judges elsewhere. We are here to defend William Clinton the president of the United States, for whom you are the only judges. You are free to criticize him, to find his personal conduct distasteful. But ask whether this is the moment when, for the first time in our history, the actions of a president have so put at risk the government the framers created that there is only one solution. You must find not merely that removal is an acceptable option, that we will be okay the day after you vote," he added in an implicit rebuttal to Lindsey Graham's powerful argument from the week before. "You must find that it's the only solution, that our democracy should not be made to sustain two more years of this president's service."

Ruff finished his prepared text, but decided he had to say one more thing. Like Bob Bauer, he had been outraged by Hyde's invocation of D-Day war heroes. Overnight, Ruff had gone back and forth about whether to challenge it and had not decided when he started speaking. But as he turned the last page, he found himself going on anyway. "I have no personal experience with war. I have only visited Normandy as a tourist. I do know this: My father was on the beach fifty-five years ago"—Ruff choked up momentarily—"and I know how he would feel if he were here. He didn't fight, no one fought, for one side of this case or the other. He fought, as all those did, for our country and our Constitution. As long as each of us—the managers, the president's counsel, the senators—does his or her constitutional duty, those who fought for the country will be proud."

Hutchinson felt stung after Ruff had finished. The zinger about Jordan being on a plane to Amsterdam hurt. How had he missed that? He had relied on the information in David Schippers's report to the committee. It did not really matter because without question Clinton knew by that point that Lewinsky might be a witness, so he already had all the incentive he needed to spur Jordan into accelerating the job hunt, even without the court order. But Hutchinson was aggravated because there was no rebuttal opportunity.

By this point, Hutchinson had grown disenchanted with Schippers anyway. He was too flamboyant, too hotheaded, too quick to declare new evidence to be "dynamite." In fact, Hutchinson was barely working with Schippers anymore, relying instead on his deputy, Susan Bogart. Still, as he digested Ruff's presentation, Hutchinson thought he detected its own flaw—the White House lawyer had flatly stated that the president could not have been witness tampering when he coached Betty Currie because she was not a witness in the Jones case and would never be named as one, let alone

subpoenaed. Hutchinson remembered that in the House investigation they
had discovered otherwise—the Jones lawyers had in fact put her on a witness
list and issued a subpoena after the Lewinsky story broke. The issue became
moot when the judge blocked them from gathering any more evidence connected to the relationship for fear of interfering with Starr's new investigation, and neither the witness list nor the subpoena had ever been made
public. Hutchinson asked Bogart, who had consulted with Jones's legal team
during the House hearings, to look into it.

That night, Hutchinson had another role to play, however. As a member
of the congressional delegation from the president's home state, he had to
serve on the escort committee for the State of the Union address. He had
considered backing out, but decided it was his duty. So when the president
approached the state delegation in the Capitol a few hours after Ruff's presentation, there was Hutchinson, the man prosecuting him, shaking his hand
and offering a polite greeting.

"Well, I see that you finally got you a good lawyer," Hutchinson told
the president with a smile, referring to the addition of Dale Bumpers that
morning.

Clinton seemed taken aback. "I think he's actually excited," the president
said of Bumpers, and then moved away.

Clinton's speech turned out to be another tour de force. While Chief Justice Rehnquist stayed away and a variety of Republicans, including Hyde,
decided not to show either, most concluded that etiquette was the better part
of valor and came anyway. From Clinton's cheery disposition and expansive
agenda, viewers might easily have forgotten that this was a president who
had just been impeached for high crimes and was on trial in the Senate. Clinton mentioned none of that. Instead, he painted a portrait of a prosperous
nation at peace and served up an ambitious plan to devote $2.7 trillion in
projected budget surpluses to Social Security. With a flourish of showman-
ship, he introduced a bevy of guests in the gallery, from home-run hitter
Sammy Sosa to civil rights legend Rosa Parks, and offered tribute to his wife,
ostentatiously mouthing "I love you" to Hillary Clinton in the gallery.

Striking a magnanimous tone intended to contrast with the partisanship
of his enemies, Clinton welcomed newly installed House Speaker Dennis
Hastert to the job and turned to shake his hand while promising cooperation. And the president made light of the obvious tension in the air, joking
that only one side of the room would applaud at a time—usually the
Democrats, as the Republicans sat on their hands. When both sides got up to
cheer a line about equal pay for women, Clinton laughed.

"That was encouraging, you know?" he said playfully. "There was more
balance on the seesaw. I like that. Let's give them a hand."

But the Republicans were not amused. The defendant in an impeachment trial was presenting his case, in effect, for more than an hour without cross-examination. Just as he had a year earlier when the scandal first broke, Clinton had used a State of the Union address to cast himself as above all the seediness that obsessed the Republicans in Congress. The lawmakers were just props in his show, and he played them masterfully. Instant polls showed that once again the public applauded Clinton and his program. The next morning, one of his fiercest critics, Christian Coalition founder Pat Robertson, would pronounce the speech a "home run" that spelled the end of the trial. "Clinton's won," he said. "They might as well dismiss the impeachment hearing and get on with something else because it's over as far as I'm concerned."

The next morning, Wednesday, January 20, President Clinton boarded *Air Force One* and left Washington for his traditional campaign-style tour to promote his State of the Union program. As a destination, his aides picked Buffalo—the home district of Congressman Jack Quinn, the moderate Republican whose support for impeachment had broken the back of the president's defenders a month earlier. White House operatives managed to pack more than eighteen thousand people into the city's hockey arena, a massive crowd even by presidential standards, to rally to the president's side along with Hillary Clinton, Vice President Gore, and Tipper Gore. The screw-you message to Quinn and the DeLay Republicans was unmistakable.

Back at the Capitol, the president's lawyers were trying a different approach with the Senate Republicans. There would be no inflammatory attacks, no overt pressure, just an appeal to those who seemed open to persuasion. Sitting on the Republican side of the chamber, some of the White House attorneys were, in fact, regularly striking up conversations with the senators during breaks. Strom Thurmond, the ancient senator from South Carolina, kept coming over to the defense table to flirt with Nicole Seligman and Cheryl Mills. "How come you're so cute?" he would ask, then clutch one of their arms. "I just love holding on to you." He even brought them candy and tangerines. The two tried to respond politely. One day, they brought brownies wrapped in tinfoil baked by a woman who had been cooking for the overworked, undernourished counsel's office, only to be stopped by Senate officials, who said food was prohibited on the floor and were surprised to hear that Thurmond had been secreting sweets to them.

Jim Ziglar, the sergeant at arms, took it upon himself to gently confront Thurmond. "Now, Senator, you've got to stop hitting on the president's lawyers."

"What do you mean?" Thurmond asked innocently.

"I know you've been bringing cookies and candy to those young lawyers."

"Oh, you caught me."

"Now, Senator, what would we do if they filed some sort of sexual harassment suit?"

A mischievous grin crossed Thurmond's face. "Now, wouldn't that be nice?"

The old-fashioned attitudes of some of the aging male senators presented other delicate challenges for the two women on the White House team. Both power players in the nation's capital, they were used to wearing pantsuits but wondered whether that would be appropriate on the Senate floor. After discussing it several times, Mills and Seligman decided to stick with skirts lest they offend even one of the crustier old senators. It was just not worth the risk, no matter how silly an issue it seemed. They were particularly worried about upsetting Robert Byrd. Once again the don't-irritate-Byrd strategy came into play.

Before Mills had her turn at the lectern, though, Greg Craig would deconstruct the perjury count for the senators on this Wednesday afternoon. Unlike Mills, Seligman, Ruff, or the others, Craig was thought of as something of an auxiliary member of the Senate club. He had worked on Capitol Hill for Senator Ted Kennedy, become friends with Senator Kent Conrad as a young man, and knew other senators from his work at the State Department. He traveled in the same circles and knew the same people. And of all the lawyers at the defense table that day—Dale Bumpers was at home working on his speech—Craig had the most political ear and voice. Indeed, as he began unwrapping his version of the case, he made the only reference to the president's strong poll numbers as a reason to acquit—a citation that other White House lawyers had objected to as crass when they read Craig's draft and thought they had succeeded in excising.

"Do not throw our politics into the darkness of endless recrimination," Craig implored the senators. "Do not inject a poison of bitter partisanship into the body politic, which, like a virus, can move through our national bloodstream for years to come with results none can know or calculate."

Craig, promising to provide the Senate with "more than one hundred percent of your minimum daily requirement for lawyering," recited a litany of complaints with the managers' case: The charges against the president were too vague and seemed to change depending on the day. The allegations misstated the president's testimony. The prosecutors were using a "bootstrapping mechanism" to try to incorporate Clinton's testimony in the Jones case as an element at the trial even though the House had specifically rejected an article of impeachment dealing with his civil deposition. With a dictionary at his side and a fourteen-minute videotape excerpt from the president's interview with the Jones lawyers, Craig defended the Clinton interpretation of "sexual relations." He even defended Clinton's "meaning of *is*" statement before the grand jury, saying the president was guilty not of perjury but "the offense of nitpicking and arguing with the prosecutors." And Craig suggested that the appropriate response to the president's misconduct was to throw him to the wolves of the criminal justice system "like any other citizen"—after he left office.

Mills went next. If she was nervous for the first major "courtroom" appearance of her career, she did not show it. Coolly, confidently, she launched into a detailed examination of some of the obstruction of justice charges against the president. She spoke slowly, taking care to enunciate each word, but each word carried with it a stiletto aimed right at the managers. Over and over, she mocked the House members; "those stubborn facts" just did not fit their allegations, she said, using the same phrase eight times, usually glaring at the prosecution table as she did, her voice dripping with contempt.

But her real mission was to demolish the argument that the case somehow turned on civil rights. Mills had been infuriated by Lindsey Graham's argument and, in the first draft of her statement, had included a slashing rejoinder that would have attacked the congressman's family. During his statement on the floor when he was talking about the progress that had been made in civil rights, Graham had noted that his parents owned a restaurant in South Carolina where blacks were not allowed to stay to drink their beer. Mills wrote a line comparing that racist practice with the policy of Clinton's grandfather, who owned one of the only stores in his Arkansas town that would cater to black customers. It was a powerful contrast, Mills thought. Too powerful, as some fellow White House aides saw it. In the end, Mills decided to take it out. In the final version she read on the floor, Mills noted the history of Clinton's family without making comparisons to Graham's. Instead, she compared Clinton to Thomas Jefferson, John F. Kennedy, and Martin Luther King Jr., all of whom strayed sexually. "We revere these men. We should. But they were not perfect men. They made human errors, but they struggled to do humanity good. I am not worried about civil rights because this president's record on civil rights, on women's rights, on all of our rights, is unimpeachable."

Mills's presentation immediately became the talk of the town. Some of her fellow White House lawyers felt it was terrible—condescending and overly melodramatic, like a high school student actor trying too hard in her stage debut. But elsewhere Mills was a huge hit. Senators gushed about her in the cloakrooms. Commentators raved about her on television. Tourists and everyday congressional aides, particularly African-Americans, flocked up to her offering praise and gratitude. She had inspired a reaction like none of the others. After she was done speaking, the White House team gathered in the vice president's office behind the Senate chamber to watch the reviews on

CNN. Craig stood closest to the television as a legal analyst panned his performance while Mills collected the plaudits. It was a humiliating moment for him, and an awkward silence filled the room.

The Senate Republicans were left dispirited by Mills. She had proved to be a powerful force and put them on the defensive. Between her and Ruff, the tide was turning; whatever momentum the managers had built was quickly dissipating. If the managers and the defense lawyers simply canceled each other out, that would be enough for Clinton to win because something dramatic had to happen to convince Democrats to buck the party line.

Unknown to either side, though, an event with that potential took place that day—Juanita Broaddrick, after years of silence, had decided to tell her story. In her home in Van Buren, Arkansas, Broaddrick taped an interview with NBC's Lisa Myers accusing Clinton of raping her. While much of official Washington by that point knew the outlines of her story, none of the senators judging the president had ever heard it from her own mouth, and even though her allegation was not technically part of the impeachment case, no one could calculate what impact it might have on public opinion if the country saw it in the middle of the trial. The question became when—or whether—NBC would air it.

Susan Collins knew none of that when she called her fellow senator Russ Feingold that night to hash over what they had heard on the floor so far. She was surprised to find that the Wisconsin Democrat shared her basic assessment—the perjury charges in Article I seemed somewhat weak, while the obstruction of justice allegations in Article II were far more troublesome. Collins and Feingold agreed to write a joint, bipartisan question about Betty Currie for the upcoming question-and-answer period.

"Although the President's lies may not meet the legal test of perjury and thus the first article may be weak, they bother me nonetheless," Collins wrote in her diary that night. "It's so tawdry, so dispiriting to hear the videotape of the President shading the truth." But, she added, "It's becoming obvious to me that the Independent Counsel's attorneys did a terrible job pinning down the President, perhaps from a misguided sense of deference. That is a major reason the perjury case is so weak."

The next morning, Thursday, January 21, anxious GOP senators began agitating for a way to put an end to the trial. "We've got to get out," Senator Craig Thomas of Wyoming said at a meeting in the office of Georgia's Senator Paul Coverdell. The same theme pervaded the Republican conference lunch meeting.

"Calm down," the conference chairman, Connie Mack, told his nervous colleagues. "We're all where we all thought we'd be."

Lott was focused on finding an endgame and holding his balky caucus together through the difficult votes to come. They needed, he said, to vote down any attempt by the Democrats to require that Clinton be found guilty beyond a reasonable doubt to be convicted, a high standard used in criminal trials but not in civil trials, and never before required in an impeachment proceeding. They also should vote against the Democratic motion to open deliberations, he said.

Susan Collins spoke up. After hearing both sides, she said, it was clear that Article II, the obstruction of justice count, was stronger than Article I, the perjury charge. They ought to focus on the obstruction allegations, she said, adding that she would vote to dismiss the other article.

It was the first crack in Republican solidarity and Lott was worried. He did not want to make it easy for any GOP senator to vote against either of the articles by separating them into distinct questions. There would be only one vote, he told the gathering—to dismiss the entire case or not. "We ought to have an all-out blitz against the motion to dismiss," he said.

Across town, Asa Hutchinson was proceeding on the assumption that they could defeat a motion to dismiss and perhaps even get permission to question witnesses. As one of the managers who would be responsible for taking any testimony, he decided to visit William G. Hundley, Vernon Jordan's attorney and law partner, to see if it would be possible to informally interview the president's friend first. Hundley, a courtly veteran of the Washington bar, politely said no, that would not be possible, and made clear that his client would not veer from his grand jury testimony in any case. Warming up to the topic, Hundley compared Jordan to another client he once represented, former attorney general John N. Mitchell, who went to prison for Richard Nixon. Jordan was the same way with Clinton, Hundley said. He would do anything for the president, even his dirty business. "I'm really surprised you people are calling Vernon. Once those White House lawyers start feeding him these softballs, he's going to have Bill Clinton up there with Abraham Lincoln."

Hutchinson arrived back at the Capitol in time to hear the White House complete its opening arguments. David Kendall went first, warning that his review of the obstruction charges would be "tedious," and he lived up to his prediction. He chastised the managers for offering one "strained theory" after another, often finding that their charts were "riddled with errors," and that the evidence actually opened up "a very large hole in their circumstantial case." Examining the various elements of obstruction individually, he offered innocent explanations for the events in question and concluded there was no trade-off for Lewinsky's silence. "Quid pro quo? No," he declared in a rhetorical refrain after each scenario.

Like Mills, Kendall initially had envisioned a provocative line of defense that worried fellow Clinton advisers. In his case, he wanted to challenge Lewinsky's credibility in certain areas of her testimony that seemed to implicate the president. But through all of the congressional proceedings, the White House had been careful never to attack Lewinsky publicly, and the advisers decided not to start now. Besides, Kendall wanted to rely heavily on her most exculpatory statement to the grand jury, and it might confuse the issue to credit part of her testimony and undermine other aspects of it. Standing in the well of the Senate, Kendall reminded the juror-judges that Lewinsky flatly denied being coerced to provide false testimony. In case any senator had missed it, he repeated it seventeen times during his presentation: "No one ever asked me to lie and I was never promised a job for my silence." Turning to the prosecution table, Kendall asked scornfully, "Is there something difficult to understand here?"

If Kendall was the mechanic, Dale Bumpers was to be the driver who powered the race car around the track. With his shock of silver hair, his deep voice, and country-lawyer mannerisms, Bumpers was the stereotypical picture of the senator. Just three weeks out of office, he spent no time on Subpart 4 of Article II, made no mention of the December 11 court order. Speaking from hand-scrawled notes on yellow legal paper and wandering around the well so far afield that his microphone kept falling off, Bumpers went straight for the hearts of his friends. He talked about his awe of the institution, the "goose bumps" he still got in the Senate chamber. He repeatedly addressed his audience as "colleagues," citing a number by name.

"The charge and the punishment are totally out of sync," Bumpers said. "When you hear somebody say, 'This is not about sex,' it's about sex." In gentler style than Kendall, he too chided the managers, attributing their excesses to "wanting to win too much." Taking direct aim at Hyde's Flanders Fields speech, Bumpers said soldiers did not fight to impeach a president for this and pointed to a handful of senators around the chamber who were war heroes themselves.

Most powerfully, Bumpers brought home the personal dimension of the case. "You pick your own adjective to describe the president's conduct. Here are some that I would use: indefensible, outrageous, unforgivable, shameless. I promise you the president would not contest any of those or any others. But there is a human element in this case that has not even been mentioned. . . . The relationship between husband and wife, father and child, has been incredibly strained, if not destroyed. There has been nothing but sleepless nights, mental agony, for this family, for almost five years, day after day, from accusations of having Vince Foster assassinated, on down."

Looking around the room, Bumpers went on, "We are, none of us, perfect. Sure, you say, he should have thought of all that beforehand. And indeed he should, just as Adam and Eve should have." Now pointing at the senators, he added, "Just as you and you and you and you and millions of other people who have been caught in similar circumstances should have thought of it before. As I say, none of us is perfect."

CHAPTER FOURTEEN

*"The horse
is stinking up the room"*

Chuck Ruff arranged the secret signal with the Senate Democratic lead-ership—and in characteristic fashion kept it so secret that he did not even tell his White House colleagues. When the Senate opened its two-day ques-tion-and-answer period on Friday, January 22, Ruff wanted the option of rebutting anything the managers might say, but the rules did not provide for any direct back-and-forth. So he and Tom Daschle's aides agreed that if he needed a chance to reply, the Senate Democrats would submit a question to the chief justice asking the White House, "Would you please comment on any of the legal or factual assertions made by the managers in their response to the previous question?" The aides would simply fill in the name of one of several "default senators," who had agreed in advance to let themselves be used in this way, such as reliable liberals Chris Dodd and Patrick Leahy. And Ruff would indicate when he needed such help simply by laying his pen down on the table in front of him on the Senate floor. The signal was so subtle that when it came time to put it into use, Senate aides sometimes missed it. "Did he move his pen?" they would ask one another. Left in the dark, Ruff's fellow White House lawyers correctly assumed he had made a deal with Senate staff and played guessing games among themselves trying to figure out what his cue was. Some wrongly speculated that it was when Ruff moved his wheelchair back from the table.

Ruff did not want to leave much to chance. Unlike the opening argu-ments, the question-and-answer session would go beyond simply reading from the script and involve at least some spontaneous back-and-forth, pre-senting obvious dangers to the White House and managers alike. The Democrats were not the only ones clandestinely rigging the process to best serve their strategic needs. Asa Hutchinson and the rest of the House team were desperate for a chance to counter the previous three days of White House arguments and turned to Senate Republicans for help. An ordinary criminal proceeding would have allowed prosecutors a chance to respond to the defense, but in the frantic rush to draft rules two weeks earlier, Senate aides had forgotten to include any rebuttal time. So the managers asked Senator Fred Thompson, who was helping to coordinate the Republican side, to plant some questions that would let them make some points. Thompson agreed to set aside the first five questions.

Under the rules, any senator could ask a question, but only by submitting it in writing to the chief justice, who would read it aloud. The rules said nothing about follow-up questions or in what order they would be asked or whether anyone could screen them for redundancy and relevance. Without much to guide them, the senators fell back on the organizational system they knew best—their political parties. Rather than allow members to send questions directly to Rehnquist, all Republicans would turn in their proposed inquiries to Trent Lott and all Democrats to Daschle. Logistically, they saw little choice; Rehnquist indicated he had no desire to winnow through the submissions, and the prospect of one hundred would-be interrogators posing random questions promised bedlam. Senator Orrin Hatch convinced Lott that the questions needed to be structured to make sure the most important areas of the case would be covered and to keep senators from asking the same question over and over. But the decision also subliminally reinforced the idea that the trial was just another party-line debate in which Democrats stuck together and Republicans did likewise. Tom Griffith, the Senate's chief lawyer, raised that concern to aides for both Lott and Daschle, only to be told there was no real choice. The preparations for the question-and-answer session became about strategy—how best to emphasize the strengths of our case and the weaknesses in theirs.

Lott had appointed Hatch, Thompson, and Senator Mike DeWine of Ohio to coordinate the questions for Republicans, and Hatch sent out his first memo soliciting proposed questions on January 14 as the opening arguments began. Within five days, they had received some fifty questions from various senators and fed them into a database so that lawyers Mike Wallace, Stewart Verdery, and others could review them. An E-mail account was set up to accept more, with a simple question mark—?—serving as the electronic address. Hatch and his staff worked up a number of their own questions, grouping them into sections—legal and constitutional matters, factual discrepancies, and so forth. The questioning was to switch off between the two parties every two hours, and Hatch wanted to develop a logical string of inquiries that would serve as the equivalent of a courtroom cross-examination.

Some of the questions submitted by senators or their aides to the Republican screening committee were clearly over the top. Senators Arlen Specter, the veteran legislator from Pennsylvania, and Jim Bunning, the baseball Hall of Famer just elected from Kentucky, jointly proposed asking "What was the specific conduct of the President and Ms. Monica Lewinsky in what the President characterized as an 'inappropriate, intimate relationship'?" While Clinton's grand jury testimony in effect raised that issue by describing their contact as "intimate" without constituting "sexual relations," GOP leadership aides knew that asking about it would just give Democrats ammunition to say the Republicans were only interested in who touched what. Scratch that question. Senators Michael Enzi of Wyoming and Bob Smith of New Hampshire sent in a sharp-edged zinger. They noted that before the grand jury Clinton had insisted his first sexual encounter with Lewinsky did not take place until 1996, even though she testified it was on November 15, 1995, after she brought him pizza during the government shutdown. Then they noted that in his Paula Jones testimony, Clinton remembered her delivering pizza. "Is it really possible," they asked, "that he remembered the pizza but forgot the intimate encounter which followed?" Clever, the leadership aides thought, but maybe too much so. Scratch that too. Then there was the one from DeWine. The Ohio senator wanted to know how White House lawyers could argue Clinton did not commit perjury when he testified that his sexual relationship with Lewinsky grew out of a friendship, given that she performed oral sex on him the first night they met. "Please explain and clarify with specificity the President's understanding of the term 'friendship' and elucidate the details of the President's 'friendship' period with Ms. Lewinsky," DeWine proposed asking. Once again, the leadership aides liked the question, but figured it could easily backfire.

A day or two before the question session was to begin, binders of 179 proposed questions were left in the Republican cloakroom with spaces for senators to fill in their names if they wanted to "ask" any of them. Near the end of one party conference that week, Lott noted that some senators had not signed on to any of the questions, let alone submitted their own, and urged all of them to do so, in order that history would record that they participated. Aides quietly steered many of the questions most likely to be asked to Senators Susan Collins, Olympia Snowe, John Chafee, and other fence-sitting moderates, hoping to make sure they felt involved.

The Democrats were going through a similar process. Bob Bauer and his fellow lawyers, Kevin Simpson and Steven Reich, collected scores of questions, sorted them into piles, put them into huge notebooks, and screened out those they considered poorly drafted or too inflammatory. Among the rejected were two rather pointed queries from newly elected senator Chuck Schumer, who sought to contrast current Republican piety with the party's own past scandals. "In light of these eloquent testimonials to the need for 'honor,' 'veracity,' and 'truthfulness' in our leaders, did any of you vote against the reelection of Newt Gingrich as Speaker of the House in January of 1997 or request his resignation upon reading the Special Counsel's report?" Schumer wanted to ask the managers, knowing that none had. One of the screeners marked "No" next to this one. Another Schumer jab: "Given your concern for the impact of President Clinton's conduct on military morale and discipline, did any of you call for President Bush's resignation when he pardoned Caspar Weinberger in 1992, while Weinberger was already under indictment for perjury?" This one was nixed as well.

The Democratic lawyers settled on what they called a "Bill Walsh strategy"—just as the famed San Francisco 49ers football coach would script out his first ten plays and call subsequent ones depending on how the game was going, they determined their first ten questions and would then leave things open to improvisation. To keep the other side from developing a rhythm, Daschle had insisted on a late switch in the format. Instead of granting each party a two-hour block at a time, every Republican question would be followed by a Democratic one and vice versa, guaranteeing instant rebuttal. The biggest debate in Daschle's office centered on whether to direct any questions to the House managers at all. Several Democrats wanted to challenge prosecutors on the flaws in their case and confront them about how they had conducted themselves. But in the end, Daschle and his advisers decided to pose no more than a few to the managers because time was limited and no follow-ups were allowed so they could not really force them to answer directly. Worse, it could just provide an opportunity for the House team to segue into some far more damaging area. Instead, the Democrats decided it was better to concentrate on sending softball questions to the White House lawyers so they could score rhetorical points.

As Friday, January 22, arrived, Republican senators were growing increasingly anxious about where the trial was headed. The president's lawyers had arrested the House team's momentum, and a number of GOP moderates, particularly from the Northeast, were struggling with deep doubts about the strength of the case. The managers began to pick up signals of where their problems lay—Susan Collins wanted to limit the scope of what witnesses could address, Fred Thompson was concerned about having too many witnesses, Democrat Richard Bryan of Nevada wanted a representative sample of witnesses, not an exhaustive list. At the Senate Republican conference lunch, the tone of the discussion turned more nervous.

"We've got to get out of here," said Bob Bennett, the lanky senator from Utah who had earlier tried to discourage his home-state House manager, Chris Cannon, from pushing for witnesses. "The horse is stinking up the room."

At 1 P.M., the senators, managers, and lawyers gathered again on the Senate floor. If the opening arguments were merely set-piece speeches, a question-and-answer period could be far more volatile, more like a debate right before an election. They could prep all they wanted, but in the end, it still required the main players to match wits and think quickly. Much as a candidate can be haunted by a single debate gaffe, the prosecutors and defense attorneys knew any ill-considered remark during the next two days could easily be used against them to ruinous effect.

From his seat on the aisle, Lott handed a sheet of paper to the deputy sergeant at arms, who delivered it to a clerk, who passed it to the chief justice. In a flat voice, Rehnquist read the first question, attributed to four bedrock conservative Republicans, Senators Wayne Allard, Jim Bunning, Paul Coverdell, and Larry Craig: "Is it the opinion of the House managers that the president's defense team, in the presentation, mischaracterized any factual or legal issue in this case? If so, please explain."

This was exactly what the managers wanted, an open-ended question intended to give them the rebuttal time they were denied during the opening arguments. Ed Bryant moved to the lectern and addressed points he argued were misconstrued by the president's team, emphasizing that this was hardly a case of he-said/she-said given the voluminous corroboration of Lewinsky's testimony. But what had clearly gotten to the managers were the attacks on their integrity. Twice in the course of a nine-minute answer Bryant brought up the White House charges that they had been "fudging the facts" and concocting a "witches' brew" of deception.

"It may be good theater, but it is simply not the case that these managers are engaged in that type of practice before the Senate and the American people," Bryant complained.

The next question came from the Democrats, relayed by Daschle to Rehnquist, and in keeping with their strategy it asked the White House lawyers if they had anything to say in response. Ruff dismissed the issue of corroboration. The evidence Bryant cited proved only what the president had already admitted—an inappropriate relationship with Lewinsky—and had no bearing on what was still in dispute, whether he had committed perjury or obstruction of justice. Aware that he had struck a nerve with his earlier zingers, Ruff said in an innocent tone that he did not mean to apply the "fudging" label to everything the managers had told the Senate. "I have never suggested that the entire presentation is so, and I made very clear in my comments to the Senate the other day the specific examples, which I think we documented quite fully," he said.

With the opening round out of the way, Asa Hutchinson finally got the chance he had been anticipating for days. Still burned at Ruff for undercutting his obstruction argument by using the Vernon Jordan trip to Amsterdam, Hutchinson had been determined to catch the White House in a blatant factual blunder, and now thanks to investigator Susan Bogart he had the documentation in front of him. In response to the second open-ended Republican question—"Please elaborate on whether the president's defense team failed to respond to any allegations made by the House managers"—Hutchinson practically leapt to the lectern, papers in hand.

Hutchinson reminded the senators that Ruff had argued that the president could not have been coaching a witness when he ran through the false statements with Betty Currie because Clinton had no reason to suspect she might be called to testify in the Jones case. Hutchinson had Ruff's quotes in case anyone had forgotten—"In the entire history of the Jones case, Ms. Currie's name had not appeared on any witness list, nor was there any reason to suspect that Ms. Currie would play a role in the Jones case," and "in the days and weeks following the deposition, the Jones lawyers never listed her, never contacted her, never added her to any witness list."

Not true, Hutchinson declared. In fact, the Jones lawyers had issued a subpoena to Currie on January 22, 1998, five days after the deposition, and put her name on a supplemental witness list on January 23. The list was sent to the president's personal lawyer, and Currie was served with the subpoena on January 27. To drive home his point, Hutchinson held up copies of the subpoena and the witness list. "Talk about prosecutorial fudging!" the manager exclaimed. "How about defense fudging?"

Hutchinson had nailed Ruff with a clean shot, one just as damning, he hoped, as the White House counsel's Amsterdam-trip rebuttal. Ruff had said there was never a subpoena, never a witness list, but there they were. Ruff was chagrined. He had not known about the subpoena or the supplemental witness list. Much as Hutchinson had drawn his information from David Schippers's report during the House hearings, Ruff had relied on Abbe Lowell's presentation. But as a seasoned courtroom practitioner, Ruff knew the best thing to do when confronted with an error was to own up to it without equivocation—and then try to pass it off as essentially irrelevant.

"I owe him indeed an explanation and he is correct in one respect," Ruff said of Hutchinson when it came his turn to respond. "I did not accurately reflect the fact that after the January twenty-first story in the *Washington Post,* the Jones lawyers did, in fact, attempt to track the entire independent counsel investigation. And I think Mr. Hutchinson will tell you, they indeed issued a long list of subpoenas. For that misleading statement, I apologize, and I trust we will hear equally candid assessments from the managers."

Still, Ruff went on, the president did not know the Jones lawyers were going to subpoena Currie when he spoke with her. It was the best answer

Ruff could give, but as the afternoon wore on, it appeared to many in the Senate chamber that the managers were having the better of the question format. For the first time, the two sides were engaging in what amounted to a direct, head-to-head debate, and some of the Democratic senators worried that the professorial style that had served Ruff so well in monologue did not match up as well against the more practiced political style of the House team's best presenters, Hutchinson, Jim Rogan, and Lindsey Graham.

After a few questions, the Senate Republicans tried to help Hutchinson explain away his flub on Jordan's flight to Amsterdam. While "the White House makes much of the fact," Hatch and Senator John Ashcroft said in a joint question, wasn't it just "a red herring" since the president's lawyer had been faxed a witness list with Lewinsky's name on it six days earlier? Now it was Hutchinson's turn to explain himself. Yes, he said, it was true that with Jordan flying to Europe at the time, the judge's order "could not have triggered any action on the eleventh. There is no question about that. That is obvious from the facts, as it was obvious when I made my presentation. The meetings on the eleventh, with Vernon Jordan and Monica Lewinsky, were triggered by the witness list coming on the fifth." Then, like Ruff, he argued that in effect it was unimportant. Jordan himself had testified that "the subpoena changed the circumstances," Hutchinson said. That meant the job search intensified as a result of Lewinsky being called as a witness.

Democrats were quick to seize on this, hoping to keep the focus on Hutchinson's mistake. Bob Bauer, sitting to Daschle's left, grabbed a beige card emblazoned with the Senate letterhead, scribbled out a question, and using one of his "default senators," signed Barbara Boxer's name to it. "In light of the confession of Manager Hutchinson that Judge Wright's order had no bearing on the 'intensity' of the job search," Rehnquist read aloud from the card, "can you comment on the balance of his claim on the previous question?"

Confession? Hutchinson did not like that and jumped to his feet. "Mr. Chief Justice, could I object to the form of the question?" he asked somewhat playfully. "That was not proper characterizing what I just stated."

Rehnquist was momentarily flummoxed: "I don't think managers—I am not sure whether the managers . . ." Then he looked down at the parliamentarian sitting in front of him. "Can the managers object to a *question?*" he asked as laughter erupted in the chamber.

"I withdraw my objection," Hutchinson said, having made his point.

"Very well," Rehnquist said. "The parliamentarian says they can only object to an answer, not to a question." Then he added in a dry aside, "Which is kind of an unusual thing, but . . ."

As senators laughed again, Daschle leaned over to Bauer. "That was kind of rough, wasn't it?" he asked quietly, meaning the phrasing of the question. Well, it wasn't supposed to be, Bauer whispered back. He had written *concession*, but his handwriting was so bad, Rehnquist read it as *confession*.

Ruff was not about to surrender to the humor of the moment when he had a chance to keep the House team on the defensive. "Whether we call it a confession or simply an acknowledgment," he said, Hutchinson's revised answer showed how the managers were trying to "bob and weave and dodge around the facts here." Ruff mocked the managers' line of argument. "If there was ever a moving target, we have just seen it in motion: 'Well, it really wasn't December eleventh, because now we know it didn't happen on December eleventh, so let's go to December nineteenth, or maybe January eighth, and somewhere in there we are going to find the right answer.' I suggest to you that that is reflective of both the difficulty we have had in coming to grips with these charges and, candidly, the difficulty that the House might have had figuring out what those charges really were."

All this jousting over details, however, was doing nothing for the one senator whose opinion the White House cared about most. To Robert Byrd, it did not matter whether Jordan flew to Holland or whether Currie had been served with a subpoena. As he saw it, the president had undeniably done the things he was accused of doing. The only real issue was whether it was worth removing him from office. Up until this point, all the questions from Democratic senators had been served up with the aim of helping the White House lawyers make a point. Byrd, though, submitted a question that cut straight to the heart of the matter. In characteristic fashion, he quoted *Federalist* No. 65, where Alexander Hamilton wrote that impeachment stemmed from "the misconduct of public men or, in other words, from the abuse or violation of some public trust."

"Putting aside the specific legal questions concerning perjury and obstruction of justice," Byrd asked, "how does the president defend against the charge that, by giving false and misleading statements under oath, such 'misconduct' abused or violated 'some public trust'?"

Ruff once again took the microphone. Even if Clinton did commit perjury and obstruction of justice, he said, it did not threaten the country. That was what the framers intended when they drafted the impeachment clause. "If we have not convinced you on the facts, I hope we will convince you that the framers would have asked: Is our system so endangered that we must not only turn the president over to the same rule of law that any other citizen would be put under, after he leaves office, but must we cut short his term and overturn the will of the nation? And in our view, in the worst-case scenario you can find, the answer to that question must still be no."

Byrd stared intently as Ruff spoke, his face betraying not a hint of reaction. He was inscrutable even to the fellow Democrats who thought they knew what he planned to do. To some of the Republicans listening, it sounded as if Byrd was truly skeptical of the White House argument, and they did not think Ruff responded persuasively. Was it possible they could win Byrd's vote? And if they did, would it provide political cover for other undecided Democrats to vote guilty as well? Even if Clinton was acquitted, winning a few Democrats might vindicate their effort as a legitimate prosecution, not just a partisan exercise.

At the House team's table, spirits were high. Finally after three days of sitting through White House arguments, the managers were taking the battle to the other side and, in their minds at least, regaining some momentum. Jim Rogan added some fire to their presentations with spirited answers to the next few questions. The Californian ridiculed the White House position that Clinton was evasive, misleading, and incomplete but did not actually lie under oath. "If anybody wants a lesson in legal schizophrenia, please read the president's trial brief," Rogan said. A few minutes later, Rogan came back to that point again. "That begs the question: What kind of oath did the president take in the civil deposition? Did he take an oath, did he raise his hand and swear to tell the truth, the evasive truth, and nothing but the evasive truth?"

If the managers harbored hopes that they had made inroads with Byrd, though, they soon learned better. Just after 3 P.M., barely two hours into the question-and-answer session, a piece of paper was pushed across their table on the Senate floor. The managers stared at it one after the other, their eyes widening. It was a news release headlined, "Statement by U.S. Senator Robert C. Byrd—a Call for Dismissal of the Charges and End of the Trial." In the statement, the West Virginia senator said he would introduce a motion to dismiss the case at the beginning of the next week.

"I plan to make this motion not because I believe that the President did no wrong," Byrd said in the statement. "In fact, I think he has caused his family, his friends, and this nation great pain. I believe that he has weakened the already fragile public trust that has been placed in his care. But I am convinced that the necessary two-thirds for conviction are not there and that they are not likely to develop. I have also become convinced that lengthening this trial will only prolong and deepen the divisive, bitter, and polarizing effect that this sorry affair has visited upon our nation." Rankled by the media-saturated atmosphere surrounding what he saw as a sacred duty, Byrd scoffed that calling witnesses would "only foster more of the same hallway press conferences and battle of press releases that are contributing to the division of our parties and our nation."

The statement electrified the Senate chamber, even though it went unmentioned in the formal proceedings, which were continuing as Rehnquist read questions aloud and the lawyers and managers stepped forward to answer. The press gallery buzzed as the news release was passed out. Lawrence Stein, the chief White House lobbyist on Capitol Hill, passed a note to Lanny Breuer, sitting at the lawyers' table on the floor, explaining what had happened. Breuer passed it along to the other lawyers. "Don't smile, don't gloat," the note said. "It's over."

Indeed, it was over, and everyone in the chamber knew it. A Democratic motion to dismiss had been inevitable, but virtually no one had anticipated that Byrd would be the sponsor. In their private party conferences, Senator Bob Torricelli, the sharply partisan New Jersey Democrat, had been pushing for that distinction, only to be put off by Daschle and other party leaders, who wanted someone with more credibility than a prominent Clinton defender. No one could be a more powerful patron of the Democratic bid to end the trial than Byrd, who was known to despise Clinton, to abhor what he had done, and to be virtually immune to the peer pressures of party politics. If Byrd, the constitutional scholar and fiercely independent soul of the Senate, had concluded that the charges could not be sustained, it meant that the Democratic caucus would hold. It meant that other Democrats who might have entertained the thought of turning against the president would not have Byrd for cover. It meant that at most there might be one or two Democrats defecting, nowhere near the twelve needed for conviction.

The managers knew that too, and Hyde could barely disguise his frustration. At every turn they had been accused of unfairness, and now here they were, not allowed to present their full case, and they were being told the trial was over before it had really begun. As the questioning continued on the floor, Hyde took advantage of a friendly inquiry from Senate Republicans to give voice to his disillusionment, sounding as if he were acknowledging defeat and offering a valedictory for their failed campaign: "We tried to be fair because we understand you need a two-thirds vote to remove the president. We needed Democratic support. So far we had none. That is okay. Let the process play itself out. But we were fair." His voice tinged with contempt, Hyde told the senators, "By dismissing the articles of impeachment before you have a complete trial, you are sending a terrible message to the people of the country. You are saying, I guess, perjury is okay, if it is about sex. Obstruction is okay, even though it is an effort to deny a citizen her right to a fair trial."

With a melodramatic flourish, Hyde played the wounded victim. "I know, oh, do I know, what an annoyance we are in the bosom of this great body. But we are a *constitutional* annoyance and I remind you of that fact."

Unbeknownst to the senators, the White House lawyers, and even most of the managers, the House team was at that very moment opening up another front just a few hundred yards away. At the federal courthouse in the shadow of the Capitol, chief U.S. district judge Norma Holloway Johnson convened an emergency hearing to decide whether Monica Lewinsky should have to talk with the managers.

Bill McCollum, the intense manager from Florida, had been pressing colleagues for days to start preparing witnesses in case they were allowed to call them during the trial. A longtime member of the naval reserves' judge advocate general corps, McCollum argued that any lawyer trying a case would talk with his witnesses before calling them to the stand; the first rule of prosecution is never ask a question to which you do not know the answer. They needed to see how Lewinsky would answer their questions, to see how cooperative she might be, to help make sure she related events in a helpful way, and to warn her that if she did not, they would have to assail her credibility. How else were they supposed to prepare unless they sat down with her?

Hyde and some of the other managers were wary. Although they were the prosecutors, they were on Senate turf now. What would a meeting really accomplish? McCollum kept pushing the point, urging David Schippers to get in touch with the witnesses and even calling Lewinsky's lawyers himself. The former intern's legal team had no interest in helping and said so. In fact, her lawyers said, the House team had no authority to talk with her outside of Starr's jurisdiction because she had an immunity agreement. So McCollum and Schippers, oblivious to the possible political fallout, turned to Starr's office for help. Within forty-eight hours they found themselves in Johnson's courtroom at five-thirty on a Friday afternoon. Lewinsky's two lead attorneys, Plato Cacheris and Jacob A. Stein, had been called away from a black-tie dinner at the downtown Mayflower Hotel and rushed over to the courthouse in their tuxedos. Starr deputy Bob Bittman asked where they had been, and Cacheris decided to yank his chain. "The White House," he said, tongue planted firmly in cheek as he watched a look of alarm momentarily cross Bittman's face.

"I'm so sorry to interfere with this black-tie affair," Johnson said when she saw the two lawyers walk into the courtroom.

"Your Honor, we always dress like this for Friday emergency hearings," replied Stein, who had cultivated a reputation as one of Washington's nattiest dressers.

The issue at hand was whether Lewinsky's immunity agreement with Starr's office required her to submit to an interview with the House managers. The agreement, which she had signed the previous July as part of her deal to avoid prosecution, stated that she agreed to "testify truthfully" in a variety of possible proceedings, including any "congressional hearings," and that she would "make herself available for any interviews upon reasonable request."

"At the time—that is, in July—that this was signed, it was absolutely con-templated that there may be some sort of proceeding in Congress," Bittman told the judge.

"The agreement has been overtaken by many events," Stein argued in response. Now that Starr's office had referred the case to the House for impeachment, its job was done and only the Senate could subpoena wit-nesses for an impeachment trial, he said. "The OIC wants to help the man-agers by ushering in Ms. Lewinsky to a private meeting, without any of the representatives of the president being there. That is a very partisan state of affairs. And the statute doesn't give them this right. Once they gave the mate-rial to the House, their role was over in this."

Johnson sounded dubious that Starr was somehow done legally just because he had made a referral to the House. "You know, I'm still handling OIC stuff," she said. "And maybe if I don't have to do that, I'd like to know what authority you're going to suggest for it."

Bittman took the cue and reinforced the point: "We are still in business, despite what many people would like, but we are. And we're still involved. And we still are involved very actively in some of the very matters that are going on in the Congress."

After a half hour, Johnson had heard all she needed. Time was short; the managers wanted to talk with Lewinsky over the weekend, before turning in their witness list to the Senate on Monday. Johnson said she would let them know her decision in the next day or so, but she tipped her hand by instruct-ing Lewinsky's lawyers to have their client get on a plane in Los Angeles just in case.

"Tell her to come on back East."

CHAPTER FIFTEEN

"This is going to be ninety white men leering at her"

As Asa Hutchinson got into the car the morning of Saturday, January 23, his aide Chris Battle thrust the newspaper at him. "Starr Tries to Force Lewinsky Interview," said the front-page headline in the *Washington Post*, "House 'Managers' Want to Talk to Her."

"Did you know about this?" Battle asked.

Hutchinson could not believe it. As he read the story, he grew more and more aggravated. What was this all about? A *Post* reporter had caught him by telephone the night before after the day's floor session ended to ask him about it, but Hutchinson did not know what she was talking about and, rather than admit that, simply offered a vague comment saying it was proper to try to prepare witnesses. He did not focus on it until the headline was staring him in the face. What a nightmare, he thought. The last thing they should be doing was getting in bed with Starr. How had this happened? Hutchinson knew the staff had been trying to make contact with Lewinsky's attorneys to see if she might be willing to be interviewed, just as he had done with Vernon Jordan's lawyer. But no one had told him they planned to recruit Starr and seek a court order forcing her to sit with them against her will. Now it was in all the newspapers and on every television broadcast.

"I'm on the evidence team!" he complained to one of the committee lawyers as soon as he arrived at the Capitol for the second day of the question-and-answer period. "I'm interviewing the witnesses! How can we be going to court with the independent counsel without me knowing about it?"

The lawyer said it was a long story. Henry Hyde had agreed to sign a letter asking Starr's office to help convince Lewinsky to cooperate but had not been told that the standoff had escalated into a court fight. David Schippers had taken it upon himself. The frustration for Hutchinson was overwhelming. The Starr intervention, coupled with Robert Byrd's announcement, had totally eclipsed his rebuttal on the Betty Currie subpoena. Hutchinson felt they had blown the White House out of the water with that, showing that the president's lawyers were every bit as fast and loose with the facts as they accused the prosecutors of being. This was a huge win and should have been a huge story. But instead, Starr and Byrd dominated the news coverage, and the Lewinsky hearing was sure to factor into the day's floor session as the senators took another crack at questioning the lawyers from both sides.

Hutchinson was right. The news of Starr's reemergence in the case threw the trial into an uproar. When the Democrats heard that the independent counsel had gone to court on the managers' behalf, they were stunned by the audacity—and overjoyed at the tactical opportunity. The managers had just given Democrats every excuse to turn attention back to their favorite issue and link the House team to its new ally—to make Starr "the fourteenth manager," as Tom Daschle put it. As long as they could focus discussion on the enormously unpopular prosecutor, they could shift scrutiny away from the president's conduct. Best yet, this appeared to be a blatant intrusion into the Senate's rightful role in running the trial, the kind of presumption that might offend Republicans as well as Democrats. Democratic lawyers Bob Bauer, Kevin Simpson, and Steven Reich happily scrapped their plans for day two of the question-and-answer session and drafted a slew of questions about the new alliance between Starr and the managers.

Indeed, the development did aggravate Senate Republicans, particularly because they had been caught unaware. Tom Griffith, the chief Senate lawyer, did not know about it until reading it in the newspaper and agreed with Democrats that it was an outrageous trampling on the privileges of the Senate. Calling Starr deputy Bob Bittman to get more details, Griffith tried to make his unhappiness clear. "I would have thought before you made representations about what the Senate meant in S. Res. 16 you would've called the Senate's lawyer," he said pointedly.

At the Republican conference meeting that morning, held at nine before the trial was to resume at ten, the senators were agitated. Not only were they blindsided on the Starr-Lewinsky hearing, they were burned up about Byrd's bombshell from the day before. Trent Lott tried to calm his anxious members: "We all knew this day had to come. On Monday, we'll have to fish or cut bait." The majority leader then laid out the possibilities for how to get through the end of the trial, including an option to go directly to final votes on the articles, forgoing Byrd's dismissal motion in exchange for calling no witnesses. Another alternative was to ram through a Republican procedural plan over the objections of the Democrats. At the moment, Lott was worried whether he could even hold his majority together to beat a motion to dismiss.

His concern only deepened when Susan Collins got up to say that the Senate should go ahead and agree with the Democrats to dismiss Article I, the perjury count. That was the charge seen as weakest by some Republicans, and throwing it out would show that they were being fair, Collins argued.

Phil Gramm disagreed. All other impeachment trials had gone the distance, he said, and this would be bad precedent for the future. What would happen, he asked, if the country had a tyrant in the White House who happened to be popular? As for Byrd, Gramm was aghast. The Byrd who issued that statement yesterday was not the master of the Senate and its history that Gramm had known. Senator Larry Craig seconded that thought and suggested they should not let Byrd deliver a lengthy speech on the floor.

Then Senator James M. Jeffords of Vermont stood up. Another of the New England moderates who had been on the fence, Jeffords now sounded as if he had made up his mind. The evidence was slim that this was a high crime, he declared. The facts of the case were terrible, he allowed, but simply not impeachable. As he listened, Lott knew what this meant—along with Collins and Ted Stevens, who had already expressed similar sentiments, Jeffords's assessment meant that there were now three Republican votes against at least one of the articles. If Lott lost three more, and Democrats stuck together, they could cobble together a fifty-one-vote majority to dismiss the case. Lott could not afford to let that happen.

When the trial resumed on the floor, Democrats immediately launched into their strategy of making the day about Starr. The first question was directed to the managers in Senator Harry Reid's name: Did they notify the White House or the Senate that they planned to go to court with Starr's office to force Monica Lewinsky to talk with them? The second Democratic question came from Senator Pat Leahy: Did they talk with any member of the Senate about this or consider that it would violate Senate rules? The third was from Senator Chris Dodd and went to the White House: Wasn't there a fundamental due-process question raised by the unilateral actions of the managers? The fourth was from Daschle, again to the White House: Shouldn't the president's lawyers be allowed to participate in any debriefing of Lewinsky? The Democrats, of course, knew the answers to all of these questions; the point was to make the managers squirm.

Bill McCollum, who had goaded the managers into interviewing Lewinsky, was sent to the lectern to defend the move: "It has everything to do with the right of anyone to prepare their witness, to get to know their witness, to shake hands, say hello, to put a face on that. It is normal practice to do this. We see in no way how that abrogates this rule, or in any way violates what you have set forth. As a matter of fact, we think we would have been incompetent and derelict as presenters of the witnesses, if we get a chance to present them, if we couldn't talk to her."

Chuck Ruff was only too happy to pounce, mocking McCollum's suggestion that the purpose was to "say hello" and pointing out that, under the terms of her immunity agreement, Lewinsky faced the possibility of imprisonment if she spurned Starr's dictates. "Can we really say that is just normal, just okay, to have one side using the might and majesty of the independent counsel's office, threatening a witness with violation of an immunity agreement if she doesn't agree to fly across the country and meet for this friendly little chat?" Ruff asked. "I think not."

After four consecutive questions on the subject, some of the Democratic aides preparing cards for Daschle to send to the lectern were raring for more. But Bauer pulled the plug, concluding they might look as if they were protesting too much if they persisted. The decision proved to be fortuitous, for the next line of inquiry would turn out to be immensely fruitful for the Democrats. Senators Herb Kohl of Wisconsin and John Edwards of North Carolina submitted an inquiry that, unlike so many of the questions, seemed less intended to make a point than to generate a more thoughtful dialogue. "Throughout this trial both sides have spoken in absolutes; that is, if the president engaged in this conduct, prosecutors claim he must be convicted and removed from office, while the president's lawyers argue that such conduct does not in any way rise to an impeachable offense. It strikes many of us as a closer call. So let me ask you this: Even if the president engaged in the alleged conduct, can reasonable people disagree with the conclusion that, as a matter of law, he must be convicted and removed from office—yes or no?"

Lindsey Graham volunteered to answer for the managers: "Absolutely." The allegations in this case "are not trivial," he said, and if the senators concluded Clinton committed perjury and obstruction of justice, he believed those counted as high crimes. "But I would be the first to admit that the Constitution is silent on this question about whether or not every high crime has to result in removal. If I was sitting where you are, I would probably get down on my knees before I made that decision. Because the impact on society is going to be real either way." He added, "You have to consider what is best for this nation."

A wave of panic washed over the managers' table. What was Graham doing? He was giving the senators an out. He was agreeing that this was a tough call. A basic rule of prosecutors was never to show a jury any hint of doubt, particularly if close to half of the jurors were already looking for reasons to acquit. They had to stop him. Steve Buyer, the hard-charging manager from Indiana, signaled that he would like to finish the answer for the managers, but Graham brushed him off.

"I will yield to Mr. Buyer in a second," Graham said, "but the point that I am trying to make, not as articulately as I can, is that I know how hard that decision is. It has also been hard for me. It has never been hard to find out whether Bill Clinton committed perjury or whether he obstructed justice. That ain't a hard one for me. But when you take the good of this nation, the upside and the downside, reasonable people can disagree on what we should do."

Democrats looked at each other, eyes widened, grins barely suppressed. Did he just say what they thought he said? Did he just say reasonable people could disagree?

Buyer jumped for the lectern as Graham sat down and tried to salvage the situation. "I would just like to remind all of you that the impeachment process is intended to cleanse the executive or the judicial office when it is plagued with such a cancer as perjury or obstruction of justice, which violates the oath required to hold those high offices. You have a duty to preserve the integrity of public office, and that is what impeachment was precisely designed to do." If the senators had any question, Buyer added, they could come up with "findings of fact," much like a civil court case, in which they could determine first whether Clinton lied under oath and obstructed justice before deciding whether to vote for conviction.

Buyer had tried to contain the damage for the managers, but it was too late. *Reasonable people can disagree.* It took only a few moments for Ruff to weave that into his answer to another question, and it would soon become the mantra for every Democrat who ran to a bank of microphones after the day's session was over. "Mr. Chief Justice, this is something I won't have an opportunity to say very often, but I believe that Mr. Manager Graham has, in fact, stated for you the essential of the role that this body must play," Ruff said at the next opportunity that presented itself on the floor. "Not only can reasonable people differ on the facts, but reasonable people may differ on the outcome. And if, indeed, reasonable people can differ, doesn't that mean, by the very statement of that proposition, that this body cannot meet its constitutional heavy mandate, which is to determine whether or not, whatever conduct you believe the president committed, as outlined by these managers over the last many days—can you legitimately determine that he ought to be removed from office?"

For the rest of the day, other managers implicitly tried to rebut their own colleague. In answer to a question about whether the views of the public should enter into the equation, Hyde tried to turn the issue into one of principle. "There are issues of transcendent importance that you have to be willing to lose your office over. I can think of several that I am willing to lose my office over. Abortion is one; national defense is another; strengthening, not emasculating, the concept of equal justice under the law. And I am willing to lose my seat any day in the week rather than sell out on those issues. Despite all the polls and all the hostile editorials, America is hungry for people who believe in something. You may disagree with us, but we believe in something."

Jim Rogan tried to turn the "reasonable people" formulation around. "Yes, reasonable minds can differ on this case as to whether the president should be removed from office," he told the senators after a recess. "But reasonable minds can only differ if those reasonable minds come to the conclusion that enforcement of the sexual harassment laws in this country are less important than the preservation of this man in the office of the presidency."

While Democrats happily piled on, they were quietly facing dissension in their own ranks. Senator Russ Feingold was pressuring Daschle to submit the question Feingold had drafted with Susan Collins. It was the only bipartisan question written through this entire two-day session, in effect reinforcing what a party-line exercise the trial had devolved into. As the day wore on, Feingold became more agitated that the question had not been asked; he was worried that they were being shut out because he and Collins had reached across the aisle. If the question was not submitted, Feingold threatened Daschle and Bauer, he would make a public issue out of it.

Finally, Daschle sent the question to the chief justice. Collins and Feingold asked the House managers if Clinton, in coaching Betty Currie, had met all of the elements of the criminal statutes on obstruction of justice and witness tampering. "We are particularly interested in your analysis of whether the Senate can infer that President Clinton intended to corruptly influence or persuade Ms. Currie to testify falsely and the weight to be given Ms. Currie's testimony in that regard," they asked.

Hutchinson happily took the question. Clinton's actions did meet all the elements of the statute, he said. In fact, a federal court recently decided a man was still guilty of witness tampering even if he did not know the person he was trying to influence was going to testify before the grand jury, as long as it was clear the person could be called. Besides, Hutchinson reminded the senators, he had shown them the subpoena for Currie yesterday. She actually was called to testify in the Jones case and Clinton had every reason to believe she would be. "The legal question is, as a prospective witness, is she covered under the obstruction of justice statute? The answer is, yes, because other people go to jail for exactly the same thing."

As the day wore on into the afternoon, the questions and the answers began taking on a numbing familiarity. By this point, the senators were already obviously debating guilt or innocence among themselves by using the lawyers for each side as proxies. "These questions are starting to get a little cruddy," Daschle told his staff. Even the chief justice, who had been uncharacteristically patient through days of oration that went well beyond time limits, finally began showing his weariness by gently cutting off managers who were rambling too long. "The chair has the view that you have answered the question," he interrupted Buyer after one such lengthy discourse.

The lawyers too were growing tired. Greg Craig slipped up during an answer to a Republican question about whether Clinton would be willing to answer a written interrogatory from the Senate about his Jones testimony. "We would be happy to take questions and get responses to you, consult the president, if you would like to submit them." It was just a brush-off answer in which Craig meant the lawyers would respond to whatever the senators wanted, but the Republicans, and even some Democrats, took him to mean that Clinton himself would respond to written questions. Craig had opened the door to what the White House had been trying to forestall from the beginning of the trial—the direct participation of the president in the proceeding. Back at the White House, the president's strategists were peeved at Craig's inartful answer as Senate Republicans immediately announced that they would submit an interrogatory to Clinton. Joe Lockhart, the White House press secretary, was dispatched to tamp down expectations, telling reporters that the president had already testified before the grand jury and would not answer any more questions.

While the question-and-answer period was wrapping up, Judge Norma Johnson sided with the managers and ordered Lewinsky to submit to an interview with the House team. Lewinsky, who had gotten on an airplane early that morning in Los Angeles, arrived back in Washington to a media mob that rushed into traffic and jostled her when she entered the Mayflower Hotel a few blocks from the White House. The scene stood in contrast to the dignified images that had been emerging from the Senate over the last few weeks, a flashback to the ugly days early in the investigation when Lewinsky was stalked everywhere she went by an unruly crowd of camera crews and photographers.

Having lost her bid to convince the judge to keep her from being dragged into the trial, Lewinsky found herself with an unanticipated ally in the Senate chamber. As Lott moved to end the Saturday session, Senator Tom Harkin tried to block adjournment in an effort to stop the Lewinsky interview. "I object," he cried out. "Mr. Chief Justice, I seek recognition." But this time, Rehnquist ignored him and adjourned the Senate at 3:55 P.M. Harkin had drafted a letter to Rehnquist asking him to quash Judge Johnson's order. Harkin raced down the aisle and tried to thrust the letter into Rehnquist's hand before the chief justice could leave the chamber, but missed him and had to settle for delivering the letter to his assistant, Jim Duff.

Harkin was not the only Democrat to continue pounding away at the issue. Democrats collected the signatures of all but one of their senators on a letter complaining about the move, and Byrd wrote his own, far more scathing missive. But Harkin was not about to leave it at that. The Iowa senator found a telephone and called over to the law firm representing Lewinsky. He finally tracked down her lawyer, Plato Cacheris, at home, and urged him to appeal the judge's order. Cacheris was noncommittal and suggested that the senator talk with his colleague, Preston Burton. Harkin then found Burton at home and began lobbying him to appeal as well.

"Call me Tom," Harkin said as he tried to establish an alliance.

"If you don't mind, sir, I'll call you Senator," Burton replied.

Harkin would not give up. He called again the next morning, Sunday, January 24, this time finding Burton at the office as he was preparing for his client's session with the managers, now scheduled for the afternoon. While reluctant to blow off a U.S. senator, Burton had to tell him they would not appeal. Lewinsky's lawyers had concluded there was little or no chance of winning anyway, and what they did not tell Harkin was they had another iron in the fire with Judge Johnson—a secret request for permission under Lewinsky's immunity agreement to conduct a television interview with Barbara Walters after the trial. The last thing they wanted to do was anger Johnson by attacking her ruling in a higher court.

For Lewinsky, who had been holed away throughout the trial in Los Angeles, far from the realpolitik in Washington, this was the moment she had dreaded. In the year since Starr's agents had first confronted her in a Virginia hotel, life had been a series of rude awakenings. She had spent countless hours glued to the television, watching people she had never met describe her as a tart and a bimbo. She had been grilled by investigators two dozen times about her most intimate moments with the president as well as everything from her troubled family history to her depression medication. Now she felt she was about to be put in a glorified glass cage for the world to stare at her again—for the sole purpose of removing the president she once thought she loved.

"All of a sudden this whole impeachment thing is back on my shoulders," she complained in a phone call to her ghostwriter, Andrew Morton, who was working on her forthcoming autobiography, intended to help defray her massive legal bills. She was convinced that "Starr thinks I'm going to turn this around for him, which I don't want to do and can't do. It's not my fault that there's not really a case here. So I'm nervous about what he will do to me if he doesn't get what he wants."

She was nervous too that she was being bugged again. As soon as she arrived at the Mayflower, she switched rooms and conducted sensitive conversations with the shower running in the bathroom to mask the sound.

*   *   *

Asa Hutchinson arrived at the House office building that Sunday unsure what to expect. He had hoped to be the one to question Lewinsky, but Hyde had instead tapped Ed Bryant, the soft-spoken manager from Tennessee. Bryant missed their prep session and arrived just in time to catch the ride from Capitol Hill to the Mayflower in vehicles provided by the Capitol Police. Like Hutchinson, Bryant was casually dressed in a sweater and slacks, the better to put a potentially hostile witness at ease. The plan originally called for Hutchinson and Bryant to go alone, but Bill McCollum showed up too; he wore a suit and tie.

Bryant was exhausted. He had just returned from a whirlwind eighteen-hour trip back home to his Tennessee district to view tornado damage. As the Senate was completing its question-and-answer period the day before, Bryant had gotten a call warning him that a home-state newspaper was preparing a scathing editorial accusing him of being more concerned with the impeachment trial than a natural disaster that had ravaged the lives of his constituents, so after the floor session he flew home to tour the wreckage and rushed right back to Washington. Now back at the Capitol, he conferred with his fellow managers. McCollum wanted to take the lead in meeting with Lewinsky, and given his seniority, neither Bryant nor Hutchinson could object. Bryant would go next and handle the bulk of the questioning, to be followed by Hutchinson, but the main purpose of the encounter was to establish a human connection with their star witness and gauge how she would come across if she were to testify before the Senate. They were a little nervous. After all this time, she was less witness than celebrity. What would she be like in person? Was she the starstruck and vulnerable young intern still harboring an impossible love for Bill Clinton? Was she the sexually seasoned woman who had eagerly pursued an affair with a married man and then relentlessly pressed him for a job in return for accepting their breakup?

They arrived at the Mayflower shortly before 3 P.M. and waded into a chaotic scene, with dozens of cameras mixed in with assorted protesters and bystanders. For all of the attention they had been getting at the Capitol, the managers had never encountered anything like this. Escorted through the crowd by the police, the managers were taken to the room chosen for the session—the Presidential Suite, complete with a backlit presidential seal etched in aqua glass inset in the floor and normally $5,000 a night. Representing Lewinsky were her lawyers, Plato Cacheris, Preston Burton, and Sydney Jean Hoffmann, and representing Starr were deputy independent counsel Bob Bittman, associate independent counsel Michael W. Emmick, and FBI special agent Patrick Fallon. Hutchinson and the other managers were not happy to see Starr's lieutenants there. After the storm generated by Starr's involvement in court over the weekend, the last thing they wanted was for him to hover over this event as well.

Before inviting Lewinsky into the room, Cacheris tried to set ground rules, employing what Hoffmann liked to call his confrontational "alpha male routine." With an amiable toughness born out of years in Washington's high-octane legal world, Cacheris had played a role in some of the capital's most celebrated cases, representing John Mitchell during Watergate, secretary Fawn Hall during Iran-contra, CIA employee Aldrich Ames during his spy case, and members of Congress during the ABSCAM and BCCI investigations. Along with Jacob Stein, Cacheris had rescued Lewinsky last summer after her first attorney, William H. Ginsburg, had bungled the case. To the lawmakers on hand today, Cacheris made clear she had no desire to appear before the Senate and demanded a letter confirming that her statements to the managers would be covered by her immunity agreement.

McCollum assured him that the conversation would be covered by immunity and that they had no desire to ask about her sexual encounters with Clinton. But when Cacheris told them he wanted the questioning to be conducted by Starr's lawyers to make sure she would retain her immunity, the managers protested. Cacheris eventually gave in after assurances that Lewinsky would be protected, that the questioning would only last a couple of hours, and that there would be no written report about it. The two sides agreed that the managers could conduct the questioning themselves and that Bittman and Fallon would leave, while Emmick would remain to observe.

The deal struck, Cacheris offered Hutchinson and the others advice on how to handle his much questioned client: "Look, you don't need to schmooze her up or soft-soap her. She's here. She'll answer your questions. You're better off going straight to that. You don't need to chat her up. Just go to the questioning."

Lewinsky was then brought into the room. In her presence, Cacheris repeated the terms of the deal, and Bittman stipulated that she had her immunity. Now it was finally time for the Starr men to leave.

"Beat it, Bittman," Cacheris said with a roguish smile.

As they began the questioning, McCollum and Bryant immediately ignored Cacheris's caveat against trying to warm up to her. After all, that was why they had come. McCollum asked her if they had been representing her story accurately on the Senate floor: "Have we been screwing it up?" Bryant asked her where she had been spending her time lately and how she was handling her newfound fame and the possible security risks. He could imagine what she was going through in terms of the celebrity, he said, recalling the media mob in front of the hotel that afternoon. "Having just been through that, I can't imagine going through that the way you have," he said.

Bryant led her through some of the facts of the case, how she got her job at the White House, the first time she ever saw the president, whether she had had any contact with anyone at the White House since the story broke (only her friend Ashley Raines, another young, low-level employee, she told them). When Bryant asked if she had voted for Clinton, her lawyers jumped in and said she was not going to answer that.

How did she think the trial should end? Bryant asked.

"I think he should be censured but not removed," she said evenly. "He's been elected twice by the people of this country." Still, she added, "as a citizen, I feel he misled the public about the nature of our relationship."

They talked about the infamous stained dress (she did not keep it as a souvenir, she insisted, but had not bothered to clean it because Linda Tripp told her she looked too fat to wear it). They talked about her subpoena in the Paula Jones case and her conversations with the president about it (she thought maybe the Jones people found her by tapping her phone). Bryant asked her if it would be hard for her if Clinton came to watch the trial while she testified—a far-fetched scenario that confused others in the room since it hardly seemed likely.

Again, Lewinsky kept her cool: "I think it's not my preference." But she added, "Look, I would do the right thing. I would tell the truth to keep my immunity."

McCollum exclaimed, "Politics be damned!"

Bryant moved into the job search and the hidden gifts. Echoing a line used by the White House lawyers, he told her, "You've given about ten different versions" of the gift exchange.

Lewinsky bristled. "I don't think I've given ten different versions."

Well, he said, Currie had testified that Lewinsky called her, not the other way around. Cell phone records showed a call from Currie to Lewinsky at 3:32 P.M. on the day in question, even though Lewinsky had said Currie had come to collect the gifts at 2 P.M.

"How do you reconcile this with that?" Bryant asked.

"It's not my job to reconcile," Lewinsky said sharply. She did not know why Currie said what she said. "I'm just telling you what I remember."

Bryant liked those answers. Lewinsky showed spirit in denying that she had given multiple accounts; that would look good in testimony, he thought. And she stuck by her story on the gifts without vacillating, even though it contradicted the president. Overall, Bryant came away pleased with the session. He had walked in afraid she would be hostile, still in love with Clinton and reluctant to say anything that might harm him. To his surprise, Lewinsky appeared relaxed and not especially unfriendly to the managers. She did not trash the president but seemed reasonably open about what he had done.

And she was playful at times. When McCollum asked about her relationship with the president, Lewinsky quipped, "I don't want to put a wrinkle in your shirt." She even joked with the Starr prosecutor who in her mind had tormented her when she was first confronted at the Ritz Carlton near the Pentagon a year earlier, telling Emmick that "we should stop meeting in hotel rooms like this." Bryant felt he had built a rapport.

He could not have been more wrong. What he missed were the rolling eyes. Lewinsky did not bond with him. She and her lawyers were contemptuous. To them, he seemed to stumble through the give-and-take. They could not believe that he would compare his moment in the public eye downstairs to the klieg-light experience she had endured for the last twelve months. He did not seem to notice the derision when she told him near the end of their session, "Let's keep this thing moving. Ask me what you've got to ask me. I'm paying these lawyers umpteen thousand dollars an hour. It's coming out of my pocket. So let's get this over with." Even Hutchinson privately thought Bryant focused too much on essentially irrelevant how-did-that-make-you-feel questions rather than on a precise interrogation that would be useful to the prosecution.

As the managers prepared to depart the Mayflower, they huddled briefly to figure out what to tell the press. McCollum suggested they should say it was "a good meeting" and that Lewinsky was "intelligent and, quite frankly, attractive." The rest of the group was aghast and immediately vetoed that description. The safest course, they decided, was to say as little as possible lest they further inflame the senators already smoldering about the interview in the first place. They got another nudge toward brevity when they reached the elevator to go downstairs and the Capitol Police officers who had accompanied them stopped to give a warning. The officers were nervous because of the size of the crowd and told the House group they could not guarantee someone with a gun was not out there. If all of a sudden the officers had to push the managers into a car to speed away from a threat, they should not be surprised.

The only shot they took came from Plato Cacheris, who had already beaten them to the cameras and pronounced the session old news. Nothing new had been said, he told reporters, and therefore there was no need to call witnesses. That was the opposite message the House team wanted to send. After departing, the managers caucused back at their House offices. Hutchinson jotted down his assessment of the witness: "She's impressive, confident. Great witness, intelligent—knows the record." But later that night, he got a telephone call from Lindsey Graham. They had lost ground on the fight for witnesses, Graham believed. The Monica Media Frenzy had turned off the moderate Republicans who wanted to avoid exactly that sort of circus in the halls of the Senate. They were going backward, not forward.

*   *   *

Troubled by the television images from the Mayflower, both Senate Republicans and Democrats met separately the next morning, Monday, January 25, to try to figure out where to go from here. The senators were weary and pessimistic. None of the options looked good.

At the Democratic caucus meeting, the senators were presented for the first time with the text of Byrd's proposed motion to dismiss. Eyes widened and heads shook as Byrd read his hastily prepared draft. His preamble included several paragraphs that condemned Clinton's behavior so harshly that by the time he moved on to the "resolved" clause, it seemed more like a motion to convict the president. The only real rationale he gave in the proposed motion for dismissing the case was the recognition that there would not be sixty-seven votes for conviction. Byrd's wording seemed to parallel the articles of impeachment themselves, the language so damning that his fellow Democrats immediately protested.

"A lot of us can't go along with this because we don't agree with this," Tom Harkin told him. Many of the things Byrd considered established fact had not been proven, Harkin argued.

"How can you vote for that and then vote to acquit?" asked Senator Pat Leahy. "With all due respect, Bob, I know you're our historian, but I've done as much work as anybody and more than most, and there's no way I'm going to say he's guilty and then vote to dismiss. I'm not going to explain that to the Senate, and I'm not going to explain that to the people of Vermont."

"I'm not comfortable with saying we're dismissing because there aren't enough votes," said Senator Chris Dodd.

The senators began proposing amendments—they could cut this section or reword that one to say something softer or add a different phrase. Time was running short; the motion had to be submitted in writing when the trial resumed that day at 1 P.M. But Daschle sat back and listened, letting the situation play out and a consensus develop on its own.

Finally, around 12:15 P.M., with just forty-five minutes before the senators were due back on the floor, Byrd stood up and surrendered: "Let's take it all out." The motion would be stripped down to the bare essentials with no garnishing: "The Senator from West Virginia, Mr. Byrd, moves that the impeachment proceedings against William Jefferson Clinton, President of the United States, be, and the same are, duly dismissed."

The other senators called out their approval as applause broke out.

Over in the Mansfield Room of the Capitol, the Republicans were struggling as well, trying to figure out where they stood on the dicey question of witnesses. Lott informed his colleagues that Daschle had offered to drop the motion to dismiss altogether if the Republicans agreed to call no witnesses.

The trial would move immediately to closing arguments and final up-or-down votes on the articles of impeachment. The Republicans were torn on how to respond. It did not sound bad to some of them. But to others, it was another cop-out.

"We've got to get this over with," said Senator Mitch McConnell.

Senator Slade Gorton suggested trying to figure out where the conference stood on witnesses first. "We have to know if people are not going to vote for witnesses. If not, we might as well take Daschle's offer."

Senator Jeff Sessions of Alabama said they should stick to procedures, call a small number of witnesses, "and we'll have done our duty."

The discussion turned to alternative ways of ending the trial. The "findings of fact" idea mentioned on the floor by manager Steve Buyer on Saturday had been floating around Senate Republican circles as well, embraced by Susan Collins and a few others, including the respected Senator Pete Domenici. The concept had some appeal—in effect, they could declare Clinton guilty of the allegations on a simple majority vote before the conclusion of the trial, even though presumably they would not muster the two-thirds necessary to remove him from office on the final votes on the articles of impeachment. Buyer had distributed a law professor's memo explaining the concept to a dozen GOP senators. Domenici rose to tell his fellow senators about the proposal and urge them to think about it.

The imperative of the moment was not to let Clinton portray an acquittal as vindication. "We have to avoid the big Rose Garden party," said Senator Fred Thompson. Senator Orrin Hatch pitched another idea: adjourn the trial with findings of fact but without taking any final votes on guilt or innocence. "We can't just acquit him," agreed Senator John Chafee of Rhode Island.

Some of the supporters of the House team came to its defense. They were not being fair to the managers, they argued. Besides, they had their own political standing to worry about. "We must have a vote on witnesses," said Phil Gramm.

Senator Pat Roberts, the sharp-tongued Kansan, offered a colorful summary of where the fifty-five Republican senators stood. "We're like fifty-five frogs in a milk can," he said, adding, "I want to be able to explain to my grandchildren how we came to the vote in which we slipped into the minority."

At 11:30 A.M., the House managers met in the Judiciary Committee conference room to haggle over the witness question again. Lindsey Graham had been one of the most interested in calling so-called pattern-and-practice witnesses—the other women who would show how Clinton's actions with Lewinsky mirrored their own experiences with him—but he was beginning to retreat. Under the present circumstances, he told fellow managers, it was probably best not to call Kathleen Willey. Steve Buyer, who had invited other

House members to look at the Juanita Broaddrick evidence in the secret vault during the impeachment debate in December, suggested that Willey's story could still be used by putting it into the record through other evidence, such as her FBI interviews or grand jury testimony. Bob Barr disagreed. He thought they should call Willey. She would make a powerful witness. She had shown through her *60 Minutes* appearance that she presented herself well, that she came across as credible. And because of that experience, she had been through the ordeal of public discussion of her case.

By this point, though, even some of the other hard-liners had decided against Willey, including Rogan, McCollum, and Charles Canady. But Rogan and Chris Cannon were still itching to challenge the restrictions imposed by the Senate. The managers, they argued, should call for fourteen witnesses and exercise the prerogatives of the House. The Senate might run the trial, but they could not tell the House how to put on their case. The other managers, while sympathetic to the argument, knew by now that such a show of defiance was pointless.

On the Senate floor, the frogs were still trying to get out of the milk can. The day's session started at 1:04 P.M., but Lott immediately recessed for an hour while he tried to broker a procedural deal with Tom Daschle. When the senators returned at 2:06 P.M., confusion reigned while they searched for some order. Finally the trial resumed with arguments on Byrd's motion to dismiss. "To dismiss the case would be unprecedented from a historical standpoint, because it has never been done before," Hutchinson told the Senate. "It would be damaging to the Constitution, because the Senate would fail to try the case. It would be harmful to the body politic, because there is no resolution of the issues of the case. But most importantly, it would show willful blindness to the evidentiary record that has thus far been presented."

Nicole Seligman handled the White House side. She had originally thought one of the senators would present the main arguments in favor of the motion, since they were the ones introducing it, only to find out later that she would carry the entire burden. As she finished preparing her remarks shortly before four that morning, Seligman discovered she was losing her voice. Rather than go to bed and nurse her throat, however, she ran through the speech at home to make sure she would finish within the one-hour limit; she had nightmares about being cut off by Rehnquist. She started at 4:17 A.M. and finished at 5:12 A.M. Just right.

Ten hours later, at 3:18 P.M., she stood at the lectern and made her argument, never stopping to sip the water that would help her raw throat for fear of throwing off the careful timing of her presentation. The case, she argued, should be dismissed because it did not rise to the level of high crimes envisioned by the framers and because the facts did not add up to the prosecution theory. "Impeachment was never meant to be just another weapon in the arsenal of partisanship. By definition, a partisan split like that which accompanied these articles from the House of Representatives creates doubt that makes plain a constitutional error of the course that we are on." She reminded the senators of Graham's statement that reasonable people could disagree. "We suggest to you that there can be no removal when even the prosecutor agrees that such reasonable doubts exist. If reasonable people can disagree, we suggest to you that reasonable senators should dismiss."

Recognizing that senators did not want to let Clinton entirely off the hook, she added, "Punishment will be found elsewhere. Judgment will be found elsewhere. Legacies will be written elsewhere. None of that will be dismissed. None of that can ever be dismissed."

She finished with six minutes to spare, but had succeeded in irritating a few of the managers. Graham used his rebuttal time to explain that he only meant that he would not question the integrity of senators who voted against conviction, not that he had any doubts about the case. "I have told you the best I can that there is no doubt these are high crimes, in my opinion," he said. "I have lost no sleep worrying about the fact that Bill Clinton may have to be removed from office because of his conduct. I have lost tons of sleep thinking he may get away with what he did. But the question was: Could you disagree with Lindsey Graham and be a good American, in essence? Absolutely."

With the arguments done, the senators would have a crack at the case for the first time as they began debating the motion to dismiss among themselves. According to long-established precedent, the Senate would deliberate behind closed doors. Harkin and his fellow Democrat Paul Wellstone wanted to conduct their discussions in public, but needed two-thirds of the Senate to suspend the rules. They did not even have a simple majority. In the first split roll call of the trial, the Senate voted 43–57 against the Harkin-Wellstone plan to keep the doors open.

At 5:50 P.M., Sergeant at Arms Jim Ziglar and his staff cleared the galleries, turned off the television cameras, and closed the doors to the public. For the next four hours, the senators talked with each other about their assessments of the case and their thoughts on how to proceed. Without the normal floodlights and the sound system used to televise their proceedings, let alone an audience, the session proved a little surreal. In the dimmed room, they gathered closer to the front so they could hear. Most spoke off-the-cuff, without prepared remarks. They addressed each other by first names rather than as "the gentleman from Nebraska" or "the gentlelady from California." The discussion struck many in the room as unusually high-minded for a group of politicians, while they struggled with what consti-

tuted an impeachable offense. But as the evening wore on, it was clear they
had no consensus. For all of the desire to keep the trial bipartisan, they were
heading inexorably toward the much feared clash between the two parties.

"The women of America will be watching to see how we treat Monica
Lewinsky," declared Senator Patty Murray.

Some twelve hours after the Senate adjourned for the night, most of them
were back at the Capitol for their morning party caucus meetings on Tuesday, January 26. At the Democratic meeting, the main topic was witnesses.
The managers were to produce their proposed witness list later this day, and
several female senators decided to make their stand against bringing Lewinsky to the floor. Murray led the charge. The senator from Washington State
reminded her colleagues that she was part of the "Year of the Woman" class
that had come to Washington in the 1992 election fueled in part by a backlash against the handling of Anita Hill and her allegations of sexual harassment during the Clarence Thomas hearings. What had alienated many
women then was how the all-male Senate Judiciary Committee had dealt
with Hill. No matter how gingerly they thought they would handle Lewinsky, Murray warned, it would look the same once again.

"Don't you understand what this is going to look like? This is going to be
ninety white men leering at her as she's being asked about her sex life."

At that point, Senator Chris Dodd piped up. "Why is everyone looking at
Kennedy?" he asked with a mischievous grin.

The room erupted in laughter, breaking the tension for a moment. But
Murray had struck a chord. One by one, other women got up and echoed her
passionate statement, including Barbara Boxer and Dianne Feinstein. They
simply could not let Lewinsky be called to testify in the well of the Senate.

Little did they know that at least some of the managers were still itching to
interview Lewinsky again in advance of any actual testimony. McCollum, who
had pushed the House team into the first encounter at the Mayflower, now
wanted to do it again. But this time, Hyde would not go along. Any more
interviews would only exacerbate the criticism they had already absorbed.

Chuck Ruff was miffed at Asa Hutchinson for showing him up on a point of
fact over the weekend the same way Ruff had undercut the Arkansas Republican a few days before. The whole White House strategy turned on showing
the Senate that the House team was twisting the facts, an approach that
would not work if it became a two-way street. Ruff had not realized that the
Paula Jones lawyers had ever put Betty Currie on a supplementary witness
list or had issued a subpoena in her name. But as he studied the issue, Ruff
realized that no one on his side had ever seen the witness list or subpoena. It

was still under seal in the courthouse in Arkansas. That must mean that Hutchinson had obtained it improperly.

Ruff had confronted Hutchinson about the matter privately, only to be brushed off. Indeed, Hutchinson had referred to the subpoena as recently as the day before in his argument against the motion to dismiss, even though Currie had not received it at the time of her conversation with the president and therefore was not a witness at that point. Now Ruff decided to turn Hutchinson in. At 9:34 A.M., Ruff faxed him a letter threatening to tell Rehnquist that the managers had violated a court-ordered seal unless the House prosecutors could prove they had not. Ruff gave Hutchinson until 10:30 A.M., less than an hour away, to respond. "In light of your continuing, inaccurate characterizations of Ms. Currie's role," Ruff wrote, they would have to use the same documents to rebut the managers' assertions and so "we intend to advise the Chief Justice of our concerns about their status so that we do not compound your violation by using them improperly in our argument." Hutchinson read the letter and decided to ignore it. Let them go to the chief justice, he thought. But just in case, he told an aide to ask the judge in the Jones case to retroactively unseal the documents.

The ten-thirty deadline came and went with no action by Ruff. Advised that the chief justice did not want to get involved in such matters, Ruff decided not to lodge a formal complaint, but to hold on to the issue in case he needed it to embarrass the managers on the floor. As the deadline passed, Hutchinson and the other managers gathered in their conference room in the Rayburn Building to make their final decisions on witnesses. By this point, the trial team had settled on three—Monica Lewinsky, Vernon Jordan, and Sidney Blumenthal. In addition, they would ask the Senate to invite Clinton to testify voluntarily. The papers had been drawn up and were ready to go. All the managers had to do was sign off on the decision. But they were still unhappy about the deal they were being forced to live with. Chris Cannon, the outspoken manager from Utah, could not believe they were simply going to swallow this.

"The question is whether we go forward with a mock trial," he said.

Lindsey Graham was in a like frame of mind. "I'd like to take Chris's idea and turn it into a motion," he said. They should vote on whether to even participate in what some of them considered a farce.

But Hyde would have none of it. He was not happy about what was happening either, but it would be ridiculous to throw a temper tantrum. Much as they hated it, they had to live within the rules and at least finish their duties with as much dignity as they could. As Cannon and Graham agitated, Hyde ignored them and tried to move the discussion to the list of proposed witnesses.

"I think we ought to vote on the motion," Cannon persisted.

"I'd like to decide which witnesses we're going to have," Hyde responded, rebuffing him.

Hyde led the group through the list. The decision on the first witness was unanimous. Despite Hyde's trepidation, everyone agreed by now that they had to call Lewinsky. The decision to force her to attend an interview had effectively closed the question, and besides, the managers who had met her felt somewhat optimistic that she might be cooperative. The second choice was not as easy. Jordan was pivotal to the case. He had obtained the job for Lewinsky at the president's behest and simultaneously set her up with an attorney to draft her false affidavit. But Bob Barr made a passionate plea not to call Jordan.

"He's a friend of the president," Barr said. "He's not going to help us. He's going to hurt us." Jordan made a living manipulating Washington, Barr said. To put somebody as smart as Jordan in a deposition where he would be in control would be inviting disaster. Better to call Betty Currie, who was not trained as an attorney and would be far less likely to hurt them on the stand, he said.

Hutchinson wanted to call Currie too, but if the choice came down to her or Jordan, he preferred to question the president's friend. Jordan was critical. They had to have him to establish the link between Clinton and the efforts to find Lewinsky a job. Bryant said all witnesses could hurt them, but Currie's testimony was already as good as it was going to get. The facts involving her conversations with Clinton were not in dispute; the only disagreement was whether the president knew at that point she might be a witness. As for the gifts, the managers preferred Lewinsky's version of events to Currie's. So, Bryant said, if Currie was called and went south on the managers, she could hurt them on the strongest elements of their case, whereas Jordan would at worst hurt them on the part of the case that was toughest to prove already— the link between the job and the affidavit. Other managers worried that calling Currie would only make them look like thirteen angry white men beating up on a sympathetic, middle-aged, churchgoing African-American woman. They remembered all too well the pictures of a frightened Currie shielding herself from the media mob at her first grand jury appearance a year ago. Jordan, at least, could take care of himself. So while other managers harbored some of the same concerns as Barr, they voted 12–1 to call Jordan.

Having expended his capital in getting Jordan on the list, Hutchinson did not feel he could now push for Currie as well, so he acquiesced as Graham and Rogan insisted on making Blumenthal their third and final witness. For one thing, the sometimes acerbic Blumenthal would not be nearly as likable a witness as the other two. For another, they said, Blumenthal could show the sinister nature of Clinton's attempts to cover up his affair with Lewinsky by testifying about how the president depicted her as a "stalker." It was important to emphasize the venality involved in the president's actions; it was not just a matter of trying to avoid embarrassing himself or his family. The team agreed and Blumenthal was approved.

Hyde started to move on, but the dissidents were not ready to give up. Barr and Cannon proposed that they name a fourth witness, Dick Morris, the president's former consultant. They knew Morris's own sexual escapades would detract from his credibility, but they argued he would be a powerful witness because of his deep knowledge of the president. Morris had spoken with David Schippers's investigators and made clear he would happily testify against his former client.

"Hell," said Barr, "we need a witness who *wants* to be a witness."

Some of the other managers agreed that Morris had said some interesting things in their interviews—tales of secret police and intimidation of women who might have come forward—but they were afraid he was *too* interesting. Morris scared some of them. If they were to call him, they would be lambasted. Besides, what did he have direct knowledge of, anyway?

They went around the table until there were six votes for Morris, including Rogan and Graham. The vote ended at that point because it was clear seven would be against. Hyde was never forced to state a vote.

In the middle of all this, the managers received a note from Senator Arlen Specter saying he wanted to meet with some of them to talk about witnesses. Hyde dispatched Graham and a couple other managers. They found Specter in his hideaway with Republican senator Jon Kyl of Arizona. With the motion for three witnesses now committed to writing and less than an hour until it had to be filed with the Senate, the two senators suddenly told the puzzled managers they could have a couple more.

"We think five is the maximum," Specter said.

While flabbergasted, the managers knew it was too late. "Look, Senator," said one of their aides, Paul McNulty, "we have to have a motion filed in your body in an hour. We don't really have a lot of flexibility."

"Don't worry about that," Specter said. "We can work around that."

No, the managers said. They had made their decision. It was done. Specter and Kyl seemed relieved.

The trial resumed at noon. The managers presented their proposal for three witnesses and an invitation to the president to testify. Given the task of arguing against the House request, David Kendall slashed away with no mercy. He displayed chart after chart showing quotes from Hyde and the other managers about why they needed no witnesses during the Judiciary Committee hearings because the record compiled by Starr was complete enough. Why should it suddenly be different in the Senate? Kendall's dagger was so sharp that when he started a sentence by saying, "Now, I don't want to be uncharitable to the House managers," senators on both sides of the aisle burst out laughing.

More ominously, though, Kendall also delivered a warning to the Senate. If it approved witnesses for the prosecution—any at all, even just three—it would let "the genie" out of the bottle and the White House would be obliged to ask for an open-ended discovery process that, as he described it, sounded as if it could last months. "We are not at all afraid of what the witnesses would say. Indeed, we know what they are going to say because it is all right there in the volumes before you." Then pointing accusatorily at the managers, Kendall added, "Let's be clear about one thing—any delay in the process necessary for us to have fair discovery is on their heads."

The managers were stung by Kendall's razor-edged performance. Hyde got up and said, "It is disturbing, it is annoying, it is irritating," when Clinton's team complained they were cut off from evidence during the House proceedings. "I pleaded with them to produce witnesses, made the subpoenas available to them. They have a positive allergy to fact witnesses." While they called academics, "you would get eye strain looking for a fact witness." Hyde explained that he considered the House hearings to be akin to a grand jury process that did not need witnesses given all the prior testimony, but the Senate was conducting a trial, and trials typically featured live testimony. All they had asked for, Hyde added, was "a pitiful three."

"I'm glad those people weren't at Valley Forge or the Alamo."

Hyde was grousing as he headed into a managers' meeting at eleven-thirty the next morning, Wednesday, January 27, ninety minutes before the senators were scheduled to vote. He was growing more discouraged with each passing day. He had not been anxious to take on this role of the president's chief prosecutor, but he knew it would become his defining legacy, like it or not. And now his fellow Republicans in the Senate were twisting the knife in his back while simultaneously offering gauze and sympathy. Usually a gentleman of equanimity, Hyde gave up trying to disguise his sense of grievance at the Senate Republicans. Hyde knew very well what the outcome of the vote would be and he used the meeting with his fellow managers to hand out assignments for the depositions—Bryant would interview Lewinsky, Hutchinson would question Jordan, and Rogan would take on Blumenthal. Unlike in the floor sessions, Hyde could have used David Schippers, but by that time the crusading chief investigator had grown so disgusted with the trial that he had all but withdrawn from active participation.

Over in the Senate chamber, the juror-judges knew which way the wind was blowing as well. Yet as they gathered on the floor for the session, which started at 1:07 P.M., the mood was sober amid anticipation for the moment of decision. Lott had spent much of the morning still searching for a way out, without success. He floated a plan to bring the trial to a conclusion by February 6 as long as the White House would agree to forgo any discovery, but Democrats were not willing to tie the president's hands before hearing from the managers' witnesses. And so the senators met on the floor for the partisan split Lott had tried so hard for so long to avert.

Rehnquist instructed the clerk to read the roll on Byrd's motion to dismiss the case.

"Mr. Abraham," the clerk intoned solemnly.

At his desk on the far side of the chamber, Republican Spencer Abraham of Michigan stood up. "Nay," he called out.

"Mr. Abraham votes nay," the clerk repeated, then called for the next vote. "Mr. Akaka."

"Aye," answered Democrat Daniel Akaka of Hawaii.

"Mr. Akaka votes aye."

The pattern continued through the roster alphabetically. One after another, a name was called, a senator rose at his or her desk, and a verdict was rendered. Some, such as Dick Durbin, Charles Grassley, and Jesse Helms, did not wait for their name to be called to stand—they moved to their feet as soon as the clerk got close. They stood rigidly formal, the men buttoning their coats for the moment of the vote, only to unbutton them the moment they were done and sit down again. Some announced their decision in a soft, even sad voice, such as Ted Kennedy, Barbara Boxer, and even Byrd. Others, such as Fred Thompson and Fritz Hollings, boomed out their answers in full senatorial baritone. The votes depended on the side of the room—from Rehnquist's right came ayes and from his left came nays.

Only twice was that rule broken. When the clerk called out "Mr. Feingold," the Democrat from Wisconsin answered, "Nay." The clerk got the same response when he came to Barbara Mikulski of Maryland, which prompted a wave of murmurs in the chamber as Boxer and Paul Sarbanes turned to gawk at Mikulski in shock. Mikulski suddenly realized she had voted the wrong way and leapt to her feet to interrupt the rest of the roll call and lodge the intended answer: "Aye." Feingold's answer, though, was intentional. A Democrat who prided himself on his maverick ways, Feingold agreed with Susan Collins and wanted to vote to dismiss only one of the two charges, perjury, but since he was not given that option, he reasoned he could not reject the entire case just yet.

"On the vote, the yeas are forty-four, the nays are fifty-six," Rehnquist announced. "The motion is not agreed to."

The clerk then went through the same process for the motion to call witnesses and came back with the same result, though in reverse—fifty-six for and forty-four against. "The motion is agreed to," Rehnquist declared.

Officially, the House team won. The case was not thrown out and they got permission to depose three witnesses. Lott had succeeded in holding his caucus together. But it was an illusory victory. In fact, at that moment, the trial was effectively over. Forty-four senators had put themselves on record saying there was not enough evidence to continue, much less convict the president—ten more than needed to block removal under the two-thirds rule in the Constitution. Barring some blockbuster new revelation, those senators had made up their minds. What was really left was to figure out how to get to the end without a partisan implosion that would crater the Senate.

The managers were dispirited. While relieved that at least they had not lost any Republicans, they knew what the vote meant. Hyde seemed particularly down, almost ready to throw in the towel. That evening, he called Asa Hutchinson with an idea. Hyde had been talking with Orrin Hatch about the senator's idea to adjourn the trial. The theory was that the Senate could quit the trial with a resolution effectively endorsing the factual basis of the House case without giving Clinton the absolution of an acquittal vote. The charges against the president would stand and the trial could be restarted if new evidence were discovered. However, Hatch had suggested that if even one Democrat were to join in the motion, they would adjourn sine die, closing down the trial for good—and eliminating the threat of the charges entirely.

Hatch had had little luck selling Lott on this idea. Lott and Hatch had a contentious relationship, particularly since 1997 when Hatch teamed up with the liberal Ted Kennedy to push through a cigarette-tax increase to expand access to health insurance for poor children. As the Lewinsky scandal unfolded in spring and summer of 1998, Hatch's Republican colleagues had grown so annoyed by his repeated discussion of forgiveness for the president if he came clean that at one senators' luncheon they reamed him for selling out the party. Judging Hatch to be a grandstander and not a team player, Lott had basically shut him out of the more central role that might have been expected of the chairman of the Judiciary Committee at a presidential impeachment trial. So Hatch had taken his adjournment plan to Hyde to see if he could win the support of the managers. Hyde was intrigued; on the face of it, it seemed to uphold the position of the House while finding an honorable way to end the trial.

Under the draft Hatch had given Hyde, the Senate would adjourn the trial after stipulating that Clinton "has given false and misleading testimony under oath in federal court proceedings and has, in several ways, impeded the justice system's search for truth," while conceding that "two-thirds of the Members present will not vote to convict and remove" the president. In some ways, it was not that different in tone from Robert Byrd's original motion to dismiss. Noting that Clinton remained subject to criminal prosecution after leaving office, the Hatch motion would conclude, "The United States Senate acknowledges, recognizes and accedes to the Articles of Impeachment passed and exhibited by the House of Representatives as the highest form of condemnation, other than removal, which can be imposed by the Congress of the United States on William Jefferson Clinton, President of the United States."

Alarmed, Hutchinson and Rogan went to see Hyde to discuss the Hatch plan and objected strenuously. They were not ready to quit like this, they told him. This was not the right way to stand up for their case. The Senate was just looking to the managers to give them political cover to cut and run. No judge would go to a prosecutor asking for permission to dismiss his case. They should not give the Senate permission to dismiss theirs. Hyde backed down, and Hutchinson and Rogan left thinking they had killed the idea.

Among the Democrats, Russ Feingold was now something of a pariah. Although they treated him politely to his face, behind his back fellow senators grumbled that he was showboating. Clinton himself applied the shiv. At a memorial service for former Florida senator and governor Lawton Chiles, held in the Russell Senate Office Building at eleven o'clock Thursday, January 28, the morning after the vote, the president eulogized the deceased in a way that contrasted his virtues with Feingold's vices, all without even mentioning the Wisconsin senator's name. "I thank him for being an early supporter of political and campaign finance reform," Clinton said of Chiles, "but . . . doing it in a way that made sense and didn't raise people's defenses. I don't think he had a sanctimonious bone in his body. . . . He didn't go around telling you how much better he was than everybody else because he only took one hundred dollars." During his campaign the previous fall, Feingold had made a point of taking no more than one hundred dollars from any donor and refusing help from national Democrats concerned he would throw away one of their seats in a fit of righteousness. He had also called for the appointment of an independent counsel to investigate possible campaign finance improprieties in the Clinton reelection campaign. Few in the audience for the Chiles service missed the president's reference.

But that was about the only thing that was obvious this day. With the critical votes behind them, Lott and Daschle were left to fashion an escape route that would lead them and their caucuses out of the political briar patch intact. The procedural resolution inspired by the joint caucus meeting in the

Old Senate Chamber had run its course. Now they needed a new set of rules to carry them through the depositions to the end of the trial. But the good will and trust that had produced the original 100–0 vote had inevitably eroded in the three weeks since then, and negotiations were not going well. That Thursday developed into an endless series of meetings in a futile quest to find a deal. The Democrats came back with a plan that essentially wiped out the language of the Republican proposal and replaced it with their own, generating plenty of grumbling among the GOP aides. Among the big points of contention were the scope of questioning to be allowed in the depositions, how much latitude to leave for further discovery, and the ability of senators to introduce alternative proposals such as the "findings of fact" promoted by Susan Collins and others. The Democrats wanted more restrictions, while the Republicans wanted to leave themselves room to maneuver if necessary.

For Lott, the problem was not just the Democrats, but his own caucus. Once again, he went into a situation doubting that he had even fifty-one votes; he had to find a way to keep his people together. By this point, the conservatives had grown increasingly restless with the way Lott was handling matters. Every time Lott sat down with Daschle alone, they felt, he would cave. After what they considered the disaster of the first resolution—no guarantee of witnesses, no rebuttal time for the managers—the conservatives were determined not to trust Lott but to make sure the rules were written the way they wanted. The grumbling had grown loud enough within the caucus that some leadership aides even privately speculated about a possible mutiny against Lott if he could not finesse the situation.

Lott met with his lawyers and several other senators, including Phil Gramm, Fred Thompson, and Slade Gorton, in his conference room that morning to go over the GOP plan. Lott's chief of staff, Dave Hoppe, sat to his right, and Senate lawyer Tom Griffith sat to his left. As they reviewed the plan line by line, a voice came from behind Lott. Eric Ueland, an aide to Don Nickles, the majority whip, was saying, "Senator, I think you need to add some language here allowing findings of fact, because as it's written now, I don't think it's allowed." Lott looked over his shoulder, appearing none too pleased.

Lott went to meet with Daschle at 11 A.M. The major point of dispute now was whether additional discovery might be allowed after the House managers finished with their first three witnesses. Feeling the pressure of his fellow Republicans, Lott was resisting any role for Democrats in making this decision, but he left his session with Daschle optimistic that he could get a deal. At noon, Lott met for lunch with his Republican conference, where he ran into a buzz saw. The animosity and mistrust in the room were palpable.

Lott started going over the latest draft of the plan, but no copies were passed out at first, a move interpreted by some more suspicious Republicans as an attempt to keep them from seeing what was being given away. When copies were eventually distributed, the senators started picking the proposal apart. What does this phrase mean? How about this clause? Gramm asked a lot of tough questions about the plan drafted by Lott's wordsmith, Elizabeth Letchworth, the Senate majority secretary.

Lott lost his temper. "Okay, fine, you guys get together with Elizabeth and you write it," he snapped. "I've got to go. There are people in my office." He turned and stormed out. Connie Mack, the chairman of the conference, chased Lott out of the room to try to calm him down.

Lott was not the only leader furious that morning. As he walked into a Democratic caucus meeting, Daschle was shown a story in *Roll Call*, the twice-a-week newspaper that covers Congress, reporting that he had applied "significant pressure" on four senators not to buck the party line. Daschle was incensed. He had bent over backward from the beginning to avoid doing anything to strong-arm Democrats. The normally mild-mannered senator was so angry he yelled at his staff.

"This is outrageous," he fumed. "We've got to fix it."

Daschle marched into the caucus and hotly denied the account. Everyone knew it was wrong, he said. He called the accusation one of the most disturbing things to happen to him in his entire career and pledged to call the four named senators, Joe Biden, Bob Graham, Evan Bayh, and John Edwards, to apologize if they felt bullied. Some of them stood up right there to say the report mischaracterized the situation.

The chaotic status of negotiations had brought the trial once again to a screeching halt. The Senate officially convened that day at 1:04 P.M., only to recess immediately pending further talks. It reconvened an hour later, then recessed again. The rest of the day continued in the same vein. Stuck in limbo was the chief justice of the United States, who took no role in the haggling and yet was forced to stick around in case white smoke did emerge. Most days when there would be a lot of down time, Rehnquist and his staff brought legal briefs to read and other court business to attend to. But with this day's long breaks, he asked for some cards and settled in for a poker game with three clerks. At one point, the Senate sergeant at arms, Jim Ziglar, walked in and found the chief justice and his fellow players, money and cards strewn all over the table.

"Chief," Ziglar said, "I'm in charge of enforcing the rules in the Senate, and gambling's not allowed. Now I'm sure that's not what it looks like. But I'm going to step out for a minute and I'll be right back." A few minutes later, Ziglar returned. They were still playing cards, but the money was gone.

Rehnquist had established a comfortable rhythm for himself by now. With the help of the parliamentarian, he was finding that he could handle most questions that came up, and he had rapidly concluded that the Senate was best left to deal with most everything without him. He adopted a hands-off, laissez-faire approach, staying out of the proceedings except when absolutely necessary. While he had agreed with Tom Harkin's initial objection about the use of the word *juror,* in recent days he had overruled other senators who objected when the White House lawyers or House managers mentioned something not formally in the record, choosing to allow the trial to continue in its relatively free flow rather than enforce a strict interpretation of the rules. And in response to Harkin's letter seeking his intervention in the Lewinsky interview with the managers, Rehnquist wrote back the day after the interview that he was not sure he had such authority and, even if he did, "I would want to use it only in a case in which its exercise were clearly warranted. The situation you pose, in my view, does not meet that criterion."

Back in their meeting room, the Republicans were in a commotion following Lott's abrupt departure. With the tablecloths still on the table from the luncheon, Fred Thompson, Slade Gorton, Don Nickles, Phil Gramm, and several aides huddled around Lott's assigned wordsmith at a computer trying to jointly dictate a resolution. The process was so frustrating that several of the aides, including Republican lawyers Stewart Verdery and Kimberly Cobb, peeled off to write their own version in Nickles's office. In the meantime, Tom Griffith, the chief Senate lawyer, met with Bob Bauer, Daschle's lawyer, trying to work out a compromise.

Finally, it became clear no deal was in the works. The Democrats met in conference and agreed to vote against the Republican plan when it came to the floor. Then Lott decided to give the Democrats one last concession— what everyone was calling the "bolt of lightning" clause. This was the provision addressing what would happen if the depositions turned up some startling new evidence that needed to be pursued despite the general reluctance to allow more discovery. Originally, Lott's plan would have allowed more discovery on a majority vote of the Senate; the Democrats had objected because that meant the Republicans could decide on their own to reopen the case. Taking a pen to the latest draft, Lott crossed out "majority vote" and wrote in "the two Leaders jointly." That meant no additional discovery could be conducted unless both Lott and Daschle agreed—in effect, giving the Democratic leader a veto.

Lott, still sore from his earlier confrontation with the Republican conference, went ahead and scheduled a vote for 5 P.M. without bothering to present the plan for the conference's approval. Around 4 P.M., Connie Mack heard from an aide that the vote was on and called Lott to ask that the conference be called to meet first, but the majority leader did not take his call. Finally, at 4:45 P.M., Mack got ahold of Lott, who reluctantly agreed to hold a meeting at 4:55 P.M. Anxious to prevent a blowup, Lott entered the conference meeting with a smile on his face, clapping his hands together in what some leadership aides called "his cheerleader bit" and presented the proposal as a done deal.

"Here's what we're going to do," he said.

By this point, the dissidents were tired and eager to get out of town for the weekend. Mollified by the target adjournment date of February 12 in Lott's plan, they were not willing to miss a plane to fight him anymore, and so they went along. Daschle got the word about the new veto power Lott had agreed to give him when the cellular telephone rang during a Democratic caucus meeting. That made the resolution far more acceptable to him. But with the day draining away and the airport beckoning, the Democrats did not bother to revisit their decision to vote against the resolution. "This is the best they can do," Daschle told the caucus.

At 5:31 P.M., the Senate returned to the floor and went through the script both sides had settled on. Daschle first offered a Democratic version of the rules, which was rejected along strict party lines, 54–44 (Republican Wayne Allard and Democrat Barbara Mikulski being absent). Then Daschle proposed that the Senate go immediately to closing arguments without witnesses, a move intended only to make a point and show that the Republicans were prolonging the trial. That failed 55–43, with Russ Feingold again breaking ranks. Finally, Lott's plan passed 54–44, and the Senate adjourned at 6:34 P.M., in time for senators to catch the evening flights out of Ronald Reagan Washington National Airport.

At the White House, aides to the president tried eagerly to use the voting to slam the trial as illegitimate, in effect painting the Senate proceeding with the same partisan veneer that had tainted the House hearings. "Clearly the bipartisanship in the Senate is dead and we've returned to an atmosphere of partisanship and partisan votes," Joe Lockhart told reporters. But in fact, at the Capitol, Daschle thought Lott had dealt with him fairly, and Daschle's fellow Senate Democrats were reasonably happy with the outcome. Because of Lott's concession, Daschle now wielded a procedural veto that would keep the trial from dragging on after the three depositions were over and all but ensure that final votes would be taken by February 12.

CHAPTER SIXTEEN

"She's the best witness
I ever saw"

Behind his back, concern was growing among some on the House team that Ed Bryant was not the right man for the job. Calm, gentle, and easygoing, Bryant was well liked among his colleagues, a solid and thoughtful contributor to the prosecution. He brought long experience to the task, having served as a judge advocate general in the army and U.S. attorney in Tennessee before being elected to the House in the Republican Revolution of 1994. Now fifty years old with graying hair, he had been picked to handle the questioning of Monica Lewinsky because of his unthreatening, kindly-uncle demeanor and the assumption that he had forged a bond with her during their earlier meeting. But this was the critical moment in the trial, the one chance the managers were likely to have to question under oath the star witness in their case against the president. She could easily shade her story to help or hurt them. They needed a home-run performance. Nothing less would do.

Quietly, Lindsey Graham and Jim Rogan were lobbying Henry Hyde to replace Bryant. Graham wanted to do the deposition himself, and Rogan backed him up. The idea was to show Lewinsky news clippings describing her as a "stalker" and worse, then ask her whether she agreed with those characterizations. Graham wanted to confront her directly with the smear campaign he believed the White House had waged against her and demonstrate that she was the victim of a malevolent president, not simply the young lover of an aging philanderer. Graham and Rogan were not the only managers worried about the choice of questioner. Bob Barr believed they should approach her in a tough manner and wanted to do it himself. Bill McCollum, who had insisted on interviewing Lewinsky informally, had definite ideas about the deposition too, insisting that it had to be more orderly and less free-flowing than their meeting with her a week earlier. Hyde, however, was nothing if not loyal to his troops and could not stomach the idea of pulling Bryant off the deposition. Tennessee gentility, Hyde hoped, might extract more from the young woman.

Having won a battle he did not realize he was in, Bryant went into the deposition with one main goal—don't make her cry. If Lewinsky became emotionally overwrought, the managers would be accused of browbeating her, and that would be the story. So with a list of questions drawn up by the prosecution staff, Bryant went in hoping to elicit the basics of her story without getting into details about the sex.

The Senate staff had set up the deposition in the same presidential suite at the Mayflower Hotel that the managers had used for their informal chat with Lewinsky. But any hopes of informality were quickly erased when Bryant and the other lawyers walked in on the morning of Monday, February 1, and saw the enormous crowd gathering for the spectacle. While reporters and cameras were barred from the event, more than forty attorneys, congressional aides, and other officials had managed to finagle their way into the secret deposition. It had become such a hot ticket that a fight erupted when a couple of aides to Senator Pat Leahy, who would be presiding over the session, arrived to find that they did not have assigned seats behind their boss.

"Goddamn it," exclaimed Bob Bauer, the lawyer for Tom Daschle brought in to mediate. "People are treating this deposition like a Beatles concert!"

As if on the Ed Sullivan soundstage, all eyes turned to the door when Lewinsky made her appearance. She had not been able to eat dinner the night before and had barely slept, but she looked poised and confident in a navy blue blazer and skirt with pearls wrapped around her neck. Several of the middle-aged male lawyers in the room were struck by how beautiful she was in person.

Lewinsky did not seem the least bit fazed by the swarm of people. She simply breezed in and confidently stuck her hand out to the first person she saw, saying, "I'm Monica Lewinsky," as if anyone did not know.

Unlike the meeting a week before, the suite was set up for a formal conference, with a long mahogany table covered by a starched white cloth positioned above the presidential seal in the floor. Lewinsky sat at one end of the table, flanked by her lawyers, Plato Cacheris, Jake Stein, Preston Burton, and Sydney Jean Hoffmann, while a video camera was set up at the other end to record her. Bryant sat in the middle of the table to her left, joined by some of the House lawyers, though not David Schippers, who did not bother to come. Clinton lawyers Nicole Seligman and Cheryl Mills sat on the opposite side, to Lewinsky's right. David Kendall did not sit at the table, but instead took a chair behind his two female colleagues. Chief Justice Rehnquist had declined to preside over the depositions on the theory that such a task went beyond his role in the trial, so Daschle and Trent Lott had assigned a half dozen senators to supervise the interviews, a pair at a time. Leahy and Senator Mike DeWine, a former prosecutor from Ohio, were first up, and they sat down at the table. A television showing Lewinsky as she was talking was set up so that others could see her. As a technician fastened a body microphone to her clothing, she was warned it would pick up every remark.

"Oh," she said mischievously, "the Linda Tripp version."

As the deposition began at 9:03 A.M., it did not take long to figure out the dynamics of the day. Bryant knew he was in trouble by the second question. The first had been to ask her to state her name for the record. The second was to ask her if she was a resident of California.

"I'm not sure exactly where I'm a resident now," she answered, "but I—that's where I'm living right now."

Bryant was alarmed. If she was quibbling over the pro forma question of where she lived, that did not bode well. Sure enough, as the session unfolded, her answers were clipped—often just a "yes" or a "no" rather than the expansive elaboration she had offered the grand jury. When Bryant misstated a point, she made sure to correct him. She quarreled with the premises of his questions. She certainly was not going out of her way to volunteer anything. When Bryant asked her to describe how her relationship began with the president, she answered curtly, "I believe I've testified to that in the grand jury pretty extensively." From Bryant's point of view, this was not the same woman he had met a week earlier.

Bryant rambled through his questions, often asking several at once and leaving many at the table confused. Cacheris repeatedly objected to the compound questions, prompting the presiding senators, DeWine and Leahy, to ask the manager to be more precise. It got to the point where Bryant stopped himself after one inquiry and announced that it was a compound question.

"I'm making my own objections now," he joked.

"We sustain those," Lewinsky interjected, prompting a wave of laughter.

Much as he tried, Bryant could not draw her out. He asked Lewinsky to describe how she viewed Clinton, but she brushed him off.

"Do you still have feelings for the president?" he asked.

"I have mixed feelings," she answered.

"What, uh—maybe you could tell us a little bit more about what those mixed feelings are."

"I think what you need to know is that my grand jury testimony is truthful irrespective of whatever those mixed feelings are in my testimony today," she replied firmly.

Bryant moved on to some of the events at the heart of the obstruction allegations, including the president's December 17, 1997, middle-of-the-night telephone call to Lewinsky warning her that she was on the witness list in the Paula Jones case and suggesting that she could file an affidavit to get out of testifying. In her proffer to the prosecutors and in her grand jury appearances, Lewinsky had said that Clinton suggested during that conversation that she could cite the "cover stories" they had used, such as explaining her visits to the Oval Office by saying she was delivering papers, even though she was not really. She told Starr's prosecutors that she understood Clinton's comments to mean she would deny their relationship under oath. But now with Bryant, she was adopting Clinton's semantical defense, maintaining that such statements would be "misleading" but "literally true."

"Did you appreciate the implications of filing a false affidavit with the court?" Bryant asked.

Lewinsky gave no ground. "I don't think I necessarily thought at that point it would have to be false, so no, probably not." In other words, if she did not think it had to be false, then Clinton could not have been suborning perjury.

Bryant tried it another way. "Did the president ever tell you, caution you, that you had to tell the truth in an affidavit?"

"Not that I recall."

"It would have been against his interest in that lawsuit for you to have told the truth, would it not?"

"I'm not really comfortable—I mean, I can tell you what would have been in my best interest, but I—"

"But you didn't file the affidavit for your best interest, did you?"

"Uh, actually, I did."

The White House lawyers had to contain their glee. She was running rings around Bryant. With every answer, it seemed, Lewinsky undermined the managers' case even more. By asserting that it was in her own interest to file a false affidavit, rather than in the president's, she again adopted a line of argument that Clinton's counsel had been using on the Senate floor. She could not have been answering better for Clinton's side if they had scripted it themselves.

Bryant grew increasingly frustrated. To demonstrate that the president had suggested Lewinsky lie in her sworn statement, he came back again to his mention of the cover stories they used.

"Now, was that in connection with the affidavit?" he asked, thinking the answer was yes.

"I don't believe so, no," she answered.

"Why would he have told you you could always say that?"

"I don't know."

At that point, Preston Burton, Lewinsky's younger attorney, who typically deferred to his senior partner, Cacheris, could not contain himself any longer. "You're asking her to speculate on someone else's testimony," he objected.

The normally placid Bryant finally snapped back. He had had about enough. Lewinsky was arguing with his questions and shading every answer in the light most favorable to the president. And her lawyers were harassing him with objections every chance they got. "Let me make a point here," he said testily. "I've been very patient in trying to get along, but as I alluded to earlier, and I said I am not going to hold a hard line to this, but I don't think the president's—the witness's lawyers ought to be objecting to this testimony. If there's an objection here, it should come from the White House side."

But Senators DeWine and Leahy did not agree. Lewinsky's lawyers were entitled to make objections.

Bryant lived up to his agreement not to get into the details of the sex between the president and the intern, but he made a faint stab at getting her to agree that Clinton had lied under oath when he denied engaging in activities that would qualify as "sexual relations" as defined by Jones's lawyers during his deposition.

"I want to refer you to the first so-called salacious occasion," he started.

"Can you call it something else?" she asked. "I mean this is—this is my relationship."

He agreed and went into the crux of the dispute. "So, if the president testifies that he did not—he was not guilty of having a sexual relationship under the Paula Jones definition even, then that testimony is not truthful, is it?"

Cacheris objected, saying his client could not know what Clinton thought. The senators overruled the objection, but Lewinsky took the cue. "I really don't feel comfortable characterizing whether what he said was truthful or not truthful," she said. She noted that the Jones definition of sex was predicated on touching with the intent to gratify or arouse sexual desire. "I'm just not comfortable commenting on someone else's intent or state of mind or what they thought."

On one subject, Bryant finally obtained firm testimony that helped his side. Asked if she had reason to doubt her recollection that Betty Currie called her to arrange pickup of the gifts, Lewinsky replied flatly, "I don't think there is any doubt in my mind."

But she remained in command of the deposition to the end. At one point, when she paused to confer with her lawyer, Senator DeWine warned her that her microphone was picking up her words. "Sorry," she said cheerily. "I was only saying nice things about you all."

At another point, Bryant tried again to elicit her thoughts about Clinton, only to have her seize control of the exchange. "I assume you think he's a very intelligent man," he said.

"I think he's an intelligent *president,*" she shot back.

Bryant knew when to quit. "Okay. Thank goodness this is confidential. Otherwise, that might be the quote of the day."

By the time Bryant was done, the White House lawyers relaxed, confident that they had little to worry about. Nicole Seligman had been tapped to cross-examine the young woman and had spent the entire weekend poring through grand jury transcripts and preparing to question Lewinsky at length if she wandered off the reservation. Under Bryant's erratic questioning, though, Lewinsky had not added anything new; the White House team knew that from the first moment Lewinsky referred back to her grand jury testimony and said she was sticking with that. And so Seligman decided to follow the old trial lawyer's credo that if you had not been hurt, freeze the record before you were.

But as she discarded the myriad questions she could have asked, Seligman did take the opportunity to pass along a message to Lewinsky. In the days leading up to the deposition, it had occurred to Seligman that this twenty-five-year-old who had fallen so hard for the president had been completely cut off from him. Lewinsky had been distraught after what she considered Clinton's dismissive treatment of her in his August 17 speech to the nation, and she was further upset that it took so long for him to apologize to her and her family in his public contrition tour that followed. Seligman realized this was a chance to reach out to her in a human way—after her testimony was over, not as a means to influence it. Would there be anything wrong in offering an apology? Seligman asked her fellow lawyers during their strategy sessions. None of the men had thought of it but, after mulling it over, they agreed.

"Ms. Lewinsky," Seligman now said, "on behalf of the president, we'd like to tell you how very sorry we all are for what you have had to go through."

With that, the deposition was over. The cameras were turned off at 3:14 P.M., and there was little question on either side about who had won this showdown. Lewinsky had dominated the session like the practiced witness she was. After two dozen other depositions, FBI interviews, and grand jury appearances, she had testifying down to an art and it showed. Bryant was on his heels the entire time. Senator Fred Thompson, who attended because he would preside at the Vernon Jordan deposition the next day, abruptly walked out partway through, disgusted by the circus atmosphere and convinced the questioning was not getting anywhere. "I can't take this anymore," he told a colleague as he left. Lewinsky was likable, at ease, and anything but a put-upon woman, Thompson concluded; she could nick up Clinton here or there, but if the public saw her, they would see her as an equal to the president, not a victim.

Tom Griffith, the chief Senate lawyer, approached Preston Burton, one of Lewinsky's attorneys, afterward and told him she would never have to worry again about work. "She's the best witness I ever saw," he said. "She wouldn't need to ever get a job. She could go into business teaching people how to testify."

That night, Griffith went back to the Capitol to brief Lott's chief aide, Dave Hoppe: It was a disaster.

Word got back pretty quickly to the other managers, and that only increased the pressure on Asa Hutchinson, set to face off against Jordan the next day. Unlike Lewinsky, Jordan was to be questioned at the Capitol in a fourth-floor room normally used for national security briefings and specially shielded from electronic surveillance. The room was set up for a committee meeting, with an imposing dais for the members and tables and chairs in the audience for everyone else. The night before the Jordan deposition, Hutchinson went to the room with Senate officials to examine the layout.

"Where will the witness sit?" Hutchinson asked.

A Senate staffer pointed up to the chairman's seat, which effectively looked down on the rest of the room.

"Where will I be?" Hutchinson asked. Down here at a table facing up to the dais, the staffer said.

Hutchinson did not like what he saw at all. Jordan would have the commanding position in their confrontation. Hutchinson decided to have his position moved closer to where Jordan would sit and asked for a tabletop lectern to be brought in so that he could stand during the questioning, which would at least put him on eye level with his witness.

Hutchinson was tending to every detail. All he had heard for more than a week was how Jordan would chew up any interrogator. Hutchinson was a little intimidated. He stayed up late at night studying the transcripts and working on his script. On the left side of each page he wrote out the questions and on the right the answers Jordan should give if he stuck to his grand jury testimony as his attorney had promised. This way Hutchinson would know if Jordan deviated and would be ready to challenge him with his prior statements. Hutchinson's main goal was simply to get Jordan to repeat on videotape his description of Clinton's involvement in the job search and the affidavit. Jordan had testified five times before the grand jury, but Hutchinson wanted to tie it all together and present it in a more coherent sequence.

When the deposition started at 9 A.M. on Tuesday, February 2, Hutchinson immediately understood what everyone had been telling him about Jordan, who wasted little time demonstrating that he was in control. Following routine legal practice, Hutchinson asked the witness to state his name for the record and asked him to confirm that this was the first time they had ever met.

"I've looked forward to this opportunity to meet you," Hutchinson said.

"I can't say the feeling is mutual," Jordan responded, deadpan, provoking laughter around the room.

Hutchinson moved on, asking Jordan about his status as a senior partner at Akin, Gump, Strauss, Hauer & Feld, one of the capital's powerhouse law firms. What did it mean to be a "rainmaker"? Hutchinson asked.

"I think even in Arkansas you understand what rainmaking is," Jordan said.

"We've read Grisham books," Hutchinson quipped back, refusing to become rattled by Jordan's condescension.

While he no longer billed by the hour, Jordan once charged as much as $500 an hour, he said in response to a question. "Not bad for a Georgia boy," Jordan added. "I'm from Georgia. You've heard of that state, I'm sure."

Hutchinson went on to establish Jordan's closeness with the president, a relationship the witness was more than happy to detail. They vacationed together, he said, played golf together, spent the holidays together. "Every year since his presidency, the Jordan family has been privileged to entertain the Clinton family on Christmas Eve," he said. Asked if he was cochairman of the Clinton transition team after the 1992 election, Jordan quickly corrected the misimpression: "I believe I was *chairman.*"

That settled, Hutchinson elicited Jordan's version of the events that led to their encounter this day, including meetings with Lewinsky, conversations with New York executives on her behalf, and discussions with the president about her. The only time Jordan appeared a bit flustered was when Hutchinson appeared to suggest that Jordan had violated his fiduciary responsibility as a board member of the companies he was referring Lewinsky to by using his position to help out the president, an implication Jordan adamantly disputed. But the influential attorney enjoyed flaunting his lifestyle, at one point describing how he took Lewinsky to meet another lawyer "in my Akin, Gump chauffeur-driven car."

Hutchinson did get Jordan to say that he was laboring for Lewinsky at Clinton's behest, a statement the manager wanted to play for the Senate to make clear that the president had been running the show. "There is no question but that through Betty Currie, I was acting on behalf of the president to get Ms. Lewinsky a job," Jordan said, to Hutchinson's satisfaction. But later in the questioning, Jordan took umbrage at the notion that he was acting on "instruction" from Clinton. "I do not view the president as giving me instructions. The president is a friend of mine, and I don't believe friends instruct friends. Our friendship is one of parity and equality."

Factually, the questions and answers followed the script Hutchinson had laid out. Jordan did not move off his story or offer any new disclosures that would change the dynamics of the trial. The only variance came when Hutchinson asked Jordan about a key breakfast the lawyer had had with Lewinsky on New Year's Eve, 1997, at the Park Hyatt Hotel, where he often ate in the morning. During an appearance before the grand jury on March 5, 1998, barely two months later, Jordan had asserted flatly, "I've never had breakfast with Monica Lewinsky." But when she finally agreed to cooperate with Ken Starr and testified later in the year, she maintained that they did have breakfast that day and that she had mentioned some notes in her apartment that she had written to Clinton. "Go home and make sure they're not there," she remembered Jordan telling her, advice she took to mean she should destroy the notes, which she then did. If her account was true and it could be proved that Jordan intended for her to discard the missives rather than turn them over in response to the subpoena from the Jones lawyers, it could be construed as destroying evidence and obstruction of justice.

Hutchinson reminded Jordan of this conflict in testimony and produced an American Express receipt from the lawyer's account showing that he had paid for two coffees, an omelette, an English muffin, and a hot cereal at the Park Hyatt on December 31, 1997, just as Lewinsky had described. Jordan abruptly reversed course. Although he did not remember the breakfast when he testified before the grand jury, he said he now accepted that they did meet that morning. "My recollection has subsequently been refreshed, and so it is undeniable that there was a breakfast in my usual breakfast place, in the corner at the Park Hyatt."

Hutchinson got excited, but did his best to hide it. This was a new admission! True, it would not alter the course of the trial, but it was striking that Jordan was now changing his story. Several people in the rows behind him exchanged notes pointing out the development to each other.

"And do you recall a discussion with Ms. Lewinsky at the Park Hyatt on this occasion in which there were notes discussed that she had written to the president?" Hutchinson pressed on.

"I am certain that Ms. Lewinsky talked to me about notes."

Certain they talked about notes? Hutchinson found that intriguing. Jordan did not remember the breakfast but now suddenly recalled what was said at it? Hutchinson kept going. "And did you make a statement to her, 'Go home and make sure they're not there'?"

"Mr. Hutchinson," Jordan said firmly, "I'm a lawyer and I'm a loyal friend, but I'm not a fool, and the notion that I would suggest to anybody that they destroy anything just defies anything that I know about myself. So the notion that I said to her go home and destroy notes is ridiculous."

"Well, I appreciate that reminder of ethical responsibilities. It was—"

Jordan interrupted, "No, it had nothing to do with ethics, as much as it's just good common sense—mother wit. You remember that in the South."

Just before 2:30 P.M., Hutchinson ended his inquiry. Senators Fred Thompson and Chris Dodd, who were presiding, turned it over to David Kendall for cross-examination. To Kendall and the rest of the White House team, Hutchinson had clearly done a far better job than Ed Bryant had done with Lewinsky the day before; their respect for Hutchinson's lawyering skills increased. Still, just as with Lewinsky, the presidential lawyers calculated that nothing Hutchinson had elicited from Jordan had changed the essential dynamics of the trial, so they decided to sit on their lead and ask just two quick questions.

By prearrangement, Jordan wanted to make a statement at the end of his deposition defending his integrity, and Kendall obligingly asked an open-ended question to let him do so. "Mr. Jordan, is there anything you think it appropriate to add to the record?"

Hutchinson objected, and Thompson asked Kendall to rephrase.

"Mr. Jordan, you were asked questions about job assistance," Kendall said. "Would you describe the job assistance you have over your career given to people who have come to you requesting help finding a job or finding employment?"

Jordan pulled notes out of his pocket and began a testimonial to his roots and sense of propriety. "Well, I've known about job assistance and have for a very long time. I learned about it dramatically when I finished at Howard University law school, 1960, to return home to Atlanta, Georgia, to look for work." Jordan went on to recall how no law firm or government agency would hire a young black lawyer. His high school bandmaster called a fraternity brother and put in a good word. As a result, he said, "I felt some responsibility to the extent that I could be helpful or got in a position to be helpful, that I would do that."

Kendall followed up to drive home the point. "Was your assistance to Ms. Lewinsky which you have described in any way dependent upon her doing anything whatsoever in the Paula Jones case?"

"No."

While Hutchinson was jousting with Jordan, the House team was facing another threat they knew nothing about. If the managers did not succeed in turning Clinton out of office, the president was vowing that day that he would do it to them. Dick Gephardt had come to the White House to let Clinton know that he would not challenge Al Gore for the Democratic presidential nomination in 2000 but would instead concentrate on retaking the House, a decision that had actually been made in November just days after the midterm election. A relieved Clinton welcomed the news and promised to do everything he could to make Gephardt the Speaker. Then, revealing a little of the anger that aides knew consumed him, Clinton made clear he had his sights set on the managers and wanted Gephardt to target the president's enemies.

"You have a chance against Barr," Clinton said of the Georgia conservative who had crusaded for impeachment before anyone else. "He only got fifty-five percent against a nobody." In fact, Clinton rattled off numbers and names of opponents in several of the managers' districts, indicating how much he had thought about it. He named four Republicans in particular he wanted to defeat—Barr, Jim Rogan, Steve Chabot of Ohio, and Jay Dickey of Arkansas. Dickey was not one of the managers, but he represented the president's hometowns of Hope and Hot Springs and Clinton felt intensely about the congressman's betrayal in voting for impeachment. Beating them, Clinton believed, would show for history's sake that their prosecution of him was illegitimate from the beginning.

With two depositions behind them, the managers had just one last shot at a witness, and this was the one Rogan and Lindsey Graham had been itching to confront. Sidney Blumenthal had a way of irritating Republicans—and more than a few Democrats—with a smug, condescending attitude, and in many ways that was what his deposition was all about. The managers had decided to call him in part because they needed a villain. The House team was counting on Blumenthal to say something outrageous during his deposition.

Just as Rogan and Graham had worked behind the scenes to replace Ed Bryant as the questioner at the Lewinsky deposition, they spent plenty of time collaborating on how to handle Blumenthal. Rogan had been assigned to do the interrogation, but he wanted Graham to do it with him, convinced that it could rattle Blumenthal because of the enmity that had developed between the two men. More than anyone else, Graham had advanced the charge that the White House had tried to smear Lewinsky, and Blumenthal resented being cast as the chief culprit in such a campaign. But Hyde had set down the rule that only one manager could do each deposition. Having blown off Bob Barr, Hyde could not very well allow Graham to participate.

The day before Blumenthal was to show up for questioning, Rogan tracked down Graham on his cellular telephone in South Carolina to suggest a plan: "Maybe I'll call in sick and you'll do it."

"No," Graham said, "you can't do that." But he had another idea. He would call Hyde and simply announce that he planned to show up at the Blumenthal deposition to share in the questioning with Rogan. He did and Hyde finally relented, but warned him not to tell anyone in advance.

The Democrats were equally aware that Blumenthal was their least sympathetic witness. While they knew they could count on him for complete loyalty to the president, they did not want him to spout off and give ammunition to the other side, so the Democratic lawyers stressed that he should restrain himself when the camera came on. In fact, they pressed the point so strongly that some Democratic strategists became worried when Blumenthal showed up so deflated, fearing that they had gone too far by undermining his confidence.

When the time came to respond, Blumenthal kept his answers short and flat, going out of his way not to be inflammatory. The central recollection the managers wanted to put on the record was the conversation Blumenthal had had with the president in the Oval Office on the evening of January 21, 1998, when Clinton tarred Lewinsky as an unstable young woman who had stalked him and fantasized a relationship with him.

"He, uh—he spoke, uh, fairly rapidly, as I recall, at that point and said that she had come on to him and made a demand for sex, that he had rebuffed her, turned her down, and that she, uh, threatened him," Blumenthal testified. "And, uh, he said that she said to him, uh, that she was called 'the stalker' by her peers and that she hated the term, and that she would claim that they had had an affair whether they had or they hadn't, and that she would tell people." Blumenthal added that he believed Clinton's account. "He was, uh, very upset. I thought he was a man in anguish."

Rogan elicited the basic elements in about an hour and turned it over to Graham. That was when the fireworks began. Graham was determined to show that the White House had deliberately spread unflattering information about Lewinsky to destroy her credibility. But the folksiness that seemed so spellbinding in his floor speeches made for sometimes meandering questions that irked the lawyers for Blumenthal and the White House, not to mention the two senators who were presiding, Arlen Specter and John Edwards. It took only two questions to start drawing indignant objections from the Democratic lawyers. Just eight minutes into the interrogation, the presiding senators had to call an off-the-record recess to confer for twenty-eight minutes about how to handle Graham's line of questioning.

The first question drew a concession Graham wanted but seemed surprised to get. "Knowing what you know now, do you believe the president lied to you about his relationship with Ms. Lewinsky?" Graham asked Blumenthal.

"I do," he answered simply.

"I appreciate your honesty," Graham said.

Over the next few hours, though, Graham could not elicit any more admissions he sought, and at one point he grew so frustrated he slammed down his notepad in aggravation. He cited news articles that quoted unnamed people at the White House describing Lewinsky as "a stalker" who was known as a flirt, wore her skirts too short, and was thought to be "a little bit weird." But Blumenthal steadfastly denied spreading negative information about Lewinsky or revealing his "stalker" discussion with the president to virtually anyone.

"I never mentioned my conversation," he testified. "I regarded that conversation as a private conversation in confidence, and I didn't mention it to my colleagues, I didn't mention it to my friends, I didn't mention it to my family, besides my wife."

"Did you mention it to any White House lawyers?" Graham asked.

"I mentioned it many months later to Lanny Breuer in preparation for one of my grand jury appearances when I knew I would be questioned about it. And I certainly never mentioned it to any reporter."

Blumenthal acknowledged discussing Lewinsky in general with reporters, but without defaming her. "I talked about Monica Lewinsky with all sorts of people—my mother, my friends—about what was in the news stories every day. Just like everyone else, but when it came to talking about her personally, I drew a line."

"So, when you talk to your mother and your friends and Mr. Lyons about Ms. Lewinsky," Graham asked, referring to Gene Lyons, an Arkansas journalist sympathetic to Clinton, "are you telling us that you have these conversations, and you know what the president has told you, and you're not tempted to tell somebody the president is a victim of this lady, out of his own mouth?"

"Not only am I not tempted, I did not."

CHAPTER SEVENTEEN

"Good God Almighty, take the vote!"

P resident Clinton was fuming. "The way they're going about this, I'll get less constitutional protection than a common criminal on the street who committed a heinous crime! And yet I've never been charged with any crime!" On the other end of the telephone line was Tom Harkin, the Iowa senator who had helped Clinton recruit Dale Bumpers to his defense team earlier in the trial. Now the president was looking for help in defeating Susan Collins's plan to adopt "findings of fact" that would allow the Senate to conclude by a mere majority vote that he had lied under oath and impeded the discovery of evidence even if it failed to convict and remove him by the two-thirds majority required by the Constitution.

By this point, Clinton knew he would not be forced out of office at the end of the trial. But this findings proposal had presented a whole new threat. The concept was similar to a process often used by regular courts in civil cases and certain criminal trials—before a final verdict is entered, a judge or jury issues findings of fact that lay down their determination about the truth of the evidence. The findings sort through the competing claims of plaintiff and defendant and conclude which are proven and which are not. Based on that established set of facts, the judge or jury then determines whether a defendant violated the law. In this case, the intent was not to help the jury reach an outcome but to lay out a permanent record of Clinton's actions. If the idea garnered bipartisan support as Collins hoped, it could negate the vindication Clinton so desperately wanted out of an acquittal vote.

In recent days, the idea had begun to catch a little fire among Republicans and even a few Democrats. Like censure, it would allow senators to express their disapproval of the president's misconduct, yet it would state legal conclusions and become part of the official trial record without the possibility of being expunged by a future Congress, as a simple resolution of reprimand might be. Clinton feared it might have a more perilous impact—it could, in effect, declare him guilty of federal crimes and provide ammunition to Starr to convict him in a regular court.

Clinton tracked down Harkin in the Democratic cloakroom during a break in the trial to vent his outrage. This was entirely unfair, he complained. The Republicans were trying to do with fifty-one votes what they could not obtain sixty-seven votes to do. Findings would amount to a criminal indictment, and yet he had not been afforded any of the customary protections of a court process, Clinton said.

"I can handle a censure if you see fit to do that," he told Harkin. "But this has implications that would treat me worse than a common criminal."

Harkin needed no convincing. He had immediately recognized the pernicious effects of the findings plan and set about trying to destroy it before it got too far. He already had made one presentation to the Democratic caucus and now spent a weekend gathering more material for his assault—he talked by phone with Laurence Tribe at Harvard and Bruce Ackerman at Yale and collected writings from Burt Neuborne at New York University, Susan Bloch at Georgetown, and Cass Sunstein at the University of Chicago questioning the constitutionality of the idea. The criticisms were straightforward. The Constitution made no provision for a two-part vote on impeachment but instead indicated clearly that a finding of guilt required a two-thirds vote and resulted in automatic expulsion from office. The president "shall be removed from Office on Impeachment for, and conviction of, Treason, Bribery, or other high Crimes and Misdemeanors," the framers wrote, adding that punishment "shall not extend further than to removal from Office, and disqualification to hold and enjoy any Office of honor, Trust or Profit under the United States."

Other Democrats were disturbed by the findings concept as well and tried to rally against it. Such a plan would "set the dangerous precedent that a Senate impeachment trial could be used for the purpose of criticizing non-impeachable conduct, thereby trivializing the constitutional impeachment process and inviting future impeachments for non-impeachable offenses," Senator Pat Leahy wrote in a memo to Tom Daschle that was made available to other Democratic senators.

But the topic was a sensitive one in the Democratic caucus. Many of the senators were eager for a bipartisan solution that would chastise Clinton. Joe Lieberman and Bob Graham had both spoken with Collins about her idea and suggested they were open to persuasion. Senate Democrats were nervous about exonerating Clinton, only to watch some explosive new allegation arise before the end of his term. By now, they knew Juanita Broaddrick had given an interview about her rape charge. Nervous NBC executives had bottled up the interview and so far it had not aired, but if it did, no one could predict the public reaction. Republicans were openly rooting for the prospect. Senator Chuck Grassley of Iowa had taken to wearing a button on the Senate floor that said, "Free Lisa Myers." So the argument that findings of fact might be bad for Clinton carried little appeal in the Democratic caucus. When Bob Bauer, Daschle's lawyer, mentioned at a caucus meeting that findings could increase the president's legal exposure once the trial ended, Senator Kent Conrad objected, "I'm hearing a lot of people talking about a strategy about defending Bill Clinton. I'm not here to defend Bill Clinton."

Still, Clinton continued to press the point with anyone who would listen. On Sunday, January 31, he invited a group of allies and advisers to Camp David to watch the Super Bowl with him, including Jesse Jackson and his two sons, lobbyists Mike Berman and Pat Griffin, Energy Secretary Bill Richardson, and lawyers Richard Ben-Veniste and Lanny Davis. The president paid little attention as John Elway led the Denver Broncos to a second straight national championship and instead talked politics with his guests in the Maryland mountains. This findings proposal was completely unfair, Clinton complained to some guests. It was rewriting the rules after the game had been played, he said. Davis, among others, volunteered to call Joe Lieberman and make that case.

In fact, Davis made it a point to launch a public crusade on the president's behalf against findings of fact. Even before the Super Bowl, he had gone on a radio station in Bangor, Maine, to attack Susan Collins's idea, comments that got back to the senator and infuriated her. Collins had been searching for a way to sanction Clinton without convicting him since before the trial began, when she had read that article back in December advocating separate votes on conviction and removal. Collins had floated it by Trent Lott, who offered encouragement, but Tom Griffith, the chief Senate lawyer, had quickly shot it down, deeming it constitutionally flawed. When her top aide's former law partner mentioned that many courts use "findings of fact," Collins seized on the concept as another possible solution.

"That's it," she said. "That's what we need to do. It would put the Senate on record. We don't let the president escape a finding that he did these things."

Others had been advocating the same idea. Steve Buyer had mentioned it on the floor, Lindsey Graham had floated it on a Sunday talk show, and Senator Pete Domenici had brought it up with the Republican caucus. During the secret morning meetings of Lott's political advisers, consultant Frank Luntz had become fixated on findings, arguing almost every day that the Republican base would revolt against their elected officials if Clinton was let off with no punishment. So Lott decided to appoint a "working group" to explore the proposal and draft possible language, headed by Domenici, the old-bull Budget Committee chairman, and Olympia Snowe, perhaps the leading moderate in the caucus and the most likely to bolt on any final votes. Collins was put on the task force along with fellow Republican senators John W. Warner of Virginia, John Ashcroft of Missouri, and Tim Hutchinson, Asa's brother.

As the working group began to meet, it found its task harder than it seemed. Some thought Lott was sincere in his interest in findings, while others suspected he had only created the group to keep possible troublemakers busy, as he often did during legislative sessions. Domenici was interested in making his mark with the findings and pushed strongly to go forward in the face of serious doubts among his peers. Tension also developed between Snowe and Collins, the two women from Maine, who seemed to be jockeying for attention in the national press as the voice of New England moderation in the Republican party. Snowe struck some as resentful that her junior colleague was grabbing so much of the spotlight, while Collins appeared disgruntled about the older woman's attempts to overshadow her. Eventually, Snowe and Collins began drafting separate versions of the findings.

Then there were the constitutional and strategic considerations. Tom Griffith, who was skeptical of innovations on the framers' work, quickly dismissed the original version of the findings that Domenici showed him because it used criminal language and had the Senate drawing legal conclusions. Concerned that their own lawyer was not on board, Lott called a meeting in his office in an attempt to get Griffith's blessing for the general concept at least. Although appointed by Lott's predecessor, Bob Dole, Griffith's role was to be the Senate's neutral arbiter, and he tried to straddle a careful line. Nothing in the Constitution prohibited the Senate from issuing findings of fact, Griffith said, but it had never been done before, and there were plenty of reasons why. Lott took that measured appraisal as an endorsement.

At 9:30 A.M. on Wednesday, January 27, just hours before the Senate would vote against dismissing the case and for calling witnesses, Domenici convened a meeting of the findings working group in Lott's conference room. With the help of Viet Dinh, a Georgetown law professor he had hired to help him, Domenici had a new draft that did not explicitly draw legal conclusions, using words like "false and misleading testimony." Since it was less objectionable, Griffith signed off on it. But as the group met again through the day, the senators were uncertain whether to go with a short, straightforward document that might have a better chance of attracting bipartisan support or a longer, more detailed version that would provide a complete catalog of Clinton's misdeeds for the history books. Snowe preferred the more concise variant, while Collins pushed for a fuller accounting. The meeting broke up inconclusively.

Over the next week, as Collins and the others continued to deliberate among themselves, they simultaneously reached out to Democrats who might come on board, but quickly ran into a cross fire by the president's allies. Aside from the public assault waged by Lanny Davis and others, the White House launched a subterranean campaign intended to keep Democratic senators away from findings. White House officials privately threatened to "amend it to death" if Republicans insisted on introducing findings of fact on the floor, ensuring that the process would degenerate into the sort of partisan mess that few senators wanted. Paul Begala, the president's counselor, and another White House aide, Jonathan Prince, collaborated on a list of their own "findings of fact" that could be proposed as amendments in any floor fight over the idea—"that the House impeached the President on the most narrow, partisan vote in history," "that Ken Starr failed to include Monica Lewinsky's direct exculpatory testimony in his Referral," "that Mr. Starr's investigation has lasted more than four years and cost American taxpayers more than 50 million dollars," and so on. Begala and Prince came up with forty-five such "findings" and faxed them to Daschle aide Joel Johnson to make their point.

At a GOP policy lunch on Tuesday, February 2, as Vernon Jordan was undergoing his interrogation elsewhere in the Capitol, Domenici stood up to sell his fellow Republicans on the findings idea, a copy of the latest draft rolled up in his hands like a college diploma. The parliamentarian had signed off on it, and Domenici told the group that he believed he had five Democratic senators interested in joining them. While he did not name them, the ones he had in mind were Joe Lieberman, Bob Graham, Russ Feingold, Bob Kerrey, and Pat Moynihan. Domenici then read his draft of the findings:

"The Senate finds that, regarding Article I, the House Managers established to the satisfaction of the Senate that: I. The President of the United States, William Jefferson Clinton, on August 17, 1998, swore to tell the truth, the whole truth, and nothing but the truth before a United States grand jury. Contrary to that oath, William Jefferson Clinton willfully provided false and misleading testimony to the grand jury." The document listed three examples. "The Senate finds that, regarding Article II, the House Managers established to the satisfaction of the Senate that: II. The President of the United States, William Jefferson Clinton, wrongfully took steps to delay the discovery and cover up the existence of evidence and testimony related to *Jones* v. *Clinton,* a civil rights lawsuit, and to a United States grand jury investigation." Six actions would be cited, including the job search, the hidden gifts, and Lewinsky's false affidavit.

Domenici said they could keep it short or list the bill of particulars, then threw the question to the assembled group. Paul Coverdell, an energetic senator from Georgia, said he preferred the shorter version because he was concerned that having a division on that would weaken them on the final vote. But there was already division. Other Republicans were not sold on the findings concept in the first place. Slade Gorton and New Hampshire's Judd Gregg both expressed worry about the effect on future presidents—this would be a floor for bad conduct, not a ceiling, they said. Besides, a decision on whether to go with a long or short version depended entirely on whether they could win over any Democrats. Despite Domenici's optimism, that remained uncertain. From the beginning, Lott had told Domenici, Collins, and the others to show him the Democratic votes. "I really want to see them put their money where their mouth is," he said regularly.

The pivotal moment came the next day at another closed-door meeting of the Republican conference that stretched on for two and a half hours. By now, most of the senators had seen the videotape of Lewinsky's deposition, and regarded it as a debacle for the House managers. It was clearly a bad idea to let her testify on the floor. Some of the Republican senators even wanted to prevent the deposition video from being released out of fear of embarrassing Ed Bryant and jeopardizing his reelection chances.

From the front of the room, Lott laid out the situation. Daschle had made clear to him that he wanted no witnesses, no video excerpts, and no findings of fact. If the Republicans would not agree, then the Democrats would vote no in a bloc. Worried that he could not command the same party unity in his own caucus, Lott was making the situation sound as ominous as he could in hopes of rallying Republicans to his side. It was all or nothing, he told the room. They all had to stick together or there would not be any of them left.

By this point, however, support for calling witnesses to the well of the Senate was quickly collapsing. The senators went around the room in a rapid-fire, round-robin discussion, each summarizing where he or she stood in just ten or fifteen seconds. Kit Bond and Phil Gramm were pro-witness and pro-video. Orrin Hatch said the House should only ask for Lewinsky. Rick Santorum wanted all three on the floor. "You can't get any worse than the video," he said. Oh, yes, you could, others countered. "Things *are* getting worse," said Slade Gorton. Don Nickles added, "We've got to finish next week—it *can* get worse." There was "an ocean of downside" in going forward with witnesses, offered Fred Thompson. "Get out of Dodge," urged Sam Brownback.

The discussion came back around to what to do after the witness issue—namely findings of fact. By this point, Domenici had abandoned the longer version in favor of a shorter, less specific draft. As many as ten Democratic senators had been on record in news accounts and public statements saying harsher things about Clinton, but the White House lobbying seemed to be paying off—one by one, Democrats were telling Domenici and Collins that they would not sign on to their findings. At this point, Fred Thompson stood and spoke out against the idea. Made famous as a lawyer for the Senate Watergate committee, Thompson had given more thought to impeachment and the constitutional prerogatives than nearly any of his colleagues, and the more he considered the findings proposal, the more uncomfortable he had become. "We have great flexibility, but we shouldn't hamper future trials by setting a floor, by saying that a future president can get away with this—lying, a cover-up," he told the Republican gathering. "That would become part of the impeachment process. It's never been done before." The only people who needed the findings were those planning to vote not guilty, he added. "You have all the elements you need to vote to convict."

After everyone had spoken, GOP aides tallied the likely lineup within their own caucus, and the disturbing count showed eight Republican supporters for findings and ten opponents. If the Republicans could not get any Democrats and their own caucus was split, then the outcome was clear: the findings proposal was dead.

While Susan Collins's efforts to orchestrate findings of fact were unraveling, Senator Dianne Feinstein was laboring hard to revive the idea of censure as a reasonable outcome to the trial. Feinstein, the California Democrat who had been so outraged because she had been at Clinton's side at the White House when he initially denied having sex with "that woman," had long since cooled down enough to turn her ire against Starr and the House Republicans instead. But she did not want Clinton to get off scot-free any more than her fellow senators across the aisle did. She felt strongly that the president had to be held accountable and censure seemed to be the only avenue open to them.

As with Collins and her findings, Feinstein knew her proposal had to be bipartisan to have any hope of passing, let alone to infuse it with any lasting meaning, and so she set about searching for a Republican to team up with. She found a willing partner in Bob Bennett, the blunt-spoken senator from Utah, who was not related to the president's lawyer with the same name. The two sounded out colleagues to see where possible votes might be and began work on some language. In trying to make it genuinely bipartisan, Feinstein and Bennett had to appeal to senators with widely divergent views of the case. Democrats resisted the idea of drawing any conclusions that sounded as if Clinton broke the law because it would seem to conflict with their not-guilty votes. Republicans, or at least those willing to consider it, did not want some weak resolution without teeth because it would not really punish Clinton but merely provide political cover for his allies to acquit him. As Feinstein and Bennett played wordsmiths, they found the tougher they made the language to attract Republicans, the more Democrats they would lose, and vice versa. And a solid core of senators refused even to consider the idea, including liberals who did not want to beat up on Clinton, conservatives who would settle for nothing less than removal, and institutionalists on both sides who harbored genuine concerns about censure's constitutionality. The negotiations were so dicey that during conversations on the floor, Senator Chuck Schumer joked that the censure resolution should say, "We not only condemn what Clinton did but anything he might do in the future."

Over several days, Feinstein and Bennett tweaked the wording until, after some twenty drafts, they had one they thought should work. It included a series of "whereas" clauses designed to excoriate Clinton for his conduct, starting off with a bare-knuckled introduction: "Whereas, William Jefferson Clinton, President of the United States, engaged in an inappropriate relationship with a subordinate employee in the White House, which was shameless, reckless and indefensible . . ." It went on to deem his conduct "unacceptable for a President of the United States" and concluded that he "has brought shame and dishonor to himself and to the Office of the President" and "violated the trust of the American people."

Those were strong words, but they did not address the legal charges included in the articles of impeachment, so Bennett convinced Feinstein to add another whereas clause that he hoped would appeal specifically to Collins and other Republican authors of the now doomed findings of fact: "Whereas, William Jefferson Clinton, President of the United States, gave false or misleading testimony and impeded discovery of evidence in judicial proceedings . . ." That did not say he committed perjury or obstruction of justice, but it came closer. The pair also included another clause intended to win over skeptics: "Whereas William Jefferson Clinton remains subject to criminal and civil actions . . ." In other words, he would not be getting away with anything if the Senate left him in office because Starr could prosecute him in criminal court or Judge Susan Webber Wright could find him in contempt.

Henry Hyde was still looking for a way out too. At a meeting of the managers on the same afternoon that the findings plan was sinking in the Senate Republican conference, Hyde again brought up Orrin Hatch's alternate proposal to adjourn without a final up-or-down vote. Asa Hutchinson, Jim Rogan, and the others made clear they were not interested. They had not come all this way for an inconclusive ending. Win or lose—and no one was fooling himself into thinking they would win—they wanted to carry their mission to completion. Hyde knew his own team was a brick wall on this point. But without their knowledge, he also tried another backdoor avenue to adjournment. Just as he had secretly reached out during the House proceedings, Hyde spoke with his Democratic friend from the Judiciary Committee, Howard Berman, and revealed that he was more open to a compromise than the younger managers. Berman passed that along to Joe Lieberman, suggesting that the senator convey this to his colleagues. For it to have any credibility, Lieberman replied, Hyde would have to tell Republican senators himself, but evidently he was not willing, since the Connecticut senator never heard from the lead manager.

At the White House, the president's aides knew that fueling the almost desperate desire to find a way to slap Clinton at the end of the trial was the widespread fear, even among some Democrats, that acquittal would set off a "Rose Garden jubilee" of celebration and claims of vindication, along the lines of the defiant "pep rally" on the South Lawn following the House impeachment vote in December. Peppered with questions about the prospect at his daily briefing, Joe Lockhart tried to dismiss it with a quick quip: "I now declare, in a postimpeachment era, this a gloat-free zone." John Podesta later found Lockhart and groused at him for the line, but it succeeded in defusing the issue for the moment.

Clinton himself did all he could to look repentant rather than jubilant the next morning, Thursday, February 4, as he used one of his favorite settings, a prayer breakfast, to talk about reconciliation. While discussing Middle East peacemaking, his own situation was clearly not far from his thoughts. "If Nelson Mandela can walk away from twenty-eight years of oppression in a little prison cell, we can walk away from whatever is bothering us," he said, citing one of his favorite aphorisms as he struggled with his own anger at his political foes. "If Leah Rabin and her family can continue their struggle for peace after the prime minister's assassination, then we can continue to believe in our better selves."

The president received a little salvation from a pair of critics at the breakfast. "Lord," Joe Lieberman prayed aloud before the audience, "may I say a special prayer at this time of difficulty for our president, that you would hear his prayers, that you help him with the work he's doing with his family and his clergy, that you accept his atonement. So, Lord, I pray that you will not only restore his soul and lead it in the paths of righteousness, but help us join with him to heal the breach, to begin the reconciliation, and restore our national soul." Congressman Steve Largent, a staunch conservative Oklahoma Republican who had voted for impeachment, shared in the themes of redemption and fellowship. "Mr. President, I may not have voted with you in the four years I've been in Congress, but I want you to know that I care for you and love you, and that's part of the mystery of Jesus."

In a final strategic retreat along the lines that Orrin Hatch had suggested separately in the Senate Republican conference, the House managers decided later that morning to ask for only one witness to be called to the floor to testify—Monica Lewinsky. Otherwise they would settle for being allowed to show videotaped portions of the other two depositions. Returning to the floor to argue the matter before the Senate, the managers described the depositions and pleaded for what they considered one last scrap. "Please allow this to be a public trial in the real sense," Rogan asked.

"The Senate has indulged the managers," Greg Craig countered on behalf of the White House. "And despite the misgivings of many senators, the Senate has leaned over backwards to accommodate the managers. We believe it is time for the Senate to say it is time to vote."

The Senate then did start voting, although these were not the final votes Craig was seeking. The Senate rejected the subpoena for Lewinsky, 70–30. In the end, all forty-five Democrats were joined by twenty-five Republicans, including the aged Strom Thurmond, who called out his answer in such an emphatic tone that laughter echoed through the chamber.

"Noooooo!" he cried.

Senator Patty Murray, the Washington State Democrat who had campaigned so vigorously against a Lewinsky appearance, now tried to prevent the videotape of her deposition from being shown either, but was dismissed even by many of her fellow Democrats. Her motion was defeated, 73–27. The countermotion to allow both sides to show excerpts of the videotapes then passed, 62–38, with two Republicans voting no and nine Democrats voting yes. But Daschle's symbolic attempt to dispense with any more proceedings and move immediately to final votes on the articles—proposed again as another symbolic jab—was rejected by the same 56–44 vote that had defeated Robert Byrd's original motion to dismiss.

After a short break to confer with his colleagues, Chuck Ruff took the microphone and asked the Senate to direct the managers to notify the White House what portions of the videotapes they intended to use. Rogan offered a pithy reply, quoting a former California judge: "I believe the appropriate legal response to your request is, that it is none of your damn business what the other side is going to put on."

As the question was put to a vote, the public, weary of the trial, made its voice heard for the first time in the form of a middle-aged man with a graying beard who suddenly jumped up in the corner gallery overlooking the chamber. "Good God Almighty!" he shouted. "Take the vote and get it over with!" Capitol Police escorted him out. Ruff's request for notice was turned down, 54–46, with Republican senator Jim Jeffords of Vermont the only member to cross party lines.

In creating the second set of trial rules, Lott and Daschle had prepared for a bolt of lightning. What they had not anticipated was the sting of a smaller spark. While the prosecution and the defense took Friday, February 5, to prepare their video highlights—using tapes delivered by Capitol Police officers who stood guard over them during the editing until the wee hours of the morning—a journalist from another country inserted himself into the proceedings to accuse Sid Blumenthal of lying during his deposition. Susan Bogart, one of the investigators for the House managers, had gotten a tip that she might be able to prove Blumenthal had spread stories about Lewinsky if she contacted his friend Christopher Hitchens, a British expatriate who wrote for *Vanity Fair* and *The Nation.* Bogart called him at 4 P.M. and asked a series of leading questions, eliciting from Hitchens a story about a lunch he and his wife, Carol Blue, had had with Blumenthal at Washington's ritzy Occidental Grill on March 19, 1998, when Blumenthal repeatedly described Lewinsky as a "stalker" and portrayed Clinton as "'the victim' of a predatory and unstable, sexually demanding young woman."

Bogart and some of the managers were excited and quickly dispatched a pair of staffers around 8 P.M. to get Hitchens to sign a sworn affidavit to that effect. The British journalist's account seemed to contradict Blumenthal's testimony from just two days earlier in which he said he had never mentioned his conversation with the president to anyone other than his wife and White House lawyers. Still, Hitchens's affidavit did not assert that Blumenthal cited his talk with Clinton specifically in terming Lewinsky a "stalker." And Blumenthal quickly denounced his former friend's account, saying he did not remember the conversation in question.

Monica Lewinsky made her only appearance on the floor of the United States Senate on Saturday, February 6, although only in four images displayed on flat screens at the front of the chamber for senators to watch. After a marathon videotape-editing session, the House team played sixteen different clips of her deposition, narrated by several managers to fill in what they saw as the darker meaning of her testimony. This was the first time Lewinsky had ever appeared before the nation as a speaking player in the drama she had helped set in motion, and the image was striking. She was calm, composed, fully in command, hardly the victimized little girl, but instead the confident witness easily parrying her interrogator.

The managers also showed Vernon Jordan eleven times and Sid Blumenthal twelve times. For good measure, they reran clips of Clinton denying any sexual relationship with Lewinsky to remind the Senate and the country of how blatant his deceptions had been. Cognizant that they had not turned up any smoking guns, the managers made the best of what they had. "You might say, 'Well, there's nothing explosive here,'" Asa Hutchinson told the senators. "Whenever you're talking about obstruction of justice, it ties together, it fits together." Lindsey Graham threw in some homespun commentary as the video ran: "Where I come from, you call somebody at two-thirty in the morning, you're up to no good."

The White House team made effective use of the videotaped testimony as well. They did not bother to show any of Blumenthal because they considered him a sideshow. They showed Jordan eight times, making clear he did not consider his actions on Lewinsky's behalf to be part of a grand conspiracy to win her silence. And they showed fourteen clips of Lewinsky, sometimes choosing the same words shown by the managers but drawing different meanings from them. Most devastating, Clinton lawyer Nicole Seligman played nearly twenty minutes of uninterrupted tape that showed just how clearly Lewinsky dominated her stammering and uncertain questioner. Seligman simply let the tape roll, and the longer it did, the more uncomfortable many senators in the chamber felt for Ed Bryant; some of the Democrats openly laughed at his stumbling.

The managers, Seligman told the Senate, had "snipped here and there in an effort to present their story" and in the process "created a profoundly erroneous impression" of what the testimony showed. Not only did Lewinsky not bolster their case, she argued, the former intern undercut it by saying she did not think she would have to lie in her Jones case affidavit and that she did not consider Clinton's mention of their "cover stories" to be a recommendation of what she should say in that affidavit. The managers, according to Seligman, glossed right over that exculpatory testimony. "We must have attended a different deposition," Seligman said pointedly. "To borrow a phrase," she said at another point, appropriating the words of Dale Bumpers, "they want to win too badly."

For all of the White House scorn, Senator Rick Santorum thought the House team made smart use of the video excerpts. In fact, the Pennsylvania Republican believed, it was the most effective presentation offered by the prosecution through the whole trial. After it was over, he wandered back into the managers' Marble Room headquarters to congratulate them—and to offer a little advice for their upcoming closing arguments.

"Do what you did today," Santorum urged. "Show us your videos. But whatever you do, don't do what you did at the beginning and have all thirteen get up and preach to us." It would only bore the senators to hear from every manager again as they did during the opening arguments, he argued. Instead, stick with the A-team.

The managers were outraged. Who was Santorum to tell them how to handle their case? An angry Bob Barr, for once echoing what others on his team felt, complained that Santorum was out of line. After all the senators had done to them, Barr told Santorum, he had a lot of nerve dictating closing arguments to them now.

Hyde was more polite but equally resistant. "Well, these guys have gone through hell with me," he told Santorum. Hyde was loath to deny them their last chance to explain themselves for history's sake. At his staff's suggestion, Hyde let one of the committee lawyers, Paul McNulty, draft a script for only the stars of the team to deliver closing arguments—Hutchinson, Rogan, Graham, and Hyde himself. But at a meeting over the weekend to lay out their plans, Hyde told the managers about McNulty's plan, politely thanked him for the effort, and then put it aside. All thirteen managers would get their chance to speak, he said.

"By God," Hyde said, "you'll be able to tell your grandchildren that you gave closing arguments in the impeachment trial of the president."

Dianne Feinstein thought she was making progress with her censure plan. By her count now, she could rely on perhaps forty of the forty-five Democratic senators and she thought she had a good shot at a number of Republicans who had expressed interest, including Susan Collins, Olympia Snowe, Slade Gorton, John Chafee, Jim Jeffords, Gordon Smith, and Mitch McConnell. Along with her partner, Bob Bennett, that would put her over the fifty-one votes she would need for a simple majority. The problem was that Phil Gramm, the scrappy boll weevil Republican senator, had decided to make it his mission to block censure because it might excuse Democratic votes for acquittal. Under the rules, Feinstein would need two-thirds, or sixty-seven votes, to suspend the rules and force a vote on censure, and that was a boundary that might be tough to cross.

On Sunday, February 7, while Clinton flew to the Middle East to attend the funeral of Jordan's King Hussein, Feinstein squared off with Gramm on *Meet the Press* on NBC. "Impeachment is about the Constitution; censure is about getting political cover," Gramm complained. "What we're really trying to do here, which is not unusual for politicians, people want to be on both sides of the issue. They want to say the president is not guilty, they want to say the president's guilty. The problem is this covering-your-fanny approach has constitutional costs. Because if we do censure the president, we establish a precedent that when a future Harry Truman fires a future General MacArthur, then Congress is going to come in, and with a lower threshold, censure the president."

Feinstein was irked. She had made perfectly clear for months that she thought Clinton was a reprobate for his conduct, and all her hard work on censure was an honest response. Sitting next to Gramm at the tiny table in the studio, she challenged his characterizations. "Most respectfully, Phil Gramm, I have never said what your motivations are," she said firmly as he looked at her with a tight smile. "The motivations for this censure are not political. And I hope you will take me at my word. It is not something to

cover one's posterior. It is something that I feel very deeply is the logical outcome of this. Now, you may differ with me, but I don't question your motivations. Please don't question ours."

When the moment finally arrived the next Monday, February 8, Hyde lived
up to his word and disregarded Rick Santorum's advice. All thirteen managers were given time as the closing arguments began on the floor, many of
them venting their frustration at the process imposed on them and baffle-
ment that the nation did not see the case as they did. They shouted, they
whispered. They cited their children and the Constitution. They virtually
pleaded with future generations to understand their cause and credit them
for waging it nobly.

In a final tactical surprise for the White House, Hyde had six of his managers give their closing speeches, then reserved two-thirds of his time so that
the remaining seven could speak after the defense lawyers. That was a lesson
from the opening arguments. This time they would have the last word.

Unlike the prosecution, Ruff chose to close the president's defense by
himself. He carefully disputed the major points one last time to give comfort
to those planning to vote for acquittal, ridiculing the prosecution theory of
the case as he went. "Nice try—no facts," he said at one point. With victory
assured, though, Ruff's more salient mission was to cast the managers as isolated and hard-hearted moralists indifferent to the broader consequences of
their lonely crusade. "I believe their vision could be too dark, a vision too little attuned to the needs of the people, too little sensitive to the needs of our
democracy. I believe it to be a vision more focused on retribution, more
designed to achieve partisan ends, more uncaring about the future we face
together. Our vision, I think, is quite different, but it is not naïve. We know
the pain the president has caused our society and his family and his friends.
But we know, too, how much the president has done for this country."

The senators found the oration impressive enough, but by now it had a
redundant flavor. Restless after so many weeks of sitting on the floor, something they rarely did in their normal senatorial lives, several members stood
and wandered to the back of the chamber during the closing arguments. As
Ruff's presentation wore on, more joined them until by 4:10 P.M. there were
fifteen senators, eight Republicans and seven Democrats, lined up together
across the aisle in the back, almost as if it were some sort of silent bipartisan
demonstration in favor of wrapping it up and getting out of town.

With the advantage of going last, the managers quarreled with a number of
Ruff's specific points about the evidence. But it did not really matter. Everyone in the room had long ago made up his or her mind. The real advantage
for the managers was that Hyde had saved all of his heavy hitters for the finale.

After his own factual summation, Hutchinson used his last appearance before the Senate to try to turn one of the Democrats' central arguments on its head. The real profile in courage here, Hutchinson suggested, would be to risk political damage by voting to convict, not to acquit, as the hero of John F. Kennedy's book did in the Andrew Johnson trial. "The question is: Will the senators of this body have the political courage to follow the facts and the law as did Senator Ross, despite enormous political pressure to ignore the facts and the law and the Constitution?"

In the back room as he worked on his final remarks, Jim Rogan caught some of the television commentary about the earlier summations and heard the managers criticized for lacking humanity. Impulsively, Rogan crossed out the first five pages of his remarks and decided to tell the story of how he first met a young Bill Clinton some twenty years earlier. "This has been a very difficult proceeding for me and for my colleagues, the House managers," Rogan told the senators off-the-cuff. "But our presence here isn't out of personal animosity toward our president. It is because we believe that, after reviewing all the evidence, the president of the United States had committed obstruction of justice and perjury, he had violated his oath of office."

Once again, the rhetorical punch was delivered by Hyde, who wrapped up the case with characteristic resonance. He quoted Horace Mann, Edward Gibbon, Saul Bellow, Charles de Gaulle, and King Edward VII, who, in response to a plea from a misjudged child, declared, "Let right be done." Hyde expressed bewilderment at the Democratic senators willing to censure the president for "shameless, reckless, and indefensible" behavior but not to remove him for it. "This entire saga has been a theater of distraction and misdirection, time-honored defense tactics when the law and the facts get in the way." He chafed at the defense charge that the managers wanted to "win too much," saying, "This surprised me because none of the managers has committed perjury nor obstructed justice and claimed false privileges. None has hidden evidence under anyone's bed nor encouraged false testimony before the grand jury. That is what you do if you want to win too badly."

As he spoke, Hyde was trying one last time to justify the managers' fervor, to explain their cause. They were not the misbegotten partisans painted by the Democrats, but rather the stouthearted soldiers following Shakespeare's King Henry V against overwhelming odds at the Battle of Agincourt. "To my House managers, your great enterprise was not to speak truth to power, but to shout it. And now let us all take our place in history on the side of honor and, oh, yes: let right be done."

At 6:30 P.M., Hyde picked up his papers, turned back toward the prosecution table, and closed the case against the president of the United States.

CHAPTER EIGHTEEN

"The most difficult, wrenching, and soul-searching vote"

Susan Collins barely made it home before her dinner guests arrived. It was Tuesday, February 9, and the Senate had just completed its first day of deliberations behind closed doors. Rushing out of the chamber, Collins made a quick stop to grab take-out food from a Japanese restaurant around the corner from her Capitol Hill apartment. An aide got sodas and a bottle of white wine. After five weeks of the impeachment trial, her refrigerator was pretty empty.

The doorbell rang and there was her unlikely visitor—Kathleen Willey, the woman who had told the world a year earlier that the president of the United States had groped her in the Oval Office suite. Collins invited Willey and her fiancé in, and they sat down around a dinner table in the living room-dining room of the apartment. In any ordinary court case, this would be clearly prohibited contact between a juror and a potential witness. But this was an impeachment trial, run by the senators as they saw fit. Nothing barred Collins or anyone else from meeting with principal characters and judging their stories for themselves. After all, every member of this jury knew the defendant, and some had talked with him at length about the case. Besides, this meeting was not Collins's idea. Willey had called the senator's office a couple of weeks earlier asking for the chance to talk with her. Originally they were going to meet at a restaurant. However, Collins decided that it might not be a good idea to be seen in public together even if there was nothing inappropriate, so she agreed to play host at home.

For Collins, the encounter came at the moment of truth. The arguments and testimony at the trial were now over. Within three days her name would be called out by the Senate clerk, and she would have to stand up next to her desk and call out "Guilty" or "Not guilty." She had long ago concluded that Article I, the perjury allegation, was not strong enough and she would vote against it. But she was still struggling with Article II, the obstruction of justice count.

As they dug into the sushi and teriyaki, Willey and her fiancé made small talk with the senator and her chief of staff, Steve Abbott, about moving to Maine. Not until dinner was over did the Richmond woman turn to the purpose of her visit. She wanted to tell Collins about what she had gone through since telling her story on *60 Minutes* the previous spring. She wanted people to understand the harassment she had endured—not the crude come-on by the president, but the various incidents that had left her scared in recent months, the dead cat, the slashed tires, the encounter with the jogger, whom she referred to as "the visitor." A reporter had shown her a picture of a member of the Clinton circle, and she said she thought he might have been the man who had confronted her outside her Richmond home the previous January before her deposition asking whether she had gotten "the message." Willey herself was unclear about how all these events were connected but found the pattern quite disturbing.

"Do you feel you're in danger?" Collins asked Willey.

"Yes."

Willey offered no comment on Clinton or what the Senate should do with him. After about two hours, she left. Collins did not know what to think. As she and Abbott chewed it over afterward, Collins said she was convinced Willey was telling the truth as she saw it, but did not know if all the things she had described were really part of an orchestrated campaign of intimidation. For all they knew, a dog could have dragged in the dead-animal skull, Collins said. And Willey had not talked about her dealings with Nathan Landow, the Maryland developer and Democratic fund-raiser she had accused of trying to influence her testimony in the Jones case. Collins knew that the Willey situation, whatever the facts, was not really before the Senate to consider, just as she could not consider Clinton's dishonest testimony in the Jones deposition because the House had rejected the article of impeachment focusing on that. But still, she could not help but find what she had heard this night troubling. Knowing what she knew, meeting a possible victim of Clinton's lechery, could Collins really vote to leave this man in the highest office of the land? Could she genuinely call him not guilty and let him get away with such revolting behavior?

The final deliberations in the case had begun behind closed doors earlier that day as Clinton returned to Washington from the funeral of King Hussein. With the television lights switched off, the Senate chamber was so dark that it was hard to see. Unlike normal jurors, most of the senators approached the lectern with their decisions already settled and prepared texts in hand, the product of weeks of research by aides, lawyers, and, in a few cases, the senators themselves. The spontaneous give-and-take of the first meeting in the

Old Senate Chamber had long since vanished. Rather than debate the case or talk through the evidence, the senators instead engaged in a series of back-to-back speeches explaining the votes about to be cast. After a time, it would begin to sound repetitive, but the dialogue still had a profound sense of purpose, and many of the senators rose to the occasion with oratory touching on accountability, constitutionality, and proportionality. They quoted Alexander Hamilton, Socrates, even the Boy Scout oath. They shared stories of personal failings and ruminated on the nexus between private sins and public trust. And they reached out to one another in hopes of avoiding the partisan explosion they had long feared.

Limited to fifteen minutes apiece, the speeches flipped back and forth between the two parties, first a Republican, followed by a Democrat, and so forth. Republicans went in order of how they had signed up to speak, while Democrats went by seniority, with the exception of Robert Byrd and Tom Daschle, who were to go last. As soon as the doors were closed, the first senator, Slade Gorton, approached the lectern and stared out at his colleagues. Gorton, who had tried to short-circuit the trial along with Joe Lieberman at the beginning, announced that while he would support conviction on Article II, he would vote against Article I, registering the first Republican defector at the very start. Phil Gramm surprised no one by announcing he would vote guilty on both counts, but reflected the sentiment of many in the chamber when he said a leader with honor "would fall on your own sword." He added: "The difference between Nixon and Clinton is that Nixon had some shame." Ted Stevens, the crusty Appropriations Committee chairman, stood up soon afterward and added another Republican no on Article I. He believed Clinton did obstruct justice and said he would vote for Article II. Yet Stevens qualified his support in a curious way: if his would be the deciding vote, he said, he would vote against Article II as well, because he did not believe the allegations, while proven, justified Clinton's removal. In effect, he said, he was voting "not guilty, but he better not do it again."

The second day of deliberations, Wednesday, February 10, offered more of the same. Democrats found reasons why Clinton's behavior was not an attack on the foundations of American democracy, while Starr's was. Republicans mostly struggled to hold their own in the face of significant doubts among their more moderate or pragmatic senators. Day two saw a tough judgment by freshman Republican Jim Bunning of Kentucky, erudition from Democrat Pat Moynihan of New York, and a spirited defense of the independent counsel law from Chuck Grassley of Iowa, the Republican who had been wearing a "Free Lisa Myers" button on the floor of the Senate in reference to NBC's never-aired interview with Juanita Broaddrick. "Mr. Chief Justice, my fellow senators, as this trial nears the end, we have to ask the question how we got here with a tragedy like this," Grassley said in the dim chamber. "There are many losers. There are no winners. There are surely no heroes. There are lots of lessons to be learned, and I think all of our prayers ought to go out to those who were ensnared in the web of controversy."

Quite a few senators had their eye on John McCain as he approached the lectern, wondering how the Arizona maverick and prospective Republican presidential candidate would go. The normally outspoken McCain had remained unusually silent through the trial, presumably uncomfortable with the topic given his own admitted adulteries that broke up his first marriage after his return from a North Vietnamese prisoner-of-war camp. Given his history and his desired future, conservatives suspected he would try to weasel his way though. But when it came time to render a verdict, McCain came down strongly against the president: "I have done things in my private life that I am not proud of. I suspect many of us have. But we are not asked to judge the president's character flaws. We are asked to judge whether the president, who swore an oath to faithfully execute his office, deliberately subverted—for whatever purpose—the rule of law." McCain said the commander in chief must be held to an even higher standard than the military. "I cannot—not in deference to public opinion, or for political considerations, or for the sake of comity and friendship—I cannot agree to expect less from the president."

At 5:45 P.M., Russ Feingold rose from his seat and headed for the front of the chamber. The only Democrat to vote against dismissing the case earlier in the trial, Feingold was the center of considerable speculation about where he might wind up at the end. He had prolonged the suspense by ordering his staff to draft both conviction and acquittal statements. Republicans were desperate for any chance to call the final vote bipartisan, and their only hopes at this point were Feingold and the mercurial Robert Byrd. If they got even a single Democratic vote, they might be able to make the argument that the case was not simply a partisan exercise by a vengeful majority.

But Feingold was to disappoint them. From the lectern, the senator from Wisconsin gave his view of the history of impeachment—the Andrew Johnson case, he said, was weak, while the Richard Nixon one was strong. Clinton's fell in the murky middle. "This is a close case. In that sense, it may be the most important of the three presidential impeachments, in terms of the law of impeachment, as we go into the future. I agree neither with the House managers who say their evidence is overwhelming, nor with the president's counsel who says the evidence against the president is nonexistent. The fact is, this is a hard case, and sometimes they say that hard cases make bad law. But we cannot afford to have this be bad law for the nation's sake."

Feingold dismissed perjury with a single sentence, deeming it unproven. "As to obstruction of justice, the president did come perilously close." Of most concern were Clinton's coaching of Betty Currie, Monica Lewinsky's false affidavit, and the hidden gifts. On Currie, Feingold concluded that Clinton could have been trying to get her to cover up for him with family and the media, not to lie in a court proceeding. And on the affidavit and the gifts, he said, Lewinsky's videotaped testimony elicited by the managers actually convinced him that there was not enough evidence to convict—she did not say the president urged her to falsify the affidavit and she seemed "indefinite" about whether it was her or Currie who initiated the meeting that transferred the gifts to the president's secretary.

"It is best not to err at all in this case," Feingold said. "But if we must err, let us err on the side of avoiding these divisions, and let us err on the side of respecting the will of the people."

At 6:07 P.M., the next Democrat to rise was Joe Lieberman. While he had been perhaps the most publicly critical of the president among his fellow Democrats six months earlier, Lieberman had tipped his hand with his attempt to short-circuit the trial and his collaboration with Dianne Feinstein on censure. But fellow senators still paid attention to Lieberman out of respect for his candor and thoughtfulness. In the end, he told his colleagues, the Senate should not substitute its judgment for that of the American people on who should lead them unless a president's continued service constituted a grave threat to the national interest. "No matter how deeply disappointed I am that our president, who has worked so successfully to lift up the lives of so many people, so lowered himself and his office, I conclude that his wrongdoing in this sordid saga does not justify making him the first president to be ousted from office in our history. I will therefore vote against both articles of impeachment."

After the day's proceedings ended, Susan Collins headed to a downtown Washington restaurant for another dinner with key players in the case—this time, Dan Gecker, Kathleen Willey's attorney, and Lisa Myers, the NBC reporter who had interviewed Juanita Broaddrick. When Willey first called and asked to meet, she had offered either to come herself or to have her lawyer talk with the senator. Collins ended up scheduling both. Gecker was especially harsh about the president, describing himself as a disillusioned Democrat who had voted for Clinton twice. He went through the same incidents Willey had related the night before and, while not suggesting Clinton was directly involved, argued they could not simply be coincidence. Where his client had remained circumspect on the trial, Gecker urged Collins to vote for conviction.

Collins returned to her apartment late and called an aide to get the latest edits of her draft statement. While she had already dismissed Article I, Collins had been under a lot of pressure to vote for conviction on Article II—from her fellow Republicans, from her constituents, and now from a woman allegedly wronged by the president. In listening to Asa Hutchinson present the case, she had been convinced that Clinton had indeed obstructed justice. Yet, sitting there alone near midnight, Collins could not convince herself that what he had done was a "high crime." She decided to vote not guilty.

She climbed out of bed barely six hours later on the morning of Thursday, February 11, fumbled into her workout clothes, and met her friend, Republican senator Kay Bailey Hutchison of Texas, for their regular walk to the Washington Monument and back. As they marched down the Mall, Hutchison warned Collins that she was considered a key swing vote on Article II. Collins nodded, but said nothing about the decision she had made. After a shower and a change of clothes, Collins headed over to the Senate chamber. Scanning the speaking list, she realized she would not have a chance to address the Senate until the end of the day, and she was leery of revealing her decision until then. But the longer she remained undeclared, the longer she was a convenient target for lobbying. Lott had never entertained hope of conviction but now wanted only to put together a simple majority vote on just one of the two articles. Collins was critical to that effort. The imperative to prevent Clinton from claiming victory had increased after a report in that morning's *New York Times* had disclosed the president's private vow to defeat the House managers in the 2000 elections. For the first time in the trial, one Republican senator after another came up to Collins on the floor to press for her support. Don Nickles, the GOP whip, and Phil Gramm, the staunch Clinton critic, each made a pitch for a guilty vote. Rick Santorum argued that all she needed to do was delete a single word from her statement—*not*. Gordon Smith, a mild-mannered Republican from Oregon, handwrote a thoughtful letter outlining why she should vote to convict.

When Mitch McConnell approached her and noted that she was in a difficult position, Collins bridled. First of all, she told him, while she had not announced her intentions, her mind was made up. Second, she added, she would cast her vote before Jim Jeffords, Richard Shelby, Olympia Snowe, and Arlen Specter, the other likely not-guilty votes, meaning she would not be the one to deny the managers the fifty-first vote.

A short while later, an aide told her Lott wanted to see her privately in the Republican cloakroom. Collins marched in, full of steam. Before Lott got out a word, she exploded, "Look, my vote is not in play. I've got to do what I think is right." She added pointedly that she resented the pressure.

To her chagrin, Lott immediately agreed. The lobbying was totally inappropriate, he said soothingly. But he needed to know which way she planned to vote. If she would support Article II, he said, she would be given one of two prestigious speaking slots just before the final vote.

Then he had better line up another senator, Collins said.

On the floor that day, the closed deliberations featured more tough assessments of the president from both sides of the aisle. Republican senator Mike Enzi of Wyoming compared Clinton to Mike Tyson, saying job performance should not be a reason to acquit. Senator Jesse Helms concluded that because of Clinton's scandals "national debate is now a national joke." But Senator Barbara Boxer, the outspoken liberal Democrat from California, apologized for voting for the independent counsel law that had led to the "Ken Starr witch-hunt" and contrasted Clinton's consensual affair with Lewinsky with the conduct of Bob Packwood, the Republican senator she had helped force from office after numerous allegations of sexual harassment. She also addressed her family connection to Clinton and denied any favoritism. "I just want to say that, yes, my daughter is married to the first lady's brother, a brother who loves and admires his sister and doesn't want to see her hurt. So, I am far from being a defender of the president's behavior."

At 1:55 P.M., following a lunch break, Senator Arlen Specter got up. Specter had been the Republicans' chief inquisitor of Anita Hill during the Clarence Thomas hearings, forever diluting his otherwise strong reputation among women's rights activists as a moderate, pro-abortion-rights GOP ally. Throughout the Lewinsky saga, he had often played the contrarian, first arguing that the House should not impeach the president but instead leave him to Starr's mercies in criminal court after leaving office, then later arguing on behalf of the managers for a full-blown trial with witnesses, including Clinton himself. As he addressed the Senate, Specter did not clear up the confusion. But he did provide a telling critique of the process they had used, saying the senators should not have held separate caucuses by party during the trial—putting his finger on one of the dynamics that had helped enforce a partisan interpretation of evidence and events.

"My position in the matter is that the case has not been proved," Specter said. "I have gone back to Scottish law where there are three verdicts—guilty, not guilty, and not proved. I am not prepared to say on this record that President Clinton is not guilty. But I am certainly not prepared to say that he is guilty. There are precedents for a senator voting 'present.' I hope that I will be accorded the opportunity to vote 'not proved' in this case."

The other senators looked at each other with quizzical gazes and scornful eye-rolling. *Not proved? Scottish law?* Senator Pat Leahy stood and asked the chief justice whether senators were allowed to vote in any way other than guilty or not guilty. The parliamentarian advised that anything but guilty would not count toward the two-thirds required for conviction.

As the afternoon wore on, a few senators decided not to speak but merely to put their statements into the written record for the archives. Others drifted in and out, despite the historic nature of what was happening around them. But most wanted to have their say, even though the only audience was their peers. For many, this was a moment to express thoughts they might not in public. At a dinner party the night before the deliberations began, Senator Bob Torricelli, one of the president's most ardent defenders on television, had shocked some of the guests when he said he could not wait until Clinton was out of office and thought what he had done to distract from his mission had been criminal. Now on the Senate floor, Torricelli revealed that private disdain to his colleagues. Clinton's conduct, he told the other senators, was a worse disappointment to Democrats than Republicans. "The president squandered his opportunity. But he can't make us cast a bad vote now." Removal was not the answer. "Clinton's not worth it. No one will even remember him."

Senator Evan Bayh, the fresh-faced, newly elected Democrat from Indiana, did little to disguise his assessment of Clinton either as he spoke without notes. After suggesting that Rehnquist write a sequel to his book on impeachment ("I know what it's going to be titled," the chief justice responded deadpan, "'Mr. Bayh, Aye; Ms. Snowe, No'"), Bayh explained why he had concluded that Clinton's offenses did not measure up to high crimes. "I might have had a different view of this case under the Twenty-fifth Amendment on mental incapacity," he said, presumably half-joking as he referred to the constitutional provision allowing for removal of a president in cases of infirmity.

The day also revealed more doubts among Republicans. Senator Olympia Snowe disclosed that she would vote against both articles, though she added, "I resent the ordeal he has put this country through." In a surprise to many, Senator John Warner of Virginia announced that he would vote against Article I, while supporting Article II. An establishment Republican, Warner had nonetheless in the past sometimes defied party convention by opposing confirmation of Robert Bork to the Supreme Court and the election of Oliver North to the Senate.

When the time finally came for Susan Collins to speak, most everyone had figured out which way she was going, but hers was still a critical voice. She had still not found the answer really, not to her satisfaction. She felt Clinton had lied to Starr's grand jury, but the questioning had not been as precise as it should have been to nail him down, and the issues in dispute were less than monumental. She concluded that Clinton had obstructed justice in the Jones case by coaching Betty Currie, hiding the gifts, and finding a job for Lewinsky, and yet it was a civil case, not a criminal investigation, and the facts that were being covered up were not issues of great moment. Crimes? Yes. High crimes? No.

"In voting to acquit the president, I do so with grave misgivings for I do not mean in any way to exonerate this man. He lied under oath; he sought to interfere with the evidence; he tried to influence the testimony of key witnesses. And, while it may not be a crime, he exploited a very young, starstruck employee whom he then proceeded to smear in an attempt to destroy her credibility, her reputation, her life. The president's actions were chillingly similar to the White House's campaign to discredit Kathleen Willey." This last sentence Collins added out of deference to her meetings with Willey and her attorney the last two days. "As much as it troubles me to acquit this president, I cannot do otherwise and remain true to my role as a senator. To remove a popularly elected president for the first time in our nation's history is an extraordinary action that should be undertaken only when the president's misconduct so injures the fabric of democracy that the Senate is left with no option but to oust the offender from the office the people have entrusted to him."

As Senator John Edwards sat and listened, he looked at his prepared remarks and decided they were inadequate to the moment. Few of the Senate juror-judges had been more attentive to the facts of the case, more analytical in their evaluations than the freshman Democrat from North Carolina. As a longtime trial lawyer and short-time senator, he viewed the trial through the prism of the courthouse where he had worked for so long. And he found plenty in the evidence to be troubled about—not just the underlying behavior, which raised moral concerns and which most Democrats preferred to focus on, but the legality of some of the president's actions. In his mind, the perjury charge was not particularly strong, but the obstruction count appeared based on legitimate questions about the president's actions. Yet like a criminal-trial juror, he was looking for proof beyond a reasonable doubt. In the end, he had doubts.

Approaching the lectern just after Collins to explain his decision, Edwards paused first to address the chief justice. "The last time I saw you before this impeachment trial you were leading a sing-along at the Fourth Circuit Judicial Conference. I thought it might be a good idea for this group."

"A healing device," Rehnquist offered. Laughter rippled through the chamber.

Edwards moved on. "I want to speak to you from the heart. I want to speak to you about a struggle, because I have been through a struggle. It is a real struggle and I suspect that there are an awful lot of you who have been through the same struggle." He dismissed the perjury article without bothering to go into detail. For the obstruction charge, though, he said he weighed each allegation according to a scale. "The one that bothers me the most" was the allegation that Clinton coached Currie. The president's assertion that he was trying to jog his memory did not wash. "I doubt if anybody buys that," Edwards said. But to prove witness tampering, the managers had to establish that he intended to influence her testimony. "If we don't know what was in his head at that moment, how can we find that the prosecution has proven intent beyond a reasonable doubt? There is an enormous difference between what has been proven and what we suspect, because I have to tell you all, I suspect a lot that has not been proven."

By contrast with the buttoned-down Edwards, Senator Ben Nighthorse Campbell offered a folksier explication. His knowledge of the law "is minimal," admitted the Colorado Republican in the bolo tie and cowboy boots, and he could not dazzle his colleagues with "forty handwritten pages" of notes taken during the trial. His basis for casting judgment was familiarity— he too was a sinner. Take the little matter of the pens they were given when they first took the oath to be impartial at the beginning of the trial. They said "*Untied* States Senate" by mistake, and the senators were asked to return them. "I am not turning mine in," Campbell said. "I want to see what it's worth. And there you have it. An imperfect senator being asked to judge an imperfect president."

Few had come to the Senate from such an imperfect background as he. "The same body where someone named Daniel Webster, John F. Kennedy, and Harry Truman once served also welcomed a mixed-blood kid from the wrong side of the tracks—the offspring of an alcoholic father and a tubercular mother, in and out of orphanages, a lawbreaker and high school dropout who lied, cheated, and stole and did many other shameful things [that] make me a poor judge indeed of someone else who used poor judgment." Turning to Clinton, Campbell said solemnly, "I genuinely like him and feel sorry for both him and his family. But after agonizing as many of my Senate friends have, I remember the first question my then nine-year-old son, Colin, asked me seventeen years ago when I told him I was going to run for public office. He asked, 'Dad, are you going to lie and stuff?' I told him, 'No, I don't have to learn how to lie'—I still remembered how to lie from my delinquent days. I'm still trying to forget it. I told him, human frailties not withstanding, elected officials should not 'lie and stuff.'" And so, Campbell said, he would have to vote guilty.

While the final speakers of the day ran through their statements, Collins was back in the cloakroom on the phone with an aide. NBC had called the office and asked for confirmation that she had announced her decision to acquit in the secret session. Collins was furious. It had to be a Democrat, she figured, because Republicans were certainly not eager to leak her defection. She marched back into the chamber and passed a note to Lott informing him. He wrote back suggesting she speak on a point of personal privilege to tell her colleagues. Collins agreed and jumped to her feet to explain what had happened. Other senators murmured at the development, disturbed that their private deliberations had been violated.

When the sun rose on Friday, February 12, only nine senators were left to speak, including Lott, Daschle, and Byrd. By now, the votes were pretty clear. Four Republicans had said they would vote no on Article I and eight on Article II. Senator Richard Shelby, an Alabama Republican who had worried party leaders by skipping daily caucus meetings, had yet to tip his hand. And then there was Arlen Specter, who wanted to vote "not proved" and therefore could not exactly be counted in either column. Lott, still desperate to find a majority vote on Article II, sent Tom Griffith, the chief Senate lawyer, to work with Specter to find a way in which his vote would not be counted against them. In the past twenty-four hours, they thought they had worked out a deal—Specter would vote "not proved" and allow himself to be counted as "present." That way, the final vote would be recorded as 50–49, with one "present" vote. That would be a majority, sort of, and perhaps enough for Lott to save face with the House managers and the party's conservative base.

At 9:44 A.M., the Senate closed its doors one last time. Five more senators delivered their remarks, and finally it was time for Byrd to speak. Although he had asked to go at the end for the Democrats, there should have been no suspense in what he would have to say. After all, he had sponsored the motion to dismiss the case earlier in the trial. Surely that meant he would vote not guilty. How could anyone deem a prosecution so meritless that it should be cast out without a full hearing and yet still think the defendant might be guilty? But this was Byrd, and nothing was ever quite so simple with him. In recent days, he had sent signals that led many in both parties to wonder which way he would vote. In an interview broadcast the previous weekend on ABC's *This Week,* Byrd had said he had no doubt that Clinton provided false testimony under oath and thought indications were that he had obstructed justice as well.

"The question is: Does this rise to the level of high crimes and misdemeanors?" he said in that television interview. "I say yes. No doubt about it in my mind. But the issue is should the president be removed? Should this president be removed? That's the issue. And the Constitution requires that if he is convicted, he is automatically removed immediately with no second chance. So, it comes down to the question—comes down to the issue, to remove or not to remove? That is the question."

Daschle was happy at least that Byrd had chosen to wait to speak until the end of the deliberations; even if he did defect, it would be too late to lead a cavalcade of other Democrats out of the stockyard. Still, Daschle wanted the caucus to be unified. If they were going out to face the political consequences of seeming to excuse Clinton's roguish conduct, the minority leader did not want to give opponents a club they could use to bash them over the head and a guilty vote by Byrd would be a mighty painful club. So when Byrd stood and walked slowly down the center aisle to the lectern, many in the chamber strained to hear his voice.

"This is my forty-seventh year in Congress," Byrd said. "I never dreamed that this day would ever come. And until six months ago I couldn't place myself in this position. I couldn't imagine that, really, an American president was about to be impeached. . . . Like so many Americans, I have been deeply torn on the matter of impeachment. I have been angry at the president, sickened that his behavior has hurt us all and led to this spectacle. I am sad for all of the actors in this national tragedy. His family and even the loyal people around him whom he betrayed—all have been hurt. All of the institutions of government—the presidency, the House of Representatives, the Senate, the system of justice and law, yes, even the media—all have been damaged by this unhappy and sorry chapter in our nation's history."

Byrd repeated what he had told ABC's Cokie Roberts: Clinton's offenses did constitute an "abuse or violation of some public trust" worthy of impeachment. But he went on. "Should Mr. Clinton be removed from office for these impeachable offenses? This question gives me great pause. The answer is, as it was intended to be by the framers, a difficult calculus. This is without question the most difficult, wrenching, and soul-searching vote that I have ever, ever cast in my forty-six years in Congress." After all the struggling, Byrd said, he had concluded that a case born in a partisan atmosphere and opposed by the public could not be sustained, no matter its merits. "In the end, the people's perception of this entire matter as being driven by political agendas all around, and the resulting lack of support for the president's removal tip the scales for allowing this president to serve out the remaining twenty-two months of his term, as he was elected to do."

By now, Byrd had rambled on well beyond his allotted fifteen minutes, but Rehnquist, who had been tougher on other less prestigious senators, did not interrupt. Byrd turned and asked how much time he had taken. Twenty-two minutes, came back the answer. Appearing slightly embarrassed, Byrd apologized and quickly finished.

Now there were just three to go. Richard Lugar of Indiana, a modest, serious-minded Republican who had once run for president himself, declared firmly that he would vote for conviction, mocking the White House defense that attributed all those suspicious events to an "'immaculate obstruction' in which jobs are found, gifts are concealed, false affidavits are filed, and the character of a witness is publicly impugned, all without the knowledge or direction of the president, who is the sole beneficiary of these actions."

Finally, it came time for Daschle and Lott to wrap up, two leaders of opposing parties with conflicting interests and yet one overriding goal—political survival with dignity. They had labored together against fantastic odds for six weeks to keep the Senate from coming apart, and each had found new respect for the other. For all of their different ideologies and styles, Daschle, as he once promised, had helped Lott to copilot the plane to a safe landing.

Daschle went first. He had a thorough analysis of the facts and law prepared for him by his lawyer, Bob Bauer, but he put it aside and spoke from his own scribblings in a more personal vein about his "sense of betrayal" by Clinton. The independent counsel had crossed the bounds of propriety, the House Judiciary Committee had relinquished its duty to conduct its own investigation, and the House as a whole had degenerated into a partisan bloodbath. "But as deeply disappointed as I am with the process, it pales in comparison to the disappointment I feel toward this president. Maybe it is because I had such high expectations. Maybe it is because he holds so many dreams and aspirations that I hold about our country. Maybe it is because he is my friend. I have never been, nor ever expect to be, so bitterly disappointed again."

Perhaps that disappointment had spurred him to ensure the Senate did not follow down the same shameful trail, he said. "The Senate has served our country well these past two months. And I now have no doubt that history will so record." He paid tribute to his partner, Trent Lott. "Perhaps more than anyone in the chamber, I can attest to his steadfast commitment to a trial conducted with dignity and in the national interest. He has demonstrated that differences—honest differences—on difficult issues need not be dissent, and in that end the Senate can transcend those differences and conclude a constitutional process that the country will respect, and I do."

With tears glistening in his eyes, Daschle reminisced about his father, who had taught him never to do anything he would not put his signature on. "I thought of that twice during these proceedings—once when we signed the oath right here, and again last night when I signed the resolution for Scott Bates," he said, referring to a Senate clerk who had died in an automobile accident during the trial. "I will hear Scott Bates's voice when I hear my name called this morning. My father passed away two years ago. He and Scott are watching now. And I believe they will say that we have a right to put our signature on this work, on what we have done in these past five weeks, for with our votes today we can turn our attention to the challenges confronting tomorrow."

Last up was Lott, who likewise extended his appreciation to "my good friend" Daschle for his cooperation and, at the same time, defended the proceeding they had cobbled together out of nothing, particularly that magic moment in the Old Senate Chamber when both parties had come together at the start. "We tried to do impartial justice—honest, fair, and quick," he said. Lott, the onetime firebrand congressman, recalled leaving the House to join the Senate and noticing how much more civil it was. "But we should lay off the House," he said, noting that it was not their fault this issue had landed in their laps. After all, he added, the independent counsel law was "not our idea," meaning Republicans. When Lott came to Clinton, he mentioned the case of a judge impeached and convicted for perjury, and the dangerous precedent set by removing judges for lying under oath but not presidents. Democrats should have no problem evicting Clinton from the White House, he said, since it would only mean that Vice President Gore would move in and carry on the same policies. But Lott's personal reference resonated the most in the chamber, at least with fellow Republicans, as he recalled that his own daughter was about the same age as the young intern Monica Lewinsky, who was used for sexual services just off the Oval Office by the president of the United States.

Finally, Lott was done and so were the deliberations.

"Let's vote," he said soberly.

"Mr. Chief Justice, members of the Senate, the Senate has met almost exclusively as a court of impeachment since January 7, 1999, to consider the articles of impeachment against the president of the United States. The Senate meets today to conclude this trial by voting on the articles of impeachment, thereby fulfilling its obligation under the Constitution. I believe we are ready to proceed to the votes on the articles. And I yield the floor."

Just after noon, Lott turned over the proceeding to the chief justice, who instructed the clerk to read Article I aloud. All one hundred senators, who had grown more relaxed and casual as the trial wore on, now sat stiffly at their desks again as they had when it had begun thirty-six days earlier. All thirteen managers were stationed at their table on the floor, as were all seven main lawyers for the president, plus a few associates and aides given chairs so they could be present for history. The galleries were packed, and for once, all of the seats set up on the floor around the edge of the chamber were filled. The high school students who worked as Senate pages were lined up against the back walls. Sitting behind the Democratic senators was a corps of the president's staunchest defenders from the House: Maxine Waters, John Lewis, Corrine Brown, and Sheila Jackson Lee.

"The question is on the first article of impeachment," Rehnquist declared.

"Senators, how say you? Is the respondent, William Jefferson Clinton, guilty or not guilty? A roll call vote is required. The clerk will call the roll."

"Mr. Abraham," the clerk called out.

Spencer Abraham stood at his desk. "Guilty."

"Mr. Abraham, guilty," the clerk repeated. "Mr. Akaka."

"Not guilty."

"Mr. Akaka, not guilty. Mr. Allard."

And so it went, just as it had during the vote on dismissal. One by one, they pronounced their verdicts. Barbara Boxer punctuated her "not guilty" forcefully. Robert Byrd mumbled his. Daschle's came out as a soft sigh. Orrin Hatch sounded resolute, if a little sad, as he declared, "Guilty." Kay Bailey Hutchison issued the same judgment in barely a whisper. Richard Shelby showed his hand, calling out, "Not guilty."

Finally, it came to Arlen Specter. "Not proved, therefore not guilty."

A rustle swept through the room, as well as a snicker or two from the galleries. The clerk had been told to expect "not proved" and to mark it as "present," per Specter's deal with Tom Griffith. But Specter had changed his mind without telling anyone. Uncertain how to record this variation, the clerk did not repeat it aloud, as he had with all the others.

A few moments later, the galleries reacted with surprised murmurs when Republicans Fred Thompson and John Warner added their "not guilty" votes, although, unlike Shelby, they had told their fellow senators during the closed sessions that they would defect on the perjury article. With Feingold's return to the party fold and the parliamentarian counting Specter as "not guilty," that meant all forty-five Democrats and ten Republicans had voted to acquit Clinton on Article I. Joining Specter, Shelby, Thompson, and Warner were Ted Stevens, John Chafee, Susan Collins, Slade Gorton, Jim Jeffords, and Olympia Snowe. The vote was completed at 12:20 P.M. A few senators got out of their seats to wander, and a low buzz hummed in the chamber as the clerks tallied the roll. Joe Lieberman went over to Shelby to congratulate him on his vote. Lott retreated to the back of the chamber to consult with Hatch.

At 12:21, the vote was in. "On this article of impeachment," Rehnquist intoned, "forty-five senators having pronounced William Jefferson Clinton, president of the United States, guilty as charged, fifty-five senators having pronounced him not guilty, two-thirds of the senators present not having pronounced him guilty, the Senate adjudges that the respondent, William Jefferson Clinton, president of the United States, is not guilty as charged in the first article of impeachment."

The faces around the room registered no reaction. Everyone knew the result before walking in, so now they were simply going through the motions of making it official: Clinton would stay in office. Indeed, Rehnquist was reading lines from a script prepared for him by staff members, who had offered him instructions on how to announce an acquittal vote and end the trial ("Chief Justice bangs the gavel," it directed) but did not even bother to outline what he should do should there be a conviction. At the White House table, the lawyers sat stone-faced, determined not to give the slightest hint of relief, much less celebration. It was, as Joe Lockhart had promised, a "gloat-free zone." At the House table, the managers stared grimly. Jim Rogan, Lindsey Graham, and a few others had taken out the long, narrow vote cards used by the Senate and were recording checks by each name for their own record of history. Asa Hutchinson sat with his left arm folded across his chest, his right hand stroking his chin.

As the clerk read the second article aloud, Lott moved to the back of the chamber to find Specter and make one last effort to salvage some measure of vindication for the House and for Republicans. "How are you going to vote on the next vote?" Lott asked Specter plaintively, still hoping for a 50–49 tally on obstruction. Would he vote some way that would be recorded as "present"?

Specter said he was going to vote the same way.

Disappointed, Lott said okay and walked away.

The clerk began calling the roll again. This time when Specter provided his own unique wording, the clerk read it back verbatim. Four other Republicans joined him in supporting acquittal on Article II—Chafee, Collins, Jeffords, and Snowe. It was a down-the-middle tie, 50–50. Lott did not get his majority.

"On this article of impeachment," Rehnquist said at 12:39 P.M., "fifty senators having pronounced William Jefferson Clinton, president of the United States, guilty as charged, fifty senators having pronounced him not guilty, two-thirds of the senators present not having pronounced him guilty, the Senate adjudges that the respondent, William Jefferson Clinton, president of the United States, is not guilty as charged in the second article of impeachment.

"The chair directs judgment to be entered in accordance with the judgment of the Senate as follows: 'The Senate, having tried William Jefferson Clinton, president of the United States, upon two articles of impeachment exhibited against him by the House of Representatives, and two-thirds of the senators present not having found him guilty of the charges contained therein: It is, therefore, ordered and adjudged that the said William Jefferson Clinton be, and he is hereby, acquitted of the charges in this said article.'"

The trial was done. President Clinton was not guilty. And more important, at least to Lott and Daschle, the Senate had survived. For the next few minutes, they celebrated. Rehnquist congratulated the senators, praising the quality of the debate and "the manner in which the majority leader and the minority leader have agreed on procedural rules in spite of the differences that separate their two parties on matters of substance." Lott and Daschle responded in kind, presenting Rehnquist with a plaque adorned with a "golden gavel" usually given to senators who had served more than one hundred hours in the presiding chair.

"I am not sure it quite reached one hundred hours, but it is close enough," Lott joked.

"It seemed like it," Rehnquist replied dryly.

At 12:43 P.M., the Senate adjourned sine die as a court of impeachment, and a squadron of six senators escorted Rehnquist from the chamber. The sergeant at arms was to similarly escort out the House managers, but Henry Hyde had already escaped through the back door and had to be called back into the chamber to repeat his exit formally down the center aisle. The White House lawyers just stood there awkwardly, unsure what to do next. Without the standing of a chief justice or a member of Congress, they were not entitled to an escort committee—even though they had just won the case.

"I'll escort you guys," Don Nickles, the majority whip, who sat in front of their table, offered cheerfully. But being lawyers and not politicians, they simply slipped quietly out the back.

The tension had broken. Six weeks of stress and uncertainty had ended. The political fratricide everyone had feared had been averted. Even though his side had not succeeded in getting even a simple majority, Lott grinned exuberantly and offered thanks to the staff. Daschle followed suit and then the two men met in the middle of the aisle to shake hands.

"We did it," Daschle said.

"We sure did," Lott answered.

A surreal postscript followed over the next twenty-five minutes. At first, this too went according to a prepared script, right down to the lines each player would utter in a parliamentary dance intended to cover both sides. Senator Dianne Feinstein, having failed to gain enough bipartisan support for her censure resolution, introduced it for a vote anyway, knowing it would fail. Senator Phil Gramm, the designated Republican censure-killer, stood up to object that the matter was out of order, and a roll call was announced. Unlike during the just-completed trial, a parade of senators sauntered casually to the front desk to record their votes. Others milled around, bantering and laughing aloud. Almost no one remained in his or her seat. Feinstein and staunch conservative John Ashcroft shook hands and talked in the center aisle. John Kerry, Chris Dodd, and Gordon Smith laughed cheerily together on the

Democratic side. Lott joked with John Edwards. Pat Moynihan combed his hair in the back of the chamber, while Bill Frist wandered up to the gallery to sit with his wife and kids. The decorum of the trial was now gone. It was back to business as usual.

A few minutes later, the vote was announced, 56–43—a majority, but not the two-thirds needed to suspend the rules. There would be no censure. But there would be one final warped act in a warped drama. A bomb threat phoned into the Capitol prompted police officers to usher senators and everyone else out of the building—a precaution so rare that longtime staffers could not remember a precedent. The senators emerged into the unseasonable 74-degree day and continued chatting on the lawn as if summer camp were ending. Daschle escaped to a museum while waiting for permission to return.

The mood was striking. Somehow, out of all this, good will had emerged among the senators from both parties. Perhaps it was all the enforced togetherness, which was so unusual in the frantic pace of ordinary legislative life. Perhaps it was the shared experience of being shot at and missed. Either way, after months of bitterness and bile, there was optimism. "Ironically, having been through this crisis may make it easier, not harder, for us to work together," Susan Collins wrote in her diary that night. "This experience has changed each of us individually, and as a Senate, forever."

Maybe. And maybe not. In modern Washington, working together went against the grain; partisanship was the tactic of the day, keeping your own caucus together and accusing the other side of politics. For all of the camaraderie of the moment, plenty of people in the room knew that working together was not necessarily in their own interests. Bob Bauer, Daschle's lawyer, who had seen the process from the beginning since his March 1998 strategy memo to Dick Gephardt advising that the Democrats transform the battle into a fight over process, watched as the high spirits flooded the chamber.

"Jesus," he said to a Democratic aide standing next to him, "how long do you think this era of good feeling will last?"

The aide did not hesitate. "Not long, I hope."

EPILOGUE

"The country didn't want an impeachment"

From the arched window of the sitting room outside her bedroom in the White House, Hillary Clinton could see a burst of sunshine warming the nation's capital. The gray gloom of winter had dissipated and springlike temperatures seemed to herald a season of renewal. At that moment, the Senate was gathering on the other end of Pennsylvania Avenue to vote to acquit her husband of the two articles of impeachment, freeing him to spend the last 708 days of his presidency rehabilitating himself. But the first lady had a new beginning of her own in mind on this Friday, February 12. Joining her for a secret meeting was Harold Ickes, the former deputy White House chief of staff who had masterminded Bill Clinton's reelection in 1996 and later explored whether the president should resign in the wake of the Starr report. Ickes had been summoned to advise Hillary Clinton about whether she should embark on a political career of her own—specifically, a campaign to join the same Senate then passing judgment on the series of events that had started when Bill Clinton cheated on her.

Hillary Clinton had her eye on the seat being vacated by retiring senator Pat Moynihan, and no one knew New York politics better than Ickes. After a couple of hours discussing the vicissitudes of running a campaign in a state where she had never lived, he and the first lady retired to the family dining room to continue the conversation over lunch. Shortly afterward, the president wandered in and planted himself at the wooden table. He set out a piece of paper on which he had scratched out a statement in longhand about the Senate verdict, a few carefully chosen words that he planned to deliver in the Rose Garden later in the afternoon. While Hillary Clinton and Ickes chatted about the New York electoral map, the president edited his statement. Occasionally he threw in his own assessment of her prospective campaign, recalling with freakish precision, for instance, how many votes he got in Herkimer County in upstate New York in 1992 and 1996. The first lady and Ickes eventually returned to the sitting room before finally wrapping up a marathon four-hour session, almost oblivious to the action taking place on the Senate floor.

The Monica Lewinsky scandal had paradoxically transformed Hillary Clinton into one of the nation's most popular political figures. The first lady who had alienated much of the public with her uncompromising and unsuccessful campaign to reshape the nation's health care system in the first Clinton term had been resurrected in the second as the wronged wife who stoically stood by her man. However unhappy she might have been at the antifeminist reasons for that image evolution, Hillary Clinton now found the door to elective office opened to her for the first time in her life even as the end of her husband's career was now in sight.

Finished with editing, the president scooped up his paper and headed over to the West Wing. Two hours after the final Senate vote, he emerged from the Oval Office into the Rose Garden, this time alone, unlike on the December impeachment day when he was surrounded by his wife, Vice President Gore, and dozens of congressional allies. Heeding the spirit of Joe Lockhart's "gloat-free zone," Clinton did his best to remain solemn and unsmiling.

"Now that the Senate has fulfilled its constitutional responsibility, bringing this process to a conclusion, I want to say again to the American people how profoundly sorry I am for what I said and did to trigger these events and the great burden they have imposed on the Congress and on the American people," he said, gripping the presidential podium. "I also am humbled and very grateful for the support and the prayers I have received from millions of Americans over this past year. Now I ask all Americans—and I hope *all* Americans—here in Washington and throughout our land—will rededicate ourselves to the work of serving our nation and building our future together. This can be and this must be a time of reconciliation and renewal for America. Thank you very much."

Clinton turned to leave and took one step before the booming voice of ABC's Sam Donaldson called after him, "In your heart, sir, can you forgive and forget?"

The president paused, looking down with a slight smile as if considering whether to take the bait, and then pivoted back to the podium. His aides tensed. He was not supposed to veer off script and detract from the carefully crafted message.

But Clinton kept to the day's theme. "I believe any person who asks for forgiveness has to be prepared to give it," he said simply, then turned away again to march back to the Oval Office.

"Do you feel vindicated, sir?" NBC's David Bloom cried out, but the president ignored him.

The answer to that last question would have to come another day. Perhaps it was fitting that Hillary Clinton's campaign for the Senate would begin the day Bill Clinton's trial ended, for in her race were the seeds of what the president hoped would be his vindication. Even though he would not be on the ballot himself, he wanted the 2000 elections to serve as his platform for political absolution. The public would decide whether to reward or punish the House managers who had so aggressively prosecuted him. The bellwether became Jim Rogan's hotly contested reelection contest, where both candidates tapped into the lingering emotions from impeachment and vast sums of money poured in from around the country to refight the battle. Yet most of the managers faced little political trouble as a result of their service; Lindsey Graham became the most popular elected official in his state, while Democrats could not even find a candidate to run against Asa Hutchinson in the president's home state. For Clinton, revenge would have to lie on other ballots. If the public were to send his wife to the Senate, install his vice president at the White House, and vault his legislative saviors into power at the Capitol, it could be portrayed as the ultimate repudiation of Tom DeLay and The Campaign. But if all three were to lose, Clinton knew he risked a historical judgment as a failed president who cost his party for years to come, a skilled leader whose own fatal flaws kept him from living up to his once-great promise.

To shore up his legacy, Clinton vowed to spend every remaining day in office focused on the duties of office. But it would not be so easy. Despite nearly unanimous desire in Washington to move on following the Senate acquittal, Clinton found it difficult to escape. Six days after the vote, he flew to New Hampshire to celebrate the seventh anniversary of one of his greatest political victories, the night he rescued his foundering presidential campaign in the 1992 primary—a campaign hobbled in the first place by revelations of Clinton's affair with Gennifer Flowers. Yet even on this bright occasion, he was confronted with the costs of his actions. Paul Begala, the tormented aide who had almost quit the previous fall, chose that moment to tell Clinton in a private huddle that he would resign now that the threat to the presidency was over. Begala could not even wait a full week to bolt. He told friends he would never look at Bill Clinton the same way again.

The day after that, Friday, February 19, the *Wall Street Journal* ran an interview with Juanita Broaddrick on its editorial pages, the first public comments by the Arkansas woman who maintained Clinton had raped her in 1978. The *Washington Post* followed with a front-page article a day later, and finally, on February 24, NBC aired Lisa Myers's month-old interview with Broaddrick on its *Dateline* newsmagazine program. "He forces me down on the bed," a teary Broaddrick recounted to Myers. "I just was very frightened and I tried to get away from him and I told him no. . . . He wouldn't listen to me." Asked about the charge at a news conference the same day, Clinton referred the question to his lawyer, David Kendall, who issued a statement calling Broaddrick's allegation "absolutely false." Neither Kendall nor any White House aides denied that Clinton and Broaddrick had met or even that they had a sexual encounter; the unspoken implication of the denial was that whatever happened between Clinton and Broaddrick in the Camelot Hotel in Little Rock that day twenty-one years earlier, it did not constitute rape. Broaddrick was not the only one to go prime-time. Lewinsky finally spoke out in a strangely bubbly interview with Barbara Walters on ABC, timed to coincide with release of her book, *Monica's Story,* and an international publicity tour. Soon, she would take to selling handbags over the Internet.

Two months to the day after his acquittal in the Senate, a federal judge handed down a different verdict. Judge Susan Webber Wright, who oversaw the Paula Jones case from start to finish, held Clinton in contempt for giving "intentionally false" testimony in his January 17, 1998, deposition when asked about his relationship with Lewinsky. Never before had a president been held in contempt of court. Wright summarily dismissed Clinton's defense against the charge that he lied under oath, writing, "There simply is no escaping the fact that the President deliberately violated this Court's discovery Orders and thereby undermined the integrity of the judicial system." While saying there were other examples of possible misconduct, she singled out two statements that were clearly false on their face—Clinton's assertion that he did not remember being alone with Lewinsky and his denial that they engaged in "sexual relations." She gave no credence to the president's later explanation that he did not interpret his encounters with Lewinsky to constitute "sexual relations," and she directly rebutted Clinton defenders who argued that testimony about Lewinsky was not material to the lawsuit in the first place. The judge, who personally supervised the president's deposition, seemed most peeved by his hairsplitting suggestion that he had tried to give misleading but literally true answers under oath because he deplored the Jones lawsuit and its sponsors. "It is simply not acceptable to employ deceptions and falsehoods in an attempt to obstruct the judicial process, understandable as his aggravation with plaintiff's lawsuit may have been," Wright wrote. She ordered the president to pay the Jones team $90,000 to compensate for his false testimony and referred him to the Arkansas Supreme Court disciplinary committee, which in May 2000 would recommend that Clinton be disbarred.

But the president remained unrepentant. In interviews after the trial, Clinton made clear he saw the impeachment process as nothing more than an illegitimate political vendetta. "I do not regard this impeachment vote as some great badge of shame," he told CBS's Dan Rather a month after the trial ended. "I do not, because it was—I do not believe it was warranted and I don't think it was right." He portrayed himself as a heroic figure for refusing to resign in the face of the charges lodged against him. "I made a personal mistake and they spent fifty million dollars trying to ferret it out and root it out, because they had nothing else to do, because all the other charges were totally false—bogus, made up—and people were persecuted because they wouldn't commit perjury against me," he told ABC's Carole Simpson in November 1999. Five months later, Ken Starr's successor as independent counsel, Robert W. Ray, suggested that he might indict Clinton after he left office, provoking a revealing public diatribe by the president. "On the impeachment, let me tell you, I am proud of what we did there, because I think we saved the Constitution of the United States," he told a newspaper editors' conference in April 2000. "I'm not ashamed of the fact that they impeached me. That was their decision, not mine. And it was wrong." He saw the impeachment merely as "one of the major chapters in my defeat of the revolution Mr. Gingrich led."

History, however, has not rendered its judgment yet and will not for years to come. The historical consensus about the validity of Andrew Johnson's impeachment shifted back and forth dramatically in the century following his trial, and Clinton may face similar swings. The first serious poll of historians after the trial placed Clinton in the mediocre middle of the presidential spectrum—ranked twenty-first out of forty-one men who have held the office. That may reflect the difficulty inherent in judging contemporary figures; nearly every other modern president was bunched around Clinton in that ranking. One category where the historians were in agreement, though, was moral leadership. Clinton was ranked dead last there, behind even Richard Nixon. Removed from the heat of the moment, much of the public in the months following the Senate trial came to accept Clinton's impeachment as an appropriate censure. A USA Today/CNN/Gallup Poll taken a year after the House vote found that 50 percent of the public approved of impeaching Clinton, compared with just 35 percent at the time. Fifty-seven percent of those interviewed still supported the Senate decision to acquit, although that was eleven percentage points lower than a year before. As time passed, the split verdict—impeachment by the House and acquittal by the Senate—struck many as perhaps the right balance. Even Newt Gingrich expressed this view in an interview on C-SPAN: "It may have had the right outcome, frankly. We sent the signal [that] presidents, even when popular, can't break the law, but at the same time I think the country didn't want an impeachment, a conviction in the Senate."

The broader question will be the impact on impeachment itself. Will the Clinton saga make it more likely in the future that a House controlled by one party will impeach a president of the other party? Or did the Senate set a higher bar for what constituted "high crimes," essentially declaring that anything less than the offenses of Watergate would not warrant removal? What role should public opinion play in deciding whether to evict a president from office? In meeting privately with Democrats just hours before the Starr report was delivered to Congress, Henry Hyde said that "it is a recipe for failure if it is partisan," and he turned out to be right. Yet looking back at the Clinton saga, partisanship clearly hurt both sides in different ways. By refusing to accept the more restricted Democratic inquiry proposal in October 1998, House Republicans launched the impeachment process on a largely party-line vote, thus guaranteeing a partisan process. In hindsight, many GOP leaders, including Hyde, rued their decision not to embrace the Democratic alternative, convinced the outcome was determined at that moment. On the other hand, by aggressively fomenting partisanship for their own purposes, Democrats polarized the situation in the House so deeply that moderate Republicans inclined to vote against impeachment once it reached the floor were turned off by what they saw as shrill politics and opted for party solidarity instead. Only afterward did Democratic strategists recognize that the partisan forces they had helped set in motion could not be throttled back when it came time for the final House vote, which may thus have contributed to Clinton's impeachment, even while ensuring eventual acquittal in the Senate.

The lesson for future presidents threatened with impeachment may be to dare Congress to follow through rather than resign. Clinton showed that a gritty defiance could carry him through the worst of political times. No matter how miserable it got, Clinton plowed forward as if nothing were happening, triumphing through adversity as he had done his entire career. Howard Baker and Fred Thompson, two Republicans who played central roles in investigating Watergate, said in separate interviews last year that had Nixon followed Clinton's example and refused to quit, they now believed he may never have been removed. "Even there, I wonder if he told Goldwater no whether that would have been enough," Thompson speculated. "I seriously doubt whether they would have convicted."

The confrontation between executive and legislative branches in 1998–99 will invariably influence the balance of power in the federal government as well, but again it may take years to evaluate just how. The Johnson trial ushered in a period of congressional dominance in Washington that prevailed until Theodore Roosevelt took office more than thirty years later. The Congress that emerged from the Clinton trial was not nearly so strong, having absorbed considerable public opprobrium for its zealous pursuit of the Lewinsky case. Still, the president found himself constrained in the aftermath of his trial as "Clinton fatigue" sapped his political authority. His legislative posture was so weakened that he could not even convince the Senate to ratify the Comprehensive Test-Ban Treaty—the first time a president had been rebuffed on a major arms control treaty since the Senate rejected the Treaty of Versailles following World War I and refused to allow the United States to join Woodrow Wilson's League of Nations. Clinton did manage to wage war successfully in Europe, leading NATO allies in a bombing campaign that drove Serbian dictator Slobodan Milosevic out of Kosovo. Yet even there, his credibility was called into constant question, and many believed his failure to win strong congressional support for the war stemmed from lingering distrust. Would that end with the Clinton era or disfigure the relationship between president and Congress for a generation? All of the major candidates to succeed him in both parties, including his own vice president, strained every political muscle to emphasize how different they would be from Clinton. In public appearances, Al Gore even took questions that never mentioned the Lewinsky ordeal and used them as opportunities to restate his deep disappointment in his political patron.

Signs pointed to a collective retreat from the edge of the political abyss, a mutual desire to forget, if not exactly forgive. In the months following the trial, Clinton and congressional leaders often acted as if it had never taken place. Sometimes it was hard to remember that it ever did. The president was still invited to deliver his State of the Union address in the same chamber where he had been impeached, and the assembled lawmakers still stood and applauded at appropriate moments. Some of the same Republicans who had pursued him so vigorously made nice on occasion. Rogan attended the White House Christmas party and had his picture taken with Clinton. DeLay even attended a White House event on adoption, long a pet cause for the foster father of two teenagers from abusive backgrounds. Clinton aides had been petrified to tell the president that the man who had called him a "sexual predator" intended to participate, and they stared as if eyeing the devil when they spotted DeLay marching down the corridors of the White House. Likewise, DeLay aides thought he was entering the den of the lions by agreeing to go. But when Clinton saw DeLay, the president went out of his way to greet his archnemesis warmly, both in private beforehand and again in front of the audience. Using golf as a metaphor for impeachment, Clinton said he had recently read a profile of the bulldog House whip. "He started grinding on my golf game and saying that I didn't count my scores and all this, and I was getting really angry. And then I get to the next part of the story, and it talks all about his experience and his commitment to adoption and to foster children, and the personal experience that he and his wife had. And my heart just melted."

Surreal as it was, the rapprochement was destined to be short-lived. Clinton left the adoption event that morning to head over to the Washington Hilton Hotel, where he addressed a meeting of the Democratic National Committee to get his party revved up for the November 2000 elections. By then, his heart had hardened and it was time for battle again. A warm-up video played for the audience ridiculed Republican leaders to the tune of "Crazy," with none other than Tom DeLay in the role of favorite villain. Clinton played to the same theme from his lectern. The other party was wrong about virtually everything, he informed the crowd of activists, about gun control, about health care, about the economy, about the debt. "They were wrong and we were right," the president declared.

Back into the breach.

ACKNOWLEDGMENTS

Any book is the collective work of untold people who have contributed ideas, knowledge, insight, and recollections. This one is no exception. Many of the key players in the drama that led to the impeachment and trial of President Clinton generously gave their time and their candor to try to make this the most complete account it could be, including quite a few who rarely spoke publicly at the time. I wish I could name them all, but I am extremely grateful for their cooperation.

My literary agent, Raphael Sagalyn, deserves special credit. He figured out what this book should be long before I did and sent me back to the drawing board repeatedly until I got it right. With infectious enthusiasm, Lisa Drew at Scribner embraced the goal of an authoritative and straightforward history of these events. No one ever had a more inspiring editor. Jake Klisivitch, Laura Wise, Elisa Rivlin, Steve Boldt, John Fontana, Kim Hilario, Jennifer Swihart, and others at Scribner helped guide me with patience, good humor, and friendship through a bewildering process. Khiota Therrien somehow managed to find time in addition to her regular job to help me with research. Ever reliable and resourceful, she came through for me time and again. Bruce Sanford introduced me to the publishing world and provided sage advice along the way.

For twelve years, I have been fortunate to work at one of the last bastions of serious journalism in the country, created and sustained by the commitment of Katharine Graham and Donald E. Graham. Our executive editor, Leonard Downie Jr., and managing editor, Steve Coll (along with his predecessor Robert G. Kaiser), have created a newsroom singularly dedicated to getting the story first and getting it right. I will always be grateful to Karen DeYoung, then assistant managing editor for national news, and her deputy, Bill Hamilton, for taking a chance with a young reporter at the White House. Thanks too to editor Maralee Schwartz for her encouragement over the years.

Several established authors at the *Washington Post* offered invaluable advice as I embarked on this project, including Bob Woodward, Rick Atkinson,

David Maraniss, and Howard Kurtz. Few first-time authors are lucky enough to have such a reservoir of talent and experience so nearby.

I especially want to thank John F. Harris, my partner on the White House beat and by far the nation's smartest and most insightful correspondent covering the presidency. Susan Schmidt, one of Washington's most dogged investigative reporters, persevered through adversity to break the biggest story of the decade and let me come along for the ride. Juliet Eilperin, who knows all the corners and crawl spaces of Capitol Hill better than its elected inhabitants, shared her energy and expertise. I also benefited during the impeachment saga from the generosity of a number of other immensely talented colleagues at the *Post,* including Lorraine Adams, Dan Balz, Ceci Connolly, Helen Dewar, Jeff Glasser, Amy Goldstein, Michael Grunwald, Guy Gugliotta, Al Kamen, Toni Locy, Ruth Marcus, Eric Pianin, Lois Romano, Lena Sun, and David Von Drehle. Appreciation is due as well to Alice Crites and the incomparable *Post* library staff, who tracked down the impossible, plus Vince Rinehart and his keen-eyed crew of copy editors, who saved me from myself too many times to count. With the blessing of Joe Elbert, the *Post*'s assistant managing editor for photography, Marylou Foy and Todd Cross helped pick out the images of impeachment for this book from the collected work of the best team of photographers in the country.

Surviving this process would not have been possible without the forbearance of my family, Ted and Martha Baker, Linda and Keith Sinrod, Karin Baker, Cindy Wallace, Mal and Inge Gross, Martha Gross, and Dan and Sylvia Baker, as well as my new family, Stephen, Lynn, Laura, Jeff, and Jennifer Glasser. The same holds true for friends John Smith, Tony Garro, Mike Allen, Tim Webster, Valerie Mann, Maria Koklanaris, Jennifer Frey, Nicole Rabner, Rajiv Chandrasekaran, Michael and Caitlin Shear, and Al and Staci Bailey.

Most of all, I am indebted to Susan Glasser, the best editor, best partner, and best friend anyone could ever have. If nothing else beneficial came out of this chapter in history, for me, at least, meeting and marrying Susan made it all worthwhile. She was the inspiration for the book and its title, not to mention the source of unwavering support through the most difficult moments. She devoted long nights and many weekends to reviewing chapters, catching mistakes, and offering numerous ways to improve the manuscript. She has made both this book and my life enormously better.

NOTES

In addition to the reporting during the events themselves, this account is based on extensive original research, including nearly 350 interviews after the end of the Senate trial as well as thousands of pages of documents never made public, such as internal memos, diaries, letters, calendars, E-mail, tape recordings, notes, speech drafts, and transcripts. In a number of cases, key players gave me free access to their confidential files. Almost 200 people took the time to sit for interviews, including more than sixty members of Congress from both parties as well as numerous senior White House officials, cabinet secretaries, and presidential lawyers. Many graciously spoke with me on several occasions, some a half dozen times or more.

Most of these subjects and sources agreed to be interviewed on condition that they not be identified, an unfortunate reality of life in modern Washington. To verify information, I tried to confirm details and recollections with multiple sources. The direct quotations that appear in this book came from transcripts, news accounts, contemporaneous notes, or the recollection of at least one person in the room at the time and often more than one. No such reconstruction of past events can be perfect, but I have labored to be as accurate as possible. Nonetheless, responsibility for any errors of fact or interpretation rests solely with me.

This book also relies on the work of other journalists, most particularly that appearing in the *Washington Post,* the *New York Times,* the *Los Angeles Times, Newsweek,* and *Time.* The impeachment Web site still maintained on washingtonpost.com (http://www.washingtonpost.com/wp-srv/politics/special/clinton/clinton.htm) provided an exhaustive archive of documents, while a similar site by MSNBC (http://archive.msnbc.com/modules/clintonunderfire/CLINTONUNDERFIRE_Front.asp) contained a useful video record of key moments. Primary source materials included the White House archives and the *Congressional Record.*

Several books contained important material as well, especially *Shadow: Five Presidents and the Legacy of Watergate* by Bob Woodward (New York: Simon & Schuster, 1999), *Truth at Any Cost: Ken Starr and the Unmaking of Bill Clin-*

ton by Susan Schmidt and Michael Weisskopf (New York: HarperCollins, 2000), *Monica's Story* by Andrew Morton (New York: St. Martin's Press, 1999), *The Corruption of American Politics* by Elizabeth Drew (Secaucus, N.J.: Birch Lane Press, 1999), *Hillary's Choice* by Gail Sheehy (New York: Random House, 1999), and *A Vast Conspiracy: The Real Story of the Sex Scandal That Nearly Brought Down a President* by Jeffrey Toobin (New York: Random House, 2000).

Because of confidentiality agreements, neither footnotes nor even extensive chapter notes are possible; however a few points should be highlighted:

Prologue: This chapter is based largely on interviews with Bob Livingston, his former aide Mark Corallo, and a number of Livingston friends and advisers. Corallo recalled the scene in the House cloakroom in vivid detail. "That was the exact exchange, word for word. I'll remember it until I die," Corallo said in one of several interviews with the author. Livingston did not recall the anecdote but did not challenge Corallo's memory. "I can't say that it happened or didn't happen. I don't remember," Livingston said. "Could it have happened? Yes." Almost a year to the day after the fact, Livingston stressed that either way, he did not regret his eventual decision. "Did I have second thoughts? I'm sure I had second thoughts. But I feel I did what I had to do. I don't regret a thing. The only thing in this whole thing I would have done differently is I would have treated my wife a little better. Let me rephrase that for the record: I would have treated my wife a *lot* better."

Chapter 1: Bob Shrum's proposed draft of President Clinton's speech was published in a collection of great speeches edited by Senator Bob Torricelli and Andrew Carroll called *In Our Own Words* (Kodansha International, 1999). Paul Begala turned over his draft to the White House Counsel's Office to prevent it from becoming public. The transcript of Clinton's grand jury session was released by the House Judiciary Committee in an appendix to the Starr report. E-mail from Tom DeLay's office was obtained by the author.

Chapter 2: Martin Frost denied suggesting to Dick Gephardt that he consider going to the White House to urge Clinton's resignation. However, several people close to Gephardt recalled the conversation.

Chapter 3: Much of the history of impeachment can be found in a paper prepared by the Congressional Research Service in 1974 as well as in William H. Rehnquist's *Grand Inquests* (New York: William Morrow, 1992). A copy of Bob Bauer's March 30, 1998, memo was obtained by the author. Through an aide, Aida Alvarez denied telling the president that women were disappointed with him. However, the quote was reported contemporaneously by the Associated Press, which based the account on a source in the room, in a story that ran on the day of the cabinet meeting.

Chapter 5: A copy of Dick Gephardt's secret censure plan was obtained by the author. The meeting between the president's lawyers and Judiciary Committee officials was reconstructed based on interviews as well as notes, including a confidential memo to the file written by David Kendall and obtained by the author. Copies of confidential reports by Republican and Democratic investigators about evidence kept at Ken Starr's office were obtained by the author.

Chapter 6: Particularly helpful in reconstructing the election and its aftermath were articles in *Newsweek* and *Time,* as well as an excellent piece by Ceci Connolly in the *Washington Post* on November 8, 1998. Campaign memos by pollsters Stan Greenberg and Frank Luntz were useful as well.

Chapter 7: A transcript of the Judiciary Committee's executive session following the Starr hearing was obtained by the author. The House Government Reform Committee ultimately released copies of the Louis Freeh and Charles LaBella documents on June 6, 2000.

Chapter 8: Early drafts of the articles of impeachment, early drafts of the proposed Clinton letter to Congress, and a copy of Lindsey Graham's handwritten suggested statement for the president were all obtained by the author.

Chapter 9: Bob Livingston and Allen Martin declined to comment on Butler Derrick's phone call, but they told at least a half dozen others who were interviewed. In addition, a former Livingston aide, Quin Hillyer, mentioned the call in a column in the *Mobile Register* on February 14, 1999. In an interview, Derrick said he called only to offer congratulations and never asked about censure or mentioned Livingston's past. "Hell, I don't know anything about Bob Livingston's personal life. I didn't know anything then and I don't know anything now. I've lived in this town for twenty-five years, and no one's ever suggested that I do things like that. I don't play that kind of dirty politics."

Chapter 11: Clinton's comments at the holiday party were reported by Elizabeth Shogren in the *Los Angeles Times* on December 22, 1998. A copy of Asa Hutchinson's original trial plan was provided to the author. *Roll Call* revealed the existence of Trent Lott's secret group of advisers during the trial.

Chapter 12: Closed meetings involving the managers and/or senators, including the session in the Old Senate Chamber, were reconstructed based on extensive interviews and notes of participants. A copy of Susan Collins's impeachment diary was provided to the author. An aide to Pat Roberts said he did not recall saying, "We've got to quit peeing down each other's legs."

Chapter 13: For an illuminating profile of Jim Rogan, see Faye Fiore's article in the *Los Angeles Times* on July 29, 1999.

Chapter 14: Copies of rejected questions by Republican and Democratic senators were obtained by the author. A transcript of Judge Norma Johnson's hearing is available from the court reporter.

Chapter 16: Transcripts of the three depositions were published in the *Congressional Record* and can be found at the washingtonpost.com Web site.

Chapter 17: Drafts of the Republican findings-of-fact proposal were obtained by the author as was a counterlist of proposed amendments faxed by Clinton aides to Tom Daschle. The draft of the Democratic censure proposal was published in the *New York Times* on February 6, 1999.

Chapter 18: The Senate conducted its final deliberations behind closed doors without reporters or television cameras present. Nonetheless, it is possible to reconstruct much of the discussion because about three-quarters of the senators later chose to insert their statements into the *Congressional Record*. In a few cases, this chapter quotes senators who did not make their comments public, including Trent Lott and Phil Gramm. In a few instances, it quotes remarks made by senators that did not appear in the authorized versions eventually inserted into the record (Ted Stevens saying Clinton "better not do it again," Evan Bayh speaking about the Twenty-Fifth Amendment, and Bob Torricelli predicting that no one would remember Clinton). Those quotes are based on notes and recollections of people in the room at the time. However, it should be noted that a Bayh spokesman said the senator did not recall making that remark.

Epilogue: The fact that Hillary Clinton met with Harold Ickes on the day of the Senate acquittal was first reported in a piece by James Bennet in the *New York Times Magazine* on May 30, 1999. President Clinton's comments were made in an interview with Dan Rather on CBS on March 31, 1999; an interview with Carole Simpson on ABC on November 5, 1999; and in an appearance at the American Society of Newspaper Editors on April 13, 2000. Newt Gingrich's comment was made during an interview with Brian Lamb aired on C-SPAN over three days, August 31–September 2, 1999. The Howard Baker and Fred Thompson comments came in interviews with the author. Charles Babington spotted the juxtaposition between Clinton's embrace of Tom DeLay at the adoption event and the video played at the DNC meeting later in the day, in the *Washington Post* on September 25, 1999.

CHRONOLOGY

Monday, Aug. 17, 1998. President Clinton appears before a grand jury via closed-circuit television to admit his relationship with Monica Lewinsky and later goes on national television to acknowledge that he had "misled people," while lashing out at Independent Counsel Kenneth W. Starr for invading his private life.

Thursday, Sept. 3. Senator Joseph Lieberman takes to the floor of the Senate to harshly denounce President Clinton's behavior as "immoral" and "deserving of public rebuke," followed quickly by Senators Daniel Patrick Moynihan and Bob Kerrey, who endorse the remarks.

Friday, Sept. 4. President Clinton issues his most direct apology yet, telling reporters traveling with him in Ireland that "I'm very sorry about it."

Wednesday, Sept. 9. Ken Starr abruptly loads thirty-six boxes into a pair of vans and delivers his impeachment referral to Capitol Hill, just hours after House Speaker Newt Gingrich, Minority Leader Richard A. Gephardt, and other leaders meet to prepare for possible arrival of a report.

Thursday, Sept. 10. President Clinton meets with his cabinet in the White House residence and is scolded by Health and Human Services secretary Donna E. Shalala for his behavior.

Friday, Sept. 11. The Starr report is released to the public and posted on the Internet shortly after the House votes 363–63 to make it public.

Monday, Sept. 14. Dick Gephardt and Senate Minority Leader Thomas A. Daschle release separate but coordinated statements calling on President Clinton to abandon legalisms and "hairsplitting" in his defense.

Wednesday, Sept. 16. The Internet magazine *Salon* reports that House Judiciary Committee chairman Henry J. Hyde had an affair thirty years before, triggering angry Republicans to blame the White House for smearing him. President Clinton, at his first news conference since the Starr report was released, brushes off talk of resignation.

Thursday, Sept. 17. The House Judiciary Committee meets in executive session to consider redactions of Starr evidence, but bogs down in partisan bickering that forces off final votes until Friday. Republicans win eleven party-line votes through the day, including rejections of Democratic attempts to delay release for seven days and give the White House a forty-eight-hour advance look at the material.

Friday, Sept. 18. The Judiciary Committee meets in closed session for a second day on redactions and agrees to release thousands of pages of documents as well as the videotape of the president's grand jury testimony.

Monday, Sept. 21. The grand jury videotape is televised live on national television. The Judiciary Committee also releases another 3,183 pages of evidence, including White House entry logs, telephone records, electronic mail, love notes, and DNA test results.

Friday, Sept. 25. The Judiciary Committee meets again in executive session to consider redactions of the final materials to be released, agreeing to make most of it public.

Wednesday, Sept. 30. Henry Hyde unveils the Republican proposal for an impeachment inquiry, adapted almost word for word from the 1974 Watergate resolution.

Friday, Oct. 2. The Judiciary Committee releases the final batch of evidence from the Starr investigation, 4,600 pages of testimony and documents that includes transcripts of Monica Lewinsky's conversations with Linda R. Tripp.

Sunday, Oct. 4. *Hustler* publisher Larry Flynt runs an ad in the *Washington Post* offering $1 million for "documentary evidence of illicit sexual relations" with a member of Congress or other high-ranking government official.

Monday, Oct. 5. The Judiciary Committee approves a resolution recommending an impeachment inquiry on a 21–16 party-line vote, after hearing initial presentations by investigators David P. Schippers and Abbe D. Lowell.

Thursday, Oct. 8. The House opens the impeachment inquiry on a largely partisan 258–176 vote, with thirty-one Democrats joining the majority. An alternative, Democrat-sponsored inquiry plan is rejected.

Thursday, Oct. 15. President Clinton wins a significant victory in budget negotiations with congressional Republicans and then heads off to open Middle East peace talks at the Wye River Conference Center in Maryland.

Tuesday, Oct. 20. Attorneys for President Clinton and Paula Jones present oral arguments before the Eighth Circuit Court of Appeals in St. Paul, Minnesota, in her attempt to resurrect her sexual harassment lawsuit. Two of the three judges appear highly skeptical of the Clinton side of the argument.

Wednesday, Oct. 21. White House attorneys meet with Judiciary Committee officials for ninety minutes to discuss procedures. White House special counsel Gregory B. Craig emerges to blast the Republicans for essentially "attacking a man who is blindfolded and handcuffed."

Tuesday, Oct. 27. Republicans begin an ad campaign approved by Newt Gingrich to attack President Clinton for his lies involving Monica Lewinsky.

Tuesday, Nov. 3. Republicans lose five House seats in the midterm elections, setting off an internal revolt against Newt Gingrich, who had predicted a twenty-seat gain earlier in the day.

Wednesday, Nov. 4. Henry Hyde meets with key aides in Chicago and then tells Judiciary Republicans they must go forward despite the disappointing election results.

Thursday, Nov. 5. At a Chicago news conference, Henry Hyde announces that Ken Starr will be asked to testify, suggesting he will be the only major witness, and sends President Clinton eighty-one questions about the case.

Friday, Nov. 6. Newt Gingrich announces that he will step down as Speaker just hours after fellow Republican Bob Livingston decides to challenge him.

Monday, Nov. 9. The Judiciary subcommittee on the Constitution holds a hearing on the history of impeachment.

Friday, Nov. 13. President Clinton and Paula Jones agree to settle their long-standing court fight for $850,000 but with no admission or apology. Ken Starr sends the Judiciary Committee additional material concerning Kathleen E. Willey, who had accused Clinton of an unwanted sexual advance.

Tuesday, Nov. 17. The Judiciary Committee releases thirty-seven audiotapes containing about twenty-two hours of taped conversations between Monica Lewinsky and Linda Tripp.

Thursday, Nov. 19. Ken Starr appears before the Judiciary Committee in a daylong session, outlining Clinton's attempts to cover up his relationship with Monica Lewinsky, while also announcing that he had found no impeachable offenses related to the Whitewater land deal, the improper collection of FBI files, or the firing of travel-office workers. The committee then meets in executive session to authorize subpoenas for Daniel Gecker, Nathan Landow, Robert S. Bennett, and Bruce R. Lindsey.

Friday, Nov. 27. The White House delivers responses to the committee's eighty-one questions, triggering Republican ire at the answers.

Tuesday, Dec. 1. The Judiciary Committee holds a hearing featuring testimony from convicted perjurers and expert witnesses. The committee authorizes subpoenas to Ken Starr, Attorney General Janet Reno, FBI Director Louis J. Freeh, and Justice Department investigator Charles LaBella for testimony or documents related to campaign-finance abuses.

Thursday, Dec. 3. Judiciary Committee officials announce that they will not address campaign finance allegations during the inquiry.

Tuesday, Dec. 8. The White House opens its defense presentation to the

Judiciary Committee with testimony from Greg Craig and a panel of experts calling the president's behavior "sinful" and "maddening" but not impeachable.

Wednesday, Dec. 9. The president's team wraps up its presentation with more experts as well as White House counsel Charles F. C. Ruff. The Judiciary Committee releases its draft of four articles of impeachment.

Thursday, Dec. 10. The Judiciary Committee begins consideration of articles of impeachment after hearing final presentations by Abbe Lowell and David Schippers.

Friday, Dec. 11. The Judiciary Committee approves the first three articles of impeachment, voting 21–16 on allegations of perjury before the grand jury and obstruction of justice and 20–17 on perjury in a civil deposition.

Saturday, Dec. 12. The Judiciary Committee approves the fourth and final article of impeachment alleging abuse of power and votes down a Democratic censure resolution. Bob Livingston, Newt Gingrich, and Henry Hyde then release a series of letters announcing that censure will not be considered on the floor.

Sunday, Dec. 13. Henry Hyde, House Majority Leader Richard K. Armey, and House Majority Whip Tom DeLay call on President Clinton to resign, just hours after the president insists that such a move "never crossed my mind."

Tuesday, Dec. 15. As President Clinton flies back to Washington from a peace mission to the Middle East, nine key uncommitted House Republicans announce they will vote for impeachment, and Congressman Jack Quinn, who had previously opposed it, declares that he will vote yes.

Wednesday, Dec. 16. President Clinton launches missile strikes against Iraq in retaliation for thwarting weapons inspectors, as ten more moderate House Republicans announce that they will vote in favor of impeachment.

Thursday, Dec. 17. Bob Livingston refuses to postpone the impeachment debate any further amid a clash about the propriety of going forward as a second wave of attacks against Iraq begins at midday. Livingston then discloses his own sexual indiscretions, telling the Republican conference that he had "on occasion strayed from my marriage."

Friday, Dec. 18. The House opens debate on impeachment, as air strikes continue against Iraq.

Saturday, Dec. 19. The House impeaches President Clinton, approving two of the four articles of impeachment and rebuffing a Democratic move to force a censure vote. Bob Livingston stuns the House by announcing his resignation on the floor. House Democrats rally to Clinton's side along with Hillary Rodham Clinton and Vice President Gore on the South Lawn of the White House.

Thursday, Jan. 7, 1999. The impeachment trial formally opens in the Senate with the reading of the charges and the swearing in of Chief Justice William H. Rehnquist and the senator-jurors. But the Senate remains deadlocked on rules and recesses for the day without an agreement.

Friday, Jan. 8. A joint closed-door party caucus meeting yields a bipartisan agreement on procedures, which then passes on the Senate floor 100–0.

Tuesday, Jan. 12. President Clinton sends a check for $850,000 to Paula Jones to finally end her case, dipping into personal funds for $375,000 of the settlement.

Thursday, Jan. 14. The trial gets under way as House managers begin three days of opening arguments with statements by Henry Hyde, F. James Sensenbrenner, Edward G. Bryant, Asa Hutchinson, and James E. Rogan.

Friday, Jan. 15. Second day of prosecution opening arguments features Bill McCollum, George W. Gekas, Steve Chabot, Chris Cannon, and Bob Barr. William Rehnquist makes his first ruling, agreeing to Senator Tom Harkin's objection to the use of the term *juror.*

Saturday, Jan. 16. House managers wrap up opening presentations, with arguments by Steve Buyer, Charles T. Canady, George Gekas, Lindsey Graham, and Henry Hyde.

Tuesday, Jan. 19. The White House begins its own opening arguments with a presentation by Chuck Ruff, just hours before President Clinton comes to the Capitol to deliver his State of the Union address in the House chamber.

Wednesday, Jan. 20. Second day of defense opening arguments features White House lawyers Greg Craig and Cheryl D. Mills.

Thursday, Jan. 21. The White House concludes its opening arguments with a legal lecture by attorney David Kendall and a populist peroration by former senator Dale Bumpers.

Friday, Jan. 22. The Senate begins a two-day question-and-answer period, as Senator Robert C. Byrd declares that he will file a motion to dismiss the case. Ken Starr's office goes to court to force Monica Lewinsky to speak with House managers.

Saturday, Jan. 23. The Senate completes its question-and-answer session as Judge Norma Holloway Johnson orders Monica Lewinsky to meet with House managers. Lewinsky returns to Washington amid a moblike media throng.

Sunday, Jan. 24. Monica Lewinsky meets at the Mayflower Hotel with Asa Hutchinson, Bill McCollum, and Ed Bryant.

Monday, Jan. 25. The Senate hears arguments from both sides on a motion to dismiss and then retreats behind closed doors to deliberate.

Tuesday, Jan. 26. The managers trim their witness list to three, Monica

Lewinsky, Vernon E. Jordan Jr., and Sidney Blumenthal, and seek a voluntary appearance by President Clinton.

Wednesday, Jan. 27. The Senate votes 56–44 to take testimony and not dismiss the case, but the back-to-back roll calls indicate that acquittal is inevitable. On both votes, Democrat Russell Feingold is the only senator to cross party lines.

Thursday, Jan. 28. The Senate approves a plan intended to end the trial within two weeks, after Republicans force their version of procedures through on a largely party-line vote.

Monday, Feb. 1. Monica Lewinsky is deposed by Ed Bryant behind closed doors and on videotape at the Mayflower Hotel, while White House lawyers pass along an apology "on behalf of the president" for all she had been put through.

Tuesday, Feb. 2. Vernon Jordan is deposed at the Capitol by Asa Hutchinson.

Wednesday, Feb. 3. Sid Blumenthal is deposed by Jim Rogan and Lindsey Graham.

Thursday, Feb. 4. The Senate votes to bar live testimony on the floor but allows video excerpts to be shown.

Saturday, Feb. 6. House managers and defense lawyers show video snippets in presentations on the Senate floor, giving the nation its first real look at Monica Lewinsky in a speaking role.

Monday, Feb. 8. Both sides present closing arguments.

Tuesday, Feb. 9. Closed-door deliberations begin after the Senate votes to open proceedings 59–41 but falls short of two-thirds required to suspend the rules.

Friday, Feb. 12. The Senate acquits President Clinton on both articles of impeachment, voting 45–55 on perjury and 50–50 on obstruction of justice. Appearing in the Rose Garden, Clinton accepts the verdict and calls on the nation to begin a period of "reconciliation and renewal."

APPENDIX ONE

Several of President Clinton's statements at key moments in the impeachment and trial saga:

<u>Statement from the Map Room</u>
<u>Following Grand Jury Testimony</u>
<u>August 17, 1998</u>

Good evening. This afternoon in this room, from this chair, I testified before the Office of Independent Counsel and the grand jury. I answered their questions truthfully, including questions about my private life, questions no American citizen would ever want to answer. Still, I must take complete responsibility for all my actions, both public and private. And that is why I am speaking to you tonight.

As you know, in a deposition in January, I was asked questions about my relationship with Monica Lewinsky. While my answers were legally accurate, I did not volunteer information. Indeed, I did have a relationship with Miss Lewinsky that was not appropriate. In fact, it was wrong. It constituted a critical lapse in judgment and a personal failure on my part for which I am solely and completely responsible.

But I told the grand jury today and I say to you now that at no time did I ask anyone to lie, to hide or destroy evidence, or to take any other unlawful action. I know that my public comments and my silence about this matter gave a false impression. I misled people, including even my wife. I deeply regret that.

I can only tell you I was motivated by many factors. First, by a desire to protect myself from the embarrassment of my own conduct. I was also very concerned about protecting my family. The fact that these questions were being asked in a politically inspired lawsuit, which has since been dismissed, was a consideration too.

In addition, I had real and serious concerns about an independent counsel investigation that began with private business dealings twenty years ago, dealings, I might add, about which an independent federal agency found no evidence of any wrongdoing by me or my wife over two years ago. The independent counsel investigation moved on to my staff and friends, then into my private life. And now the investigation itself is under investigation.

This has gone on too long, cost too much, and hurt too many innocent people. Now, this matter is between me, the two people I love most—my wife and our daughter—and our God. I must put it right, and I am prepared to do whatever it takes to do so. Nothing is more important to me personally. But it is private, and I intend to reclaim my family life for my family. It's nobody's business but ours. Even presidents have private lives.

It is time to stop the pursuit of personal destruction and the prying into private lives and get on with our national life. Our country has been distracted by this matter for too long, and I take my responsibility for my part in all of this. That is all I can do. Now it is time—in fact, it is past time—to move on. We have important work to do—real opportunities to seize, real problems to solve, real security matters to face.

And so tonight, I ask you to turn away from the spectacle of the past seven months, to repair the fabric of our national discourse, and to return our attention to all the challenges and all the promise of the next American century.

Thank you for watching. And good night.

Statement in the Rose Garden
Prior to Vote by House Judiciary Committee
December 11, 1998

Good afternoon. As anyone close to me knows, for months I have been grappling with how best to reconcile myself to the American people, to acknowledge my own wrongdoing and still to maintain my focus on the work of the presidency.

Others are presenting my defense on the facts, the law, and the Constitution. Nothing I can say now can add to that.

What I want the American people to know, what I want the Congress to know, is that I am profoundly sorry for all I have done wrong in words and deeds. I never should have misled the country, the Congress, my friends, or my family. Quite simply, I gave in to my shame. I have been condemned by my accusers with harsh words. And while it's hard to hear yourself called deceitful and manipulative, I remember Ben Franklin's admonition that our critics are our friends, for they do show us our faults.

Mere words cannot fully express the profound remorse I feel for what our country is going through and for what members of both parties in Congress are now forced to deal with. These past months have been a torturous process of coming to terms with what I did. I understand that accountability demands consequences, and I'm prepared to accept them. Painful as the condemnation of the Congress would be, it would pale in comparison to the consequences of the pain I have caused my family. There is no greater agony.

Like anyone who honestly faces the shame of wrongful conduct, I would give anything to go back and undo what I did. But one of the painful truths I have to live with is the reality that that is simply not possible. An old and dear friend of mine recently sent me the wisdom of a poet who wrote, "The moving finger writes and having writ, moves on. Nor all your piety nor wit shall lure it back to cancel half a line. Nor all your tears wash out a word of it."

So nothing, not piety, nor tears, nor wit, nor torment can alter what I have done. I must make my peace with that. I must also be at peace with the fact that the public consequences of my actions are in the hands of the American people and their representatives in the Congress. Should they determine that my errors of word and deed require their rebuke and censure, I am ready to accept that.

Meanwhile, I will continue to do all I can to reclaim the trust of the American people and to serve them well. We must all return to the work, the vital work, of strengthening our nation for the new century. Our country has wonderful opportunities and daunting challenges ahead. I intend to seize those opportunities and meet those challenges with all the energy and ability and strength God has given me. That is simply all I can do—the work of the American people.

Thank you very much.

Statement on the South Lawn with House Democrats Following Impeachment December 19, 1998

Let me begin by expressing my profound and heartfelt thanks to Congressman Gephardt and the leadership and all the members of the Democratic caucus for what they did today. I thank the few brave Republicans who withstood enormous pressures to stand with them for the plain meaning of the Constitution and for the proposition that we need to pull together, to move beyond partisanship, to get on with the business of our country.

I thank the millions upon millions of American citizens who have expressed their support and their friendship to Hillary, to me, to our family, and to our administration during these last several weeks. The words of the members here with me and others who are a part of their endeavor in defense of our Constitution were powerful and moving, and I will never forget them.

The question is, what are we going to do now? I have accepted responsibility for what I did wrong in my personal life, and I have invited members of Congress to work with us to find a reasonable bipartisan and proportionate response. That approach was rejected today by Republicans in the House, but I hope it will be embraced by the Senate. I hope there will be a constitutional and fair means of resolving this matter in a prompt manner.

Meanwhile, I will continue to do the work of the American people. We still, after all, have to save Social Security and Medicare for the twenty-first century. We have to give all our children world-class schools. We have to pass a patients' bill of rights. We have to make sure the economic turbulence around the world does not curb our economic opportunity here at home. We have to keep America the world's strongest force for peace and freedom. In short, we have a lot to do before we enter the twenty-first century. And we still have to keep working to build that elusive one America I have talked so much about.

For six years now, I have done everything I could to bring our country together across the lines that divide us, including bringing Washington together across party lines. Out in the country, people are pulling together. But just as America is coming together, it must look—from the country's point of view—like Washington is coming apart.

I want to echo something Mr. Gephardt said. It is something I have felt strongly all my life. We must stop the politics of personal destruction. We must get rid of the poisonous venom of excessive partisanship, obsessive animosity, and uncontrolled anger. That is not what America deserves. That is not what America is about. We are doing well now. We are a good and decent country but we have significant challenges we have to face. In order to do it right, we have to have some atmosphere of decency and civility, some presumption of good faith, some sense of proportionality and balance in bringing judgment against those who are in different parties.

We have important work to do. We need a constructive debate that has all the different voices in this country heard in the halls of Congress. I want the American people to know today that I am still committed to working with people of good faith and good will of both parties to do what's best for our country, to bring our nation together, to lift our people up, to move us all forward together.

It's what I've tried to do for six years. It's what I intend to do for two more until the last hour of the last day of my term.

So with profound gratitude for the defense of the Constitution and the best in America that was raised today by the members here and those who joined them, I ask the American people to move with me—to go on from here to rise above the rancor, to overcome the pain and division, to be a repairer of the breach—all of us—to make this country as one America, what it can and must be for our children in the new century about to dawn.

Thank you very much.

Statement in the Rose Garden
Following Acquittal by the Senate
February 12, 1999

Now that the Senate has fulfilled its constitutional responsibility, bringing this process to a conclusion, I want to say again to the American people how profoundly sorry I am for what I said and did to trigger these events and the great burden they have imposed on the Congress and the American people.

I also am humbled and very grateful for the support and the prayers I have received from millions of Americans over this past year.

Now I ask all Americans, and I hope all Americans—here in Washington and throughout our land—will rededicate ourselves to the work of serving our nation and building our future together. This can be and this must be a time of reconciliation and renewal for America.

Thank you very much.

Question from the press: In your heart, sir, can you forgive and forget?

Clinton: I believe any person who asks for forgiveness has to be prepared to give it.

APPENDIX TWO

Text of the four articles of impeachment passed by the House Judiciary Committee on December 11 and 12, 1998. On December 19, the full House approved Article I and Article III, while rejecting Article II and Article IV. When passed on to the Senate, Article III became Article II. The Senate voted to acquit President Clinton on both remaining articles on February 12, 1999.

Resolved, that William Jefferson Clinton, President of the United States, is impeached for high crimes and misdemeanors, and that the following articles of impeachment be exhibited to the United States Senate:

Articles of impeachment exhibited by the House of Representatives of the United States of America in the name of itself and of the people of the United States of America, against William Jefferson Clinton, President of the United States of America, in maintenance and support of its impeachment against him for high crimes and misdemeanors.

Article I

In his conduct while President of the United States, William Jefferson Clinton, in violation of his constitutional oath faithfully to execute the office of President of the United States and, to the best of his ability, preserve, protect, and defend the Constitution of the United States, and in violation of his constitutional duty to take care that the laws be faithfully executed, has willfully corrupted and manipulated the judicial process of the United States for his personal gain and exoneration, impeding the administration of justice, in that:

On August 17, 1998, William Jefferson Clinton swore to tell the truth, the whole truth, and nothing but the truth before a Federal grand jury of the United States. Contrary to that oath, William Jefferson Clinton willfully provided perjurious, false, and misleading testimony to the grand jury concerning one or more of the following: (1) the nature and details of his relationship with a subordinate Government employee; (2) prior perjurious, false, and misleading testimony he gave in a Federal civil rights action brought against him;

438

(3) prior false and misleading statements he allowed his attorney to make to a Federal judge in that civil rights action; and (4) his corrupt efforts to influence the testimony of witnesses and to impede the discovery of evidence in that civil rights action.

In doing this, William Jefferson Clinton has undermined the integrity of his office, has brought disrepute on the Presidency, has betrayed his trust as President, and has acted in a manner subversive of the rule of law and justice, to the manifest injury of the people of the United States.

Wherefore, William Jefferson Clinton, by such conduct, warrants impeachment and trial, and removal from office and disqualification to hold and enjoy any office of honor, trust, or profit under the United States.

Article II

In his conduct while President of the United States, William Jefferson Clinton, in violation of his constitutional oath faithfully to execute the office of President of the United States and, to the best of his ability, preserve, protect, and defend the Constitution of the United States, and in violation of his constitutional duty to take care that the laws be faithfully executed, has willfully corrupted and manipulated the judicial process of the United States for his personal gain and exoneration, impeding the administration of justice, in that:

(1) On December 23, 1997, William Jefferson Clinton, in sworn answers to written questions asked as part of a Federal civil rights action brought against him, willfully provided perjurious, false, and misleading testimony in response to questions deemed relevant by a Federal judge concerning conduct and proposed conduct with subordinate employees.

(2) On January 17, 1998, William Jefferson Clinton swore under oath to tell the truth, the whole truth, and nothing but the truth in a deposition given as part of a Federal civil rights action brought against him. Contrary to that oath, William Jefferson Clinton willfully provided perjurious, false, and misleading testimony in response to questions deemed relevant by a Federal judge concerning the nature and details of his relationship with a subordinate Government employee, his knowledge of that employee's involvement and participation in the civil rights action brought against him, and his corrupt efforts to influence the testimony of that employee.

In all of this, William Jefferson Clinton has undermined the integrity of his office, has brought disrepute on the Presidency, has betrayed his trust as President, and has acted in a manner subversive of the rule of law and justice, to the manifest injury of the people of the United States.

Wherefore, William Jefferson Clinton, by such conduct, warrants impeachment and trial, and removal from office and disqualification to hold and enjoy any office of honor, trust or profit under the United States.

Article III
(Article II in the Senate)

In his conduct while President of the United States, William Jefferson Clinton, in violation of his constitutional oath faithfully to execute the office of President of the United States and, to the best of his ability, preserve, protect, and defend the Constitution of the United States, and in violation of his constitutional duty to take care that the laws be faithfully executed, has prevented, obstructed, and impeded the administration of justice, and has to that end engaged personally, and through his subordinates and agents, in a course of conduct or scheme designed to delay, impede, cover up, and conceal the existence of evidence and testimony related to a Federal civil rights action brought against him in a duly instituted judicial proceeding.

The means used to implement this course of conduct or scheme included one or more of the following acts:

(1) On or about December 17, 1997, William Jefferson Clinton corruptly encouraged a witness in a Federal civil rights action brought against him to execute a sworn affidavit in that proceeding that he knew to be perjurious, false, and misleading.

(2) On or about December 17, 1997, William Jefferson Clinton corruptly encouraged a witness in a Federal civil rights action brought against him to give perjurious, false, and misleading testimony if and when called to testify personally in that proceeding.

(3) On or about December 28, 1997, William Jefferson Clinton corruptly engaged in, encouraged, or supported a scheme to conceal evidence that had been subpoenaed in a Federal civil rights action brought against him.

(4) Beginning on or about December 7, 1997, and continuing through and including January 14, 1998, William Jefferson Clinton intensified and succeeded in an effort to secure job assistance to a witness in a Federal civil rights action brought against him in order to corruptly prevent the truthful testimony of that witness in that proceeding at a time when the truthful testimony of that witness would have been harmful to him.

(5) On January 17, 1998, at his deposition in a Federal civil rights action brought against him, William Jefferson Clinton corruptly allowed his attorney to make false and misleading statements to a Federal judge characterizing an affidavit, in order to prevent questioning deemed

relevant by the judge. Such false and misleading statements were subsequently acknowledged by his attorney in a communication to that judge.

(6) On or about January 18 and January 20–21, 1998, William Jefferson Clinton related a false and misleading account of events relevant to a Federal civil rights action brought against him to a potential witness in that proceeding, in order to corruptly influence the testimony of that witness.

(7) On or about January 21, 23, and 26, 1998, William Jefferson Clinton made false and misleading statements to potential witnesses in a Federal grand jury proceeding in order to corruptly influence the testimony of those witnesses. The false and misleading statements made by William Jefferson Clinton were repeated by the witnesses to the grand jury, causing the grand jury to receive false and misleading information.

In all of this, William Jefferson Clinton has undermined the integrity of his office, has brought disrepute on the Presidency, has betrayed his trust as President, and has acted in a manner subversive of the rule of law and justice, to the manifest injury of the people of the United States.

Wherefore, William Jefferson Clinton, by such conduct, warrants impeachment and trial, and removal from office and disqualification to hold and enjoy any office of honor, trust or profit under the United States.

Article IV

Using the powers and influence of the office of President of the United States, William Jefferson Clinton, in violation of his constitutional oath faithfully to execute the office of President of the United States and, to the best of his ability, preserve, protect, and defend the Constitution of the United States, and in disregard of his constitutional duty to take care that the laws be faithfully executed, has engaged in conduct that resulted in misuse and abuse of his high office, impaired the due and proper administration of justice and the conduct of lawful inquiries, and contravened the authority of the legislative branch and the truth-seeking purpose of a coordinate investigative proceeding in that, as President, William Jefferson Clinton refused and failed to respond to certain written requests for admission and willfully made perjurious, false, and misleading sworn statements in response to certain written requests for admission propounded to him as part of the impeachment inquiry authorized by the House of Representatives of the Congress of the United States.

William Jefferson Clinton, in refusing and failing to respond, and in making perjurious, false, and misleading statements, assumed to himself functions and judgments necessary to the exercise of the sole power of impeachment vested by the Constitution in the House of Representatives and exhibited contempt for the inquiry.

In doing this, William Jefferson Clinton has undermined the integrity of his office, has brought disrepute on the Presidency, has betrayed his trust as President, and has acted in a manner subversive of the rule of law and justice, to the manifest injury of the people of the United States.

Wherefore, William Jefferson Clinton, by such conduct, warrants impeachment and trial, and removal from office and disqualification to hold and enjoy any office of honor, trust or profit under the United States.

VOTES

	HOUSE	**SENATE**
Article I	228–206	45–55
	Passed	Failed
	(All but five Republicans	(Ten Republicans
	voted yes, while all but	joined all forty-five Democrats
	five Democrats voted no)	in voting not guilty)
Article II	205–229	
	Failed	
	(All but five Democrats	
	voted no, while twenty-eight	
	Republicans broke ranks)	
Article III	221–212	50–50
(Article II in	Passed	Failed
the Senate)	(All but five Democrats	(Five Republicans
	voted no, while all but twelve	joined all forty-five Democrats
	Republicans voted yes)	in voting not guilty)
Article IV	148–285	
	Failed	
	(Only one Democrat voted	
	yes, while eighty-one	
	Republicans voted no)	

APPENDIX THREE

Text of the proposed censure resolution drafted by Congressman Rick Boucher of Virginia and endorsed by the House Democratic leadership. The House Judiciary Committee rejected it 22–16 on December 12, 1998, and the House Republican leadership refused to allow a vote on it on the floor when articles of impeachment went before the full body on December 19.

That it is the sense of Congress that—
1. on January 20, 1993, William Jefferson Clinton took the oath prescribed by the Constitution of the United States faithfully to execute the office of President; implicit in that oath is the obligation that the President set an example of high moral standards and conduct himself in a manner that fosters respect for the truth; and William Jefferson Clinton has egregiously failed in this obligation, and through his actions has violated the trust of the American people, lessened their esteem for the office of President, and dishonored the office which they have entrusted to him;
2. (A) William Jefferson Clinton made false statements concerning his reprehensible conduct with a subordinate;
   (B) William Jefferson Clinton wrongly took steps to delay discovery of the truth; and
   (C) in as much as no person is above the law, William Jefferson Clinton remains subject to criminal and civil penalties; and
3. William Jefferson Clinton, President of the United States, by his conduct has brought upon himself, and fully deserves, the censure and condemnation of the American people and the Congress; and by his signature on this Joint Resolution, acknowledges this censure and condemnation.

APPENDIX FOUR

Text of the proposed censure resolution drafted by Senators Dianne Feinstein, a California Democrat, and Robert F. Bennett, a Utah Republican, and introduced on the Senate floor on February 12, 1999. The Senate voted 56–43 to consider the resolution, but fell short of the two-thirds majority required to suspend the rules. Instead, Feinstein inserted the resolution in the form of a statement into the Congressional Record with the signatures of thirty-eight senators, including twenty-nine Democrats and nine Republicans.

Whereas William Jefferson Clinton, President of the United States, engaged in an inappropriate relationship with a subordinate employee in the White House, which was shameful, reckless, and indefensible;

Whereas William Jefferson Clinton, President of the United States, deliberately misled and deceived the American people, and people in all branches of the United States government;

Whereas William Jefferson Clinton, President of the United States, gave false or misleading testimony and his actions have had the effect of impeding discovery of evidence in judicial proceedings;

Whereas William Jefferson Clinton's conduct in this matter is unacceptable for a President of the United States, does demean the Office of the President as well as the President himself, and creates disrespect for the laws of the land;

Whereas President Clinton fully deserves censure for engaging in such behavior;

Whereas future generations of Americans must know that such behavior is not only unacceptable but also bears grave consequences, including loss of integrity, trust, and respect;

Whereas William Jefferson Clinton remains subject to criminal actions in a court of law like any other citizen;

Whereas William Jefferson Clinton's conduct in this matter has brought shame and dishonor to himself and to the Office of the President; and

Whereas William Jefferson Clinton through his conduct in this matter has violated the trust of the American people;

*   *   *

Now therefore, be it resolved that:

The United States Senate does hereby censure William Jefferson Clinton, President of the United States, and does condemn his wrongful conduct in the strongest terms; and

Now be it further resolved that:

The United States Senate recognizes the historic gravity of this bipartisan resolution, and trusts and urges that future congresses will recognize the importance of allowing this bipartisan statement of censure and condemnation to remain intact for all time; and

Be it further resolved that:

The Senate now move on to other matters of significance to our people, to reconcile differences between and within the branches of government, and to work together—across party lines—for the benefit of the American people.

INDEX

Abbott, Steve, 396
ABC, 89, 224, 306, 307, 405, 406, 414, 416, 417
Abercrombie, Neil, 53
abortion rights, 51, 77, 143, 283
Abourezk, James, 262
Abraham, Spencer, 360, 409
abuse of office, 189
    in articles of impeachment, 190, 193
    in Starr report, 80, 81, 91
    see also Article IV
Ackerman, Bruce, 266, 269–70, 381
Ackerman, Gary L., 128
Adams, Gerry, 200
Adams, John, 84
Afghanistan, U.S. bombing of, 26, 47, 50
AFL-CIO, 52, 65, 66, 222, 226
Africa, bombing of U.S. embassies in, 25
African-Americans, 56, 116, 147, 153, 316–17, 322, 357
    Clinton's support among, 76–77, 115
AFSCME, 65
Air Force One, 38, 46, 57, 94, 227, 320
Akaka, Daniel K., 288, 289, 360, 409
Akin, Gump, Strauss, Hauer & Feld, 374
Alabama, 81, 352, 405
Alaska, 276
Albright, Madeleine, 58, 72, 73, 227, 267
Allard, Wayne, 331, 366, 409
Alvarez, Aida, 75
American Conservative Union, 155
American Federation of Teachers, 65
Ames, Aldrich, 348
Arafat, Yasser, 134, 227
Archer, Bill, 153
Arizona, 151, 152, 285, 358, 398
Arkansas, 37, 74, 109, 158, 241, 294, 311, 323, 377
    Asa Hutchinson and, 93–95, 124, 183, 355, 374
    Clinton as attorney general of, 16, 138

Clinton as governor of, 73, 88, 103, 138, 307, 314, 315
    Hillary Clinton's bar membership in, 45
    state troopers of, 35
Arkansas, University of, 94
Arkansas state troopers, 35
Armey, Dick, 43, 50, 67, 72, 220, 226, 235, 237, 247, 256
articles of impeachment, 239
    drafting of, 188–94
    House Judiciary Committee vote on, 206, 209–16
    House vote on, 251–53, 442
    Senate vote on, 408–10, 442
    texts of, 438–42
Article I (House and Senate), 193, 323, 324, 340–41, 395, 397, 400, 403–4, 405
    findings of fact and, 384
    House Judiciary Committee vote on, 210–14
    House vote on, 251–52, 442
    Senate vote on, 408–9, 442
    text of, 438–39
Article II (House), 193
    House Judiciary Committee vote on, 214
    House rejection of, 252, 265, 442
    text of, 439–40
Article III (House) (Senate Article II), 190, 265, 323, 324, 325, 395, 397, 400, 401, 404, 405
    findings of fact and, 384
    House Judiciary Committee vote on, 214
    House vote on, 252, 442
    Senate vote on, 410, 442
    text of, 440–41
Article IV (House), 193, 252
    House Judiciary Committee vote on, 214–16, 217
    House rejection of, 252, 253, 442
    text of, 441–42
Ashcroft, John, 333, 383, 411

Associated Press, 269
Atlanta, Ga., 150, 376
attorney-client privilege, 26, 28, 37, 175–76

Babbitt, Bruce, 74
Baesler, Scotty, 53
Baghdad, 233–34, 248
Baker, Howard H., Jr., 19, 64, 164, 418
Baker, Nancy Kassebaum, 164
Baldwin, Tammy, 141
Bank of the United States, 288
Barber, Ben, 279
Barr, Robert L., Jr., 11, 162, 189, 211–12,
    241–42, 260, 309, 353, 377
  as manager in Senate trial, 272, 287, 296,
    309, 357–58, 367, 391
Barrett, Thomas, 216, 315
Battalino, Barbara, 184
Battle, Chris, 125, 339
Bauer, Robert F., 11, 85–86, 91, 111–12, 114,
    117, 130, 136, 293, 295, 305, 313,
    318, 329, 333–34, 340, 342, 344, 365,
    368, 382, 407, 412
Bayh, Evan, 262, 364, 402
Begala, Paul, 11, 55, 79–80, 158, 180, 194,
    311, 384
  attorney retained by, 19
  and Clinton's post–grand jury television
    speech, 24–25, 26, 30, 31, 33
  Clinton's responsibility as viewed by,
    118–19
  leak of speech draft of, 207–9
  low morale of, 37, 96, 130
  resignation of, 415
Bennett, Jackie M., Jr., 70, 71
Bennett, Robert F., 286, 330, 386–87, 392
Bennett, Robert S., 37, 86, 100, 108, 117,
    134, 166, 175, 176, 177, 299, 386
Ben-Veniste, Richard, 165, 198, 382
Berger, Samuel R. "Sandy," 26, 227, 242
Berman, Howard L., 11, 65, 87, 123, 125,
    131, 168, 175, 204, 211–12, 213,
    387–88
Berman, Mike, 165, 382
Berry, Marsha, 47
Bible, 74, 76
Biden, Joseph R., Jr., 96, 276, 278, 291, 303,
    364
Bilbray, Brian, 142
bills of attainder, 113
bin Laden, Osama, 25, 49, 50
bipartisanship, 18, 21, 77, 80, 113, 167, 196,
    235, 250–51, 259, 263, 269, 276, 280,
    283, 284–86, 292, 294, 344, 380, 381,
    383, 393, 411
  Clinton's pledge of, 7, 19

in House Judiciary Committee, 68, 101–2,
    110, 124, 126, 131
in previous impeachments, 84
see also partisanship
Bisek, Callista, 156
Bittman, Robert J., 28, 337–38, 340, 347,
    348
blacks, see African-Americans
"blind memos," 305
Bloch, Susan, 381
Bloodworth-Thomason, Linda, 33
Bloom, David, 414
Blue, Carol, 390
Blue Dogs, 53, 116, 123, 125, 126
Blumenthal, Sidney, 11, 25, 99, 162, 208,
    273
  in Senate trial, 356, 357–58, 359, 377–79,
    390, 391
Bob Jones University, 93–94
Boehlert, Sherwood L., 220, 263
Bogart, Susan, 231, 318, 332, 390
"bolt of lightning" clause, 365
Bond, Kit, 385
Bonior, David E., 53, 63
Bonner, Robert, 273
Bono, Mary, 11, 102, 132, 150–51, 152, 176,
    186, 260
Bono, Sonny, 132, 150, 260
Bork, Robert H., 18, 402
Bosnia, 38
Boucher, Rick, 11, 115–16, 122, 123–24, 125,
    129, 168, 193, 204, 216, 315
Bowles, Erskine B., 11, 20, 31, 33, 37–40, 55,
    59–60, 64, 74–75, 96, 99, 118, 119,
    133, 182
  Clinton's relationship with, 37–38, 39–40
Bowles, Sam, 38
Boxer, Barbara, 333, 355, 360, 401, 409
Boys Nation, 255
breach, see bipartisanship; partisanship
"breakfast club," 131, 168, 204
Breaux, John, 117
Breuer, Lanny A., 11, 89, 267, 271, 301, 316,
    336, 379
Britton, Nan, 34
Broaddrick, Juanita ("Jane Doe No. 5"), 11,
    110, 183, 191, 242, 243, 252, 271,
    353
  Clinton accused of rape by, 16–17, 109,
    231–32, 323, 415–16
  NBC interview with, 323, 381–82, 397,
    399, 415–16
Brophy, Susan, 95, 200, 222, 225–26
Brown, Corrine, 128, 408
Brownback, Sam, 385
Browner, Carol M., 75

Browning, Dolly Kyle, 11, 138, 191, 274
Bryan, Richard, 48, 330
Bryant, Edward G., 11, 272, 276, 277, 296,
    303, 331, 377
    Lewinsky questioned by, 347, 349, 350,
    359, 367–72, 376, 377, 391
BTU tax, 48
Buffalo, N.Y., 221–22, 226, 320
Bullfeathers restaurant, 78, 132
Bumpers, Dale, 11, 311, 314–15, 316, 319,
    321, 325–26, 380, 391
Bunning, Jim, 328–29, 331, 397
Burton, Dan, 99, 156, 218
Burton, Preston, 346, 347, 368, 370–71, 373
Bush, George, 38
Bush, George W., 151
Buyer, Steve, 11, 102, 132, 176, 231, 252,
    260, 311, 342–43, 345, 352–53, 382
Byrd, Robert C., 11, 110, 202, 245, 262, 263,
    275
    Clinton as viewed by, 48, 334–35
    Clinton's resignation favored by, 63
    as key to Clinton's acquittal, 272
    political career of, 289
    in Senate trial, 289–90, 303, 316, 321,
    334–35, 336, 339–40, 341, 346, 351,
    353, 354–55, 360, 362, 389, 397, 398,
    405–6, 409

cabinet, Clinton's meeting with, 72–76
Cacheris, Plato, 11, 177, 337, 346, 347, 348,
    350, 368, 370, 371
Cahill, Mary Beth, 143
Calhoun, John C., 288
California:
    Democratic Party in, 53, 64, 65, 76, 87,
    112, 116, 120, 123, 126, 128, 131,
    204, 211, 386, 401
    Republican Party in, 102, 142, 161, 211,
    224, 307–8
Callahan, H. L. "Sonny," 81, 151
Campaign, The, 72, 114, 200, 217, 223, 250,
    257, 415
    naming of, 45
    organization of, 43–44, 45
campaign finance scandals, 183–84, 185
Campbell, Ben Nighthorse, 404
Campbell, Tom, 224
Camp David, 382
Campolo, Tony, 252–53
Canady, Charles T., 11, 127, 135, 162, 190,
    210, 237, 272, 311, 353
Cannon, Chris, 11, 97, 161, 216, 286–87,
    309, 330, 353, 356–57, 358
Capitol Police, 71, 257, 309, 350, 389, 390
Caribou, Maine, 283

Carle, Robin H., 80
Carpenter-McMillan, Susan, 166
Carter, Jimmy, 111, 263
Carville, James, 11, 20, 23, 24, 31, 56,
    125–26, 127, 177, 203
    attack dog role of, 32
Castle, Michael N., 201, 202, 221, 229, 231,
    263
cast of characters, 11–13
CBS, 89, 99, 416
censure of Clinton, 19, 59, 60, 108, 144, 165,
    167, 176, 186, 209, 216, 220, 221,
    222, 241, 268, 380
    as acceptable to Clinton, 203, 219, 381
    Boucher's proposed resolution on, 192–94,
    200, 217, 443
    Carter and Ford's support for, 263
    DeLay's opposition to, 114, 130, 204,
    217–19
    Democratic opposition to, 130, 168
    Feinstein and Bennett's proposed resolu-
    tion on, 386–87, 392–93, 411–12,
    444–45
    fine proposed with, see censure-plus plan
    Gephardt's secret plans for, 111–14, 130,
    166, 167–68
    House rejection of vote on, 251
    Lewinsky's support for, 349
    Livingston's eleventh-hour near-agreement
    on, 15–18, 21–22, 242
    public opinion on, 221, 224–25
    Ruff's offers of, 195–96, 203
censure of Jackson, 255, 288–89
censure-plus plan, 113, 114, 130, 184, 202,
    229
    Clinton's opposition to, 165, 166, 168
Central Intelligence Agency (CIA), 189, 205,
    228, 235, 348
Chabot, Steve, 162, 309, 377
Chafee, John, 284, 329, 352, 392, 409, 410
Chase, Samuel, 84
Chenoweth, Helen, 99, 156, 218
Chicago, Ill., 85, 118, 147, 149
Chiles, Lawton, 362
China, People's Republic of, 108, 183
Christenson, Arne, 99, 157
Christian Coalition, 144, 320
Christian right, 223, 230
chronology of events, 427–32
Chubb Group Insurance, 299
Chung, Johnny, 183
cigars, 77, 82, 90, 101, 136, 147
Clay, Henry, 288
Cleveland, Grover, 34, 83
Cleveland, Ohio, focus groups in, 128
Clifford, Clark, 111

Clinton, Bill:
apologies made by, 25, 34, 52, 55, 62, 72–76, 79, 89, 97, 194–95, 207, 212, 254, 255, 372
as attorney general of Arkansas, 16, 138
bipartisanship pledge of, 7, 19
censure of, see censure of Clinton
civil deposition in Jones case made by, 26, 28, 29, 39, 80, 89, 90, 112, 167, 180–81, 186, 191, 192, 195, 198, 252, 264, 273, 304, 321, 329, 416
"compartmentalizing" ability of, 35–36
contempt citation of, 416
criminal prosecution as prospect for, 194, 196, 202, 263, 269
departures by staff members of, 118–19, 130, 415
domestic agenda of, 133, 208
elections and, see specific elections
electronic monitoring of, 30
emotional effects of scandal and impeachment on, 35–36, 56, 58, 59, 79, 131, 201, 219, 226–27, 233, 253, 264
"finger-wagging" denial by, 33, 145, 304
"forgiveness" speech of, 56
fund-raising by, 72, 91
as golfer, 37, 56, 181, 419
as governor of Arkansas, 73, 88, 103, 138, 307, 314, 315
grand jury testimony of, 23, 24, 26, 27–29, 31, 36, 40, 41, 80, 90–91, 93, 97–98, 100, 101, 102, 105–7, 112–13, 121, 132, 167, 170, 191, 193, 195, 210, 224, 252, 265, 304, 322, 329, 345, 402
history of womanizing by, 34–35, 74, 88, 103, 138, 273, 315, 322
House Judiciary Committee's written questions submitted to, 147–49, 179–81, 201, 215, 229
lawyers vs. political advisors of, 30–31, 32, 33, 36, 96, 105
legacy and place in history of, 251, 264, 271, 415, 417
legalisms used in defense of, 26, 29, 33, 89, 90, 91–92, 113, 180, 195
medical questions about, 49
military strikes ordered by, 15, 26, 47, 50
morale problems among staff of, 37, 45–46, 64, 96, 118, 130, 271
nature of alleged offenses of, see obstruction of justice; perjury
opinion poll standings of, 18, 19, 47, 57, 70, 102, 107, 125, 127, 223, 224–25, 320, 321, 417

overseas trips of, 57–59, 60, 61, 206, 216, 219, 220, 224, 225, 226–27, 232, 264, 392, 396
physical appearance of, 28, 253
policy victories won by, 133
at prayer breakfast, 78–79
rape allegations made against, see Broaddrick, Juanita
Republican animosity toward, 19, 21, 42, 258, 271, 312
revenge against Republicans sought by, 376–77, 415
rumors about, 57, 138–39, 294, 315
"secret police" rumors about, 124
sense of victimhood of, 29, 32, 34, 54, 73, 74–75, 77, 97, 131, 253, 416–17
split within legal team of, 36–37, 96
statement after impeachment of, 255–56, 435–37
statement after Senate acquittal of, 413–14, 437
statement before House Judiciary Committee vote on, 211–13, 434–35
State of the Union addresses of, 38, 39, 40, 114, 298, 300, 316, 319–20, 419
televised speech of, after grand jury testimony, 24–25, 30–34, 41, 42, 43, 433–34
temper of, 30, 105, 106, 219
weakened political authority of, 419
weekly political strategy sessions of, 206
Clinton, Chelsea, 46, 47, 100, 207
Clinton, Hillary Rodham, 11, 32, 34, 36, 38, 65, 77, 88, 94, 95, 124, 140, 205, 255, 256, 320, 413–14
bill for Clinton's misdeeds paid by, 113, 299
censure opposed by, 130
Clinton's relationship with, 46, 47, 49, 50, 56–57, 104, 131, 143, 246, 253–54, 319
effect of scandal on, 23, 33, 47, 104
Lewinsky affair revealed to, 24
popularity of, 414
right wing blamed by, 104–5
role in Clinton's defense played by, 33, 104, 125, 172, 245–46
Senate run planned by, 140, 413, 415
Watergate role of, 45, 84, 202
Whitewater investigation and, 33, 140
Clinton, Roger, 94, 138
CNBC, 207, 296
CNN, 30, 63, 80, 323
Cobb, Kimberly, 365
Coble, Howard, 216
Cochran, Thad, 279

Coelho, Tony, 85
Cohen, Bill, 227, 228, 235, 282–83
Collins, Susan M., 11, 282–83, 284, 301, 306,
    308, 323, 324, 329, 330, 340–41, 344,
    352, 360, 363, 380, 381, 382, 383,
    385, 386, 392, 395–96, 399–401,
    402–3, 404–5, 409, 410, 412
Colmer, William M., 261
Colorado, 53, 404
Committee on Reconstruction, 83–84
common-law privileges, 175
Comprehensive Test Ban Treaty, 419
Condit, Gary, 123
Congress, U.S.:
    privileges recognized by, 175
    Republican control of, 37, 48–49
    separation-of-powers doctrine and, 298
    see also House of Representatives, U.S.;
        Senate, U.S.
Congressional Black Caucus, 36, 76, 115
Congressional Research Service, 269
Connecticut, 41, 59, 61, 128, 151, 229, 230,
    231, 234, 241, 242, 262, 263
Conrad, Kent, 97, 321, 382
Constitution, U.S., 61, 128, 149, 175–77,
    241, 246, 254, 266, 273, 310, 318,
    353, 383, 387, 392, 417
    on bills of attainder, 113
    Fifth Amendment of, 175, 177
    privileges in, 175
    provisions for impeachment and removal
        from office in, 52, 82–84, 162, 164,
        189, 190, 259, 267, 361, 405; see also
        "high crimes and misdemeanors"
    separation-of-powers doctrine in, 298
    Twentieth Amendment of, 269
Constitutional Convention (1787), 82–83
Conyers, John, Jr., 11, 67, 68, 69, 71–72, 86,
    87, 116, 120–21, 122, 137, 163, 170,
    200, 213, 216, 241, 246, 247, 248,
    315
Corallo, Mark, 16–17, 22, 153, 154, 237
Corr, Bill, 267
Coulson, Beth, 138
Council of Conservative Citizens, 241–42
Covenant, Sword and Arm of the Lord, 94
Coverdell, Paul, 323, 331, 384–85
Covington & Burling, 316
Craig, Derry, 87
Craig, Gregory B., 12, 96–97, 129, 130–31,
    134, 135–36, 171, 172, 182, 185–87,
    195, 202, 230, 233, 246
    Clinton as viewed by, 88–89, 264–65
    Clinton's legal defense team joined by,
        87–89, 95–96
    defense strategy of, 265

House Judiciary Committee appearance of,
    197–200
legal career of, 88
role in Clinton's defense played by, 266
in Senate trial, 269–70, 278, 300–301,
    306, 310, 315, 316, 321–22, 345,
    389
Craig, Larry, 331, 341
Crowley, Candy, 80
Currie, Betty, 12, 39, 87, 149, 172, 253, 254,
    265, 273, 307, 323, 334, 339, 349,
    355–56, 357, 371, 374
    Clinton's coaching of, 81, 89, 91, 167,
        181, 186, 193, 304, 318–19, 332, 344,
        399, 402, 404
Cutler, Lloyd N., 12, 111–12, 114, 130,
    164–65, 166, 187, 195, 203
Czechoslovakia, 100

Daley, William, 72, 73
D'Amato, Al, 140, 200–201, 220
Danforth, Jack, 202
Danner, Pat, 53, 123
Daschle, Thomas A., 12, 40–41, 85, 87, 89,
    91–92, 109, 110, 117–18, 133, 232
    background and political career of, 262
    as liaison between Clinton and Senate
        Democrats, 41, 48, 60, 245
    Lott and, 260–62, 407, 410–11
    and Senate trial, 268, 269, 271–72, 274,
        276, 280–81, 283–84, 285–86, 288,
        289, 292, 293, 295, 297, 305, 308,
        309, 310, 311, 312, 313, 316, 327,
        328, 330, 331, 333–34, 336, 340, 341,
        342, 344, 353, 362–66, 368, 381, 385,
        389–90, 397, 405, 406, 407–8, 409,
        411
Dash, Samuel, 177
Dateline, 415–16
Davis, Jefferson, 279
Davis, Lanny J., 165, 382, 384
Davis, Thomas M., III, 250
DeFazio, Peter, 53
DeGette, Diana, 53
Delahunt, William D., 116, 131, 168, 169
DeLauro, Rosa, 128, 241
Delaware, 96, 201, 229, 276
DeLay, Tom, 12, 16, 19, 20, 21, 22, 43–45,
    72, 114, 130, 146, 147, 181, 200, 201,
    204, 223, 224, 226, 230, 231, 233,
    234, 236, 237, 239, 256, 301, 320,
    415, 419, 420
    background and political career of, 44–45
    censure opposed by, 114, 130, 204,
        217–19, 229
    Clinton as viewed by, 42, 43, 44

DeLay, Tom (*cont.*)
    efforts to remove Clinton orchestrated by,
        43–45, 177–79
    Livingston's resignation and, 243–45,
        249–50, 257
    nickname of, 44
Democratic Governors Association, 103
Democratic National Committee, 420
Democratic Party:
    centrism and, 37, 59; *see also* New Democ-
        rats
    Clinton's relationship with members of, 41,
        47–49, 51–55, 57, 59–62, 63–66, 72,
        76–77, 96–97, 103–5, 109–10,
        123–29, 249, 271–72, 314
    conservative wing of, *see* Blue Dogs
    diversity and, 116
    interest groups and, 65–66
    liberal wing of, 53, 54, 116, 123, 129, 161
    meeting of House members of, 76–77
    1998 election victories of, 140–47, 168
    senior House members of, *see* Old Bulls
    see also specific elections, individuals and
        states
Derrick, Butler, 218, 229
DeWine, Mike, 293, 328, 329, 369, 371
Dickey, Jay, 231–32, 377
Dingell, John D., 65, 69
Dinh, Viet, 383
DiVall, Linda, 298
DNA evidence, 23, 26, 40, 42, 81, 118, 173
Doar, John, 121
Dodd, Chris, 262, 291, 327, 341, 355, 376,
    411
Dole, Bob, 208, 229, 262, 263, 271, 308,
    383
Domenici, Pete V., 12, 276, 281, 352, 382,
    383, 384, 385
Donaldson, Sam, 414
Douglass, Linda, 307
Dove, Bob, 267, 310
Dow Jones Industrial Average, 57
Drinan, Robert F., 198
Drudge, Matt, 294
Duberstein, Ken, 187
Dublin, 61
Dudas, Jon, 305
Duff, Jim, 267, 268, 310, 345
Durbin, Richard J., 109, 305, 313, 360

Echaveste, Maria, 75
Edwards, John, 262, 342, 364, 378, 403–4,
    412
Eighth U.S. Circuit Court of Appeals, 108,
    134
Eisenhower, Dwight D., 34

elections, U.S.:
    of 1972, 97
    of 1974, 126
    of 1988, 34–35, 51, 262
    of 1992, 32, 35, 37–38, 103, 127, 307,
        355, 415
    of 1994, 48–49, 124, 146, 158, 254, 262,
        286, 367
    of 1996, 38, 49, 65, 108, 206, 208, 229
    of 1998, 21, 51, 85, 134, 140–47, 152,
        161–62, 163, 298, 377
    of 2000, 85, 376–77, 415, 420
Elmendorf, Steve, 52–53, 65, 86, 87, 158, 163
Emanuel, Rahm, 12, 25, 30, 31, 32, 33, 37,
    55, 64, 96, 118, 119, 125–26, 130
Emerson, Jo Ann, 152
Emily's List, 143
Emmick, Michael W., 347, 348, 350
energy (BTU) tax, 48
Ensign, John, 141
Environmental Protection Agency, 75
Enzi, Mike, 329, 401
Epstein, Julian, 12, 86–87, 101, 102, 103,
    116, 128, 164, 168, 185, 200, 203,
    209, 213, 233, 253
Era of Good Feelings, 146
Eshoo, Anna G., 64
executive privilege, 91, 121–22, 175, 190,
    214–15
Exner, Judith Campbell, 34

Face the Nation, 89
"Factual Inaccuracies in House Managers' Pre-
    sentation (Day One)," 305
Faircloth, Lauch, 140
Fallon, Patrick, 347, 348
Fazio, Vic, 65, 112, 126–27, 142
federal budget, 133, 134, 144
    balancing of, 38, 39, 158
Federal Bureau of Investigation (FBI), 110,
    127, 137, 138, 170, 172, 173, 189,
    205, 273, 347, 353, 372
federal government, 1995 shutdown of, 21, 42
Federalist papers, 83, 222, 310, 317, 334
Feingold, Russell, 12, 59, 62, 63, 262, 305,
    323, 344, 360, 362, 366, 384, 398–99
Feinstein, Dianne, 12, 63, 109, 314, 355, 399
    censure proposal by Bennett and, 386–87,
        392–93, 411–12, 444–45
    Clinton's credibility as viewed by, 48
Feldman, Sandy, 65
fetal-tissue research, 38
Fifth Amendment, 175, 177
"Fighting Ninth" district, 115
Filegate, 24
"finger-wagging" denial, 33, 145, 304

Fisher, James A., 134
Florida, 72, 73, 127, 128, 192, 209, 237, 248, 262, 284, 362
Flowers, Gennifer, 32, 35, 42, 415
Flynt, Larry, 120, 202, 228–29, 236, 259, 260, 296
Foley, Mark, 248
Forbes, Michael P., 151, 182, 221, 227
Ford, Gerald R., 263, 298
Ford, James David, 238
Ford House Office Building, 71, 85, 93
Foster, Vince, 325
Fox, Jon D., 140, 224
Fox News, 106, 124
Frank, Barney, 12, 87, 102, 123, 209, 211, 213, 216
Freeh, Louis J., 183, 184, 185, 273
"Free Lisa Myers" button, 382, 397
Freeman, Sharee, 184
free-trade legislation, 38, 51
Frist, Bill, 412
Frost, Martin, 53, 241, 246

"Gaining the Edge" (Greenberg), 143–44
Gang of Six, 276, 281
Ganske, Greg, 242
Gaylord, Joe, 141, 145, 157
Gecker, Daniel, 175, 176, 177, 273, 274, 399
Gekas, George W., 97, 214–15, 216, 272, 309, 311
Georgetown University, 77
George Washington University, 157
Georgia, 141, 150, 152, 156, 162, 211, 241, 323, 374, 384
Gephardt, Richard A., 12, 21, 41, 42, 62, 63, 65, 67, 76, 85–86, 90–92, 93, 102, 103, 127, 133, 136, 143, 158–59, 162–63, 164, 176, 217, 228, 232, 233, 234, 236, 245, 248, 254, 255, 259, 305, 412
    background and political career of, 51
    Clinton's relationship with, 51–52, 53, 64
    Gingrich's meetings with, 67–70, 71–72, 107–8
    in House impeachment debate, 240–41
    impeachment inquiry strategy of, 114–15, 116, 117, 123, 124, 125, 128, 129, 130, 132
    on Livingston's resignation, 250–51
    Lowell hired by, 86–87
    secret censure plans of, 111–14, 130, 166, 167–68
    2000 election goal of, 376–77
gerrymandering, 225
Giancana, Sam, 85

Gillespie, Ed, 275
Gilman, Benjamin A., 224, 263
Gingrich, Marianne, 140, 156
Gingrich, Newt, 12, 38, 43, 44, 50, 67–70, 77, 78, 87, 132, 160, 163, 165, 186, 187, 218, 219, 224, 229, 235–36, 238, 242, 243–44, 245, 256, 262, 330, 417
    Clinton's actions as viewed by, 145, 152, 156
    dinosaur skull in office of, 67
    ethics investigation conducted on, 70, 128, 239
    extramarital affair of, 98–99, 156
    Gephardt's meetings with, 67–70, 71–72, 107–8
    Livingston's relationship with, 20, 153, 154, 156
    1997 coup attempted against, 45
    1998 election and, 140–42, 143
    ousted as House Speaker, 17, 21, 141–42, 146–47, 149–59
Ginsburg, William H., 348
Giuliani, Rudolph, 273
Glazier, Mitch, 147–48, 184, 188–90, 192, 210
Glendening, Parris N., 62
Glenn, John, 311, 314
Glickman, Dan, 74, 131, 223
Goldberg, Adam, 215
Goldberg, Don, 215
Goldberg, Lucianne, 137, 163
Goldwater, Barry, 19
Goode, Virgil H., Jr., 252
Goodlatte, Bob, 210
Gore, Albert, Jr., 12, 51, 65, 66, 73, 108, 227, 263, 282, 376, 414, 419
    Clinton supported by, 76, 223, 225, 226, 253, 254, 255, 320
Gore, Tipper, 320
Gorton, Slade, 12, 263, 268, 271, 274, 275, 284, 290–91, 293, 352, 363, 365, 385, 392, 397, 409
Graham, Bob, 48, 59, 262, 364, 381, 384
Graham, Lindsey O., 12, 102–3, 121, 127, 130–31, 160, 174, 176, 181, 185–86, 192–93, 194, 196, 211–12, 213, 214, 241, 252, 260, 272, 273, 297, 309, 311–12, 317, 322, 333, 342–43, 350, 352, 354, 356, 358, 367, 377, 382, 391, 392, 410, 415
    threatened "outing" of, 259
Gramm, Phil, 12, 269, 291–92, 293, 341, 352, 363, 364, 365, 385, 392, 397, 400, 411
Grand Inquests (Rehnquist), 267

grand jury, 81, 173, 205
    Clinton's closed-circuit testimony before,
        23, 26, 27–29, 31, 36, 40, 41, 80,
        90–91, 93, 97–98, 100, 101, 102,
        105–7, 112–13, 121, 132, 167, 170,
        191, 193, 195, 210, 224, 252, 265,
        304, 322, 329, 345, 402
    Jordan's testimony before, 91
    Lewinsky's appearances before, 50, 81, 102,
        172, 369–70
Grant, Ulysses S., 300
Grassley, Charles, 360, 397–98
Green, Tom, 86
Greenberg, Stan, 127–28, 143–44
Greenwood, Jim, 234, 263
Gregg, Judd, 310, 385
Griffin, Pat, 382
Griffith, Thomas B., 12, 267, 268, 274, 292,
        293, 310, 328, 340, 363, 365, 373,
        382, 383, 405, 409
Griscom, Tom, 275

Hall, Fawn, 348
Hall, Ralph M., 53, 123, 252
Hamilton, Alexander, 83, 84, 265, 334
Hamilton, Jim, 165, 198
Hamilton, Lee, 141
Hammerschmidt, John Paul, 94, 95
Hannan, Philip, 154
Harding, Warren G., 34
Harkin, Tom, 12, 293, 309–11, 314, 345–46,
        351, 354, 365, 380–81
Hart, Gary, 35
Hastert, J. Dennis, 178, 319
    chosen as House Speaker, 245, 256–57
Hatch, Orrin G., 12, 41, 42, 196, 286–87,
        328, 352, 361–62, 385, 387, 388, 409
    Clinton schooled on repentance by, 89–90
Havel, Vaclav, 100, 107
Hawaii, 53, 289, 360
Hays, Paul, 239
Hayworth, J. D., 152
helicopter walks, choreographing of, 45–46
Helms, Jesse, 360, 401
Henry, Ann, 95
Herman, Alexis M., 74
"high crimes and misdemeanors," 15, 91,
        121–22, 125, 136, 268, 298, 311, 354,
        403, 405, 418
    lack of definition of, 82–84, 123, 135, 162,
        198–99
Hill, Anita F., 56, 355, 401
Hinckley, John W., Jr., 88
Hirschfeld, Abe, 117, 118, 134, 166
Hirschmann, Susan, 179
Hitchens, Christopher, 390

Hoffmann, Sydney Jean, 347, 348, 368
Hollings, Fritz, 63, 314, 360
Holtzman, Elizabeth, 198
Hoover, Herbert, 83
Hoppe, David, 267, 293, 310, 363, 373
Houghton, Amo, 229, 252
House Judiciary Committee, 43, 45, 65, 67,
        76, 77, 78, 80, 83, 84, 93, 132, 142,
        160–87, 231, 235, 252, 261, 266
    articles of impeachment drafted by, 188–94
    articles of impeachment voted on by, 206,
        209–16
    bipartisanship and, 68, 101–2, 110, 124,
        126, 131
    chief investigators hired by, 67, 84–87,
        119–20
    Clinton's defense presented before,
        197–200, 202–3
    diversity of Democratic members of, 116
    Gecker's deposition for, 177
    impeachment inquiry opened by, 120–30
    investigators' summations before, 205–6
    meeting between Clinton's lawyers and,
        134–36
    partisanship and, 68, 72, 87, 101–2,
        107–8, 110, 115, 121, 123, 127,
        129–30, 136, 162–64, 169–70, 174,
        214, 216, 259–60
    political polarity and reelection of members
        of, 161–62
    Senate impeachment trial prosecuted by
        managers from, 259–60, 269, 270,
        272–75, 276–78, 280, 281, 286–88,
        294, 300–305, 321, 331, 341–46,
        355–58, 387, 388–89, 391–94
    size of, 209
    Starr report testimony redacted by, 101–2,
        107, 110
    Starr's appearance before, 148, 160, 163,
        168–74, 177, 205
    subpoenas voted on by, 174–76
    Tripp's tapes released by, 167
    videotape of Clinton's grand jury testimony
        released by, 97–98, 102, 106
    written questions submitted to Clinton by,
        147–49, 179–81, 201, 215, 229
House majority whip, ranking of, 44
House of Representatives, U.S., 15, 18, 20, 44,
        50, 51, 62–63, 67, 70, 78, 94–95, 122,
        132, 143, 201, 222, 376, 418
    Appropriations Committee of, 20–21, 146,
        153, 154
    Clinton's relationship with Democratic
        members of, 48–49, 51–53, 63–65, 72,
        76–77, 103–5, 123–29, 249
    history of impeachments by, 83–84

impeachment debate in, 235–36, 238–42, 246–52
impeachment inquiry vote passed by, 125–30
impeachment vote of, 251–53, 442
independent counsel's obligation to, 62
International Affairs Committee of, 224
lame-duck status of, 182, 266, 269–70, 297
longest-serving member of, 65
meetings of Democratic members of, 76–77
1998 election results in, 146
power of impeachment held by, 62, 82, 189
Rules Committee of, 68, 78
Speaker of, *see* Speaker of the House
Starr report released by, 80
unofficial impeachment tally of, 178
Ways and Means Committee of, 86, 153, 257
Hoyer, Steny H., 59
Huang, John, 184, 185
Hubbell, Webster, 108
Hundley, William G., 324
Hussein, Saddam, 15, 227, 228, 234, 240
Hussein ibn Talal, King of Jordan, 392, 396
Hustler, 120, 202, 228, 236, 296
Hutchinson, Asa, 12, 97–98, 99, 102, 103, 117, 121, 127, 130–31, 166–67, 174, 175–76, 204–5, 214, 241, 260, 383, 415
    background and political career of, 93–95
    Broaddrick questioned by, 183
    encounters between Clinton and, 93, 94
    as manager in Senate trial, 266, 272–73, 276, 277, 296, 297, 300, 301, 302, 303–4, 305, 306–7, 311, 312, 317, 324, 327, 331–32, 333, 334, 339–40, 344, 347, 350, 353, 355–56, 357, 359, 361, 362, 373–76, 387, 390–91, 392, 394, 400, 410
    Morris's meeting with, 124–25
    Roger Clinton prosecuted by, 94
Hutchinson, Susan Burrell, 94
Hutchinson, Tim, 93, 94–95, 266, 383
Hutchison, Kay Bailey, 400
Hyde, Henry J., 12, 43, 67, 68, 69, 70, 71–72, 80, 93, 97, 102, 107, 119, 120, 122, 134, 136–37, 139, 147–50, 156, 159, 160, 161, 169, 173, 174, 181, 182, 185, 188, 190, 191–92, 200, 203–4, 205, 206, 209, 210, 211, 212, 214–15, 217, 218, 219, 220, 223, 231, 232, 250, 256, 310, 319, 339, 418
    background and political career of, 77

Clinton as viewed by, 77–78, 99, 239–40
    Cutler's meeting with, 164–65
    impeachment inquiry strategy of, 116–17, 123, 124, 126, 128, 129
    revelation of adultery of, 98–99, 102
    Ruff's censure offer and, 195–96
    Schippers hired by, 84–85
    and Senate trial, 259, 260, 269, 270, 272–73, 274, 275–78, 280, 287, 288, 295, 296, 301, 311, 312, 318, 325, 336, 337, 343–44, 347, 355, 356–58, 359, 361, 367–68, 377, 387–88, 392, 393–94, 411
Hyde, Jeanne Simpson, 77, 98

Ickes, Harold M., 12, 65–66, 143, 413–14
Idaho, 99
Illinois, 45, 109, 140, 164, 178, 237, 245, 248, 305, 313
impeachment, 82–84
    of Andrew Johnson, 18, 83–84, 188, 189, 238, 248, 251, 266, 267, 298, 398, 417
    Constitution on, *see* Constitution, U.S.
    future of, 417–18
    history of, 83–84
    House's "sole Power of," 62, 82, 189
    independent counsel's obligation regarding, 62
    Nixon and, 18, 19, 45, 83, 84, 116, 120, 121, 134, 188–89, 192, 198, 202, 205, 211, 235, 261, 270, 398
    Reagan and, 19
impeachment of Clinton, 60, 61, 85, 109–10, 162, 279
    alternatives to, *see* censure of Clinton; resignation of Clinton
    beginning of inquiry into, 114–17
    canvassing undecided House members on, 219–28
    Clinton on, 416–17
    consequences of, 18, 417–19
    as coup attempt, 107, 128, 241
    Democrats in favor of, 53, 104, 129
    drafting of charges in, 188–94
    Gephardt's early mention of, 52
    growing probability of, 181–87
    House debate on, 235–36, 238–42, 246–52
    House's vote to launch inquiry into, 125–30
    impeachment trial held before, 259
    improvisational nature of, 19–20
    as 1998 election issue, 143–46
    Nixon's impeachment proceedings used as model for, 45, 107, 116, 123, 134–35, 188–89, 190, 192, 270

impeachment of Clinton (*cont.*)
  public opinion on, 127–28, 165, 197,
    224–25, 298
  Senate trial of, 259
  sex vs. power as motive in, 18, 254, 325
  unofficial vote count taken on, 178
  see also articles of impeachment; *specific*
    articles
independent counsel:
  establishment of, 18
  obligation of, 62
  see also Starr, Kenneth W.; Starr report
Indiana, 63, 97, 99, 102, 140, 141, 186, 197,
  230–31, 262, 342, 402, 406
Inglis, Bob, 199, 213
Inslee, Jay, 144
interest groups, 65–66
Internal Revenue Service (IRS), 146, 189,
  205
International Monetary Fund (IMF), 133
Internet, 98, 137, 142, 416
  Starr report released on, 76, 80, 88, 97,
    100, 128
Iowa, 22, 51, 97, 242, 293, 309, 346, 380,
  397
Iran-contra affair, 19, 64, 169, 205, 348
Iraq, bombing of, 15, 166, 227, 228, 229, 232,
  233–34, 235–36, 242, 248, 257–58,
  261
Ireland, Northern, 57, 60, 61, 200, 267
Ireland, Republic of, 57, 61, 62
"is," Clinton's query on meaning of, 29, 304
Isenbergh, Joseph, 283
Israel, 133, 219, 220, 226, 227

Jackson, Andrew, censure of, 255, 288–89
Jackson, Jesse, 52, 382
Jackson, Jesse, Jr., 248, 382
Jane Does, 231, 294
  No. 5, *see* Broaddrick, Juanita
Jaworski, Leon, 62, 171
Jefferson, Thomas, 84, 322
Jeffords, James T., 341, 389, 392, 400, 409,
  410
Jenkins, Bill, 186
Jenkins, Marilyn Jo, 138
Jenner, Albert, 121
Jennings, Peter, 306–7
Jewish members, on House Judiciary Commit-
  tee, 116
Johnson, Andrew, 279, 295, 394, 418
  impeachment of, 18, 83–84, 188, 189,
    238, 248, 251, 266, 267, 298, 398,
    417
Johnson, Joel P., 295
Johnson, Lyndon B., 34, 300

Johnson, Nancy, 227, 234
Johnson, Norma Holloway, 12, 183, 184–85,
  337–38, 345, 346
Joint Chiefs of Staff, U.S., 228, 235
Joint Committee for the Study of Presidential
  Privileges, 113
Jones, Paula, 12, 23, 37, 108–9, 138, 171,
  175, 190, 204, 241, 252, 294, 303,
  318–19, 338, 355–56, 370, 376, 391,
  396
  civil deposition of Clinton in suit of, 26,
    28, 29, 39, 80, 89, 90, 112, 167,
    180–81, 186, 191, 192, 195, 198,
    214, 252, 264, 273, 304, 321, 329,
    416
  Clinton's financial settlement with, 100,
    108, 117, 134, 165–66, 298–99
  sexual harassment suit of, 35, 81, 105, 273,
    311
Jordan, Jim, 102
Jordan, Vernon E., Jr., 12, 149, 172, 273, 306,
  324, 332, 333, 334, 339, 384
  Clinton's friendship with, 47, 49, 76, 357,
    374
  grand jury testimony of, 91
  Lewinsky aided in job search by, 47, 81,
    137, 303, 304, 317, 318, 357, 374,
    376
  in Senate trial, 356–57, 359, 372, 373–76,
    390, 391
Justice Department, U.S., 85, 86, 183–84,
  185, 202, 206

Kadzik, Peter J., 165
Kansas, 285, 352
Kantor, Mickey, 12, 24, 25, 30–31, 33, 37
Kaptur, Marcy, 53, 63
Kendall, David E., 12, 26, 28, 31, 32, 37, 64,
  77, 78, 79, 89, 90, 96, 105, 106, 180,
  181, 186, 194, 195, 197, 198, 266,
  416
  as lawyer for both Clintons, 24, 36
  in Senate trial, 278, 301, 310, 316,
    324–25, 358–59, 368, 376
  Starr questioned by, 171–74
  Starr's letter from, 62–63, 69
  Starr's "walk in the woods" with, 27
Kennan, George, 88
Kennedy, Edward M., 55, 88, 110, 279, 292,
  293, 321, 355, 360, 361
Kennedy, Jim, 215
Kennedy, John F., 34, 75, 241, 248, 255, 279,
  322, 394
Kennedy, Joseph P., II, 248
Kennedy, Patrick J., 241–42
Kennedy, Robert F., 85

Kentucky, 22, 53, 140, 141, 274, 329, 397
Kerrey, Bob, 48, 60–61, 262, 302, 384
Kerry, John, 411
King, John, 30
King, Larry, 63
King, Martin Luther, Jr., 56, 322
King, Peter T., 12, 200–202, 206, 208,
    220–21, 223, 226, 252, 257, 258
Kohl, Herb, 342
Kosovo, 419
Kremlin, 57–58
Kundanis, George, 53
Kyl, Jon, 285, 293, 297, 358

LaBella, Charles G., 183, 184, 185
labor unions, 65–66, 115, 221–22, 223,
    226
LaHood, Ray, 238, 239, 247, 251
Landow, Nathan, 175, 176, 396
Lapin, Daniel, 224
Largent, Steve, 388
Lawrence, Shelia Davis, 138
Leahy, Patrick J., 327, 341, 351, 368, 369,
    371, 381, 401–2
    Clinton admonished by, 54–55
Lee, Robert E., 300
Lee, Sheila Jackson, 76, 116, 168, 216, 408
Lehman, Kathryn, 218–19
Letchworth, Elizabeth, 364
Levin, Carl, 109, 276, 278
Lewinsky, Monica S., 12, 16, 24–25, 33, 35,
    51, 55, 68, 72, 79, 80, 90, 100, 101,
    103, 112, 135, 138, 145, 148, 149,
    171, 189, 190, 195, 203, 205, 206,
    225, 229, 239, 241, 253, 263, 264,
    289, 297, 318, 324–25, 331, 333, 352,
    375, 378–79, 384, 401, 402–3
    affidavit filed in Jones suit by, 81, 175, 304,
        349, 370, 391, 399
    blue dress of, 26, 40, 81, 118, 173, 205,
        349; see also DNA evidence
    Clinton appraised by, 371–72
    Clinton's civil deposition in Jones case
        regarding, 28, 29, 39, 80, 89, 90, 167,
        180–81, 214, 264, 273, 304, 321, 329,
        416
    Clinton's coaching of, 91, 193
    Clinton's gifts to, 28, 80, 81, 181, 265,
        304, 349, 357, 371, 399, 402
    Clinton's grand jury testimony regarding,
        23, 26, 27–29, 80, 90–91, 105–7, 210,
        265, 304, 322, 329
    in Clinton's post-grand jury television
        speech, 33–34
    grand jury appearances of, 50, 81, 102,
        172, 369–70
    House managers' questioning of, 337–38,
        339–40, 341–42, 345–50, 367–73,
        385
    Jordan's aid in finding job for, 47, 81, 137,
        303, 304, 317, 318, 357, 374, 376
    media appearances of, 416
    media obsession with, 58–59, 147, 345,
        350
    private deposition before Starr's prosecutors
        given by, 62
    rejection of Senate subpoena for, 389
    Starr report on Clinton's sexual relationship
        with, 81–82, 101
    Tripp's tape recordings of, 167
    as witness in Senate trial, 272, 273, 274,
        277, 355, 356–57, 359, 367–73
Lewis, Ann, 143
Lewis, John, 56, 408
Lieberman, Joseph I., 13, 63, 109, 129
    Clinton criticized by, 41, 42, 48, 54,
        59–62, 88, 207, 263, 291
    and Senate trial, 268, 271, 274, 275, 276,
        278, 284, 290, 293, 297, 381, 382,
        384, 388, 397, 399, 409
Limbaugh, Rush, 134
Lincoln, Abraham, 83, 300
Linder, John, 141
Lindsey, Bruce R., 13, 107, 124, 158, 172,
    175, 176, 301–2, 315
    Clinton's relationship with, 36–37
Little Rock, Ark., 88, 109, 138, 416
Livingood, Wilson, 71, 80
Livingston, Bob, 13, 20–22, 146–47, 160,
    163, 182, 216, 221, 233, 234–35, 238,
    241, 256, 257, 259
    background of, 17, 20
    DeLay's anti-censure moves and, 217–19
    in eleventh-hour moment of doubt, 15–18,
        242
    Gingrich's relationship with, 20, 153, 154,
        156
    as House Appropriations Committee chair-
        man, 20–21, 146, 153, 154
    marital infidelities of, 15, 22, 155, 218,
        228–29, 236–37, 239
    political career and reputation of, 20
    resignation of, 22, 242, 243–45, 246–50,
        254
    as slated to become House Speaker, 15, 16,
        17, 21–22, 150–56, 158, 186, 217,
        244, 247
Livingston, Bonnie, 20, 155
Livingston, Susie, 155
Lockhart, Joe, 13, 30, 36, 80, 105, 182, 207,
    227–28, 249, 265, 345, 366, 388, 410,
    414

Lofgren, Zoe, 116, 120, 164, 216, 247
Lott, Trent, 13, 38, 43, 50, 196, 235
    background and political career of, 261–62
    Daschle and, 260–62, 407, 410–11
    Senate trial and, 267, 268–69, 270, 271,
        272, 274–76, 280–81, 283–84,
        285–88, 289, 292, 293, 294, 297, 309,
        310, 311–12, 314, 324, 328, 331, 340,
        341, 345–50, 353, 360, 361, 362–66,
        368, 382, 383, 385, 389–90, 400–401,
        405, 407–8, 409, 410, 411, 412
Louisiana, 117
Lowell, Abbe D., 13, 67–68, 69, 71, 93, 103,
        108, 109, 119–20, 135, 162, 163, 164,
        167, 171, 176, 184–85, 213, 305, 332
    Gephardt's hiring of, 86–87
    House Judiciary Committee statements of,
        121, 122, 205
    Starr report reviewed by, 90–91
Lugar, Richard, 406–7
Luntz, Frank, 146, 275, 382
Lyons, Gene, 379

MacArthur, Douglas, 83
McAuliffe, Terence R., 13, 52, 56, 104, 142,
        143, 253, 298, 315
McCain, John, 398
McCarthy, Carolyn, 53
McCollum, Bill, 13, 119, 192, 213, 252, 296,
        309, 313, 337, 341–42, 347, 348, 349,
        350, 353, 355, 367
McConnell, Mitch, 274, 275, 291, 352, 392,
        400
McCurry, Michael, 13, 25, 30, 31, 36, 37, 46,
        47, 49–50, 58, 64, 100, 105, 106, 118,
        119, 130, 182
McEntee, Gerald, 52, 65, 143
McHale, Paul, 47–48, 63, 168, 252
McHugh, John N., 221
Mack, Connie, 284, 290, 323, 364, 365–66
McKeon, Buck, 151
McMillan, William N., III, 166
McNulty, Paul J., 98, 119, 135, 358, 392
McQuillan, Laurence, 58, 59
Madison, James, 265
Maine, 282, 283, 383
Malcolm, Ellen, 143
Mandela, Nelson, 56, 264, 388
Manzullo, Don, 237
Mariano, E. Connie, 49
marijuana eradication program, 94
Marshall, Capricia, 46
Martha's Vineyard, 31, 46, 47, 49, 50, 54, 55,
        56, 57
Martin, Allen, 155, 218, 219
Martinez, Matthew G., 53

Maryland, 59, 62, 133, 175, 222, 252, 360
Massachusetts, 87, 102, 116, 123, 131, 169,
        198, 202, 248, 291
Mattoon, Dan, 256
Mayflower Hotel, 346–47, 350, 351, 355, 368
media, 18–19, 34, 50, 89, 99–100, 265, 271,
        309
    Lewinsky as obsession of, 58–59, 147, 345,
        350
Meehan, Martin, 130–31, 171, 216, 247
Meet the Press, 392
Mellman, Mark, 25, 143
Menendez, Robert, 241
Mercer, Lucy, 34
Metropolitan Club, 111, 114
Michel, Bob, 187
Michigan, 53, 63, 65, 67, 109, 141, 276, 360,
        409
Middle East, 133–34, 206, 216, 219, 220,
        224, 225, 226, 232, 233, 264, 388,
        392
Mikulski, Barbara, 360, 366
Mikva, Abner J., 99
Miller, George, 53
Mills, Cheryl D., 13, 79, 89, 195, 215, 301,
        316–17, 368
    Clintons' relationship with, 36–37, 316
    in Senate trial, 316–17, 320–21, 322–23,
        324
Milosevic, Slobodan, 419
Mississippi, 53, 140, 252, 274, 279
Mississippi, University of, 261
Missouri, 41, 53, 123, 152, 383
Mitchell, George J., 64, 263, 266–67, 271,
        311, 314
Mitchell, John N., 324, 348
Molinari, Susan, 152
Monica's Story (Lewinsky), 416
Monroe, James, 146
Monroe, Marilyn, 34
Mooney, Thomas E., Sr., 13, 70, 71, 103, 119,
        134–36, 147, 184, 195, 200, 210, 212
Moore, Kiki, 165
Moran, James P., Jr., 63, 103–5, 126
Morella, Constance A., 222–23, 252
Morris, Dick, 38, 49, 124–25, 273, 358
Morton, Andrew, 346
Moschella, William E., 184
Moscow, Clinton at news conference in,
        57–59, 60
Moynihan, Daniel Patrick, 48, 61, 262, 271,
        384, 397, 412, 413
MSNBC, 71, 207
Murray, Patty, 63, 142, 355, 389
Muskie, Ed, 97
Myers, Lisa, 71, 323, 382, 397, 399, 415

Nadler, Jerrold, 116, 128, 210, 215, 250
NAFTA (North American Free Trade Agreement), 51
National Enquirer, 260
National Republican Congressional Committee (NRCC), 141, 145
National Republican Senatorial Committee, 291
NATO, 419
NBC, 207, 392, 404, 414
    Broaddrick's interview on, 323, 381–82, 397, 399, 415–16
Nebraska, 60, 262
Netanyahu, Benjamin, 134, 219, 227
Neuborne, Burt, 381
Nevada, 63, 141, 262, 330
New Democrats, 53, 59, 64
New Hampshire, 32, 51, 279, 291, 310, 329, 385, 415
New Jersey, 59, 140, 241, 336
Newman, Paul, 230
New Mexico, 223, 231, 276
New Orleans, La., 20
New York:
    Democratic Party in, 53, 61, 116, 121, 128, 198, 210, 250, 262, 271, 397
    Hillary Clinton and, 140, 413, 415
    Republican Party in, 44, 140, 151, 152, 182, 200, 201, 220, 221–22, 226, 229, 252
New Yorker, 25, 38
New York Times, 24, 30, 47, 106, 229, 263, 400
Ney, Bob, 221
Nichols, Laura, 91, 158, 248
Nickles, Don, 269, 271, 280, 283, 298, 310, 363, 365, 385, 400, 411
Nixon, Richard M., 75, 164, 184, 249, 254, 324, 397, 417
    Ford's pardoning of, 298
    impeachment proceedings faced by, 18, 19, 45, 83, 84, 116, 120, 121, 134, 188–89, 192, 198, 202, 205, 211, 235, 261, 270, 398
    resignation of, 19, 48, 84, 220
North, Oliver, 169, 316, 402
North American Free Trade Agreement (NAFTA), 51
North Carolina, 31, 37, 38, 76, 140, 162, 169, 216, 262, 342, 403
North Dakota, 97, 382
Northern Ireland, 57, 60, 61, 200, 267
Northup, Anne, 22, 141, 221
NRCC (National Republican Congressional Committee), 141, 145

oath of office, presidential, 17, 273, 303
Obey, David R., 21, 53
obstruction of justice, 16, 112, 139, 148, 156, 178, 183, 243, 265, 303, 316, 344, 369–70, 375, 399
    addressed in articles of impeachment, 189; *see also* Article III
    Starr report's allegations of, 80, 81, 91
Office of Government Ethics, 113–14
Ohio, 53, 63, 162, 311, 328, 329, 369, 377
Oklahoma, 93, 153, 269, 388
Old Bulls, 65, 69, 150, 276, 306
Old Executive Office Building, 95
Old Senate Chamber, 280, 288–92
"Operation Breakout," 145
Oregon, 53
Oval Office, 18, 23, 34, 36, 40, 50, 81, 82, 95, 126, 127, 183, 212, 249, 252, 254, 370, 378, 408
Owens, Wayne, 198

Packard, Ron, 151
Packwood, Bob, 401
Palmer, Scott, 178–79
Paone, Marty, 293
Pappas, Michael, 140
Parks, Rosa, 319
Parsons, Pam, 184
partisanship, 15, 234, 238–39, 241, 249, 252, 254, 255, 263, 271, 280, 289, 301, 338, 417
    in House Judiciary Committee, 68, 72, 87, 101–2, 107–8, 110, 115, 121, 123, 127, 129–30, 136, 162–64, 169–70, 174, 214, 216, 259–60
    in Senate trial, 284, 294–95, 313, 321, 328, 344, 354–55, 360, 361, 363, 366, 401, 412
    triumph of, 19, 158, 412
    see also bipartisanship
Paster, Howard, 65
Paxon, Bill, 13, 44, 141, 152, 154–55, 220, 256, 257
Pease, Ed, 97, 186, 231
Pelosi, Nancy, 128
Penn, Mark, 143, 144, 181, 206, 208, 225
Pennsylvania, 50, 97, 140, 234, 252, 269, 276, 286, 328
People for the American Way, 223
Perelman, Ron, 273, 304
perjury, 16, 30, 89, 109, 112, 121, 148–49, 156, 167, 178, 184, 185, 198, 220, 224, 240, 243, 247, 264, 273, 315, 316, 360, 399, 403, 408
    addressed in articles of impeachment, 189–93

perjury (*cont.*)
   in Starr report, 80, 81, 90–91
   see also Article I; Article II; Article IV
Persian Gulf War, 47, 132, 260
Phoenix Park, 61
Pickering, John, 84
pledge of allegiance, 246
Podesta, John D., 13, 25, 30, 32, 33, 36, 37,
     48, 55, 88, 95, 96, 99, 111, 130, 143,
     165, 180, 195, 207–9, 223, 227, 232,
     233, 246, 248, 249, 253, 254, 255,
     258, 273, 294, 295, 315, 388
   Democratic support for Clinton rounded
     up by, 63–65
   promoted to White House chief of staff,
     181–82
police officers, 55
   Capitol, 71, 257, 309, 350, 389, 390
Porter, John, 221
"Positive Points About Independent Counsel
     Ken Starr," 169
Presidential Medal of Freedom, 308
presidential oath of office, 17, 273, 303
presidents:
   infidelities of, 34
   post-presidency benefits of, 113
   separation-of-powers doctrine and, 298
President's Room, 300
Prince, Jonathan, 182, 194, 195, 384
Profiles in Courage (Kennedy), 248
"protective function privilege," 113

Quinn, Jack, 13, 182, 201, 208, 221–22,
     225–26, 320

Radical Republicans, 83
Raines, Ashley, 349
Ramadan, 227, 257
Rangel, Charles, 245–46, 249, 253, 256–57
Rather, Dan, 416
Ray, Robert W., 417
Reagan, Ronald, 19, 51, 64, 88, 202, 312
Reconstruction, 83
Reed, Ralph, 144
Rehnquist, William H., 13, 266, 319
   as presiding officer at Senate trial, 266,
     267–68, 270, 281–82, 295, 300–301,
     302, 303, 308, 310, 328, 331,
     333–34, 344–45, 356, 360–61,
     364–65, 368, 401–2, 403, 406,
     408–9, 411
   robe worn by, 281–82
Reich, Steven, 167, 305, 329, 340
Reid, Harry, 63, 141, 262, 311, 341
Reilly, Mame, 104
Reno, Janet, 171

Republican Party:
   animosity toward Clinton in, 19, 21, 42,
     258, 271, 312
   Congress controlled by, 37, 48–49
   conservative wing of, 16, 45, 269, 276,
     286, 306, 308, 331
   deals cut between Clinton and, 49, 74
   gerrymandering and, 225
   moderate wing of, 16, 47, 194, 197–98,
     201, 206–7, 208, 220–32, 234, 269,
     282–83, 284, 320, 341, 350, 383
   1998 election losses of, 140–47
   Nixon's resignation and, 19, 48
   range of stances on Clinton in, 43
   revenge sought by Clinton against,
     376–77, 415
   see also specific elections, individuals and states
"requests for admission," 147
resignation, 98
   of Livingston, 22, 242, 243–45, 246–50,
     254
   of Nixon, 19, 48, 84, 220
resignation of Clinton, 59, 60, 87, 244, 247,
     249
   Clinton on, 100, 220, 256
   as DeLay's goal, 44, 220
   Democrats in favor of, 47–48, 53, 63, 96,
     104, 314
   as option, 19, 41
"Response to Recent Attacks on Judge Starr's
     Investigation," 169
Reuters, 58
Revlon, 137, 273, 304
Rhode Island, 241, 284, 352
Rhodes, John J., 19
Ricchetti, Steven, 95, 96, 194, 226, 267, 271
Richards, Ann, 143
Richardson, Bill, 39, 63, 64, 96, 206, 223, 382
Riggs, Frank, 142, 221
Riley, Richard W., 72
Rivera, Geraldo, 207, 296
Rivera Live, 207, 296
Rivers, Lynn, 53
Roberts, Cokie, 406
Roberts, Pat, 285, 352
Robertson, Pat, 320
Rodino, Peter W., Jr., 108, 116, 120, 123, 188,
     189
Roemer, Tim, 63–64, 96–97, 196–97, 201
Rogan, James E., 13, 102, 142, 160, 161, 162,
     211, 213, 252, 297, 415, 419
   background and political career of, 307–8
   as manager in Senate trial, 272, 276, 277,
     287, 296, 303, 304–5, 307, 311, 313,
     333, 335, 344, 353, 358, 359, 362,
     367, 377, 387, 389, 392, 394, 410

Rogers, Ed, 275
Roll Call, 264
Roosevelt, Franklin D., 27, 34, 65, 243
Roosevelt, Theodore, 251, 418
Ross, Edward G., 279
Rostenkowski, Dan, 86
Rouse, Pete, 91
Rubin, Bob, 75–76
Rudman, Warren, 202
Rudy, Tony C., 42, 44, 178, 179, 204
Ruff, Charles F. C., 13, 25, 26, 27, 30, 36, 62,
    64, 77, 78, 89, 95, 96, 105, 109, 130,
    134–35, 195, 198, 199, 203–4, 207,
    208, 212, 214–15, 263
  censure offers of, 195–96, 203
  Clinton's relationship with, 28, 36
  legal career of, 28
  in Senate trial, 278, 293, 295, 297,
    300–301, 306, 310, 316, 317–18, 321,
    323, 327, 331–33, 334–35, 342, 343,
    355–56, 389, 393
  wheelchair of, 28, 300, 317
rule of law, 15, 17, 121, 240, 247, 398
Russia, 55, 56, 57–59, 60

Saddam Hussein, 15, 227, 228, 234, 240
St. Clair, James, 134
St. Paul, Minn., 134
Salmon, Matt, 151
Salon, 98, 99, 102
Santorum, Rick, 13, 276, 286, 287–88, 292,
    303, 385, 391–92, 400
Sarajevo, Clintons' visit to, 38
Sarbanes, Paul, 360
Scanlon, Michael P., 42, 43, 44, 179, 204
Schippers, David P., 13, 67–68, 87, 93, 119,
    127, 135, 139, 147, 160–61, 166, 174,
    184, 185, 191–92, 195, 209, 210, 231,
    252, 318, 332, 337, 339, 358, 359,
    368
  Clinton's actions as viewed by, 139
  House Judiciary Committee statements of,
    121–22, 205–6
  Hyde's hiring of, 84–85
  legal career of, 85
  and Senate trial, 273, 274–75
  Willey questioned by, 182–83
Schippers, Tom, 85
Schmelzer, Ranit, 91
Schumer, Charles E., 121, 165, 171, 213, 295,
    309, 313, 329–30, 387
Scott, Bobby, 116, 117, 163–64, 171, 204,
    209, 216
Scott, Hugh, 19
Scottish law, 401
Secret Service, 18, 27, 81, 87, 88, 113, 273

Seligman, Nicole K., 13, 26, 27, 36, 105, 106,
    180, 301, 316, 320–21, 353–54, 368,
    372, 391
Senate, U.S., 18, 129, 182, 196, 200, 201,
    261, 262, 413, 419
  Clinton's relationship with Democratic
    members of, 41, 48, 54–55, 59–62, 63,
    64, 65, 96, 109–10, 249, 314
  history of impeachment trials in, 83–84,
    267
  Jackson censured by, 255, 288–89
  legacy of desks in, 279
  Rules Committee of, 274
  trial of impeached officeholder as responsi-
    bility of, 82
Senate trial, 41, 202, 259–78, 279–99,
    300–326, 327–38, 339–66, 367–79,
    380–94, 395–412
  Blumenthal's deposition in, 377–79, 390,
    391
  Byrd's motion to dismiss filed in, 335–36,
    341, 351, 353, 354–55, 360, 362,
    389
  ceremonial opening of, 281–82
  Clinton acquitted in, 18, 19, 409–10
  Clinton's acquittal foreseen in, 262–63,
    276, 278, 290, 359, 361, 409–10
  Clinton's defense team in, 301–2, 310–11,
    314–16, 319, 380
  Clinton's direct participation as issue in,
    345, 356
  closing arguments in, 391, 393–94
  defense presentation in, 316–18, 321–23
  defense strategy in, 265–67, 269–72,
    305–6
  final deliberations in, 396–99, 401–8
  final plan for, 294
  "findings of fact" proposal in, 352, 363,
    380–86
  Gorton-Lieberman plan for, 268–69, 271,
    274, 275, 284, 290
  House managers' evidence team and,
    272–73, 276, 296
  joint caucus hearing and, 280–81, 283–84,
    285–86, 288–93, 313, 362–63
  Jordan's deposition in, 372, 373–76, 390,
    391
  Lewinsky interviewed by House managers
    for, 337–38, 339–40, 341–42,
    345–50
  Lewinsky's deposition in, 367–73, 385,
    390, 391
  lodging of charges in, 280
  misprint on ceremonial pen used in, 282,
    404
  opening arguments presented in, 324–25

Senate trial (*cont.*)
  partisanship in, 284, 294–95, 313, 321,
    328, 344, 354–55, 360, 361, 363, 366,
    401, 412
  prosecution presentation in, 302–5, 309
  race and, 316–17
  Rehnquist as presiding officer of, 266,
    267–68, 270, 281–82, 295, 300–301,
    302, 303, 308, 310, 328, 331, 333–34,
    344–45, 356, 360–61, 364–65, 368,
    401–2, 403, 406, 408–10, 411
  seating plan for, 295, 301
  terms used for senators in, 309–10, 311,
    365
  tip sheet on decorum for, 308
  two-stage vote as possibility in, 283
  two-thirds majority required to uphold
    impeachment in, 44, 82, 335, 361
  video presentations in, 303, 385, 389,
    390–91
  vote taken in, 408–12, 442
  witness issue in, 269, 270, 272–73,
    274–75, 277, 278, 281, 286, 287, 288,
    290, 293–94, 297, 312–13, 330, 350,
    351, 352–53, 355, 356–59, 361, 385,
    388–89
  wrangling over end plans for, 351–66
  written questions submitted in, 302,
    327–36, 341–45
Sensenbrenner, F. James, 175, 203, 213, 302,
    303, 305, 306, 310
separation-of-powers doctrine, 298
"sequential caucus," 262
Serbia, 419
Sessions, Jeff, 297, 298, 352
"sexual relations," defining of, 26, 28, 29, 81,
    82, 89, 91, 264, 322, 329, 371, 416
Shalala, Donna E., 13, 72, 73, 74–75, 76
Shays, Betsy, 232
Shays, Christopher, 13, 151, 221, 229–30,
    231, 232, 242–43, 252
Shelby, Richard, 400, 405, 409
Shelton, Hugh, 228, 235
Shrum, Robert, 24, 25, 86
Simpson, Alan, 262
Simpson, Carole, 417
Simpson, Kevin, 167, 185, 305, 313, 329,
    340
Sirica, John J., 62
60 Minutes, 183, 353, 396
"six-year itch" elections, 146
Skaggs, David E., 53
Slater, Rodney, 74
Slaughter, Louise M., 53
Small Business Administration, 38, 73, 75
Smith, Craig, 104, 142, 143

Smith, Erik, 248
Smith, Gordon, 392, 400, 411
Smith, Guy, 164
Smith, Lamar, 213
Smith, Linda, 142
Smith, Robert C., 279, 329
Smith, William Kennedy, 88
Smithsonian Institution, 67
Snodgrass, Cherie, 98–99
Snodgrass, Fred, 98–99
Snowe, Olympia, 284, 329, 382–83, 392, 400,
    402, 409, 410
Solomon, Gerald B. H., 68
Sosa, Sammy, 319
Sosnik, Douglas B., 13, 25, 30, 31–32, 33, 45,
    46, 48, 64, 78–79, 96, 105, 106, 107,
    130, 143, 158, 207, 226, 249, 253,
    258, 265, 272
  as Clinton's senior advisor, 119
Souder, Mark, 221, 230–31, 252
South Carolina, 94, 102, 199, 213, 218, 259,
    311, 322, 377
South Dakota, 40, 262
Speaker of the House, 44, 152
  ranking of, 257
  selection process for, 142
Specter, Arlen, 13, 50, 269, 284, 297, 298,
    303, 328, 358, 378, 400
  "not proved" votes of, 401, 405, 409, 410
Stanford University, 47
Stanton, Edwin M., 83, 188
Stark, Fortney H. "Pete," 53
Starr, Kenneth W., 13, 19, 23, 24, 25, 26, 27,
    28, 29, 30, 32, 35, 43, 52, 53, 54, 58,
    59, 67, 70, 71, 73, 76–77, 85, 87, 94,
    97, 109, 112, 114, 117, 120, 122, 125,
    131, 135, 149, 184, 185, 186, 196,
    198, 202, 206, 223, 301, 319, 338,
    339, 340, 341, 347–48, 359, 375, 384,
    386, 387, 401, 417
  cost and length of investigation conducted
    by, 29, 68, 229
  Hillary Clinton and, 33
  House Judiciary Committee appearance of,
    148, 160, 163, 168–74, 177, 205
  Kendall's letter to, 62–63, 69
  legal career of, 169
  range covered by investigation led by, 127
Starr report, 60, 67, 79–82, 85, 87, 112, 121,
    132
  Clinton-Lewinsky relationship detailed in,
    81–82, 90, 101
  Clinton's response to, 79–80
  delivery of boxes of evidence from, 70–72
  eleven counts against Clinton outlined in,
    80–81, 135

release of, 68–69, 71–72, 76, 78, 80, 97, 100, 128
secret evidence and, 16, 87, 93, 101–2, 103, 107, 110, 137–39, 231–32, 252
State Department, U.S., 88, 100, 321
State Farm Insurance, 299
State of the Union addresses, Clinton's, 38, 39, 40, 114, 298, 300, 316, 319–20, 419
Steele, Julie Hiatt, 172
Stein, Jacob A., 337–38, 348, 368
Stein, Lawrence, 63, 336
Stenholm, Charles W., 123, 252
Stevens, Ted, 13, 276, 277, 278, 281, 284, 293, 302, 306, 341, 397, 409
Stevens, Thaddeus, 83–84, 280
stock market, 1998 tumble of, 57, 58
Stratman, Sam, 98, 102, 147
Sudan, 26, 47, 50
Summersby, Kay, 34
Sumner, Charles, 279, 288, 291
Sunstein, Cass, 381
Super Tuesday, 51
Supreme Court, U.S., 107, 170, 266, 311–12, 402
Sweeney, John, 52–53, 65, 66, 143

Talbott, David, 98
Taylor, Gene, 53, 252
Taylor, Peggy, 226
teachers, 55
    hiring program for, 133
Tenet, George J., 228, 235
Tennessee, 123, 164, 186, 272, 276, 303, 347, 367
Tenure of Office Act, 83
Texas, 16, 37, 43, 44, 53, 76, 116, 123, 143, 151, 213, 216, 241, 252, 269, 291, 400
This Week, 89, 405
Thomas, Clarence, 18, 56, 355, 401
Thomas, Craig, 323
Thomason, Harry, 33
Thompson, Fred D., 123, 276, 281, 293, 328, 330, 352, 360, 363, 365, 372, 376, 385–86, 409, 418
302's, 137
Thurmond, Strom, 282, 295, 320–21, 389
Tiefer, Charles, 269
Tonry, Richard, 20
Torricelli, Robert G., 59, 109, 117, 309, 336, 402
Toward Tradition, 224
Tower, John, 18
town hall meetings, 230
Towson, Md., focus groups in, 128

Traficant, James A., Jr., 53
Travelgate, 24, 170, 172
"triangulation" strategy, 49
Tribe, Laurence, 120, 381
Tripp, Linda, 13, 105, 122, 137, 163, 167, 205, 297, 349, 369
Truman, Harry S, 83
Tsongas, Paul, 103
Tucker, Jim Guy, 94
Tulane University, 20
Turton, Dan, 248
Twentieth Amendment, 269
Tyler, John, 83

überlawyer, 64
Ueland, Eric, 310, 363
United Nations, 39, 106–7, 166, 227
Utah, 41, 89, 97, 118, 161, 198, 216, 286, 330, 356, 386

Verdery, Stewart, 328, 365
Vermont, 54, 341, 351, 389
Virginia, 43, 63, 103, 115, 116, 126, 168, 173, 197, 210, 250, 252, 315, 383, 402
Voting Rights Act (1965), 300

Wag the Dog, 50, 227, 233
Walker, Bob, 78, 152–53, 155, 157
"walk-in" privilege, 95
Wallace, Mike, 274, 293, 310, 328
Wall Street Journal, 114, 415
Walsh, Bill, 330
Walters, Barbara, 346, 416
Warner, John W., 383, 402, 409
Washington, 63, 142, 144, 263, 355, 389
Washington, D.C., scandal culture of, 18–19, 38
Washington, George, 17
Washington Post, 24, 39, 52, 120, 178, 224, 332, 339, 415
Watergate scandal, 18, 48, 62, 68, 82, 107, 108, 116, 126, 171, 188–89, 205, 236, 241, 418
    bipartisanship as lesson of, 19, 68
    current holdovers from, 28, 84, 120–21, 134, 164, 177, 198, 202, 210, 276, 287, 348, 386
    see also impeachment, Nixon and
Waters, Maxine, 13, 76, 116, 120, 209, 211, 216, 241, 247, 408
Watt, Mel, 76, 162, 169, 209
Watts, J. C., 153, 237
Weber, Vin, 157, 186–87
Webster, Daniel, 279, 288, 291, 292
Weicker, Lowell P., 202, 229–30

Weinberger, Caspar, 330
Weld, William F., 202–3
welfare reform, 74, 76
Wellstone, Paul, 310, 354
West Virginia, 110, 202, 290
Wexler, Anne, 165
Wexler, Robert, 209, 216
White, Rick, 144
White Citizens Council, 241
White House:
    Christmas parties at, 196–97, 419
    Democratic rally held at, 245–46, 249,
        253–54, 262, 388
    electronic monitoring of Clinton's location
        in, 30
    F. D. Roosevelt on, 243
    West Wing of, 95, 142–43, 271
    see also Oval Office
White House Counsel's Office, 114
Whitewater investigation, 24, 33, 38, 94,
        107–8, 127, 140, 170, 172, 200
Wiggins, Charles E., 184
Wilentz, Sean, 198–99
Willey, Kathleen E., 13, 127, 137, 172, 175,
        177, 182–83, 273, 274, 297, 352–53,
        395–96, 399, 403
Williams, Margaret A., 143
Williams & Connolly, 24, 79, 180, 271

Wilson, Heather, 223, 231
Wilson, Woodrow, 298, 419
Wisconsin, 53, 141, 175, 216, 262, 305, 315,
        323, 342, 360
Wisconsin, University of, 74
"wise men," 19, 164, 187, 239
Wisenberg, Solomon L., 27, 29
Witt, James Lee, 74
women, 355
    Clinton's support among, 75, 102, 128
women's organizations, 65, 143
Woodward, Bob, 57
Worcester, Mass., Clinton's day trip to, 55
World Bank, 36
Wright, Betsey, 35
Wright, Jim, 18, 43, 86, 158, 264
Wright, Susan Webber, 204, 273, 274, 333,
        387, 416
Wye River accords, 133–34
Wyoming, 38, 323, 329, 401

Yale Law School, 88, 266, 269
Yeltsin, Boris, 57, 58, 60

Zeldin, Michael, 86
Ziegler, Ron, 37
Ziglar, James W., 268, 279, 295, 320–21, 354,
        364